AF826600

# CBSE Board Exams 2023

*i Succeed*

# 15 Sample Question Papers

As Per Latest CBSE Sample Paper Issued on 16 Sep. 2022

# Mathematics

## Class 10 (Basic)

# CBSE Board Exams 2023

*i Succeed*

# 15 Sample Question Papers

As Per Latest CBSE Sample Paper Issued on 16 Sep. 2022

# Mathematics

## Class 10 (Basic)

*Authors*
**Tanmay Batra**
**Naveen Kishore**

**arihant**
**Arihant Prakashan** (School Division Series)

CBSE Board Exams 2023

**arihant**

**Arihant Prakashan** (School Division Series)



**Administrative & Production Offices**

**Regd. Office**

'Ramchhaya' 4577/15, Agarwal Road, Darya Ganj, New Delhi -110002
Tele: 011- 47630600, 43518550

**Head Office**

Kalindi, TP Nagar, Meerut (UP) - 250002
Tel: 0121-7156203, 7156204

**Sales & Support Offices**

Agra, Ahmedabad, Bengaluru, Bareilly, Chennai, Delhi, Guwahati, Hyderabad, Jaipur, Jhansi, Kolkata, Lucknow, Nagpur & Pune.

**PRICE** ₹250.00

**PO No :** TXT-XX-XXXXXXX-X-XX

Published by Arihant Publications (India) Ltd.

For further information about the books published by Arihant, log on to www.arihantbooks.com or e-mail at info@arihantbooks.com

Follow us on

9 789327 195583

# REAL PRACTICE

*A Key to Achieve Perfection*

Practice is the key to achieve perfection; one should practice to achieve perfection in any field and school examinations are not an exception to this fact. Constant practice can help one to overcome his weakness. The practice done in a right way with proper guidelines helps to attain grasp over the subject and result in a 'Perfect Performance'.

Sample paper is a must have study resource for each and every student, as it helps them to make themselves acquainted with the real exam paper pattern. They can check and update different aspects like enough speed to complete the paper within the prescribed time limit, identifying those topics/chapter, they are not comfortable with, polishing their skills of writing the answer as per the need of the question, etc.

*iSucceed* 15 Sample Question Papers will serve the above cited purpose in a perfect manner. This book will help you to master all the skills required to attempt the CBSE Class X Examination Paper perfectly. This series is not just another Sample Paper series in the market, there are some special features associated with *iSucceed* which make it stand apart.

**Some of them are :**

- A special section at the start, **The Qualifying Round** to give you an assessment of your Chapterwise Knowledge before attempting the full length Sample Question Papers.
- For Step-by-Step Upgradation, Sample Question Papers grouped into **Three Stages: Stage I, II & III**. Through these stages one can enhance his/her performance gradually .
- All Sample Papers strictly following the **Latest CBSE Sample Paper Pattern 2023**.
- At the end, there are fully solved **Latest CBSE Sample Paper** & a separate sample paper for **One Day Before Exam.**
- Solutions given with each question has Stepwise Marking & strictly follows the **CBSE Marking Scheme**.
- **Online Guidance** is available for unsolved Sample Question Papers.

To gain maximum benefit from Sample Papers, it is advised that you attempt the papers at a stretch in 3 hours without any help.

Although, We have put our best efforts to preparing this book, but if any error or discrepancy has skipped our attention, or you have any suggestion, send your feedbacks. We will welcome your feedback. We thank everyone involved in the process of preparing this book and especially acknowledge the contribution of
Er. Ashwani (Project Head). With the hope that this book will be of great help to the students, we wish great success to our readers.

*Authors*
Tanmay Batra
Naveen Kishore

# STAGES
## of Real Practice

# SAMPLE QUESTION PAPERS

## a need of the students

It is a question which may rise in the mind of the students that inspite of all the Classroom studies, reading good books, completing homework, etc.

Why there is a need of separate book having simulated Sample Question Papers ?

The answer will be, YES it is needed.

Following points will successfully explain the need of Sample Question Papers

- *iSucceed* 15 Sample Question Papers help you to practice for the CBSE Class 10th Examination 2021 and finally will make you getting high end success.
- This series is not just another Sample Papers series in the market but there are some special features associated with *iSucceed* Series books which make them stand apart from others.

### TAKING THE SAMPLE QUESTION PAPERS

In order to maximise the benefits of the Sample Question Papers, it is recommended that you take these Papers under conditions similar to the conditions under which the real examinations are administered.

T ry to take the Sample Papers in a quiet atmosphere with few interruptions and limit yourself to the three hour time period allotted for the real examination. You will find your results to be more useful if you refer to the answer key only after you have completed the Sample Question Papers.

### PURPOSE OF SAMPLE QUESTION PAPERS

The Sample Question Papers are designed to provide an additional resource to help you effectively prepare for the School Examinations. The primary purpose of the Sample Question Papers is to help you become familiar with the structure and content of the examination. It is also intended to help you to identify the areas in which you need to focus on your studies.

### INCORPORATING SAMPLE QUESTION PAPERS *IN YOUR STUDY PLAN*

Adequate preparation prior to taking the real examination is strongly recommended. How much preparation and study you need depends on how comfortable and knowledgeable you are with the content of the examination.

The Sample Question Papers may be used as one indicator of potential strengths and weaknesses in your knowledge of the content in the examination. Because of the similarities in the format and difficulty level between the Sample Question Papers and real examinations, it is possible to predict precisely how you might score in the examination. So, by incorporating the Sample Question Papers in your study plan you can assess yourself from the examination point of view in a better and realistic manner.

To Give You Interactive &

# STEP-BY-STEP PRACTICE

*iSucceed books have been divided in*

## 3 STAGES

### STAGE I *(Sample Papers 1 to 5)*

The solution to individual question has been given with the question itself, by attempting this stage you can practice along with the learning. If you have any doubt while solution any question you can refer the solution instantly, in this way you will learn and will be able to make your concepts clear.

### STAGE II *(Sample Papers 6 to 10)*

The solution to the questions has been given at the end of the question paper. You can check what you have learnt in the Stage I. This is the stage which will seriously assess your knowledge, if you go through this stage without referring to the solution, then you can be sure of getting a high end success in the exam.

### STAGE III *(Sample Papers 11 to 15)*

No solution to the questions has been given, But Online guidelines has been provided this stage. You are advised to attempt this stage within the prescribed time limit of three hours (however, we advice you to attempt all the Sample Question Papers in the prescribed time limit), this is the stage of real assessment. If you find yourself in problem while solving some of the questions, then attempt the same question again and again till you get it correct.

*"After going through all the three stages, you will find yourself confident about the coming examination and will come out with the flying colours."*

Attempting the

# EXAMINATION PAPER

*The examination question papers contains different types of questions, like Objective Questions, Very Short Answer Type Questions, Short Answer Type Questions and Long Answer Type Questions, etc. Each type of question is to be dealt with in different way, which are discussed below.*

## OBJECTIVE QUESTIONS AND SHORT ANSWER TYPE QUESTIONS

Attempt all the questions. Always keep in mind that Objective Questions do not involve very lengthy answers. Always read these types of questions very carefully and understand the demand of the question and answer accordingly. If you cannot answer a question, leave it and return to it when you have completed the other questions. Use your spare time at the end of the examination to check your answers.

## LONG ANSWER TYPE QUESTIONS

Once you reach on descriptive questions section, go through the question paper and choose a question you feel confident about. You need not to start with first question. Read the question twice, look at the mark allocation for each part and then decide exactly what is required to secure the marks.

## WHILE ATTEMPTING THE EXAMINATION PAPER

Follow the instructions in the question carefully responding to words and phrases such as describe and give a reason for.

- Do not rush, this is a major cause of mistakes, particularly of misreading the question. The time allocated for the examination is adequate for the candidates to complete the paper.
- Leave the hardest questions or parts of questions to be tackled at the end.
- If you finish early, take the opportunity to check through your answers. Ask yourself, have I answered the question and have I made sufficient points to be awarded the marks?

## TIPS

- Take reasonable care that your writing is legible- which cannot be read, cannot be marked.
- Do not rewrite the information given in the question and expect to gain marks.

"Too many candidates write at length without answering the question properly. Never forget marks are not awarded for correct subject, but for correct subject that answers the question most appropriately."

*We are sure that using the above tips and advices you will surely be able to improve your grades in the examination.*

# COURSE STRUCTURE
## (2022-23)

**Time: 3 Hrs** **Total Marks : 80**

| Units | Unit Name | Marks |
|---|---|---|
| I | Number Systems | 06 |
| II | Algebra | 20 |
| III | Coordinate Geometry | 06 |
| IV | Geometry | 15 |
| V | Trigonometry | 12 |
| VI | Mensuration | 10 |
| VII | Statistics & Probability | 11 |
| | Total | 80 |

## Unit I NUMBER SYSTEMS

**1. *Real Numbers***

Fundamental Theorem of Arithmetic - statements after reviewing work done earlier and after illustrating and motivating through examples, Proofs of irrationality of $\sqrt{2}$, $\sqrt{3}$, $\sqrt{3}$ Decimal representation of rational numbers interms of terminating/non-terminating recurring decimals.

## Unit II ALGEBRA

**1. *Polynomials***

Zeros of a polynomial. Relationship between zeros and coefficients of quadratic polynomials.

**2. *Pair of Linear Equations in Two Variables***

Pair of linear equations in two variables and graphical method of their solution, consistency/inconsistency.

Algebraic conditions for number of solutions. Solution of a pair of linear equations in two variables algebraically - by substitution, by elimination. Simple situational problems. Simple problems on equations reducible to linear equations.

**3. *Quadratic Equations***

Standard form of a quadratic equation $ax^2 + bx + c = 0$, $(a \neq 0)$. Solutions of quadratic equations (only real roots) by factorization, and by using quadratic formula. Relationship between discriminant and nature of roots.

**4. *Arithmetic Progressions***

Motivation for studying Arithmetic Progression Derivation of the $n$th term and sum of the first $n$ terms of A.P.

## Unit III COORDINATE GEOMETRY

**1. *Lines (In two-dimensions)***

**Review** : Concepts of coordinate geometry, graphs of linear equations. Distance formula. Section formula (internal division).

## Unit IV GEOMETRY

### 1. *Triangles*

Definitions, examples, counter examples of similar triangles.

I. (Prove) If a line is drawn parallel to one side of a triangle to intersect the other two sides at distinct points, then the other two sides are divided in the same ratio.

II. (Motivate) If a line divides two sides of a triangle in the same ratio, then the line is parallel to the third side.

III. (Motivate) If in two triangles, the corresponding angles are equal, then their corresponding sides are proportional and the triangles are similar.

IV. (Motivate) If the corresponding sides of two triangles are proportional, then their corresponding angles are equal and the two triangles are similar.

V. (Motivate) If one angle of a triangle is equal to one angle of another triangle and the sides including these angles are proportional, then two triangles are similar.

VI. (Motivate) If a perpendicular is drawn from the vertex of the right angle of a right angled triangle to the hypotenuse, then the triangles on each side of the perpendicular are similar to the whole triangle and to each other.

VIII. (Prove) In a right angled triangle, the square on the hypotenuse is equal to the sum of the squares on the other two sides.

### 2. *Circles*

Tangents to a circle at point of contact.

I. (Prove) The tangent at any point of a circle is perpendicular to the radius through the point of contact.

II. (Prove) The lengths of tangents drawn from an external point to circle are equal.

### 3. *Constructions*

I. Division of a line segment in a given ratio (internally).

II. Tangent to a circle from a point outside it.

## Unit V TRIGONOMETRY

### 1. *Introduction to Trigonometry*

Trigonometric ratios of an acute angle of a right angled triangle. Proof of their existence (well-defined). Values (with proofs) of the trigonometric ratios of 30°, 45° and 60°. Relationships between the ratios.

### 2. *Trigonometric Identities*

Proofs and applications of the identity $\sin^2 A + \cos^2 A = 1$. Only simple identities to be given.

### 3. *Heights and Distances : Angle of Elevation, Angle of Depression*

Simple problems on heights and distances. Problems should not involve more than two right triangles. Angles of elevation/depression should be only 30°, 45°, 60°.

## Unit VI MENSURATION

**1. *Areas Related to Circles***

Motivate the area of a circle; area of sectors and segments of a circle. Problems based on areas and perimeter /circumference of the above said plane figures. (In calculating area of segment of a circle, problems should be restricted to central angle of 60°, 90° only. Plane figures involving triangles, simple quadrilaterals and circle should be taken.)

**2. *Surface Areas and Volumes***

I. Surface areas and volumes of combinations of any two of the following: cubes, cuboids, spheres, hemispheres and right circular cylinders/cones.

II. Problems involving converting one type of metallic solid into another and other mixed problems. (Problems with combination of not more than two different solids be taken.)

## Unit VII STATISTICS AND PROBABILITY

**1. *Statistics***

Mean, median and mode of grouped data (bimodal situation to be avoided).

**2. *Probability***

Classical definition of probability. Simple problems on finding the probability of an event.

# QUESTION PAPER DESIGN

## Mathematics (Basic)

Marks : 80 Duration : 3 Hours

| S. N. | Typology of Questions | Total Marks | % Weightage (approx.) |
|---|---|---|---|
| 1 | **Remembering:** Exhibit memory of previously learned material by recalling facts, terms, basic concepts, and answers.<br>**Understanding:** Demonstrate understanding of facts and ideas by organizing, comparing, translating, interpreting, giving descriptions, and stating main ideas. | 60 | 75 |
| 2 | **Applying:** Solve problems to new situations by applying acquired knowledge, facts, techniques and rules in a different way. | 12 | 15 |
| 3 | **Analysing :** Examine and break information into parts by identifying motives or causes. Make inferences and find evidence to support generalizations<br>**Evaluating :** Present and defend opinions by making judgments about information, validity of ideas, or quality of work based on a set of criteria.<br>**Creating :** Compile information together in a different way by combining elements in a new pattern or proposing alternative solutions. | 8 | 10 |
| | **Total** | **80** | **100** |

| **INTERNAL ASSESSMENT** | **20 MARKS** |
|---|---|
| Pen Paper Test and Multiple Assessment (5+5) | 10 Marks |
| Portfolio | 05 Marks |
| Lab Practical (Lab activities to be done from the prescribed books) | 05 Marks |

# Qualifying ROUND

## Chapter 1 Real Numbers

### Multiple Choice Questions (1 mark each)

**1.** The greatest number which on dividing 1659 and 2036 leaves remainders 8 and 4, respectively is

(a) 124 (b) 129 (c) 127 (d) 305

**2.** 144 L of liquid $P$ and 216 L of liquid $Q$ are to be packed in containers of the same size. The minimum number of containers required are

(a) 6 (b) 5 (c) 10 (d) 15

**3.** Three numbers are in the ratio 3 : 4 : 5 and their LCM is 1200. Then, their HCF is

(a) 40 (b) 60 (c) 20 (d) 120

**4.** For some integer $q$, every odd integer is of the form

(a) $q$ (b) $q+1$ (c) $2q$ (d) $2q+1$

**5.** Two positive integers $p$ and $q$ can be expressed as $p = ab^2$ and $q = a^2b$, $a$ and $b$ are prime numbers. The LCM of $p$ and $q$ is

(a) $ab$ (b) $a^2b^2$ (c) $a^3b$ (d) $ab^3$

### Short Answer Type (I) Questions (2 marks each)

**6.** Find the number nearest to 110000 but greater than 100000 which is exactly divisible by each of 8, 15 and 21.

**7.** Find the prime factorisation of 2475.

**8.** Explain why $7 \times 11 \times 13 + 13$ is a composite number?

**9.** Can the number $8^n$, $n$ being a natural number, end with the digit 0? Give reason.

**10.** There is a circular path around a sports field. Sonia takes 18 min to drive one round of the field, while Ravi takes 12 min for the same. Suppose they both start at the same point and at the same time and go in the same direction. After how many minutes will they meet again at the starting point?

**11.** Three sets of English, Hindi and Mathematics books have to be stacked in such a way that all the books are stored topicwise and the height of each stack is same. The number of English books is 96, the number of Hindi books is 240 and the number of Mathematics books is 336. Assuming that the books are of same thickness. Determine the number of stacks of English, Hindi and Mathematics books.

### Short Answer Type (II) Questions (3 marks each)

**12.** Two tankers contain 850 L and 680 L of petrol, respectively. Find the maximum capacity of a container which can measure the petrol of either tanker an exact number of times.

**13.** If $n$ is an odd integer, then show that $n^2 - 1$ is divisible by 8.

### Long Answer Type Questions (5 marks each)

**14.** Prove that $7 - 5\sqrt{3}$ is an irrational number.

**15.** Find the largest number that divides 1251, 9377 and 15628 leaving remainders 1, 2 and 3, respectively.

### Answers

| | | | | |
|---|---|---|---|---|
| **1.** (c) | **2.** (b) | **3.** (c) | **4.** (d) | **5.** (b) |
| **6.** 109200 | **7.** $3^2 \times 5^2 \times 11$ | **9.** No | **10.** 36 | |
| **11.** 48 | **12.** 170 L | **15.** 625 | | |

***Detailed solutions are given on page 181.***

# Chapter 2 **Polynomials**

### Multiple Choice Questions (1 mark each)

**1.** Zeroes of a polynomial $p(y)$ is......... of the point, where the graph intersects the $Y$-axis.

(a) abscissa (b) ordinate
(c) Both (a) and (b) (d) None of these

**2.** If one zero of the polynomial $x^2 - 8x + k = 0$ is the HCF of (6, 12), then the value of $k$ is

(a) 6 (b) 12 (c) 24 (d) None of these

**3.** If $a$ and $b$ are the zeroes of the polynomial $px^2 - 5x + q$, then the values of $p$ and $q$, if $a + b = ab = 10$, are

(a) 5 and 1/2 (b) 5 and 2 (c) 1/2 and 5 (d) 10 and 1

**4.** If one root of the polynomial $p(x) = 5x^2 + 13x + k$ is reciprocal of the other, then the value of $k$ is

(a) 3 (b) 1 (c) 5 (d) 4

**5.** If 2 is a zero of polynomial $p(x) = ax^2 - 3(a+2) - 4$, then the value of $a$ is

(a) 10 (b) 9 (c) 12 (d) 8

### Short Answer Type (I) Questions (2 marks each)

**6.** If one of the zeroes of the quadratic polynomial $f(x) = 4x^2 - 8kx - 9$ is equal in magnitude but opposite in sign of the other, then find the value of $k$.

**7.** If sum and product of zeroes are 8 and –3 respectively, then find the quadratic polynomial.

**8.** If $\alpha$ and $\beta$ are the zeroes of the quadratic polynomial $x^2+5x-10$, then find the values of $\alpha^2+\beta^2$.

**9.** Find the zeroes of the quadratic polynomial $7y^2-\frac{11}{3}y-\frac{2}{3}$ and verify the relationship between the zeroes and their coefficients.

**10.** If one zero of the polynomial $(a^2+4)x^2+9x+4a$ is the reciprocal of the other, then find the value of $a$.

## Short Answer Type (II) Questions (3 marks each)

**11.** If $\alpha$ and $\beta$ are zeroes of the polynomial $f(x)=x^2-5x+k$ such that $\alpha-\beta=1$, then find the value of $k$.

**12.** If the zeroes of the polynomial $ax^2+bx+b=0$ are in the ratio $m:n$, then find the value of $\sqrt{\frac{m}{n}}+\sqrt{\frac{n}{m}}$.

## Long Answer Type Questions (5 marks each)

**13.** If $\alpha$ and $\beta$ are the zeroes of the polynomials $ax^2+bx+c$, then find the other polynomial whose zeroes are $\frac{\alpha^2}{\beta}$ and $\frac{\beta^2}{\alpha}$.

**14.** If $\alpha$ and $\beta$ are the zeroes of the quadratic polynomial $f(x)=kx^2+4x+4$ such that $\alpha^2+\beta^2=24$, find the values of $k$.

**15.** If $\alpha$ and $\beta$ are the zeroes of a quadratic polynomial $3x^2-6x+4$, find the value of

$$\left(\frac{\alpha}{\beta}+\frac{\beta}{\alpha}\right)+2\left(\frac{1}{\alpha}+\frac{1}{\beta}\right)+3\alpha\beta.$$

## Answers

| | | | | |
|---|---|---|---|---|
| **1.** (b) | **2.** (b) | **3.** (c) | **4.** (c) | **5.** (a) |
| **6.** $k=0$ | **7.** $x^2-8x-3$ | **8.** 45 | **9.** $\frac{2}{3}$ and $\frac{-1}{7}$ | **10.** 2 |
| **11.** $k=6$ | **12.** $-\sqrt{\frac{b}{a}}$ | **13.** $x^2+\frac{b}{a^2c}(b^2-3ac)x+\frac{c}{a}$ | **14.** $k=\frac{2}{3}$ and $k=-1$ | **15.** 8 |

*Detailed solutions are given on page 182.*

# Chapter 3 Pair of Linear Equations in Two Variables

## Multiple Choice Questions
(1 mark each)

**1.** The pair of linear equations $x+2y=5$ and $3x+12y=10$ has

(a) unique solution (b) no solution
(c) more than two solutions (d) infinitely many solutions

**2.** Which of the following pairs has a unique solution?

(a) $2x + y = 3$ and $x + 2y = 5$ (b) $2x + 4y = 6$ and $4x + 8y = 12$
(c) $4x + 8y = 14$ and $8x + 16y - 9 = 0$ (d) $x + 5y - 3 = 0$ and $3x + 15y - 9 = 0$

**3.** The pair of equations $x=-2$ and $x=3$ has

(a) unique solution (b) infinitely many solutions
(c) no solution (d) two solutions

**4.** If a pair of linear equations is inconsistent, then the lines representing them will be

(a) parallel (b) coincident
(c) intersecting or coincident (d) intersecting

**5.** A man rows upstream at 7 km/h and downstream at 10 km/h. Then, the man's speed in still water and the rate of current respectively, are

(a) 6.5 km/h and 3.5 km/h (b) 8.5 km/h and 1.5 km/h
(c) 6 km/h and 4 km/h (d) 7 km/h and 3 km/h

## Short Answer Type (I) Questions
(2 marks each)

**6.** Write the nature of the graph of the equations $6x-2y+9=0$ and $3x-y+12=0$.

**7.** If $47x+31y=18$ and $31x+47y=60$, then find the value of $x+y$.

**8.** 7 audio cassettes and 3 video cassettes cost ₹ 1110. 5 audio cassettes and 4 video cassettes cost ₹ 1350. Find the cost of an audio cassette and a video cassette.

**9.** For all real values of $c$, the pair of equations $x-2y=8$, $5x+10y=c$ has a unique solution. Justify whether it is true or false.

**10.** Find the values of $\alpha$ and $\beta$ for which the following system of linear equations has infinite number of solutions.

$$2x+3y=7 \text{ and } 2\alpha x+(\alpha+\beta)y=28.$$

**11.** In the given figure, $ABCD$ is a rectangle. Find the values of $x$ and $y$.

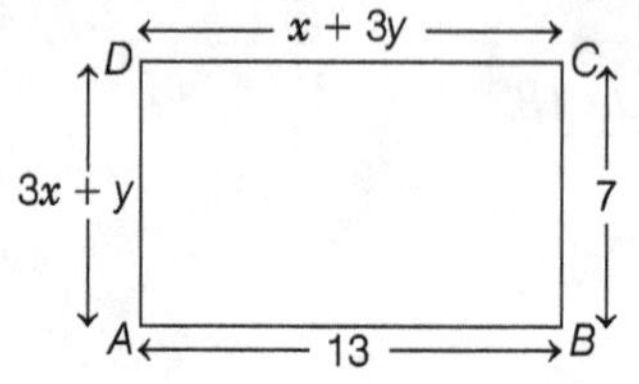

## Short Answer Type (II) Questions (3 marks each)

**12.** Solve the following system of equations for $x$ and $y$ by using the method of elimination

$$0.4x+0.3y=1.7 \text{ and } 0.7x-0.2y=0.8$$

**13.** A lending library has a fixed charge for the first three days and an additional charge for each day thereafter and Saritha paid ₹ 27 for a book kept for seven days, while Susy paid ₹ 21 for the book she kept for five days. Find the fixed charge and the charge for each extra day.

**14.** The sum of the digits of a two-digit number is 12. The number obtained by interchanging its digits exceeds the given number by 18. Find the number.

## Long Answer Type Questions (5 marks each)

**15.** The numerator of a fraction is 4 less than the denominator. If the numerator is decreased by 2 and the denominator is increased by 1, then the denominator is eight times the numerator. Find the fraction.

**16.** Draw the graph of the pair of equations $2x+y=4$ and $2x-y=4$. Write the vertices of the triangle formed by these lines and the $Y$-axis. Find the area of this triangle.

### Answers

| | | | | |
|---|---|---|---|---|
| **1.** (a) | **2.** (a) | **3.** (c) | **4.** (a) | **5.** (b) |
| **6.** Parallel | **7.** $x+y=1$ | | | |
| **8.** The cost of one audio and one video cassette are ₹ 30 and ₹ 300, respectively. | | | | |
| **9.** True | **10.** $\alpha=4$ and $\beta=8$ | **11.** $x=1$ and $y=4$ | | **12.** $x=2$ and $y=3$ |
| **13.** Fixed charge for first three days = ₹ 15 and extra charge for each day = ₹ 3. | | | | |
| **14.** 57 | **15.** $\frac{3}{7}$ | **16.** 8 sq units | | |

*Detailed solutions are given on page 184.*

# Chapter 4 Quadratic Equations

## Multiple Choice Questions (1 mark each)

**1.** If the equation $x^2-bx+1=0$ does not possess real roots, then

(a) $-3<b<3$ (b) $-2<b<2$ (c) $b>2$ (d) $b<-2$

**2.** If $p$ and $q$ are the roots of the equation $x^2-px+q=0$, then the value of $p$ and $q$

(a) $p=1$ and $q=0$ (b) $p=0$ and $q=1$ (c) $p=-2$ and $q=0$ (d) $p=-2$ and $q=1$

**3.** The equation $k^2x^2+kx+1=0$ has

(a) one real root (b) two real roots (c) no real roots (d) None of these

**4.** If $ax^2+bx+c=0$ has equal roots, then value of $c$ is

(a) $\frac{4a}{b}$ (b) $\frac{b^2}{4a}$ (c) $\frac{a^2}{4a}$ (d) $\frac{4b^2}{a}$

## Short Answer Type (I) Questions (2 marks each)

**5.** If $x=2$ is a root of the equation $kx^2+2x-3=0$, then find the value of $k$.

**6.** Find the roots of the equation $9x^2-3x-2=0$.

**7.** Find the roots of the quadratic equation $2x^2-7x+3=0$ by using the quadratic formula.

**8.** Find the roots of the equation $\sqrt{3}x^2+10x+7\sqrt{3}=0$.

## Short Answer Type (II) Questions (3 marks each)

**9.** Solve the following equation for $x$, $\frac{x+1}{x-1}+\frac{x-2}{x+2}=3$.

**10.** $\frac{3}{x+1}+\frac{4}{x-1}=\frac{29}{4x-1}$, $x\neq 1,-1,\frac{1}{4}$

**11.** Solve the quadratic equation $x^2+\left(\frac{a}{a+b}+\frac{a+b}{a}\right)x+1=0$ by factorisation method.

## Long Answer Type Question (5 marks each)

**12.** Find the value of $k$ for which the quadratic equation $(3k+1)x^2+2(k+1)x+1=0$, has equal roots . Also find these roots.

### Answers

| | | | | |
|---|---|---|---|---|
| **1.** (b) | **2.** (a) | **3.** (c) | **4.** (b) | **5.** $k=-\frac{1}{4}$ |
| **6.** $x=-\frac{1}{3}$ and $x=\frac{2}{3}$ | | **7.** $3, \frac{1}{2}$ | **8.** $x=-\frac{7}{\sqrt{3}}, -\sqrt{3}$ | |
| **9.** $x=-5$ and $x=2$ | | **10.** $x=4$ and $x=-7$ | | |
| **11.** $x=-\frac{a}{a+b}$ or $x=-\frac{a+b}{a}$ | | **12.** For $k=0$, roots are $-1$ and $-1$ and for $k=1$, roots are $-\frac{1}{2}$ and $-\frac{1}{2}$ | | |

*Detailed solutions are given on page 186.*

# Chapter 5 **Arithmetic Progression (AP)**

## Multiple Choice Questions (1 mark each)

**1.** In an AP, if $d=-3$, $n=8$, $a_n=5$, then $a$ is

(a) 20 (b) 30 (c) 26 (d) 24

**2.** The number of terms in the AP 7, 11, 15, ..., 139 is

(a) 34 (b) 36 (c) 31 (d) 35

**3.** The sum of first 30 positive integers divisible by 6 is

(a) 2860 (b) 2790 (c) 3069 (d) 3142

**4.** Which term of the AP 20, 17, 14, ... is first negative term?
(a) 8th (b) 6th (c) 9th (d) 7th

## Short Answer Type (I) Questions
(2 marks each)

**5.** Find the common difference of an AP sequence $a_n = 4n + 5$.

**6.** Write an AP having 4 as the first term and $-3$ as the common difference.

**7.** Which term of the AP 3,15, 27, 39, ... will be 120 more than its 21st term?

**8.** If four numbers in AP are such that their sum is 50 and the greatest number is 4 times the least, then find the numbers.

**9.** Find the sum of all natural numbers between 200 and 1502 which are exactly divisible by 3.

**10.** Ramkali saved ₹ 5 in the first week of a year and then increased her weekly savings by ₹ 1.75. If in the $n$th week, her weekly saving become ₹ 20.75, then find the value of $n$.

## Short Answer Type (II) Questions
(3 marks each)

**11.** How many terms of the AP $-6, -\frac{11}{2}, -5, \ldots$ are needed to give the sum $-25$?

**12.** Find the sum of $n$ terms of the sequence $\{a_n\}$, where $a_n = 5 - 6n,\ n \in N$.

## Long Answer Type Questions
(5 marks each)

**13.** The 8th term of an AP is zero. Prove that its 38th term is triple its 18th term.

**14.** The sum of $n$, $2n$, $3n$ terms of an AP are $S_1, S_2, S_3$, respectively.
Prove that $S_3 = 3(S_2 - S_1)$.

### Answers

| | | | | |
|---|---|---|---|---|
| **1.** (c) | **2.** (a) | **3.** (b) | **4.** (a) | **5.** 4 |
| **6.** 4, 1, −2, −5, ... | **7.** 31st term | **8.** 5, 10, 15, 20 | **9.** 369117 | **10.** $n = 10$ |
| **11.** 5 or 20 | **12.** $n(2 - 3n)$ | | | |

*Detailed solutions are given on page 187.*

# Chapter 6 Triangles

## Multiple Choice Questions
(1 mark each)

**1.** In the given figure, $AB \| DC$ and diagonals $AC$ and $BD$ intersect at $O$. If $AO = (3x - 1)$ cm, $BO = (2x + 1)$ cm, $OC = (5x - 3)$ cm and $OD = (6x - 5)$ cm, then find the value of $x$.

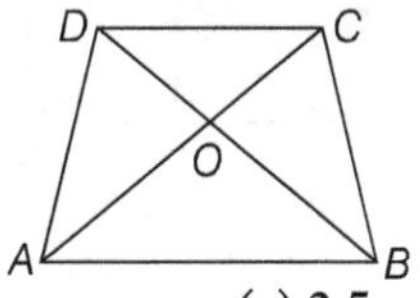


(a) 2 (b) 3 (c) 2.5 (d) 3.5

**2.** If $\Delta ABC$ and $\Delta DEF$ are similar such that $3AB = DE$ and $BC = 6$ cm, then $EF$ is

(a) 12 cm (b) 6 cm (c) 15 cm (d) 18 cm

**3.** Two poles of height 6 m and 11 m stand vertically upright on a plane ground. If the distance between their foot is 12 m, the distance between their tops is

(a) 12 m (b) 14 m (c) 13 m (d) 11 m

**4.** If $E$ is a point on side $CA$ of an equilateral $\Delta ABC$ such that $BE \perp CA$, then find the value of $AB^2 + BC^2 + CA^2$.

(a) $3BE^2$ (b) $BE^2$ (c) $4BE^2$ (d) $6BE^2$

**5.** $\Delta ABC$ is a right triangle, right angled at $A$ and $AD \perp BC$. If $AB = c$ and $AC = b$, then $AD$ is equal to

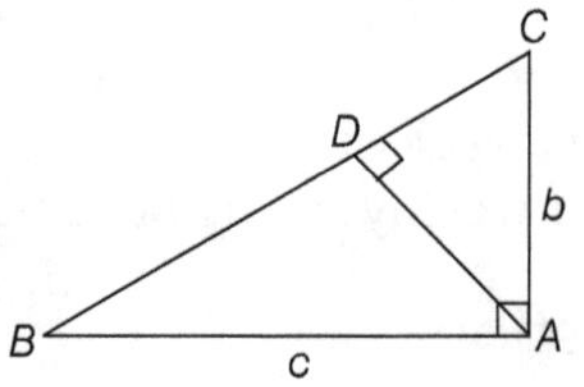


(a) $\frac{bc}{\sqrt{b^2 + c^2}}$ (b) $\frac{bc}{b^2 + c^2}$ (c) $\frac{b^2c}{\sqrt{b^2 + c^2}}$ (d) None of these

## Short Answer Type (I) Questions

(2 marks each)

**6.** In a $\Delta ABC$, it is given that $AB = \sqrt{3}$ cm, $AC = 2$ cm and $AD$ is the bisector of $\angle A$. Then, find $BD : DC$.

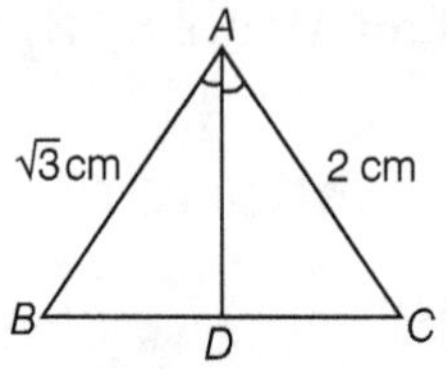


**7.** In the given figure, $PQ \parallel BC$, find $AQ$.

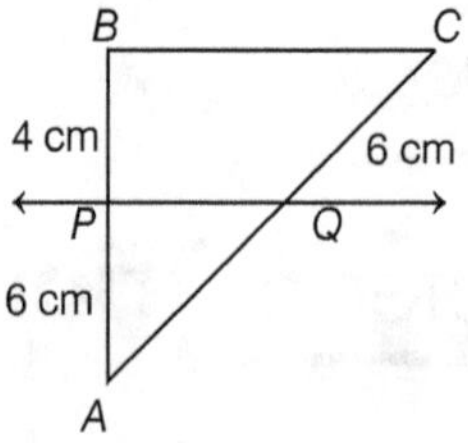


**8.** In the given figure, $DE \parallel AC$ and $DC \parallel AP$. Prove that $\frac{BE}{EC} = \frac{BC}{CP}$.

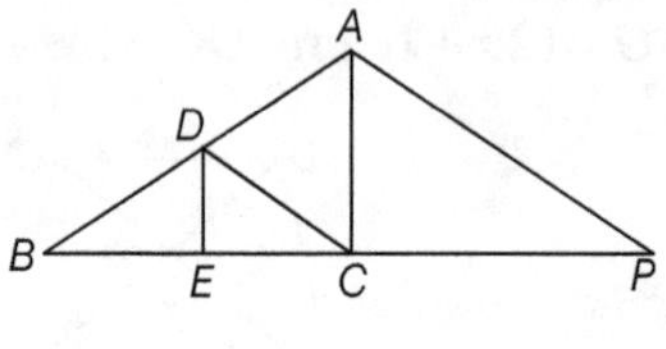

**9.** In given figure, $\Delta ODC \sim \Delta OBA$, $\angle BOC = 125°$ and $\angle CDO = 70°$.
Find $\angle DOC$, $\angle DCO$ and $\angle OAB$.

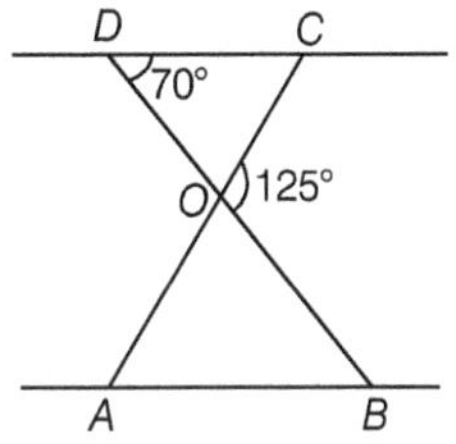


**10.** The hypotenuse of a right angled triangle is 6 m more than twice of the shortest side. If 3rd side is 2 m less than the hypotenuse, find the sides of the triangle.

## Short Answer Type (II) Questions (3 marks each)

**11.** In the given figure, $ACB$ is a right angled triangle, right angled at $C$ and $DE \perp AB$. Prove that $\Delta ACB \sim \Delta AED$ and hence find the lengths of $DE$ and $AE$.

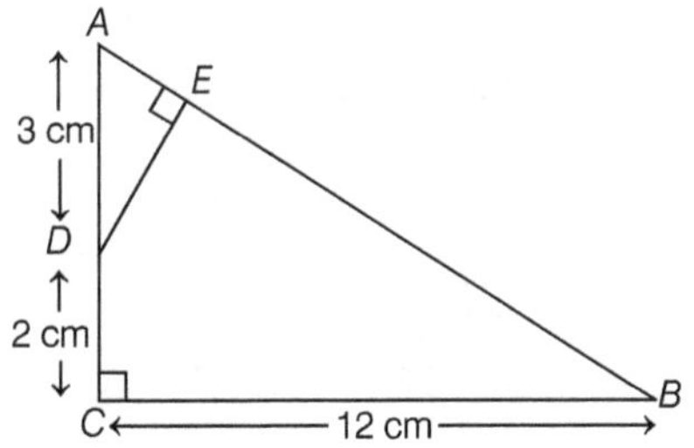


**12.** In the given figure, $\angle ABC = \angle AED$.

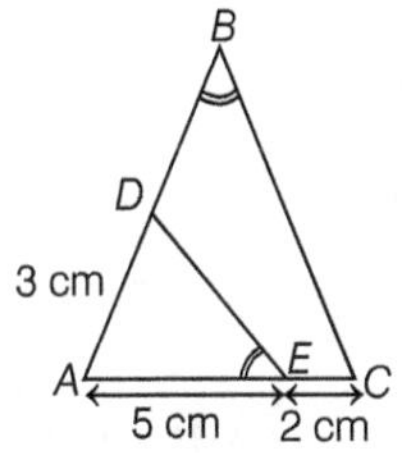


(i) Explain, why $\Delta ABC$ and $\Delta AED$ are similar?
(ii) Given, $AD$ = 3 cm, $AE$ = 5 cm and $EC$ = 2cm. Calculate $BD$.

**13.** In $\Delta PQR$, $D$ and $S$ are points on the sides $PQ$ and $PR$ respectively, such that $DS \parallel QR$. If $PD = 4x - 3$, $PS = 8x - 7$, $QD = 3x - 1$ and $RS = 5x - 3$, then find the value of $x$.

**14.** In the given figure, $D$ and $E$ are two points on $AB$ such that $AD = BE$. If $DP \parallel BC$ and $EQ \parallel AC$, then prove that $PQ \parallel AB$.

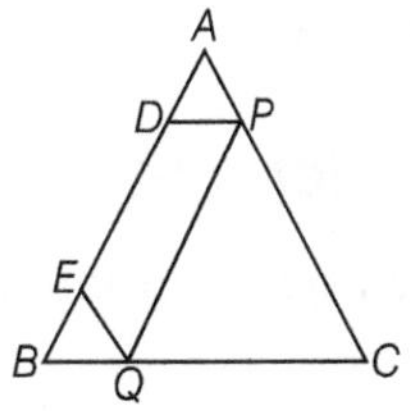

## Long Answer Type Questions (5 marks each)

**15.** In the given figure, $AB = 8$ cm, $BC = 3$ cm and $BE$ is parallel to $CD$.

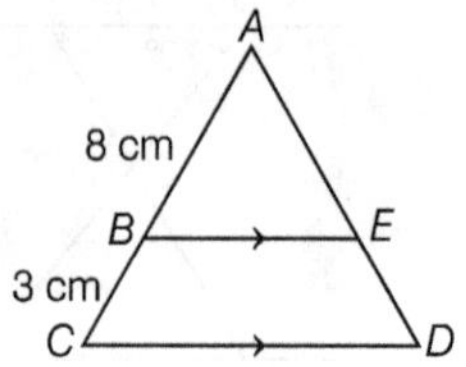


(i) Find $\frac{BE}{CD}$.

(ii) What is the special name given to the quadrilateral $BCDE$?

**16.** $CD$ and $GH$ are respectively the bisectors of $\angle ACB$ and $\angle EGF$ such that $D$ and $H$ lie on sides $AB$ and $FE$ of $\Delta ABC$ and $\Delta EFG$, respectively. If $\Delta ABC \sim \Delta FEG$, show that

(i) $\frac{CD}{GH} = \frac{AC}{FG}$ (ii) $\Delta DCB \sim \Delta HGE$ (iii) $\Delta DCA \sim \Delta HGF$.

**17.** Sides $AB$ and $AC$ and median $AD$ of $\Delta ABC$ are respectively proportional to sides $PQ$ and $PR$ and median $PM$ of another $\Delta PQR$. Show that $\Delta ABC \sim \Delta PQR$.

## Answers

| | | | | |
|---|---|---|---|---|
| **1.** (a) | **2.** (d) | **3.** (c) | **4.** (c) | **5.** (a) |
| **6.** $\sqrt{3}:2$ | **7.** 9 cm | **9.** $\angle DOC = \angle DCO = \angle OAB = 55°$ | | **10.** 26 m, 10 m, 24 m |
| **11.** $DE = \frac{36}{13}$ cm and $AE = \frac{15}{13}$ cm | | **12.** (ii) $BD = 8\frac{2}{3}$ cm | | **13.** $x = 1$ |
| **15.** (i) $\frac{8}{11}$ (ii) Trapezium | | | | |

*Detailed solutions are given on page 189.*

# Chapter 7 **Coordinate Geometry**

## Multiple Choice Questions (1 mark each)

**1.** If distance between the points (2, 3) and ($x$, 0) is 3, then $x$ is equal to

(a) 2 (b) 3 (c) –2 (d) –3

**2.** If $A(-1, 2)$, $B(0, 0)$ and $C(2, 1)$ are the vertices of a $\Delta ABC$, then the length of median through the vertex $A$ is

(a) 5 units (b) 10 units (c) $\frac{5}{2}$ units (d) $\frac{3}{2}$ units

## Short Answer Type (I) Questions (2 marks each)

**3.** If $A$ is a point on $Y$-axis, whose ordinate is 4 and coordinates of point $B$ are (–3, 1), then find the distance $AB$.

**4.** If $\left(3, \frac{3}{4}\right)$ is the mid-point of the line segment joining the points $(k, 0)$ and $\left(7, \frac{3}{2}\right)$, then find the value of $k$.

**5.** The coordinates of one end point of a diameter of a circle are $(4, -1)$ and the coordinates of the centre of the circle are $(1, -3)$. Find the coordinates of the other end of the diameter.

**6.** If the point $B(-2, 4)$ divides internally the line segment joining the points $A(2, 5)$ and $C(x, y)$ in the ratio of 3 : 4, find the value of $x^2 + y^2$.

**7.** Find a relation between $x$ and $y$, such that the point $(x, y)$ is equidistant from the points $(3, 6)$ and $(-3, 4)$.

**8.** Find the ratio in which the line segment joining $A(1, -5)$ and $B(-4, 5)$ is divided by the $X$-axis.

**9.** Point $P$ divides the line segment joining the points $A(-1, 3)$ and $B(9, 8)$ such that $\frac{AP}{BP} = \frac{k}{1}$. If the $P$ lies on the line $x - y + 2 = 0$, find the value of $k$.

## Short Answer Type (II) Questions (3 marks each)

**10.** Show that the points (3, 2), (0, 5), (–3, 2) and (0, –1) are the vertices of a square.

**11.** If $(a, b)$ is the mid-point of the line segment joining the points $A(10, -6)$ and $B(k, 4)$ and $a - 2b = 18$, then find the value of $k$ and the distance $AB$.

**12.** A point $A$ is at a distance of $\sqrt{10}$ units from the point (4, 3). Find the coordinates of point $A$, if its ordinate is twice its abscissa.

## Long Answer Type Questions (5 marks each)

**13.** Find the coordinates of the points of trisection of the line segment joining $(-2, -3)$ and $(4, -1)$.

**14.** The two opposite vertices of a square are $(-1, 2)$ and $(3, 2)$. Find the coordinates of the other two vertices.

### Answers

| | | | | |
|---|---|---|---|---|
| **1.** (a) | **2.** (c) | **3.** $3\sqrt{2}$ units | **4.** $k = -1$ | **5.** $(-2, -5)$ |
| **6.** $\frac{548}{3}$ | **7.** $3x + y - 5 = 0$ | **8.** 1:1 | **9.** $\frac{2}{3}$ | **11.** $k = 22$ and $AB = 2\sqrt{61}$ units |
| **12.** (3, 6) and (1, 2) | | **13.** $\left(2, -\frac{5}{3}\right)$ and $\left(0, -\frac{7}{3}\right)$ | | **14.** (1, 0) and (1, 4) |

*Detailed solutions are given on page 192.*

# Chapter 8 **Introduction to Trigonometry**

## Multiple Choice Questions (1 mark each)

**1.** If $\sin\theta + \sin^2\theta = 1$, then $\cos^2\theta + \cos^4\theta$ is equal to

(a) $-1$ (b) 1 (c) 0 (d) $\frac{1}{2}$

**2.** If $\sin\theta = \frac{1}{2}$ and $\theta$ is an acute angle, then $(3\cos\theta - 4\cos^3\theta)$ is equal to

(a) 0 (b) $\frac{1}{2}$ (c) $\frac{1}{6}$ (d) $-1$

3. If $\tan\theta = \frac{12}{5}$, then the value of $\frac{1+\cos\theta}{1-\cos\theta}$ is

(a) $\frac{4}{9}$ (b) $\frac{9}{4}$ (c) 25 (d) $\frac{169}{14}$

4. The value of $\frac{\sin 30^\circ - \sin 90^\circ + 2\cos 0^\circ}{\tan 30^\circ \tan 60^\circ}$ is

(a) $\frac{3}{2}$ (b) $\frac{1}{2}$ (c) $\frac{-3}{2}$ (d) $\frac{-1}{2}$

## Short Answer Type (I) Questions

(2 marks each)

5. If $x = 30^\circ$, verify that $\sin 3x = 3\sin x - 4\sin^3 x$.

6. If $\cos 2x = \cos 60^\circ \cos 30^\circ + \sin 60^\circ \sin 30^\circ$, then find the value of $x$.

7. If $a\cos\theta + b\sin\theta = t$ and $a\sin\theta - b\cos\theta = s$, then prove that $a^2 + b^2 = s^2 + t^2$.

8. If $\cos\theta\left(\frac{1}{1-\sin\theta} - \frac{1}{1+\sin\theta}\right)$ can be written in the form $k\tan\theta$, then find the value of $k$.

9. If $\sin A = \frac{3}{4}$, then calculate $\cos A$ and $\tan A$.

10. Prove that $4(\sin^4 30^\circ + \cos^4 60^\circ) - 3(\cos^2 45^\circ - \sin^2 90^\circ) = 2$.

11. Prove that $\left(\frac{1+\sin\theta-\cos\theta}{1+\sin\theta+\cos\theta}\right)^2 = \frac{1-\cos\theta}{1+\cos\theta}$.

## Short Answer Type (II) Questions

(3 marks each)

12. Prove that $2\sec^2\theta - \sec^4\theta - 2\operatorname{cosec}^2\theta + \operatorname{cosec}^4\theta = \cot^4\theta - \tan^4\theta$.

13. If $\tan^2\theta = 1 - t^2$, prove that $\sec\theta + \tan^3\theta \operatorname{cosec}\theta = (2 - t^2)^{3/2}$.

14. Show that $\frac{2 - \operatorname{cosec}^2 A}{\operatorname{cosec}^2 A + 2\cot A} = \frac{\sin A - \cos A}{\sin A + \cos A}$.

15. Find acute angles $A$ and $B$, if $\sin(A + 2B) = \frac{\sqrt{3}}{2}$ and $\cos(A + 4B) = 0$, $A > B$.

## Long Answer Type Questions

(5 marks each)

16. Prove that $\sec^4\theta(1 - \sin^4\theta) - 2\tan^2\theta = 1$

17. If $\operatorname{cosec}\theta - \sin\theta = a$ and $\sec\theta - \cos\theta = b$, then prove that $a^2b^2(a^2 + b^2 + 3) = 1$.

18. Prove that $\frac{\cot^2 A(\sec A - 1)}{1+\sin A} = \frac{1-\sin A}{\cos A(1+\cos A)}$.

## Answers

| | | | | |
|---|---|---|---|---|
| **1.** (b) | **2.** (a) | **3.** (b) | **4.** (a) | **6.** $x = 15°$ |
| **8.** $k = 2$ | **9.** $\cos A = \frac{\sqrt{7}}{4}$ and $\tan A = \frac{3}{\sqrt{7}}$ | | **15.** $A = 30°$ and $B = 15°$ | |

*Detailed solutions are given on page 195.*

# Chapter 9 Some Applications of Trigonometry

## Multiple Choice Questions (1 mark each)

**1.** The height of a tower is $\frac{100}{\sqrt{3}}$ m. The angle of elevation of its top from a point 100 m away from its foot is

(a) 60° (b) 30°
(c) 75° (d) 45°

**2.** From the ground, the angle of elevation of a clock tower is 30°. On moving 20 m nearer, the angle of elevation increases to 60° the height of the clock tower is

(a) $\frac{10}{\sqrt{3}}$ m (b) $10\sqrt{3}$ m
(c) $20\sqrt{3}$ m (d) 10 m

**3.** The angle of depression from the top of a tower to a point 30 m from its base is 45°. Then, the height of the tower is

(a) 20 m (b) 30 m
(c) 40 m (d) 15 m

## Short Answer Type (I) Questions (2 marks each)

**4.** The angle of depression from the top of a tower 40 m high, to a point on the ground is 30°. Find the distance of the point from the top of the tower.

**5.** Find the length of the shadow on the ground of a pole of height 18 m when the angle of elevation $\theta$ of the sun is such that $\tan\theta = \frac{6}{7}$.

**6.** If two towers of heights $x$ m and $y$ m subtend angles of 45° and 60°, respectively at the centre of a line joining their feet, then find the ratio of $(x + y) : y$.

**7.** The angle of elevation of the top of a hill from the foot of a tower is 60° and the angle of elevation of the top of the tower from the foot of the hill is 30°. If the tower is 65 m high, how high is the hill?

**8.** At sometime of the day, the length of the shadow of a tower is equal to its height. Then, find the sun's altitude at that time.

**9.** A statue 2.4 m tall stands on the top of pedestal. From a point on the ground, the angle of elevation of the top of the statue is 60° and from the same point the angle of elevation of the top of the pedestal is 45°. Find the height of the pedestal.

## Short Answer Type (II) Questions

(3 marks each)

**10.** From the top of a tower $h$ m high, the angle of depression of two objects which are in line with the foot of the tower, are $\alpha$ and $\beta (\beta > \alpha)$. Show that the distance between the two objects is $h(\cot\alpha - \cot\beta)$.

**11.** From an aeroplane vertically above a straight horizontal road, the angles of depression of two consecutive mile stones on opposite sides of the aeroplane are observed to be $\alpha$ and $\beta$. Show that the height in miles of aeroplane above the road is given by $\dfrac{\tan\alpha\tan\beta}{\tan\alpha + \tan\beta}$.

**12.** Two pillars of equal height are on either sides of a road, which is 100 m wide. The angles of the top of the pillars are 60° and 30° at a point on the road between the pillars. Find the position of the point between the pillars. Also, find the height of each pillar.

## Long Answer Type Questions

(5 marks each)

**13.** An aeroplane flying horizontally at a height of 2500 m above the ground is observed at an elevation of 60° and after 15 s, the elevation is observed to be 30°. Find the speed (in km/h) of the aeroplane.

**14.** From a point, 36 m above the surface of a lake, the angle of elevation of a bird is observed to be 30° and angle of depression of its image in the water is observed to be 60°. Find the actual height of the bird above the surface of the lake.

### Answers

| | | | |
|---|---|---|---|
| **1.** (b) | **2.** (b) | **3.** (b) | **4.** 80 m |
| **5.** 21 m | **6.** $(1+\sqrt{3}):\sqrt{3}$ | **7.** 195 m | **8.** $\theta = 45°$ |
| **9.** $12(\sqrt{3}+1)$ m | **12.** 25 m, 43.3 m | **13.** 692.8 km/h | **14.** 72 m |

***Detailed solutions are given on page 198.***

# Chapter 10 **Circles**

## Multiple Choice Questions

(1 mark each)

**1.** The length of the tangent to a circle from a point $P$, which is 13 cm away from the centre is 12 cm. The diameter of the circle is

(a) 6 cm
(b) 10 cm
(c) 5 cm
(d) 8 cm

**2.** If tangents $PA$ and $PB$ from a point $P$ to a circle with centre $O$ are inclined to each other at angle of 80°, then $\angle POA$ is equal to

(a) 50°
(b) 60°
(c) 70°
(d) 80°

**3.** In the given figure, $PQ$ is a tangent at point $R$ of a circle with centre $O$ and $\angle QRB = 30°$, then $\angle PRA$ is equal to

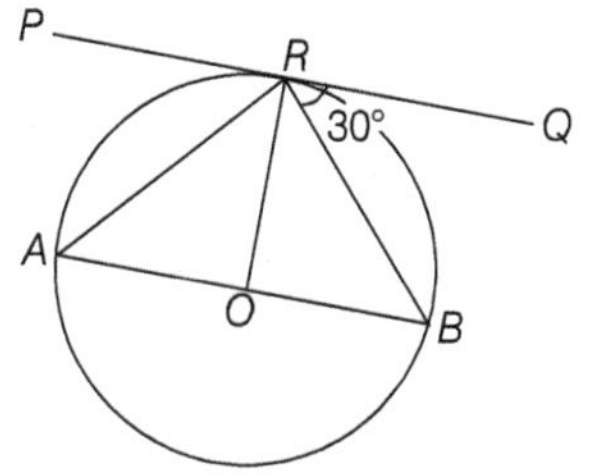


(a) 30°
(b) 90°
(c) 120°
(d) 60°

**4.** In the given figure, $\Delta PQR$ is circumscribing a circle, then the length of $QR$ is

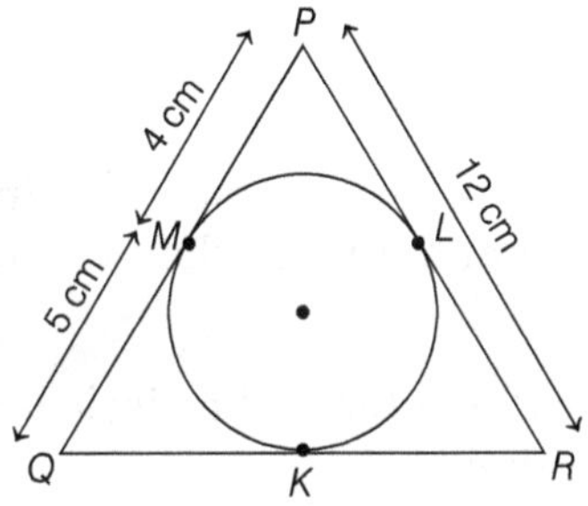


(a) 13 cm
(b) 10 cm
(c) 15 cm
(d) 18 cm

## Short Answer Type (I) Questions

(2 marks each)

**5.** A point $A$ is 10 cm from the centre of the circle. The length of the tangent drawn from $A$ to the circle is 8 cm. Find the radius of the circle.

**6.** $AB$ is a tangent drawn from a point $A$ to a circle with centre $O$ and $BOC$ is a diameter of the circle such that $\angle AOC = 130°$, find $\angle OAB$.

**7.** Two circles of radii 5 cm and 3 cm are concentric. Calculate the length of the chord of the outer circle which touches the inner circle.

**8.** The incircle of an isosceles $\Delta ABC$, in which $AB = AC$, touches the sides $BC$, $CA$ and $AB$ at $D$, $E$ and $F$, respectively. Prove that $BD = CD$.

**9.** In the given figure, $PA$ is a tangent to the circle with center $O$. If $BC = 3$ cm, $AC = 4$ cm and $\Delta ACB \sim \Delta PAO$, then find $OA$ and $\frac{OP}{AP}$.

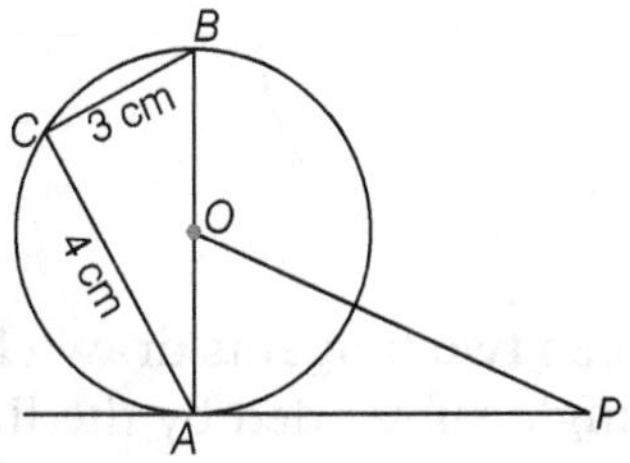

**10.** If two circles touch each other at the point $C$. Prove that the common tangent to the circles at $C$, bisects the common tangent $PQ$.

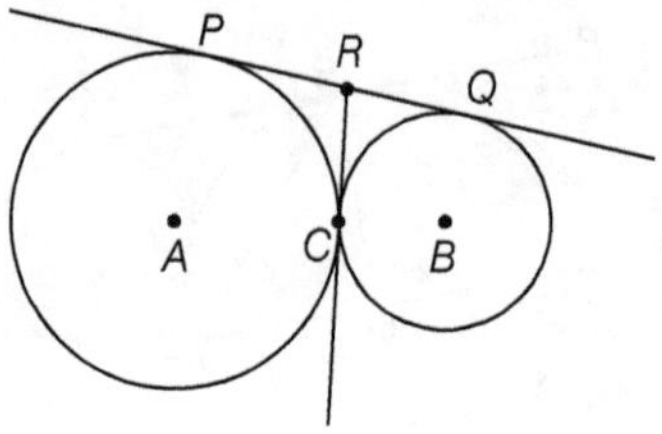


## Short Answer Type (II) Questions

(3 marks each)

**11.** If $a, b$ and $c$ are the sides of a right angled triangle, where $c$ is hypotenuse, then prove that the radius $r$ of the circle which touches the sides of the triangle is given by $r = \frac{a+b-c}{2}$.

**12.** The length of common chord of two intersecting circles is 30 cm. If the diameters of these two circles are 50 cm and 34 cm, then calculate the distance between their centres.

**13.** In the given figure, $AB$ is a diameter of the circle with centre $O$ and $AT$ is a tangent. Calculate the numerical value of $x$.

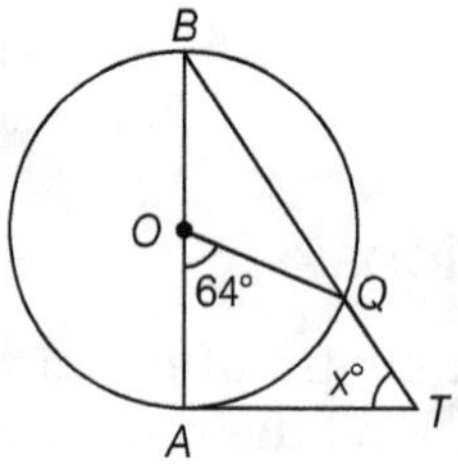


**14.** Two tangents $PA$ and $PB$ are drawn to the circle with centre $O$, such that $\angle APB = 120°$. Prove that $OP = 2AP$.

## Long Answer Type Questions

(5 marks each)

**15.** In the given figure, $AB$ is the diameter of a circle with centre $O$ and $QC$ is a tangent to the circle at $C$. If $\angle CAB = 30°$, then find $\angle CQA$ and $\angle CBA$.

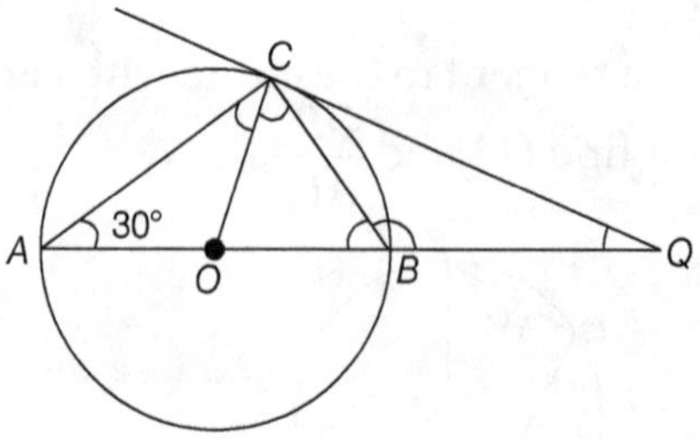


**16.** Prove that the angle between two tangents drawn from an external point to a circle is supplementary to the angle subtended by the line segment joining the points of contact at the centre.

**17.** In the given figure, $PT$ is a tangent and $PAB$ is a secant. If $PT = 6$ cm and $AB = 5$ cm, then find the length of $PA$.

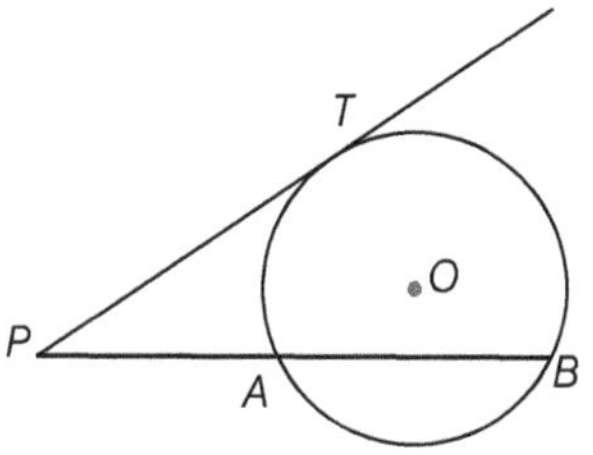


## Answers

| | | | | |
|---|---|---|---|---|
| **1.** (b) | **2.** (a) | **3.** (d) | **4.** (a) | **5.** 6 cm |
| **6.** 40° | **7.** 8 cm | **9.** $OA = 2.5$ cm and $\frac{OP}{AP} = \frac{5}{4}$ | **12.** 28 cm | |
| **13.** 58° | **15.** $\angle CQA = 30°$ and $\angle CBA = 60°$ | **17.** 4 cm | | |

*Detailed solutions are given on page 201.*

# Chapter 11 **Areas Related to Circles**

## Multiple Choice Questions (1 mark each)

**1.** The area of a quadrant of a circle whose circumference is 44 cm is

(a) $\frac{77}{4}$ cm$^2$ (b) 77 cm$^2$ (c) 154 cm$^2$ (d) $\frac{77}{2}$ cm$^2$

**2.** The area of a segment of a circle of radius is 21 cm, if the arc of the segment has a measure of 60° is (take $\sqrt{3} = 1.73$)

(a) 45.27 cm$^2$ (b) 40 cm$^2$ (c) 40.8 cm$^2$ (d) None of these

**3.** The radius of a bicycle wheel is 14 cm. The distance covered by the wheel after making 50 complete rotations is

(a) 88 cm (b) 2200 cm (c) 440 cm (d) 4400 cm

**4.** A race track is in the form of a ring whose inner and outer circumference are 437 m and 503 m, respectively. The width of the track is

(a) 10.5 m (b) 20.5 m (c) 21 m (d) 30 m

**5.** If the perimeter and area of a circle are numerically equal, then the radius of the circle is

(a) 1 unit (b) $\pi$ (c) 2 units (d) $\frac{1}{\pi}$

## Short Answer Type (I) Questions (2 marks each)

**6.** The length of the minute hand of a clock is 14 cm. Find the area swept out by the minute hand in 1 h.

**7.** If the radius of protractor is 3.5 cm, then find the perimeter of protractor.

**8.** The radius of a circle is halved. What is the ratio of the areas of the new circle to the area of the given circle?

**9.** An umbrella has 8 ribs which are equally spaced (see the figure). Assuming umbrella to be a flat circle of radius 45 cm, find the area between the two consecutive ribs of the umbrella.

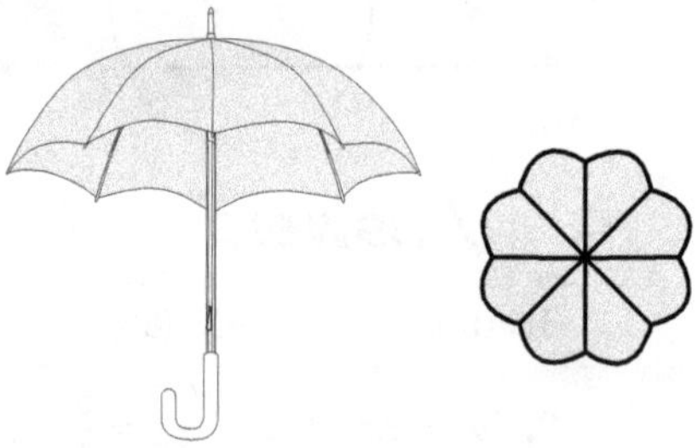

**10.** A bucket is raised from a well by means of a rope which is wound around a wheel of diameter 77 cm. If the bucket ascents in 1 min 28 s with a uniform speed of 1.1 m/s, then calculate the number of complete revolutions the wheel makes in raising the bucket.

**11.** A cow is tied with a rope of length 14 m at the corner of a rectangular field of dimensions 20 m $\times$ 16 m. Find the area of the field in which the cow can graze.

## Short Answer Type (II) Questions (3 marks each)

**12.** The circumference of a circle exceeds the diameter by 24.6 cm. Find the circumference of the circle. ($\pi = 3.14$)

**13.** In the given figure, *OACB* is a quadrant of a circle with centre *O* and radius 3.5 cm. Then, find the area of the quadrant *OACB*.

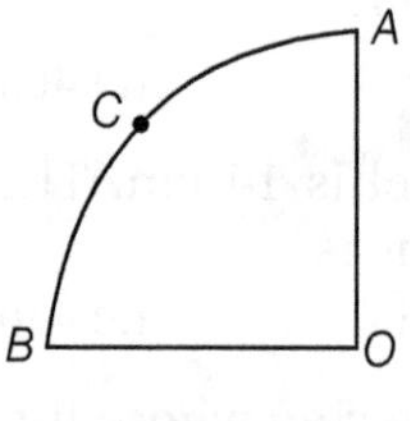


**14.** *AB* and *CD* are respectively arcs of two concentric circles of radii 21 cm and 7 cm with centre *O* (see the figure). If $\angle AOB = 30°$, then find the area sector *OAB* and sector *COD*.

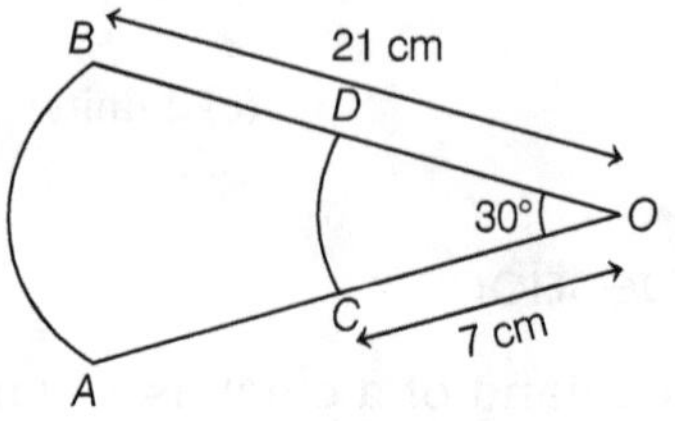

**15.** A brooch is made with silver wire in the form of a circle with diameter 35 mm. The wire is also used in making 5 diameters which divide the circle into 10 equal sectors as shown in the figure.

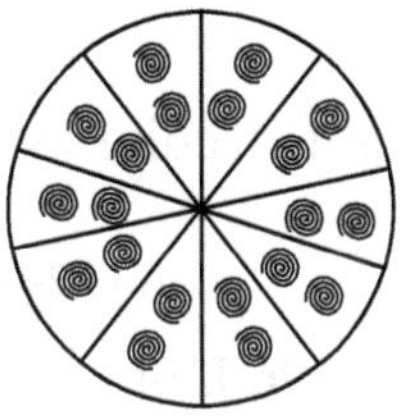

Find

(i) the total length of the silver wire required.

(ii) the area of each sector of the brooch.

## Long Answer Type Questions (5 marks each)

**16.** In figure, $AOB$ is a flower bed in the shape of a sector of a circle of radius 40 m and $\angle AOB = 60°$. Also, a 15 m wide concrete track is made as shown in the figure. Flower bed is made at the rate of ₹ 2.40 per $m^2$ and rate of making the concrete track is ₹ 20 per $m^2$. Find the total amount spent for the job. [take, $\pi = 3.14$]

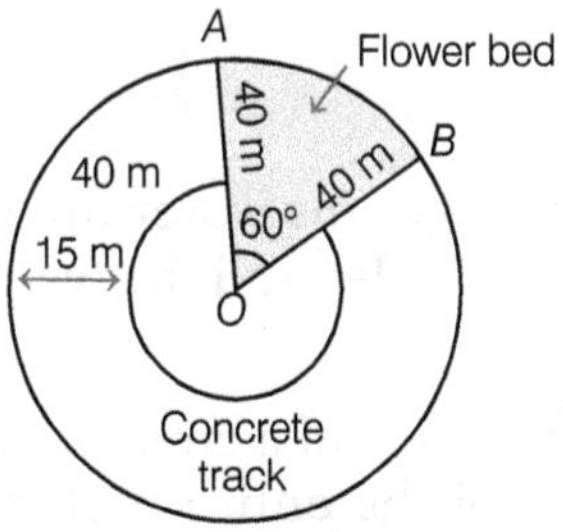


**17.** A chord of a circle of radius 15 cm subtends an angle of 60° at the centre. Find the areas of the corresponding minor and major segments of the circle.
[take, $\pi = 3.14$ and $\sqrt{3} = 1.73$]

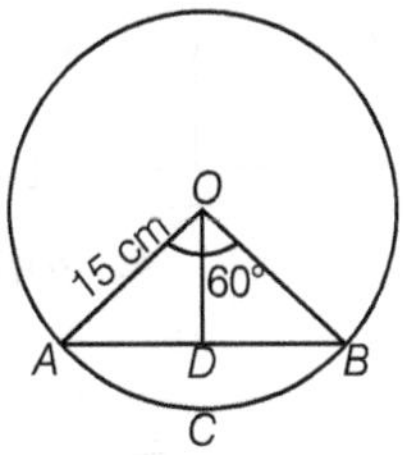


## Answers

| | | | | |
|---|---|---|---|---|
| **1.** (d) | **2.** (b) | **3.** (d) | **4.** (a) | **5.** (c) |
| **6.** 616 $cm^2$ | **7.** 18 cm | **8.** 1 : 4 | **9.** $\frac{22275}{28}$ $cm^2$ | |
| **10.** 40 | **11.** 154 $m^2$ | **12.** 36.04 cm | **13.** 9.625 $cm^2$ | |
| **14.** 115.50 $cm^2$, 12.83 $cm^2$ | | **15.** 285 mm, $\frac{385}{4}$ $mm^2$ | | |
| **16.** ₹ 53034.60 | | **17.** 20.43 $cm^2$, 686.06 $cm^2$ | | |

*Detailed solutions are given on page 204.*

# Chapter 12 **Surface Areas and Volumes**

## Multiple Choice Questions (1 mark each)

**1.** The diameter of the base of a right circular cylinder is 21 cm and its height is 14 cm. Its curved surface area is

(a) 1060 $cm^2$ (b) 508 $cm^2$ (c) 924 $cm^2$ (d) 624 $cm^2$

**2.** A cylindrical vessel contains 49.896 L of liquid. Cost of painting its curved surface area at 2 paise/sq cm is ₹ 95.04. Then, its total surface area is

(a) 5724 $cm^2$ (b) 7524 $cm^2$ (c) 5742 $cm^2$ (d) None of these

**3.** A piece of metal pipe is 77 cm long with internal diameter of the cross-section as 4 cm. If the outer diameter is 4.5 cm and the metal weights 8 gm/$cm^3$, the weight of the pipe is

(a) 2.057 kg (b) 20.57 kg (c) 205.7 kg (d) None of these

**4.** The curved surface area of a right circular cone is 12320 $cm^2$. If its radius is 56 cm, find its slant height.

(a) 35 cm (b) 70 cm (c) 55 cm (d) $\frac{35}{2}$ cm

## Short Answer Type (I) Questions (2 marks each)

**5.** The cylinder of radius 12 cm contains water up to the height of 20 cm. One piece of iron ball is dropped into the cylinder and the water level raised by 6.75 cm. Find the radius of spherical piece.

**6.** A wooden toy rocket is in the shape of a cone mounted on a cylinder as shown in the following figure. The height of the entire rocket is 26 cm, while the height of the conical part is 6 cm. The base of the conical portion has a diameter of 5 cm, while the base diameter of the cylindrical portion is 3 cm. Find the volume of the solid figure. [take $\pi = 3.14$]

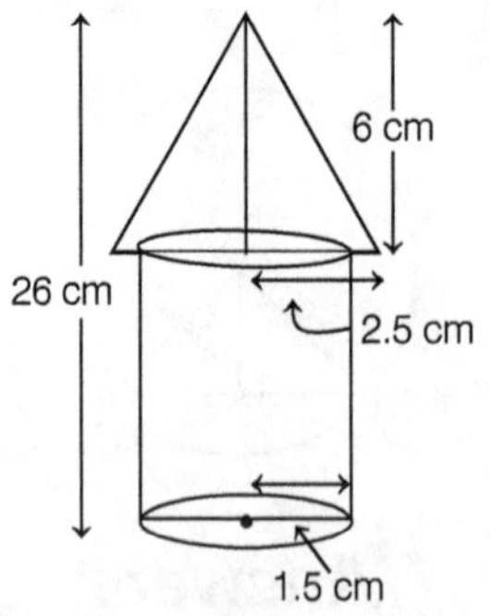


**7.** A semi-circular sheet of metal of diameter 28 cm is bent into an open conical cup. Find the depth and capacity of the cup.

**8.** A hemispherical bowl of diameter 7.2 cm is filled completely with tomato sauce. This sauce is poured into an inverted cone of radius 4.8 cm. Find the height of the cone.

**9.** The rain water from a roof 22 m × 20 m drain into a conical vessel having diameter of base as 2 m and height 3.5 m. If the vessel is just full, then find the rainfall.

**10.** From a solid cube of side 7 cm, a conical cavity of height 7 cm and radius 3 cm is hollowed out. Find the volume of the remaining solid.

## Short Answer Type (II) Questions (3 marks each)

**11.** A vessel is in the form of a hollow hemisphere mounted by a hollow cylinder. The diameter of the hemisphere is 14 cm and the total height of the vessel is 13 cm. Find the inner surface area of the vessel.

**12.** A metallic cylinder has radius 3 cm and height 5 cm. It is made of metal $A$. To reduce its weight, a conical hole is drilled in the cylinder, as shown and it is completely filled with a lighter metal $B$. The conical hole has a radius of 3/2 cm and its depth is 8/9 cm. Calculate the ratio of the volume of the metal $A$ to the volume of the metal $B$ in the solid.

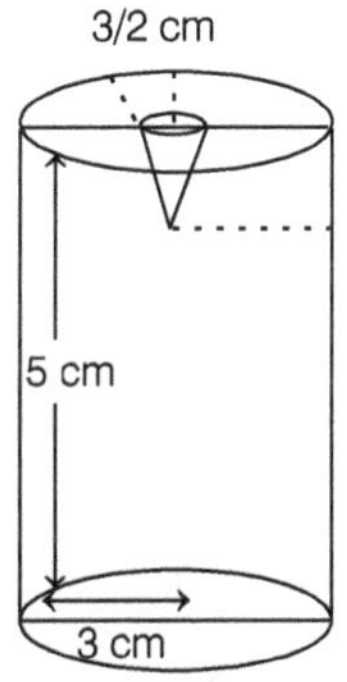


**13.** The internal and external diameters of a hollow hemispherical vessel are 35 cm and 39 cm respectively. Find the volume of the vessel and its outer curved surface area.

**14.** A Joker's cap is in the form of a right circular cone of base radius 8 cm and height 15 cm. Find the area of the sheet required to make 10 such caps.

## Long Answer Type Questions (5 marks each)

**15.** A toy is in the form of a cone mounted on a hemisphere with the same radius. The radius of the conical portion is 4 cm and its height is 3 cm. Calculate the surface area and volume of the toy. [take $\pi = 3.14$]

**16.** A building is in the form of a cylinder surmounted by a hemispherical vaulted dome which contains 17.7 $m^3$ of air and its internal diameter is equal to the height of the crown of the vault above the floor. Find the height of the building. [take, $\pi = 22/7$]

**17.** A spherical glass vessel has a cylinderical neck 9 cm long and 3 cm in diameter and the diameter of the spherical part is 10 cm. How much water can be stored in the glass vessel.

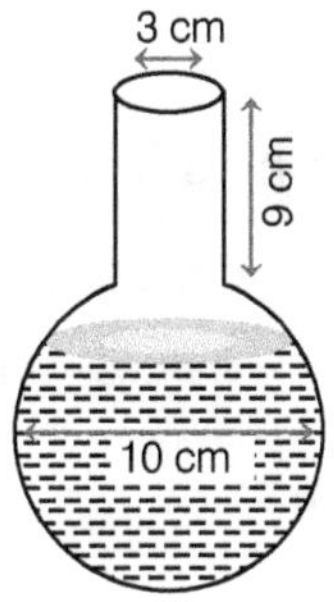

## Answers

| | | | | |
|---|---|---|---|---|
| **1.** (c) | **2.** (b) | **3.** (a) | **4.** (b) | |
| **5.** 9 cm | **6.** 180.55 $cm^3$ | **7.** 622.16 $cm^3$ | **8.** $h = 4.05$ cm | **9.** 0.83 cm |
| **10.** 277 $cm^3$ | **11.** 572 $cm^2$ | **12.** 66.5:1 | **13.** 89833.33 $cm^3$, 9560.57 $cm^2$ | |
| **14.** 4274.2 $cm^2$ | **15.** 163.28 $cm^2$ and 184.21 $cm^3$ | | **16.** 3 m (approx.) | **17.** 186.91 $\pi$ $cm^3$ |

*Detailed solutions are given on page 207.*

# Chapter 13 **Statistics**

## Multiple Choice Questions (1 mark each)

**1.** The mean of five numbers is 10. If each number is decreased by 3, mean of the new number is

(a) 13 (b) 10 (c) 7 (d) None of these

**2.** The median of a data is 20. If each item is increased by 2, the new median will be

(a) 40 (b) 10 (c) 22 (d) None of these

**3.** If the mean of the following distribution is 2.6, then the value of $y$ is

| Variable ($x$) | 1 | 2 | 3 | 4 | 5 |
|---|---|---|---|---|---|
| Frequency | 4 | 5 | $y$ | 1 | 2 |

(a) 3 (b) 8 (c) 13 (d) 24

**4.** If median $= 145$ and mean $= 148.5$, then mode is equal to

(a) 138 (b) 137.5 (c) 139.5 (d) 140.5

**5.** The arithmetic mean of 1, 2, 3, 4, ……, 10 is

(a) 5.5 (b) 7 (c) 5.1 (d) 10

## Short Answer Type (I) Questions (2 marks each)

**6.** The mean of 6, $6 + 2x$, 5 and $8 + 3x$ is 20. Find the value of $x$.

**7.** The mean of 20 observations is 12. If each observation is increased by 5, then find the new mean.

**8.** The following table shows the heights (in cm) of 50 girls of Class X of a school.

| Height (in cm) | 120-130 | 130-140 | 140-150 | 150-160 | 160-170 | Total |
|---|---|---|---|---|---|---|
| Number of girls | 2 | 8 | 12 | 20 | 8 | 50 |

Find the mean of the above data by deviation method.

**9.** Calculate the median for the following data

| Class interval | 130-139 | 140-149 | 150-159 | 160-169 | 170-179 | 180-189 | 190-199 |
|---|---|---|---|---|---|---|---|
| Frequency | 4 | 9 | 18 | 28 | 24 | 10 | 7 |

**10.** The following data gives the distribution of total household expenditure (in ₹) of manual workers in a city.

| Expenditure (in ₹) | 1000-1500 | 1500-2000 | 2000-2500 | 2500-3000 | 3000-3500 | 3500-4000 | 4000-4500 | 4500-5000 |
|---|---|---|---|---|---|---|---|---|
| Frequency | 24 | 40 | 33 | 28 | 30 | 22 | 16 | 7 |

Find the mode from the above data.

## Short Answer Type (II) Questions (3 marks each)

**11.** The mean of the following frequency table is 50 but the frequencies $f_1$ and $f_2$ in class intervals 20-40 and 60-80 are missing. Find the missing frequencies.

| Class interval | 0-20 | 20-40 | 40-60 | 60-80 | 80-100 | Total |
|---|---|---|---|---|---|---|
| Frequency | 17 | $f_1$ | 32 | $f_2$ | 19 | 120 |

**12.** Consider the following frequency distribution

| Classes | 0-5 | 6-11 | 12-17 | 18-23 | 24-29 |
|---|---|---|---|---|---|
| Frequency | 13 | 10 | 15 | 8 | 11 |

Find the upper limit of median class.

## Long Answer Type Questions (5 marks each)

**13.** The following table gives the literacy rate of 35 cities. Find the mean literacy rate.

| Literacy rate (in %) | 45-55 | 55-65 | 65-75 | 75-85 | 85-95 |
|---|---|---|---|---|---|
| Number of cities | 3 | 10 | 11 | 8 | 3 |

**14.** The median of the distribution given below is 14.4. Find the values of $x$ and $y$, if the total frequency is 20.

| Class interval | 0-6 | 6-12 | 12-18 | 18-24 | 24-30 |
|---|---|---|---|---|---|
| Frequency | 4 | $x$ | 5 | $y$ | 1 |

**15.** Find the mean, mode and median of the following data.

| Classes | 0-10 | 10-20 | 20-30 | 30-40 | 40 50 | 50-60 | 60-70 |
|---|---|---|---|---|---|---|---|
| Frequency | 3 | 4 | 7 | 15 | 10 | 7 | 4 |

## Answers

| | | | | |
|---|---|---|---|---|
| **1.** (c) | **2.** (c) | **3.** (b) | **4.** (a) | **5.** (a) |
| **6.** 11 | **7.** 17 | **8.** 149.8 | **9.** 166.29 | **10.** 1847.825 |
| **11.** $f_1 = 28$ and $f_2 = 24$ | | **12.** 17.5 | **13.** 69.43% | **14.** $x = 4$ and $y = 6$ |
| **15.** (i) 37.4, (ii) 36.15, (iii) 37.3 | | | | |

*Detailed solutions are given on page 210.*

# Chapter 14 **Probability**

## Multiple Choice Questions

(1 mark each)

**1.** A number is selected from the numbers 1, 2, 3, 4, ..., 25. What is the probability that the number selected is a multiple of 5?

(a) $\frac{1}{25}$ (b) $\frac{1}{5}$ (c) $\frac{4}{5}$ (d) $\frac{4}{25}$

**2.** A bag contains 8 red, 2 black and 5 white balls. One ball is drawn at random. The probability that the ball drawn is not white is

(a) $\frac{1}{2}$ (b) $\frac{2}{3}$ (c) $\frac{1}{4}$ (d) $\frac{2}{5}$

**3.** A number is selected at random from the numbers 3, 5, 5, 7, 7, 7, 9, 9, 9, 9. The probability that the selected number is their average is

(a) $\frac{1}{10}$ (b) $\frac{3}{10}$ (c) $\frac{7}{9}$ (d) $\frac{9}{10}$

**4.** The probability of getting a number less than 5 in a single throw of a die is

(a) $\frac{1}{3}$ (b) $\frac{2}{3}$ (c) 0 (d) $\frac{1}{6}$

## Short Answer Type (I) Questions

(2 marks each)

**5.** Answer the following statements.

(i) Write the probability of a sure event.

(ii) Write the probability of an event which is impossible.

(iii) For an event $E$, write a relation representing the range of values of $P(E)$.

**6.** Two dice are rolled once. Find the probability of getting such numbers on the two dice, whose product is 12.

**7.** It is given that in a group of 3 students, the probability of 2 students not having the same birthday is 0.992. What is the probability that the 2 students have the same birthday?

**8.** 17 cards numbered 1, 2, 3 ... 16, 17 are put in a box and mixed throughly. A card is drawn at random from the box. Find the probability that it is an odd numbered card.

**9.** What is the probability that an ordinary year has 53 Sundays?

**10.** A box contains 5 red marbles, 8 white marbles and 4 green marbles. One marble is taken out of the box at random. What is the probability that the marble taken out will be

(i) red? (ii) white? (iii) not green?

**11.** 12 defective pens are accidentally mixed with 132 good ones. It is not possible to just look at a pen and tell whether it is defective or not. One pen is taken out at random from this lot. Determine the probability that the pen taken out is a good one.

**12.** Find the probability that a number selected at random from the numbers 3, 4, 5, ..., 25 is prime.

## Short Answer Type (II) Questions (3 marks each)

**13.** Find the probability that a number selected at random from the numbers 1, 2, 3, 4, 5 ..., 35 is a

(i) multiple of 7 (ii) multiple of 3 or 5

**14.** A box contains 90 discs which are numbered from 1 to 90. If one disc is drawn at random from the box, find the probability that it bears

(i) a two digit number (ii) a perfect square number (iii) a number divisible by 5.

**15.** Suppose you drop a dice at random on the rectangular region shown in figure. What is the probability that it will land inside the circle with diameter 1 m?

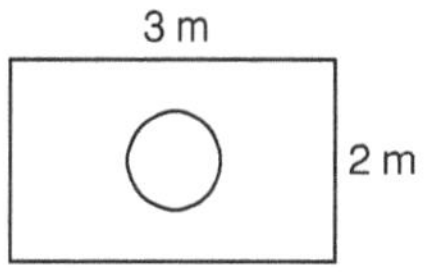


**16.** Two dice are thrown simultaneously. What is the probability that the sum of the numbers appearing on the dice is

(i) 7? (ii) a prime number? (iii) 1?

## Long Answer Type Questions (5 marks each)

**17.** Cards numbered 1, 2, 3, 4, 5,...., 17 are put in a box and mixed thoroughly. One person draws a card from the box. Find the probability that the number on the card is

(i) an odd number. (ii) a prime number. (iii) divisible by 3.
(iv) divisible by 2 and 3 both. (v) a multiple of 3 or 5.

**18.** One card is drawn from a well-shuffled deck of 52 cards. Find the probability of getting

(i) a king of red colour. (ii) a face card.
(iii) a red face card. (iv) the jack of heart.

**19.** Neha, Lata and Sonia were fighting to get first chance in a game. Neha says,"Let us toss two coins. If head appears on both, Lata will take first chance. If first tail appears on both, Sonia will take first chance and if one head and one tail appears, I will get the chance."

(i) What is the probability of Neha getting the first chance?
(ii) What is the probability of Lata getting the first chance?
(iii) What is the probability of Sonia getting the first chance.
(iv) Is her decision fair?

## *Answers*

| | | | | |
|---|---|---|---|---|
| **1.** (b) | **2.** (b) | **3.** (b) | **4.** (b) | **5.** (i) 1 (ii) 0 (iii) $0 \le P(E) \le 1$ |
| **6.** $\frac{1}{9}$ | **7.** 0.008 | **8.** $\frac{9}{17}$ | **9.** $\frac{1}{7}$ | **10.** (i) $\frac{5}{17}$ (ii) $\frac{8}{17}$ (iii) $\frac{13}{17}$ |
| **11.** $\frac{11}{12}$ | **12.** $\frac{8}{23}$ | **13.** (i) $\frac{1}{7}$ (ii) $\frac{16}{35}$ | **14.** (i) $\frac{9}{10}$ (ii) $\frac{1}{10}$ (iii) $\frac{1}{5}$ | |
| **15.** $\frac{\pi}{24}$ | **16.** (i) $\frac{1}{6}$ (ii) $\frac{5}{12}$ (iii) zero | | **17.** (i) $\frac{9}{17}$ (ii) $\frac{7}{17}$ (iii) $\frac{5}{17}$ (iv) $\frac{2}{17}$ (v) $\frac{7}{17}$ | |
| **18.** (i) $\frac{1}{26}$ (ii) $\frac{3}{13}$ (iii) $\frac{3}{26}$ (iv) $\frac{1}{52}$ | | | **19.** (i) $\frac{1}{2}$ (ii) $\frac{1}{4}$ (iii) $\frac{1}{4}$ (iv) No | |

*Detailed solutions are given on page 212.*

CBSE Board Exams 2023

# SAMPLE QUESTION PAPERS

STAGE - I (1-5)
STAGE - II (6-10)
STAGE - III (11-15)

Stage 1

# SAMPLE QUESTION PAPER 1

## Mathematics (Basic)

Time : **3 hrs** Max. Marks : **80**

### Instructions

1. This question paper has 5 Sections A, B, C, D and E.
2. Section A has 20 Multiple Choice Questions (MCQs) carrying 1 mark each.
3. Section B has 5 Short Answer-I (SA-I) Type Questions carrying 2 marks each.
4. Section C has 6 Short Answer-II (SA-II) Type Questions carrying 3 marks each.
5. Section D has 4 Long Answer (LA) Type Questions carrying 5 marks each.
6. Section E has 3 Case Based integrated units of assessment (4 marks each) with sub-parts of the values of 1, 1 and 2 marks each respectively.
7. All questions are compulsory. However, an internal choice in 2 questions of 2 marks, 2 questions of 3 marks and 2 questions of 5 marks has been provided. An internal choice has been provided in the 2 marks questions of Section E.
8. Draw neat figures wherever required. Take $\pi = 22/7$ wherever required if not stated.

## Section-A

**Section A consists of 20 questions of 1 mark each**

**1.** The probability of an impossible event is

(a) 0 (b) $\frac{1}{2}$

(c) 1 (d) None of these

***Sol.*** (a) The probability of an impossible event is 0.

**2.** A die is thrown once. The probability of getting a number greater than 4 is

(a) $\frac{1}{2}$ (b) $\frac{2}{3}$

(c) $\frac{1}{3}$ (d) 1

***Sol.*** (c) On a die, there are six numbers 1, 2, 3, 4, 5 and 6.

$\therefore$ Total number of possible outcomes = 6

Number on dice which are greater than 4 = 5, 6

$\therefore$ Favourable number of elementary events = 2

$\therefore$ Required probability $= \frac{2}{6} = \frac{1}{3}$

**3.** The value of $\sin^2\theta + \frac{1}{1+\tan^2\theta}$ is

(a) $2\sin^2\theta$ (b) 1

(c) $\sin^2\theta - \cos^2\theta$ (d) 0

**Sol.** (b) We have, $\sin^2\theta + \dfrac{1}{1+\tan^2\theta}$

$$= \sin^2\theta + \frac{1}{\sec^2\theta} \quad [\because \sec^2 A = 1 + \tan^2 A]$$

$$= \sin^2\theta + \cos^2\theta \quad \left[\because \sec A = \frac{1}{\cos A}\right]$$

$$= 1 \quad [\because \sin^2 A + \cos^2 A = 1]$$

**4.** The area of a sector of a circle of radius 5 cm formed by an arc of length 3.5 cm, is

(a) 16.5 $cm^2$ (b) 17.5 $cm^2$
(c) 19.62 $cm^2$ (d) 8.75 $cm^2$

**Sol.** (d) We know that area of sector $A$ of radius $r$ and length of arc $l$ is given by

$$A = \frac{1}{2}lr$$

$$\therefore \quad A = \frac{1}{2} \times 3.5 \times 5$$

$$= 8.75 \text{cm}^2$$

**5.** If a cylinder is covered by two hemispherical lid of equal shape, then the total curved surface area of the new object will be (where $r$ is the radius and $h$ is the height of cylinder)

(a) $4\pi rh + 2\pi r^2$ (b) $4\pi rh - 2\pi r^2$
(c) $2\pi rh + 4\pi r^2$ (d) $2\pi rh + 4\pi r$

**Sol.** (c)

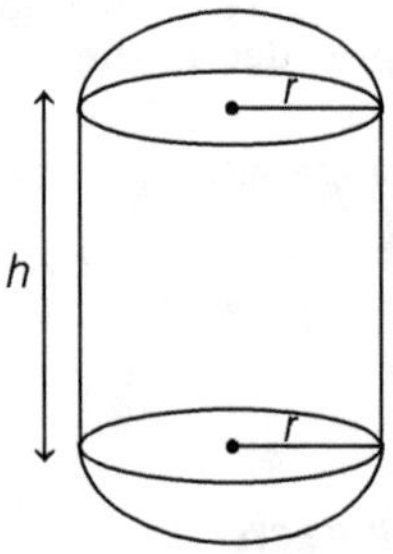


Total curved surface area

= Curved surface area of cylinder + 2 × Curved surface area of hemispheres

$$= 2\pi rh + 2 \times (2\pi r^2)$$

$$= 2\pi rh + 4\pi r^2$$

**6.** If radius of circle is 8 cm and tangent is drawn from an external point to the circle is 15 cm, the distance from centre of circle to the external point is

(a) $\sqrt{241}$ cm (b) 17 cm
(c) 10 cm (d) None of these

**Sol.** (b) Given, $OQ = 8$ cm and $PQ = 15$ cm.

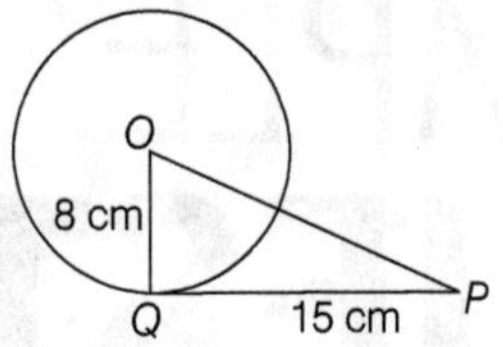


In right angled $\Delta OPQ$, using Pythagoras theorem

$$OP = \sqrt{OQ^2 + QP^2} = \sqrt{8^2 + 15^2}$$

$$= \sqrt{64 + 225} = \sqrt{289} = 17 \text{ cm}$$

**7.** Suppose mean of 10 observations is 12.5 and each observation is multiplied by 5, then what is the new mean?

(a) 50 (b) 62.5 (c) 60 (d) 48.2

**Sol.** (b) Let 10 observations be $x_1, x_2, x_3, \ldots, x_{10}$

Given, $\dfrac{x_1 + x_2 + x_3 + \ldots + x_{10}}{10} = 12.5$ ...(i)

Now, if each observation multiplied by 5, then new mean = $\dfrac{5x_1 + 5x_2 + \ldots + 5x_{10}}{}$

$$= \frac{5(x_1 + x_2 + \ldots + x_{10})}{10} \quad \text{[using Eq. (i)]}$$

$$= 5 \times 12.5 = 62.5$$

**8.** In $\Delta ABC$, right angled at $A$ and $AB = 5$, $AC = 12$ and $BC = 13$, then find the value of $\sin B$ and $\tan B$.

(a) $\dfrac{12}{5}$ and $\dfrac{5}{13}$ (b) $\dfrac{5}{13}$ and $\dfrac{5}{12}$
(c) $\dfrac{12}{13}$ and $\dfrac{12}{5}$ (d) $\dfrac{13}{5}$ and $\dfrac{12}{13}$

**Sol.** (c) With reference to $\angle B$, we have

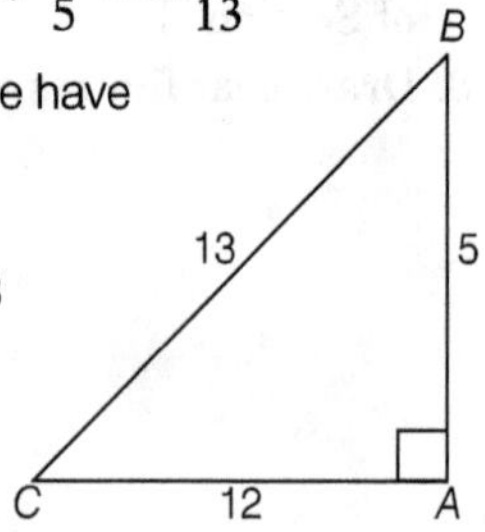


Base = $AB = 5$,
perpendicular = $AC = 12$
and hypotenuse = $BC = 13$

$$\therefore \quad \sin B = \frac{AC}{BC} = \frac{12}{13}$$

$$\text{and } \tan B = \frac{AC}{AB} = \frac{12}{5}$$

**9.** Find the value of $3\sin 30° - 4\sin^3 60°$.

(a) $3 - \sqrt{3}$ (b) $\dfrac{3(1-\sqrt{3})}{2}$
(c) $\dfrac{3\sqrt{3}-1}{2}$ (d) $-\dfrac{3}{2}$

**Sol.** (b) $3\sin 30° - 4\sin^3 60°$

$$= 3 \times \frac{1}{2} - 4\left(\frac{\sqrt{3}}{2}\right)^3 = \frac{3}{2} - 4 \times \frac{3\sqrt{3}}{8}$$

$$= \frac{3}{2} - \frac{3\sqrt{3}}{2} = \frac{3 - 3\sqrt{3}}{2} = \frac{3(1-\sqrt{3})}{2}$$

**10.** If median $=143$ and mean $=143.06$, then the mode is

(a) 143.18 (b) 142.94
(c) 142.88 (d) 143

***Sol.*** (c) We know that

$$\text{Mode} = 3\,(\text{Median}) - 2\,(\text{Mean})$$
$$= 3(143) - 2(143.06)$$
$$= 429 - 286.12 = 142.88$$

**11.** If the lines given by $4x + ky = 1$ and $6x - 10y = 14$ has unique solution, then the value of $k$ is

(a) $\frac{20}{3}$
(b) $-\frac{5}{7}$
(c) $-15$
(d) all real values except $-\frac{20}{3}$

***Sol.*** (d) The given equations can be re-written as

$$4x + ky - 1 = 0 \text{ and } 6x - 10y - 14 = 0$$

On comparing with $a_1x + b_1y + c_1 = 0$ and $a_2x + b_2y + c_2 = 0$, we get

$$a_1 = 4,\ b_1 = k,\ c_1 = -1$$

and $a_2 = 6,\ b_2 = -10,\ c_2 = -14$

For unique solution,

$$\frac{a_1}{a_2} \neq \frac{b_1}{b_2}$$
$$\Rightarrow \frac{4}{6} \neq \frac{k}{-10}$$
$$\Rightarrow k \neq -\frac{20}{3}$$

Thus, given lines have a unique solution for all real values of $k$, except $-\frac{20}{3}$.

**12.** Which term of the AP : 21, 18, 15, ... is $-81$?

(a) 34 (b) 36 (c) 35 (d) 33

***Sol.*** (c) Given, AP is 21, 18, 15, ...

Here, $a = 21$ and $d = 18 - 21 = -3$

Let $n$th term of given AP be $-81$.

Then, $a_n = -81$

$\Rightarrow a + (n-1)d = -81 \quad [\because a_n = a + (n-1)d]$ ...(i)

On putting the values of $a$ and $d$ in Eq. (i), we get

$$21 + (n-1)\times(-3) = -81$$
$$\Rightarrow 21 - 3n + 3 = -81$$
$$\Rightarrow 24 - 3n = -81$$
$$\Rightarrow -3n = -81 - 24$$
$$\therefore n = \frac{-105}{-3} = 35$$

Hence, 35th term of given AP is $-81$.

**13.** The distance between the points $A(x_1, y_1)$ and $B(x_2, y_2)$ is

(a) $\sqrt{(x_1 + x_2) + (y_1 + y_2)}$
(b) $\sqrt{(x_1 + x_2)^2 + (y_1 + y_2)^2}$
(c) $\sqrt{(x_1 - x_2)^2 + (y_1 - y_2)^2}$
(d) $\sqrt{(x_1 - x_2) + (y_1 - y_2)}$

***Sol.*** (c) $AB = \sqrt{(x_1 - x_2)^2 + (y_1 - y_2)^2}$

**14.** If $a = 2$ and 20th term $= 62$, then the sum of first 20 terms of an AP is

(a) 1200 (b) 640 (c) 600 (d) 1280

***Sol.*** (b) Given, $a = 2$, $a_{20} = 62$ and $n = 20$

Now, sum of first 20 terms

$$S_{20} = \frac{20}{2}(2 + 62) \quad \left[\because S_n = \frac{n}{2}(a + a_n)\right]$$
$$= 10 \times 64 = 640$$

**15.** The product of the HCF and LCM of two prime numbers $a$ and $b$ is

(a) $\frac{a}{b}$ (b) $a - b$ (c) $a + b$ (d) $a \times b$

***Sol.*** (d) HCF $(a, b) = 1$

LCM $(a, b) = ab$

$\therefore$ HCF $(a, b) \times$ LCM $(a, b) = 1 \times ab = ab$

**16.** If the product of the zeroes of the polynomial $mx^2 - 6x - 6$ is $-3$, then the value of $m$ is

(a) 6 (b) 2 (c) $-2$ (d) $-3$

***Sol.*** (b) Let $\alpha$ and $\beta$ be the zeroes of $(mx^2 - 6x - 6)$.

Here, $a = m$, $b = -6$ and $c = -6$

Given, $\alpha\beta = -3$

$$\therefore \frac{c}{a} = -3 \Rightarrow \frac{-6}{m} = -3 \Rightarrow m = 2$$

**17.** The solution of $2x^2 - 5x - 3 = 0$ is

(a) $-\frac{1}{2}, 3$ (b) $1, -3$
(c) $-1, 3$ (d) $-1, \frac{1}{2}$

***Sol.*** (a) Given, $2x^2 - 5x - 3 = 0$

Splitting the middle term, we get

$$2x^2 - 6x + x - 3 = 0$$
$$\Rightarrow 2x(x - 3) + 1(x - 3) = 0$$
$$\Rightarrow (x - 3)(2x + 1) = 0$$
$$\Rightarrow x = -\frac{1}{2}, 3$$

**18.** If in $\Delta ABC$ and $\Delta DEF$, $\frac{AB}{DE} = \frac{BC}{FD}$, then they will be similar, when

(a) $\angle B = \angle E$ (b) $\angle A = \angle D$
(c) $\angle B = \angle D$ (d) $\angle A = \angle F$

***Sol.*** (c) Given, in $\Delta ABC$ and $\Delta DEF$, $\frac{AB}{DE} = \frac{BC}{FD}$

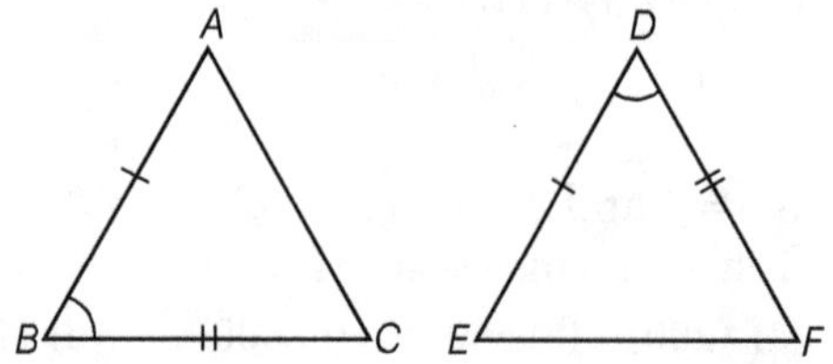


$\Delta ABC$ and $\Delta EDF$ will be similar, if

$\angle B = \angle D$ [by SAS similarity criterion]

**Directions** *In the question number 19 and 20, a statement of Assertion (A) is followed by a statement of Reason (R). Choose the correct option.*

**19. Assertion (A)** The value of $\sin 60° \cos 30° + \sin 30° \cos 60°$ is 1.

**Reason (R)** $\sin 90° = 1$ and $\cos 90° = 0$

(a) Both Assertion (A) and Reason (R) are true and Reason (R) is the correct explanation of Assertion (A)
(b) Both Assertion (A) and Reason (R) are true but Reason (R) is not the correct explanation of Assertion (A)
(c) Assertion (A) is true but Reason (R) is false
(d) Assertion (A) is false but Reason (R) is true

***Sol.*** (b) **Assertion** $\sin 60° \cos 30° + \sin 30° \cos 60°$

$$= \frac{\sqrt{3}}{2}\left(\frac{\sqrt{3}}{2}\right) + \left(\frac{1}{2}\right)\left(\frac{1}{2}\right) = \frac{3}{4} + \frac{1}{4} = \frac{4}{4} = 1$$

So, Assertion is true.

**Reason** We know, $\sin 90° = 1$ and $\cos 90° = 0$

So, Reason is true.

But Reason is not the correct explanation of Assertion.

**20. Assertion (A)** The system of equations $2x + 3y + 5 = 0$ and $4x + ky + 7 = 0$ is inconsistent when $k = 6$.

**Reason (R)** The system of equations $a_1x + b_1y + c_1 = 0$ and $a_2x + b_2y + c_2 = 0$ is inconsistent when $\frac{a_1}{a_2} = \frac{b_1}{b_2} \neq \frac{c_1}{c_2}$.

(a) Both Assertion (A) and Reason (R) are true and Reason (R) is the correct explanation of Assertion (A)
(b) Both Assertion (A) and Reason (R) are true but Reason (R) is not the correct explanation of Assertion (A)
(c) Assertion (A) is true but Reason (R) is false
(d) Assertion (A) is false but Reason (R) is true

***Sol.*** (a) **Assertion (A)**

Here, $a_1 = 2, b_1 = 3, c_1 = 5$

and $a_2 = 4, b_2 = 6, c_2 = 7$ $[\because k = 6]$

So, $\frac{a_1}{a_2} = \frac{b_1}{b_2} \neq \frac{c_1}{c_2}$ $\left[\because \frac{2}{4} = \frac{3}{6} \neq \frac{5}{7}\right]$

So, the given system of equations has no solution (i.e. inconsistent).

So, the Assertion is true.

**Reason (R)** $a_1x + b_1y + c_1 = 0$

and $a_2x + b_2y + c_2 = 0$

We know, for the system of equations to be inconsistent,

$$\frac{a_1}{a_2} = \frac{b_1}{b_2} \neq \frac{c_1}{c_2}$$

So, both Assertion and Reason are true and Reason is a correct explanation of Assertion.

## Section-B

**Section B consists of 5 questions of 2 marks each**

**21.** Prove that the line segment joining the point of contact of two parallel tangents to a circle is a diameter of the circle.

***Sol.*** **Given** $AB$ and $CD$ are two parallel tangents at the point $P$ and $Q$ of a circle with centre $O$.

**To prove** $POQ$ is a diameter of the circle.

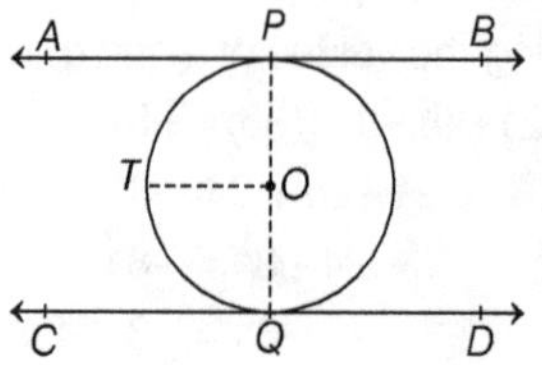


(1)

**Construction** Join $OP$ and $OQ$ and draw $OT \parallel AB$.

**Proof** $\angle APO + \angle TOP = 180°$ [$\because OT \parallel AB$]

$\Rightarrow$ $90° + \angle TOP = 180°$ [$\because OP \perp AB$]

$\Rightarrow \angle TOP = 180° - 90° = 90°$

Similarly, $\angle TOQ = 90°$

$\therefore$ $\angle TOP + \angle TOQ = 90° + 90° = 180°$

Since, $POQ$ is a straight line.

Hence, $POQ$ is a diameter of the circle with centre $O$. **Hence proved.** (1)

**22.** What is the probability that a number selected from the numbers 1, 2, 3, ..., 25 is a prime number, when each of the given numbers is equally likely to be selected?

*Or*

A letter is chosen at random from the letters of word 'ASSASSINATION'. Find the probability that the letter chosen is a (i) vowel (ii) consonant.

***Sol.*** Out of 25 numbers, 1, 2, 3, ..., 25 one number can be chosen in 25 ways.

$\therefore$ Total number of elementary events = 25 (1)

The number selected will be a prime number, if it is chosen from the numbers

2, 3, 5, 7, 11, 13, 17, 19, 23.

$\therefore$ Favourable number of elementary events = 9

Hence, required probability $= \frac{9}{25}$ (1)

*Or*

There are 13 letters in the word 'ASSASSINATION' out of which one letter can be chosen in 13 ways.

$\therefore$ Total number of elementary events = 13

(i) There are 6 vowels in the word 'ASSASSINATION'. So, there are 6 ways of selecting a vowel.

$\therefore$ Probability of selecting a vowel $= \frac{6}{13}$ (1)

(ii) We have, probability of selecting a consonant

= 1 − Probability of selecting a vowel

$= 1 - \frac{6}{13} = \frac{7}{13}$ (1)

**23.** Find the sum of first 15 even natural numbers.

***Sol.*** The sequence goes like this

2, 4, 6, 8, ...

Here, $4-2 = 6-4 = 8-6 = 2$

So, it is an AP with first term, $a = 2$,

common difference, $d = 4 - 2 = 2$

and total number of terms, $n = 15$ (1)

$\therefore$ Sum of first 15 even natural numbers

$$S_{15} = \frac{n}{2}[2a + (n-1)d] = \frac{15}{2}[2 \times 2 + (15-1)2]$$

$$\left[\because S_n = \frac{n}{2}\{2a + (n-1)d\}\right]$$

$$= \frac{15}{2}[4 + 28] = \frac{15}{2} \times 32 = 240$$ (1)

**24.** If one root of the quadratic equation $2x^2 + kx - 6 = 0$ is 2, find the value of $k$. Also, find the other root.

***Sol.*** Since, $x = 2$ is a root of the equation

$$2x^2 + kx - 6 = 0$$

$\therefore$ $2 \times 2^2 + 2k - 6 = 0$

$\Rightarrow$ $8 + 2k - 6 = 0$

$\Rightarrow$ $2k + 2 = 0 \Rightarrow k = -1$ (1)

On putting $k = -1$ in the equation $2x^2 + kx - 6 = 0$, we get

$$2x^2 - x - 6 = 0 \Rightarrow 2x^2 - 4x + 3x - 6 = 0$$

$\Rightarrow$ $2x(x-2) + 3(x-2) = 0 \Rightarrow (x-2)(2x+3) = 0$

$\Rightarrow$ $x - 2 = 0$ or $2x + 3 = 0$

$\Rightarrow$ $x = 2$ or $-\frac{3}{2}$

Hence, the other root is $-\frac{3}{2}$. (1)

**25.** Prove that $\cot A + \tan A = \sec A \operatorname{cosec} A$.

*Or* Evaluate $\cos^2 30° + \sin^2 45° - \frac{1}{3}\tan^2 60°$.

***Sol.*** LHS $= \cot A + \tan A = \frac{\cos A}{\sin A} + \frac{\sin A}{\cos A}$

$$\left[\because \cot\theta = \frac{\cos\theta}{\sin\theta}, \tan\theta = \frac{\sin\theta}{\cos\theta}\right]$$

$$= \frac{\cos^2 A + \sin^2 A}{\sin A \cdot \cos A} = \frac{1}{\cos A \cdot \sin A}$$

$[\because \sin^2\theta + \cos^2\theta = 1]$ (1)

$$= \frac{1}{\sin A} \cdot \frac{1}{\cos A} = \operatorname{cosec} A \sec A$$

$$\left[\because \operatorname{cosec}\theta = \frac{1}{\sin\theta} \text{ and } \sec\theta = \frac{1}{\cos\theta}\right]$$

= RHS **Hence proved.** (1)

*Or*

We have, $\cos^2 30° + \sin^2 45° - \frac{1}{3}\tan^2 60°$

$$= \left(\frac{\sqrt{3}}{2}\right)^2 + \left(\frac{1}{\sqrt{2}}\right)^2 - \frac{1}{3}(\sqrt{3})^2$$ (1)

$$\left[\because \cos 30° = \frac{\sqrt{3}}{2}, \sin 45° = \frac{1}{\sqrt{2}} \text{ and } \tan 60° = \sqrt{3}\right]$$

$$= \frac{3}{4} + \frac{1}{2} - \frac{3}{3} = \frac{3+2}{4} - 1 = \frac{5}{4} - 1 = \frac{5-4}{4} = \frac{1}{4}$$ (1)

# Section-C

**Section C consists of 6 questions of 3 marks each**

**26.** In the given figure, two chords $AB$ and $CD$ intersect each other at the point $P$. Prove that

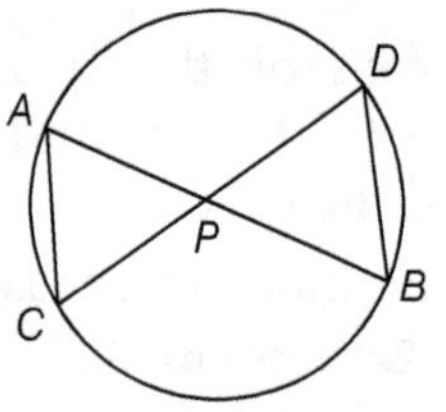


(i) $\Delta APC \sim \Delta DPB$ (ii) $AP \cdot PB = CP \cdot DP$

***Sol.*** **Given** In figure, two chords $AB$ and $CD$ intersect each other at point $P$.

**To prove** (i) $\Delta APC \sim \Delta DPB$

(ii) $AP \cdot PB = CP \cdot DP$

**Proof**

(i) In $\Delta APC$ and $\Delta DPB$,

$\angle APC = \angle DPB$ [vertically opposite angles]

and $\angle CAP = \angle BDP$ [angles in the same segment]

$\therefore$ $\Delta APC \sim \Delta DPB$ [by AA similarity criterion] (1)

(ii) We have, $\Delta APC \sim \Delta DPB$ [proved in part (i)]

$\therefore \quad \frac{AP}{DP} = \frac{CP}{BP}$ (1)

[$\because$ if two triangles are similar, then the ratio of their corresponding sides is equal]

$\therefore \quad AP \cdot BP = CP \cdot DP$

or $\quad AP \cdot PB = CP \cdot DP$ **Hence proved.** (1)

**27.** A circle is inscribed in a $\Delta ABC$ having sides 8 cm, 10 cm and 12 cm as shown in figure. Find $AD$, $BE$ and $CF$.

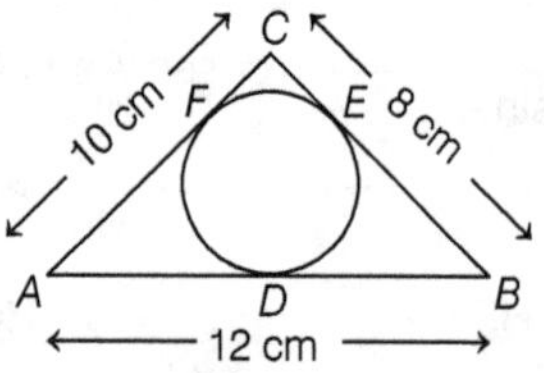


***Sol.*** Given, a circle is inscribed in the triangle, whose sides are $BC = 8$ cm, $AC = 10$ cm and $AB = 12$ cm.

Let $AD = AF = x$, $BD = BE = y$

and $CE = CF = z$

[$\because$ the length of two tangents drawn from an external point to a circle are equal]

We have, $AB = 12$

$\Rightarrow \quad AD + DB = 12$

$\Rightarrow \quad x + y = 12$ ...(i)

$AC = 10$

$\Rightarrow \quad AF + FC = 10$

$\Rightarrow \quad x + z = 10$ ...(ii)

and $\quad BC = 8$

$\Rightarrow \quad CE + EB = 8$

$\Rightarrow \quad z + y = 8$ ...(iii) (1)

On adding Eqs. (i), (ii) and (iii), we get

$2(x + y + z) = 12 + 10 + 8$

$\Rightarrow \quad x + y + z = \frac{30}{2} = 15$ ...(iv)

On putting $x + y = 12$ from Eq. (i) in Eq. (iv), we get

$12 + z = 15$

$\Rightarrow \quad z = 3$

On putting $z + y = 8$ from Eq. (iii) in Eq. (iv), we get

$x + 8 = 15$

$\Rightarrow \quad x = 7$ (1)

On putting $x + z = 10$ from Eq. (ii) in Eq. (iv), we get

$10 + y = 15$

$\Rightarrow \quad y = 5$

Hence, $AD = 7$ cm, $BE = 5$ cm and $CF = 3$ cm (1)

**28.** Prove that $\frac{\sin A + \cos A}{\sin A - \cos A} + \frac{\sin A - \cos A}{\sin A + \cos A} = \frac{2}{\sin^2 A - \cos^2 A}$

*Or*

Prove that $\frac{\sin\theta - \cos\theta + 1}{\sin\theta + \cos\theta - 1} = \frac{1}{\sec\theta - \tan\theta}$, using the identity $\sec^2\theta = 1 + \tan^2\theta$.

***Sol.*** LHS $= \frac{\sin A + \cos A}{\sin A - \cos A} + \frac{\sin A - \cos A}{\sin A + \cos A}$

$= \frac{(\sin A + \cos A)^2 + (\sin A - \cos A)^2}{(\sin A - \cos A)(\sin A + \cos A)}$ (1)

$= \frac{\left[\begin{array}{r}\sin^2 A + 2\sin A\cos A + \cos^2 A + \sin^2 A \\ - 2\sin A\cos A + \cos^2 A\end{array}\right]}{\sin^2 A - \cos^2 A}$

[$\because (a \pm b)^2 = a^2 + b^2 \pm 2ab$] (1)

$= \frac{2\sin^2 A + 2\cos^2 A}{\sin^2 A - \cos^2 A} = \frac{2(\sin^2 A + \cos^2 A)}{\sin^2 A - \cos^2 A}$

$= \frac{2}{\sin^2 A - \cos^2 A}$ [$\because \sin^2\theta + \cos^2\theta = 1$]

= RHS **Hence proved.** (1)

*Or*

$$\text{LHS} = \frac{\sin\theta - \cos\theta + 1}{\sin\theta + \cos\theta - 1} = \frac{\tan\theta - 1 + \sec\theta}{\tan\theta + 1 - \sec\theta}$$

[dividing numerator and denominator by $\cos\theta$]

$$= \frac{(\tan\theta + \sec\theta) - 1}{(\tan\theta - \sec\theta) + 1}$$

$$= \frac{[(\tan\theta + \sec\theta) - 1][\tan\theta - \sec\theta]}{[(\tan\theta - \sec\theta) + 1][\tan\theta - \sec\theta]}$$

[multiplying and dividing by $(\tan\theta - \sec\theta)$] (1)

$$= \frac{(\tan^2\theta - \sec^2\theta) - (\tan\theta - \sec\theta)}{(\tan\theta - \sec\theta + 1)(\tan\theta - \sec\theta)}$$

[$\because (a-b)(a+b) = a^2 - b^2$]

$$= \frac{-1 - \tan\theta + \sec\theta}{(\tan\theta - \sec\theta + 1)(\tan\theta - \sec\theta)}$$

[$\because \tan^2 A - \sec^2 A = -1$] (1)

$$= \frac{-(\tan\theta - \sec\theta + 1)}{(\tan\theta - \sec\theta + 1)(\tan\theta - \sec\theta)}$$

$$= \frac{-1}{\tan\theta - \sec\theta}$$

$$= \frac{1}{\sec\theta - \tan\theta} = \text{RHS}$$ **Hence proved.** (1)

**29.** Circular footpath of width 2 m is constructed at the rate of ₹ 20 per $m^2$ around a circular park of radius 1500 m.

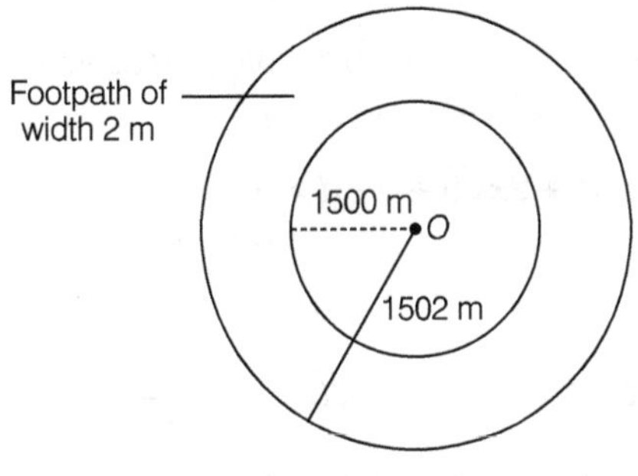


Contractor Ravi was assigned for constructing this footpath. Then, he proposed a estimate of ₹ 377051.2. Is his estimation right? Explain.

***Sol.*** Yes, radius of the park, i.e. inner radius of the park $r = 1500$ m

Width of the footpath around the park = 2 m

Let $R$ be the outer radius of the park including the footpath.

Then, $R = 1500 + 2 = 1502$ m (1)

Now, area of footpath $= \pi R^2 - \pi r^2$

$= \pi(R^2 - r^2) = 3.14[(1502)^2 - (1500)^2]$ (1)

$= 3.14[(1502 + 1500)(1502 - 1500)]$

$= 3.14 \times 6004 = 18852.56\, m^2$

$\therefore$ Total cost of construction of the footpath at the rate of ₹ 20 per $m^2 = 20 \times 18852.56$

= ₹ 377051.2 (1)

**30.** Find the roots of the following equation $\frac{1}{x+4} - \frac{1}{x-7} = \frac{11}{30}, x \neq -4, 7.$

*Or*

Solve for $x$, $2\left(\frac{2x+3}{x-3}\right) - 25\left(\frac{x-3}{2x+3}\right) = 5.$

***Sol.*** Given equation is $\frac{1}{x+4} - \frac{1}{x-7} = \frac{11}{30}, x \neq -4, 7$

$\Rightarrow \frac{(x-7)-(x+4)}{(x+4)(x-7)} = \frac{11}{30}$

$\Rightarrow \frac{x-7-x-4}{x^2 - 7x + 4x - 28} = \frac{11}{30}$

$\Rightarrow \frac{-11}{x^2 - 3x - 28} = \frac{11}{30}$

$\Rightarrow \frac{-1}{x^2 - 3x - 28} = \frac{1}{30}$

$\Rightarrow -30 = x^2 - 3x - 28$

$\Rightarrow x^2 - 3x + 2 = 0$ (1)

On comparing with the standard quadratic equation $ax^2 + bx + c = 0$, we get

$a = 1,\ b = -3$ and $c = 2$

By using quadratic formula, we get

$$x = \frac{-b \pm \sqrt{b^2 - 4ac}}{2a}$$

$$= \frac{-(-3) \pm \sqrt{(-3)^2 - 4(1)(2)}}{2 \times 1}$$ (1)

$$= \frac{3 \pm \sqrt{9-8}}{2} = \frac{3 \pm \sqrt{1}}{2} = \frac{3 \pm 1}{2}$$

$\Rightarrow x = \frac{3+1}{2}$ or $x = \frac{3-1}{2} \Rightarrow x = \frac{4}{2}$ or $x = \frac{2}{2}$

$\therefore x = 2$ or $x = 1$

Hence, the roots of the given equation are 2 and 1. (1)

*Or*

Let $\frac{2x+3}{x-3} = y$ ...(i)

Then, $\frac{x-3}{2x+3} = \frac{1}{y}$ (1/2)

Therefore, the given equation reduces to

$$2y - 25\frac{1}{y} = 5$$

$\Rightarrow 2y^2 - 25 = 5y$

$\Rightarrow 2y^2 - 5y - 25 = 0$

$\Rightarrow 2y^2 - 10y + 5y - 25 = 0$ [by factorisation method]

$\Rightarrow 2y(y-5) + 5(y-5) = 0$

$\Rightarrow (y-5)(2y+5) = 0$

$\Rightarrow y = 5$ or $y = \frac{-5}{2}$ (1)

Now, putting $y = 5$ in Eq. (i), we get

$$\frac{2x+3}{x-3} = \frac{5}{1}$$

$\Rightarrow 5x - 15 = 2x + 3$

$\Rightarrow 3x = 18$

$\Rightarrow x = 6$ (1/2)

Again, putting $y = -\frac{5}{2}$ in Eq. (i), we get

$$\frac{2x+3}{x-3} = -\frac{5}{2}$$

$\Rightarrow -5x + 15 = 4x + 6$

$\therefore 9x = 9$

$\Rightarrow x = 1$

Hence, the values of $x$ are 1 and 6. (1)

**31.** The Resident Welfare Association of a colony decided to build two straight paths in their neighbourhood park such that they do not cross each other, to plant trees along the boundary lines of each path. One of the members of association, Sarika suggested that the paths should be constructed represented by the two linear equations $x - 3y = 2$ and $-2x + 6y = 5$. Check whether the two paths will cross each other or not.

***Sol.*** Given, linear equations are

$x - 3y = 2$

$\Rightarrow x - 3y - 2 = 0$ ...(i)

and $-2x + 6y = 5$

$\Rightarrow -2x + 6y - 5 = 0$ ...(ii)

Here, $a_1 = 1,\ b_1 = -3,\ c_1 = -2$

and $a_2 = -2,\ b_2 = 6,\ c_2 = -5$ (1)

Now, $\frac{a_1}{a_2} = \frac{1}{-2} = -\frac{1}{2},\ \frac{b_1}{b_2} = \frac{-3}{6} = -\frac{1}{2}$

and $\frac{c_1}{c_2} = \frac{-2}{-5} = \frac{2}{5}$

Here, $\frac{a_1}{a_2} = \frac{b_1}{b_2} \neq \frac{c_1}{c_2}$ (1)

So, the paths represented by the equations are parallel, i.e. not cross (intersect) each other. (1)

# Section-D

**Section D consists of 4 questions of 5 marks each**

**32.** Prove that, if $a, b, c$ and $d$ are positive rationals such that, $a + \sqrt{b} = c + \sqrt{d}$, then either $a = c$ and $b = d$ or $b$ and $d$ are squares of rationals.

*Or*

In a seminar, the number of participants, in Hindi, English and Mathematics are 60, 84 and 108 respectively. Find the number of rooms required, if in each room the same number of participants are to be seated and all of them bring the same subject.

***Sol.*** Given, $a + \sqrt{b} = c + \sqrt{d}$

If $a = c$, then $a + \sqrt{b} = a + \sqrt{d}$

$\Rightarrow \sqrt{b} = \sqrt{d}$

$\Rightarrow b = d$ [squaring both sides]

If $a \neq c$, then there exists a positive rational number $x$ such that, $a = c + x$.

Now, $a + \sqrt{b} = c + \sqrt{d}$

$\Rightarrow c + x + \sqrt{b} = c + \sqrt{d}$ [$\because a = c + x$]

$\Rightarrow x + \sqrt{b} = \sqrt{d}$ ...(i) (1)

$\Rightarrow (x + \sqrt{b})^2 = (\sqrt{d})^2$ [squaring both sides]

$\Rightarrow x^2 + b + 2x\sqrt{b} = d$

$\Rightarrow x^2 + 2x\sqrt{b} + b - d = 0$

[$\because (A+B)^2 = A^2 + B^2 + 2AB$]

$\Rightarrow 2x\sqrt{b} = d - b - x^2$

$\therefore \sqrt{b} = \frac{d - b - x^2}{2x}$

Since, $d$, $x$ and $b$ are rational numbers and $x > 0$.

So, $\frac{d - b - x^2}{2x}$ is a rational.

Then, $\sqrt{b}$ is a rational number. (2)

Hence, $b$ is the square of a rational number.

From Eq. (i), we get

$\sqrt{d} = x + \sqrt{b}$

Also, $\sqrt{d}$ is a rational.

So, $d$ is the square of a rational number.

Hence, either $a = c$ and $b = d$ or $b$ and $d$ are the squares of rationals. **Hence proved.** (2)

*Or*

The number of participants in each room must be the HCF of 60, 84 and 108. (1)

Now, prime factors of numbers 60, 84 and 108 are

$$60 = 2^2 \times 3 \times 5,$$
$$84 = 2^2 \times 3 \times 7$$
and $$108 = 2^2 \times 3^3$$

HCF of (60, 84, 108) $= 2^2 \times 3 = 12$ **(2)**

Therefore, in each room maximum 12 participants can be seated.

$\therefore$ Total number of participants $= 60 + 84 + 108 = 252$

$\therefore$ Number of rooms required $= \dfrac{252}{12} = 21$ **(2)**

**33.** The median of the distribution given below is 14.4. Find the values of $x$ and $y$, if the total frequency is 20.

| Class interval | 0-6 | 6-12 | 12-18 | 18-24 | 24-30 |
|---|---|---|---|---|---|
| Frequency | 4 | $x$ | 5 | $y$ | 1 |

***Sol.*** Table for cumulative frequency is given below

| Class interval | Frequency | Cumulative frequency |
|---|---|---|
| 0-6 | 4 | $4 + 0 = 4$ |
| 6-12 | $x$ | $4 + x = (4 + x)\,(cf)$ |
| 12-18 | $5\,(f)$ | $5 + (4 + x) = 9 + x$ |
| 18-24 | $y$ | $y + (9 + x) = 9 + x + y$ |
| 24-30 | 1 | $1 + (9 + x + y) = 10 + x + y$ |

**(1)**

Since, $N = 20$

$\therefore \quad 10 + x + y = 20$

$\Rightarrow \quad x + y = 20 - 10$

$\Rightarrow \quad x + y = 10$ ...(i)

Also, we have, median = 14.4

which lies in the class interval 12-18. **(1)**

$\therefore$ The median class is 12-18, such that

$l = 12, f = 5, cf = 4 + x$ and $h = 6$

$$\therefore \quad \text{Median} = l + \left(\frac{\frac{N}{2} - cf}{f}\right) \times h$$ **(1)**

$$\Rightarrow \quad 14.4 = 12 + \left[\frac{10 - (4 + x)}{5}\right] \times 6$$

$$\Rightarrow \quad 14.4 - 12 = \frac{6 - x}{5} \times 6$$

$$\Rightarrow \quad 2.4 = \frac{36 - 6x}{5}$$

$$\Rightarrow \quad 12 = 36 - 6x$$

$\Rightarrow \quad 6x = 24 \Rightarrow x = 4$ **(1)**

Now, put the value of $x$ in Eq. (i), we get

$$4 + y = 10 \Rightarrow y = 10 - 4 = 6$$

Thus, $x = 4$ and $y = 6$ **(1)**

**34.** Find the length of the median drawn through $A$ on $BC$ of a $\Delta ABC$, whose vertices are $A(7, -3)$, $B(5, 3)$ and $C(3, -1)$ and also find the distance of the point $A(7, -3)$ from the origin.

*Or*

Find the centre of a circle passing through the points $(6, -6)$, $(3, -7)$ and $(3, 3)$.

***Sol.*** The median from a vertex of a triangle bisects the opposite side, to that vertex. So, let $AD$ be the median through $A$, then $D$ be the mid-point of the side $BC$.

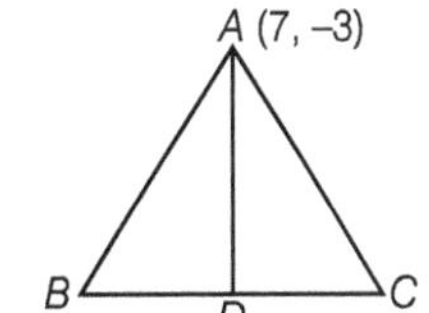


Now, coordinates of $D = \left(\dfrac{5+3}{2}, \dfrac{3-1}{2}\right) = (4, 1)$ **(2)**

$\left[\because \text{coordinates of mid-point of line segment joining } (x_1, y_1) \text{ and } (x_2, y_2) = \left(\dfrac{x_1 + x_2}{2}, \dfrac{y_1 + y_2}{2}\right)\right]$

and length of median $AD$ is given by

$$AD = \sqrt{(x_2 - x_1)^2 + (y_2 - y_1)^2}$$ [by distance formula] **(1)**

$$= \sqrt{(4-7)^2 + (1+3)^2} = \sqrt{(-3)^2 + (4)^2}$$

$= \sqrt{9 + 16} = \sqrt{25} = 5$ units **(1)**

Also, $OA = \sqrt{(0-7)^2 + (0+3)^2}$

$= \sqrt{49 + 9} = \sqrt{58}$ units **(1)**

*Or*

Let $C(x, y)$ be the centre of the circle passing through the points $P(6, -6)$, $Q(3, -7)$ and $R(3, 3)$.

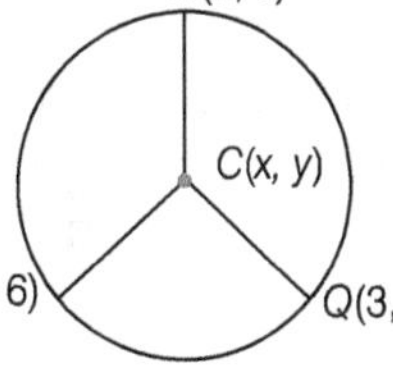


**(2)**

Then, $PC = QC = CR$ [radii of circle]

Now, $PC = QC$

$\Rightarrow \quad PC^2 = QC^2$ [squaring both sides]

$\Rightarrow (x - 6)^2 + (y + 6)^2 = (x - 3)^2 + (y + 7)^2$

$\left[\because \text{distance} = \sqrt{(x_2 - x_1)^2 + (y_2 - y_1)^2}\right]$

$\Rightarrow x^2 - 12x + 36 + y^2 + 12y + 36$

$= x^2 - 6x + 9 + y^2 + 14y + 49$

$[\because (a - b)^2 = a^2 + b^2 - 2ab]$ **(1)**

$\Rightarrow -12x + 6x + 12y - 14y + 72 - 58 = 0$

$\Rightarrow \quad -6x - 2y + 14 = 0$

$\Rightarrow \quad 3x + y - 7 = 0$ [dividing by − 2] ...(i)

and $\quad QC = CR$

$\Rightarrow \quad QC^2 = CR^2$ [squaring both sides]

$\Rightarrow (x-3)^2 + (y+7)^2 = (x-3)^2 + (y-3)^2$

$\Rightarrow \quad (y+7)^2 = (y-3)^2$ (1)

$\Rightarrow \quad y^2 + 14y + 49 = y^2 - 6y + 9$

$\Rightarrow \quad 20y + 40 = 0$

$\Rightarrow \quad y = -\frac{40}{20} = -2$ ...(ii)

On putting $y = -2$ in Eq. (i), we get

$3x - 2 - 7 = 0$

$\Rightarrow \quad 3x = 9$

$\Rightarrow \quad x = 3$

Hence, the centre of circle is (3, − 2). (1)

**35.** A hemispherical bowl of internal diameter 36 cm contains liquid. This liquid is filled into 72 cylindrical bottles of diameter 6 cm. Find the height of each bottle, if 10% liquid is wasted in this transfer.

***Sol.*** Given, diameter of hemispherical bowl = 36 cm

$\Rightarrow$ Radius $(r) = 18$ cm

Volume of liquid in the bowl $= \frac{2}{3}\pi r^3$

$= \frac{2}{3} \times \pi \times 18 \times 18 \times 18$

$= 3888\pi \text{ cm}^3$ (1)

Amount of the liquid wasted $= 3888\pi \times \frac{10}{100}$

$= \frac{3888\,\pi}{10} \text{ cm}^3$ (1)

Liquid transferred into the bottles

$= 3888\pi - \frac{3888\pi}{10} \text{ cm}^3$

$= \frac{34992\pi}{10} \text{ cm}^3$ ...(i)

Also, given diameter of bottle = 6 cm

$\Rightarrow$ Radius $(r) = 3$ cm (1)

Let $h$ be the height of the bottle.

Volume of bottle $= \pi r^2 h = \pi \times 3 \times 3 \times h = 9\pi h \text{ cm}^3$

Volume of 72 such bottles $= 72 \times 9\pi h \text{ cm}^3$

$= 648\pi h \text{ cm}^3$ (1)

Now, volume of 72 bottles

= Volume of liquid transferred into the bottles

$\Rightarrow \quad 648\pi h = \frac{34992\pi}{10}$ [using Eq. (i)]

$\Rightarrow \quad h = 5.4$ cm

$\therefore$ Height of each bottle is 5.4 cm. (1)

# Section-E

**Case study based questions are compulsory**

**36. Roller Coaster Polynomials**

Polynomials are everywhere. They play a key role in the study of algebra in analysis and on the whole many mathematical problems involving them.

Since, polynomial are used to describe curves of various types engineers use polynomials to graph the curves on roller coasters.

On the basis of above information, answer the following questions.

(i) If the roller coaster is represented by the following graph $y = p(x)$, then name the type of the polynomial it traces. (1)

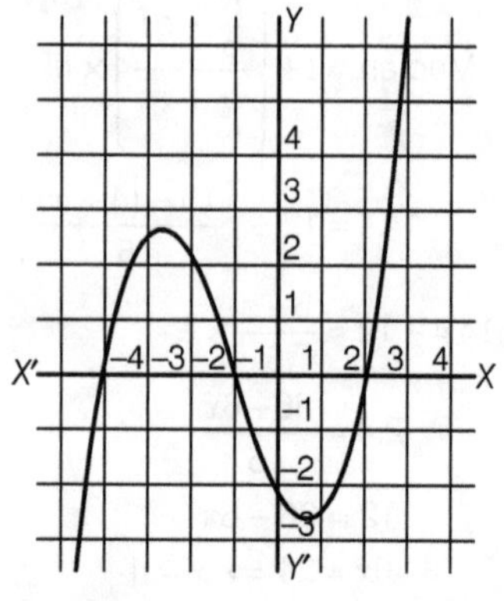


(ii) In the graph shown above, find the zeroes of $y = p(x)$. (1)

(iii) If $p(x)=2x^3-5x^2-14x+8$, then find the sum and product of zeroes. (2)

*Or*

Find a quadratic polynomial, the sum and product of whose roots are −3 and 2, respectively. (2)

**Sol.** (i) Since, graph of given polynomial intersect X-axis at 3 points. So, it has three zeroes.
Hence, it is a cubic polynomial.

(ii) The graph of given polynomial intersect X-axis at points −4, −1 and 2. So, zeroes of given polynomial are −4, −1 and 2.

(iii) On comparing given polynomial $2x^3-5x^2-14x+8$ with $ax^3+bx^2+cx+d$, we get

$$a=2, b=-5, c=-14 \text{ and } d=8$$

Sum of roots, $\alpha+\beta+\gamma=\frac{-b}{a}$

$$=\frac{-(-5)}{2}=\frac{5}{2}$$

Product of roots, $\alpha\beta\gamma=\frac{-d}{a}=\frac{-8}{2}=-4$

*Or*

Sum of roots, $\alpha+\beta=-3=\frac{-b}{a}$

and product of roots, $\alpha\beta=2=\frac{c}{a}$

∴ Quadratic polynomial is $x^2+3x+2$.

**37.** Ritu is studying in X standard. She observes two poles $AB$ and $DC$ and the heights of these poles are $a$ m and $b$ m respectively, shown as figure below.

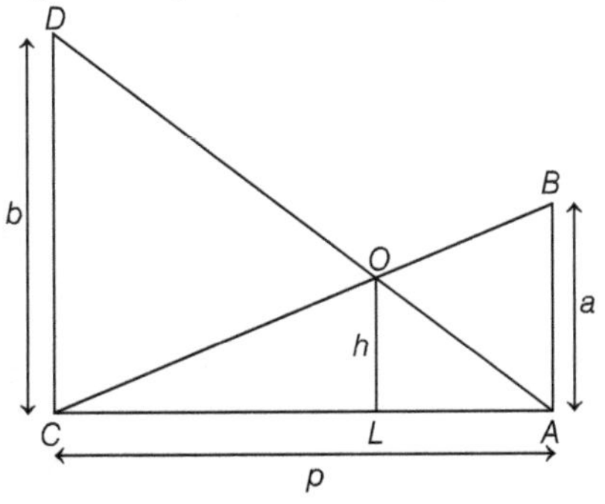


These poles are $p$ m apart and $O$ is the point of intersection of the lines joining the top of each pole to the foot of opposite pole and the distance between point $O$ and $L$ is $h$. Few questions came to his mind while observing the poles. Give answer to his questions by looking at figure.

(i) If $CL=x$, then find $x$ in terms of $a$, $b$ and $h$. (1)

(ii) If $AL=y$, then find $y$ in terms of $a$, $b$ and $h$. (1)

(iii) Find $h$ in terms of $a$ and $b$. (2)

*Or*

If $a=5$ m and $b=10$ m, then find $h$. (2)

**Sol.** (i) In $\Delta ABC$ and $\Delta LOC$, we have

$$\angle CAB=\angle CLO=90^\circ$$

$$\angle C=\angle C \quad \text{[common]}$$

∴ By AA-criterion of similarity,

$$\Delta CAB \sim \Delta CLO$$

$$\Rightarrow \quad \frac{CA}{CL}=\frac{AB}{LO}$$

$$\Rightarrow \quad \frac{p}{x}=\frac{a}{h} \Rightarrow x=\frac{ph}{a} \quad \text{...(i)}$$

(ii) In $\Delta ALO$ and $\Delta ACD$, we have

$$\angle ALO=\angle ACD=90^\circ$$

$$\angle A=\angle A \quad \text{[common]}$$

$$\therefore \Delta ALO \sim \Delta ACD \quad \text{[by AA similarity criterion]}$$

$$\Rightarrow \quad \frac{AL}{AC}=\frac{OL}{DC}$$

$$\Rightarrow \quad \frac{y}{p}=\frac{h}{b} \Rightarrow y=\frac{ph}{b} \quad \text{...(ii)}$$

(iii) From Eqs. (i) and (ii), we get

$$x+y=\frac{ph}{a}+\frac{ph}{b}=ph\left(\frac{1}{a}+\frac{1}{b}\right)$$

$$\Rightarrow \quad p=ph\left(\frac{a+b}{ab}\right) \quad [\because x+y=CL+LA=p]$$

$$\Rightarrow \quad h=\frac{ab}{a+b}\text{ m}$$

*Or*

If a = 5 m and b = 10 m.

Then, $h=\frac{ab}{a+b}=\frac{5\times 10}{5+10}=\frac{50}{15}=\frac{10}{3}$ m

**38.** Sara is studying in X standard. She is making a figure to understand trigonometric ratio as shown below.

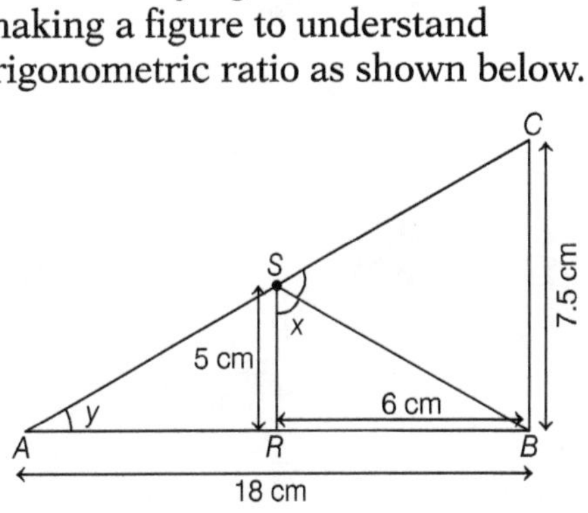

In $\Delta ABC$, $\angle B$ is right angled, $\Delta BSC$ is right angled at $S$ and $\Delta BRS$ is right angled at $R$. $AB = 18$ cm, $BC = 7.5$ cm, $RS = 5$ cm, $RB = 6$ cm, $\angle BSR = x$ and $\angle SAB = y$.

Give answers to her questions by looking at the figure.

(i) What is the length of $AS$? (1)

(ii) Find $\tan x$. (1)

(iii) Find $\sec x$. (2)

*Or* Find $\operatorname{cosec} x$. (2)

***Sol.*** (i) We have, $AR = AB - RB = 18 - 6 = 12$ cm

In $\Delta ARS$, by using Pythagoras theorem

$$AS^2 = AR^2 + RS^2$$

$$= (12)^2 + (5)^2 = 144 + 25 = 169$$

$$\Rightarrow \quad AS = \sqrt{169} = 13\text{ cm}$$

(ii) In $\Delta BRS$,

$$\tan x = \frac{\text{Perpendicular}}{\text{Base}} = \frac{BR}{RS} = \frac{6}{5}$$

(iii) We know that

$$\sec x = \sqrt{1 + \tan^2 x}$$

$$= \sqrt{1 + \left(\frac{6}{5}\right)^2}$$

$$= \sqrt{1 + \frac{36}{25}}$$

$$= \sqrt{\frac{61}{25}} = \frac{\sqrt{61}}{5}$$

*Or*

We know that

$$\operatorname{cosec} x = \sqrt{1 + \cot^2 x}$$

$$= \sqrt{1 + \frac{1}{\tan^2 x}}$$

$$= \sqrt{1 + \left(\frac{5}{6}\right)^2}$$

$$= \sqrt{\frac{36 + 25}{36}} = \sqrt{\frac{61}{36}} = \frac{\sqrt{61}}{6}$$

# SAMPLE QUESTION PAPER 2

## Mathematics (Basic)

Time : **3 hrs** Max. Marks : **80**

### Instructions

1. This question paper has 5 Sections A, B, C, D and E.
2. Section A has 20 Multiple Choice Questions (MCQs) carrying 1 mark each.
3. Section B has 5 Short Answer-I (SA-I) Type Questions carrying 2 marks each.
4. Section C has 6 Short Answer-II (SA-II) Type Questions carrying 3 marks each.
5. Section D has 4 Long Answer (LA) Type Questions carrying 5 marks each.
6. Section E has 3 Case Based integrated units of assessment (4 marks each) with sub-parts of the values of 1, 1 and 2 marks each respectively.
7. All questions are compulsory. However, an internal choice in 2 questions of 2 marks, 2 questions of 3 marks and 2 questions of 5 marks has been provided. An internal choice has been provided in the 2 marks questions of Section E.
8. Draw neat figures wherever required. Take $\pi = 22/7$ wherever required if not stated.

## Section-A

**Section A consists of 20 questions of 1 mark each**

**1.** The mid-point of line segment joining origin and $(-4, -2)$ is

(a) (2, 1) (b) (1, 2) (c) (−4, −2) (d) (−2, −1)

***Sol.*** (d) The mid-point of line segment joining (0, 0) and $(-4, -2)$ is $\left(\frac{0-4}{2}, \frac{0-2}{2}\right)$ i.e. $(-2, -1)$.

**2.** The value of $\tan 45° \cos 60° + \sin 60° \cot 60°$ is

(a) $\frac{1}{2}$ (b) 2 (c) 1 (d) $\frac{1}{2}(\sqrt{3}+1)$

***Sol.*** (c) $\tan 45° \cos 60° + \sin 60° \cot 60°$

$$= 1 \times \frac{1}{2} + \frac{\sqrt{3}}{2} \times \frac{1}{\sqrt{3}} = \frac{1}{2} + \frac{1}{2} = 1$$

**3.** The discriminant of the quadratic equation $2x^2 - \sqrt{5}x + 1 = 0$ is

(a) −3 (b) $\sqrt{-3}$ (c) 1 (d) −1

***Sol.*** (a) Given equation, $2x^2 - \sqrt{5}x + 1 = 0$

On comparing it with $ax^2 + bx + c = 0$, we get

$$a = 2, b = \sqrt{5} \text{ and } c = 1$$

$\therefore$ $D = (-\sqrt{5})^2 - 4(2)(1)$ $[\because D = b^2 - 4ac]$

$$= 5 - 8 = -3$$

**4.** The acute angle $\theta$ satisfying $\sqrt{3}\sin\theta = \cos\theta$ is

(a) 70° (b) 30°
(c) 45° (d) 60°

***Sol.*** (b) We have, $\sqrt{3}\sin\theta = \cos\theta$

$\Rightarrow \quad \dfrac{\sin\theta}{\cos\theta} = \dfrac{1}{\sqrt{3}}$

$\Rightarrow \quad \tan\theta = \dfrac{1}{\sqrt{3}}$

$\Rightarrow \quad \tan\theta = \tan 30°$

$\therefore \quad \theta = 30°$

**5.** In $\Delta DEW$, $AB \| EW$. If $AD = 4$ cm, $DE = 12$ cm and $DW = 24$ cm, then the value of $DB$ is

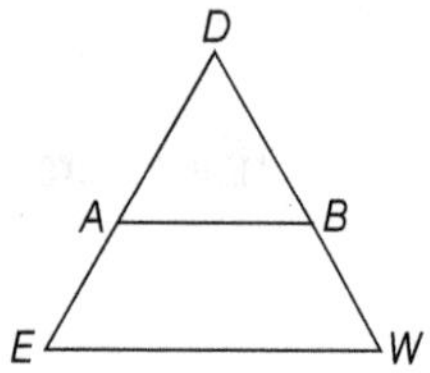


(a) 16 cm (b) 4 cm
(c) 12 cm (d) 8 cm

***Sol.*** (d) Given, $AB \| EW$

$\therefore \quad \dfrac{DA}{AE} = \dfrac{DB}{BW}$ [by Thale's theorem]

$\Rightarrow \quad \dfrac{DA}{DE - DA} = \dfrac{DB}{DW - DB}$

$\Rightarrow \quad \dfrac{4}{12-4} = \dfrac{DB}{24 - DB}$

$\Rightarrow \quad \dfrac{4}{8} = \dfrac{DB}{24 - DB}$

$\Rightarrow \quad 24 - DB = 2DB$

$\Rightarrow \quad 24 = 3DB$

$\Rightarrow \quad DB = \dfrac{24}{3} = 8\,\text{cm}$

**6.** An unbiased die is thrown, the probability of getting an even number is

(a) 1 (b) $\frac{1}{2}$
(c) $\frac{3}{4}$ (d) $\frac{1}{3}$

***Sol.*** (b) Let $A$ be the event 'getting an even number.' Clearly, event $A$ occurs, if we obtain any one of 2, 4, 6 as an outcome.

$\therefore$ Number of outcomes favourable to $A = 3$

Hence, $P(A) = \dfrac{3}{6} = \dfrac{1}{2}$

**7.** A pendulum swings through an angle of 30° and describes an arc 4.4 cm in length, then the length of the pendulum is

(a) 8.4 cm (b) 4.4 cm (c) 10.2 cm (d) 6.8 cm

***Sol.*** (a) Length of the arc $= \dfrac{\theta}{360°} \times 2\pi r$

$\Rightarrow \quad 4.4 = \dfrac{30°}{360°} \times 2 \times \dfrac{22}{7} \times r$

$\Rightarrow \quad 4.4 = \dfrac{1}{12} \times \dfrac{44}{7} \times r$

$\Rightarrow \quad r = \dfrac{4.4 \times 12 \times 7}{44} = 8.4\,\text{cm}$

**8.** If $\alpha, \beta$ are the zeroes of the polynomial $p(x) = 4x^2 + 3x + 7$, then the value of $\alpha\beta$ is

(a) $\frac{3}{4}$ (b) $-\frac{3}{4}$ (c) $\frac{7}{4}$ (d) $\frac{7}{3}$

***Sol.*** (c) We know that

$\text{Product of zeroes} = \dfrac{\text{Constant term}}{\text{Coefficient of } x^2}$

$\therefore \quad \alpha\beta = \dfrac{7}{4}$

**9.** A card is drawn from a well-shuffled deck of 52 cards. The probability of getting a king of red colour is

(a) $\frac{1}{52}$ (b) $\frac{1}{13}$ (c) $\frac{1}{26}$ (d) $\frac{3}{52}$

***Sol.*** (c) Total number of cards = 52

Kings which are red in colour = 2

$P(\text{king of red colour}) = \dfrac{2}{52} = \dfrac{1}{26}$

**10.** If point $P$ lies inside the circle, then the number of tangent(s) drawn from point $P$ are

(a) 0 (b) 1 (c) 2 (d) $\infty$

***Sol.*** (a) If point $P$ lies inside the circle, then no tangent can be drawn.

**11.** For what value of $k$, if 3 is a zero of the polynomial $2x^2 + x + k$?

(a) −15 (b) −9 (c) −18 (d) −21

***Sol.*** (d) Let $f(x) = 2x^2 + x + k$ ...(i)

Given, 3 is a zero of the polynomial $f(x)$.

Therefore, put $x = 3$ in Eq. (i) and consider $f(3) = 0$

$\therefore \quad f(3) = 2(3)^2 + 3 + k = 0$

$\Rightarrow \quad 2 \times 9 + 3 + k = 0$

$\Rightarrow \quad 18 + 3 + k = 0 \Rightarrow k = -21$

**12.** The formula for finding mean by direct method is $\frac{\Sigma(A \times B)}{\Sigma A}$, where $B$ and $A$ are respectively

(a) class mark, frequency of the class
(b) average frequency, class size
(c) class size, average frequency
(d) frequency of the class, class mark

***Sol.*** (a) Class mark, frequency of the class

$$\bar{x} = \frac{\Sigma fx}{\Sigma f} = \frac{\Sigma(A \times B)}{\Sigma A},$$

where $B$ is the class mark.

Class mark $= \frac{1}{2}$ (upper limit + lower limit)

and $A$ is the frequency of the class.

**13.** The 17th term of an AP exceeds its 10th term by 7. Then, the common difference is

(a) 1 (b) $\frac{7}{8}$ (c) 2 (d) $\frac{7}{6}$

***Sol.*** (a) Let $d$ be the common difference of the AP.
According to the question,

$$a_{17} - a_{10} = 7$$

$\Rightarrow$ $(a + 16d) - (a + 9d) = 7 \Rightarrow 7d = 7 \Rightarrow d = 1$

**14.** The mode of the following data is

| $x_i$ | 10 | 14 | 18 | 21 | 25 |
|---|---|---|---|---|---|
| $y_i$ | 10 | 15 | 7 | 9 | 9 |

(a) 16 (b) 14 (c) 12 (d) 10

***Sol.*** (b) The mode is the most frequent observation.
Here, the mode is 14 with a frequency of 15.

**15.** Solve $(x + 2)(3x - 5) = 0$.

(a) $2, \frac{5}{3}$ (b) $2, \frac{3}{2}$ (c) $-2, 5$ (d) $-2, \frac{5}{3}$

***Sol.*** (d) $(x + 2)(3x - 5) = 0$

$\Rightarrow$ $x + 2 = 0$ or $3x - 5 = 0$

$\Rightarrow$ $x = -2$ or $x = \frac{5}{3}$

Hence, the roots of the given equation are $-2$ and $\frac{5}{3}$.

**16.** The roots of the equation $2x^2 - 6x + 7 = 0$ are

(a) real, unequal and rational
(b) real, unequal and irrational
(c) real and equal
(d) imaginary

***Sol.*** (d) Given, equation $2x^2 - 6x + 7 = 0$
On comparing it with $ax^2 + bx + c = 0$, we get

$$a = 2, b = -6 \text{ and } c = 7$$

$\therefore$ $D = b^2 - 4ac = (-6)^2 - 4(2)(7)$
$= 36 - 56 = -20 < 0$

So, the roots are imaginary.

**17.** A ladder 15 m long makes an angle of 60° with the wall. The height of the point, where the ladder touches the wall, is

(a) $15\sqrt{3}$ m (b) $\frac{15\sqrt{3}}{2}$ m
(c) $\frac{15}{2}$ m (d) 15 m

***Sol.*** (c) Given, $\angle ABC = 60°$
In $\Delta ABC$, $\angle BAC + \angle ABC + \angle ACB = 180°$

$\Rightarrow$ $\angle BAC = 180° - 90° - 60° = 30°$

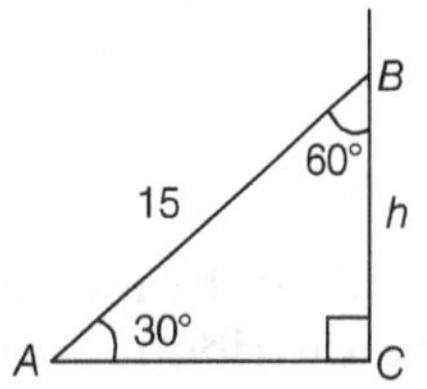


So, $\sin 30° = \frac{BC}{AB} = \frac{h}{15}$

$\Rightarrow$ $\frac{1}{2} = \frac{h}{15} \Rightarrow h = \frac{15}{2}$ m

**18.** In a right circular cone, the cross-section made by a plane parallel to the base is

(a) sphere (b) hemisphere
(c) circle (d) semi-circle

***Sol.*** (c) Circle

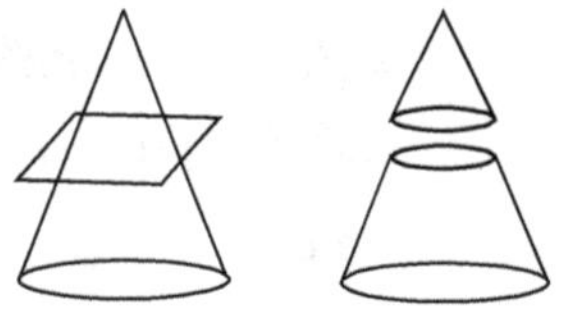

**Directions** *In the question number 19 and 20, a statement of Assertion (A) is followed by a statement of Reason (R). Choose the correct option.*

**19. Assertion (A)** The system of equations $x + y - 8 = 0$ and $x - y - 2 = 0$ has a unique solution.

**Reason (R)** The system of equations $a_1x + b_1y + c_1 = 0$ and $a_2x + b_2y + c_2 = 0$ has a unique solution, when $\frac{a_1}{a_2} = \frac{b_1}{b_2}$.

(a) Both Assertion (A) and Reason (R) are true and Reason (R) is the correct explanation of Assertion (A)

(b) Both Assertion (A) and Reason (R) are true but Reason (R) is not the correct explanation of Assertion (A)
(c) Assertion (A) is true but Reason (R) is false
(d) Assertion (A) is false but Reason (R) is true

**Sol.** (c) **Assertion** Given $x+y-8=0$ and $x-y-2=0$

Here, $a_1=1, b_1=1, c_1=8$

and $a_2=1, b_2=-1, c_2=-2$

So, $\frac{a_1}{a_2}=\frac{1}{1}, \frac{b_1}{b_2}=\frac{1}{-1}$ and $\frac{c_1}{c_2}=\frac{-8}{-2}=4$

$\because \frac{a_1}{a_2}\neq\frac{b_1}{b_2}$

So, the system of equations has a unique solution and the Assertion is true.

**Reason** For equations to have a unique solution, $\frac{a_1}{a_2}$ should not be equal to $\frac{b_1}{b_2}$.

$\therefore$ The given Reason is false.

**20. Assertion (A)** If the median and mode of a frequency distribution are 150 and 154 respectively, then its mean is 148.

**Reason (R)** Mean, median and mode of a frequency distribution are related as

Mode = 3 Median −2 Mean

(a) Both Assertion (A) and Reason (R) are true and Reason (R) is the correct explanation of Assertion (A)
(b) Both Assertion (A) and Reason (R) are true but Reason (R) is not the correct explanation of Assertion (A)
(c) Assertion (A) is true but Reason (R) is false
(d) Assertion (A) is false but Reason (R) is true

**Sol.** (a) Reason is clearly true.

Using the relation given in reason, we have

$$2 \text{ Mean} = 3 \text{ Median} - \text{Mode}$$
$$= 3\times150-154$$
$$=296$$

$\therefore$ Mean $=\frac{296}{2}=148$, which is true.

Thus, both Assertion and Reason are true and Reason is the correct explanation of Assertion.

# Section-B

**Section B consists of 5 questions of 2 marks each**

**21.** If $x=a\cos\theta$ and $y=b\sin\theta$, then find $b^2x^2+a^2y^2$.

**Sol.** Given, $x=a\cos\theta$ and $y=b\sin\theta$

$\therefore b^2x^2+a^2y^2=b^2(a\cos\theta)^2+a^2(b\sin\theta)^2$ (1)

$=a^2b^2\cos^2\theta+a^2b^2\sin^2\theta$

$=a^2b^2(\cos^2\theta+\sin^2\theta)$

$=a^2b^2(1)$ $[\because \cos^2 A+\sin^2 A=1]$

$=a^2b^2$ (1)

**22.** Show that $\frac{2}{5\sqrt{3}}$ is an irrational number.

*Or*

Show that $6-2\sqrt{3}$ is irrational.

**Sol.** Let us assume that $\frac{2}{5\sqrt{3}}$ is a rational number.

$\therefore \frac{2}{5\sqrt{3}}=\frac{p}{q}$, where $p, q$ $(q\neq0)$ are integers and $p, q$ are coprimes. (1)

$\Rightarrow \frac{2q}{5p}=\sqrt{3}$

Since, 2, 5, $p$ and $q$ are integers.

$\therefore \frac{2q}{5p}$ is rational, so $\sqrt{3}$ is rational.

But this contradicts the fact that $\sqrt{3}$ is irrational.

Hence, $\frac{2}{5\sqrt{3}}$ is an irrational number.

**Hence proved.** (1)

*Or*

Let us assume that $6-2\sqrt{3}$ is rational number.

Then, it will be of the form $\frac{a}{b}$, where $a, b$ are coprime integers and $b\neq0$.

Now, $6-2\sqrt{3}=\frac{a}{b}$

On rearranging, we get

$$6-\frac{a}{b}=2\sqrt{3}$$ (1)

Since, 6 and $\frac{a}{b}$ are rational. So, their difference will be rational.

$\therefore 2\sqrt{3}$ is rational.

But we know that, $\sqrt{3}$ is irrational.

So, this contradicts the fact that $\sqrt{3}$ is irrational.

Therefore, our assumption is wrong.

Hence, $6-2\sqrt{3}$ is irrational. **Hence proved.** (1)

**23.** If $\alpha$ and $\beta$ are the zeroes of the polynomial $p(x) = 5x^2 - 7x + 1$, then find the value of $\frac{1}{\alpha} + \frac{1}{\beta}$.

***Sol.*** We have, $p(x) = 5x^2 - 7x + 1$, whose zeroes are $\alpha$ and $\beta$.

$\therefore$ Sum of zeroes, $\alpha + \beta = -\frac{\text{Coefficent of } x}{\text{Coefficent of } x^2}$

$= -\frac{(-7)}{5} = \frac{7}{5}$ ...(i) (1)

and product of zeroes, $\alpha\beta = \frac{\text{Constant term}}{\text{Coefficent of } x^2}$

$= \frac{1}{5}$ ... (ii)

Now, $\frac{1}{\alpha} + \frac{1}{\beta} = \frac{\beta + \alpha}{\alpha\beta} = \frac{7/5}{1/5}$

[from Eqs. (i) and (ii)]

$= 7$ (1)

**24.** Solve for $x$:

$$\frac{1}{x+1} + \frac{2}{x+2} = \frac{4}{x+4}, \; x \neq -1, -2, -4$$

***Sol.*** We have, $\frac{1}{x+1} + \frac{2}{x+2} = \frac{4}{x+4}$

$\Rightarrow \quad \frac{(x+2)+2(x+1)}{(x+1)(x+2)} = \frac{4}{x+4}$ (1)

$\Rightarrow \quad (x+4)(3x+4) = 4(x^2 + 3x + 2)$

$\Rightarrow \quad x^2 - 4x - 8 = 0$

On comparing it with $ax^2 + bx + c = 0$, we get

$a = 1, b = -4$ and $c = -8$

$\therefore \quad x = \frac{-b \pm \sqrt{b^2 - 4ac}}{2a}$

$\Rightarrow \quad x = \frac{-(-4) \pm \sqrt{16 - 4(1)(-8)}}{2} = \frac{4 \pm \sqrt{48}}{2}$

$\Rightarrow \quad x = 2 \pm 2\sqrt{3}$ (1)

**25.** In the given figure, if $DEFG$ is a square and $\angle BAC = 90°$, then show that $DE^2 = BD \times EC$.

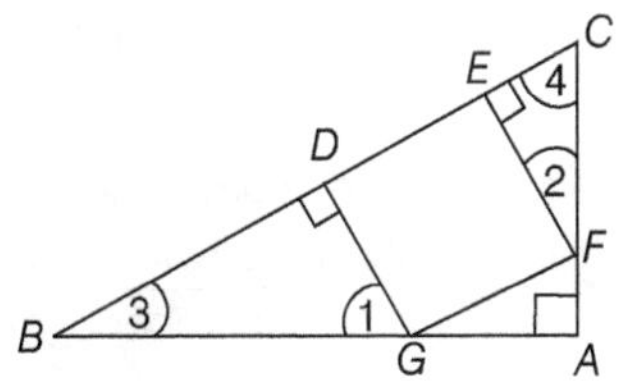


***Sol.*** $\because \quad \Delta AGF \sim \Delta DBG$ ...(i)

[by AA similarity criterion]

Now, in $\Delta AGF$ and $\Delta EFC$, we get

$\angle FAG = \angle CEF$ [each 90°]

and $\angle AFG = \angle ECF$

[corresponding angles because $GF \parallel BC$ and $AC$ is the transversal]

$\therefore \quad \Delta AGF \sim \Delta EFC$ ...(ii) (1)

From Eqs. (i) and (ii), we get

$\Delta DBG \sim \Delta EFC$

$\Rightarrow \quad \frac{BD}{EF} = \frac{DG}{EC}$

$\Rightarrow \quad \frac{BD}{DE} = \frac{DE}{EC}$ [$\because$ $DEFG$ is a square]

$\therefore \quad DE^2 = BD \times EC$ **Hence proved.** (1)

*Or*

In an isosceles right angled triangle, if the hypotenuse is $6\sqrt{2}$ cm, find the length of the sides of the triangle.

***Sol.*** Let $\Delta ABC$ be an isosceles right angled triangle, right angled at $B$ having $AB = BC$.

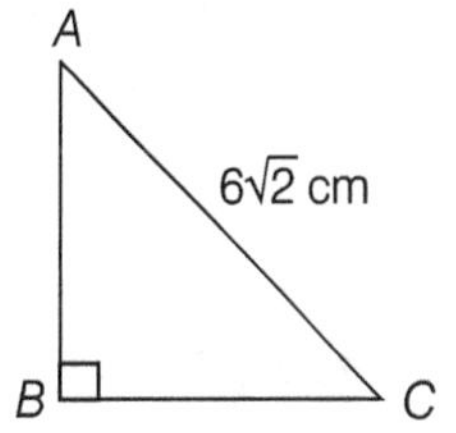


(1)

In right angled $\Delta ABC$,

$AC^2 = AB^2 + BC^2$

[by Pythagoras theorem]

$\Rightarrow \quad (6\sqrt{2})^2 = AB^2 + AB^2$ [$\because$ $BC = AB$]

$\Rightarrow \quad 36 \times 2 = 2AB^2$

$\Rightarrow \quad AB^2 = 36$

On taking square root both sides, we get

$AB = 6$ cm

Hence, the length of equal sides of triangle is 6 cm. (1)

# Section-C

**Section C consists of 6 questions of 3 marks each**

**26.** The cost of fencing a circular field at the rate of ₹ 36 per m is ₹ 11880. The field is to be ploughed at the rate of ₹ 0.60 per $m^2$. Find the cost of ploughing the field. [Take, $\pi = 22/7$]

***Sol.*** Length of the fence of a circular field

$$= \frac{\text{Total cost}}{\text{Rate}} = \frac{11880}{36} = 330 \text{ m}$$

So, the circumference of the field is 330 m.

Let $r$ be the radius of the field, then

$\therefore$ $2\pi r = 330$

[$\because$ circumference of circular field $= 2\pi r$]

$\Rightarrow$ $2 \times \frac{22}{7} \times r = 330$

$\Rightarrow$ $r = \frac{330 \times 7}{2 \times 22} = 52.5 \text{ m}$

So, the radius of the field is 52.5 m. (1)

Now, area of the field $= \pi r^2 = \frac{22}{7} \times 52.5 \times 52.5$

$= 22 \times 7.5 \times 52.5 \text{ m}^2$

Given, cost of ploughing 1 $m^2$ of the field = ₹ 0.60

So, total cost of ploughing the field

$= 0.6 \times 22 \times 7.5 \times 52.5$

= ₹ 5197.5 (1)

**27.** In the given figure, if $PQ = PR$ prove that $QT = TR$ i.e. $QR$ is bisected at $T$.

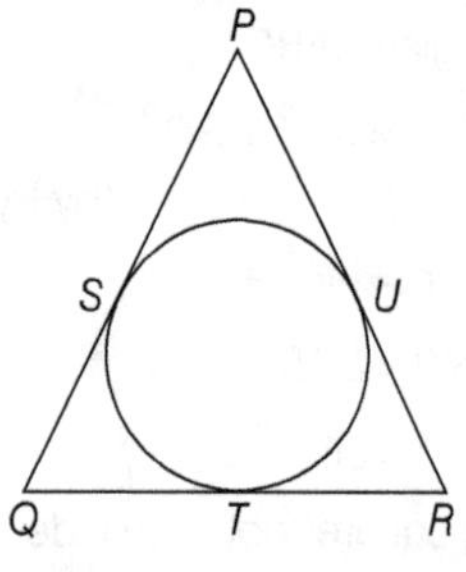


***Sol.*** **Given** A circle inscribed in a $\Delta PQR$ such that $PQ = PR$

**To prove** $QT = TR$

**Proof** We know that the tangents from an external points to a circle are equal in length.

$PS = PU$ [tangents from $P$] ...(i)

$QS = QT$ [tangents from $Q$] ...(ii)

$RT = RU$ [tangents from $R$] ...(iii)

Now, $PQ = PR$ [given] (1½)

$\Rightarrow$ $PQ - PS = PR - PS$

[subtracting $PS$ from both sides]

$\Rightarrow$ $PQ - PS = PR - PU$ [from Eq. (i)]

$\Rightarrow$ $QS = RU$

$\Rightarrow$ $QT = RU$ [from Eq. (ii)]

$\Rightarrow$ $QT = RT$ [from Eq. (iii)]

**Hence proved.** (1½)

**28.** A die is thrown once. Find the probability of getting

(i) an even prime number.

(ii) a number divisible by 2.

*Or*

A card is drawn at random from a well-shuffled pack of 52 cards. Find the probability that the card drawn is neither a red card nor a queen.

***Sol.*** There are 6 possible outcomes (1, 2, 3, 4, 5 and 6) in a single throw of a die.

(i) We know that even prime number is only 2.

So, number of favourable outcomes = 1

$\therefore P$ (getting an even prime number) $= \frac{1}{6}$ (1½)

(ii) The numbers divisible by 2 are 2, 4 and 6.

So,number of favourable outcomes = 3

$\therefore$ $P$ (getting a number divisible by 2)

$= \frac{3}{6} = \frac{1}{2}$ (1½)

*Or*

Number of red cards = 26

Number of queens = 4

But, out of these 4 queens, 2 are red.

$\therefore$ Number of queens which are not red = 2

Now, number of cards which are red or queen

$= 26 + 2 = 28$ (1)

$\therefore$ $P$ (getting either red card or queen)

$$= \frac{\text{Number of card which are red or queen}}{\text{Total number of cards}}$$

$= \frac{28}{52} = \frac{7}{13}$ (1)

Now, $P$ (not getting either red card or queen)

$= 1 - P$ (getting either red card or queen)

$= 1 - \frac{7}{13} = \frac{13-7}{13} = \frac{6}{13}$ (1)

**29.** The following table shows the age distribution of cases of a certain disease admitted during a year in a particular hospital.

| Age (in yr) | 5-14 | 15-24 | 25-34 | 35-44 | 45-54 | 55-64 |
|---|---|---|---|---|---|---|
| Number of cases | 6 | 11 | 21 | 23 | 14 | 5 |

Find the average age for which maximum cases occurred.

***Sol.*** Here, class intervals are not in inclusive form.

So, we first convert them in inclusive form by subtracting $h/2$ from the lower limit and adding $h/2$ to the upper limit of each class, where $h$ is the difference between the lower limit of a class and the upper limit of the preceding class.

The given frequency distribution in inclusive form is as follows.

| Age (in yr) | 4.5-14.5 | 14.5-24.5 | 24.5-34.5 | 34.5-44.5 | 44.5-54.5 | 54.5-64.5 |
|---|---|---|---|---|---|---|
| Number of cases | 6 | 11 | 21 | 23 | 14 | 5 |

(1)

We observe that the class 34.5-44.5 has the maximum frequency.

So, it is the modal class such that

$$l = 34.5, h = 10, f_1 = 23, f_0 = 21 \text{ and } f_2 = 14$$

$$\therefore \quad \text{Mode} = l + \frac{f_1 - f_0}{2f_1 - f_0 - f_2} \times h,$$

$$\Rightarrow \quad \text{Mode} = 34.5 + \frac{23-21}{46-21-14} \times 10$$

$$= 34.5 + \frac{2}{11} \times 10 = 36.31 \qquad (1)$$

**30.** Solve for $x$ and $y$ using elimination method

$$10x + 3y = 75,\ 6x - 5y = 11$$

*Or*

Solve for $x$ and $y$ using substitution method

$$11x + 15y + 23 = 0,\ 7x - 2y - 20 = 0$$

***Sol.*** The given equations are

$$10x + 3y = 75 \qquad \ldots(\text{i})$$

$$6x - 5y = 11 \qquad \ldots(\text{ii})$$

Multiplying Eq. (i) by 5 and Eq. (ii) by 3, we get

$$50x + 15y = 375 \qquad \ldots(\text{iii})$$

$$18x - 15y = 33 \qquad \ldots(\text{iv})\ (1)$$

Adding Eqs. (iii) and (iv), we get

$$68x = 408$$

$$\Rightarrow \quad x = \frac{408}{68} \Rightarrow x = 6 \qquad (1)$$

Putting $x = 6$ in Eq. (i), we get

$$(10 \times 6) + 3y = 75$$

$$\Rightarrow \quad 60 + 3y = 75$$

$$\Rightarrow \quad 3y = 75 - 60$$

$$\Rightarrow \quad 3y = 15$$

$$\Rightarrow \quad y = 5$$

$$\therefore \quad x = 6 \text{ and } y = 5 \qquad (1)$$

*Or*

The given equations are

$$11x + 15y + 23 = 0 \qquad \ldots(\text{i})$$

$$7x - 2y - 20 = 0 \qquad \ldots(\text{ii})$$

Multiplying Eq. (i) by 2 and Eq. (ii) by 15 and adding the results, we get

$$22x + 105x = -46 + 300$$

$$\Rightarrow \quad 127x = 254$$

$$\Rightarrow \quad x = \frac{254}{127} = 2 \qquad (1)$$

Putting $x = 2$ in Eq. (i), we get

$$22 + 15y = -23$$

$$\Rightarrow \quad 15y = -23 - 22$$

$$\Rightarrow \quad 15y = -45$$

$$\Rightarrow \quad y = \frac{-45}{15} \Rightarrow y = -3$$

Hence, $x = 2$ and $y = -3$ (2)

**31.** Two pillars of equal height are on either sides of a road, which is 100 m wide. The angles of the top of the pillars are 60° and 30° at a point on the road between the pillars. Find the position of the point between the pillars. Also, find the height of each pillar.

***Sol.*** Let $AB$ and $CD$ be two pillars of equal height $h$ and distance between them be $BD = 100$ m.

Let $E$ be a point on the road such that $BE = x$, $DE = (100 - x)$, $\angle AEB = 60°$ and $\angle CED = 30°$.

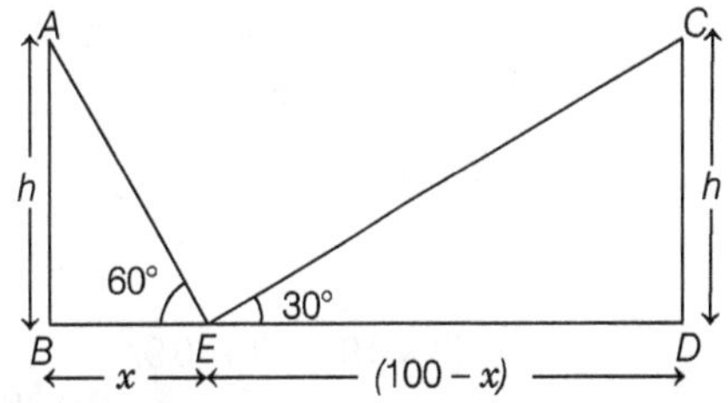


In right angled $\Delta ABE$,

$$\frac{AB}{BE} = \tan 60°$$

$$\Rightarrow \quad \frac{h}{x} = \sqrt{3} \qquad [\because \tan 60° = \sqrt{3}]$$

$$\Rightarrow \quad h = \sqrt{3}x \qquad \ldots(\text{i})\ (1)$$

In right angled $\Delta CDE$,

$$\frac{CD}{DE} = \tan 30°$$

$$\Rightarrow \quad \frac{h}{100 - x} = \frac{1}{\sqrt{3}} \quad \left[\because \tan 30° = \frac{1}{\sqrt{3}}\right]$$

$$\Rightarrow \quad h = \frac{100 - x}{\sqrt{3}} \quad \text{...(ii) (1)}$$

From Eqs. (i) and (ii), we get

$$\sqrt{3}x = \frac{100 - x}{\sqrt{3}}$$

$$\Rightarrow \quad 3x = 100 - x$$

$$\Rightarrow \quad 4x = 100$$

$$\therefore \quad x = 25$$

On putting $x = 25$ in Eq. (i), we get

$$h = \sqrt{3} \times 25$$
$$= 25 \times 1.732$$
$$= 43.3 \text{ m}$$

Hence, height of each pillar is 43.3 m and position of the point from pillar making an angle of 60° is 25 m. (1)

# Section-D

**Section D consists of 4 questions of 5 marks each**

**32.** From a solid cylinder whose height is 2.8 cm and diameter is 1.8 cm, a conical cavity of the same height and same diameter is hollowed out. Find the total surface area of the remaining solid to the nearest $cm^2$.

*Or* Water in a canal, 6 m wide and 1.5 m deep is flowing with a speed of 10 km/h. How much area will it irrigate in 30 min, if 8 cm of standing water is needed?

***Sol.*** Let $S$ be the total surface area of the remaining solid.

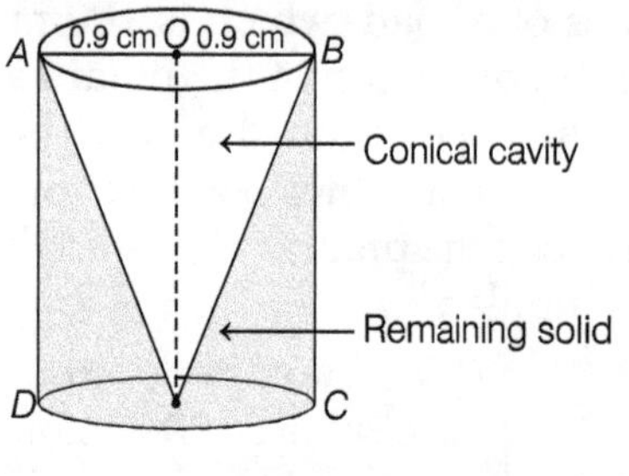


(1)

Then, $S$ = Curved surface area of the cylinder + Area of the base of the cylinder + Curved surface area of the cone

$$= 2\pi rh + \pi r^2 + \pi rl \quad (1)$$

$$= \pi[2rh + r^2 + r\sqrt{r^2 + h^2}] \quad [\because l = \sqrt{h^2 + r^2}]$$

$$= \frac{22}{7}[2 \times 0.9 \times 2.8 + (0.9)^2 + 0.9\sqrt{(0.9)^2 + (2.8)^2}]$$

$$\left[\because r = \frac{1.8}{2} = 0.9 \text{ cm and } h = 2.8 \text{ cm}\right] \quad (1)$$

$$= \frac{22}{7}[5.04 + 0.81 + 0.9\sqrt{0.81 + 7.84}]$$

$$= \frac{22}{7}[5.85 + 0.9\sqrt{8.65}]$$

$$= \frac{22}{7}[5.85 + 0.9 \times 2.94]$$

$$= \frac{22}{7} \times [5.85 + 2.64] = \frac{186.78}{7} = 26.68 \text{ cm}^2 \quad (2)$$

*Or*

Given, speed of flow of water = 10 km/h

$$= 10 \times 1000 \text{ m/h} \quad [\because 1 \text{ km} = 1000 \text{ m}]$$

$\Rightarrow$ Length of water flow in 1 h = $10 \times 1000$ m

$\Rightarrow$ Length of water flow in 30 min $\left(\text{i.e. in } \frac{1}{2}\text{h}\right)$

$$= \frac{1}{2} \times 10 \times 1000$$
$$= 5000 \text{ m} \quad (1)$$

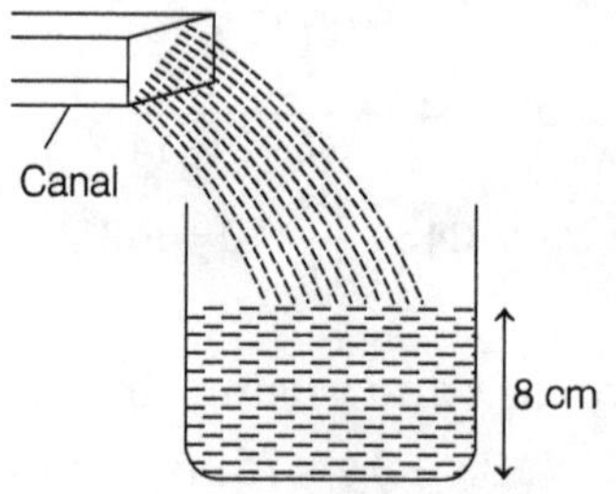


(1)

Now, volume of water flowing in 30 min

= Volume of cuboid of length 5000 m, width 6 m and depth 1.5 m

$$= 500 \times 6 \times 1.5 \text{ m}^3 = 45000 \text{ m}^3 \quad (1)$$

Hence, the required area covered for irrigation with 8 cm or $\frac{8}{100}$ m of standing water

$$= \frac{45000}{8} \times 100$$
$$= 562500 \text{ m}^2$$
$$= \frac{562500}{10000} \text{ hec} \quad [\because 1 \text{ hec} = 10000 \text{ m}^2]$$
$$= 56.25 \text{ hec} \quad (2)$$

**33.** Draw the graphs of the equations $5x - y = 5$ and $3x - y = 3$. Determine the coordinates of the vertices of the triangle formed by these lines and Y-axis.

***Sol.*** Given, equations are $5x - y = 5$ ...(i)

and $3x - y = 3$ ...(ii)

Table for $5x - y = 5$ or $y = 5x - 5$ is

| x | 1 | 0 |
|---|---|---|
| y | 0 | −5 |
| **Points** | A (1, 0) | B (0, − 5) |

Plot the points A(1, 0) and B(0, − 5) on a graph paper and join these points to form line AB. (1)

Table for $3x - y = 3$ or $y = 3x - 3$ is

| x | 1 | 0 |
|---|---|---|
| y | 0 | −3 |
| **Points** | A (1, 0) | C (0, −3) |

Plot the points A (1, 0) and C (0, −3) on the same graph paper and join these points to form line AC. (1)

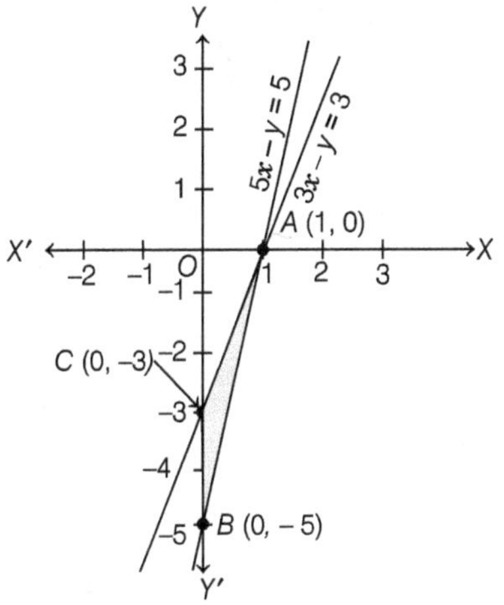


(2)

Hence, the triangle formed by given lines is $\Delta ABC$ whose vertices are A(1, 0), B(0, − 5) and C(0, − 3). (1)

**34.** If the sum of the first $n$ terms of an AP is $4n - n^2$, then what is the first term (i.e. $S_1$). What is the sum of first two terms? Find the $n$th term.

*Or*

The first and the last term of an AP are 5 and 45 respectively. If the sum of all its terms is 400, find its common difference.

***Sol.*** Given, the sum of first $n$ terms,

$$S_n = 4n - n^2 \quad ...(i)$$

On putting $n = 1$ in Eq. (i), we get

$$S_1 = 4 \times 1 - 1^2 = 4 - 1 = 3 \quad (1)$$

Thus, first term = 3

On putting $n = 2$ in Eq. (i), we get

$$S_2 = 4 \times 2 - 2^2 = 8 - 4 = 4$$

Thus, sum of first two terms = 4 (1)

Now, on replacing $n$ by $n - 1$ in Eq. (i), we get

$$S_{n-1} = 4(n-1) - (n-1)^2$$
$$= 4n - 4 - n^2 + 2n - 1$$
$$= -n^2 + 6n - 5 \quad (1)$$

$\therefore$ $n$th term $= S_n - S_{n-1}$

$$= 4n - n^2 - (-n^2 + 6n - 5)$$
$$= 4n - n^2 + n^2 - 6n + 5 = 5 - 2n \quad (2)$$

*Or*

Let $a$ and $d$ be the first term and common difference of an AP.

Then, $a = 5, T_n = 45$

$\Rightarrow$ $45 = a + (n-1)d$ $[\because T_n = a + (n-1)d]$

$\Rightarrow$ $45 = 5 + (n-1)d$

$\Rightarrow$ $40 = (n-1)d$ ...(i) (1)

We know that sum of $n$ terms of an AP is

$$S_n = \frac{n}{2}[2a + (n-1)d] \quad (1)$$

$\Rightarrow$ $400 = \frac{n}{2}[2 \times 5 + 40]$ [from Eq. (i)]

$\Rightarrow$ $800 = n[50]$

$\Rightarrow$ $n = \frac{800}{50} = 16$ ...(ii) (1)

Put $n = 16$ in Eq. (i) we get

$(16-1)d = 40$

$\Rightarrow$ $15d = 40$

$\Rightarrow$ $d = \frac{40}{15} = \frac{8}{3}$ (2)

**35.** Diagonals $AC$ and $BD$ of a trapezium $ABCD$ with $AB \| DC$ intersect each other at the point $O$. Using similarity criterion for two triangles, show that $\frac{OA}{OC} = \frac{OB}{OD}$.

***Sol.*** **Given** ABCD is a trapezium in which AB || DC.

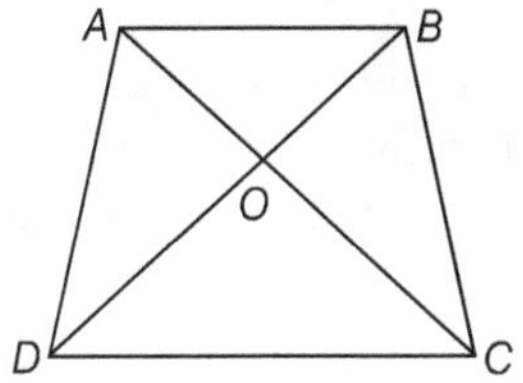

**To prove** $\frac{OA}{OC} = \frac{OB}{OD}$ (2)

**Proof** In $\Delta OAB$ and $\Delta ODC$, we have

$$AB \parallel DC$$

Then, $\angle OAB = \angle OCD$ [alternate interior angles]

$\angle AOB = \angle DOC$

[vertically opposite angles]

and $\angle ABO = \angle CDO$ [alternate interior angles]

$\therefore$ $\Delta OAB \sim \Delta OCD$ [by AAA similarity criterion]

(2)

Hence, $\frac{OA}{OC} = \frac{OB}{OD}$

[ if two triangles are similar, then their corresponding sides are proportional]

**Hence proved.** (1)

# Section-E

**Case study based questions are compulsory**

**36.** A Ferris wheel (or a big wheel in the United Kingdom) is an amusement ride consisting of a rotating upright wheel with multiple passenger-carrying components (commonly referred to as passenger cars, cabins, tubs, capsules, gondolas, or pods) attached to the rim in such a way that as the wheel turns, they are kept upright, usually by gravity.

After taking a ride in Ferris wheel, Aarti came out from the crowd and was observing her friends who were enjoying the ride. She was curious about the different angles and measures that the wheel will form. She forms the figure as given below.

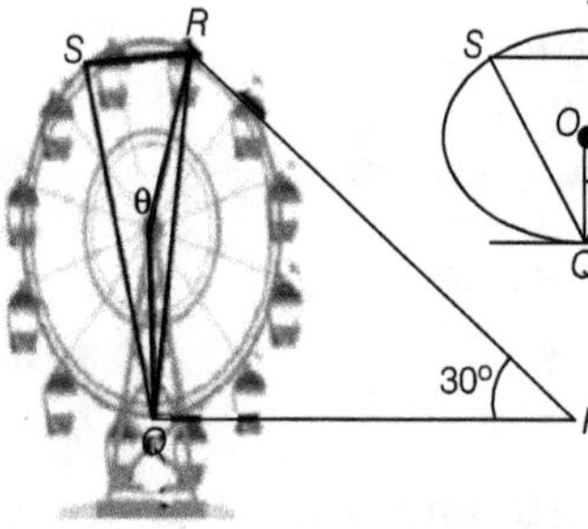


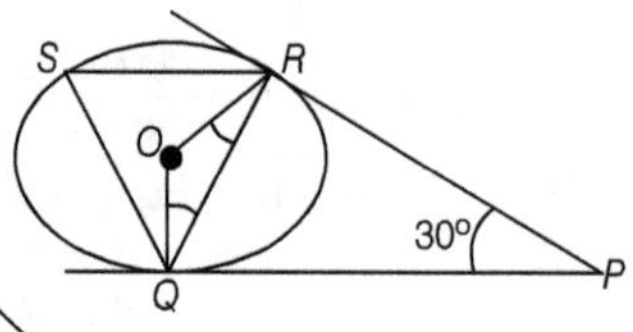


On the basis of above information, answer the following questions.

(i) In the given figure, find $\angle ROQ$. (1)

(ii) In the given figure, find $\angle RSQ$. (1)

(iii) In the given figure, find $\angle RQP$. (2)

*Or*

In the given figure, two circles touch each other at $C$ and $AB$ is a tangent to both the circles. Find $\angle ACB$. (2)

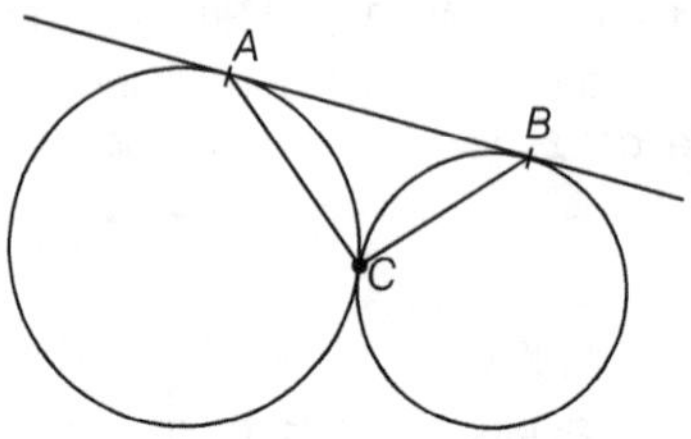


***Sol.*** (i) In quadrilateral $PQOR$, we have

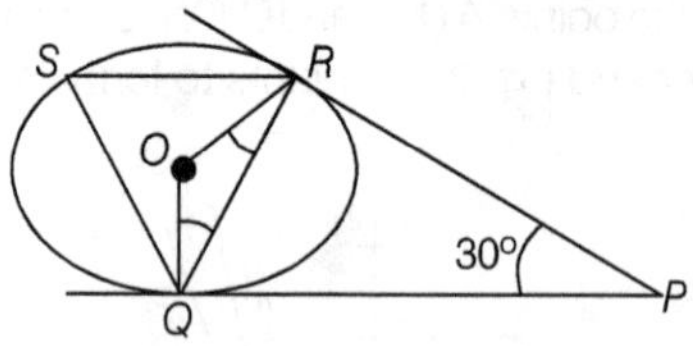


$$\angle QPR + \angle PRO + \angle PQO + \angle ROQ = 360^\circ$$

$\Rightarrow$ $30^\circ + 90^\circ + 90^\circ + \angle ROQ = 360^\circ$

[$\because$ radius is always perpendicular to the tangent at point of contact]

$\Rightarrow$ $\angle ROQ = 360^\circ - 210^\circ = 150^\circ$

(ii) We know that angle subtended by an arc at centre is double the angle subtended by it at any other part of the circle.

$$2\angle RSQ = \angle ROQ$$

$$\angle RSQ = \frac{1}{2} \times 150^\circ = 75^\circ$$

(iii) In $\Delta QOR$, $OQ = OR$ [radii]

$\therefore$ $\angle ORQ = \angle OQR$

Now, $\angle ROQ + \angle ORQ + \angle OQR = 180^\circ$

$\Rightarrow$ $2\angle OQR = 180^\circ - 150^\circ$

$\Rightarrow$ $2\angle OQR = 30^\circ$

$\Rightarrow$ $\angle OQR = 15^\circ$

Again, $\angle OQP = 90^\circ$

[$\because OQ \perp QP$]

$\Rightarrow$ $\angle OQR + \angle RQP = 90^\circ$

$\Rightarrow$ $\angle RQP = 90^\circ - 15^\circ = 75^\circ$

*Or*

Draw a tangent to the circles at point $C$. Let it meets $AB$ at $P$.

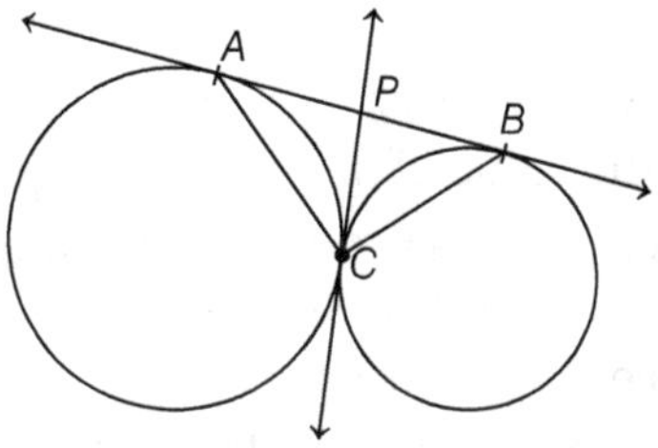


Then, $PA = PC$ and $PB = PC$

[the tangents from an external points to a circle are equal in length]

$$PA = PC \Rightarrow \angle PAC = \angle PCA$$
$$PB = PC \Rightarrow \angle PBC = \angle PCB$$
$$\therefore \quad \angle PAC + \angle PBC = \angle PCA + \angle PCB = \angle ACB$$
$$\Rightarrow \angle PAC + \angle PBC + \angle ACB = 2\angle ACB$$
$$\Rightarrow 180^\circ = 2\angle ACB$$
$$\Rightarrow \angle ACB = 90^\circ$$

**37.** A group of students of class X visited India Gate on an educational trip. The teacher and students had interest in history as well. The teacher narrated that India Gate, official name Delhi Memorial, originally called All-India War Memorial, monumental sandstone arch in New Delhi, dedicated to the troops of British India who died in wars fought between 1914 and 1919. The teacher also said that India Gate, which is located at the eastern end of the Rajpath (formerly called the Kingsway), is about 138 ft (42 m) in height.

On the basis of above information, answer the following questions.

(i) What is the angle of elevation, if they are standing at a distance of 42 m away from the monument? (1)

(ii) They want to see the gate at an angle of elevation 60°. So, they want to know the distance where they should stand and hence find the distance. (1)

(iii) The shadow of the gate when the Sun's altitude is 30° is found to be 30 m longer than when it was 60°. Find the sum of length of its shadow. (2)

*Or*

If a 1.5 m tall girl stands at a distance of 3 m from a lamp-post and casts a shadow of length 4.5 m on the ground, then find the height of the lamp-post. (2)

***Sol.*** (i) Let $AB$ be the monument of height 42 m and $C$ is the point where they are standing. Such that, $BC = 42$ m.

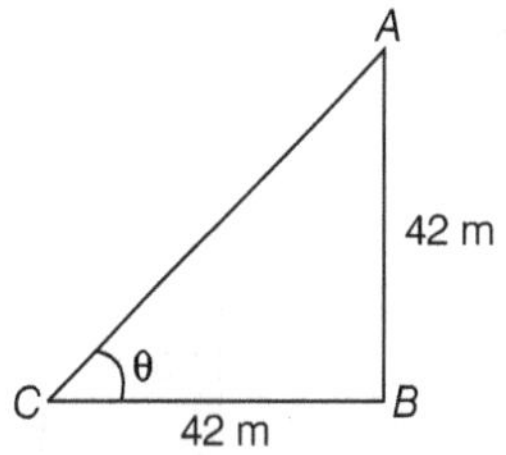


Now, in $\Delta ABC$,

$$\tan\theta = \frac{AB}{BC} \quad \left[\because \tan\theta = \frac{\text{Perpendicular}}{\text{Base}}\right]$$
$$\Rightarrow \tan\theta = \frac{42}{42} = 1$$
$$\Rightarrow \tan\theta = 1$$
$$\Rightarrow \theta = 45^\circ$$

(ii) In $\Delta ABC$,

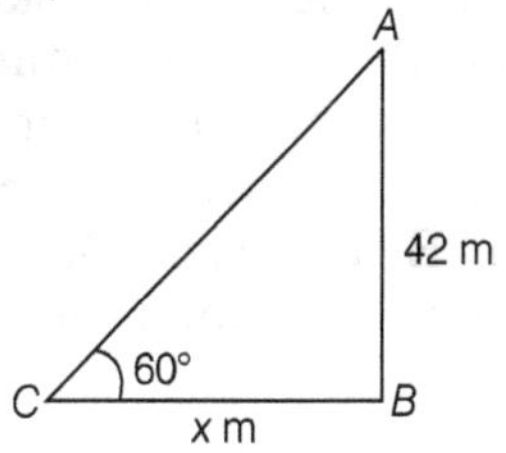


$$\tan 60^\circ = \frac{AB}{BC} \quad \left[\because \tan\theta = \frac{\text{Perpendicular}}{\text{Base}}\right]$$
$$\Rightarrow \sqrt{3} = \frac{42}{BC}$$
$$\Rightarrow BC = \frac{42}{\sqrt{3}} = \frac{42\sqrt{3}}{3} = 14\sqrt{3}$$
$$= 14 \times 1.73 = 24.22 \text{ m}$$

(iii) Let $AB$ be the gate and let $BC$ and $BD$ be the lengths of its shadows when $\angle ACB = 60^\circ$ and $\angle ADB = 30^\circ$.

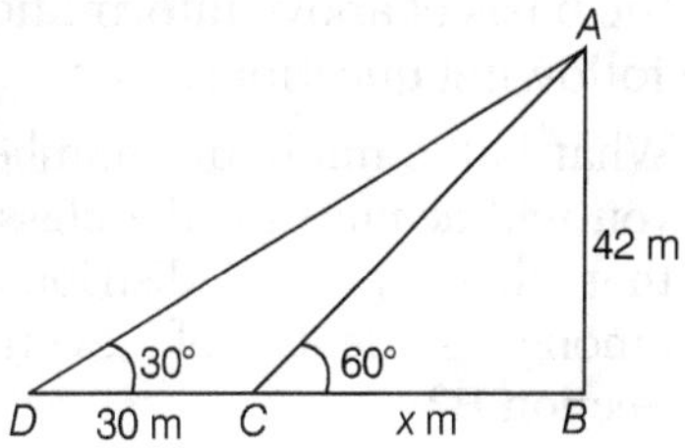

In right $\Delta CBA$, $\tan 60° = \frac{AB}{BC} = \frac{42}{x}$

$\Rightarrow \quad \sqrt{3} = \frac{42}{x} \Rightarrow x = \frac{42\sqrt{3}}{3} = 14\sqrt{3}$ m

$\therefore$ Lengths of its shadows are $14\sqrt{3}$ m and $(30 + 14\sqrt{3})$ m.

So, the sum of lengths of its shadows

$= (30 + 28\sqrt{3})$ m

*Or*

Let *AB* be the lamp-post and *CD* be the girl.

Let *CE* be the shadow of *CD*.

Then, *CD* = 1.5 m, *CE* = 4.5 m and *AC* = 3 m

Let *AB* = *h*

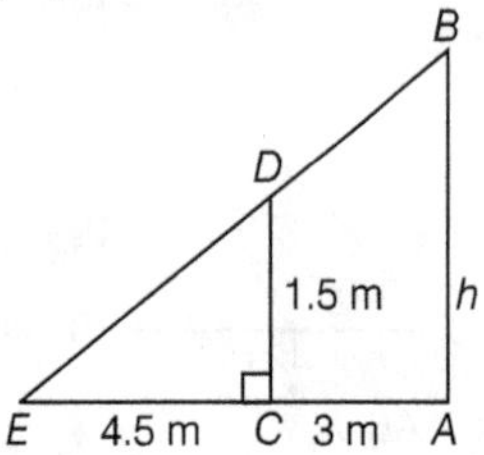


Now, $\Delta AEB$ and $\Delta CED$ are similar.

$\therefore \quad \frac{AB}{CD} = \frac{AE}{CE} \Rightarrow \frac{AB}{AE} = \frac{CD}{CE}$

$\Rightarrow \quad \frac{h}{(3 + 4.5)} = \frac{1.5}{4.5} = \frac{1}{3} \Rightarrow h = \frac{1}{3} \times 7.5 = 2.5$

Hence, the height of the lamp-post is 2.5 m.

**38.** To enhance the reading skills of grade X students, the school nominates you and two of your friends to set up a class library. There are two sections- Section A and Section B of grade X. There are 32 students in section A and 36 students in section B.

On the basis of above information, answer the following questions.

(i) What is the minimum number of books you will acquire for the class library, so that they can be distributed equally among students of Section A or Section B? (1)

(ii) Express 36 as product of it primes. (1)

(iii) Find the HCF of the numbers 867 and 255. (2)

*Or*

If LCM of 12 and 42 is $10m + 4$, then find the value of $m$. (2)

***Sol.*** (i) Given, number of students in Section A = 32

Number of students in Section B = 36

The minimum number of books to be acquired for the class library = LCM of (32, 36)

$= 2 \times 2 \times 2 \times 2 \times 2 \times 3 \times 3$

$= 2^5 \times 3^2$

$= 32 \times 9$

$= 288$

(ii) The prime factors of 36 are

$36 = 2 \times 2 \times 3 \times 3 = 2^2 \times 3^2$

(iii) We find HCF (867, 255) by using the following steps

**Step 1** Since, 867 > 255, we divide 867 by 255 to get 3 as quotient and 102 is remainder.

By Euclid's division lemma, we get

$867 = 255 \times 3 + 102$

```
255) 867 (3
     -765
     102) 255 (2
          -204
           51) 102 (2
               -102
                  0
```

**Step 2** Since, the remainder $102 \neq 0$, we divide 255 by 102 to get 2 as quotient and 51 as remainder.

By Euclid's division lemma, we get

$255 = 102 \times 2 + 51$

**Step 3** Since, the remainder $51 \neq 0$, we divide 102 by 51 to get 2 as quotient and 0 as remainder.

Since, the remainder is 0, our procedure stops and the last divisor is the required HCF.

$\therefore$ HCF (867, 255) = 51

*Or*

Given, LCM (12, 42) = $10m + 4$

Factors of $12 = 2 \times 2 \times 3$

and factors of $42 = 2 \times 3 \times 7$

Now, LCM (12, 42) $= 2 \times 2 \times 3 \times 7 = 84$

$\therefore \quad 84 = 10m + 4$

$\Rightarrow \quad 84 - 4 = 10m$

$\therefore \quad m = \frac{80}{10} = 8$

# SAMPLE QUESTION PAPER 3

## Mathematics (Basic)

Time : **3 hrs** Max. Marks : **80**

### Instructions

1. This question paper has 5 Sections A, B, C, D and E.
2. Section A has 20 Multiple Choice Questions (MCQs) carrying 1 mark each.
3. Section B has 5 Short Answer-I (SA-I) Type Questions carrying 2 marks each.
4. Section C has 6 Short Answer-II (SA-II) Type Questions carrying 3 marks each.
5. Section D has 4 Long Answer (LA) Type Questions carrying 5 marks each.
6. Section E has 3 Case Based integrated units of assessment (4 marks each) with sub-parts of the values of 1, 1 and 2 marks each respectively.
7. All questions are compulsory. However, an internal choice in 2 questions of 2 marks, 2 questions of 3 marks and 2 questions of 5 marks has been provided. An internal choice has been provided in the 2 marks questions of Section E.
8. Draw neat figures wherever required. Take $\pi = 22/7$ wherever required if not stated.

## Section-A

**Section A consists of 20 questions of 1 mark each**

**1.** The length of the shadow on the ground of a pole of height 18m when the angle of elevation $\theta$ of the sun is such that $\tan\theta = \frac{6}{7}$, is

(a) 24 m
(b) 21 m
(c) 15.42 m
(d) None of the above

***Sol.*** (b) Let $AB$ be the length of the shadow and height of the pole $BC = 18$ m and elevation $\angle BAC = \theta$.

In right angled $\Delta ABC$,

$$\tan\theta = \frac{BC}{AB} \qquad \left[\because \tan\theta = \frac{\text{perpendicular}}{\text{base}}\right]$$

$$\Rightarrow \quad \frac{6}{7} = \frac{18}{AB} \qquad \left[\tan\theta = \frac{6}{7}, \text{given}\right]$$

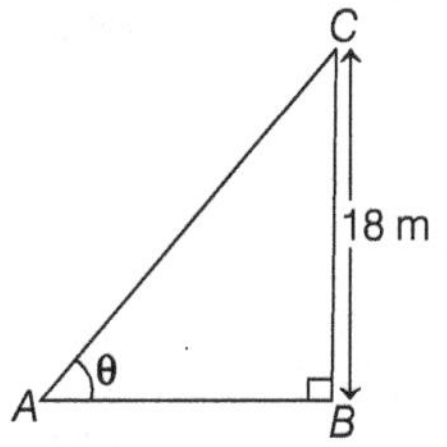


$$\Rightarrow 6 \times AB = 18 \times 7$$

$$\Rightarrow \quad AB = \frac{18 \times 7}{6} = 21$$

Hence, the length of the shadow is 21 m.

**2.** The pair of equations $x+2y-5=0$ and $-4x-8y+20=0$ has

(a) unique solution
(b) exactly two solutions
(c) infinitely many sulutions
(d) no solution

**Sol.** (c) Here, $\frac{a_1}{a_2}=\frac{1}{-4}, \frac{b_1}{b_2}=\frac{2}{-8}=\frac{1}{-4}$ and $\frac{c_1}{c_2}=\frac{-5}{20}=\frac{-1}{4}$

This shows, $\frac{a_1}{a_2}=\frac{b_1}{b_2}=\frac{c_1}{c_2}$

∴ The pair of equations has infinitely many solutions.

**3.** The probability of getting a face card from a pack of card, is

(a) $\frac{2}{13}$ (b) $\frac{3}{13}$ (c) $\frac{4}{13}$ (d) $\frac{1}{13}$

**Sol.** (b) The total number of cards in a pack of cards is 52.
The total number of face cards in a pack of cards = 12

∴ Probability of getting a face card $=\frac{12}{52}=\frac{3}{13}$

**4.** If the perimeter of a semi-circular protractor is 72 cm, then its radius is

(a) 14 cm (b) 23 cm
(c) 12 cm (d) None of these

**Sol.** (a) Let the radius of the protractor be $r$ cm.
Then, perimeter of protractor $=(\pi r+2r)=72$

$\Rightarrow (\pi+2)r=72$

$\Rightarrow \left(\frac{22}{7}+2\right)r=72$

$\Rightarrow \frac{36}{7}r=72$

$\Rightarrow r=72\times\frac{7}{36}=14\text{cm}$

**5.** The coordinate of point $A$, where $AB$ is the diameter of a circle whose centre is (2, −3) and the point $B$ is (1, 4), is

(a) (3, −10) (b) (1, −7)
(c) (1, 2) (d) (2, 7)

**Sol.** (a) Let the coordinates of point $A$ be $(x, y)$. As, $AB$ is the diameter and $O$ is the centre of a circle. Then, $O$ will be the mid-point of $AB$.

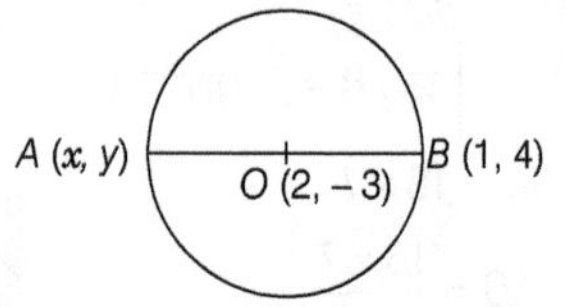


∴ Coordinates of $O$
= Coordinates of mid-point of $AB$

$\Rightarrow (2,-3)=\left(\frac{x+1}{2},\frac{y+4}{2}\right)$

On comparing both sides, we get

$2=\frac{x+1}{2}$ and $-3=\frac{y+4}{2}$

$\Rightarrow x+1=4$ and $y+4=-6$

$\therefore x=3$ and $y=-10$

Hence, the coordinates of point $A$ are (3, – 10).

**6.** The value of $\tan 60°\cot 30°+\tan 30°\cot 60°$ is

(a) 4 (b) 2 (c) $\frac{10}{3}$ (d) 5

**Sol.** (c) $\tan 60°\cot 30°+\tan 30°\cot 60°$

$=\sqrt{3}\times\sqrt{3}+\frac{1}{\sqrt{3}}\times\frac{1}{\sqrt{3}}$

$=3+\frac{1}{3}=\frac{9+1}{3}=\frac{10}{3}$

**7.** The value of $x$ for which $2x$, $x+10$ and $3x+2$ are in AP is

(a) 2 (b) 6 (c) 4 (d) 8

**Sol.** (b) Since, $2x$, $x+10$ and $3x+2$ are in AP.

$\therefore (x+10)-2x=(3x+2)-(x+10)$

[common difference must be same]

$\Rightarrow -x+10=2x-8$

$\Rightarrow 3x=18$

$\therefore x=6$

**8.** If $\Delta ABC \sim \Delta DFE$, $\angle A=30°$, $\angle C=50°$, then the value of $\angle F$ is

(a) 80° (b) 100° (c) 30° (d) 50°

**Sol.** (b) In $\Delta ABC$, $\angle A+\angle B+\angle C=180°$

$\Rightarrow 30°+\angle B+50°=180°$

$\Rightarrow \angle B=100°$

Since, $\Delta ABC \sim \Delta DFE$

$\therefore \angle F=\angle B=100°$ [by CPCT]

**9.** The graph of a polynomial $f(x)$ is as shown in figure, the number of zeroes of $f(x)$ is

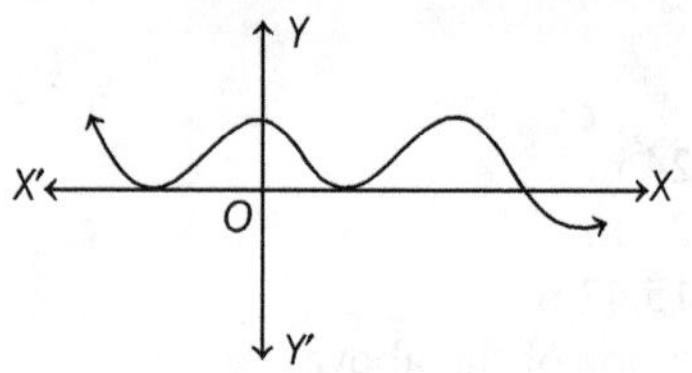


(a) 1 (b) 2 (c) 3 (d) 4

**Sol.** (c) The number of zeroes of $f(x)$ is 3, as the graph of $f(x)$ intersects the $X$-axis at three points.

**10.** The distance between the points (2, 3) and (4, 1), is

(a) $\sqrt{2}$ units (b) 2 units
(c) $2\sqrt{2}$ units (d) 4 units

**Sol.** (c) Let $A$ (2, 3) and $B$ (4, 1) be the given points. Here, $x_1 = 2, y_1 = 3$ and $x_2 = 4, y_2 = 1$

Now, $AB = \sqrt{(x_2 - x_1)^2 + (y_2 - y_1)^2}$ [by distance formula]

$= \sqrt{(4-2)^2 + (1-3)^2} = \sqrt{(2)^2 + (-2)^2}$

$= \sqrt{4+4} = \sqrt{8} = 2\sqrt{2}$ units

**11.** Express 120 as the product of primes.

(a) $2^2 \times 3 \times 5$ (b) $2^3 \times 3 \times 5$
(c) $2^3 \times 5$ (d) $2 \times 3 \times 5$

**Sol.** (b)

| | |
|---|---|
| 2 | 120 |
| 2 | 60 |
| 2 | 30 |
| 3 | 15 |
| 5 | 5 |
| | 1 |

$\therefore$ Product of 120 $= 2 \times 2 \times 2 \times 3 \times 5 = 2^3 \times 3 \times 5$

**12.** If $DA$ and $DB$ are two tangents to a circle with centre $O$ such that $\angle AOB = 110°$, then the value of $\angle ADB$, is

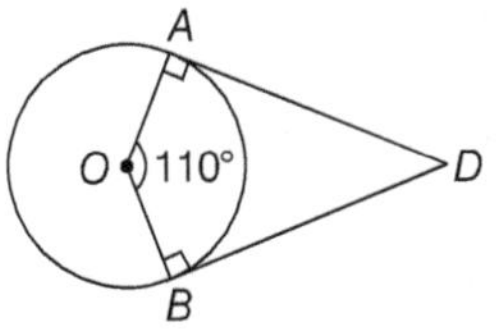


(a) 70° (b) 80° (c) 100° (d) 60°

**Sol.** (a) Clearly, $\angle OAD = 90°$ and $\angle OBD = 90°$

$\Rightarrow \angle AOB + \angle ADB = 180°$

$\Rightarrow 110° + \angle ADB = 180°$

$\Rightarrow \angle ADB = 180° - 110° = 70°$

**13.** If the mean of the first $n$ natural numbers is 18, then the value of $n$ is

(a) 18 (b) 32 (c) 36 (d) 35

**Sol.** (d) We know that the sum of first $n$ natural numbers is given by $S_n = \frac{n(n+1)}{2}$

$\therefore$ Mean of first $n$ natural numbers $= \frac{[n(n+1)]/2}{n}$

$= \frac{n+1}{2}$

Given, mean of first $n$ natural numbers = 18

$\Rightarrow \frac{n+1}{2} = 18$

$\Rightarrow n + 1 = 36$

$\Rightarrow n = 35$

**14.** The area of the sector of a circle having radius $R$ making an angle of $x$, is

(a) $\frac{x}{180°} \times \pi R^2$ (b) $\frac{x}{360°} \times 2\pi R$
(c) $\frac{x}{180°} \times 2\pi R^2$ (d) $\frac{x}{360°} \times \pi R^2$

**Sol.** (d) $\therefore$ Area $= \frac{x}{360°} \times \pi R^2$

**15.** The LCM of $(2 \times 3^2 \times 5)$ and $(2^2 \times 3 \times 5^3)$ is

(a) 4500 (b) 30 (c) 900 (d) 1500

**Sol.** (a) LCM = Product of the greatest power of each prime factor involved in the number

$= 2^2 \times 3^2 \times 5^3 = 4 \times 9 \times 125 = 4500$

**16.** If 2 is a root of the equation $kx^2 - x - 2 = 0$, then the value of $k$, is

(a) 2 (b) 0 (c) 1 (d) 4

**Sol.** (c) Since, $x = 2$ is a root of the equation.

$\therefore k(2)^2 - 2 - 2 = 0$

$\Rightarrow 4k - 2 - 2 = 0$

$\Rightarrow 4k - 4 = 0$

$\Rightarrow k = 1$

**17.** The roots of the equation $2x^2 - 3x = 0$ is

(a) $0, \frac{-2}{3}$ (b) $0, \frac{3}{2}$ (c) 0, 3 (d) 0, 2

**Sol.** (b) Given, $2x^2 - 3x = 0$

$\Rightarrow x(2x - 3) = 0$

$\Rightarrow x = 0$ or $2x - 3 = 0$

$\Rightarrow x = 0$ or $x = \frac{3}{2}$

Hence, the roots are $0, \frac{3}{2}$.

**18.** In $\Delta ABC$, $AD$ is the internal bisector of $\angle A$. If $BD = 5$ cm and $BC = 7.5$ cm, then the value of $AB : AC$ is

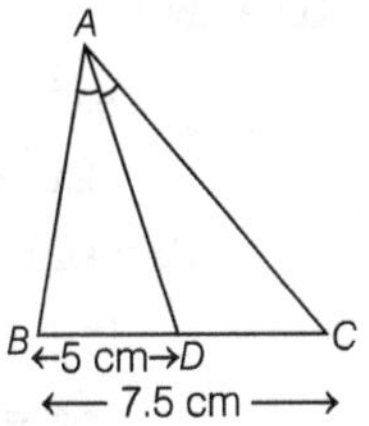


(a) 2 : 1 (b) 2 : 4 (c) 1 : 4 (d) 3 : 2

**Sol.** (a) Given, $AD$ is a internal bisector of $\angle A$.

Therefore, $\frac{AB}{AC}=\frac{BD}{DC}=\frac{BD}{(BC-BD)}$

$$=\frac{5}{(7.5-5)}=\frac{5}{2.5}=\frac{2}{1}=2:1$$

**Directions** *In the question number 19 and 20, a statement of Assertion (A) is followed by a statement of Reason (R). Choose the correct option.*

**19.** **Assertion (A)** The point $(-1, 6)$ divides the line segment joining the points $(-3, 10)$ and $(6, -8)$ in the ratio $2:7$ internally.

**Reason (R)** Given three points i.e. $A$, $B$, $C$ from an equilateral triangle, then $AB=BC=CA$.

(a) Both Assertion (A) and Reason (R) are true and Reason (R) is the correct explanation of Assertion (A)

(b) Both Assertion (A) and Reason (R) are true but Reason (R) is not the correct explanation of Assertion (A)

(c) Assertion (A) is true but Reason (R) is false

(d) Assertion (A) is false but Reason (R) is true

**Sol.** (b) **Assertion** Coordinates of the point which divides the line segment joining the points $(-3, 10)$ and $(6, -8)$ in the ratio $2:7$,

$$(x, y)=\left(\frac{2\times6+7\times(-3)}{2+7}, \frac{2\times(-8)+7\times(10)}{2+7}\right)$$

$$=\left(\frac{12-21}{9}, \frac{-16+70}{9}\right)=\left(-1, \frac{54}{9}\right)=(-1, 6)$$

So, the Assertion is true.

**Reason** Since, in equilateral triangle $ABC$, all sides are equal.

So, $AB=BC=CA$

So, the Reason is true but it is not the correct explanation of Assertion.

**20.** **Assertion (A)** If $\Delta ABC$ and $\Delta PQR$ are congruent triangles, then they are also similar triangles.

**Reason (R)** All congruent triangles are similar but the similar triangles need not be congruent.

(a) Both Assertion (A) and Reason (R) are true and Reason (R) is the correct explanation of Assertion (A)

(b) Both Assertion (A) and Reason (R) are true but Reason (R) is not the correct explanation of Assertion (A)

(c) Assertion (A) is true but Reason (R) is false

(d) Assertion (A) is false but Reason (R) is true

**Sol.** (a) Clearly, Assertion is true.

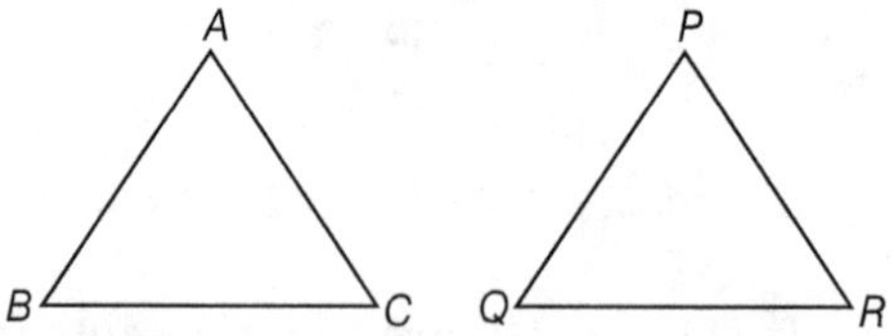


So, Reason is also true and it is the correct explanation of Assertion.

## Section-B

**Section B consists of 5 questions of 2 marks each**

**21.** Solve for $x$

$$\frac{2x}{x-3}+\frac{1}{2x+3}+\frac{3x+9}{(x-3)(2x+3)}=0, x\neq3, -\frac{3}{2}$$

**Sol.** Given, $\frac{2x}{x-3}+\frac{1}{2x+3}+\frac{3x+9}{(x-3)(2x+3)}=0$

$\Rightarrow$ $\frac{2x(2x+3)+x-3+3x+9}{(x-3)(2x+3)}=0$

$\Rightarrow$ $4x^2+6x+x-3+3x+9=0$ (1)

$\Rightarrow$ $4x^2+10x+6=0$

$\Rightarrow$ $2x^2+5x+3=0$

$\Rightarrow$ $2x^2+2x+3x+3=0$

$\Rightarrow$ $(x+1)(2x+3)=0$

$\Rightarrow$ $x=-1$ or $x=-\frac{3}{2}$

As, $x\neq\frac{-3}{2}$

Hence, $x=-1$. (1)

**22.** Show that

$$2(\cos^2 45^\circ+\tan^2 60^\circ)-6(\sin^2 45^\circ-\tan^2 30^\circ)=6.$$

*Or*

Prove that

$$\frac{\sin^2 A}{\cos^2 A}+\frac{\cos^2 A}{\sin^2 A}=\frac{1}{\sin^2 A\cos^2 A}-2.$$

**Sol.** We have,

$$\text{LHS}=2(\cos^2 45^\circ+\tan^2 60^\circ)-6(\sin^2 45^\circ-\tan^2 30^\circ)$$

$$= 2\left\{\left(\frac{1}{\sqrt{2}}\right)^2 + (\sqrt{3})^2\right\} - 6\left\{\left(\frac{1}{\sqrt{2}}\right)^2 - \left(\frac{1}{\sqrt{3}}\right)^2\right\} \quad (1)$$

$$= 2\left(\frac{1}{2} + 3\right) - 6\left(\frac{1}{2} - \frac{1}{3}\right) = 1 + 6 - 3 + 2 = 6 = \text{RHS} \quad (1)$$

*Or*

We have,

$$\text{LHS} = \frac{\sin^2 A}{\cos^2 A} + \frac{\cos^2 A}{\sin^2 A} = \frac{\sin^4 A + \cos^4 A}{\sin^2 A \cos^2 A}$$

[taking LCM]

$$= \frac{(\sin^2 A)^2 + (\cos^2 A)^2 + 2\sin^2 A\cos^2 A - 2\sin^2 A\cos^2 A}{\sin^2 A\cos^2 A} \quad (1)$$

$$= \frac{(\sin^2 A + \cos^2 A)^2 - 2\sin^2 A\cos^2 A}{\sin^2 A\cos^2 A}$$

$$= \frac{1 - 2\sin^2 A\cos^2 A}{\sin^2 A\cos^2 A}$$

$$= \frac{1}{\sin^2 A\cos^2 A} - 2 = \text{RHS}$$

**Hence proved.** (1)

**23.** In the given figure, $O$ is the centre of the circle, $PT$ is the tangent drawn from the point $P$ to the circle and $PAB$ passes through the centre $O$ of the circle.

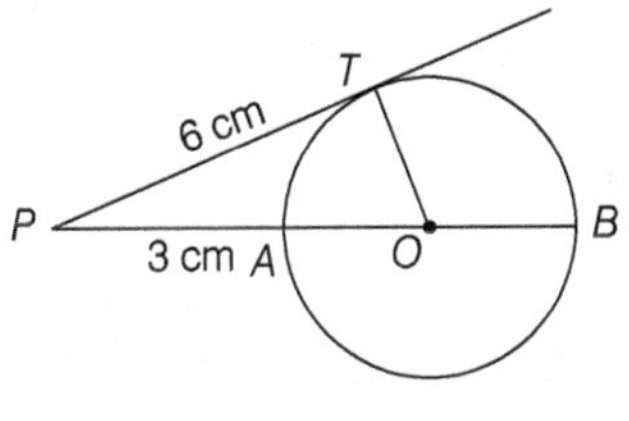


If $PT = 6$ cm and $PA = 3$ cm, then find the radius of the circle.

***Sol.*** Let the radius of circle be $r$ cm.

Then, $OA = OT = r$ cm ...(i)

Since, $PT$ is a tangent to circle at $T$ and $OT$ is a radius.

So, $OT \perp PT$

$\therefore$ $\angle OTP = 90°$ (1/2)

In right angled $\Delta OTP$,

$$OP^2 = OT^2 + PT^2$$

[by Pythagoras theorem]

$\Rightarrow$ $(PA + OA)^2 = OT^2 + 6^2$

$\Rightarrow$ $(3 + r)^2 = r^2 + 36$

[from Eq. (i) and $PA = 3$ cm, $PT = 6$ cm, (given)] (1/2)

$\Rightarrow$ $r^2 + 6r + 9 - r^2 - 36 = 0$

[$\because (a + b)^2 = a^2 + b^2 + 2ab$]

$\Rightarrow$ $6r - 27 = 0$

$\Rightarrow$ $r = \frac{27}{6} = 4.5$

Hence, the radius of the circle is 4.5 cm. (1)

**24.** In the given figure, $PQ \parallel NO$.

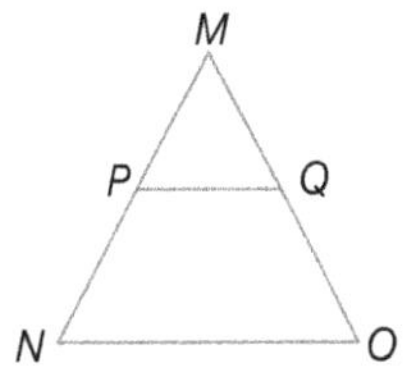


If $\frac{MP}{PN} = \frac{4}{13}$ and $MO = 20.4$ cm, then find $MQ$.

***Sol.*** In $\Delta MNO$, we have $PQ \parallel NO$

$\Rightarrow$ $\frac{MP}{PN} = \frac{MQ}{QO}$

[by basic proportionality theorem] (1/2)

$\Rightarrow$ $\frac{MP}{PN} = \frac{MQ}{MO - MQ}$ [$\because QO = MO - MQ$]

$\Rightarrow$ $\frac{4}{13} = \frac{MQ}{20.4 - MQ}$ (1/2)

[given, $\frac{MP}{PN} = \frac{4}{13}$ and $MO = 20.4$ cm]

$\Rightarrow$ $4(20.4 - MQ) = 13MQ$

$\Rightarrow$ $81.6 - 4MQ = 13MQ$

$\Rightarrow$ $81.6 = 17MQ$

$\therefore$ $MQ = 4.8$ cm (1)

**25.** Find the ratio in which the line segment joining $A(1, -5)$ and $B(-4, 5)$ is divided by the $X$-axis.

*Or* Find the coordinates of points on the $X$-axis which are at the distance of 17 units from the point $(11, -8)$.

***Sol.*** For any point on $X$-axis, $y = 0$.

Let the ratio be $k : 1$, then by section formula, the coordinates of the point which divides $AB$ in the ratio $k : 1$ are $\left(\frac{-4k + 1}{k + 1}, \frac{5k - 5}{k + 1}\right)$ (1)

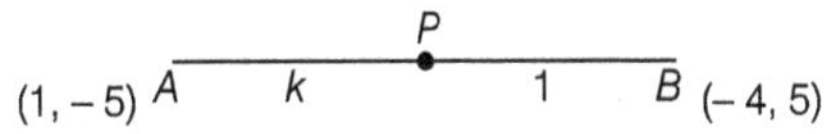


Thus, point lies on the $X$-axis, and we know that on the $X$-axis, the ordinate is zero.

$\therefore$ $\frac{5k - 5}{k + 1} = 0$

$\Rightarrow$ $5k - 5 = 0 \Rightarrow k = 1$

Therefore, the required ratio is 1:1. (1)

*Or*

Let $P(x, 0)$ be the point on $X$-axis.

Take other point $(11, -8)$ as $Q$.

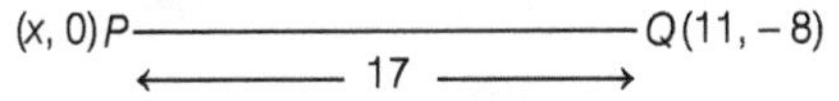


$\therefore$ $PQ = 17$

$\Rightarrow \sqrt{(11-x)^2+(-8-0)^2}=17$

[$\because$ by using distance formula,

distance $=\sqrt{(x_2-x_1)^2+(y_2-y_1)^2}$]

On squaring both sides, we get

$(11-x)^2+(-8)^2=289$ (1)

$\Rightarrow 121+x^2-22x+64-289=0$

$\Rightarrow x^2-22x-104=0$

$\Rightarrow x^2-26x+4x-104=0$ [splitting middle term]

$\Rightarrow x(x-26)+4(x-26)=0$

$\Rightarrow (x-26)(x+4)=0$

$\Rightarrow x-26=0$ or $x+4=0$

$\Rightarrow x=26$ or $x=-4$

When $x=26$, then $P=(26, 0)$.

When $x=-4$, then $P=(-4, 0)$.

So, points are (26, 0) and (–4, 0). (1)

# Section-C

**Section C consists of 6 questions of 3 marks each**

**26.** A circle with diameter 20 cm is drawn somewhere on a rectangular piece of paper with length 40 cm and width 30 cm. This paper is kept horizontal on table top and a die, very small in size, is dropped on the rectangular paper without seeing towards it. If the die falls and lands on the paper only, then find the probability that it will fall and land inside the circle.

***Sol.*** $\because$ Area of rectangle paper $=40\times 30=1200$ cm$^2$ (1/2)

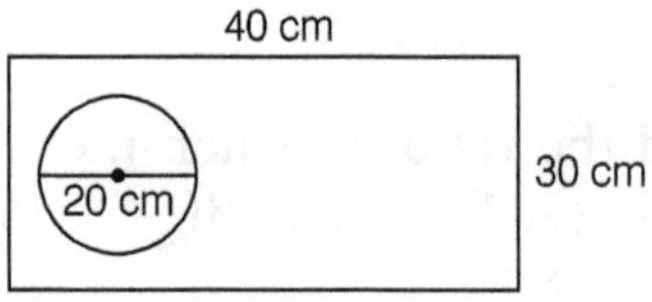


$\therefore$ Area of circle $=\pi r^2$

$=\frac{22}{7}\times 10\times 10=\frac{2200}{7}$ cm$^2$ (1)

$\therefore$ Total possible outcomes = Area of rectangle paper and number of favourable outcomes

= Area of circle (1/2)

$\therefore$ $P$ (die will fall inside the circle)

$=\frac{\text{Area of circle}}{\text{Area of rectangle paper}}$

$=\frac{2200}{7\times 1200}=\frac{11}{42}$ (1)

**27.** If 6th term of an AP is –10 and its 10th term is –26, then find the 15th term of an AP.

***Sol.*** We know that $n$th term of an AP is given by

$T_n=a+(n-1)d$

$\therefore$ 6th term, $T_6=-10$

$\Rightarrow a+5d=-10$ ...(i)

and 10th term, $T_{10}=-26$

$\Rightarrow a+9d=-26$ ...(ii) (1/2)

On subtracting Eq. (i) from Eq. (ii), we get

$4d=-16 \Rightarrow d=-4$ (1/2)

On substituting $d=-4$ in Eq. (i), we get

$a+5(-4)=-10$

$\Rightarrow a-20=-10$

$\Rightarrow a=-10+20 \Rightarrow a=10$ (1)

Now, 15th term, $T_{15}=a+14d=10+14(-4)$

$=10-56=-46$

Hence, 15th term of the AP is –46. (1)

**28.** Prove that

$$\cot^2 A\left(\frac{\sec A-1}{1+\sin A}\right)+\sec^2 A\left(\frac{\sin A-1}{1+\sec A}\right)=0.$$

*Or*

Prove that

$$\sqrt{\frac{\operatorname{cosec} A-1}{\operatorname{cosec} A+1}}+\sqrt{\frac{\operatorname{cosec} A+1}{\operatorname{cosec} A-1}}=2\sec A.$$

***Sol.*** LHS $=\cot^2 A\left(\frac{\sec A-1}{1+\sin A}\right)+\sec^2 A\left(\frac{\sin A-1}{1+\sec A}\right)$

$$=\frac{\left[\cot^2 A(\sec A-1)(1+\sec A)+\sec^2 A(\sin A-1)(1+\sin A)\right]}{(1+\sin A)(1+\sec A)}$$ (1)

$$=\frac{\cot^2 A(\sec^2 A-1)+\sec^2 A(\sin^2 A-1)}{(1+\sin A)(1+\sec A)}$$

[$\because (a-b)(a+b)=a^2-b^2$]

$$=\frac{\cot^2 A\tan^2 A-\sec^2 A(1-\sin^2 A)}{(1+\sin A)(1+\sec A)}$$

[$\because 1+\tan^2\theta=\sec^2\theta$]

$$=\frac{\cot^2 A\tan^2 A-\sec^2 A\cos^2 A}{(1+\sin A)(1+\sec A)}$$ (1)

[$\because \sin^2\theta+\cos^2\theta=1$]

$$=\frac{1-1}{(1+\sin A)(1+\sec A)}=0=\text{RHS}$$

[$\because \cot\theta\tan\theta=1$ and $\sec\theta\cos\theta=1$]

**Hence proved.** (1)

*Or*

$$\text{LHS} = \sqrt{\frac{\text{cosec } A - 1}{\text{cosec } A + 1}} + \sqrt{\frac{\text{cosec } A + 1}{\text{cosec } A - 1}}$$

$$= \frac{\left[(\sqrt{\text{cosec } A - 1})(\sqrt{\text{cosec } A - 1}) + (\sqrt{\text{cosec } A + 1})(\sqrt{\text{cosec } A + 1})\right]}{(\sqrt{\text{cosec } A + 1})(\sqrt{\text{cosec } A - 1})}$$

$$= \frac{(\sqrt{\text{cosec } A - 1})^2 + (\sqrt{\text{cosec } A + 1})^2}{(\sqrt{\text{cosec } A + 1})(\sqrt{\text{cosec } A - 1})} \quad (1)$$

$$= \frac{(\text{cosec } A - 1) + (\text{cosec } A + 1)}{\sqrt{\text{cosec}^2 A - 1}}$$

$[\because (\sqrt{a})^2 = a$ and $\sqrt{a+b} \times \sqrt{a-b} = \sqrt{a^2 - b^2}]$

$$= \frac{2 \text{cosec } A}{\sqrt{\cot^2 A}} \quad [\because \text{cosec}^2\theta = 1 + \cot^2\theta] \ (1)$$

$$= \frac{2 \text{ cosec } A}{\cot A} = \frac{2}{\sin A} \times \frac{\sin A}{\cos A}$$

$$\left[\because \text{cosec } \theta = \frac{1}{\sin\theta} \text{ and } \cot\theta = \frac{\cos\theta}{\sin\theta}\right]$$

$$= \frac{2}{\cos A} = 2\sec A \quad \left[\because \frac{1}{\cos\theta} = \sec\theta\right]$$

= RHS **Hence proved.** (1)

**29.** In the following figure, $CM$ and $RN$ are respectively the medians of $\Delta ABC$ and $\Delta PQR$. If $\Delta ABC \sim \Delta PQR$, prove that

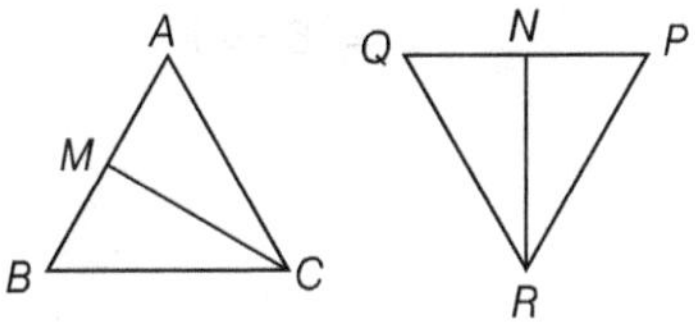


(i) $\Delta AMC \sim \Delta PNR$ (ii) $\frac{CM}{RN} = \frac{AB}{PQ}$

***Sol.*** **Given** $\Delta ABC$ and $\Delta PQR$

$CM$ is the median of $\Delta ABC$ and $RN$ is the median of $\Delta PQR$.

Also, $\Delta ABC \sim \Delta PQR$

**To prove** (i) $\Delta AMC \sim \Delta PNR$ (ii) $\frac{CM}{RN} = \frac{AB}{PQ}$

**Proof**

(i) Given, $\Delta ABC \sim \Delta PQR$

$$\therefore \quad \frac{AB}{PQ} = \frac{BC}{QR} = \frac{AC}{PR} \quad \ldots(i)$$

[$\because$ in similar triangles, corresponding sides are proportional]

and $\angle A = \angle P, \angle B = \angle Q$ and $\angle C = \angle R$ ...(ii)

[$\because$ in similar triangles, corresponding angles are equal] (1/2)

We know that the median bisects the opposite side.

$\therefore \quad AM = MB$

$\Rightarrow \quad AB = 2\,AM$

and $\quad PN = NQ$

$\Rightarrow \quad PQ = 2PN$ (1/2)

From Eq. (i), we have

$$\frac{AB}{PQ} = \frac{AC}{PR}$$

$$\Rightarrow \quad \frac{2AM}{2PN} = \frac{AC}{PR}$$

$$\Rightarrow \quad \frac{AM}{PN} = \frac{AC}{PR} \quad \ldots(iii)$$

In $\Delta AMC$ and $\Delta PNR$, we have

$\angle A = \angle P$ [from Eq. (ii)]

and $\frac{AM}{PN} = \frac{AC}{PR}$ [from Eq. (iii)]

So, $\Delta AMC \sim \Delta PNR$

[by SAS similarity criterion] (1)

(ii) We have, $\Delta AMC \sim \Delta PNR$

$$\Rightarrow \quad \frac{AM}{PN} = \frac{AC}{PR} = \frac{CM}{RN}$$

[$\because$ triangles are similar, so corresponding sides will be proportional]

$$\therefore \quad \frac{CM}{RN} = \frac{AC}{PR}$$

$$\Rightarrow \quad \frac{CM}{RN} = \frac{AB}{PQ} \quad \text{[from Eq. (i)]}$$

**Hence proved.** (1)

**30.** Prove that $\sqrt{n}$ is not a rational number, if $n$ is not a perfect square.

*Or*

The length, breadth and height of a room are 8 m 25 cm, 6 m 75 cm and 4 m 50 cm, respectively. Find the length of the longest rod that can measure the three dimensions of the room exactly.

***Sol.*** Let $\sqrt{n}$ be a rational number.

Then, assume $\sqrt{n} = \frac{p}{q}$

[where $p, q$ are coprime and $q \neq 0$]

$$\Rightarrow \quad n = \frac{p^2}{q^2} \quad \text{[squaring both sides]}$$

$$\Rightarrow \quad p^2 = nq^2 \quad \ldots(i)$$

$\Rightarrow$ $n$ divides $p^2$

$\Rightarrow$ $n$ divides $p$ [by using theorem]...(ii) (1)

Let $p = nm$

$\Rightarrow p^2 = n^2m^2$ [squaring both sides]

On putting the value of $p^2$ in Eq. (i), we get

$$n^2m^2 = nq^2$$

$\Rightarrow$ $q^2 = nm^2$

$\Rightarrow$ $n$ divides $q^2$

$\Rightarrow$ $n$ divides $q$ ...(iii) (1)

From Eq. (ii), $n$ divides $p$ and from Eq. (iii) $n$ divides $q$.
It means $n$ is a common factor of both $p$ and $q$.
This contradicts the assumption that $p$ and $q$ are coprime.
So, our supposition is wrong.
Hence, $\sqrt{n}$ cannot be a rational number. (1)

*Or*

Given, length of the room = 8 m 25 cm

= 825 cm [$\because$ 1m = 100 cm]

Breadth of the room = 6m 75cm = 675cm
and height of the room = 4m 50 cm = 450cm
Clearly, the length of the longest rod (in cm) is the HCF of 825, 675 and 450. (1)

Now,

| | |
|---|---|
| 3 | 825 |
| 5 | 275 |
| 5 | 55 |
| 11 | 11 |
| | 1 |

| | |
|---|---|
| 3 | 675 |
| 3 | 225 |
| 3 | 75 |
| 5 | 25 |
| 5 | 5 |
| | 1 |

| | |
|---|---|
| 2 | 450 |
| 3 | 225 |
| 3 | 75 |
| 5 | 25 |
| 5 | 5 |
| | 1 |

Thus, $825 = 3 \times 5^2 \times 11$,

$675 = 3^3 \times 5^2$

and $450 = 2 \times 3^2 \times 5^2$ (1)

Now, HCF (825, 675, 450)

= Product of the smallest power of each common prime factor

$= 3 \times 5^2$

$= 75$

Hence, the required length of the longest rod is 75 cm. (1)

**31. If 2 is a root of the quadratic equation $3x^2 + px - 8 = 0$ and the quadratic equation $4x^2 - 2px + k = 0$ has equal roots, find the value of $k$.**

***Sol.*** Given, 2 is a root of the quadratic equation $3x^2 + px - 8 = 0$.

So, it satisfies the given equation.

$\therefore$ $3(2)^2 + p(2) - 8 = 0$

$\Rightarrow$ $12 + 2p - 8 = 0$

$\Rightarrow$ $2p = -4$

$\Rightarrow$ $p = -2$ (1)

Put $p = -2$ in the second given equation $4x^2 - 2px + k = 0$, we get

$$4x^2 - 2(-2)x + k = 0 \Rightarrow 4x^2 + 4x + k = 0$$

It is given that, this equation has equal roots.

$\therefore$ $b^2 - 4ac = 0$ (1)

On comparing with $ax^2 + bx + c = 0$, we get

$a = 4, b = 4$ and $c = k$.

$\therefore$ $(4)^2 - 4 \times 4 \times k = 0$

$\Rightarrow$ $16 - 16k = 0$

$\Rightarrow$ $16k = 16 \Rightarrow k = 1$ (1)

# Section-D

**Section D consists of 4 questions of 5 marks each**

**32. From a well-shuffled deck of 52 cards, one card is drawn. Find the probability that the card drawn is**

(i) a queen of black colour.
(ii) a card with number 5 or 6.
(iii) a card with number less than 8.
(iv) a card with number between 2 and 9.
(v) a face card

*Or*

Cards numbered 1, 2, 3, 4, 5, ..., 17 are put in a box and mixed thoroughly. One person draws a card from the box. Find the probability that the number on the card is

(i) an odd number.
(ii) a prime number.
(iii) divisible by 2 and 3 both.
(iv) a multiple of 3 or 5.

***Sol.*** Since, one card is drawn from 52 well-shuffled cards.

$\therefore$ Total number of possible outcomes = 52

(i) Since, there are two queens of black colour.

$\therefore$ $P$ (getting a queen of black colour)

$$= \frac{2}{52} = \frac{1}{26}$$ (1)

(ii) In each suit, there are two cards with number 5 and 6. So, total such cards are 4 times 2 = 8

$\therefore$ $P$ (getting a card with number 5 or 6)

$$= \frac{8}{52} = \frac{2}{13} \quad (1)$$

(iii) In each suit, there are six cards with number less than 8, namely 2, 3, 4, 5, 6 and 7

$\therefore$ $P$ (getting a card with number less than 8)

$$= \frac{4 \times 6}{52} = \frac{24}{52} = \frac{6}{13} \quad (1)$$

(iv) In each suit, there are six cards with number between 2 and 9, namely 3, 4, 5, 6, 7, 8.

$\therefore$ $P$ (getting a card with number between 2 and 9)

$$= \frac{4 \times 6}{52} = \frac{24}{52} = \frac{6}{13} \quad (1)$$

(v) In a pack of cards, there are 12 face cards.

$\therefore$ $P$ (getting a face card) $= \frac{12}{52} = \frac{3}{13}$ (1)

*Or*

There are 17 cards numbered 1, 2, 3, 4, 5,...,17 in a box.

Out of 17 cards, one card can be drawn in 17 ways.

$\therefore$ Total number of outcomes = 17 (1)

(i) There are nine odd numbered cards, namely 1, 3, 5, 7, 9, 11, 13, 15 and 17.

$\therefore$ Number of favourable outcomes = 9

Hence, $P$ (getting an odd number)

$$= \frac{\text{Number of favourable outcomes}}{\text{Total number of outcomes}} = \frac{9}{17} \quad (1)$$

(ii) There are seven prime numbered cards, namely 2, 3, 5, 7, 11, 13 and 17.

$\therefore$ Number of favourable outcomes = 7

Hence, $P$ (getting a prime number)

$$= \frac{\text{Number of favourable outcomes}}{\text{Total number of outcomes}} = \frac{7}{17} \quad (1)$$

(iii) If a number is divisible by 2 and 3 both, then it must be a multiple of 6. In cards bearing number 1, 2, 3, 4, ..., 17, there are only 2 cards which bear a number divisible by 2 and 3 both, i.e. by 6. These cards bearing numbers 6 and 12.

$\therefore$ Number of favourable outcomes = 2

Hence, $P$ (getting a card bearing number divisible by 2 and 3 both)

$$= \frac{\text{Number of favourable outcomes}}{\text{Total number of outcomes}} = \frac{2}{17} \quad (1)$$

(iv) There are 7 numbered cards, which are multiple of 3 or 5 namely, 3, 5, 6, 9, 10, 12 and 15.

$\therefore$ Number of favourable outcomes = 7

Hence, $P$ (getting a card bearing a number multiple of 3 or 5)

$$= \frac{\text{Number of favourable outcomes}}{\text{Total number of outcomes}} = \frac{7}{17} \quad (1)$$

**33. The angle of elevation of the top of a tower from certain point is 30°. If the observer moves 20 m towards the tower, the angle of elevation of the top increases by 15°. Find the height of the tower.**

***Sol.*** Let the height of the tower $PR$ be $h$ m, the angle of elevation at point $Q$ is 30° i.e. $\angle PQR = 30°$ and $S$ be the position of observer after moving 20 m towards the tower.

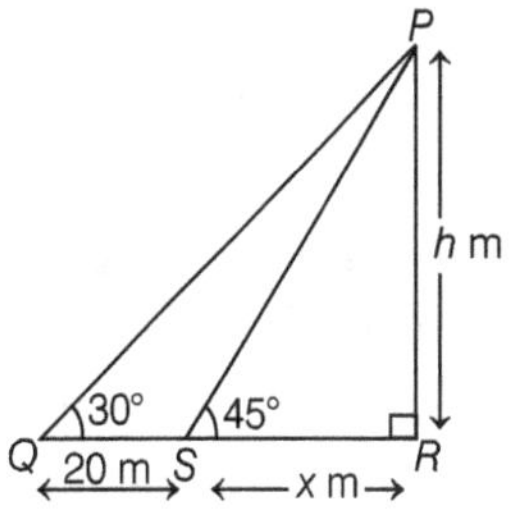


According to the question,

$$\angle PSR = \angle PQR + 15°$$

$$\Rightarrow \quad \angle PSR = 30° + 15°$$

$$\Rightarrow \quad \angle PSR = 45° \quad (1)$$

Now, in right angled $\Delta PRS$,

$$\tan 45° = \frac{PR}{SR} = \frac{h}{x} \quad \left[\because \tan\theta = \frac{\text{Perpendicular}}{\text{Base}}\right]$$

$$\Rightarrow \quad \tan 45° = \frac{h}{x}$$

$$\Rightarrow \quad 1 = \frac{h}{x} \quad [\because \tan 45° = 1]$$

$$\Rightarrow \quad x = h \quad \ldots\text{(i)} \ (1)$$

and in right angled $\Delta PRQ$,

$$\tan 30° = \frac{PR}{QR} = \frac{PR}{QS + SR} \quad [\because QR = QS + SR]$$

$$\Rightarrow \quad \frac{1}{\sqrt{3}} = \frac{h}{20 + x} \quad \left[\because \tan 30° = \frac{1}{\sqrt{3}}\right]$$

$$\Rightarrow \quad 20 + x = \sqrt{3}h \quad (1)$$

$$\Rightarrow \quad 20 + h = \sqrt{3}h \quad [\text{from Eq. (i)}]$$

$$\Rightarrow \quad \sqrt{3}h - h = 20$$

$$\Rightarrow \quad h(\sqrt{3} - 1) = 20$$

$$\Rightarrow h = \frac{20}{\sqrt{3} - 1} \times \frac{\sqrt{3} + 1}{\sqrt{3} + 1} \quad [\text{by rationalising}] \ (1)$$

$$\Rightarrow h = \frac{20(\sqrt{3} + 1)}{3 - 1}$$

$$= \frac{20(\sqrt{3} + 1)}{2}$$

$$= 10(\sqrt{3} + 1)\,\text{m}$$

Hence, the required height of the tower is $10(\sqrt{3} + 1)$ m. (1)

**34.** A wooden article was made by scooping out a hemisphere from each end of a solid cylinder, as shown in figure.

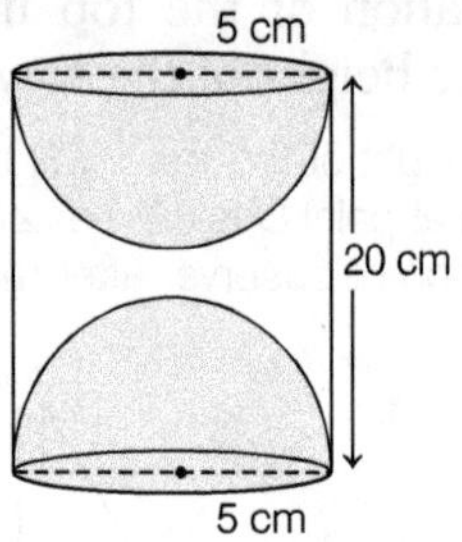


If the height of the cylinder is 20 cm and its base is of radius 5 cm, find the total surface area of the article.

*Or*

The volume of two spheres are in the ratio 64 : 27. Find their radii, if the sum of their radii is 21 cm.

***Sol.*** Given, base radius of cylinder, $r = 5$ cm and its height, $h = 20$ cm

Also, radius of hemisphere, $r = 5$ cm (1)

Now, total surface area of the article

= Curved surface area of the cylinder + 2 (Surface area of a hemisphere)

$$= 2\pi rh + 2(2\pi r^2) = 2\pi r(h + 2r) \quad (2)$$

$$= 2 \times \frac{22}{7} \times 5(20 + 2 \times 5)$$

$$= \frac{220}{7} \times (20 + 10) = \frac{220 \times 30}{7}$$

$$= \frac{6600}{7} = 942.86\ \text{cm}^2 \quad (2)$$

*Or*

Let the volume of two spheres are $V_1$ and $V_2$, respectively and corresponding radii are $r_1$ and $r_2$.

Given, $\frac{V_1}{V_2} = \frac{64}{27} \Rightarrow \frac{\frac{4}{3}\pi r_1^3}{\frac{4}{3}\pi r_2^3} = \left(\frac{4}{3}\right)^3$

$\left[\because \text{volume of the sphere } (V) = \frac{4}{3}\pi r^3\right]$ (1)

$\Rightarrow \frac{r_1^3}{r_2^3} = \left(\frac{4}{3}\right)^3 \Rightarrow \left(\frac{r_1}{r_2}\right)^3 = \left(\frac{4}{3}\right)^3$

$\Rightarrow \frac{r_1}{r_2} = \frac{4}{3}$ [taking cube root]

$\Rightarrow r_1 = \frac{4}{3} r_2$ ...(i) (1)

Also given, sum of their radii = 21 cm

$\therefore r_1 + r_2 = 21$ ...(ii) (1)

From Eqs. (i) and (ii), we get

$\frac{4}{3} r_2 + r_2 = 21$

$\Rightarrow \frac{4r_2 + 3r_2}{3} = 21$

$\Rightarrow 7r_2 = 21 \times 3$

$\Rightarrow r_2 = 3 \times 3$

$\Rightarrow r_2 = 9$ cm (1)

On putting $r_2 = 9$ cm in Eq. (i), we get

$$r_1 = \frac{4}{3} \times 9 = 12 \text{ cm}$$

Hence, the radii of the two spheres are 12 cm and 9 cm. (1)

**35.** Find the mean of the following frequency distribution using step-deviation method.

| Marks obtained | Number of students |
|---|---|
| Less than 10 | 14 |
| Less than 20 | 22 |
| Less than 30 | 37 |
| Less than 40 | 58 |
| Less than 50 | 67 |
| Less than 60 | 75 |

***Sol.*** The given data may be written as

| Class | Frequency |
|---|---|
| 0-10 | 14 |
| 10-20 | 22 − 14 = 8 |
| 20-30 | 37 − 22 = 15 |
| 30-40 | 58 − 37 = 21 |
| 40-50 | 67 − 58 = 9 |
| 50-60 | 75 − 67 = 8 |

(1)

Here, $h = 10$

Let assumed mean $(A)$ = Mid-value of (30-40) = 35 (1/2)

Table for deviation and their product with corresponding frequency is given below

| Class | Frequency $(f_i)$ | Mid-value $(x_i)$ | $d_i = x_i - A$ | $f_i d_i$ |
|---|---|---|---|---|
| 0-10 | 14 | 5 | − 30 | − 420 |
| 10-20 | 8 | 15 | − 20 | − 160 |
| 20-30 | 15 | 25 | − 10 | − 150 |
| 30-40 | 21 | 35 (A) | 0 | 0 |
| 40-50 | 9 | 45 | 10 | 90 |
| 50-60 | 8 | 55 | 20 | 160 |
| **Total** | $\Sigma f_i = 75$ | | | $\Sigma f_i d_i = -480$ |

(2)

Here, $h = 10$, $\Sigma f_i = 75$, $\Sigma f_i d_i = -480$ and $A = 35$

$$\therefore \text{Mean, } \bar{x} = \left\{A + \frac{\Sigma f_i d_i}{\Sigma f_i}\right\} = 35 + \frac{(-480)}{75} \quad (1/2)$$

$$= 35 + (-6.4) = 35 - 6.4 = 28.6 \quad (1)$$

# Section-E

**Case study based questions are compulsory**

**36.** Pankaj's father gave him some money to buy avocado from the market at the rate of $p(x)=x^2-24x+128$.

Let $\alpha$, $\beta$ are the zeroes of $p(x)$.

On the basis of above information, answer the following questions.

(i) Find the value of $\alpha$ and $\beta$, where $\alpha<\beta$. (1)

(ii) Find the value of $p(2)$. (1)

(iii) If $\alpha$ and $\beta$ are zeroes of $x^2+88x+125$, then find the value of $\frac{1}{\alpha}+\frac{1}{\beta}$. (2)

*Or*

If sum of zeroes of $q(x)=kx^2+2x+3k$ is equal to their product, then find the value of $k$. (2)

***Sol.*** (i) We have, $p(x)=x^2-24x+128$

$\Rightarrow \quad p(x)=x^2-16x-8x+128$

$\Rightarrow \quad p(x)=x(x-16)-8(x-16)$

$\Rightarrow \quad p(x)=(x-16)(x-8)$

So, the zeroes of $p(x)$ are given by $p(x)=0$

$\Rightarrow (x-16)(x-8)=0$

$\Rightarrow (x-16)=0$ and $(x-8)=0$

$\Rightarrow x=16$ and $x=8$

So, the values of $\alpha$ and $\beta$ are 8 and 16, respectively. [$\because 8<16$]

(ii) $p(2)=(2)^2-24(2)+128$

$=4-48+128=132-48=84$

(iii) Let $q(x)=x^2+88x+125$

Sum of roots $=\alpha+\beta=-88$

and product of roots $=\alpha\beta=125$

$\therefore \frac{1}{\alpha}+\frac{1}{\beta}=\frac{\beta+\alpha}{\alpha\beta}=\frac{-88}{125}$

*Or*

Given, $q(x)=kx^2+2x+3k$

Sum of zeroes of $q(x)=\frac{-2}{k}$

Product of zeroes of $q(x)=\frac{3k}{k}=3$

According to the question,

$$\frac{-2}{k}=3 \Rightarrow k=\frac{-2}{3}$$

**37.** A test consists of 'True' or 'False' questions. One mark is awarded for every correct answer while $\frac{1}{4}$ mark is deducted for every wrong answer. A student knew answers to some of the questions. Rest of the questions he attempted by guessing. He answered 120 questions and got 90 marks.

| Type of question | Marks given for correct answer | Marks deducted for wrong answer |
|---|---|---|
| True/False | 1 | 0.25 |

On the basis of above information, answer the following questions.

(i) If answer to all questions he attempted by guessing were wrong, then how many questions did he answer correctly? (1)

(ii) How many questions did he guess? (1)

(iii) If answer to all questions he attempted by guessing were wrong and answered 80 correctly, then how many marks he got? (2)

*Or* If answer to all questions he attempted by guessing were wrong, then how many questions answered correctly to score 95 marks? (2)

***Sol.*** Let the number of questions whose answer is known to the student be $x$ and questions attempted by guessing be $y$.

Then, $\quad x+y=120 \quad$ ...(i)

and $\quad x-\frac{1}{4}y=90 \Rightarrow 4x-y=360 \quad$ ...(ii)

On adding Eqs. (i) and (ii), we get

$$5x=480 \Rightarrow x=\frac{480}{5}=96$$

Put $x=96$ in Eq. (i), we get

$$96+y=120 \Rightarrow y=120-96=24$$

(i) He answered 96 questions correctly.

(ii) He guesses only 24 questions.

(iii) In out of 120 questions attempted 80 answered are correct and 40 guessing answered are wrong.

Then, he got the marks $=80-\frac{1}{4}$ of 40

$=80-\frac{1}{4}\times 40$

$=80-10=70$

*Or*

According to the given condition,

$$x - \frac{1}{4} \text{ of } (120 - x) = 95$$

$$\Rightarrow \quad x - \frac{1}{4} \times (120 - x) = 95$$

$$\Rightarrow \quad 4x - 120 + x = 380$$

$$\Rightarrow \quad 5x = 500$$

$$\Rightarrow \quad x = 100$$

Hence, he answered correctly 100 questions to score 95 marks.

**38.** Varun has been selected by his School to design logo for Sports Day T-shirts for students and staff. The logo design is as given in the figure and he is working on the fonts and different colours according to the theme.

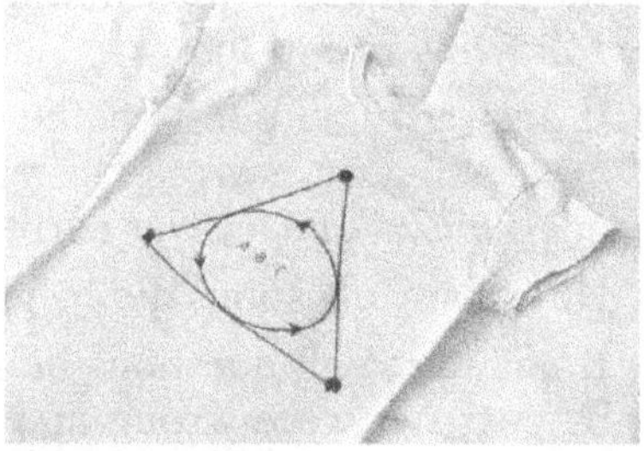

In given figure, a circle with centre $O$ is inscribed in a $\Delta ABC$, such that it touches the sides $AB$, $BC$ and $CA$ at points $D$, $E$ and $F$, respectively. The lengths of sides $AB$, $BC$ and $CA$ are 12 cm, 8 cm and 10 cm, respectively.

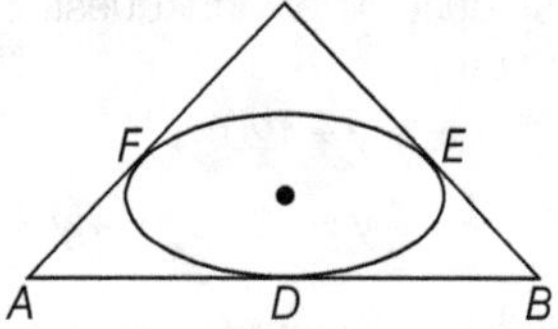


On the basis of above information, answer the following questions.

(i) Find the length of $AD$. (1)

(ii) Find the length of $BE$. (1)

(iii) If radius of the circle is 4 cm, Find the area of $\Delta ABC$. (2)

*Or*

If radius of the circle is 4 cm, Find the area of $\Delta OFC$. (2)

***Sol.*** Let $AD = x = AF$ [$\because$ lengths of tangents drawn from an external point to a circle are equal]

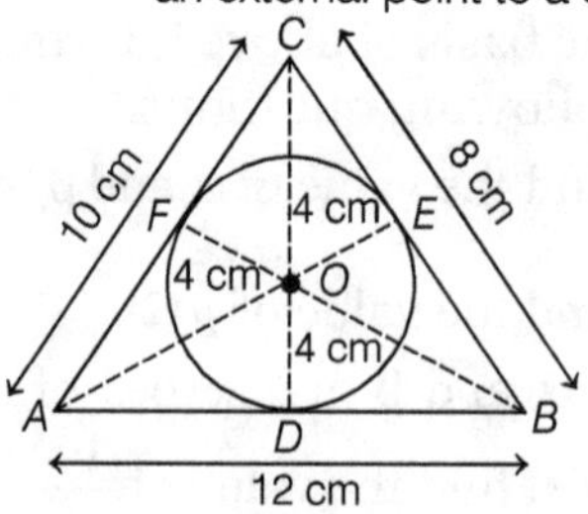


Then, $BD = BE = AB - AD = 12 - x$

and $CF = CE = AC - AF = 10 - x$

Now, $BC = BE + CE$

$$\Rightarrow \quad 8 = 12 - x + 10 - x$$

$$\Rightarrow \quad 2x = 14 \Rightarrow x = 7$$

(i) $AD = x = 7$ cm

(ii) $BE = 12 - x = 12 - 7 = 5$ cm

(iii) $\text{ar}(\Delta OAB) = \frac{1}{2} \times AB \times OD$

$$= \frac{1}{2} \times 12 \times 4 = 24 \text{ cm}^2$$

$$\text{ar}(\Delta OAC) = \frac{1}{2} \times AC \times OF = \frac{1}{2} \times 10 \times 4 = 20 \text{ cm}^2$$

$$\text{ar}(\Delta OBC) = \frac{1}{2} \times BC \times OE = \frac{1}{2} \times 8 \times 4 = 16 \text{ cm}^2$$

$$\text{ar}(\Delta ABC) = \text{ar}(\Delta OAB) + \text{ar}(\Delta OAC) + \text{ar}(\Delta OBC)$$

$$= 24 + 20 + 16 = 60 \text{ cm}^2$$

*Or*

$$CF = 10 - x = 10 - 7 = 3 \text{ cm}$$

$$\therefore \text{ Area of } \Delta OCF = \frac{1}{2} \times CF \times OF$$

$$= \frac{1}{2} \times 3 \times 4 = 6 \text{ cm}^2$$

# SAMPLE QUESTION PAPER 4

## Mathematics (Basic)

Time : **3 hrs** Max. Marks : **80**

### Instructions

1. This question paper has 5 Sections A, B, C, D and E.
2. Section A has 20 Multiple Choice Questions (MCQs) carrying 1 mark each.
3. Section B has 5 Short Answer-I (SA-I) Type Questions carrying 2 marks each.
4. Section C has 6 Short Answer-II (SA-II) Type Questions carrying 3 marks each.
5. Section D has 4 Long Answer (LA) Type Questions carrying 5 marks each.
6. Section E has 3 Case Based integrated units of assessment (4 marks each) with sub-parts of the values of 1, 1 and 2 marks each respectively.
7. All questions are compulsory. However, an internal choice in 2 questions of 2 marks, 2 questions of 3 marks and 2 questions of 5 marks has been provided. An internal choice has been provided in the 2 marks questions of Section E.
8. Draw neat figures wherever required. Take $\pi = 22/7$ wherever required if not stated.

## Section-A

**Section A consists of 20 questions of 1 mark each**

**1.** If the product of zeroes of the polynomial $f(x) = ax^3 - 6x^2 + 11x - 6$ is 4, then the value of $a$ is

(a) $\frac{3}{2}$ (b) $\frac{11}{4}$

(c) 3 (d) None of these

***Sol.*** (a) Let $\alpha, \beta, \gamma$ are the zeroes of the polynomial $f(x)$.

Now, we have

$$\alpha\beta\gamma = 4 \Rightarrow \frac{-(-6)}{a} = 4$$

$$\therefore \quad a = \frac{6}{4} = \frac{3}{2}$$

**2.** If $0° < \theta < 90°$, then the value of $\theta$ in $\tan 5\theta = 1$ is

(a) 6° (b) 12°

(c) 9° (d) 0°

***Sol.*** (c) We have,

$$\tan 5\theta = 1$$

$$\Rightarrow \tan 5\theta = \tan 45°$$

$$\Rightarrow 5\theta = 45°$$

$$\Rightarrow \theta = \frac{45°}{5} = 9°$$

**3.** If the general term of an AP is $4n+3$, then its common difference ($d$) is

(a) 7 (b) 11 (c) 4 (d) 15

**Sol.** (c) Given, $T_n = 4n + 3$

$$T_1 = 4(1) + 3 = 7$$
$$T_2 = 4(2) + 3 = 11$$
$$T_3 = 4(3) + 3 = 15$$
$$T_3 - T_2 = T_2 - T_1 = 4$$

Hence, $d$ is 4.

**4.** If one of the zeroes of a quadratic polynomial $(k-1)x^2 + kx + 1$ is $-3$, then the value of $k$ is

(a) 1 (b) $\frac{1}{3}$ (c) $\frac{2}{3}$ (d) $\frac{4}{3}$

**Sol.** (d) Let $p(x) = (k-1)x^2 + kx + 1$

Since, $-3$ is a zero of polynomial.

$\therefore p(-3) = 0$

$\therefore (k-1)(-3)^2 + k(-3) + 1 = 0$

$\Rightarrow 9(k-1) - 3k + 1 = 0$

$\Rightarrow 9k - 9 - 3k + 1 = 0$

$\Rightarrow 6k - 8 = 0 \Rightarrow 6k = 8$

$\therefore k = \frac{8}{6} \Rightarrow k = \frac{4}{3}$

**5.** The area of a quadrant of a circle whose circumference is 20 cm, is

(a) $\frac{400}{\pi}\text{cm}^2$ (b) $\frac{100}{\pi}\text{cm}^2$

(c) $\frac{200}{\pi}\text{cm}^2$ (d) $\frac{800}{\pi}\text{cm}^2$

**Sol.** (a) Given, the circumference of a quadrant is 20 cm

$\Rightarrow \frac{2\pi r}{4} = 20$

$\Rightarrow \pi r = 40$

$\Rightarrow r = \frac{40}{\pi}$

Now, area of a quadrant $= \frac{\pi r^2}{4} = \frac{\pi}{4} \times \left(\frac{40}{\pi}\right)^2$

$= \frac{\pi}{4} \times \frac{1600}{\pi^2}$

$= \frac{400}{\pi}\text{cm}^2$

**6.** The median and mode of a frequency distribution are 32 and 38 respectively, then the mean is

(a) 34 (b) 29

(c) 20 (d) 35

**Sol.** (b) $\because$ Mode = 3 Median − 2 Mean

$\Rightarrow 38 = 3 \times 32 - 2 \times \text{Mean}$

$\Rightarrow 2\,\text{Mean} = 3 \times 32 - 38 = 96 - 38 = 58$

$\Rightarrow \text{Mean} = \frac{58}{2} = 29$

**7.** In a throw of a die, the probability of getting a prime number, is

(a) $\frac{2}{3}$ (b) $\frac{1}{2}$ (c) $\frac{1}{3}$ (d) $\frac{5}{6}$

**Sol.** (b) Total number of possible outcomes = 1, 2, 3, 4, 5, 6

Let $E$ = Event of getting a prime number = 2, 3, 5

$\therefore P(E) = \frac{3}{6} = \frac{1}{2}$

**8.** If $PA$ and $PB$ are two tangents to a circle with centre $O$ such that $\angle AOB = 115°$, then the value of $\angle APB$ is

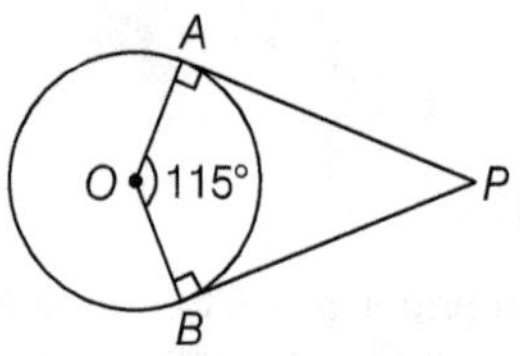


(a) 57.5° (b) 65° (c) 75° (d) 55°

**Sol.** (b) Given, $\angle OAP = 90°$

$\angle OBP = 90°$

$\therefore \angle AOB + \angle APB = 180°$

$\Rightarrow 115° + \angle APB = 180°$

$\Rightarrow \angle APB = 180° - 115° = 65°$

**9.** In the given figure, $PQ \parallel BC$, find $AQ$.

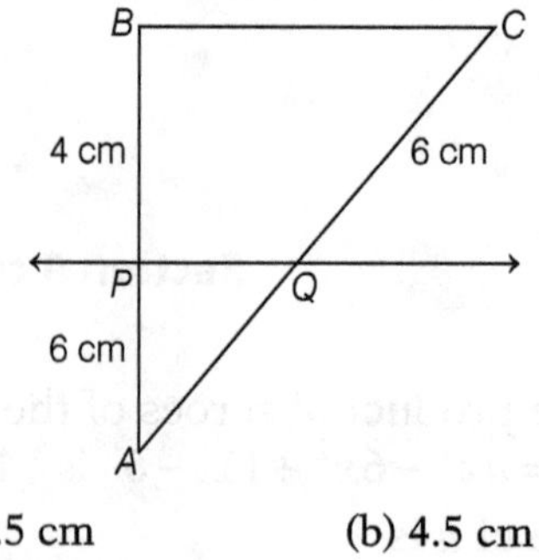


(a) 3.5 cm (b) 4.5 cm

(c) 9 cm (d) 9.5 cm

**Sol.** (c) In $\Delta ABC$, we have

$PQ \parallel BC$

$\Rightarrow \frac{AQ}{QC} = \frac{AP}{PB}$ [by Thales theorem]

$\Rightarrow \frac{AQ}{6} = \frac{6}{4}$

$\Rightarrow AQ = \frac{6 \times 6}{4} = 9\,\text{cm}$

**10.** Given that $\sin A = \frac{\sqrt{3}}{2}$ and $\cos B = \frac{\sqrt{3}}{2}$, the value of $(A+B)$ is

(a) 60° (b) 105° (c) 75° (d) 90°

***Sol.*** (d) Given, $\sin A = \frac{\sqrt{3}}{2}$ and $\cos B = \frac{\sqrt{3}}{2}$

$\Rightarrow \quad \sin A = \sin 60° \quad \left[\because \sin 60° = \frac{\sqrt{3}}{2}\right]$

and $\quad \cos B = \cos 30° \quad \left[\because \cos 30° = \frac{\sqrt{3}}{2}\right]$

$\Rightarrow \quad A = 60°$ and $B = 30°$

$\therefore \quad A + B = 60° + 30° = 90°$

**11.** The angle of elevation of the sun when the shadow of a 10 m long pole is $10\sqrt{3}$ m is

(a) 60° (b) 30°
(c) 45° (d) None of these

***Sol.*** (b) Let the angle of elevation of the sun be θ from $\Delta PQR$.

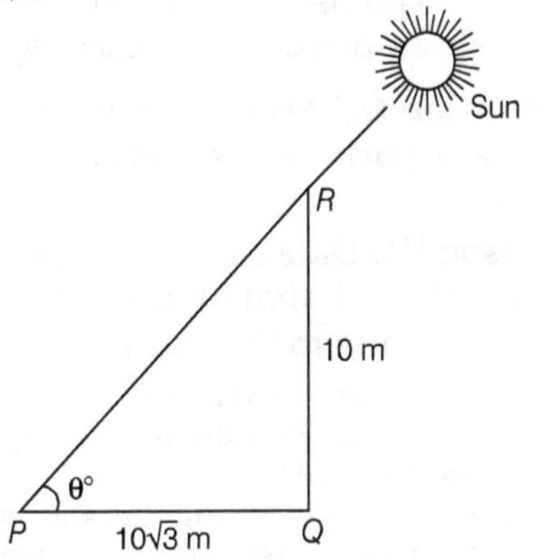


In $\Delta PQR$, $\tan\theta = \frac{QR}{QP} = \frac{10}{10\sqrt{3}} = \frac{1}{\sqrt{3}} \Rightarrow \theta = 30°$

**12.** In $\Delta ABC$ it is given that, $\frac{AB}{AC} = \frac{BD}{DC}$, if $\angle B = 60°$ and $\angle C = 60°$, then $\angle BAD$ is equal to

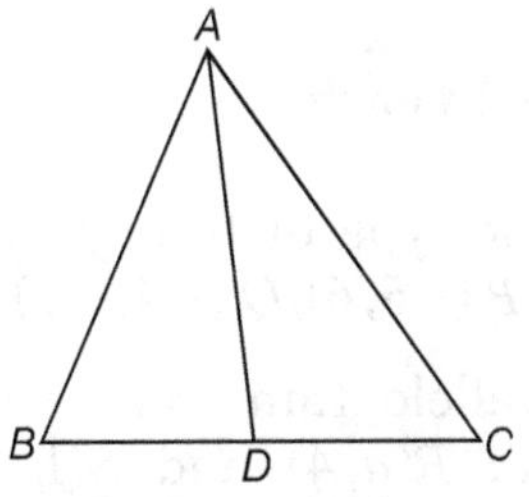


(a) 30° (b) 40° (c) 45° (d) 50°

***Sol.*** (a) Given, in $\Delta ABC$, $\frac{AB}{AC} = \frac{BD}{DC}$

$\angle B = 60°$ and $\angle C = 60°$

We know that sum of angles of a triangle is 180°.

In $\Delta ABC$, $\quad \angle A + \angle B + \angle C = 180°$

$\Rightarrow \quad \angle A + 60° + 60° = 180°$

$\Rightarrow \quad \angle A = 180° - 120° = 60°$

Now, $\quad \frac{AB}{AC} = \frac{BD}{DC}$ [given]

Therefore, $AD$ bisects $BC$.

[by angle bisector theorem]

Then, $\angle BAC = \frac{1}{2}\angle A = 30°$.

Hence, the value of $\angle BAD$ is 30°.

**13.** The graph of the equations, $x = y$ and $x - 2 = y - 2$ are two lines which are

(a) coincident
(b) parallel
(c) intersecting exactly at one point
(d) perpendicular to each other

***Sol.*** (a) We have, $x = y$ and $x - 2 = y - 2 \Rightarrow x = y$

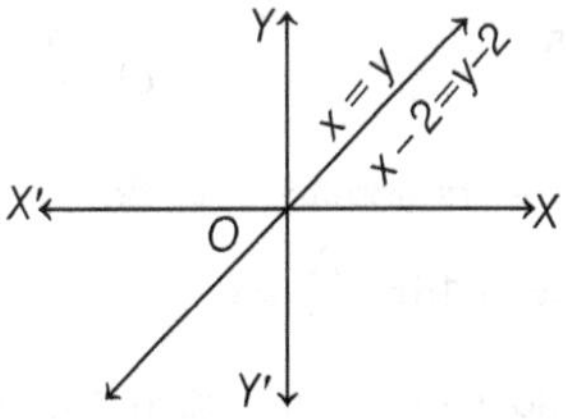


On graphical representation, we get a pair of coincident lines.

**14.** The probability that it will rain tomorrow is 0.3. What is the probability that it will not rain tomorrow?

(a) 0.3 (b) 0.2 (c) 0.7 (d) 0.07

***Sol.*** (c) Let $A$ be the event of rain tomorrow.

Then, $\quad P(A) = 0.3$

We know that

$P(A) + P(\bar{A}) = 1$

Then, probability that it will not rain tomorrow

$= 1 - 0.3 = 0.7$

**15.** The smallest number by which $\sqrt{27}$ should be multiplied so as to get a rational number is

(a) $\sqrt{27}$ (b) $3\sqrt{3}$ (c) $\sqrt{3}$ (d) 3

***Sol.*** (c) As, $\sqrt{27} = \sqrt{3 \times 3 \times 3} = 3\sqrt{3}$

So, if we multiply it by $\sqrt{3}$ it will become

$3\sqrt{3} \times \sqrt{3} = 3 \times 3 = 9$

i.e a rational number.

**16.** The product of the HCF and LCM of the smallest prime number and the smallest composite number is

(a) 2 (b) 4 (c) 6 (d) 8

**Sol.** (d) Smallest prime number = 2
Smallest composite number = 4
Since, product of HCF and LCM
= Product of numbers
$\therefore$ HCF $\times$ LCM = $2 \times 4 = 8$

**17.** Which of the following is not a quadratic equation?

(a) $x^2 - 4x + 10 = 0$ (b) $(x+2)^2 = 2(x+7)$
(c) $(\sqrt{3}x+7)^2 = 3x^2+5$ (d) $(x-3)^2 + 2 = 7x + 16$

**Sol.** (c) From option (c), $(\sqrt{3}x+7)^2 = 3x^2+5$

$\Rightarrow \quad 3x^2 + 49 + 14\sqrt{3}x = 3x^2 + 5$

$\Rightarrow \quad 14\sqrt{3}x + 44 = 0$

$\because$ The highest power of $x$ is 1, so it is a linear equation.

**18.** If one root of the equation $5x^2 + 15x + \frac{25}{4} = 0$ is $-\frac{1}{2}$, then the other root is

(a) $-\frac{5}{2}$ (b) $\frac{1}{2}$ (c) $-\frac{2}{2}$ (d) $-\frac{3}{2}$

**Sol.** (a) Given, quadratic equation

$$5x^2 + 15x + \frac{25}{4} = 0$$

We know that if $\alpha$ and $\beta$ are roots of quadratic equation, then

$$\alpha + \beta = -\frac{b}{a}$$

Here, $\alpha = -\frac{1}{2}$ and $a = 5, b = 15$

Then, $\alpha + \beta = -\frac{15}{5} = -3 \Rightarrow \beta = -3 + \frac{1}{2}$

$\therefore \quad \beta = -\frac{5}{2}$

**Directions** *In the question number 19 and 20, a statement of Assertion (A) is followed by a statement of Reason (R). Choose the correct option.*

**19. Assertion (A)** If the median of the given data 26, 29, 42, 53, $x$, $x+4$, 70, 75, 80, 92 is 68, then the value of $x$ is 66.

**Reason (R)** When the number of observations ($n$) is odd, the median is the value of $\left(\frac{n+1}{2}\right)$th observation.

(a) Both Assertion (A) and Reason (R) are true and Reason (R) is the correct explanation of Assertion (A)
(b) Both Assertion (A) and Reason (R) are true but Reason (R) is not the correct explanation of Assertion (A)
(c) Assertion (A) is true but Reason (R) is false
(d) Assertion (A) is false but Reason (R) is true

**Sol.** (b) Given, number of observations is 10 (even).

$\therefore$ Median $= \frac{x + (x+4)}{2} = \frac{2x+4}{2} = x + 2$

$\Rightarrow \quad 68 = x + 2 \Rightarrow x = 66$

So, Assertion (A) is true.

Clearly, Reason (R) is also true. But Reason (R) is not the correct explanation of Assertion (A).

**20. Assertion (A)** Frequency is the number of times a particular observation occurs in data.

**Reason (R)** Data can be grouped into class intervals such that all observations in that range belong to the class.

(a) Both Assertion (A) and Reason (R) are true and Reason (R) is the correct explanation of Assertion (A)
(b) Both Assertion (A) and Reason (R) are true but Reason (R) is not the correct explanation of Assertion (A)
(c) Assertion (A) is true but Reason (R) is false
(d) Assertion (A) is false but Reason (R) is true

**Sol.** (b) Both Assertion (A) and Reason (R) are correct but Reason (R) is not the correct explanation of Assertion (A).

# Section-B

**Section B consists of 5 questions of 2 marks each**

**21.** Sohan and Rohan are friends. They were both born in 1993. What is the probability that they have the same birthday?

**Sol.** The year 1993 is a non-leap year. Both friends can have their birthday on any one of the 365 days. So, total number of outcomes = 365 (1)

Favourable outcomes = 1

$\therefore \quad P(E) = \frac{1}{365}$ (1)

**22.** Find the type of triangle formed by the points $P(-5, 6)$, $Q(-4, -2)$ and $R(7, 5)$.

*Or* A parallelogram has vertices $P(1, 4)$, $Q(7, 11)$, $R(a, 4)$ and $S(1, -3)$. Find the value of $a$.

**Sol.** Given, vertices of triangle are $P(-5, 6)$, $Q(-4, -2)$ and $R(7, 5)$.

Now, $PQ = \sqrt{(x_2 - x_1)^2 + (y_2 - y_1)^2}$ [by distance formula]

$= \sqrt{(-4+5)^2 + (-2-6)^2}$

$= \sqrt{1+64} = \sqrt{65}$ units (1/2)

$QR = \sqrt{(7+4)^2 + (5+2)^2}$

$= \sqrt{121+49}$

$= \sqrt{170}$ units (1/2)

and $PR = \sqrt{(7+5)^2 + (5-6)^2}$

$= \sqrt{144+1} = \sqrt{145}$ units (1/2)

Here, $PQ \neq QR \neq PR$

Hence, the given triangle is a scalene triangle. (1/2)

*Or*

Let $P(1, 4)$, $Q(7, 11)$, $R(a, 4)$ and $S(1, -3)$ be the vertices of a parallelogram $PQRS$, respectively.

Join $PR$ and $QS$. Let $PR$ and $QS$ intersect at the point $T$.

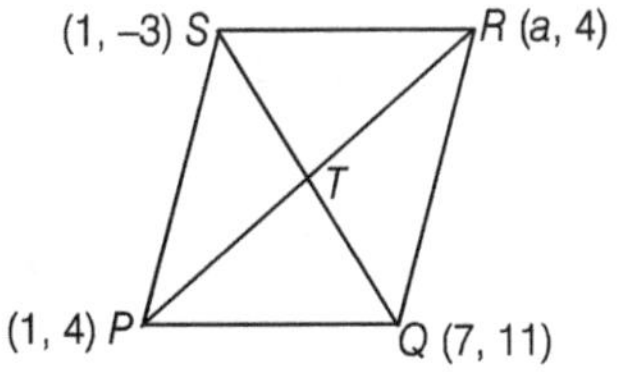


(1)

We know that the diagonals of a parallelogram bisect each other.

So, $T$ is the mid-point of $PR$ as well as that of $QS$.

$\therefore$ Mid-point of $PR$ = Mid-point of $QS$

$\Rightarrow \left(\frac{1+a}{2}, \frac{4+4}{2}\right) = \left(\frac{7+1}{2}, \frac{11-3}{2}\right)$

$\Rightarrow \left(\frac{1+a}{2}, 4\right) = (4, 4)$

On comparing $x$-coordinate from both sides, we get

$\frac{1+a}{2} = 4 \Rightarrow 1+a = 8 \Rightarrow a = 7$

Hence, the value of $a$ is 7. (1)

**23.** Two buildings $ABC$ and $PQR$ are constructed in triangular shapes are similar as shown in the below figure

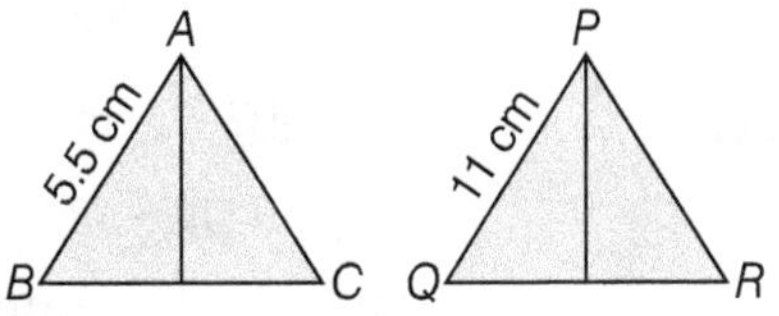


If perimeter of $\Delta ABC$ is 70 cm, then find the perimeter of $\Delta PQR$.

***Sol.*** Given, $\Delta ABC \sim \Delta PQR$ with $AB = 5.5$ cm and $PQ = 11$ cm

Since, $\Delta ABC \sim \Delta PQR$, so corresponding sides are proportional.

$\therefore \frac{AB}{PQ} = \frac{BC}{QR} = \frac{AC}{PR} = \frac{5.5}{11} = \frac{55}{110} = \frac{1}{2}$

$\Rightarrow \frac{AB}{PQ} = \frac{1}{2}, \frac{BC}{QR} = \frac{1}{2}$ and $\frac{AC}{PR} = \frac{1}{2}$ (1)

$\Rightarrow AB = \frac{1}{2}PQ, BC = \frac{1}{2}QR$ and $AC = \frac{1}{2}PR$

Also, given perimeter of $\Delta ABC = 70$ cm

$\Rightarrow AB + BC + CA = 70$

$\Rightarrow \frac{1}{2}PQ + \frac{1}{2}QR + \frac{1}{2}PR = 70$

$\therefore PQ + QR + PR = 140$ cm

Hence, perimeter of $\Delta PQR$ is 140 cm (1)

**24.** Find the zeroes of the polynomial $f(x) = 8x^2 - 2$ and verify the relationship between zeroes and its coefficients.

***Sol.*** Given, polynomial is

$f(x) = 8x^2 - 2 = (2\sqrt{2}x)^2 - (\sqrt{2})^2$

$= (2\sqrt{2}x - \sqrt{2})(2\sqrt{2}x + \sqrt{2})$

$[\because a^2 - b^2 = (a-b)(a+b)]$

To determine zeroes, put $f(x) = 0$

$\Rightarrow (2\sqrt{2}x - \sqrt{2})(2\sqrt{2}x + \sqrt{2}) = 0$

$\Rightarrow x = \frac{1}{2}$ and $x = -\frac{1}{2}$

Hence, zeroes of $f(x)$ are $\frac{1}{2}$ and $-\frac{1}{2}$. (1)

Now, sum of zeroes $= \frac{1}{2} - \frac{1}{2} = 0$

$= -\frac{\text{Coefficient of } x}{\text{Coefficient of } x^2}$

and product of zeroes $= \frac{1}{2}\left(-\frac{1}{2}\right)$

$= -\frac{1}{4} \times \frac{2}{2} = -\frac{2}{8}$

$= \frac{\text{Constant term}}{\text{Coefficient of } x^2}$

Hence, its verify the relationship between zeroes and coefficient. (1)

**25.** A circus artist is climbing a 40 m long rope, which is tightly stretched and tied from the top of a vertical pole to the ground. Find the height of the pole, if the angle made by the rope with the ground level is 60°.

*Or*

**A kite is flying at a height of 30 m from the level ground, attached to string inclined at 30° to the horizontal. Find the length of the string.**

**Sol.** Let $BC$ be the vertical pole and $AB$ be the rope which is tightly stretched and tied from the top of pole to the ground.

Then, $AB = 40$ m

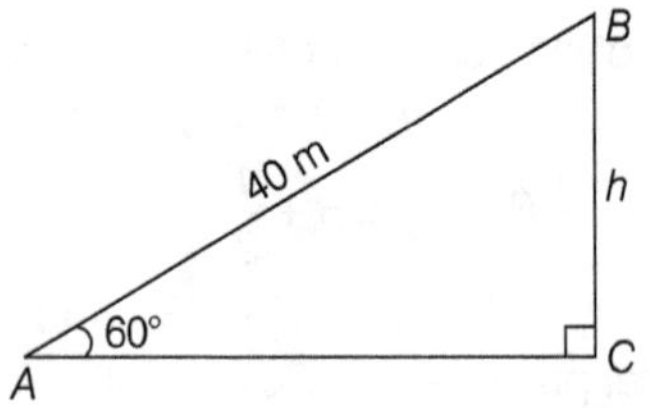


Let $h$ m be the height of the vertical pole $BC$.
Then, angle of elevation $= \angle BAC = 60°$ (given). (1)
From right angled $\Delta ABC$, we get

$$\sin 60° = \frac{BC}{AB} \Rightarrow \frac{\sqrt{3}}{2} = \frac{h}{40} \Rightarrow h = 20\sqrt{3}$$

Hence, the height of the pole is $20\sqrt{3}$ m. (1)

*Or*

Let $P$ be the kite and the height of the kite, $MP = 30$ m.
Let the string be held at the point $O$,
then $\angle MOP = 30°$ (given)
and $OP$ is the length of the string.

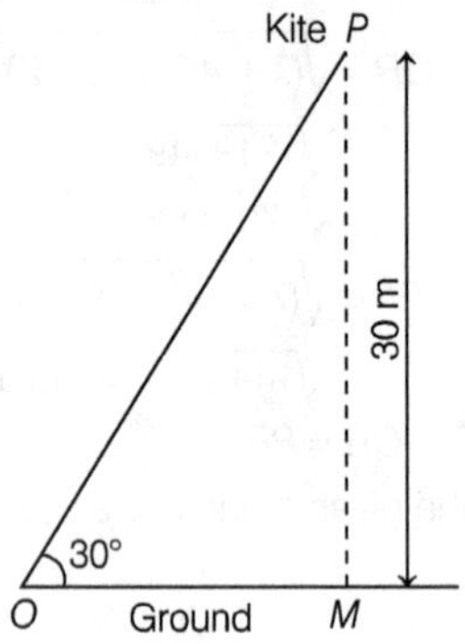


(1)

From right angled $\Delta OMP$,

$$\sin 30° = \frac{MP}{OP} \Rightarrow \frac{1}{2} = \frac{30}{OP}$$

$$\Rightarrow \quad OP = 60 \text{ m}$$

Hence, the length of the string is 60 m. (1)

# Section-C

**Section C consists of 6 questions of 3 marks each**

**26.** The given figure represents a hemisphere surmounted by a conical block of wood. The diameter of their bases is 10 cm each and the slant height of the cone is 13 cm.

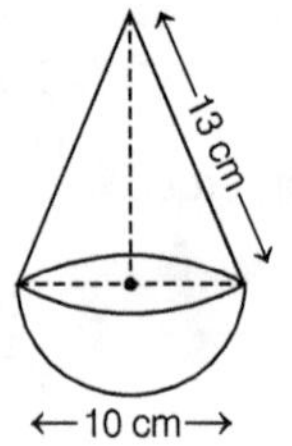


Calculate
(i) the height of the cone.
(ii) the volume of the solid.

**Sol.** Given, diameter of the base $(d) = 10$ cm

$\therefore$ Radius of the base $(r) = \frac{10}{2} = 5$ cm

Slant height of the cone $(l) = 13$ cm

(i) Let the height of the cone $= h$

We know that

$l^2 = r^2 + h^2$ [using Pythagoras theorem]

$\Rightarrow (13)^2 = (5)^2 + h^2$

$\Rightarrow 169 = 25 + h^2$

$\Rightarrow h^2 = 169 - 25 = 144$

$\therefore h = \sqrt{144} = 12$ cm

[taking positive square root]

Hence, height of the cone is 12 cm. (1½)

(ii) Volume of solid = Volume of hemisphere + Volume of cone

$$= \frac{2}{3}\pi r^3 + \frac{1}{3}\pi r^2 h$$

$$= \frac{1}{3}\pi r^2 (2r + h)$$

$$= \frac{1}{3} \times \frac{22}{7} \times 5 \times 5 (2 \times 5 + 12)$$

$[\because r = 5 \text{ cm and } h = 12 \text{ cm}]$

$$= \frac{22 \times 25}{21}(10 + 12)$$

$$= \frac{22 \times 25}{21}(22) = \frac{12100}{21}$$

$$= 576.19 \text{ cm}^3$$

Hence, the volume of solid is 576.19 $\text{cm}^3$. (1½)

**27.** Calculate the mode for the following frequency distribution

| Class | 0-10 | 10-20 | 20-30 | 30-40 | 40-50 | 50-60 | 60-70 | 70-80 |
|---|---|---|---|---|---|---|---|---|
| Frequency | 5 | 8 | 7 | 12 | 28 | 20 | 10 | 10 |

***Sol.*** As the class 40-50 has maximum frequency, so it is the modal class.

$\therefore l = 40, h = 10, f_1 = 28, f_0 = 12$ and $f_2 = 20$. (1)

Mode, $M_0 = l + \left\{h \times \frac{f_1 - f_0}{(2f_1 - f_0 - f_2)}\right\}$

$= 40 + \left\{10 \times \frac{(28-12)}{(2\times 28 - 12 - 20)}\right\}$ (1)

$= 40 + \left\{10 \times \frac{16}{24}\right\} = 40 + \frac{20}{3}$

$= 40 + 6.67 = 46.67$

Hence, mode is 46.67. (1)

**28.** Solve the following quadratic by factorisation

$$\frac{1}{x+4} - \frac{1}{x+7} = \frac{3}{10}, \; x \neq -4, -7$$

*Or*

Using quadratic formula, solve for $x$.

$$9x^2 - 3(a+b)x + ab = 0$$

***Sol.*** Given, $\frac{1}{x+4} - \frac{1}{x+7} = \frac{3}{10}$

$\therefore \frac{x+7-(x+4)}{(x+7)(x+4)} = \frac{3}{10}$

$\Rightarrow \frac{3}{(x^2+11x+28)} = \frac{3}{10}$

$\Rightarrow \frac{1}{x^2+11x+28} = \frac{1}{10}$ (1½)

$\Rightarrow x^2 + 11x + 28 = 10$

$\Rightarrow x^2 + 11x + 18 = 0$

$\Rightarrow x^2 + 9x + 2x + 18 = 0$

$\Rightarrow x(x+9) + 2(x+9) = 0$

$\Rightarrow (x+9)(x+2) = 0$

$\Rightarrow x = -9, -2$ (1½)

*Or*

Given, equation is $9x^2 - 3(a+b)x + ab = 0$.

On comparing with $Ax^2 + Bx + C = 0$, we get

$A = 9, B = -3(a+b)$ and $C = ab$

Discriminant, $D = B^2 - 4AC$

$= 9(a+b)^2 - 4(9)(ab)$

$= 9\{(a+b)^2 - 4ab\}$

$= 9(a-b)^2$

$[\because (a+b)^2 - 4ab = (a-b)^2]$ (1)

Therefore, the two real roots of the equation are given by

$x = \frac{-B \pm \sqrt{D}}{2A}$ [by quadratic formula]

$= \frac{3(a+b) \pm 3(a-b)}{18}$

$= \frac{(a+b) \pm (a-b)}{6}$ (1)

$\Rightarrow x = \frac{(a+b)+(a-b)}{6}$

or $x = \frac{(a+b)-(a-b)}{6}$

$\Rightarrow x = \frac{2a}{6}$ or $x = \frac{2b}{6}$

$\therefore x = \frac{a}{3}$ or $x = \frac{b}{3}$

Hence, the two roots are $\frac{a}{3}$ and $\frac{b}{3}$. (1)

**29.** Prove that

$$\frac{(1+\cot A + \tan A)(\sin A - \cos A)}{\sec^3 A - \text{cosec}^3 A} = \sin^2 A \cdot \cos^2 A$$

***Sol.*** LHS $= \frac{(1+\cot A + \tan A)(\sin A - \cos A)}{\sec^3 A - \text{cosec}^3 A}$

$= \frac{\left(1 + \frac{\cos A}{\sin A} + \frac{\sin A}{\cos A}\right)(\sin A - \cos A)}{[(\sec A - \text{cosec } A)(\sec^2 A + \sec A \text{cosec } A + \text{cosec}^2 A)]}$ (1)

$\left[\because \cot\theta = \frac{\cos\theta}{\sin\theta}, \tan\theta = \frac{\sin\theta}{\cos\theta} \text{ and } a^3 - b^3 = (a-b)(a^2+b^2+ab)\right]$

$= \frac{\frac{(\sin A\cos A + \cos^2 A + \sin^2 A)(\sin A - \cos A)}{\sin A\cos A}}{(\sec A - \text{cosec } A)\left(\frac{1}{\cos^2 A} + \frac{1}{\cos A\sin A} + \frac{1}{\sin^2 A}\right)}$

$= \frac{(\sin A\cos A + 1)\left(\frac{\sin A}{\sin A\cos A} - \frac{\cos A}{\sin A\cos A}\right)}{(\sec A - \text{cosec } A)\left(\frac{\sin^2 A + \sin A\cos A + \cos^2 A}{\sin^2 A\cos^2 A}\right)}$

$[\because \sin^2\theta + \cos^2\theta = 1]$ (1)

$= \frac{(\sin A\cos A + 1)(\sec A - \text{cosec } A)}{(\sec A - \text{cosec } A)(1 + \sin A\cos A)} \times \sin^2 A\cos^2 A$

$[\because \sin^2\theta + \cos^2\theta = 1]$

$= \sin^2 A\cos^2 A =$ RHS **Hence proved.** (1)

**30.** Find the largest positive integer that will divide 398, 436 and 542 leaving remainders 7, 11 and 15, respectively.

**Or** There are 156, 208 and 260 students in groups $A, B$ and $C$, respectively. Buses are to be hired to take them for a field trip. Find the minimum number of buses to be hired, if the same number of students should be accommodated in each bus.

**Sol.** It is given that when dividing 398 by the required number, then there is a remainder of 7. This means that $398-7=391$ is exactly divisible by the required number. In other words, required number is a factor of 391. (1)

Similarly, the required positive integer is a factor of $436-11=425$ and $542-15=527$.

Clearly, required number is the HCF of 391, 425 and 527. (1)

Using prime factorisations of 391, 425 and 527 as follows

$391=17\times23,\ 425=5^2\times17$ and $527=17\times31$

$\therefore$ HCF of 391, 425 and 527 = 17

Hence, 17 is the required number. (1)

*Or*

Given numbers are 156, 208 and 260.

The prime factor of given numbers are

$156=2^2\times3\times13,\ 208=2^4\times13$

and $260=2^2\times5\times13$

$\therefore$ HCF of (156, 208, 260) $=2^2\times13=52$ (2)

Thus, HCF of 156, 208 and 260 is 52.

Hence, the minimum number of buses

$=\frac{156}{52}+\frac{208}{52}+\frac{260}{52}$

$=3+4+5=12$ (1)

**31.** In a circle of radius 21 cm, an arc subtends an angle of 45° at the centre. Find the length of the arc and using it, find the area of the sector.

**Sol.** Given, $r=21$ cm and $\theta=45°$

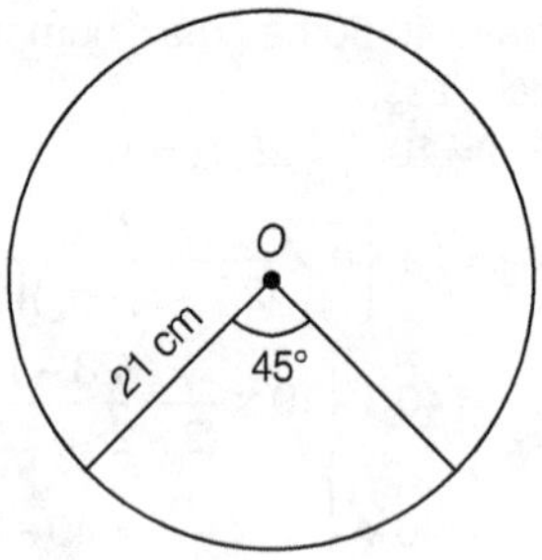


(1)

$\therefore$ Arc length $=\frac{\theta}{360°}\times2\pi r$

$=\frac{45°}{360°}\times2\times\frac{22}{7}\times21$

$=\frac{1}{4}\times22\times3$

$=16.5$ cm (1)

Now, area of sector $=\frac{1}{2}\times l\times r$ [where $l$ = arc length]

$=\frac{1}{2}\times16.5\times21$

$=173.25\text{ cm}^2$ (1)

## Section-D

**Section D consists of 4 questions of 5 marks each**

**32.** If $D$ is a point on the side $BC$ of $\Delta ABC$ such that $\angle ADC=\angle BAC$, prove that $CA^2=CB\times CD$.

**Or** In a $\Delta ABC$, $AD$ is the median of $BC$ and $E$ is the mid-point of $AD$. If $BE$ produced, it meets $AC$ in $F$. Prove that $AF=\frac{1}{3}AC$.

**Sol.** Draw $\Delta ABC$ such that $D$ is a point on $BC$ and join $AD$.

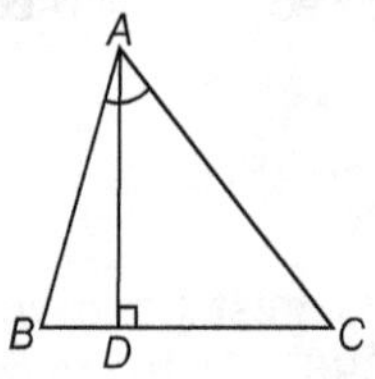


(1)

In $\Delta ABC$ and $\Delta DAC$, we have

$\angle BAC=\angle ADC$ [given] (1)

and $\angle ACB=\angle DCA$ [common angle]

$\therefore$ $\Delta ABC\sim\Delta DAC$ [by AA similarity criterion]

$\Rightarrow$ $\frac{AC}{DC}=\frac{CB}{CA}$ (1)

[since, corresponding sides of two similar triangles are proportional]

or $\frac{CA}{CD}=\frac{CB}{CA}$ (1)

$\Rightarrow$ $CA\times CA=CB\times CD$

$\Rightarrow$ $CA^2=CB\times CD$ **Hence proved.** (1)

*Or*

**Given** In $\Delta ABC$, mid-point of $BC$ is $D$ and mid-point of $AD$ is $E$.

**Construction** Draw $DG \parallel BF$.

**To Prove** $AF = \frac{1}{3} AC$

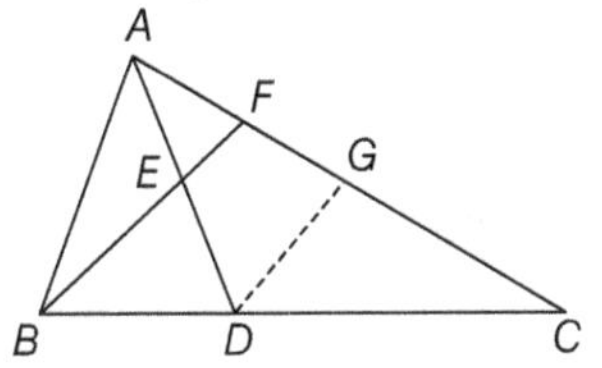


(1)

**Proof** In $\Delta CBF$, $DG \parallel BF$

$\therefore \quad \frac{CG}{GF} = \frac{CD}{BD}$

[by Basic proportionality theorem] (1)

$\Rightarrow \quad \frac{CG}{GF} = 1 \quad$ [$\because D$ is mid-point of $BC$]

$\Rightarrow \quad CG = GF \quad \ldots$(i)

In $\Delta ADG$, $EF \parallel DG$

$\therefore \quad \frac{AE}{ED} = \frac{AF}{FG}$

[by Basic proportionality theorem] (1)

$\Rightarrow \quad 1 = \frac{AF}{FG} \quad$ [$\because E$ is mid-point of $AD$]

$\Rightarrow \quad AF = FG \quad \ldots$(iii) (1)

From Eqs. (i) and (ii), we get

$AF = FG = CG$

$\therefore \quad AF = \frac{1}{3} AC \quad$ **Hence proved.** (1)

**33.** Determine the ratio in which the line $x + 2y - 3 = 0$ divides the line segment joining the points $A(2, -1)$ and $B(3, 5)$.

***Sol.*** Let the line $x + 2y - 3 = 0$ divides the line segment joining the points $A(2, -1)$ and $B(3, 5)$ in the ratio $\lambda : 1$ at the point $P$.

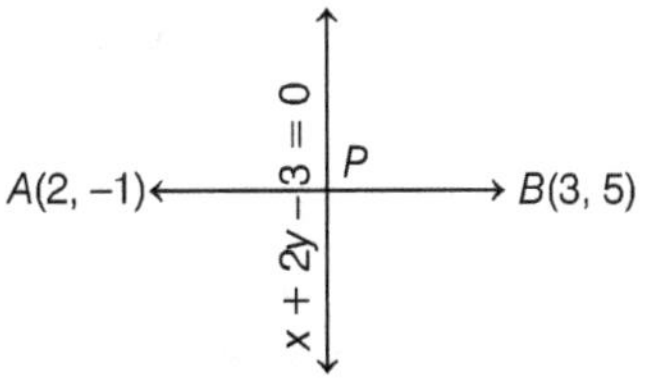


(1)

$\therefore$ Coordinates of $P = \left( \frac{3\lambda + 2}{\lambda + 1}, \frac{5\lambda - 1}{\lambda + 1} \right)$

$\left[ \begin{array}{l} \because \text{ using section formula} \\ \text{i.e.} \left( \frac{m_1 x_2 + m_2 x_1}{m_1 + m_2}, \frac{m_1 y_2 + m_2 y_1}{m_1 + m_2} \right) \end{array} \right]$ (1)

But $P$ lies on $x + 2y - 3 = 0$.

So, coordinates of $P$ satisfy the equation $x + 2y - 3 = 0$.

$\therefore \quad \frac{3\lambda + 2}{\lambda + 1} + 2\left( \frac{5\lambda - 1}{\lambda + 1} \right) - 3 = 0$ (1½)

$\Rightarrow \quad 3\lambda + 2 + 10\lambda - 2 = 3\lambda + 3$

$\Rightarrow \quad 10\lambda = 3$

$\Rightarrow \quad \lambda = \frac{3}{10}$

So, the point $P$ divides the line segment in the ratio 3 : 10. (1½)

**34.** The angle of depressions of two consecutive kilometre stones of the road, which are situated on opposite sides of an aeroplane, from an aeroplane fly vertically of the horizontal road are $\alpha$ and $\beta$. Prove that height of an aeroplane is $\frac{\tan \alpha \cdot \tan \beta}{\tan \alpha + \tan \beta}$.

*Or*

An aeroplane is flying above two houses and minimum distance between houses is 300 m. If at any time from the one side of aeroplane, the angle of depressions of two houses are 45° and 60°, respectively. Find, how much the height of the aeroplane?

***Sol.*** Let $A$ be an aeroplane flies above $h$ km from the road and angles of depressions on both sides of road $B$ and $C$ from $A$ are $\alpha$ and $\beta$, respectively.

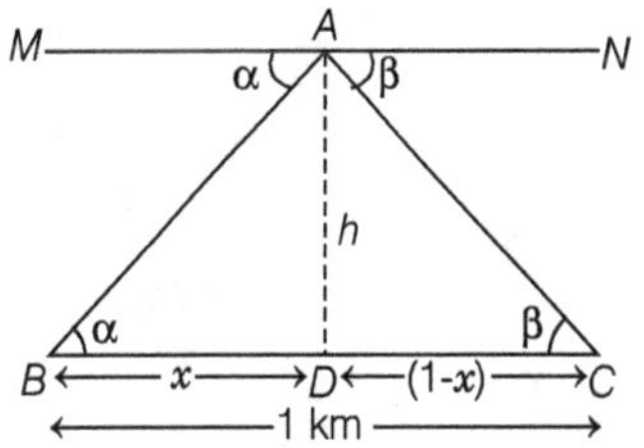


$\because$ Distance between two stones $B$ and $C$ = 1 km [given]

Now, $\quad MN \parallel BC$

$\therefore \quad \angle MAB = \angle ABD = \alpha \quad$ [alternate angles]

and $\quad \angle NAC = \angle ACD = \beta \quad$ [alternate angles] (1)

Let $BD = x$ km, then $DC = (1 - x)$ km

In right angled $\Delta ADB$,

$\tan \alpha = \frac{\text{Perpendicular}}{\text{Base}} = \frac{AD}{BD}$

$\Rightarrow \quad \tan \alpha = \frac{h}{x}$

$\Rightarrow \quad h = x \tan \alpha$

[using cross-multiplication] ...(i) (1)

In right angled $\Delta ADC$,

$\tan \beta = \frac{\text{Perpendicular}}{\text{Base}} = \frac{AD}{DC}$

$\Rightarrow \quad \tan\beta = \dfrac{h}{(1-x)}$

$\Rightarrow \quad \tan\beta = \dfrac{x\tan\alpha}{(1-x)}$ [from Eq. (i)] (1)

$\Rightarrow \tan\beta(1-x) = x\tan\alpha$ [using cross-multiplication]

$\Rightarrow \tan\beta - x\tan\beta = x\tan\alpha$

$\Rightarrow \quad \tan\beta = x\tan\alpha + x\tan\beta$ [on transposition]

$\Rightarrow \quad \tan\beta = x(\tan\alpha + \tan\beta)$

$\Rightarrow \quad x = \dfrac{\tan\beta}{\tan\alpha + \tan\beta}$ ...(ii) (1)

On putting the value of $x$ in Eq. (i), we get

$$h = \frac{\tan\beta}{\tan\alpha + \tan\beta}\cdot\tan\alpha = \frac{\tan\alpha\cdot\tan\beta}{\tan\alpha + \tan\beta}$$

Hence, the height of aeroplane is $\dfrac{\tan\alpha\cdot\tan\beta}{\tan\alpha + \tan\beta}$.

**Hence proved.** (1)

*Or*

Let $D$ be an aeroplane flying at height $h$ m. $A$ and $B$ are two houses and distance between them is $AB = 300$ m. The angles of depression from $D$ to $A$ and $B$ are 45° and 60°, respectively.

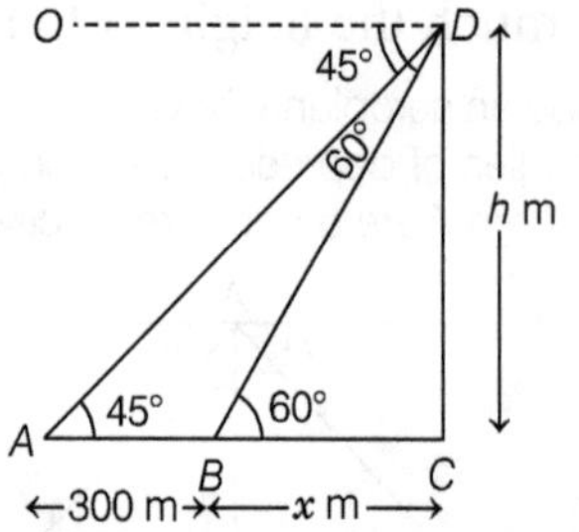


$\therefore \quad \angle ODA = 45°$ and $\angle ODB = 60°$ (1)

Now, draw $OD \parallel AC$.

Then, $\angle DAC = \angle ODA = 45°$ [alternate angles]

and $\angle DBC = \angle ODB = 60°$ [alternate angles]

Again, let $BC = x$ m.

Then, $AC = AB + BC = (300 + x)$ m

In right angled $\Delta DCB$,

$$\tan 60° = \frac{DC}{BC} \quad \left[\because \tan\theta = \frac{\text{perpendicular}}{\text{base}}\right]$$

$\Rightarrow \quad \sqrt{3} = \dfrac{h}{x}$ $[\because \tan 60° = \sqrt{3}]$

$\Rightarrow \quad x = \dfrac{h}{\sqrt{3}}$ ...(i) (1)

In right angled $\Delta DCA$,

$$\tan 45° = \frac{DC}{AC}$$

$\Rightarrow \quad 1 = \dfrac{DC}{AB + BC}$

$\Rightarrow \quad 1 = \dfrac{h}{300 + x}$ $[\because \tan 45° = 1]$

$\Rightarrow \quad 300 + x = h$ [using cross-multiplication] (1)

On putting the value of $x$ from Eq. (i), we get

$$300 + \frac{h}{\sqrt{3}} = h$$

$\Rightarrow \quad 300 = h - \dfrac{h}{\sqrt{3}}$ [on transposition]

$\Rightarrow \quad \dfrac{\sqrt{3}h - h}{\sqrt{3}} = 300$

$\Rightarrow \quad \dfrac{h(\sqrt{3}-1)}{\sqrt{3}} = 300$

$\therefore \quad h = \dfrac{300\sqrt{3}}{(\sqrt{3}-1)} = \dfrac{300\sqrt{3}}{(\sqrt{3}-1)} \times \dfrac{(\sqrt{3}+1)}{(\sqrt{3}+1)}$

[on rationalisation ] (1)

$= \dfrac{300\sqrt{3}(\sqrt{3}+1)}{(\sqrt{3})^2 - (1)^2}$ $[\because (a-b)(a+b) = a^2 - b^2]$

$= \dfrac{300\sqrt{3}(\sqrt{3}+1)}{3-1} = \dfrac{300(3+\sqrt{3})}{2}$

$= 150(3 + 1.732) = 150 \times 4.732$ $[\because \sqrt{3} = 1.732]$

$= 709.800 \approx 709.8$

Hence, the height of an aeroplane is 709.8 m. (1)

**35.** Two circles with centres $O$ and $O'$ of radii 3 cm and 4 cm, respectively intersect at two points $P$ and $Q$ such that $OP$ and $O'P$ are two perpendicular tangents to the two circles. Find the length of the common chord $PQ$.

***Sol.*** Here, two circles of radii

$OP = 3$ cm and $PO' = 4$ cm

These two circles intersect at $P$ and $Q$.

Here, $OP$ and $PO'$ are two tangents drawn at point $P$.

But these two tangents make an angle 90°.

Join $OO'$ and $PN$.

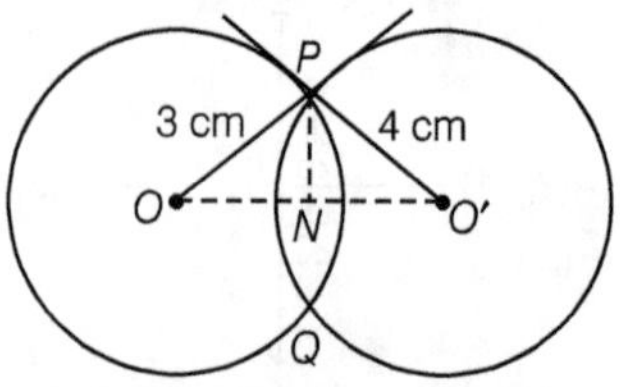


(1)

In right $\Delta OPO'$,

$$(OO')^2 = (OP)^2 + (PO')^2$$

[by Pythagoras theorem]

$$= (3)^2 + (4)^2 = 25$$

$\Rightarrow \quad OO' = 5$ cm (1)

Also, $\quad PN \perp OO'$

Let $ON = x$, then $NO' = 5 - x$

In right angled $\Delta OPN$,

$$(OP)^2 = (ON)^2 + (NP)^2$$

$\Rightarrow$ $(NP)^2 = 3^2 - x^2 = 9 - x^2$ ...(i) (1)

and in right angled $\Delta PNO'$,

$$(PO')^2 = (PN)^2 + (NO')^2$$

$\Rightarrow$ $(4)^2 = (PN)^2 + (5 - x)^2$

$\Rightarrow$ $(PN)^2 = 16 - (5 - x)^2$ ...(ii)

From Eqs. (i) and (ii), we get

$$9 - x^2 = 16 - (5 - x)^2$$

$\Rightarrow$ $7 + x^2 - (25 + x^2 - 10x) = 0$

$\Rightarrow$ $10x = 18$

$\Rightarrow$ $x = 1.8$ (1)

Again, in right angled $\Delta OPN$,

$$OP^2 = (ON)^2 + (NP)^2$$

$\Rightarrow$ $3^2 = (1.8)^2 + (NP)^2$

$\Rightarrow$ $(NP)^2 = 9 - 3.24 = 5.76$

$\Rightarrow$ $(NP) = 2.4$

$\therefore$ Length of common chord,

$PQ = 2PN = 2 \times 2.4 = 4.8$ cm (1)

# Section-E

**Case study based questions are compulsory**

**36.** India's literacy rate has increased six times since the end of the British rule in 1947. From 12% to 74% in recent times. Yet India has the world's largest population of illiterate people according to a report of oxfam.

Ram asks the labour to dig a well up to a depth of 10 m. Labour charges ₹ 150 for first metre and ₹ 50 for each subsequent metres. As labour was uneducated, he claims ₹ 550 for the whole work.

On the basis of above information, answer the following questions.

(i) What should be the actual amount to be paid to the labour? (1)

(ii) How much money will Ram save, if labour agrees with ₹ 550? (1)

(iii) If the $n$th term of an AP is $(4n - 10)$, then find its 16th term. (2)

*Or*

Find the middle term of the AP 10, 7, 4, ..., (−62). (2)

***Sol.*** (i) Labour charges for each subsequent metres are 150, 150 + 50, 150 + 2 × 50 + 150 + 3 × 50, .... i.e. 150, 200, 250, 300....

Thus, amount of labour charge form an AP with

$$a = 150 \text{ and } d = 50$$

Total depth = 10 m

$\therefore$ Labour charge for 10 m depth

$$= 150 + (10 - 1) \times 50 = 600$$

Hence, ₹ 600 should be paid to the labour.

(ii) Ram saves = 600 − 550 = ₹ 50

(iii) First term, $a = 4(1) - 10 = 4 - 10 = -6$

Second term, $b = 4(2) - 10 = 8 - 10 = -2$

$\therefore$ Common difference, $d = b - a = -2 - (-6)$
$= -2 + 6 = 4$

So, 16th term $= a + (n - 1)d$
$= -6 + (16 - 1) \times 4$
$= -6 + 60 = 54$

*Or*

Given, $n$th term of the AP = −62

Here, $a = 10, d = 7 - 10 = -3$

$\therefore$ $a + (n - 1)d = -62$

$\Rightarrow$ $10 + (n - 1)(-3) = -62$

$\Rightarrow$ $10 - 3n + 3 = -62$

$\Rightarrow$ $3n = 13 + 62$

$\Rightarrow$ $n = \frac{75}{3} = 25$

So, there are total 25 terms.

Middle term of the AP $= \left(\frac{25 + 1}{2}\right)$th term
= 13th term

So, 13th term $= 10 + (13 - 1) \times (-3)$
$= 10 - 36$
$= -26$

**37.** Mathematics teacher of class-X of a school organized a colouring activity to understand geometrical figures. He is interested to make decorative block that shown in the following figure, which is made up of two solids, a cube and a hemisphere.

The base of the block is a cube with edge 12 cm and the hemisphere fixed on the top has a diameter of 4.2 cm. $\left[\text{take, } \pi = \frac{22}{7}\right]$

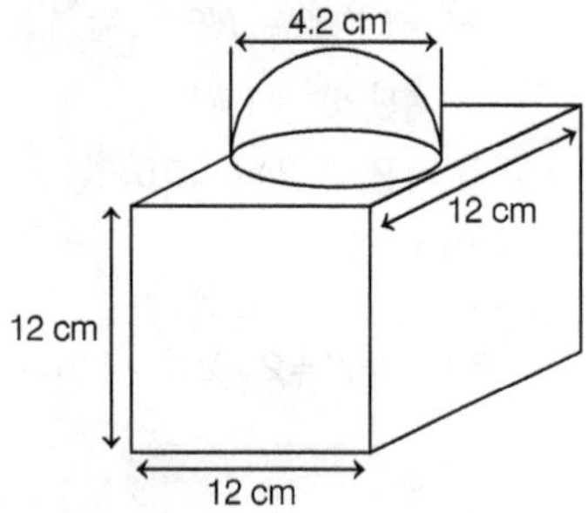


On the basis of above information, answer the following questions.

(i) Find the base area of the cube. (1)

(ii) What is the radius of hemispherical portion? (1)

(iii) Find the total surface area of hemisphere and total surface area of the cube. (2)

*Or*

Find the total surface area to be covering the packing paper. (2)

***Sol.*** (i) Base area of cube = $(\text{Side})^2$

$= (12)^2 = 144 \text{ cm}^2$

(ii) Radius of hemispherical portion $= \frac{4.2}{2} = 2.1$ cm

(iii) Total surface area of hemisphere $= 3\pi r^2$

$= 3 \times \frac{22}{7} \times (2.1)^2 = 3 \times \frac{22}{7} \times 2.1 \times 2.1$

$= 41.58 \text{ cm}^2$

Total surface area of cube = $6\,(\text{edge})^2$

$= 6 \times (12)^2 = 6 \times 144$

$= 864 \text{ cm}^2$

*Or*

Total surface area to covering the packing paper of the decorative block

= Total surface area of cube

− Area of base of hemisphere block

+ Curved surface area of hemisphere

$= 864 - \pi r^2 + 2\pi r^2$

$= 864 + \pi r^2$

$= 864 + \frac{22}{7} \times (2.1)^2$

$= 864 + \frac{22}{7} \times 2.1 \times 2.1$

$= 864 + 13.86$

$= 877.86 \text{ cm}^2$

**38.** Palak went to a mall with her mother and enjoys rides on the giant wheel and plays hoopla (a game in which you throw a ring on the items kept in stall and if the ring covers any object completely you get it). The number of times she played hoopla is half the number of times she rides the giant wheel. If each ride costs ₹ 3 and a game of hoopla costs ₹ 4 and she spent ₹ 20 in the fair.

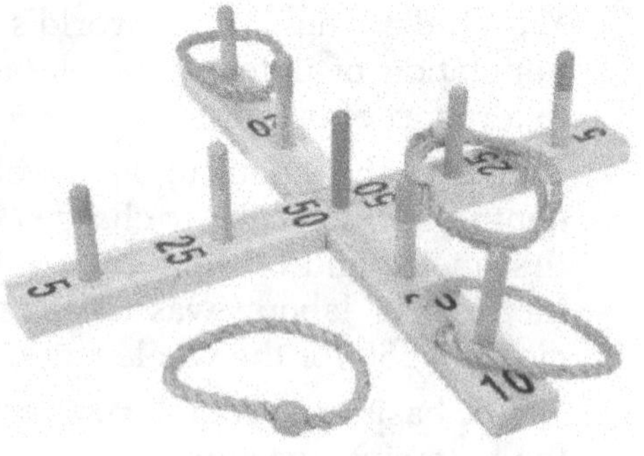

On the basis of above information, answer the following questions.

(i) Write the representation of given statement algebraically. (1)

(ii) Graphically, if the pair of equations intersect at one point, then check the pair is consistent or inconsistent. (1)

(iii) Find the intersection point of two lines. (2)

*Or*

Find the intersection points of the line $3x + 4y = 20$ on $X$ and $Y$-axes. (2)

***Sol.*** (i) Let $x$ be the number of rides on the giant wheel and $y$ be the number of times hoopla played by Palak.

Then, $y = \frac{x}{2}$ and $3x + 4y = 20$

Rewrite the above equations to represent algebraically

$$x - 2y = 0 \quad \ldots\text{(i)}$$

$$3x + 4y = 20 \quad \ldots\text{(ii)}$$

(ii) If the pair of equations intersect at only one point. Then the pair of equations has a unique solution and hence consistent.

(iii) From Eq. (i), $x = 2y$

Put $x = 2y$ in Eq. (ii), we get

$$3(2y) + 4y = 20$$

$$\Rightarrow \quad 10y = 20$$

$$\Rightarrow \quad y = 2$$

$$\Rightarrow \quad x = 2 \times 2 = 4$$

Hence, the intersection point is (4, 2).

*Or*

For intersection point of the line $3x + 4y = 20$ on $X$-axis.

Put $y = 0$ in Eq. (ii), we get

$$3x + 0 = 20$$

$$x = \frac{20}{3}$$

$\therefore$ The intersection point is $\left(\frac{20}{3}, 0\right)$.

For intersection point of the line $3x + 4y = 20$ on $Y$-axis.

Put $x = 0$ in Eq. (ii), we get

$$0 + 4y = 20 \Rightarrow y = 5$$

$\therefore$ The intersection point is (0, 5).

# SAMPLE QUESTION PAPER 5

## Mathematics (Basic)

Time : **3 hrs** Max. Marks : **80**

### Instructions

1. This question paper has 5 Sections A, B, C, D and E.
2. Section A has 20 Multiple Choice Questions (MCQs) carrying 1 mark each.
3. Section B has 5 Short Answer-I (SA-I) Type Questions carrying 2 marks each.
4. Section C has 6 Short Answer-II (SA-II) Type Questions carrying 3 marks each.
5. Section D has 4 Long Answer (LA) Type Questions carrying 5 marks each.
6. Section E has 3 Case Based integrated units of assessment (4 marks each) with sub-parts of the values of 1, 1 and 2 marks each respectively.
7. All questions are compulsory. However, an internal choice in 2 questions of 2 marks, 2 questions of 3 marks and 2 questions of 5 marks has been provided. An internal choice has been provided in the 2 marks questions of Section E.
8. Draw neat figures wherever required. Take $\pi = 22/7$ wherever required if not stated.

## Section-A

**Section A consists of 20 questions of 1 mark each**

**1.** Which of the following is not a polynomial?

(a) $2x^{-3} - 5 + 3x^{-1}$ (b) $x^3 + 2x - 9$

(c) $(x-2)^2 + 3x$ (d) $\frac{(2x+10)}{x+5} \times (x^2 - 25)$

***Sol.*** (a) A polynomial is an algebraic expression containing two or more terms.

Also, it requires the exponents of the variables in the each term should be positive integer.

(a) $2x^{-3} - 5 + 3x^{-1}$, it is not polynomial, because it has negative power in second term.

(b) $x^3 + 2x - 9$, it is a polynomial.

(c) $(x-2)^2 + 3x = x^2 + 4 - 4x + 3x$

$= x^2 - x + 4$, it is a polynomial.

(d) $\frac{2x+10}{x+5} \times (x^2 - 25) = \frac{2(x+5)}{(x+5)} \times (x^2 - 25)$

$= 2x^2 - 50$, it is a polynomial.

**2.** If $\Delta ABC$ is an isosceles triangle, right angled at $C$, with $AC = 2$ cm, then the length of hypotenuse is

(a) 4 cm (b) 2 cm (c) $2\sqrt{2}$ cm (d) $2\sqrt{3}$ cm

**Sol.** (c) Given, $\Delta ACB$ right angled at $C$.

We have, $AC = CB = 2$ cm

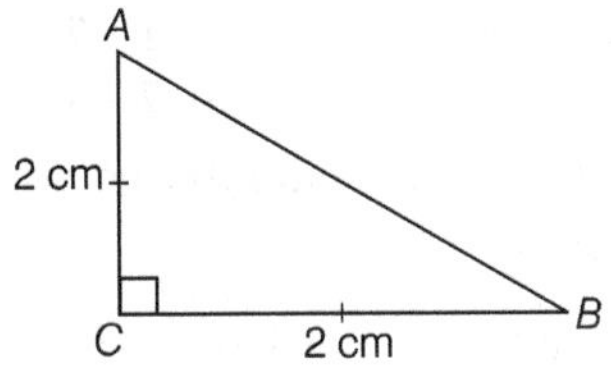


By Pythagoras theorem,

$$(AB)^2 = (AC)^2 + (CB)^2 = 2^2 + 2^2 = 4 + 4$$

$\Rightarrow \quad (AB)^2 = 8$

$\Rightarrow \quad AB = 2\sqrt{2}$ cm

$\therefore$ Hypotenuse $(AB) = 2\sqrt{2}$ cm

**3.** The distance between two parallel tangents to a circle of radius 7 cm is

(a) 7 cm (b) 14 cm (c) 3.5 cm (d) 49 cm

**Sol.** (b) The distance between two parallel tangents to a circle of radius 7 cm is $2 \times 7 = 14$ cm.

**4.** The angle of elevation of a ladder leaning against a wall is 60° and the foot of the ladder is 12 m away from the wall. The length of the ladder is

(a) $8\sqrt{3}$ cm (b) $12\sqrt{2}$ cm
(c) 12 cm (d) 24 cm

**Sol.** (d) Let length of ladder is $AC$ is $l$ m.

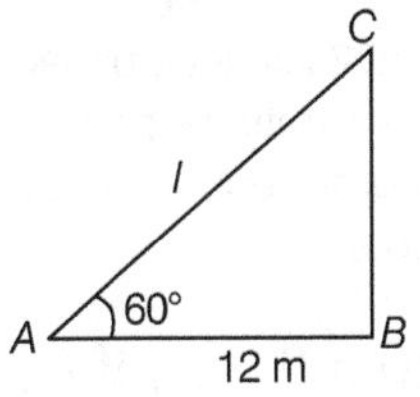


In right $\Delta ABC$,

$$\cos 60^\circ = \frac{AB}{AC} \Rightarrow \frac{1}{2} = \frac{12}{l}$$

$$\Rightarrow \quad l = \frac{12}{1/2} \Rightarrow l = 24 \text{ m}$$

**5.** The area of the shaded portion, is

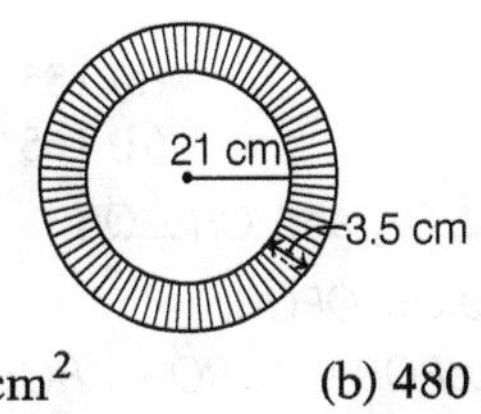


(a) 500 $cm^2$ (b) 480 $cm^2$
(c) 520 $cm^2$ (d) 550 $cm^2$

**Sol.** (a) Radius of the smaller circle = 21 cm

Radius of the bigger circle = 21 + 3.5 = 24.5 cm

$\therefore$ Area of the path $= [\pi(24.5)^2 - \pi(21)^2]$

$$= \pi[(24.5)^2 - (21)^2]$$
$$= \pi(24.5 + 21)(24.5 - 21)$$
$$= \frac{22}{7} \times 45.5 \times 3.5$$
$$= 500.5 \text{ cm}^2$$

**6.** If $\sin\theta = \frac{a}{b}$, then the value of $\sec\theta + \tan\theta$ is

(a) 1 (b) $\sqrt{\frac{b+a}{b-a}}$

(c) $\sqrt{\frac{a+b}{a-b}}$ (d) $\frac{b^2 - a^2 + ab}{b(\sqrt{b^2 - a^2})}$

**Sol.** (b) Given, $\sin\theta = \frac{a}{b}$

$\therefore \quad \sec\theta = \frac{b}{\sqrt{b^2 - a^2}}$ and $\tan\theta = \frac{a}{\sqrt{b^2 - a^2}}$

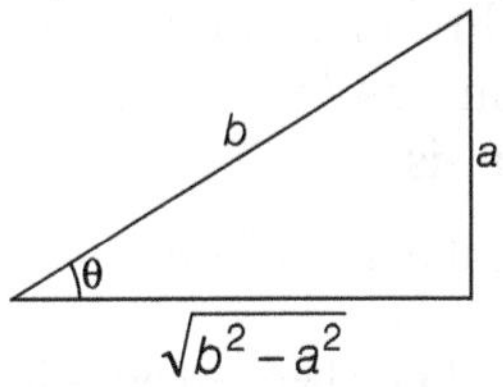


$$\therefore \sec\theta + \tan\theta = \frac{b}{\sqrt{b^2 - a^2}} + \frac{a}{\sqrt{b^2 - a^2}}$$
$$= \frac{a + b}{\sqrt{b^2 - a^2}}$$
$$= \frac{a + b}{\sqrt{(b - a)(b + a)}}$$
$$= \sqrt{\frac{b + a}{b - a}}$$

**7.** If $47x + 31y = 18$ and $31x + 47y = 60$, then the value of $x + y$ is

(a) 1 (b) 2 (c) 36 (d) 78

**Sol.** (a) Given, $47x + 31y = 18$ ...(i)

and $31x + 47y = 60$ ...(ii)

On adding Eqs. (i) and (ii), we get

$$78x + 78y = 78$$

$\Rightarrow \quad x + y = 1$ [divide both sides by 78]

**8.** The values of $t$, if $(t + 4)x^2 + (t + 1)x + 1 = 0$ has real and equal roots, are

(a) −5, +3 (b) −3, −5 (c) 5, 3 (d) −3, 5

**Sol.** (d) Discriminant $= b^2 - 4ac = (t + 1)^2 - 4(t + 4) \times 1$

$$= t^2 - 2t - 15$$

For equal roots, discriminant = 0

$\therefore \quad t^2 - 2t - 15 = 0$

$\Rightarrow \quad t^2 - 5t + 3t - 15 = 0$

$\Rightarrow \quad t(t-5) + 3(t-5) = 0$

$\Rightarrow \quad (t+3)(t-5) = 0$

$\Rightarrow \quad t = 5 \text{ or } t = -3$

Hence, the values of $t$ is 5, −3.

**9.** The value of $\dfrac{2\sin 30°}{1-\cos^2 60°}$ is

(a) $4\sqrt{3}$ (b) $\dfrac{4}{3}$ (c) 4 (d) $\dfrac{4}{\sqrt{3}}$

***Sol.*** (b) $\dfrac{2\sin 30°}{1-\cos^2 60°} = \dfrac{2 \times \frac{1}{2}}{1-\left(\frac{1}{2}\right)^2}$

$= \dfrac{1}{1-\frac{1}{4}} = \dfrac{1}{3/4} = \dfrac{4}{3}$

**10.** The value of $k$ for which the system of equations $x + ky = 0, 2x - y = 0$ has unique solution, is

(a) All real numbers except $\dfrac{1}{2}$

(b) All real numbers except $-\dfrac{1}{2}$

(c) All real numbers except 0

(d) None of the above

***Sol.*** (b) Given system of equations is

$x + ky = 0$ and $2x - y = 0$

On comparing these equations with

$a_1x + b_1y + c_1 = 0$ and $a_2x + b_2y + c_2 = 0$, we get

$a_1 = 1, b_1 = k, c_1 = 0$

and $a_2 = 2, b_2 = -1, c_2 = 0$

Condition for unique solution,

$\dfrac{a_1}{a_2} \neq \dfrac{b_1}{b_2} \Rightarrow \dfrac{1}{2} \neq \dfrac{k}{-1} \Rightarrow k \neq -\dfrac{1}{2}$

**11.** Two unbiased coins are tossed simultaneously. The probability of getting no head, is

(a) 1 (b) $\dfrac{1}{2}$ (c) $\dfrac{1}{4}$ (d) $\dfrac{3}{4}$

***Sol.*** (c) Total number of elementary events = 4

($HT, TH, HH, TT$)

No head is obtained i.e. $TT$

∴ Favourable number of elementary elements = 1

∴ Required probability $= \dfrac{1}{4}$

**12.** The value(s) of $a$, if the distance between the points $(a, -1)$ and $(3, 2)$ is 5, is/are

(a) 7 only (b) 1, −7

(c) −6, −7 (d) 7, −1

***Sol.*** (d) Let $A(a, -1)$ and $B(3, 2)$ be the given points,

then $AB = 5$

$\Rightarrow \quad \sqrt{(a-3)^2 + (-1-2)^2} = 5$

$\Rightarrow \quad (a-3)^2 + (-3)^2 = 25$

$\Rightarrow \quad a^2 + 9 - 6a + 9 = 25$

$\Rightarrow \quad a^2 - 6a + 18 - 25 = 0$

$\Rightarrow \quad a^2 - 6a - 7 = 0$

$\Rightarrow \quad (a-7)(a+1) = 0$

$\Rightarrow \quad a = 7 \text{ or } a = -1$

**13.** The nature of the roots of the equation $3x^2 + 6x + 1 = 0$ is

(a) real, unequal and rational

(b) real and unequal

(c) real, unequal and irrational

(d) imaginary

***Sol.*** (c) Given, $3x^2 + 6x + 1 = 0$

$a = 3, b = 6$ and $c = 1$

Discriminant, $D = b^2 - 4ac$

$= (6)^2 - 4 \times 3 \times 1$

$= 36 - 12$

$= 24 > 0$

We know that 24 is not a perfect square, so the roots will contain an irrational part.

Hence, the given equation has two distinct real and irrational roots.

**14.** In the given figure, if $PQR = 25°$, then the value of $\angle POR$ is

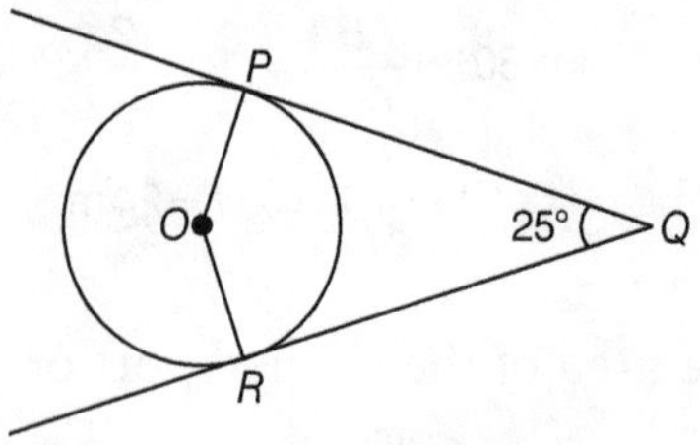


(a) 135° (b) 155°

(c) 145° (d) 165°

***Sol.*** (b) ∵ $OP \perp QP$ and $OR \perp QR$

In quadrilateral $OPQR$,

$\angle OPQ + \angle PQR + \angle QRO + \angle ROP = 360°$

$\Rightarrow \quad 90° + 25° + 90° + \angle ROP = 360°$

$\Rightarrow \quad \angle ROP = 360° - 180° - 25°$

$= 155°$

**15.** In the given figure, $DE \| BC$. If $AD = 5$ cm, $BD = 8$ cm and $AE = 10$ cm, the the value of $EC$ is

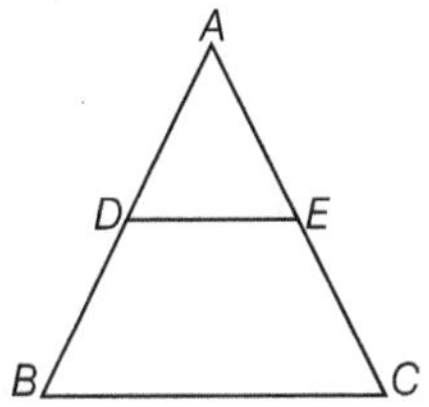


(a) 8 cm (b) 16 cm
(c) 4 cm (d) 5 cm

***Sol.*** (b) In $\Delta ABC$, $DE || BC$

Let $EC = x$ cm,

then $\frac{AD}{DB} = \frac{AE}{EC}$

[by basic proportionality theorem]

$\Rightarrow \frac{5}{8} = \frac{10}{x}$

$\Rightarrow x = \frac{10 \times 8}{5}$

$= 16 \text{cm}$

$\therefore EC = 16 \text{cm}$

**16.** The area of the triangle formed by the lines $2x + 3y = 12$, $x - y - 1 = 0$ and $X$-axis (as shown in figure), is

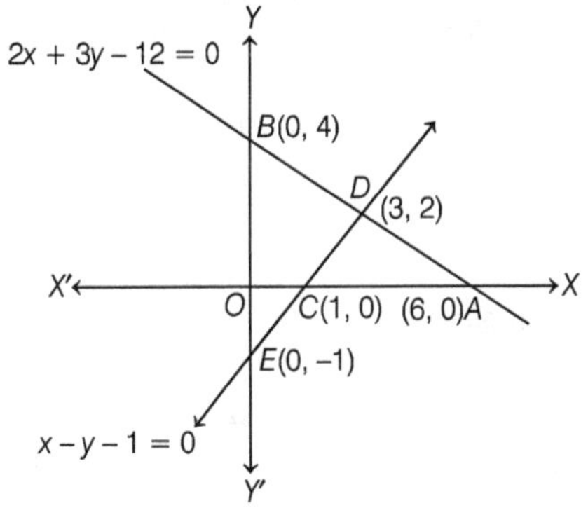


(a) 7 sq units (b) 5 sq units
(c) 6.5 sq units (d) 6 sq units

***Sol.*** (b) From the figure, the required triangle is $\Delta ACD$.

Here, base of triangle $= 6 - 1 = 5$

Height of triangle $= 2$

We know that,

Area of $\Delta ACD = \frac{1}{2} \times \text{base} \times \text{height}$

$= \frac{1}{2} \times 5 \times 2$

$= 5 \text{ sq units}$

**17.** Check the relation between the following triangles

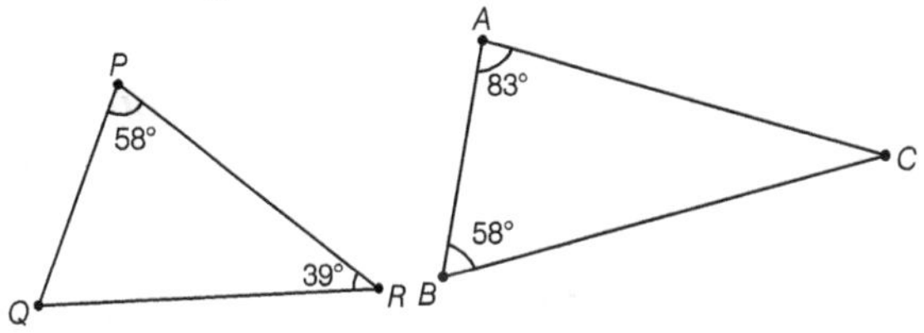


(a) similar by SAS (b) similar by AAA
(c) similar by SSS (d) similar by ASS

***Sol.*** (b) In $\Delta ABC$, $\angle A + \angle B + \angle C = 180°$

[sum of all angles of a triangle is 180°]

$83° + 58° + \angle C = 180°$

$\Rightarrow \angle C = 180° - (83° + 58°)$

$\Rightarrow \angle C = 39°$

Now, In $\Delta PQR$,

$\angle P + \angle Q + \angle R = 180°$

$\Rightarrow 58° + \angle Q + 39° = 180°$

$\Rightarrow \angle Q = 180° - (58° + 39°)$

$\Rightarrow \angle Q = 83°$

Now, In $\Delta ABC$ and $\Delta QPR$,

$\angle A = \angle Q = 83°$

$\angle B = \angle P = 58°$

$\angle C = \angle R = 39°$

$\therefore \Delta ABC \sim \Delta QPR$ [by AAA similarity criterion]

**18.** The sum of the numerator and denominator of a fraction $\frac{x}{y}$ is 8. If the denominator is increased by 1, the fraction becomes $\frac{1}{2}$. The situation can be represented algebraically as

(a) $x + y = 8$ and $\frac{x+1}{y} = \frac{1}{2}$

(b) $x + y = 8$ and $\frac{x}{y} + 1 = \frac{1}{2}$

(c) $\frac{x}{y} = 8$ and $\frac{x}{y+1} = \frac{1}{2}$

(d) $x + y = 8$ and $\frac{x}{y+1} = \frac{1}{2}$

***Sol.*** (d) We have numerator and denominator of the fraction be $x$ and $y$ respectively.

Sum of numerator and denominator = 8

i.e. $x + y = 8$

Since, denominator is increased by 1

i.e New, denominator $= y + 1$

$\therefore$ New fraction is $\frac{x}{y+1} = \frac{1}{2}$

Hence, algebraically the situation can be represented as

$$x + y = 8 \text{ and } \frac{x}{y+1} = \frac{1}{2}$$

**Directions** *In the question number 19 and 20, a statement of Assertion (A) is followed by a statement of Reason (R). Choose the correct option.*

**19.** **Assertion (A)** If length of a tangent from an external point to a circle is 18 cm, then length of the other tangent from the same point is 18 cm.

**Reason (R)** Length of the tangents of drawn from an external point to a circle are equal.

(a) Both Assertion (A) and Reason (R) are true and Reason (R) is the correct explanation of Assertion (A)

(b) Both Assertion (A) and Reason (R) are true but Reason (R) is not the correct explanation of Assertion (A)

(c) Assertion (A) is true but Reason (R) is false

(d) Assertion (A) is false but Reason (R) is true

***Sol.*** (a) Both Assertion (A) and Reason (R) are true and Reason (R) is the correct explanation of Assertion (A).

**20.** **Assertion (A)** $ABCD$ is a trapezium with $DC \| AB$. $E$ and $F$ are points on $AD$ and $BC$ respectively such that $EF \| AB$. Then, $\frac{AE}{ED} = \frac{BF}{FC}$.

**Reason (R)** Any line parallel to parallel sides of a trapezium divides the non-parallel sides proportionally.

(a) Both Assertion (A) and Reason (R) are true and Reason (R) is the correct explanation of Assertion (A)

(b) Both Assertion (A) and Reason (R) are true but Reason (R) is not the correct explanation of Assertion (A)

(c) Assertion (A) is true but Reason (R) is false

(d) Assertion (A) is false but Reason (R) is true

***Sol.*** (a) Given, $EF \| AB$

$\therefore \quad OE \| AB \| CD \quad [\because AB \| CD]$

In $\Delta ACD$,

$$\frac{AE}{ED} = \frac{AO}{OC} \quad \text{[by BPT]} \dots \text{(i)}$$

Similarly in $\Delta ABC$,

$$\frac{AO}{OC} = \frac{BF}{FC} \quad \dots \text{(ii)}$$

From Eqs. (i) and (ii),

$$\frac{AE}{ED} = \frac{BF}{FC}$$

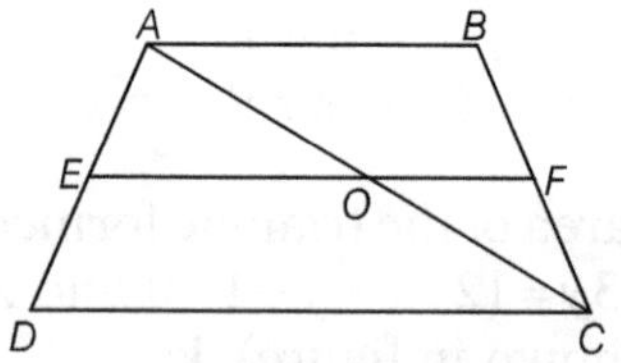


$\therefore$ Any line parallel to parallel sides of a trapezium divides the non-parallel sides proportionally.

Both Statement I and II are True and Statement II is the correct explanation of Statement I.

## Section-B

**Section B consists of 5 questions of 2 marks each**

**21.** A teacher of Class X write some information about the tour on blackboard as follows

Tours of the national capital and the white house begin at 8:30 am at a tour agency. Tours for the national capital leave every 15 min. Tours for the white house leave every 20 min. How many minutes after do the tours leave at the same time?

***Sol.*** Required time = LCM (15, 20). (1)

By using prime factorisation method,

Now, $15 = 3 \times 5$

and $20 = 2 \times 2 \times 5 = 2^2 \times 5$

$\therefore$ LCM (15, 20) $= 2^2 \times 3 \times 5 = 60$ min

In every 60 min, tour leaves at the same time. (1)

**22.** Find the value of $x$ in $\sqrt{3} \tan 2x = \cos 60° + \sin 45° \cos 45°$.

*Or*

In a triangle $ABC$ right angled at $C$, if $\tan A = \frac{1}{\sqrt{3}}$, find the value of $\sin A \cos B$.

***Sol.*** Given, $\sqrt{3} \tan 2x = \cos 60° + \sin 45° \cos 45°$

$$\therefore \quad \sqrt{3} \tan 2x = \frac{1}{2} + \frac{1}{\sqrt{2}} \times \frac{1}{\sqrt{2}} \quad (1)$$

$$\Rightarrow \quad \tan 2x = \frac{1}{\sqrt{3}}\left(\frac{1}{2} + \frac{1}{2}\right)$$

$$\Rightarrow \quad \tan 2x = \frac{1}{\sqrt{3}} \Rightarrow \tan 2x = \tan 30°$$

$$\Rightarrow \quad 2x = 30° \Rightarrow x = 15° \quad (1)$$

*Or*

Given, $\tan A = \frac{1}{\sqrt{3}} \Rightarrow A = 30°$

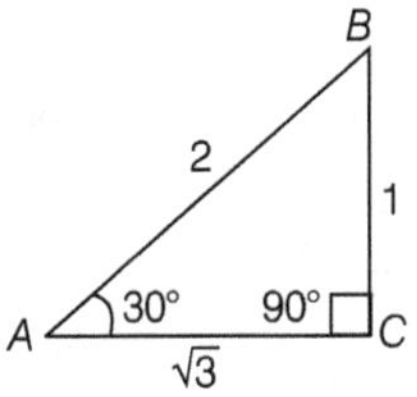


$\Rightarrow \quad \tan A = \frac{BC}{AC} = \frac{1}{\sqrt{3}}$

$\Rightarrow \quad BC = k, AC = \sqrt{3}k$

In right $\Delta ABC$,

$AB = \sqrt{(AC)^2 + (BC)^2}$

$= \sqrt{(\sqrt{3}k)^2 + (k)^2} = \sqrt{3k^2 + k^2} = 2k$ (1)

In right $\Delta ABC$, $\angle A + \angle B + \angle C = 180°$

$\Rightarrow \quad \angle B = 180° - (30° + 90°) = 60°$

Now, $\cos B = \frac{BC}{AB} = \frac{1}{2}$

Now, $\sin A \cos B = \sin 30° \times \frac{1}{2} = \frac{1}{2} \times \frac{1}{2} = \frac{1}{4}$ (1)

**23.** The following table shows the heights (in cm) of 50 girls of Class X of a school.

| Height (in cm) | 120-130 | 130-140 | 140-150 | 150-160 | 160-170 | Total |
|---|---|---|---|---|---|---|
| Number of girls | 2 | 8 | 12 | 20 | 8 | 50 |

Find the mean of the above data.

***Sol.*** Let assumed mean, $A = 145$

Table for deviation is given below

| Height (in cm) | Number of girls ($f_i$) | Class marks $x_i$ | $d_i = x_i - A$ | $f_i d_i$ |
|---|---|---|---|---|
| 120-130 | 2 | 125 | −20 | −40 |
| 130-140 | 8 | 135 | −10 | −80 |
| 140-150 | 12 | 145 = A | 0 | 0 |
| 150-160 | 20 | 155 | 10 | 200 |
| 160-170 | 8 | 165 | 20 | 160 |
| **Total** | $\Sigma f_i = 50$ | | | $\Sigma f_i d_i = 240$ |

(1)

Here, $\Sigma f_i = 50$ and $\Sigma f_i d_i = 240$

$\therefore$ Mean $= A + \frac{\Sigma f_i d_i}{\Sigma f_i} = 145 + \frac{240}{50}$

$= 145 + 4.8 = 149.8$ (1)

**24.** The difference between two numbers is 26 and one number is three times the other number. Find the numbers.

***Sol.*** Let the two numbers be $x$ and $y$ $(x > y)$.

According to the question,

$x - y = 26$ ...(i)

and $\quad x = 3y$ ...(ii)

On substituting the value of $x$ from Eq. (ii) in Eq. (i), we get $\quad 3y - y = 26$

$\Rightarrow \quad 2y = 26 \Rightarrow y = 13$ (1)

On substituting $y = 13$ in Eq. (ii), we get

$x = 3 \times 13 \Rightarrow x = 39$

Hence, the two numbers are 39 and 13. (1)

**25.** If the 3rd and 9th terms of an AP are 4 and − 8 respectively, then which term of this AP is zero?

*Or* Find the common difference of an AP, whose first term is 1/2 and the 8th term is 17/6. Also, find the ratio of 4th term and 50th term.

***Sol.*** Let $a$ be the first term and $d$ be the common difference of an AP.

$\because$ The $n$th term of an AP is $a_n = a + (n-1)d$

$\therefore \quad a_3 = a + 2d = 4 \quad [\because a_3 = 4, \text{given}]$...(i)

and $\quad a_9 = a + 8d = -8 \quad [\because a_9 = -8, \text{given}]$...(ii)

On subtracting Eq. (i) from Eq. (ii), we get

$6d = -12 \Rightarrow d = \frac{-12}{6} = -2$ (1/2)

On putting the value of $d$ in Eq. (i), we get

$a + 2 \times (-2) = 4 \Rightarrow a - 4 = 4 \Rightarrow a = 4 + 4 = 8$ (1/2)

Let the $n$th term of this AP be zero,

i.e. $\quad a_n = 0$

$\Rightarrow \quad a + (n-1)d = 0$

$\Rightarrow \quad 8 + (n-1)(-2) = 0 \quad [\because a = 8, d = -2]$

$\Rightarrow \quad (n-1)(-2) = -8$

$\Rightarrow \quad n - 1 = \frac{-8}{-2} = 4$

$\therefore \quad n = 4 + 1 = 5$

Hence, 5th term of this AP is zero. (1)

*Or*

Let $a$ be the first term and $d$ be the common difference of an AP.

Then, $n$th term, $T_n = a + (n-1)d$

Given, 8th term, $T_8 = \frac{17}{6} \Rightarrow a + 7d = \frac{17}{6}$

$\Rightarrow \quad \frac{1}{2} + 7d = \frac{17}{6} \quad \left[\because a = \frac{1}{2}\right]$

$\Rightarrow \quad 7d = \frac{17}{6} - \frac{1}{2} \Rightarrow 7d = \frac{14}{6} \Rightarrow d = \frac{1}{3}$ (1)

Now, 4th term, $T_4 = a + 3d = \frac{1}{2} + 3\left(\frac{1}{3}\right) = \frac{1}{2} + 1 = \frac{3}{2}$

and 50th term, $T_{50} = a + 49d = \frac{1}{2} + 49 \times \frac{1}{3} = \frac{101}{6}$

$\therefore$ Required ratio $= \frac{3/2}{101/6} = \frac{3}{2} \times \frac{6}{101} = 9 : 101$ (1)

# Section-C

**Section C consists of 6 questions of 3 marks each**

**26.** If $\alpha$ and $\beta$ are zeroes of the polynomial $x^2-2x-15$, then form a quadratic polynomial whose zeroes are $2\alpha$ and $2\beta$.

***Sol.*** Let $p(x)=x^2-2x-15$

On comparing with $ax^2+bx+c$, we get

$a=1, b=-2$ and $c=-15$ (1/2)

Given, $\alpha$ and $\beta$ are the zeroes of $p(x)$.

$\therefore$ Sum of zeroes, $(\alpha+\beta)=-\frac{b}{a}$

$\Rightarrow \quad \alpha+\beta=-\frac{(-2)}{1}$

$\Rightarrow \quad \alpha+\beta=2$ ...(i) (1/2)

and product of zeroes, $(\alpha\cdot\beta)=\frac{c}{a}$

$\Rightarrow \quad \alpha\beta=\frac{-15}{1}$

$\Rightarrow \quad \alpha\beta=-15$ ...(ii) (1/2)

We have to form a polynomial whose zeroes are $2\alpha$ and $2\beta$.

$\therefore$ Sum of zeroes $=2\alpha+2\beta=2(\alpha+\beta)$

$=2\times2=4$ [using Eq. (i)]

and product of zeroes $=2\alpha\cdot2\beta$ (1/2)

$=4\alpha\beta=4\times(-15)$

$=-60$ [using Eq. (ii)]

$\therefore$ Required polynomial

$=x^2-$ (Sum of zeroes) $x$ + (Product of zeroes)

$=x^2-4x+(-60)=x^2-4x-60$ (1)

**27.** A health officer took an initiative of organising a medical camp in a remote village. The medical checkup of 400 students of the age group of 10 yr and their heights were recorded as follows

| Height (in cm) | Frequency |
|---|---|
| 160-162 | 15 |
| 163-165 | 117 |
| 166-168 | 136 |
| 169-171 | 118 |
| 172-174 | 14 |

Then, find the median height of students.

***Sol.*** The given series is in inclusive form. Converting it to exclusive form and preparing the cumulative frequency table is given below

| Class interval | Frequency ($f_i$) | Cumulative frequency |
|---|---|---|
| 159.5-162.5 | 15 | 15 |
| 162.5-165.5 | 117 | 132 |
| 165.5-168.5 | 136 | 268 |
| 168.5-171.5 | 118 | 386 |
| 171.5-174.5 | 14 | 400 |
| **Total** | $N=\Sigma f_i=400$ | |

(1)

Here, $N=400$

Now, $\frac{N}{2}=\frac{400}{2}=200$

The cumulative frequency just greater than 200 is 268 and the corresponding class is 165.5-168.5.

Thus, the median class is 165.5-168.5.

$\therefore l=165.5, h=3, f=136$ and $C=132$ (1/2)

$\therefore$ Median $=l+\left\{h\times\frac{\frac{N}{2}-C}{f}\right\}$ (1/2)

$=165.5+\left\{3\times\frac{200-132}{136}\right\}$

$=165.5+\frac{3\times68}{136}=165.5+1.5=167$

Hence, the median height is 167 cm. (1)

**28.** Find the sum of first 22 terms of an AP in which 3rd term is 7 and 7th term is two more than thrice of its 3rd term.

*Or*

Anjali started work in 2001 at an annual salary of ₹ 5000 and received a ₹ 200 raise each year. In what year did his annual salary will reach ₹ 8000?

***Sol.*** Let $a$ be the first term and $d$ be the common difference of an AP.

Then, $a_3=7$ and $a_7=3a_3+2$

$\Rightarrow \quad a+(3-1)d=7$

and $\quad a+(7-1)d=3[a+(3-1)d]+2$

$[\because a_n=a(n-1)d]$ (1)

$\Rightarrow a+2d=7$ and $a+6d=3[a+2d]+2$

$\Rightarrow a+2d=7$ and $2a+2=0$

$\Rightarrow a+2d=7$ and $a=-1$

Put the value of $a$, we get

$\Rightarrow \quad -1+2d=7$

$\Rightarrow \quad 2d=8$

$\Rightarrow \quad d=4$ (1)

∴ Sum of first 22 terms,

$$S_{22} = \frac{22}{2}[2 \times (-1) + (22-1) \times 4]$$

$$\left[\because S_n = \frac{n}{2}[2a + (n-1)d]\right]$$

$$= 11[-2 + 84] = 11 \times 82 = 902 \quad (1)$$

*Or*

Annual salary received by Anjali in 2001, 2002, 2003, ..... is ₹ 5000, ₹ 5200, ₹ 5400, ..... .

Clearly, it is an arithmetic progression with first term $a = 5000$ and common difference, $d = 200$.

Suppose Anjali annual salary reaches to ₹ 8000 in $n$th years. (1)

Then, $n$th term of the above AP = ₹ 8000

$\Rightarrow \quad a + (n-1)d = 8000$

$\Rightarrow 5000 + (n-1)200 = 8000 \Rightarrow (n-1)200 = 3000$

$\Rightarrow \quad n - 1 = \frac{3000}{200}$

$\Rightarrow \quad n - 1 = 15 \Rightarrow n = 16$ (1)

Thus 16th annual salary received by Anjali will be ₹ 8000. This means that after 15 yr i.e. in the year 2016 his annual salary will reach to ₹ 8000. (1)

**29.** In the given figure, $AB$ is a diameter of the circle with centre $O$ and $AT$ is a tangent. Calculate the numerical value of $x$.

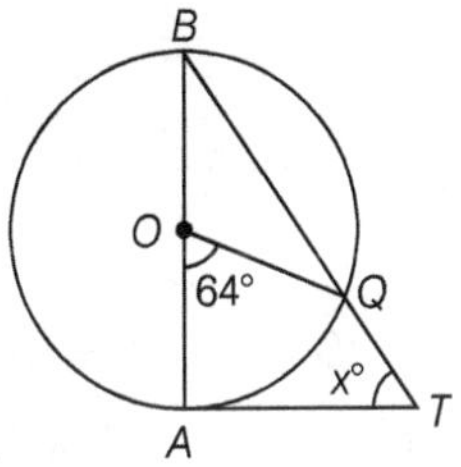


***Sol.*** **Given** $O$ is the centre of a circle $AB$ is diameter and $AT$ is tangent at $A$. Also, $\angle AOQ = 64°$

$\because$ $OA$ is radius and $AT$ is tangent.

$\therefore \quad \angle OAT = 90°$

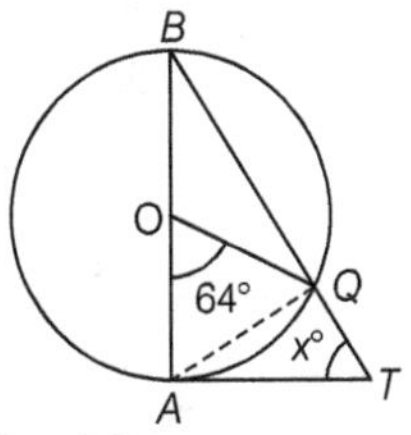


(1)

Also, $\angle AOQ = 64°$ [given]

$\therefore \quad \angle BOQ = 180° - \angle AOQ$

$= 180° - 64° = 116°$ ...(i)

[linear pair axiom]

But $\quad OB = OQ$ [radii]

$\Rightarrow \quad \angle OQB = \angle OBQ$

[$\because$ angle opposite to equal sides of a triangle are equal]

But $\angle OBQ + \angle OQB + \angle BOQ = 180°$

[by angle sum property of a triangle] (1)

$\Rightarrow \quad \angle OBQ + \angle OQB = 180° - 116° = 64°$

[using Eq. (i)]

$\Rightarrow \quad \angle OBQ + \angle OBQ = 64°$

$\Rightarrow \quad \angle OBQ = 32°$

$\therefore \quad \angle OQB = 32° \quad [\because \angle OBQ = \angle OQB]$

Now, in $\Delta BAT$,

$\angle ABT + \angle BAT + \angle ATB = 180°$

$\Rightarrow \quad 32° + 90° + x° = 180°$

$[\because \angle BAT = \angle OAT = 90°]$

$\Rightarrow \quad x° = 180° - 32° - 90°$

$\Rightarrow \quad x° = 58°$ (1)

**30.** A window of a house is $h$ m above the ground. From the window, the angles of elevation and depression of the top and the bottom of another house situated on the opposite side of the lane are found to be $\alpha$ and $\beta$, respectively. Prove that the height of the other house is $h(1 + \tan\alpha\cot\beta)$ m.

*Or*

A balloon is connected to an electric pole. It is inclined at 60° to the horizontal by a cable of length 215 m. Determine the height of the balloon from the ground. Also, find the height of the balloon, if the angle of inclination is changed from 60° to 30°.

***Sol.*** Let $B$ be the position of the window.

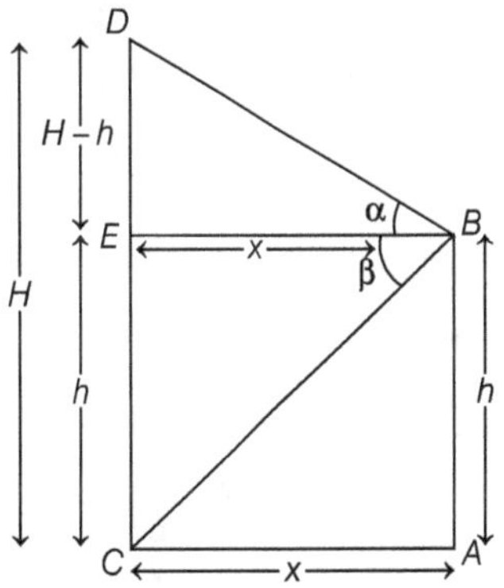


(1/2)

$\therefore AB = h$ metre

Let $CD = H$ metre be the height of another house which is situated on the opposite side of the lane.

From the position of window $B$, the elevation and depression are $\angle EBD = \alpha$ and $\angle EBC = \beta$

Draw a perpendicular line $BE$ to the $CD$. (1/2)

Let $AC = BE = x$

In right angled $\Delta EBD$,

$$\tan\alpha = \frac{ED}{BE}$$

$$\Rightarrow \quad \tan\alpha = \frac{H-h}{x}$$

$$x = (H-h)\cot\alpha \quad \text{...(i)} \quad (1)$$

In right angled $\Delta ABC$,

$$\tan\beta = \frac{AB}{CA}$$

$$\Rightarrow \quad \tan\beta = \frac{h}{x}$$

$$\Rightarrow \quad \tan\beta = \frac{h}{(H-h)\cot\alpha} \quad \text{[from Eq. (i)]}$$

$$(H-h) = h\tan\alpha\cot\beta$$

$$\therefore \quad H = h(1+\tan\alpha\cot\beta) \quad (1)$$

*Or*

Let $D$ be the position of the balloon, when it is inclined at angle of 60° and $AB$ be the height of the pole.

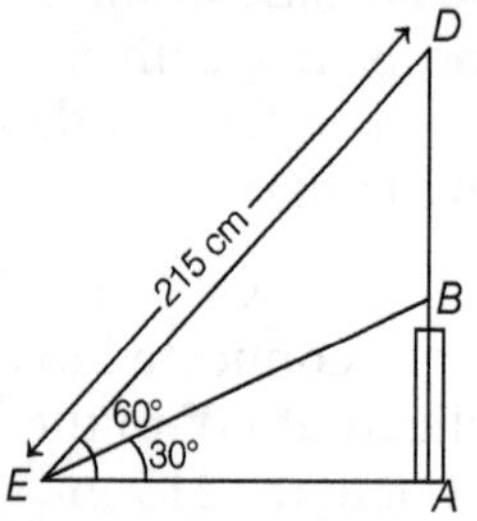


(1/2)

Given, length of cable,

$$DE = 215\,\text{m}$$

In right angled $\Delta EAD$,

$$\sin 60^\circ = \frac{AD}{ED}$$

$$\Rightarrow \quad \frac{\sqrt{3}}{2} = \frac{AD}{215} \quad \left[\because \sin 60^\circ = \frac{\sqrt{3}}{2}\right]$$

$$\Rightarrow \quad AD = \frac{215\sqrt{3}}{2}\,\text{m} \quad (1/2)$$

Hence, initial height of the balloon from the ground is $\frac{215\sqrt{3}}{2}$ m.

Again, in right angled $\Delta EAD$,

$$\cos 60^\circ = \frac{AE}{DE} = \frac{AE}{215}$$

$$\Rightarrow \quad \frac{1}{2} = \frac{AE}{215}$$

$$\Rightarrow \quad AE = \frac{215}{2}\,\text{m} \quad (1)$$

In right angled $\Delta EAB$,

$$\tan 30^\circ = \frac{AB}{AE}$$

$$AB = \frac{215}{2\sqrt{3}} = \frac{215\sqrt{3}}{6}\,\text{m} \quad (1)$$

**31. A chord $AC$ of a circle of radius 10 cm makes a right angle at the centre. Find the areas of the minor segment and major sector of the circle. ($\pi = 3.14$)**

***Sol.*** Given, radius of a circle $AO = 10$ cm

A perpendicular is drawn from centre of circle to the chord of the circle, which bisects the chord.

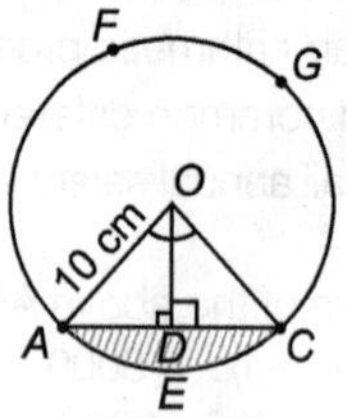


$$\therefore \quad AD = DC$$

Also, $\angle AOD = \angle COD = 45^\circ$

$$\therefore \quad \angle AOC = \angle AOD + \angle COD = 45^\circ + 45^\circ = 90^\circ$$

In right angled $\Delta AOD$,

$$\sin 45^\circ = \frac{AD}{AO}$$

$$\Rightarrow \quad \frac{1}{\sqrt{2}} = \frac{AD}{10}$$

$$\Rightarrow \quad AD = 5\sqrt{2}\text{ cm}$$

and $\cos 45^\circ = \frac{OD}{AO}$

$$\Rightarrow \quad \frac{1}{\sqrt{2}} = \frac{OD}{10}$$

$$\Rightarrow \quad OD = 5\sqrt{2}\text{ cm} \quad (1)$$

Now, $AC = 2\,AD = 2 \times 5\sqrt{2} = 10\sqrt{2}$ cm

Now, area of $\Delta AOC = \frac{1}{2} AC \times OD$

$$= \frac{1}{2} \times 10\sqrt{2} \times 5\sqrt{2} = 50\text{ cm}^2$$

Now, area of sector $= \frac{\theta\pi r^2}{360^\circ}$

$$= \frac{90}{360} \times 3.14 \times (10)^2 = \frac{314}{4} = 78.5\text{ cm}^2 \quad (1)$$

(i) $\therefore$ Area of minor segment $AEC$

= Area of sector $OAEC$ – Area of $\Delta AOC$

$= 78.5 - 50 = 28.5\text{ cm}^2$

(ii) $\therefore$ Area of major sector $OAFGCO$ = Area of circle – Area of sector $OAEC$

$= \pi r^2 - 78.5 = 3.14 \times (10)^2 - 78.5$

$= 314 - 78.5 = 235.5\text{ cm}^2$ (1)

# Section-D

**Section D consists of 4 questions of 5 marks each**

**32.** An aeroplane is flying 30 min late from its initial starting time and the speed of aeroplane is increased by 250 km/h to reach the distance of 1500 km. Find the usual speed of aeroplane.

*Or*

A rectangular park is to be designed whose breadth is 3 m less than its length. Its area is to be 4 sq m more than the area of a park that has already been made in the shape of an isosceles triangle with its base as the breadth of the rectangular park and of altitude 12 m. Find its length and breadth.

***Sol.*** Let the usual speed of aeroplane be $x$ km/h

Then, increased speed of aeroplane $= (x + 250)$ km/h

$\because$ Total distance = 1500 km [given]

$\therefore$ Time taken to cover 1500 km by usual speed

$$= \frac{1500}{x}\text{ km}$$

$$\left[\because \text{speed} = \frac{\text{distance}}{\text{time}} \Rightarrow \text{time} = \frac{\text{distance}}{\text{speed}}\right] \quad (1)$$

and time taken to cover 1500 km after increased the speed $= \dfrac{1500}{x + 250}$ km

According to the question,

$$\frac{1500}{x} - \frac{1500}{x + 250} = \frac{1}{2} \quad \left[\because 30 \text{ min} = \frac{1}{2}\text{ h}\right] \quad (1)$$

$$\Rightarrow 1500\left[\frac{1}{x} - \frac{1}{x + 250}\right] = \frac{1}{2}$$

$$\Rightarrow 1500\left[\frac{x + 250 - x}{x(x + 250)}\right] = \frac{1}{2} \quad \text{[taking LCM]}$$

$$\Rightarrow \frac{1500 \times 250}{x^2 + 250x} = \frac{1}{2}$$

$$\Rightarrow x^2 + 250x = 750000$$

[using cross-multiplication] (1)

$$\Rightarrow x^2 + 250x - 750000 = 0$$

By using factorisation method,

$$x^2 + (1000 - 750)x - 750000 = 0 \quad (1)$$

$[\because 750000 \times 1 = 750000$ and $1000 \times 750 = 750000$, $1000 - 750 = 250]$

$$\Rightarrow x^2 + 1000x - 750x - 750000 = 0$$

$$\Rightarrow x(x + 1000) - 750(x + 1000) = 0$$

$$\Rightarrow (x + 1000)(x - 750) = 0$$

$$\Rightarrow x + 1000 = 0 \text{ and } x - 750 = 0$$

$$\Rightarrow x = -1000 \text{ and } x = 750$$

$$\therefore x = 750$$

$[\because$ speed cannot be negative$]$

Hence, the usual speed of an aeroplane is 750 km/h. (1)

*Or*

Let breadth of the rectangular park be $x$ m.

So, its length $= (x + 3)$ m

Therefore, the area of the rectangular park

$= \text{Length} \times \text{Breadth}$

$= x \times (x + 3) = (x^2 + 3x)\text{m}^2$ (1)

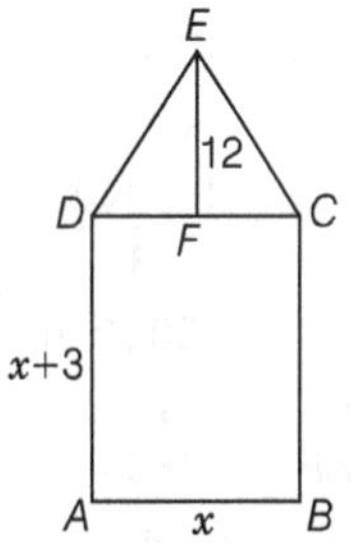


In the figure, $AB = DC = x$ (1)

Now, area of $\Delta DEC = \dfrac{1}{2} \times DC \times EF$

$= \dfrac{1}{2} \times x \times 12 = 6x\text{m}^2$

According to the given condition,

Area of rectangular park = Area of an isosceles triangle + 4

$$\Rightarrow x^2 + 3x = 6x + 4 \Rightarrow x^2 - 3x - 4 = 0 \quad (1)$$

By using quadratic formula,

$$x = \frac{-(-3) \pm \sqrt{(-3)^2 - 4 \times 1 \times (-4)}}{2(1)}$$

$$= \frac{3 \pm \sqrt{9 + 16}}{2} = \frac{3 \pm 5}{2} = \frac{8}{2} \text{ or } -\frac{2}{2} = 4 \text{ or } -1 \quad (1)$$

But $x \neq -1$ $[\because x$ cannot be negative$]$

Therefore, $x = 4$,

So, the breadth of the park = 4 m

and its length will be = 4 + 3 = 7 m (1)

**33.** An army pilot is flying an aeroplane at an altitude of 1800 m observes some suspicious activity of two ships which are sailing towards it in the same directions and immediately report it to the navy chief. The angles of depression of the ships as observed from the aeroplane are 60° and 30°, respectively. Find the distance between two ships.

**Sol.** Let the aeroplane is at $B$ and let the two ships are at point $C$ and $D$ such that their angles of depression from $B$ are 60° and 30°, respectively.

We have, $AB = 1800$ m. (1)

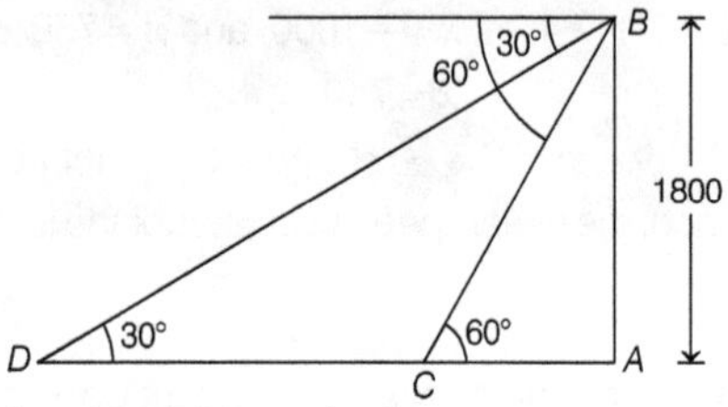


(1)

Now, in $\Delta BAC$, we have

$$\tan 60° = \frac{AB}{AC} \quad \left[\because \tan\theta = \frac{\text{perpendicular}}{\text{base}}\right]$$

$$\Rightarrow \sqrt{3} = \frac{1800}{AC} \quad [\because \tan 60° = \sqrt{3}]$$

$$\Rightarrow AC = \frac{1800}{\sqrt{3}} \times \frac{\sqrt{3}}{\sqrt{3}}$$

$$= \frac{1800\sqrt{3}}{3}$$

$$= 600\sqrt{3} \text{ m} \quad (1)$$

and in $\Delta BAD$, we have

$$\tan 30° = \frac{AB}{AD} = \frac{1800}{AC + CD} \quad [\because AD = AC = CD]$$

$$\Rightarrow \frac{1}{\sqrt{3}} = \frac{1800}{600\sqrt{3} + CD} \quad \left[\because \tan 30° = \frac{1}{\sqrt{3}}\right]$$

$$\Rightarrow CD + 600\sqrt{3} = 1800\sqrt{3}$$

$$\Rightarrow CD = 1800\sqrt{3} - 600\sqrt{3}$$

$$= 1200\sqrt{3} \text{ m}$$

Hence, the distance between the two ships is $1200\sqrt{3}$ m. (2)

**34.** A die is thrown once. Find the probability of getting

(i) a even prime number.

(ii) a number lying between 2 and 6.

(iii) an odd prime number.

*Or*

One card is drawn from a well-shuffled deck of 52 cards. Find the probability of getting

(i) a king of red colour.

(ii) a face card.

(iii) the jack of heart.

(iv) a spade.

**Sol.** On a die, there are six numbers 1, 2, 3, 4, 5 and 6.

$\therefore$ Total number of possible outcomes = 6 (1/2)

(i) Let $E_1$ = Event of getting a even prime number

Then, $E_1$ would consist of one outcome namely 2.

$\therefore$ Number of outcome favourable to $E_1 = 1$

Probability of getting a prime number,

$$P(E_1) = \frac{1}{6} \quad (1½)$$

(ii) Let $E_2$ = Event of getting a number lying between 2 and 6

Then, $E_2$ would consist of three outcomes, namely 3, 4 and 5.

$\therefore$ Number of outcomes favourable to $E_2 = 3$

Probability of getting a number lying between 2 and 6,

$$P(E_2) = \frac{3}{6} = \frac{1}{2} \quad (1½)$$

(iii) Let $E_3$ = Event of getting an odd prime number

Favourable outcomes = 3, 5

$\therefore$ Number of favourable outcomes = 2

Probability of getting an odd number,

$$P(E_3) = \frac{2}{6} = \frac{1}{3} \quad (1½)$$

*Or*

Total number of cards in one deck of cards is 52.

$\therefore$ Total number of outcomes = 52 (1)

(i) Let $E_1$ = Event of getting a king of red colour

$\therefore$ Number of outcomes favourable to $E_1 = 2$

[$\because$ there are four kings in a deck of playing cards out of which two are red and two are black]

Hence, probability of getting a king of red colour,

$$P(E_1) = \frac{2}{52} = \frac{1}{26} \quad (1)$$

(ii) Let $E_2$ = Event of getting a face card

$\therefore$ Number of outcomes favourable to $E_2 = 12$

[$\because$ in a deck of cards, there are 12 face cards, namely 4 kings, 4 jacks, 4 queens]

Hence, probability of getting a face card,

$$P(E_2) = \frac{12}{52} = \frac{3}{13} \quad (1)$$

(iv) Let $E_4$ = Event of getting a jack of heart

$\therefore$ Number of outcomes favourable to $E_4 = 1$

[$\because$ there are four jack cards in a deck, namely 1 of heart, 1 of club, 1 of spade and 1 of diamond]

Hence, probability of getting a jack of heart,

$$P(E_4) = \frac{1}{52} \quad (1)$$

(iv) Let $E_5$ = Event of getting a spade

$\therefore$ Number of outcomes favourable to $E_5 = 13$

[$\because$ in a deck of cards, there are 13 spades, 13 clubs, 13 hearts and 13 diamonds]

Hence, probability of getting a spade,

$$P(E_5) = \frac{13}{52} = \frac{1}{4} \quad (1)$$

**35.** A container shape like a right circular cylinder having diameter 12 cm and height 15 cm is full of ice-cream. The ice-cream is to be filled into cones of height 12 cm and diameter 6 cm, having a hemispherical shape on the top.
Find the number of such cones which can be filled with ice-cream.

***Sol.*** Let $V_1$ be the volume of the given ice-cream container.

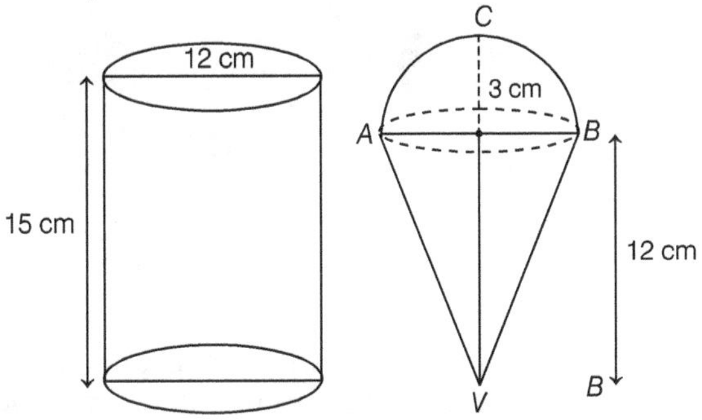


Then, $V_1 = \frac{2}{3}\pi r^3 + \frac{1}{3}\pi r^2 h$

$$= \pi\left[\frac{2}{3} \times (3)^3 + \frac{1}{3} \times 3^2 \times 12\right]$$

$$= \pi\,[18 + 36] = 54\pi \text{ cm}^3 \quad (1)$$

Let $V_2$ be the volume of ice-cream filled in the shape of circular cylinder having diameter 12 cm and height = 15 cm (1)

$\therefore \quad V_2 = \pi r_1^2 h_1$

$$= \pi(6)^2(15)$$

$$= 540\,\pi \quad (1)$$

Let the total number of cones that can be filled with ice-cream given in the container be $n$. Then,

Volume of ice-cream in $n$ cones

= Volume of ice-cream in the container

$\Rightarrow \quad nV_1 = V_2$ (1)

$\Rightarrow \quad n \times 54\pi = 540\pi$

$\Rightarrow \quad n = 10$ (1)

# Section-E

**Case study based questions are compulsory**

**36.** A student of Class X standard observing a girl of height 120 cm walking away from the base of lamp-post at a speed of 2.0 m/s. If the lamp is 5 m above and $x$ be the length of her shadow after 6s.

The figure is shown below

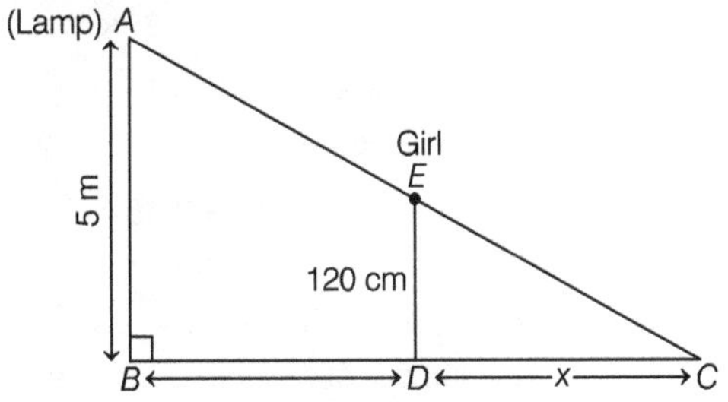


Give answer to his questions by looking at the figure.

(i) Find the distance of girl from lamp-post after 6s. (1)

(ii) Which is the correct similarity criteria application for $\Delta ABC$ and $\Delta EDC$. (1)

(iii) Find the ratio of the squares of sides $ED$ and $AB$. (2)

*Or*

Find the length of her shadow after 6s. (2)

***Sol.*** (i) Distance of the girl from lamp-post after 6 s,

$$BD = 2.0 \times 6$$

$$= 12 \text{ m}$$

(ii) In $\Delta ABC$ and $\Delta EDC$

$$\angle B = \angle D = 90°$$

$$\angle C = \angle C \quad \text{[common angle]}$$

$\therefore$ By AA similarity criterion

$$\Delta ABC \sim \Delta EDC$$

(iii) $$\left(\frac{ED}{AB}\right)^2 = \left(\frac{12}{5}\right)^2$$

$$= \frac{1.44}{25} \times \frac{4}{4}$$

$$= \frac{5.76}{100}$$

$$= 0.0576$$

*Or*

From (ii), we have $\Delta ABC \sim \Delta EDC$

$\Rightarrow \quad \frac{BC}{DC} = \frac{AB}{ED}$

$\Rightarrow \quad \frac{12 + x}{x} = \frac{5}{1.2}$

$\Rightarrow \quad 14.4 + 1.2x = 5x$

$\Rightarrow \quad 3.8x = 14.4$

$\Rightarrow \quad x = \frac{14.4}{3.8} = 3.8 \text{ m}$ [approx]

**37.** Class X students of a school in Gomtinagar have been alloted a rectangular plot of a land for gardening activity. Sapling of roses are planted on the boundary at a distance of 1m from each other. There is a triangular grassy fountain in the plot as shown in the figure. The students are to sow seeds of flowering plants on the remaining area of the plot.

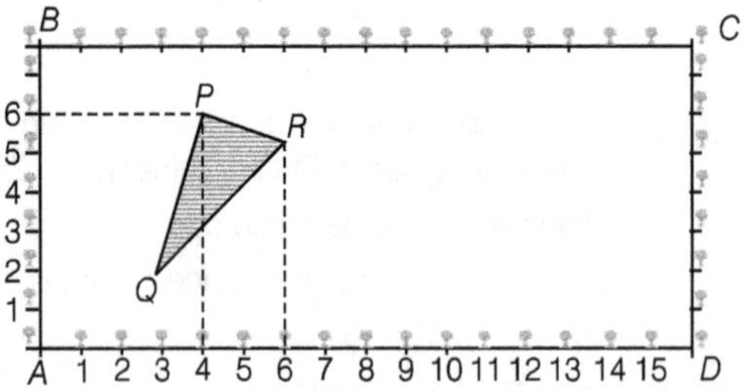


Considering $A$ as origin answer the following questions

(i) What are the coordinates of $R$? (1)

(ii) Find the distance between points $Q$ and $R$. (1)

(iii) What is $\Delta PQR$? (2)

*Or* What is the centroid of $\Delta PQR$? (2)

***Sol.*** (i) The coordinates of $R$ is (6, 5) as the point is 6 units on $X$-axis and 5 units on $Y$-axis.

(ii) The coordinates of $Q$ are (3, 2) and $R$ are (6, 5).

$\therefore$ The distance between points $Q$ and $R$ is

$$QR = \sqrt{(6-3)^2 + (5-2)^2}$$

$$= \sqrt{(3)^2 + (3)^2} = \sqrt{9+9} = 3\sqrt{2} \text{ units}$$

(iii) Since, coordinates of vertices of a $\Delta PQR$ are $P(4, 6), Q(3, 2)$ and $R(6, 5)$.

Now, $PQ = \sqrt{(3-4)^2 + (2-6)^2}$

$= \sqrt{(-1)^2 + (-4)^2}$

$= \sqrt{1+16} = \sqrt{17}$ units

$PR = \sqrt{(6-4)^2 + (5-6)^2}$

$= \sqrt{(2)^2 + (-1)^2}$

$= \sqrt{4+1} = \sqrt{5}$ units

and $QR = 3\sqrt{2}$

Here, $PQ \neq QR \neq PR$

Hence, $\Delta PQR$ is a scalene triangle.

*Or*

The centroid of $\Delta PQR$ is $\left(\frac{4+3+6}{3}, \frac{6+2+5}{3}\right)$

i.e. $\left(\frac{13}{3}, \frac{13}{3}\right)$.

**38.** A vegetable seller has 420 potatoes and 130 tomatoes. He wants to stack them in such a way that each stack has same number and they take up the least area of the tray.

Based on the above information of a vegetable shop, answer the following questions

(i) Find the product of exponents of the prime factors of total number of vegetables. (1)

(ii) What is the number of vegetables that can be placed in each stack for this purpose? (1)

(iii) Find the sum of exponents of the prime factors of the number of vegetables that can be placed in each stack for this purpose. (2)

*Or* What is the total number of rows in which they can be placed? (2)

***Sol.*** (i) Since, total number of vegetables is 550

Prime factorisation of $550 = 2 \times 5 \times 5 \times 11$

$= 2^1 \times 5^2 \times 11^1$

The exponents are 1, 2 and 1.

$\therefore$ Product of exponents $= 1 \times 2 \times 1 = 2$

(ii) Prime factor of $420 = 2^2 \times 3 \times 5 \times 7$

and $130 = 2 \times 5 \times 13$

$\therefore$ HCF $(420, 130) = 2 \times 5 = 10$

So, the number of vegetables that can be placed in each stack for this purpose is 10.

(iii) The number of vegetables that can be placed in each stack = 10

Prime factor of $10 = 2^1 \times 5^1$

The exponents are 1 and 1.

$\therefore$ Sum of exponents $= 1 + 1 = 2$

*Or*

Total number of vegetables = 550

Number of vegetables that can be placed in each stack = 10

$\therefore$ Number of rows of vegetables $= \frac{550}{10} = 55$

**Stage 2**

# SAMPLE QUESTION PAPER 6

## Mathematics (Basic)

Time : **3 hrs** Max. Marks : **80**

## Instructions

1. This question paper has 5 Sections A, B, C, D and E.
2. Section A has 20 Multiple Choice Questions (MCQs) carrying 1 mark each.
3. Section B has 5 Short Answer-I (SA-I) Type Questions carrying 2 marks each.
4. Section C has 6 Short Answer-II (SA-II) Type Questions carrying 3 marks each.
5. Section D has 4 Long Answer (LA) Type Questions carrying 5 marks each.
6. Section E has 3 Case Based integrated units of assessment (4 marks each) with sub-parts of the values of 1, 1 and 2 marks each respectively.
7. All questions are compulsory. However, an internal choice in 2 questions of 2 marks, 2 questions of 3 marks and 2 questions of 5 marks has been provided. An internal choice has been provided in the 2 marks questions of Section E.
8. Draw neat figures wherever required. Take $\pi = 22/7$ wherever required if not stated.

## Section-A

**Section A consists of 20 questions of 1 mark each**

**1.** The HCF of $3 \times 5^3$ and $3^2 \times 5^2$ is

(a) $3^2 \times 5^2$ (b) $3 \times 5$ (c) $3^2 \times 5^3$ (d) $3 \times 5^2$

**2.** In the given figure, the value of $BP$ is

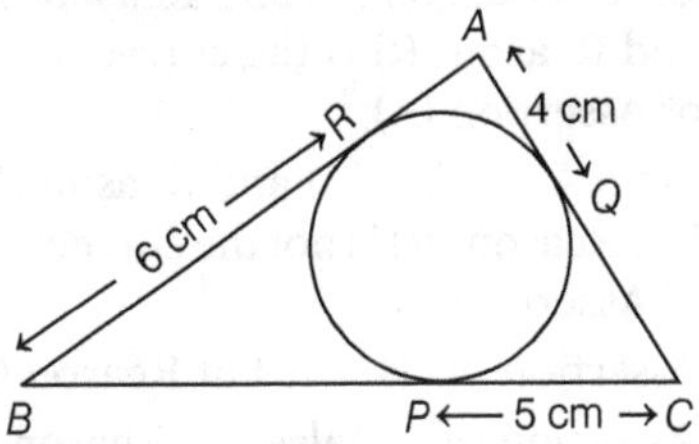


(a) 9 cm (b) 8 cm (c) 6 cm (d) 11 cm

**3.** The sum of the exponents of the prime factors in the prime factorisation of 196, is

(a) 3 (b) 4 (c) 2 (d) 5

**4.** For what values of $k$, the pair of linear equations $x + 2y = 3$ and $5x + ky + 7 = 0$ represents intersecting lines?

(a) $R$ (b) $R - \{10\}$
(c) 10 (d) None of these

**5.** The perpendicular distance of the point $P(4, 2)$ from the $X$-axis is

(a) 4 units (b) 6 units (c) 2 units (d) 8 units

**6.** The values of $x$ and $y$ in the given figure are

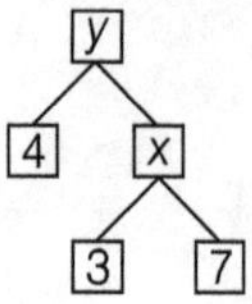


(a) 10 and 14 (b) 21 and 84
(c) 21 and 25 (d) 10 and 40

**7.** A card is drawn from a deck of 52 cards. The event $E$ is that card which is not an ace of heart. The number of outcomes favourable to $E$ is

(a) 4 (b) 13 (c) 48 (d) 51

**8.** If the distance between the points $(4, p)$ and $(1, 0)$ is 5 units, then the value of $p$ is

(a) $\sqrt{9}$ (b) $\sqrt{16}$ (c) $\sqrt{25}$ (d) $\sqrt{24}$

**9.** $1+\cot^2\theta$ is equal to

(a) $\sin^2\theta$ (b) $\tan^2\theta$
(c) $\text{cosec}^2\theta$ (d) $\sec^2\theta$

**10.** If $\sin\theta = \frac{a}{b}$, then $\cos\theta$ is equal to

(a) $\frac{\sqrt{b-a}}{b}$ (b) $\frac{b-a}{b}$
(c) $\frac{\sqrt{b^2-a^2}}{b}$ (d) $\frac{b^2-a^2}{b}$

**11.** For any two similar triangles, which of the following statements are valid?

(a) Their sides are proportional
(b) Their sides are equal
(c) Their sides are parallel
(d) None of the above

**12.** If $\Delta ABC \sim \Delta DEF$, such that $DE = 3AB$ and $BC = 6$ cm, then the length of $EF$ is

(a) 8 cm (b) 16 cm (c) 18 cm (d) 26 cm

**13.** If in a lottery, there are 5 prizes and 20 blanks, then the probability of getting a prize is

(a) $\frac{2}{5}$ (b) $\frac{4}{5}$ (c) $\frac{1}{5}$ (d) 1

**14.** The sum and the product of the zeroes of polynomial $6x^2-5$, respectively are

(a) 0 and $\frac{-6}{5}$ (b) 0 and $\frac{6}{5}$
(c) 0 and $\frac{5}{6}$ (d) 0 and $\frac{-5}{6}$

**15.** For the equation $y = a + \frac{b}{x}$, where $a$ and $b$ are real numbers, if $y = 1$ when $x = -1$ and $y = 5$ when $x = -5$, then $a + b$ is equal to

(a) $-1$ (b) 0
(c) 11 (d) 10

**16.** If arithmetic mean of $a$, $a+2$, $a+4$, $a+6$ and $a+8$ is 12, then $a$ is equal to

(a) 10 (b) 8
(c) 5.6 (d) 10.4

**17.** If we cut a cone in two parts by a plane parallel to the base, then the bottom part left over is the

(a) cone (b) frustum of cone
(c) cylinder (d) sphere

**18.** A tangent intersects the circle at

(a) one point (b) two distinct points
(c) at the circle (d) does not intersect

**Directions** *In the question number 19 and 20, a statement of Assertion (A) is followed by a statement of Reason (R). Choose the correct option.*

**19. Assertion (A)** Class width
= Upper class limit – Lower class limit
**Reason (R)** Class mark
= (Upper class limit + Lower class limit)/2

(a) Both Assertion (A) and Reason (R) are true and Reason (R) is the correct explanation of Assertion (A)
(b) Both Assertion (A) and Reason (R) are true but Reason (R) is not the correct explanation of Assertion (A)
(c) Assertion (A) is true but Reason (R) is false
(d) Assertion (A) is false but Reason (R) is true

**20. Assertion (A)** Angles in the same segment of a circle are equal.
**Reason (R)** In cyclic quadrilateral, opposite angles are complementary.

(a) Both Assertion (A) and Reason (R) are true and Reason (R) is the correct explanation of Assertion (A)
(b) Both Assertion (A) and Reason (R) are true but Reason (R) is not the correct explanation of Assertion (A)
(c) Assertion (A) is true but Reason (R) is false
(d) Assertion (A) is false but Reason (R) is true

# Section-B

**Section B consists of 5 questions of 2 marks each**

**21.** 17 cards numbered 1, 2, 3, ......, 17 are put in a box and mixed thoroughly. One person drawns a card from the box. Find the probability that the number on card is divisible by 3 and 2 both.

*Or*

Two unbiased coins are tossed simultaneously. Find the probability of getting atleast one head.

**22.** In two concentric circles, prove that a chord of larger circle which is tangent to smaller circle is bisected at the point of contact.

**23.** If $\frac{x \operatorname{cosec}^2 30° \sec^2 45°}{8 \cos^2 45° \sin^2 60°} = \tan^2 60° - \tan^2 30°$, then find the value of $x$.

*Or* Prove that $\frac{1}{1+\sin\theta} + \frac{1}{1-\sin\theta} = 2\sec^2\theta$.

**24.** If the perimeter of a semi-circular protractor is 108 cm, find the diameter of the protractor.

**25.** Find the solution of the equation

$$\frac{16}{x} - 1 = \frac{15}{x+1}, x \neq 0, -1$$

# Section-C

**Section C consists of 6 questions of 3 marks each**

**26.** On diwali, Pawan purchases a decorative block as shown in figure is made of two solids; a cube and a hemisphere. The base of the block is the cube with edge of 5 cm and the hemisphere attached on the top has a diameter of 4.2 cm. If the block is to be painted, then find the total area to be painted by him. [take, $\pi = 22/7$]

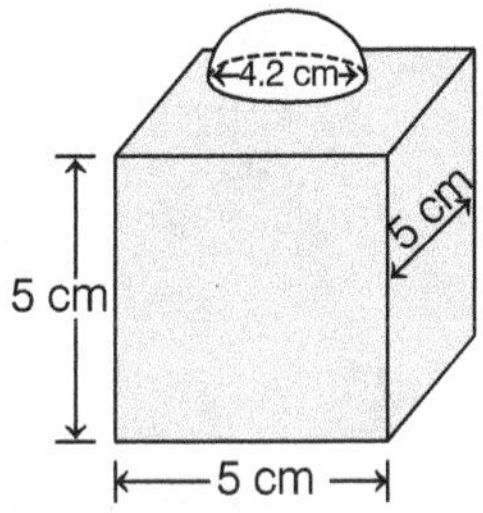


**27.** In a two-digit number, the ten's digit is three times the unit's digit. When the number is decreased by 54, the digits are reversed. Find the number.

**28.** The sum of the reciprocals of Rehman's ages, (in yr) 3 yr ago and 5 yr from now is $\frac{1}{3}$. Find his present age.

**29.** In $\Delta ABC$, points $P$ and $Q$ are on $CA$ and $CB$, respectively such that $CA = 16$ cm, $CP = 10$ cm, $CB = 30$ cm and $CQ = 25$ cm. Is $PQ \parallel AB$?

*Or* In the given figure of $\Delta ABC$, $DE \parallel AC$. If $DC \parallel AP$, where point $P$ lies on $BC$ produced, then prove that $\frac{BE}{EC} = \frac{BC}{CP}$.

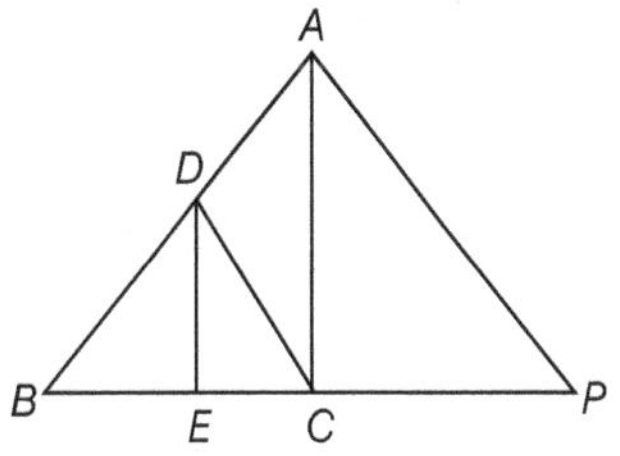


**30.** Evaluate the value of $\frac{\sin 30° + \tan 45° - \operatorname{cosec} 60°}{\sec 30° + \cos 60° + \cot 45°}$.

*Or* In $\Delta ABC$, if $AB = BC$, $\angle B = 90°$, then find the value of the following

(i) $\sin A$ (ii) $\cos A$

**31.** There is a circular path around a sports field. Sonia takes 18 min to drive one round of the field, while Ravi takes 12 min for the same. Suppose they both start at the same point and at the same time and go in the same direction. After how many minutes will they meet again at the starting point?

# Section-D

### Section D consists of 4 questions of 5 marks each

**32.** Find the sum of first 50 terms of an AP, whose second and third terms are 14 and 18 respectively.

*Or*

If the 5th term of an AP is 31 and 25th term is 140 more than 5th term, find the AP.

**33.** Find the median for the following data.

| Class interval | Frequency |
|---|---|
| 130-139 | 4 |
| 140-149 | 9 |
| 150-159 | 18 |
| 160-169 | 28 |
| 170-179 | 24 |
| 180-189 | 10 |
| 190-199 | 7 |

**34.** A 1.2 m tall girl spots a balloon moving with the wind in a horizontal line at a height of 88.2 m from the ground. The angle of elevation of the balloon from the eyes of the girl at any instant is 60°. After sometime, the angle of elevation reduces to 30° (see the figure). Find the distance travelled by the balloon during the interval.

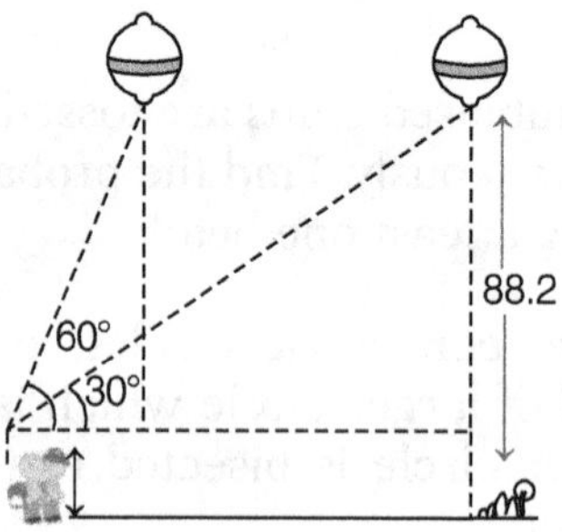


**35.** $BL$ and $CM$ are medians of $\Delta ABC$ right angled at $A$.

Prove that $4(BL^2 + CM^2) = 5BC^2$.

*Or*

In right angle $\Delta ABC$, $\angle B = 90°$. If $D$ is mid-point of side $BC$, prove that $AC^2 = 4AD^2 - 3AB^2$.

# Section-E

### Case study based questions are compulsory

**36.** Mathematics teacher of a school took her X standard students for drill practice. Teacher interest for students are standing in rows and columns in their playground for a drill practice. $A, B, C$ and $D$ are the positions of four students as shown in figure.

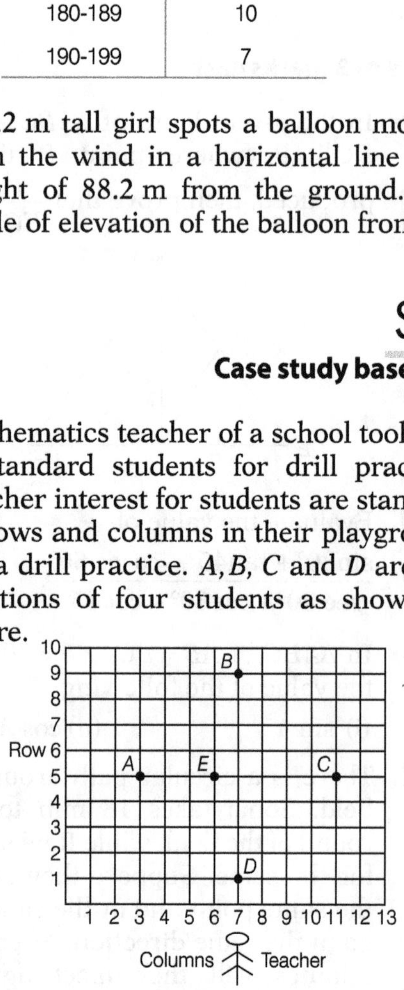


Considering $O$ as origin.

On the basis of above information, answer the following questions.

(i) What are the coordinates of $A$? (1)

(ii) What is the ratio in which $E$ divides $AC$? (1)

(iii) Find the distance between $A$ and $D$. (2)

*Or* Find the coordinates of mid-point of $DC$. (2)

**37.** Heena hold a Japanese fan in her hand as shown in the figure.

It is shaped like a sector of a circle and made of a thin material such as paper or feather. The inner and outer radii are 6 cm and 10 cm respectively. The fan has three colours i.e. Pink, Blue and Black.

On the basis of above information, answer the following questions.

(i) If the region containing blue colour makes an angle of 80° at the centre, then find the area of the region having blue colour. (1)

(ii) If the region containing black colour makes an angle of 40° at the centre, then find the area of the region having black colour. (1)

(iii) If the region containing pink colour makes an angle of 30° at the centre, then find the perimeter of the region containing pink colour. (2)

*Or*

Find the area of the region having radius 6 cm. (2)

**38.** Due to heavy storm an electric wire got bent as shown in the figure. It followed a mathematical shape.

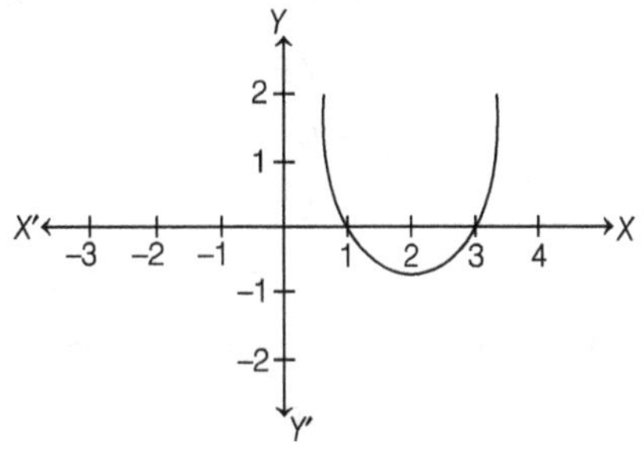


On the basis of above information, answer the following questions.

(i) Name the shape in which the wire is bent. (1)

(ii) Find the zeroes of the polynomial. (1)

(iii) What will be the expression of the polynomial? (2)

*Or* If one zero of $3x^2+8x+k$ be the reciprocal of the other, then find the value of $k$. (2)

# SOLUTIONS

**1.** (d) HCF of $3\times5^3$ and $3^2\times5^2$

= Product of each common prime factor which contain smallest power in the numbers

$=3\times5^2$

**2.** (c) Since, tangents drawn from an external point to a circle are equal in length.

$\therefore\ BP = BR \Rightarrow BP = 6\text{ cm}$

**3.** (b)

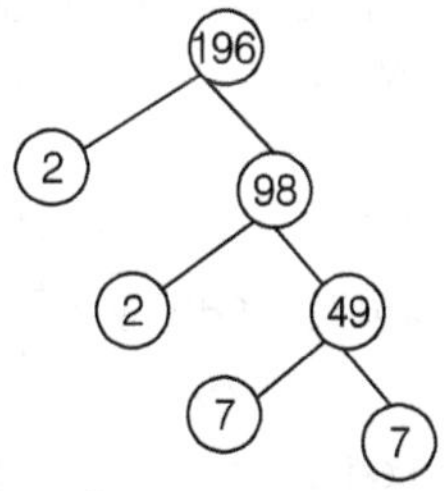


$\therefore\ 196 = 2^2\times7^2$

$\therefore$ Required sum $= 2+2 = 4$

**4.** (b) Given, pair of linear equations is

$x+2y=3$ and $5x+ky+7=0$

On comparing with standard equations, we get

$a_1 = 1, b_1 = 2, c_1 = -3$

and $a_2 = 5, b_2 = k, c_2 = 7$

The condition for intersecting lines is

$$\frac{a_1}{a_2} \neq \frac{b_1}{b_2}$$

$$\therefore\quad \frac{1}{5} \neq \frac{2}{k}$$

$$\Rightarrow\quad k \neq 10$$

Hence, the value of $k$ is $R-\{10\}$.

**5.** (c) Firstly, plot the point $P(4, 2)$

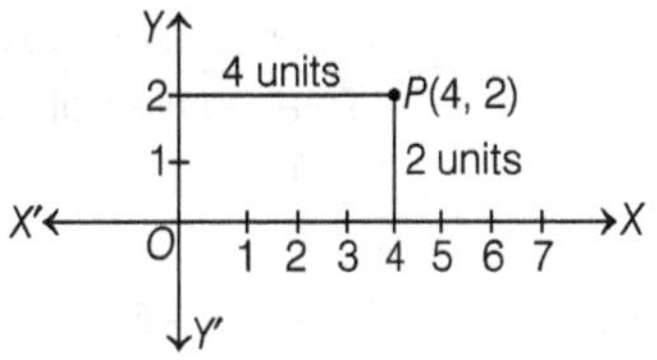


Hence, the distance from $P$ to the $X$-axis is 2 units.

**6.** (b) Given,

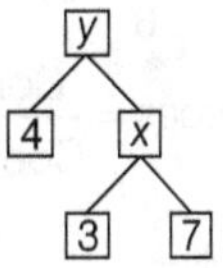


Here, $x = 3\times7 = 21$ and $y = 4\times x = 4\times21 = 84$

**7.** (d) In a deck of 52 cards, there are 13 cards of heart and 1 of them is ace of heart.
So, number of favourable outcomes to $E = 52 - 1 = 51$

**8.** (b) Let the given coordinates $A(4, p)$ and $B(1, 0)$

$\therefore \quad AB = 5$

$\Rightarrow \quad \sqrt{(4-1)^2 + (p-0)^2} = 5$

$\Rightarrow \quad 9 + p^2 = 25$

$\Rightarrow \quad p^2 = 16 \Rightarrow p = \sqrt{16}$

**9.** (c) We know, by trigonometric identities,
$$1 + \cot^2\theta = \text{cosec}^2\theta$$

**10.** (c) We know, $\sin^2\theta + \cos^2\theta = 1$

$\Rightarrow \quad \left(\frac{a}{b}\right)^2 + \cos^2\theta = 1$

$\Rightarrow \quad \cos^2\theta = 1 - \frac{a^2}{b^2}$

$\Rightarrow \quad \cos^2\theta = \frac{b^2 - a^2}{b^2}$

$\Rightarrow \quad \cos\theta = \frac{\sqrt{b^2 - a^2}}{b}$

**11.** (a) Two triangles are said to be similar, if
(i) their corresponding angles are equal.
(ii) their corresponding sides are proportional.

**12.** (c) Since, $\Delta ABC \sim \Delta DEF$

$\therefore \quad \frac{AB}{DE} = \frac{BC}{EF}$ [by BPT]

$\Rightarrow \quad \frac{AB}{3AB} = \frac{6}{EF}$

$\Rightarrow \quad EF = 3 \times 6 = 18 \text{ cm}$

**13.** (c) Total number of outcomes $= 5 + 20 = 25$
Number of favourable outcomes $= 5$
$\therefore$ Required probability
$$= \frac{\text{Number of favourable outcomes}}{\text{Total number of outcomes}}$$
$$= \frac{5}{25} = \frac{1}{5}$$

**14.** (d) Given, polynomial is $6x^2 - 5$

$\therefore$ Sum of zeroes $= -\frac{\text{Coefficient of } x}{\text{Coefficient of } x^2}$

$= -\frac{0}{6} = 0$

$\therefore$ Product of zeroes $= \frac{\text{Constant term}}{\text{Coefficient of } x^2} = \frac{-5}{6}$

**15.** (c) Given, $y = a + \frac{b}{x}$

Put $x = -1$ and $y = 1$ in above equation.

$1 = a + \frac{b}{-1} \Rightarrow a - b = 1$ ...(i)

Put $x = -5$ and $y = 5$ in the given equation.

$5 = a + \frac{b}{-5} \Rightarrow 25 = 5a - b$ ...(ii)

On subtracting Eq. (i) from Eq. (ii), we get

$4a = 24 \Rightarrow a = 6$

Now, $a - b = 1$ [from Eq. (i)]

$b = a - 1$ [$\because a = 6$]

$\therefore \quad b = 6 - 1 = 5$

$\therefore \quad a + b = 6 + 5 = 11$

**16.** (b) We know that $\text{AM} = \frac{\text{Sum of terms}}{\text{Number of terms}}$

$\Rightarrow \quad \frac{a + a + 2 + a + 4 + a + 6 + a + 8}{5} = 12$

$\Rightarrow \quad 5a + 20 = 60$

$\Rightarrow \quad 5a = 40$

$\Rightarrow \quad a = 8$

**17.** (b)

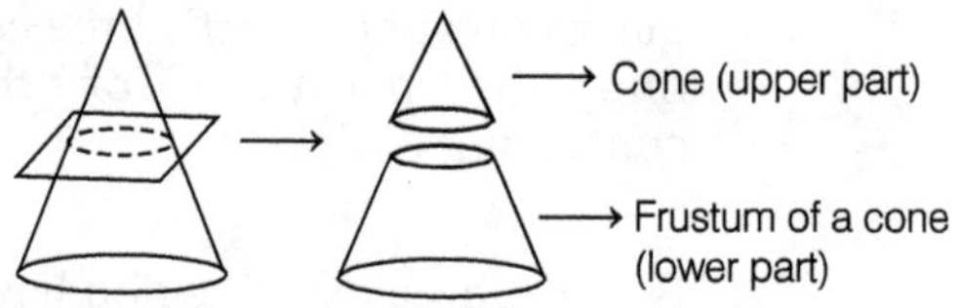


**18.** (a) A tangent touches the circle on its boundary at only one point.

**19.** (b) Both Assertion and Reason are correct but Reason is not the correct explanation of Assertion.

**20.** (c) Clearly, Assertion is true.
Reason is not true, as in cyclic quadrilateral, opposite angles are supplementary i.e. sum of opposite angles is equal to 180°.

**21.** Out of 17 cards, in the box, one card can be drawn in 17 ways.
$\therefore$ Total number of possible outcomes $= 17$ **(1/2)**
If a number is divisible by both 3 and 2, then it is a multiple of 6. In cards bearing number 1, 2, 3, ..., 17, there are only 2 cards which bear a number multiple of 6, i.e. 6 and 12. **(1)**
$\therefore$ Number of favourable outcomes $= 2$
Hence, required probability $= \frac{2}{17}$ **(1/2)**

*Or*

If two unbiased coins are tossed simultaneously we obtain any one of the following as an outcome.
$$HH, HT, TH, TT$$
$\therefore$ Total number of elementary events $= 4$ **(1/2)**
Atleast one head is obtained, if any one of the following elementary events happens:
$$HH, HT, TH$$
$\therefore$ Favourable number of elementary events $= 3$ **(1)**
Hence, required probability $= \frac{3}{4}$ **(1/2)**

**22.** Let $O$ be the common centre of two concentric circles, and let $AB$ be a chord of the larger circle touching the smaller circle at $P$.
Join $OP$.

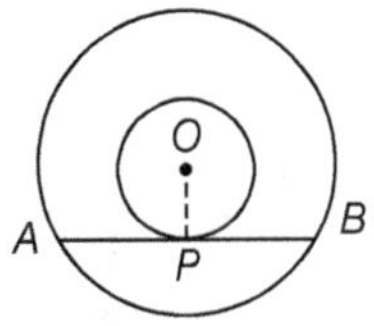


Since, $OP$ is the radius of the smaller circle and $AB$ is a tangent to this circle at a point $P$.

$\therefore \quad OP \perp AB$ **(1)**

We know that, the perpendicular drawn from the centre of a circle to any chord of the circle, bisects the chord.

So, $AP = BP$

Hence, $AB$ is bisected at $P$. **Hence proved. (1)**

**23.** Given, $\frac{x \operatorname{cosec}^2 30° \sec^2 45°}{8\cos^2 45° \sin^2 60°} = \tan^2 60° - \tan^2 30°$

$$\Rightarrow \frac{x \times (2)^2 \times (\sqrt{2})^2}{8 \times \left(\frac{1}{\sqrt{2}}\right)^2 \times \left(\frac{\sqrt{3}}{2}\right)^2} = (\sqrt{3})^2 - \left(\frac{1}{\sqrt{3}}\right)^2$$ **(1)**

$$\Rightarrow \frac{x \times 4 \times 2}{8 \times \frac{1}{2} \times \frac{3}{4}} = 3 - \frac{1}{3}$$

$$\Rightarrow x \times \frac{8}{3} = \frac{8}{3}$$

$$\Rightarrow x = 1$$ **(1)**

*Or*

We have,

$$\text{LHS} = \frac{1}{1+\sin\theta} + \frac{1}{1-\sin\theta}$$

$$= \frac{(1-\sin\theta)+(1+\sin\theta)}{(1+\sin\theta)(1-\sin\theta)}$$ **(1)**

$$= \frac{2}{1-\sin^2\theta} = \frac{2}{\cos^2\theta}$$

$$= 2\sec^2\theta = \text{RHS}$$ **Hence proved. (1)**

**24.** Let the radius of the semi-circular protractor be $r$ cm.

Then, its perimeter $= \frac{2\pi r}{2} + 2r$

$\therefore \quad \pi r + 2r = 108$ [given] **(1)**

$\Rightarrow \quad \frac{22}{7}r + 2r = 108$

$\Rightarrow \quad 36r = 108 \times 7$

$\Rightarrow \quad r = 21$

$\therefore$ Diameter of the semi-circular protractor $= 2r$

$= (2 \times 21)$ cm

$= 42$ cm **(1)**

**25.** Given, equation is $\frac{16}{x} - 1 = \frac{15}{x+1}, x \neq 0, -1$

$\Rightarrow \quad \frac{16-x}{x} = \frac{15}{x+1}$ **(1)**

$\Rightarrow \quad (16-x)(x+1) = 15x$

$\Rightarrow \quad 16x + 16 - x^2 - x = 15x$

$\Rightarrow \quad x^2 = 16$

$\Rightarrow \quad x = \pm 4$ **(1)**

**26.** Given, edge of cube = 5 cm
and diameter of hemisphere = 4.2 cm
Clearly, total surface area of the cube = 6 (Edge)$^2$

$= 6 \times 5 \times 5$

$= 150 \text{ cm}^2$ **(1/2)**

Now, area to be painted on the cube

= Total surface area of cube − Base area of hemisphere

$= 150 - \pi r^2$

$= 150 - \frac{22}{7} \times \frac{4.2}{2} \times \frac{4.2}{2}$

$= 150 - 13.86$

$= 136.14 \text{ cm}^2$ **(1)**

Area to be painted on the hemisphere

= Curved surface area of hemisphere

$= 2\pi r^2 = 2 \times \frac{22}{7} \times \frac{4.2}{2} \times \frac{4.2}{2}$

$= 27.72 \text{ cm}^2$ **(1)**

$\therefore$ Total area to be painted

= Area to be painted on the cube + Area to be painted on the hemisphere

$= 136.14 + 27.72$

$= 163.86 \text{ cm}^2$ **(1/2)**

**27.** Let the digit in unit's place be $x$ and the digit in ten's place be $y$.

Then, number $= 10y + x$

According to the given condition, $y = 3x$ ...(i)

Number obtained by reversing the digits

$= 10x + y$ **(1)**

If the number is decreased by 54, the digits are reversed.

$\Rightarrow \quad 10y + x - 54 = 10x + y$

$\Rightarrow \quad 9x - 9y = -54$

$\Rightarrow \quad x - y = -6$ ...(ii)

[dividing both sides by 9] **(1)**

On putting $y = 3x$ from Eq. (i) in Eq. (ii), we get

$x - 3x = -6$

$\Rightarrow \quad x = 3$

On putting $x = 3$ in Eq. (i), we get

$y = 9$

Hence, number $= 10y + x = 10 \times 9 + 3 = 93$ **(1)**

**28.** Let the present age of Rehman $= x$ yr

$\therefore$ Rehman's age, 3 yr ago $= (x - 3)$ yr

Rehman's age, after 5 yr $= (x + 5)$ yr

According to the question, $\frac{1}{x-3} + \frac{1}{x+5} = \frac{1}{3}$ (1)

$\Rightarrow \frac{x+5+x-3}{(x-3)(x+5)} = \frac{1}{3}$

$\Rightarrow \frac{2x+2}{x^2+2x-15} = \frac{1}{3}$

$\therefore 6x + 6 = x^2 + 2x - 15$

$\Rightarrow x^2 + 2x - 6x - 15 - 6 = 0$ (1)

$\Rightarrow x^2 - 4x - 21 = 0$

$\Rightarrow x^2 - (7x - 3x) - 21 = 0$

[by factorisation method]

$\Rightarrow x^2 - 7x + 3x - 21 = 0$

$\Rightarrow x(x-7) + 3(x-7) = 0$

$\Rightarrow (x-7)(x+3) = 0$

$\therefore x - 7 = 0 \Rightarrow x = 7$

or $x + 3 = 0 \Rightarrow x = -3$

which is not possible because age cannot be negative.

So, present age of Rehman is 7 yr. (1)

**29.** Given, $CQ = 25$ cm, $CB = 30$ cm, $CP = 10$ cm and $CA = 16$ cm

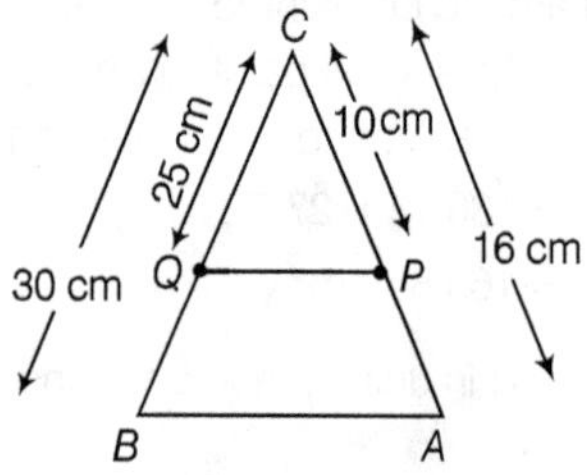


(1)

Here, $\frac{CQ}{CB} = \frac{25}{30} = \frac{5}{6}$

and $\frac{CP}{CA} = \frac{10}{16} = \frac{5}{8}$

$\Rightarrow \frac{CQ}{CB} \neq \frac{CP}{CA}$ (1)

$\Rightarrow \frac{CB}{CQ} \neq \frac{CA}{CP}$

$\Rightarrow \frac{CB}{CQ} - 1 \neq \frac{CA}{CP} - 1$

$\Rightarrow \frac{CB-CQ}{CQ} \neq \frac{CA-CP}{CP}$

$\Rightarrow \frac{QB}{CQ} \neq \frac{PA}{CP}$ or $\frac{CQ}{QB} \neq \frac{CP}{PA}$

Hence, by converse of basic proportionality theorem, $PQ$ is not parallel to $AB$. (1)

*Or*

Given, in $\Delta ABC$, $DE \parallel AC$ [given]

So, $\frac{BE}{EC} = \frac{BD}{DA}$ ...(i)

[by basic proportionality theorem]

Also, in $\Delta ABP$, $DC \parallel AP$ [given]

So, $\frac{BC}{CP} = \frac{BD}{DA}$ ...(ii) (1½)

[by basic proportionality theorem]

From Eqs. (i) and (ii), we get

$\frac{BE}{EC} = \frac{BC}{CP}$ **Hence proved.** (1½)

**30.** $\frac{\sin 30° + \tan 45° - \text{cosec } 60°}{\sec 30° + \cos 60° + \cot 45°}$

$= \frac{\frac{1}{2} + \frac{1}{1} - \frac{2}{\sqrt{3}}}{\frac{2}{\sqrt{3}} + \frac{1}{2} + 1} = \frac{\frac{\sqrt{3} + 2\sqrt{3} - 4}{2\sqrt{3}}}{\frac{4 + \sqrt{3} + 2\sqrt{3}}{2\sqrt{3}}}$

$= \frac{3\sqrt{3} - 4}{4 + 3\sqrt{3}} \times \frac{4 - 3\sqrt{3}}{4 - 3\sqrt{3}}$ (1½)

[multiply by $4 - 3\sqrt{3}$ in numerator and denominator both]

$= \frac{12\sqrt{3} - 27 - 16 + 12\sqrt{3}}{16 - 27}$

$= \frac{24\sqrt{3} - 43}{-11}$

$= \frac{43 - 24\sqrt{3}}{11}$ (1½)

*Or*

Given, in $\Delta ABC$, $\angle B = 90°$ and $AB = BC$

$\therefore \angle ACB = \angle BAC$

[angles opposite to two equal sides are equal]

In $\Delta ABC$, $\angle ABC + \angle ACB + \angle BAC = 180°$

[$\because$ sum of all angles of a triangle is 180°]

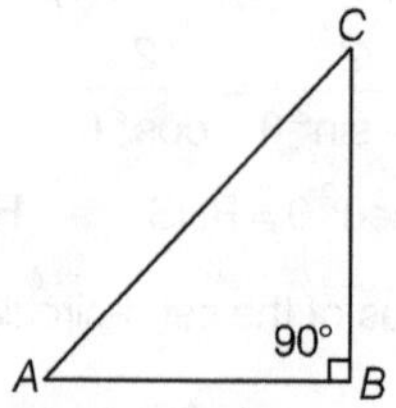


Let $\angle ACB = \angle BAC = x$

$\therefore 90° + x + x = 180°$

$\Rightarrow 2x = 90°$

$\Rightarrow x = 45°$

$\therefore \angle ACB = \angle BAC = 45°$ (1)

(i) $\sin A = \sin 45° = \frac{1}{\sqrt{2}}$ $\left[\because \sin 45° = \frac{1}{\sqrt{2}}\right]$ (1)

(ii) $\cos A = \cos 45° = \frac{1}{\sqrt{2}}$ $\left[\because \cos 45° = \frac{1}{\sqrt{2}}\right]$ (1)

**31.** Time taken by Sonia to drive one round of the field $= 18$ min

Time taken by Ravi to drive one round of the field $= 12$ min

The LCM of 18 and 12 gives the exact number of minutes after which they will meet at the starting point again.

Now, $18 = 2 \times 3 \times 3 = 2 \times 3^2$

and $12 = 2 \times 2 \times 3 = 2^2 \times 3$ (1½)

$\therefore$ LCM of 18 and 12 $= 2^2 \times 3^2$

$= 2 \times 2 \times 3 \times 3 = 36$

Hence, Sonia and Ravi will meet again at the starting point after 36 min. (1½)

**32.** Let $a$ and $d$ be the first and common difference of an AP.

Given, $a_2 = 14$ and $a_3 = 18$

$\Rightarrow a + (2-1)d = 14$ and $a + (3-1)d = 18$

$\Rightarrow a + d = 14$ ... (i)

and $a + 2d = 18$ ... (ii) (1)

On subtracting Eq. (i) from Eq. (ii), we get

$d = 18 - 14$

$\Rightarrow d = 4$ (1)

Put $d = 4$ in Eq. (i), we get

$a + 4 = 14$

$\Rightarrow a = 14 - 4 = 10$ (1)

Now, sum of first 50 terms of an AP is

$S_{50} = \frac{n}{2}[2a + (n-1)d]$

$= \frac{50}{2}[2 \times 10 + (50-1) \times 4]$

$= 25[20 + 49 \times 4]$

$= 25[20 + 196] = 25 \times 216 = 5400$ (2)

*Or*

Let $a$ and $d$ be the first term and common difference of an AP.

Given, $a_5 = 31$ and $a_{25} = 140 + a_5$

$\Rightarrow a + (5-1)d = 31$ and $a + (25-1)d = 140 + 31$

$\Rightarrow a + 4d = 31$ ... (i)

and $a + 24d = 171$ ...(ii) (1)

On subtracting Eq. (i) from Eq. (ii), we get

$20d = 171 - 31$

$\Rightarrow 20d = 140$

$\Rightarrow d = 7$ (1)

Put $d = 7$ in Eq. (i), we get

$a + 4 \times 7 = 31$

$\Rightarrow a = 31 - 28 = 3$ (1)

$\because$ The AP series is $a, a+d, a+2d, a+3d, \ldots$

i.e. $3, 3+7, 3+2\times 7, 3+3\times 7, \ldots$

or 3, 10, 17, 24, .... (2)

**33.** Here, given the frequency distributive table is not in continuous classes, so we convert it into continuous classes for finding, the median. For this, subtract 0.5 from lower limit of each class interval and add 0.5 to upper limit of each class interval as shown in the table given below (1)

| Class interval | Frequency | Cumulative frequency |
|---|---|---|
| 129.5-139.5 | 4 | 4 |
| 139.5-149.5 | 9 | 13 |
| 149.5-159.5 | 18 | 31 (*cf*) |
| 159.5-169.5 | 28 (*f*) | 59 |
| 169.5-179.5 | 24 | 83 |
| 179.5-189.5 | 10 | 93 |
| 189.5-199.5 | 7 | 100 |

(1)

Here, $n = 100$

$\Rightarrow \frac{n}{2} = \frac{100}{2} = 50$

The cumulative frequency just greater than 50 is 59 and its corresponding class is 159.5-169.5.

Now, $l = 159.5, f = 28, cf = 31$ and $h = 10$ (1)

$\therefore$ Median $= l + \left(\frac{n/2 - cf}{f}\right) \times h$

$= 159.5 + \frac{50 - 31}{28} \times 10$

$= 159.5 + \frac{19}{28} \times 10$

$= 159.5 + 6.79$

$= 166.29$ (2)

**34.** Let $AD = 1.2$ m be the height of girl standing on the horizontal line $AB$ and let $FH = EB = 88.2$ m be the height of balloon from the line $AB$.

At the eyes of the girl, the angles of elevation are $\angle FDC = 60°$ and $\angle EDC = 30°$.

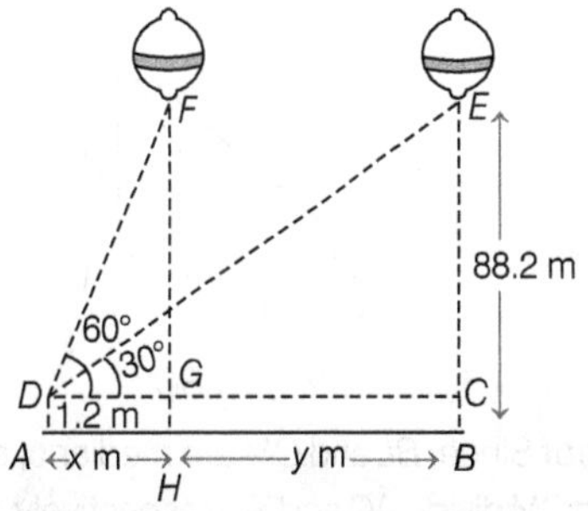


Now, $FG = EC = 88.2 - 1.2 = 87$ m (1)

Let the distance travelled by the balloon,

$HB = y$ m

and $AH = x$ m.

$\therefore DG = AH = x$ m

and $GC = HB = y$ m

In right angled $\Delta FGD$,

$$\tan 60^\circ = \frac{FG}{DG}$$

$$\Rightarrow \quad \sqrt{3} = \frac{87}{x} \quad [\because \tan 60^\circ = \sqrt{3}]$$

$$\Rightarrow \quad x = \frac{87}{\sqrt{3}} \quad \ldots(i)\ (1)$$

In right angled $\Delta ECD$,

$$\tan 30^\circ = \frac{EC}{DC}$$

$$\Rightarrow \quad \frac{1}{\sqrt{3}} = \frac{87}{DG + GC}$$

$$\left[\because \tan 30^\circ = \frac{1}{\sqrt{3}} \text{ and } DC = DG + GC\right]$$

$$\Rightarrow \quad \frac{1}{\sqrt{3}} = \frac{87}{x+y} \quad (1)$$

$$\Rightarrow \quad x + y = 87\sqrt{3} \quad \ldots(ii)$$

On putting $x = \frac{87}{\sqrt{3}}$ from Eq. (i) in Eq. (ii), we get

$$\frac{87}{\sqrt{3}} + y = 87\sqrt{3}$$

$$\Rightarrow \quad y = 87\left(\sqrt{3} - \frac{1}{\sqrt{3}}\right) \quad (1)$$

$$\Rightarrow \quad y = \frac{87\,(3-1)}{\sqrt{3}}$$

$$= \frac{87 \times 2}{\sqrt{3}} \times \frac{\sqrt{3}}{\sqrt{3}}$$

$$= \frac{87 \times 2\sqrt{3}}{3} \quad \text{[rationalising]}$$

$$= 29 \times 2\sqrt{3}$$

$$= 58\sqrt{3}\text{ m}$$

Hence, the distance travelled by the balloon during the interval is $58\sqrt{3}$ m. (1)

**35.** **Given** $BL$ and $CM$ are medians of $\Delta ABC$ right angled at $A$.

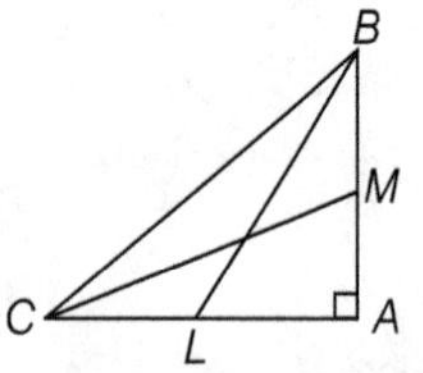


**To show** $4(BL^2 + CM^2) = 5BC^2$

**Proof** Since, $BL$ and $CM$ are medians, so the lines $BL$ and $CM$ divide $AC$ and $AB$ respectively, into two equal parts.

$$\therefore \quad CL = AL = \frac{AC}{2} \quad \ldots(i)$$

$$\text{and} \quad AM = BM = \frac{AB}{2} \quad \ldots(ii)$$

In $\Delta BAC$, $\angle A = 90^\circ$ (1)

Using Pythagoras theorem, we get

$$BC^2 = AB^2 + AC^2 \quad \ldots(iii)$$

In $\Delta BAL$, $\angle A = 90^\circ$

Using Pythagoras theorem, we get

$$BL^2 = AB^2 + AL^2 \quad (1)$$

$$\Rightarrow \quad BL^2 = AB^2 + \left(\frac{AC}{2}\right)^2 \quad \text{[from Eq. (i)]}$$

$$\Rightarrow \quad BL^2 = AB^2 + \frac{AC^2}{4} \quad (1)$$

$$\Rightarrow \quad 4BL^2 = 4AB^2 + AC^2 \quad \ldots(iv)$$

In $\Delta MAC$, $\angle A = 90^\circ$

Using Pythagoras theorem, we get

$$CM^2 = AC^2 + AM^2$$

$$\Rightarrow \quad CM^2 = AC^2 + \left(\frac{AB}{2}\right)^2 \quad \text{[from Eq. (ii)]}$$

$$\Rightarrow \quad 4CM^2 = 4AC^2 + AB^2 \quad \ldots(v)\ (1)$$

On adding Eqs. (iv) and (v), we get

$$4(BL^2 + CM^2) = 5(AC^2 + AB^2)$$

$$\Rightarrow \quad 4(BL^2 + CM^2) = 5\,BC^2 \quad \text{[from Eq. (iii)]}$$

**Hence proved.** (1)

*Or*

**Given** $\Delta ABC$ is a right angled triangle, $\angle B = 90^\circ$ and $BD = DC$.

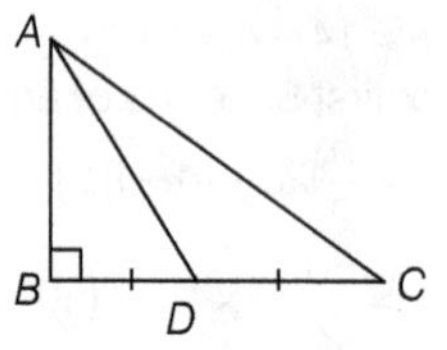


(1)

**To show** $AC^2 = 4AD^2 - 3AB^2$.

**Proof** In $\Delta ABC$,

$$AC^2 = AB^2 + BC^2$$

[by Pythagoras theorem] ...(i) (1)

Now, $BD = DC$ [given]

$$\therefore \quad BD = DC = \frac{1}{2}BC \Rightarrow BC = 2BD \quad \ldots(ii)$$

Put $BC = 2BD$ in Eq. (i), we get

$$AC^2 = AB^2 + (2BD)^2 = AB^2 + 4BD^2$$

$$\Rightarrow \quad 4BD^2 = AC^2 - AB^2 \quad \ldots(iii)\ (1)$$

In $\Delta ABD$,

$$AD^2 = AB^2 + BD^2$$

$$\Rightarrow \quad BD^2 = AD^2 - AB^2 \quad \ldots(iv)$$

$$\Rightarrow \quad 4BD^2 = 4AD^2 - 4AB^2$$

From Eqs. (iii) and (iv), we get

$$AC^2 = AB^2 + 4AD^2 - 4AB^2$$

$$\Rightarrow \quad AC^2 = AB^2 + 4AD^2 - 4AB^2$$

$$\therefore \quad AC^2 = 4AD^2 - 3AB^2$$ **Hence proved.** (2)

**36.** (i) The coordinates of $A$ are (3, 5).

(ii) $AE = 6 - 3 = 3$ units

and $EC = 11 - 6 = 5$ units

$\therefore$ Required ratio $= \frac{AE}{EC} = \frac{3}{5}$

(iii) Coordinates of $D$ are (7, 1)

and coordinates of $A$ are (3, 5)

$\therefore AD = \sqrt{(7-3)^2 + (1-5)^2}$

$= \sqrt{16+16}$

$= \sqrt{32} = 4\sqrt{2}$ units

*Or*

Coordinates of $C$ are (11, 5)

and coordinates of $D$ are (7, 1).

$\therefore$ Coordinates of mid-point of $DC$

$$= \left(\frac{11+7}{2}, \frac{5+1}{2}\right) = (9, 3)$$

**37.** (i) From the figure,

Area of the region having blue colour

$$= \frac{80^\circ}{360^\circ}\pi(10)^2 - \frac{80^\circ}{360^\circ} \times \pi(6)^2$$

$$= \frac{80^\circ}{360^\circ} \times \frac{22}{7} \times [(10)^2 - (6)^2]$$

$$= \frac{80^\circ}{360^\circ} \times \frac{22}{7} \times 16 \times 4$$

$[\because a^2 - b^2 = (a+b)(a-b)]$

$$= \frac{112640}{2520}$$

$= 44.69 \text{cm}^2$

(ii) Similarly,

Area of the region having black colour

$$= \frac{40^\circ}{360^\circ} \times \frac{22}{7} \times 16 \times 4$$

$$= \frac{56320}{2520} = 22.34 \text{cm}^2$$

(iii) Similarly,

Perimeter of the region having pink colour
$= 2(10 - 6)$ + length of arc having radius 6 cm
+ length of arc having radius 10 cm.

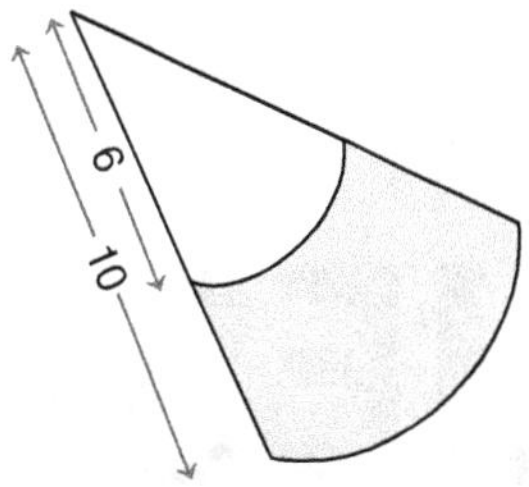


$$= 8 + \frac{30^\circ}{360^\circ} \times 2 \times \frac{22}{7} \times 6 + \frac{30^\circ}{360^\circ} \times 2 \times \frac{22}{7} \times 10$$

$$= 8 + \frac{7920}{2520} + \frac{13200}{2520}$$

$= 8 + 3.142 + 5.238 = 16.38$ cm

*Or*

Total angle $= 80^\circ + 40^\circ + 30^\circ = 150^\circ$

$\therefore$ Area of the region

$$= \frac{150^\circ}{360^\circ} \times \frac{22}{7} \times 6 \times 6$$

$$= \frac{118{,}800}{2520} = 47.14 \text{cm}^2$$

**38.** (i) Wire is bent in the shape of parabola.

(ii) Since, graph intersects $X$-axis at points 1 and 3, so zeroes are 1 and 3.

(iii) Expression of the polynomial,

$$p(x) = (x-1)(x-3)$$

$$= x^2 - 3x - x + 3 = x^2 - 4x + 3$$

*Or*

Given, polynomial is $3x^2 + 8x + k$

Let one zero of given polynomial is $\alpha$, then other zero will be $\frac{1}{\alpha}$.

$\because$ Product of zeroes $= \frac{\text{Constant term}}{\text{Coefficient of } x^2}$

$\therefore \quad \alpha \times \frac{1}{\alpha} = \frac{k}{3}$

$\Rightarrow \quad k = 3$

# SAMPLE QUESTION PAPER 7

## Mathematics (Basic)

Time : **3 hrs** Max. Marks : **80**

### Instructions

1. This question paper has 5 Sections A, B, C, D and E.
2. Section A has 20 Multiple Choice Questions (MCQs) carrying 1 mark each.
3. Section B has 5 Short Answer-I (SA-I) Type Questions carrying 2 marks each.
4. Section C has 6 Short Answer-II (SA-II) Type Questions carrying 3 marks each.
5. Section D has 4 Long Answer (LA) Type Questions carrying 5 marks each.
6. Section E has 3 Case Based integrated units of assessment (4 marks each) with sub-parts of the values of 1, 1 and 2 marks each respectively.
7. All questions are compulsory. However, an internal choice in 2 questions of 2 marks, 2 questions of 3 marks and 2 questions of 5 marks has been provided. An internal choice has been provided in the 2 marks questions of Section E.
8. Draw neat figures wherever required. Take $\pi = 22/7$ wherever required if not stated.

## Section-A

**Section A consists of 20 questions of 1 mark each**

**1.** If HCF of 306 and 657 is 9, then the LCM is

(a) 19428 (b) 27352
(c) 22338 (d) None of these

**2.** A point $P$ is 13 cm from the centre of the circle. The length of the tangent drawn from $P$ to the circle is 12 cm. Then, the radius of the circle is

(a) 3 cm (b) 5 cm (c) 9 cm (d) 7 cm

**3.** The prime factorisation of 351 is

(a) $3^3 \times 13$ (b) $3^3$ (c) $3^2 \times 5$ (d) $3^2 \times 5^2$

**4.** A standard deck of 52 cards is shuffled. Ritu draws a single card from the deck at random. The probability that the card is jack, is

(a) $\frac{1}{2}$ (b) $\frac{1}{52}$
(c) $\frac{3}{52}$ (d) $\frac{1}{13}$

**5.** If $d_i = x_i - 20$, $\Sigma f_i d_i = 300$ and $\Sigma f_i = 40$, then the value of $\bar{x}$ is

(a) 20.3 (b) 32 (c) 27.5 (d) 22.9

**6.** The discriminant of the quadratic equation $6x^2 - 7x + 2 = 0$ is

(a) $\sqrt{41}$ (b) $\frac{1}{12}$
(c) 5 (d) None of these

**7.** The first term of an AP is −7 and the common difference is 5. Its 18th term is

(a) 97 (b) 92
(c) 83 (d) 78

**8.** $C$ is the mid-point of $PQ$, if $P$ is $(4, x)$, $C$ is $(y, -1)$ and $Q$ is $(-2, 4)$, then $x$ and $y$ respectively are

(a) − 6 and 1 (b) − 6 and 2
(c) 6 and − 1 (d) 6 and − 2

**9.** The radius of a wheel is 0.25 m. The number of approximate revolutions it will make to travel a distance of 11 km, is

(a) 5000 (b) 7000
(c) 6000 (d) 1000

**10.** If 2 is a zero of polynomial $f(x) = 4x^2 + 4x - 4a$, then the value of $a$ is

(a) 6 (b) 2 (c) 4 (d) 8

**11.** The value of $x$ in the given figure is

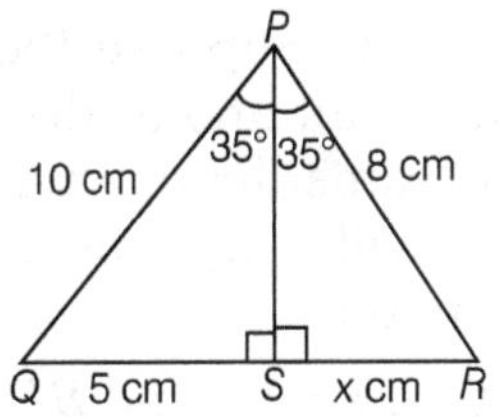


(a) 5 cm (b) 4 cm
(c) 2 cm (d) 3 cm

**12.** The coordinates of the point which divides the line segment joining the points (4, − 3) and (8, 5) in the ratio 1 : 3 internally are

(a) (4, 3) (b) (7, 3) (c) (3, 5) (d) (5, − 1)

**13.** If $\tan(3x + 30°) = 1$, then the value of $x$ is

(a) 3 (b) 5 (c) 10 (d) 0

**14.** If a pair of linear equations is consistent, then the lines will be

(a) always coincident
(b) parallel
(c) always intersecting
(d) intersecting or coincident

**15.** The LCM and HCF of two non-zero positive numbers are equal, then the numbers must be

(a) prime (b) coprime
(c) composite (d) equal

**16.** The mean of the following distribution is

| $x_i$ | 12 | 14 | 18 | 20 |
|---|---|---|---|---|
| $f_i$ | 3 | 5 | 8 | 7 |

(a) 19.5 (b) 18 (c) 16.95 (d) 15.24

**17.** A fair dice is rolled. Probability of getting a number greater than 3 is

(a) 0 (b) $\frac{1}{3}$ (c) $\frac{1}{4}$ (d) $\frac{1}{2}$

**18.** If $2\cos 3\theta = \sqrt{3}$, then the value of $\theta$ is

(a) 60° (b) 30° (c) 10° (d) 15°

**Directions** *In the question number 19 and 20, a statement of Assertion (A) is followed by a statement of Reason (R). Choose the correct option.*

**19.** **Assertion (A)** A coin is tossed 30 times and head appears 20 times. Then, the probability of getting a tail is $\frac{1}{3}$.

**Reason (R)** Probability of happening of an event = Number of trials in which the event happened / Total number of trials.

(a) Both Assertion (A) and Reason (R) are true and Reason (R) is the correct explanation of Assertion (A)
(b) Both Assertion (A) and Reason (R) are true but Reason (R) is not the correct explanation of Assertion (A)
(c) Assertion (A) is true but Reason (R) is false
(d) Assertion (A) is false but Reason (R) is true

**20.** **Assertion (A)** If $S_n$ is the sum of the first $n$ terms of an AP, then its $n$th term is given by $a_n = S_n - S_{n-1}$.

**Reason (R)** The 8th term of the AP : 3, 8, 13, ..., is 43.

(a) Both Assertion (A) and Reason (R) are true and Reason (R) is the correct explanation of Assertion (A)
(b) Both Assertion (A) and Reason (R) are true but Reason (R) is not the correct explanation of Assertion (A)
(c) Assertion (A) is true but Reason (R) is false
(d) Assertion (A) is false but Reason (R) is true

# Section-B

**Section B consists of 5 questions of 2 marks each**

**21.** Two dice are thrown simultaneously. Find the probability of getting a multiple of 2 on one die and a multiple of 3 on the other die.

*Or* Suppose you drop a die at random on the rectangular region shown in figure.

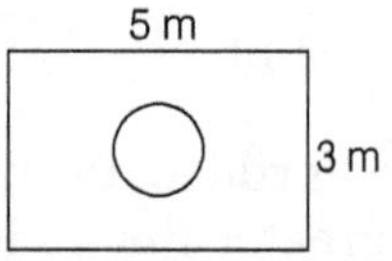


What is the probability that it will land inside the circle of diameter 2 m?

**22.** Prove that $(1+\tan^2\theta)(1+\sin\theta)(1-\sin\theta)=1$.

*Or*

Determine the value of $x$, such that $2\operatorname{cosec}^2 30^\circ + x\sin^2 60^\circ - \frac{3}{4}\tan^2 30^\circ = 10$.

**23.** If the 3rd and 9th terms of an AP are 4 and $-8$ respectively, which term of this AP is zero?

**24.** The quadratic equation $x^2-3x+p=0$ has distinct real roots, then find the value of $p$.

**25.** If two tangents inclined at an angle of 60° are drawn to a circle of radius 5 cm, then find the length of each tangent.

# Section-C

**Section C consists of 6 questions of 3 marks each**

**26.** In the given figure $AOB$ is a flower bed in the shape of a sector of a circle of radius 80 m and $\angle AOB = 60^\circ$. Also a 30 m wide concrete track is made as shown in the figure.

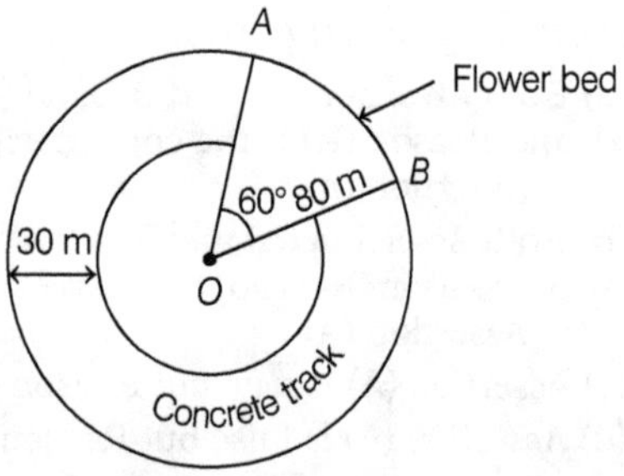


Two friends Vicky and Love went to the concrete track. Love said that area of the track is 10205 m$^2$. Is he right? Explain.

**27.** Prove that

$$\sin\theta(1+\tan\theta)+\cos\theta(1+\cot\theta) = \sec\theta + \operatorname{cosec}\theta$$

*Or* If $\sin\theta+\cos\theta=\sqrt{3}$, then prove that $\tan\theta+\cot\theta=1$.

**28.** Prove that $\sqrt{3}$ is an irrational.

*Or*

There is a circular path around a sports field, Sania takes 18 min to drive one round of the field, while Ravi takes 12 min for the same. Suppose they both start at the same point and at the same time and go in the same direction. After how many minutes will they meet again at the starting point?

**29.** In $\Delta ABC$, $\angle B = 90^\circ$ and $BD \perp AC$. If $AC = 10$ cm and $AD = 4$ cm, then find the value of $BD$.

**30.** In the given figure, $PP'$ and $QQ'$ are the two common tangents of the two circles. Show that $PP' = QQ'$.

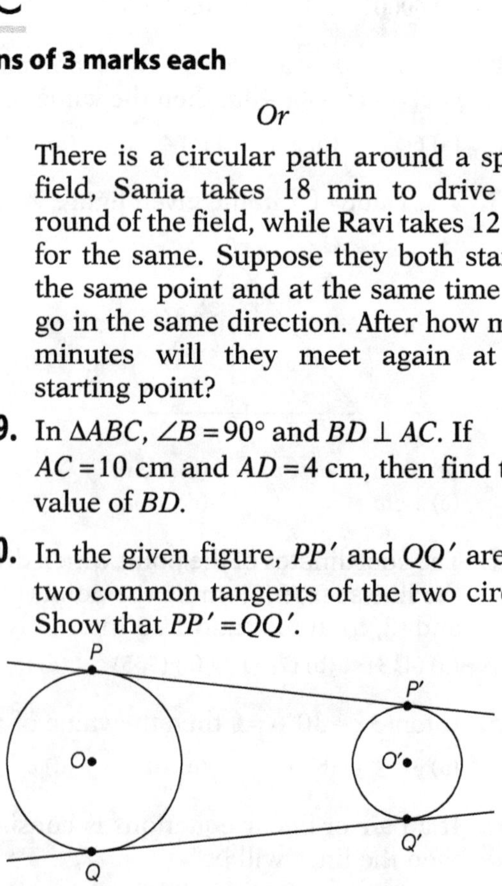


**31.** Solve for $x$, $2\left(\frac{2x+3}{x-3}\right) - 25\left(\frac{x-3}{2x+3}\right) = 5$.

# Section-D

**Section D consists of 4 questions of 5 marks each**

**32.** A tent is in the form of a cylinder on which a cone is surmounted. If height and diameter of cylindrical portion are 2.1 m and 4 m and slant height of cone is 2.8 m, find the area of used canvas in making this tent. Also, find the volume of air within tent.

*Or*

From a solid cylinder whose height is 12 cm and diameter is 10 cm, a conical cavity of same height and same diameter is hollowed out. Find the volume and total surface area of the remaining solid.

**33.** From the top of a 7m high building the angle of elevation of the top of a cable tower is 60° and the angle of depression of its foot is 45°. Determine the height of the tower.

**34.** The following table shows the age distribution of cases of a certain disease admitted during a year in a particular hospital.

| Age (in years) | 5-14 | 15-24 | 25-34 | 35-44 | 45-54 | 55-64 | Total |
|---|---|---|---|---|---|---|---|
| Number of cases | 6 | 11 | 21 | 23 | 14 | 5 | 80 |

Find the modal age.

*Or*

If the median of the distribution given below is 30, find the values of $x$ and $y$.

| Class interval | 0-10 | 10-20 | 20-30 | 30-40 | 40-50 | 50-60 | Total |
|---|---|---|---|---|---|---|---|
| Number of students | 5 | $x$ | 20 | 15 | $y$ | 5 | 60 |

**35.** In the given figure, $AD$ is the bisector of $\angle BAC$ of $\Delta ABC$.

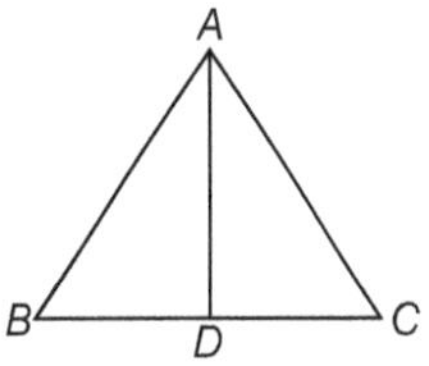


Prove that $\frac{BD}{DC} = \frac{AB}{AC}$.

# Section-E

**Case study based questions are compulsory**

**36.** Vikas is working with TCS and he is sincere and dedicated to his work. He pay all his taxes on time and invest the some amount of his salary in funds for his future.

He invested some amount at the rate of 12% simple interest and some other amount at the rate of 10% simple interest. He received yearly interest of ₹ 130. But, if he interchange the amounts invested, he would have received ₹ 4 more as interest.

On the basis of above information, answer the following questions.

(i) Consider the amount invested at 12% be $p$ and at 10% be $q$. Then, formulate the required linear equation for first condition. (1)

(ii) Now, formulate the linear equation for the second condition? (1)

(iii) Find the value of $p$ and $q$. (2)

*Or* Draw the graph of the two equations that are formed. (2)

**37.** A teacher of class X draw the three graphs of a quadratic polynomials on the board as shown below.

I.

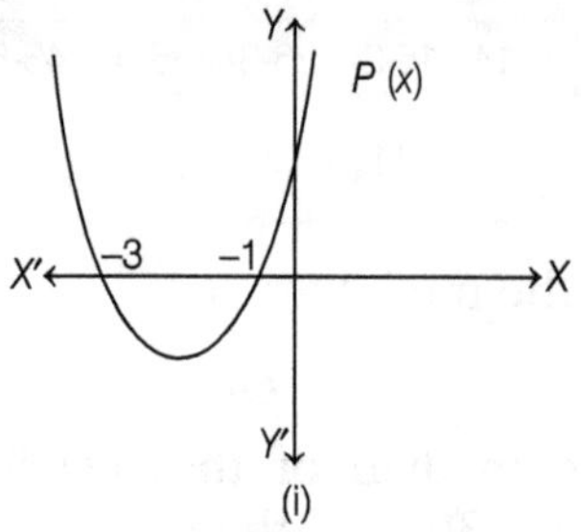


II.

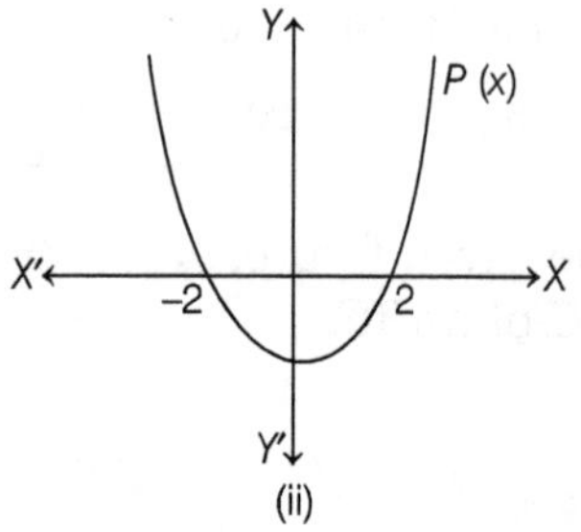


III.

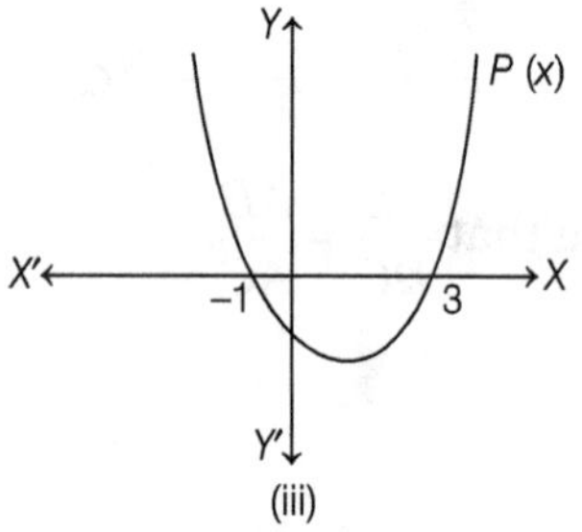


Answer the following questions which are based on the above graphs.

(i) Write the zeroes of polynomial $P(x)$ in graph I. (1)

(ii) Write zeroes of polynomial $P(x)$ in graph II. (1)

(iii) Write the polynomial $P(x)$ for graph (I). (2)

*Or* Find the value of $(a+b)$ for which $p(x) = x^2 + ax - b$ in graph (III). (2)

**38.** Walking is a good habit for human beings to improve health and stamina. In this order Ayush starts walking from his house to office. Instead of going to the office directly he goes to bank first, from there he leaves his daughter to school and then reaches the office, [assume that all distances covered are in straight lines] if the house is situated at (2, 4), bank at (5, 8), school at (13, 14) and office at (13, 26) and the coordinates are in kilometre.

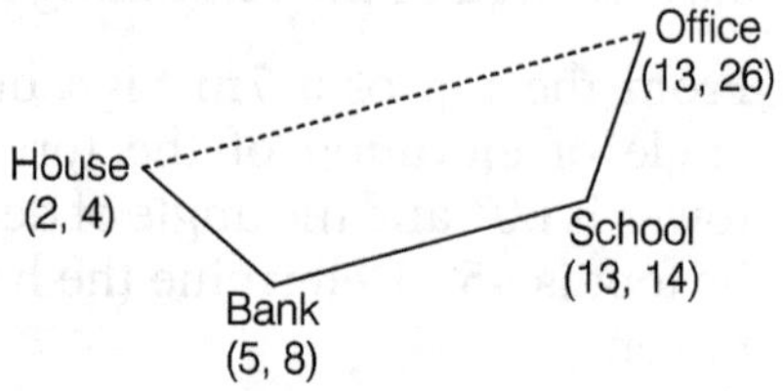


On the basis of above information, answer the following questions.

(i) Find the distance between bank and office. (1)

(ii) Find the shortest distance between house and office. (1)

(iii) Find the extra distance travelled by Ayush in reaching his office. (2)

*Or*

If on the shortest path from house to office, a point divides the path in the ratio 4 : 3. Find the coordinates of that point. (2)

# SOLUTIONS

**1.** (c) Given, HCF of 306 and 657 = 9

We know that

LCM × HCF = Product of two numbers

$\Rightarrow \quad LCM \times 9 = 306 \times 657$

$\Rightarrow \quad LCM = \dfrac{306 \times 657}{9} = 34 \times 657 = 22338$

$\therefore$ LCM of 306 and 657 = 22338

**2.** (b) Since, tangent to a circle is perpendicular to the radius through the point of contact.

$\therefore \quad \angle OTP = 90°$

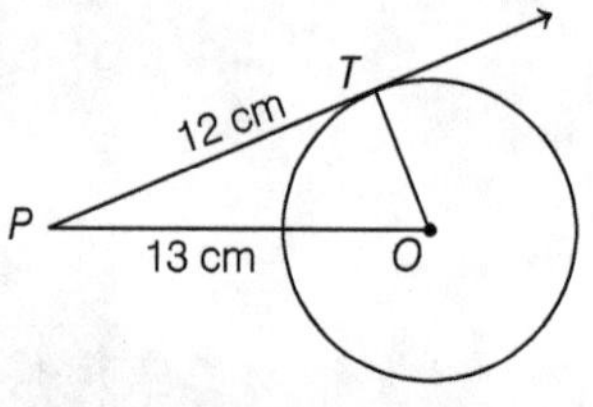


In right angled $\Delta OTP$, we have

$OP^2 = OT^2 + PT^2 \Rightarrow 13^2 = OT^2 + 12^2$

$\Rightarrow \quad OT^2 = 13^2 - 12^2 = (13-12)(13+12) = 25$

$\Rightarrow \quad OT = 5\,cm$

**3.** (a) We have, $351 = 3 \times 3 \times 3 \times 13$

$\therefore \quad 351 = 3^3 \times 13$

**4.** (d) Number of possible outcomes in a deck of cards $= 52$

Number of favourable outcomes to the events of selecting a jack = 4

$\therefore$ Required probability

$$= \frac{\text{Number of favourable to the events}}{\text{Number of possible outcomes}}$$

$$= \frac{4}{52} = \frac{1}{13}$$

**5.** (c) Given, $\Sigma f_i d_i = 300$, $\Sigma f_i = 40$ and $d_i = x_i - 20$

We know that $d_i = x_i - a$

On comparing, we get $a = 20$

$$\therefore \quad \bar{x} = a + \left\{\frac{\Sigma f_i d_i}{\Sigma f_i}\right\}$$

$$= 20 + \frac{300}{40}$$

$$= 20 + \frac{30}{4} = 20 + 7.5 = 27.5$$

**6.** (d) Given, $6x^2 - 7x + 2 = 0$ ...(i)

On comparing Eq. (i) with $ax^2 + bx + c = 0$, we get

$a = 6, b = -7$ and $c = 2$

We know that $D = b^2 - 4ac = (-7)^2 - 4(6)(2)$

$= 49 - 48 = 1$

Hence, the value of discriminant is 1.

**7.** (d) We have, $a$ = first term $= -7$ and $d = 5$

$\therefore \quad a_{18} = a + (18 - 1)d \quad [\because a_n = a + (n-1)d]$

$\Rightarrow \quad a_{18} = a + 17d$

$= -7 + 17 \times 5$

$= -7 + 85 = 78$

**8.** (a) Given, $C$ is the mid-point of $PQ$ i.e. $P(4, x)$ and $Q(-2, 4)$.

Therefore, $(y, -1) = \left(\frac{4-2}{2}, \frac{x+4}{2}\right)$

$\Rightarrow \quad (y, -1) = \left(1, \frac{x+4}{2}\right)$

On equating the coordinates, we get

$y = 1$ and $-1 = \frac{x+4}{2}$

$\therefore \quad x = -6$ and $y = 1$

**9.** (b) The distance covered in one revolution is equal to the circumference of the wheel.

$\because$ Circumference of wheel $= 2\pi r$

$$= 2 \times \frac{22}{7} \times 0.25 = \frac{11}{7}$$

$\therefore$ Number of revolutions

$$= \frac{\text{Distance covered by wheel}}{\text{Circumference of wheel}}$$

$$= \frac{11 \times 1000}{11/7} = 7000$$

**10.** (a) Given, polynomial is $f(x) = 4x^2 + 4x - 4a$.

Since, 2 is a zero of the given polynomial.

$\therefore \quad f(2) = 0$

$\Rightarrow \quad 4(2)^2 + 4(2) - 4a = 0 \quad$ [putting $x = 2$]

$\Rightarrow \quad 16 + 8 - 4a = 0$

$\Rightarrow \quad 4a = 24$

$\Rightarrow \quad a = \frac{24}{4} = 6$

**11.** (b) In $\Delta PSQ$ and $\Delta PSR$,

$\angle QPS = \angle SPR = 35°$

$\angle PSQ = \angle PSR \quad [\because PS \perp QR]$

From AA similarity,

$\Delta PSQ \sim \Delta PSR$

$\therefore \quad \frac{PQ}{PR} = \frac{SQ}{SR}$

$\Rightarrow \quad \frac{10}{8} = \frac{5}{x} \Rightarrow x = 4\text{ cm}$

**12.** (d) Given, $(x_1, y_1) = (4, -3)$ and $(x_2, y_2) = (8, 5)$

Let $(x, y)$ be the coordinates of the point which divides the line joining the points $(x_1, y_1)$ and $(x_2, y_2)$ in ratio $m : n = 1 : 3$ internally.

So, $(x, y) = \left(\frac{mx_2 + nx_1}{m+n}, \frac{my_2 + ny_1}{m+n}\right)$

$$= \left(\frac{1(8) + 3(4)}{1+3}, \frac{1(5) + 3(-3)}{1+3}\right)$$

$$= \left(\frac{20}{4}, \frac{-4}{4}\right) = (5, -1)$$

**13.** (b) We have, $\tan(3x + 30°) = 1$

$\Rightarrow \quad \tan(3x + 30°) = \tan 45° \quad [\because \tan 45° = 1]$

$\Rightarrow \quad 3x + 30° = 45°$

$\Rightarrow \quad 3x = 45° - 30° = 15°$

$\Rightarrow \quad x = 5°$

**14.** (d) If a pair of linear equations is consistent, then it has unique solution or infinitely solutions.

For unique solution,

$$\frac{a_1}{a_2} \neq \frac{b_1}{b_2}$$

$\therefore$ The lines will be intersecting.

For infinitely solutions,

$$\frac{a_1}{a_2} = \frac{b_1}{b_2} = \frac{c_1}{c_2}$$

$\therefore$ The lines will be coincident.

**15.** (d) Given, LCM and HCF are equal.
Let two non-zero positive numbers are $p$ and $q$.
Then, HCF $(p, q) =$ LCM $(p, q)$ [given]
Let HCF $(p, q) = k$

$\Rightarrow \quad p = ka$ and $q = kb$

where, $a$ and $b$ are natural numbers.

$\because$ HCF $\times$ LCM = product of numbers

$$k \times k = ka \times kb \Rightarrow a \times b = 1$$

$\therefore a = b = 1$, as they are natural numbers.
Hence, $p = q$ or the number must be equal.

**16.** (c) $\Sigma f_i x_i = 3\times12 + 5\times14 + 8\times18 + 7\times20$

$= 36 + 70 + 144 + 140$

$= 390$

$\therefore$ Mean $= \dfrac{\Sigma f_i x_i}{\Sigma f_i} = \dfrac{390}{3+5+8+7}$

$= \dfrac{390}{23} = 16.95$

**17.** (d) Favourable outcomes = 4, 5, 6
Total number of outcomes = 6

$\therefore \quad P = \dfrac{3}{6} = \dfrac{1}{2}$

**18.** (c) We have, $2\cos 3\theta = \sqrt{3}$

$\Rightarrow \quad \cos 3\theta = \dfrac{\sqrt{3}}{2}$

$\Rightarrow \quad \cos 3\theta = \cos 30° \quad \left[\because \cos 30° = \dfrac{\sqrt{3}}{2}\right]$

$\Rightarrow \quad 3\theta = 30°$

$\because 3\theta$ and $30°$ are acute angles.

$\therefore \quad \theta = 10°$

**19.** (a) Total number of times in which tail appeared $= 30 - 20 = 10$

$\therefore$ Probability of getting a tail $= \dfrac{10}{30} = \dfrac{1}{3}$

So, the given Assertion is true.
Also, the given Reason is also true and it is the correct explanation of Assertion.

**20.** (c) $n$th term of an AP is given by

$$a_n = a + (n-1)d$$

Sum of $n$ terms of an AP

$$S_n = \frac{n}{2}[2a + (n-1)d] \quad \text{...(i)}$$

Sum of $n-1$ terms of an AP

$$S_{n-1} = \frac{n-1}{2}[2a + (n-2)d] \quad \text{...(ii)}$$

On subtracting Eq. (ii) from Eq. (i), we get

$$S_n - S_{n-1} = \frac{n}{2}[2a + (n-1)d] - \frac{n-1}{2}[2a + (n-2)d]$$

$$= na + \frac{n}{2}(n-1)d - (n-1)a - \frac{(n-1)(n-2)d}{2}$$

$$= a[n-(n-1)] + \frac{(n-1)d}{2}[n-(n-2)]$$

$$= a(1) + \frac{(n-1)d}{2}(2) = a + (n-1)d = a_n$$

$\therefore$ The given Assertion is true.
Now, for AP 3, 8, 13, ...

$a = 3$ and $d = 5$

$a_8 = 3 + (8-1)5 = 3 + 7\times5 = 38 \neq 43$

So, the given Reason is false.

**21.** Here, two dice are thrown, so possible outcomes are

(1, 1), (1, 2), (1, 3), (1, 4), (1, 5), (1, 6)
(2, 1), (2, 2), (2, 3), (2, 4), (2, 5), (2, 6)
(3, 1), (3, 2), (3, 3), (3, 4), (3, 5), (3, 6)
(4, 1), (4, 2), (4, 3), (4, 4), (4, 5), (4, 6)
(5, 1), (5, 2), (5, 3), (5, 4), (5, 5), (5, 6)
(6, 1), (6, 2), (6, 3), (6, 4), (6, 5) and (6, 6)

$\therefore$ Total number of outcomes = 36 (1)

Let $E$ = Event of getting a multiple of 2 on one die and a multiple of 3 on the other die.
Here, multiples of 2 are 2, 4 and 6 and multiples of 3 are 3 and 6.
So, favourable outcomes for event $E$ are (2, 3), (4, 3), (6, 3), (2, 6), (4, 6), (6, 6), (3, 2), (3, 4), (3, 6), (6, 2) and (6, 4).

$\therefore$ Number of outcomes favourable to $E = 11$

$\therefore$ Required probability $= P(E)$

$= \dfrac{\text{Number of favourable outcomes to } E}{\text{Total number of outcomes}} = \dfrac{11}{36}$ (1)

*Or*

Area of rectangle $= 5\times3 = 15\,\text{m}^2$

and area of circle of radius 1 m $= \pi(1)^2 = \pi\,\text{m}^2$

$\left[\because \text{diameter} = 2\text{m} \Rightarrow \text{radius} = \dfrac{2}{2} = 1\text{m}\right]$ (1)

Now, probability that the die land inside the circle

$= \dfrac{\pi}{15}$ (1)

**22.** LHS $= (1 + \tan^2\theta)(1 + \sin\theta)(1 - \sin\theta)$

$= (1 + \tan^2\theta)(1 - \sin^2\theta)$ (1)

$= \sec^2\theta \times \cos^2\theta$

$[\because \sec^2\theta - \tan^2\theta = 1 \text{ and } \sin^2\theta + \cos^2\theta = 1]$

$= \dfrac{\cos^2\theta}{\cos^2\theta} = 1 \quad \left[\because \sec\theta = \dfrac{1}{\cos\theta}\right]$

**Hence proved.** (1)

*Or*

Given, $2\operatorname{cosec}^2 30° + x\sin^2 60° - \dfrac{3}{4}\tan^2 30° = 10$

$\Rightarrow \quad 2(2)^2 + x\left(\dfrac{\sqrt{3}}{2}\right)^2 - \dfrac{3}{4}\left(\dfrac{1}{\sqrt{3}}\right)^2 = 10$

$\left[\because \operatorname{cosec} 30° = 2, \sin 60° = \dfrac{\sqrt{3}}{2} \text{ and } \tan 30° = \dfrac{1}{\sqrt{3}}\right]$

$\Rightarrow \quad 8+\frac{3x}{4}-\frac{3}{4}\times\frac{1}{3}=10$

$\Rightarrow \quad 8+\frac{3x}{4}-\frac{1}{4}=10$

$\Rightarrow \quad \frac{3x}{4}=10+\frac{1}{4}-8$ (1)

$\Rightarrow \quad \frac{3x}{4}=2+\frac{1}{4}$

$\Rightarrow \quad \frac{3x}{4}=\frac{8+1}{4}$

$\Rightarrow \quad \frac{3x}{4}=\frac{9}{4}$

$\Rightarrow \quad 3x=9$

$\therefore \quad x=3$ (1)

**23.** Let $a$ be the first term and $d$ be the common difference of an AP.

$\because$ The $n$ th term of an AP is $a_n = a+(n-1)d$

$\therefore \quad a_3 = a+2d \Rightarrow a+2d=4$

[$\because a_3 = 4$ (given)] ...(i)

and $\quad a_9 = a+8d \Rightarrow a+8d=-8$

[$\because a_9 = -8$ (given)] ...(ii)

On subtracting Eq. (i) from Eq. (ii), we get

$6d=-12$

$\Rightarrow \quad d=\frac{-12}{6}=-2$

$\therefore$ From Eq. (i), $a+2\times(-2)=4$

$\Rightarrow \quad a-4=4$

$\Rightarrow \quad a=4+4=8$ (1)

Let the $n$th term of an AP is zero.

Then, $\quad a_n=0$

$\Rightarrow \quad a+(n-1)d=0$

$\Rightarrow \quad 8+(n-1)(-2)=0$

$\Rightarrow \quad (n-1)(-2)=-8$

$\Rightarrow \quad n-1=\frac{-8}{-2}=4$

$\Rightarrow \quad n=4+1=5$

Hence, 5th term of an AP is zero. (1)

**24.** Given quadratic equation is $x^2-3x+p=0$

On comparing with $ax^2+bx+c=0$, we get

$a=1, b=-3$ and $c=p$

The condition for distinct real roots is

$b^2-4ac>0$ (1)

$\Rightarrow \quad (-3)^2-4(1)(p)>0$

$\Rightarrow \quad 9-4p>0$

$\Rightarrow \quad 9>4p$

$\Rightarrow \quad 4p<9$

$\Rightarrow \quad p<\frac{9}{4}$ (1)

**25.** In the given figure, $OA = 5$ cm and $\angle APB = 60°$

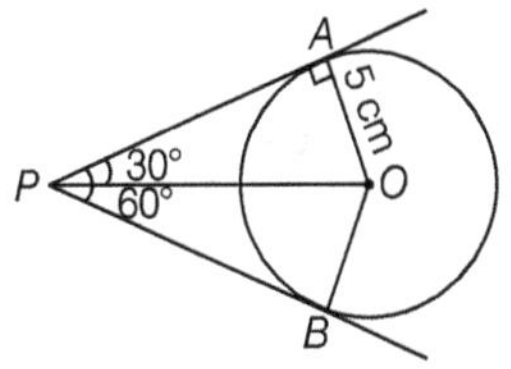


(1)

In $\Delta APO$, $\quad \angle PAO = 90°$

[$\because$ the tangent at any point of a circle is perpendicular to the radius through the point of contact]

Since, $\quad \angle APB = 60°$

$\Rightarrow \quad \angle APO = \frac{60°}{2}=30°$

$\therefore \quad \tan 30° = \frac{AO}{AP}$

$\Rightarrow \quad \frac{1}{\sqrt{3}}=\frac{5}{AP}$

$\Rightarrow \quad AP = 5\sqrt{3}$ cm $= BP$

[$\because$ lengths of tangent drawn from an external point to the circle are equal]

Hence, the length of each tangent is $5\sqrt{3}$ cm. (1)

**26.** Given, radius of circle = 80 m

and angle of sector = 60°

$\therefore$ Angles for the major sectors of both the circles at $\theta$ is same i.e. 300°.

Radius of inner circle = 80 − 30 = 50 m (1)

$\therefore$ Area of concrete track

$=\frac{300°}{360°}\times\pi\times(80)^2-\frac{300°}{360°}\times\pi\times 50^2$ (1)

[$\because$ area of track = area of outer sector − area of inner sector]

$=\frac{5}{6}\times\pi\times(6400-2500)$

$=\frac{5}{6}\times 3.14\times 3900$

$=10205\text{ m}^2$

Yes, Love is right. (1)

**27.** LHS $=\sin\theta(1+\tan\theta)+\cos\theta(1+\cot\theta)$

$=\sin\theta\left(1+\frac{\sin\theta}{\cos\theta}\right)+\cos\theta\left(1+\frac{\cos\theta}{\sin\theta}\right)$

$\left[\because \tan\theta=\frac{\sin\theta}{\cos\theta}, \cot\theta=\frac{\cos\theta}{\sin\theta}\right]$ (1)

$=\sin\theta\left(\frac{\cos\theta+\sin\theta}{\cos\theta}\right)+\cos\theta\left(\frac{\sin\theta+\cos\theta}{\sin\theta}\right)$

$=(\cos\theta+\sin\theta)\left(\frac{\sin\theta}{\cos\theta}+\frac{\cos\theta}{\sin\theta}\right)$ (1)

$=(\cos\theta+\sin\theta)\left(\frac{\sin^2\theta+\cos^2\theta}{\cos\theta\sin\theta}\right)$

$= (\cos\theta + \sin\theta)\left(\frac{1}{\cos\theta\sin\theta}\right)$ $[\because \sin^2\theta + \cos^2\theta = 1]$

$= \frac{\cos\theta}{\cos\theta\sin\theta} + \frac{\sin\theta}{\cos\theta\sin\theta} = \frac{1}{\sin\theta} + \frac{1}{\cos\theta}$

$= \text{cosec}\,\theta + \sec\theta = \text{RHS}$

$\left[\because \sin\theta = \frac{1}{\text{cosec}\,\theta}, \cos\theta = \frac{1}{\sec\theta}\right]$

**Hence proved.** (1)

*Or*

Given, $\sin\theta + \cos\theta = \sqrt{3}$

$\Rightarrow (\sin\theta + \cos\theta)^2 = (\sqrt{3})^2$ [squaring both sides]

$\Rightarrow (\sin^2\theta + \cos^2\theta) + 2\sin\theta\cos\theta = 3$ (1)

$\Rightarrow 1 + 2\sin\theta\cos\theta = 3$

$[\because \sin^2\theta + \cos^2\theta = 1]$

$\Rightarrow 2\sin\theta\cos\theta = 2$

$\Rightarrow \sin\theta\cos\theta = 1 \Rightarrow \sin\theta\cos\theta = \sin^2\theta + \cos^2\theta$

$\Rightarrow 1 = \frac{\sin^2\theta + \cos^2\theta}{\sin\theta\cos\theta}$

[dividing both sides by $\sin\theta\cos\theta$]

$\Rightarrow 1 = \frac{\sin^2\theta}{\sin\theta\cos\theta} + \frac{\cos^2\theta}{\sin\theta\cos\theta}$

$\Rightarrow 1 = \frac{\sin\theta}{\cos\theta} + \frac{\cos\theta}{\sin\theta} \Rightarrow 1 = \tan\theta + \cot\theta$

$\left[\because \frac{\sin\theta}{\cos\theta} = \tan\theta, \frac{\cos\theta}{\sin\theta} = \cot\theta\right]$

**Hence proved.** (2)

**28.** Let $\sqrt{3}$ be rational in the simplest form of $\frac{p}{q}$, where $p$ and $q$ are integers and having no common factor other than 1 and $q \neq 0$, i.e. $\sqrt{3} = \frac{p}{q}$

On squaring both sides, we get

$3 = \frac{p^2}{q^2} \Rightarrow 3q^2 = p^2$ ...(i)

Since, $3q^2$ is divisible by 3.

$\therefore p^2$ is also divisible by 3.

$\Rightarrow p$ is divisible by 3. ...(ii) (1/2)

Let $p = 3c$ for some integer $c$.

On putting $p = 3c$ in Eq. (i), we get

$3q^2 = (3c)^2$

$\Rightarrow 3q^2 = 9c^2 \Rightarrow q^2 = 3c^2$ (1/2)

Since, $3c^2$ is divisible by 3.

$\therefore q^2$ is divisible by 3.

$\Rightarrow q$ is divisible by 3. ...(iii) (1)

From Eqs. (ii) and (iii), we get 3 is a common factor of $p$ and $q$. But this contradict our assumption that $p$ and $q$ are having no common factor other than 1.

Therefore, our assumption that $\sqrt{3}$ is rational, is wrong.

Hence, $\sqrt{3}$ is an irrational. **Hence proved.** (1)

*Or*

Time taken by Sania to drive one round of the field = 18 min

Time taken by Ravi to drive one round of the field = 12 min (1)

The LCM of 18 and 12 gives the exact number of minutes after which they will meet at the starting point again. (1)

Now, $18 = 2 \times 3 \times 3 = 2 \times 3^2$

and $12 = 2 \times 2 \times 3 = 2^2 \times 3$

$\therefore$ LCM of 18 and 12 $= 2^2 \times 3^2 = 4 \times 9 = 36$

Hence, Sania and Ravi will meet again at the starting point after 36 min. (1)

**29.** Given, $AC = 10$ cm, $AD = 4$ cm

$CD = AC - AD = 10 - 4 = 6$ cm

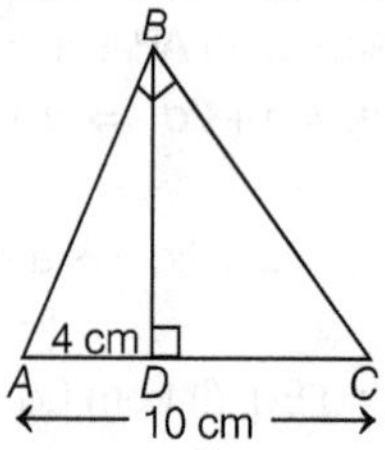


In $\Delta ABC$ and $\Delta ADB$

$\angle BAC = \angle BAD$

$\angle ABC = \angle ADB$ [each 90° angle]

$\therefore \Delta ABC \sim \Delta ADB$

[by $AA$ similarity criterion] ... (i) (1)

In $\Delta ABC$ and $\Delta BDC$,

$\angle ABC = \angle BDC$ [each 90° angle]

$\angle ACB = \angle BCD$

$\therefore \Delta ABC \sim \Delta BDC$

[by $AA$ similarity criterion] ... (ii) (1)

From Eqs. (i) and (ii), $\Delta ADB \sim \Delta BDC$

$\therefore \frac{BD}{CD} = \frac{AD}{BD}$ [by CPCT]

$\Rightarrow BD^2 = AD \cdot CD$

$= 4 \times 6 = 24$ cm

$\Rightarrow BD = 2\sqrt{6}$ cm (1)

**30.** Produce $PP'$ and $QQ'$ to meet at point $R$ (say).

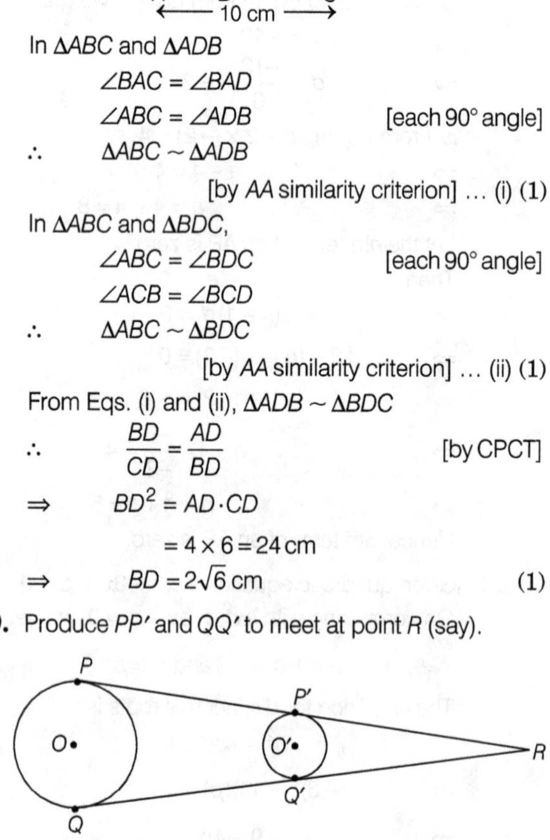


$\therefore RP = RQ$ (1½)

[$\because R$ is an external point and lengths of tangents drawn from an external point to a circle are equal]

$\Rightarrow RP' + P'P = RQ' + Q'Q$

$\Rightarrow P'P = Q'Q$ $[\because RP' = RQ']$ (1½)

**31.** Given, $2\left(\frac{2x+3}{x-3}\right)-25\left(\frac{x-3}{2x+3}\right)=5$

Let $\frac{2x+3}{x-3}=y$ ...(i)

Then, $\frac{x-3}{2x+3}=\frac{1}{y}$

Therefore, the given equation reduces to

$$2y-25\frac{1}{y}=5$$

$\Rightarrow$ $2y^2-25=5y$

$\Rightarrow$ $2y^2-5y-25=0$

$\Rightarrow$ $2y^2-10y+5y-25=0$

$\Rightarrow$ $2y(y-5)+5(y-5)=0$

$\Rightarrow$ $(y-5)(2y+5)=0 \Rightarrow y=5$

or $y=\frac{-5}{2}$ (1)

Now, putting $y=5$ in Eq. (i), we get

$$\frac{2x+3}{x-3}=\frac{5}{1} \Rightarrow 5x-15=2x+3$$

$\Rightarrow$ $3x=18 \Rightarrow x=6$ (1)

Again, putting $y=-\frac{5}{2}$ in Eq. (i), we get

$$\frac{2x+3}{x-3}=-\frac{5}{2}$$

$\Rightarrow$ $-5x+15=4x+6$

$\therefore$ $9x=9 \Rightarrow x=1$

Hence, the values of $x$ are 1 and 6. (1)

**32.** Given, a tent which is combination of a cylinder and a cone.

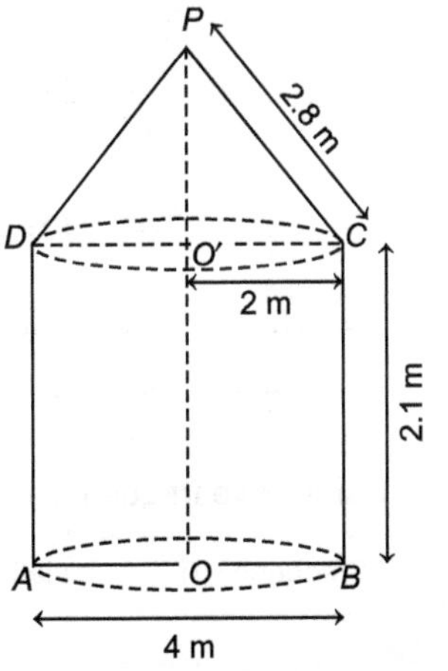


(1)

Also, we have slant height ($l$) of the cone = 2.8 m

Radius of the cone, $r$ = Radius of cylinder

$$=\frac{\text{Diameter}}{2}$$

$$=\frac{4}{2}=2\text{ m}$$

and height of the cylinder, $h_1=2.1$ m

$\therefore$ Required surface area of the tent

= Surface area of cone + Surface area of cylinder

$=\pi rl+2\pi rh_1$ (1)

$=\pi r(l+2h_1)$

$=\frac{22}{7}\times 2\times(2.8+2\times 2.1)$

$=\frac{44}{7}(2.8+4.2)$

$=\frac{44}{7}\times 7=44\text{ m}^2$ (1)

Now, height of cone,

$h_2=\sqrt{(PC)^2-(O'C)^2}$

$=\sqrt{(2.8)^2-(2)^2}$

$=\sqrt{7.84-4}=\sqrt{3.84}=1.96$ (1)

Now, the volume of air within tent

= Volume of tent

= Volume of cone + Volume of cylinder

$=\frac{1}{3}\pi r^2h_2+\pi r^2h_1$

$=\pi\left[\frac{1}{3}\times(2)^2\times 1.96+(2)^2\times 2.1\right]$

$=\frac{22}{7}\left[\frac{7.84}{3}+8.4\right]$

$=\frac{22}{7}[2.61+8.4]$

$=\frac{11.01\times 22}{7}=\frac{242.22}{7}=34.60\text{ m}^3$ (1)

*Or*

Given, diameter of the cylinder = 10 cm

$\therefore$ Radius of the cylinder, $r=\frac{10}{2}=5$ cm

and height of the cylinder, $h=12$ cm

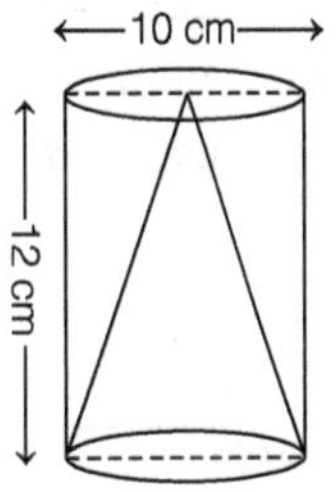


(1)

$\therefore$ Volume of the cylinder $=\pi r^2h=\frac{22}{7}\times 5\times 5\times 12$

$=\frac{6600}{7}\text{ cm}^3$

and volume of the cone $=\frac{1}{3}\pi r^2h$

$=\frac{1}{3}\times\frac{22}{7}\times 5\times 5\times 12$

$=\frac{2200}{7}\text{ cm}^3$ (1)

Now, volume of remaining solid

$= \text{Volume of the cylinder} - \text{Volume of the cone}$

$= \frac{6600}{7} - \frac{2200}{7} = \frac{4400}{7} = 628.57 \text{ cm}^3$

Since, slant height of the cone,

$l = \sqrt{r^2 + h^2} = \sqrt{(5)^2 + (12)^2}$

$= \sqrt{169} = 13 \text{ cm}$ (1)

$\therefore$ Curved surface area of the cone $= \pi r l$

$= \frac{22}{7} \times 5 \times 13$

$= \frac{1430}{7} \text{ cm}^2$

Clearly, curved surface area of the cylinder

$= 2\pi r h = 2 \times \frac{22}{7} \times 5 \times 12$

$= \frac{2640}{7} \text{ cm}^2$ (1)

and area of upper base of the cylinder $= \pi r^2$

$= \frac{22}{7} \times 5 \times 5$

$= \frac{550}{7} \text{ cm}^2$

Now, total surface area of the remaining solid

= Curved surface area of the cylinder

+ Curved surface area of the cone

+ Area of upper base of the cylinder

$= \frac{2640}{7} + \frac{1430}{7} + \frac{550}{7}$

$= \frac{4620}{7} = 660 \text{ cm}^2$ (1)

**33.** Let $AD = 7$m be the height of the building and $BC = h$ be the height of the cable tower. From the top of the building $D$, the angles of elevation and depression are $\angle CDE = 60°$ and $\angle EDB = 45°$, respectively.

From the point $D$, draw a line $DE \parallel AB$. (1)

Then, $\angle EDB = \angle ABD = 45°$ [alternate angles]

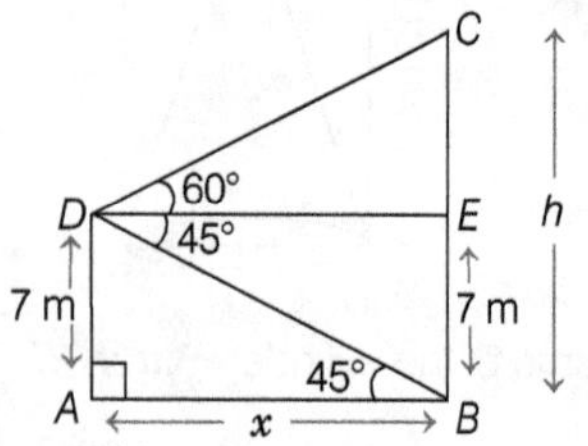


(1)

Also, let $AB = DE = x$ be the distance between building and tower.

In right angled $\Delta BAD$,

$\tan 45° = \frac{P}{B} = \frac{AD}{AB} \Rightarrow 1 = \frac{7}{x}$

[$\because \tan 45° = 1$] (1)

$\Rightarrow \quad x = 7 \text{ m}$ ...(i)

and in right angled $\Delta CED$,

$\tan 60° = \frac{CE}{DE} = \frac{CB - BE}{AB}$ [$\because CE = CB - BE$]

$\Rightarrow \quad \sqrt{3} = \frac{h-7}{x}$ [$\because \tan 60° = \sqrt{3}$](1)

$\Rightarrow \quad h - 7 = x\sqrt{3}$

$\Rightarrow \quad h = x\sqrt{3} + 7$

$\Rightarrow \quad h = 7\sqrt{3} + 7$ [from Eq. (i)]

$\Rightarrow \quad h = 7(\sqrt{3} + 1) \text{ m}$

Hence, the height of the tower is $7(\sqrt{3} + 1)$ m. (1)

**34.** As, the distribution is discontinuous, so firstly we will convert it into a continuous distribution by using adjustment factor of $\frac{15-14}{2} = 0.5$, hence we get the following table

| **Age** (in years) | **Number of cases** |
|---|---|
| 4.5-14.5 | 6 |
| 14.5-24.5 | 11 |
| 24.5-34.5 | 21 |
| 34.5-44.5 | 23 |
| 44.5-54.5 | 14 |
| 54.5-64.5 | 5 |
| **Total** | 80 |

(2)

As, the class 34.5-44.5 has maximum frequency, so it is the modal class.

Here, $l = 34.5, f_1 = 23, f_2 = 14, f_0 = 21$ and $h = 10$

$\therefore \quad \text{Mode} = l + \left(\frac{f_1 - f_0}{2f_1 - f_0 - f_2}\right) \times h$ (1)

$= 34.5 + \left(\frac{23 - 21}{2 \times 23 - 21 - 14}\right) \times 10$

$= 34.5 + \frac{2}{46 - 35} \times 10 = 34.5 + \frac{20}{11}$

$= 34.5 + 1.82 = 36.32$ (approx)

Hence, the modal age is 36.32 yr. (2)

*Or*

**Cumulative frequency table**

| **Class interval** | **Frequency** ($f$) | **Cumulative frequency** ($cf$) |
|---|---|---|
| 0-10 | 5 | 5 |
| 10-20 | $x$ | $5 + x$ |
| 20-30 | 20 | $25 + x$ |
| 30-40 | 15 | $40 + x$ |
| 40-50 | $y$ | $40 + x + y$ |
| 50-60 | 5 | $45 + x + y$ |
| **Total** | $\Sigma f_i = 60$ | |

(2)

$\because$ Median = 30

So, it lies in the interval 20-30.

Thus, 20-30 is the median class.

$\therefore\ l = 20, h = 10, f = 20, cf = 5 + x, N = 60$

$$\because \quad \text{Median} = l + \frac{\frac{N}{2} - cf}{f} \times h$$

$$\therefore \quad 30 = 20 + \frac{\frac{60}{2} - (5 + x)}{20} \times 10$$

$$\Rightarrow \quad 10 = \frac{30 - 5 - x}{2}$$

$$\Rightarrow \quad 20 = 25 - x \Rightarrow x = 5 \quad (2)$$

Also, we have

$$60 = 45 + x + y$$

$$\Rightarrow \quad 15 = x + y$$

$$\Rightarrow \quad 15 = 5 + y \Rightarrow y = 10$$

Hence, the value of $x$ and $y$ are 5 and 10. (1)

**35.** **Given** In the given figure, $AD$ is the bisector of $\angle BAC$ of $\Delta ABC$.

$\therefore\ \angle BAD = \angle CAD$

**To prove** $\frac{BD}{DC} = \frac{AB}{AC}$

**Construction** Now, draw $CT \parallel DA$ to meet $BA$ produced at $T$.

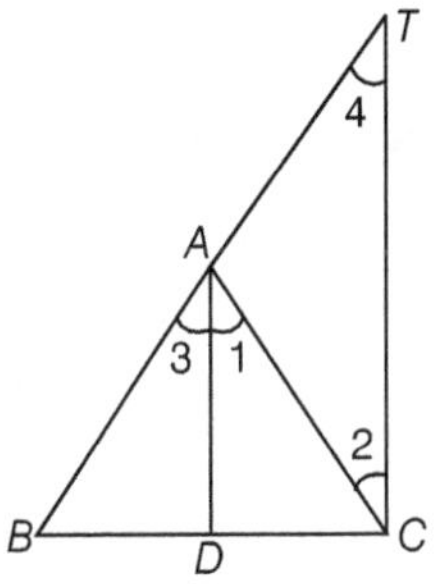


(1)

**Proof** $\because$ $CT \parallel DA$

and transversal $AC$ intersects them.

$\therefore\ \angle 1 = \angle 2$ [alternate interior angles] ...(i)

Also, $CT \parallel DA$ (1)

and transversal $BT$ intersects them.

$\therefore\ \angle 3 = \angle 4$ [corresponding angles] ...(ii)

But $\angle 1 = \angle 3$ [given]

$\Rightarrow\ \angle 1 = \angle 4$ [from Eq. (ii)] ...(iii)

From Eqs. (i) and (iii), we get

$\angle 2 = \angle 4 \Rightarrow AT = AC$ (1)

[since, sides opposite to equal angles of a triangle are also equal] ...(iv)

In $\Delta BCT$, $AD \parallel CT$

$$\therefore \quad \frac{BD}{DC} = \frac{AB}{AT} \quad \text{[by BPT]}$$

$$\Rightarrow \quad \frac{BD}{DC} = \frac{AB}{AC} \quad \text{[from Eq. (iv)]}$$

**Hence proved.** (2)

**36.** (i) Vikas received ₹ 130 as profit.

$\therefore$ According to the situation,

$$\frac{12}{100}p + \frac{10}{100}q = 130 \Rightarrow 12p + 10q = 13000$$

(ii) Vikas received ₹ 4 extra, if he interchange the investment amount.

$\therefore$ According to the situation,

$$\frac{10}{100}p + \frac{12}{100}q = 130 + 4 \Rightarrow 10p + 12q = 13400$$

(iii) From above situations, we have

$$12p + 10q = 13000 \quad ...(i)$$

and $$10p + 12q = 13400 \quad ...(ii)$$

Adding Eqs. (i) and (ii), we get

$$22p + 22q = 26400 \Rightarrow p + q = 1200 \quad ...(iii)$$

Now, subtracting Eq. (ii) from Eq. (i), we get

$$2p - 2q = -400 \Rightarrow p - q = -200 \quad ...(iv)$$

Now, on adding Eqs. (iii) and (iv), we get

$$2p = 1000 \Rightarrow p = ₹500$$

Putting the value of $p$ in Eq. (iii)

$$q = 1200 - 500 = ₹\,700$$

*Or*

Two equations are

$$12p + 10q = 13000 \quad ...(i)$$

and $$10p + 12q = 13400 \quad ...(ii)$$

For Eq. (i), $12p + 10q = 13000$

| | | |
|---|---|---|
| $p$ | 0 | 500 |
| $q$ | 1300 | 700 |

For Eq. (ii),

$$10p + 12q = 13400$$

| | | |
|---|---|---|
| $p$ | 0 | 500 |
| $q$ | 1116.6 | 700 |

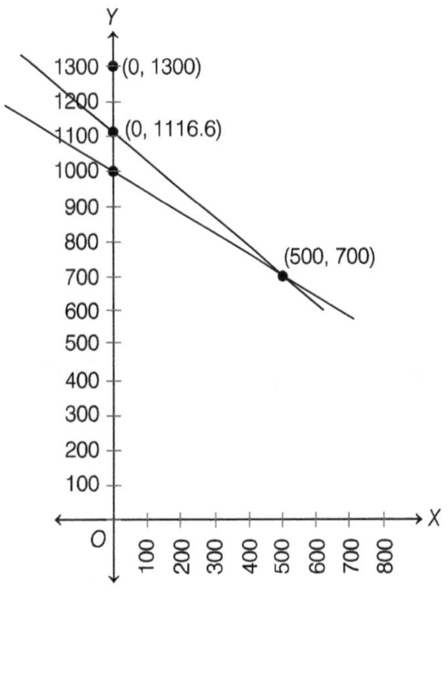

**37.** (i) From the graph I, we have

Zeroes of $P(x) = -3, -1$

(ii) From the graph II, we have

Zeroes of $P(x) = -2, 2$

(iii) In graph I, sum of zeroes $= -3 - 1 = -4$

and product of zeroes $= (-3)(-1) = 3$

$\therefore$ Polynomial $P(x)$ will be

$x^2$ – (Sum of zeroes) $x$ + Product of zeroes

$$= x^2 + 4x + 3$$

*Or*

From the graph III, we have

Zeroes of $p(x) = -1, 3$

Sum of zeroes $= 2 = \frac{-a}{1}$

$\Rightarrow \quad a = -2$

and product of zeroes $= -3 = -b$

$\Rightarrow \quad b = 3$

$\therefore a + b = -2 + 3 = 1$

**38.** (i) Required distance $= \sqrt{(13-5)^2 + (26-8)^2}$

$= \sqrt{8^2 + 18^2}$

$= \sqrt{64 + 324} = \sqrt{388}$

$= 2\sqrt{97}$ km

(ii) Required distance $= \sqrt{(13-2)^2 + (26-4)^2}$

$= \sqrt{11^2 + 22^2} = \sqrt{121 + 484}$

$= \sqrt{605} = 24.6$ km

(iii) Extra distance

= Distance from house to bank
+ Distance from bank to school
+ Distance from school to office
– Distance from house to office

$$= \sqrt{(5-2)^2 + (8-4)^2} + \sqrt{(13-5)^2 + (14-8)^2} + \sqrt{(13-13)^2 + (26-14)^2} - \sqrt{(13-2)^2 + (26-4)^2}$$

$$= \sqrt{9+16} + \sqrt{64+36} + \sqrt{0+144} - \sqrt{121+484}$$

$$= \sqrt{25} + \sqrt{100} + \sqrt{144} - \sqrt{605}$$

$= 5 + 10 + 12 - 24.6$

$= 27 - 24.6$

$= 2.4$ km

*Or*

Let the coordinates of the required point be $x, y$.

Then, by section formula,

$$(x, y) = \left(\frac{4\times13+3\times2}{4+3}, \frac{4\times26+3\times4}{4+3}\right)$$

$$= \left(\frac{52+6}{7}, \frac{104+12}{7}\right)$$

$$\Rightarrow \quad (x, y) = \left(\frac{58}{7}, \frac{116}{7}\right)$$

$\therefore$ The coordinates of the point are $\left(\frac{58}{7}, \frac{116}{7}\right)$.

# SAMPLE QUESTION PAPER 8

## Mathematics (Basic)

Time : **3 hrs** Max. Marks : **80**

### Instructions

1. This question paper has 5 Sections A, B, C, D and E.
2. Section A has 20 Multiple Choice Questions (MCQs) carrying 1 mark each.
3. Section B has 5 Short Answer-I (SA-I) Type Questions carrying 2 marks each.
4. Section C has 6 Short Answer-II (SA-II) Type Questions carrying 3 marks each.
5. Section D has 4 Long Answer (LA) Type Questions carrying 5 marks each.
6. Section E has 3 Case Based integrated units of assessment (4 marks each) with sub-parts of the values of 1, 1 and 2 marks each respectively.
7. All questions are compulsory. However, an internal choice in 2 questions of 2 marks, 2 questions of 3 marks and 2 questions of 5 marks has been provided. An internal choice has been provided in the 2 marks questions of Section E.
8. Draw neat figures wherever required. Take $\pi = 22/7$ wherever required if not stated.

## Section-A

**Section A consists of 20 questions of 1 mark each**

**1.** If the HCF of 45 and 55 is 5, LCM of 45 and 55 is $99 \times a$, then the value of $a$ is

(a) 25 (b) 49 (c) 5 (d) 7

**2.** The prime factorisation of 1350 is

(a) $2\times3^3$ (b) $2\times3\times5$
(c) $2\times3^2\times5$ (d) $2\times3^3\times5^2$

**3.** If the probability of Sania winning a tennis match is 0.63, then probability of her losing the match is

(a) 0.63 (b) 1 (c) 0 (d) 0.37

**4.** The graph of a polynomial $p(x)$ is shown below. The number of zeroes of $p(x)$ is

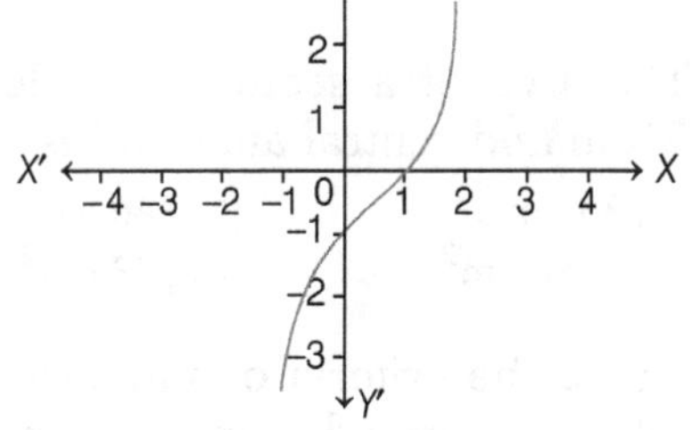


(a) 1 (b) 2 (c) 3 (d) 4

**5.** If 2 is a zero of polynomial $p(x) = 4x^2 + 2x - 5a$, then the value of $a$ is

(a) $-\frac{5}{2}$ (b) 4
(c) 2 (d) 6

**6.** $7 + 5\sqrt{8}$ is

(a) rational (b) irrational
(c) prime (d) integer

**7.** The distance of the point (20, 15) from the origin is

(a) $\sqrt{35}$ units (b) 25 units
(c) $\sqrt{5}$ units (d) 7 units

**8.** The mid-point of the line segment joining the points (–7, 9) and (–3, 5) is

(a) $\left(\frac{5}{2}, \frac{7}{2}\right)$ (b) (2, 7)
(c) (–5, 7) (d) (5, 2)

**9.** If the lines given by $2x + ky = 1$ and $3x - 5y = 7$ has unique solution, then the value of $k$ is

(a) $-\frac{10}{3}$
(b) All real values
(c) $\frac{10}{3}$
(d) All real values, except $-\frac{10}{3}$

**10.** The value of $2\sin^2 30° - 3\cos^2 45° + \tan^2 60°$ is

(a) 0 (b) 2
(c) $\frac{9}{2}$ (d) $-\frac{2}{3}$

**11.** The ratio of the length of a rod and its shadow is $\sqrt{3} : 1$. Then, the angle of elevation of the Sun, is

(a) 45° (b) 40°
(c) 30° (d) 60°

**12.** The area of a sector of circle of radius 21cm and central angle 90° is

(a) 33 $cm^2$ (b) 346.5 $cm^2$
(c) 1386 $cm^2$ (d) 693 $cm^2$

**13.** Name the criteria of similarity by which following triangles are similar.

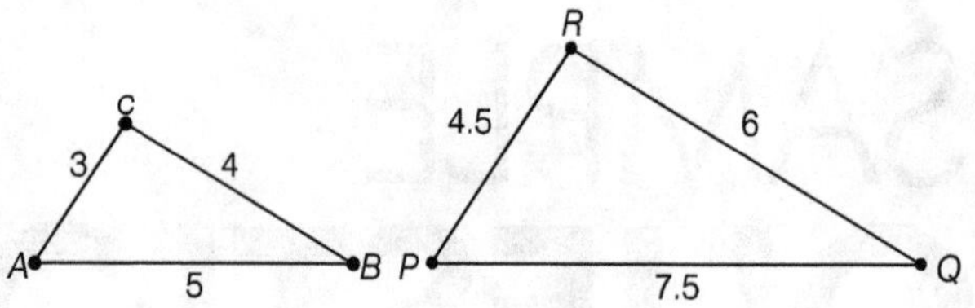


(a) SSS (b) SAS (c) AAA (d) ASA

**14.** The radius of the wheel of a bus is 20 cm. If the speed of the bus is 30 km/h, then how many revolutions will the wheel make in 1 min?

(a) 390 (b) 398 (c) 326 (d) 450

**15.** In an arithmetic progression, if $a = 5$, $d = -7$ and $n = 6$, then $a_n$ is

(a) –17
(b) 18
(c) Cannot be determined
(d) –30

**16.** If $a = 10$ and $d = 7$, then first four terms will be

(a) 10, 3, –4, –11 (b) 3, 10, 17, 24
(c) 10, 17, 24, 31 (d) 7, 17, 27, 37

**17.** If a number $x$ is added to twice its square, then the resultant is 21. Then the quadratic representation of this statement is

(a) $2x^2 - x + 21 = 0$ (b) $2x^2 + x - 21 = 0$
(c) $2x^2 - x - 20 = 0$ (d) None of these

**18.** Which of the following equation has root as 3?

(a) $x^2 - 5x + 6 = 0$
(b) $-x^2 + 3x - 3 = 0$
(c) $\sqrt{2}x^2 - \frac{3}{\sqrt{2}}x + 1 = 0$
(d) $3x^2 - 3x + 3 = 0$

**Directions** *In the question number 19 and 20, a statement of Assertion (A) is followed by a statement of Reason (R). Choose the correct option.*

**19.** **Assertion (A)** Three consecutive terms $k$, $2k + 1$, $5k - 2$ form an AP, then $k$ is equal to 2.

**Reason (R)** In an AP : $a, a + d, a + 2d \ldots$, the sum of $n$ terms of AP is

$$S_n = \frac{n}{2}[a + (n - 1)d]$$

(a) Both Assertion (A) and Reason (R) are true and Reason (R) is the correct explanation of Assertion (A)
(b) Both Assertion (A) and Reason (R) are true but Reason (R) is not the correct explanation of Assertion (A)
(c) Assertion (A) is true but Reason (R) is false
(d) Assertion (A) is false but Reason (R) is true

**20.** **Assertion (A)** $x^3 + x$ has only one real zero.

**Reason (R)** A polynomial of $n$th degree must have $n$ real zeroes.
(a) Both Assertion (A) and Reason (R) are true and Reason (R) is the correct explanation of Assertion (A)
(b) Both Assertion (A) and Reason (R) are true but Reason (R) is not the correct explanation of Assertion (A)
(c) Assertion (A) is true but Reason (R) is false
(d) Assertion (A) is false but Reason (R) is true

# Section-B

**Section B consists of 5 questions of 2 marks each**

**21.** Find the radius of a circle, if the length of tangent from a point at distance of 13 cm from the centre of the circle is 12 cm.

**22.** Prove that
$$\tan^2\theta + \cot^2\theta + 2 = \sec^2\theta \operatorname{cosec}^2\theta.$$

*Or* Prove that $(\operatorname{cosec} A - \sin A)(\sec A - \cos A) = \sin A \cos A.$

**23.** A teacher told his students to write a quadratic polynomial whose sum and product of the zeroes are −3 and 2, then students write the polynomial $x^2 + 3x + 2$. Is it right? Justify your answer.

**24.** If the mean of the following distribution is 6, find the value of $p$.

| $x$ | 2 | 4 | 6 | 10 | $p + 5$ |
|---|---|---|---|---|---|
| $f$ | 3 | 2 | 3 | 1 | 2 |

**25.** Solve the quadratic equation $\frac{x+3}{x-2} - \frac{1-x}{x} = \frac{17}{4}$ by factorisation method.

*Or* If −4 is a root of the quadratic equation $x^2 + px - 4 = 0$ and the quadratic equation $x^2 + px + k = 0$ has equal roots, find the value of $k$.

# Section-C

**Section C consists of 6 questions of 3 marks each**

**26.** Find the sum of series
$$7 + 10\frac{1}{2} + 14 + \ldots + 84.$$

**27.** Prove that
$$\sin^6\theta + \cos^6\theta + 3\sin^2\theta\cos^2\theta = 1.$$

*Or* Prove that
$$\frac{\tan\theta}{1-\cot\theta} + \frac{\cot\theta}{1-\tan\theta} = 1 + \sec\theta \operatorname{cosec}\theta.$$

**28.** Find the largest positive integer that will divide 444, 486 and 604 leaving remainders 7, 11 and 15 respectively.

**29.** In the given figure, $PT$ and $PS$ are tangents to a circle from a point $P$ such that $PT = 4$ cm and $\angle TPS = 60°$. Find the length of chord $TS$. How many line segment of same length $TS$ can be drawn in the circle?

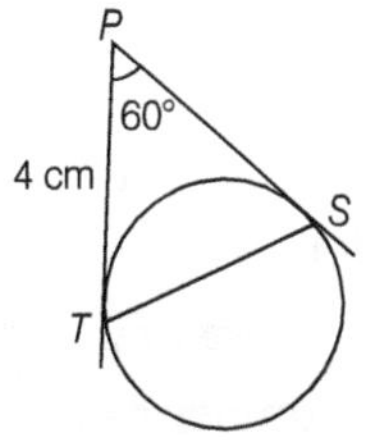


*Or*

$AB$ is a diameter and $AC$ is a chord of a circle such that $\angle BAC = 30°$. If the tangent at $C$ intersects $AB$ produced in $D$, prove that $BC = BD$.

**30.** A Rafree is standing on the side of the athletic track and kept a stopwatch, which is used to find the time that it took a group of students to run 200 m.

In different time intervals, different number of students completed the race are given in the table as shown below

| Time (in seconds) | 0-50 | 50-100 | 100-150 | 150-200 |
|---|---|---|---|---|
| Number of students | 10 | 15 | 7 | 8 |

Find mode of the given data.

**31.** From the given figures, find $\angle P$.

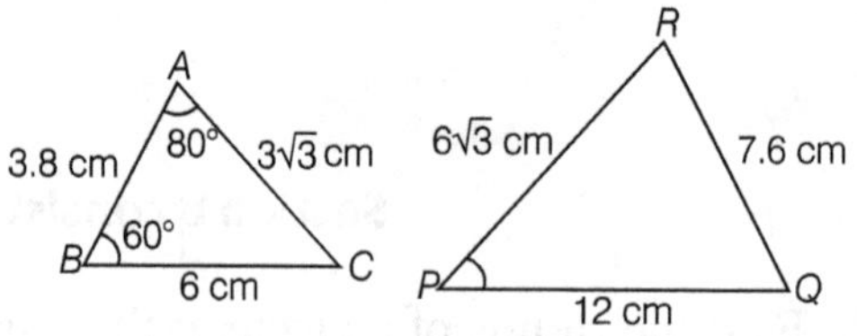


## Section-D

**Section D consists of 4 questions of 5 marks each**

**32.** A straight highway leads to the foot of a national communication and telecasting tower. A watchman standing at the top of the tower observes a car at an angle of depression of 30° which is approaching the foot of the tower with a uniform speed. Two minutes later, the angle of depression was found to be 60°. Find the time taken by the car to reach the foot of the tower from this point. The watchman suspects that some terrorist are approaching the tower. It needs half a minute for the watchman to inform the security staff to be on the alert.

**33.** $ABC$ is an isosceles triangle with $AB = AC$ and $D$ is a point on $AC$ such that

$BC^2 = AC \times DC$ prove that $BD = BC$.

**34.** In a single throw of two dice, find the probability of

(i) a doublet.

(ii) a number less than 3 on each die.

(iii) an odd number as a sum.

(iv) an odd number on a die and a number less than or equal to 4 on other die.

*Or*

From a pack of 52 playing cards jacks, queens, kings and aces of red colour are removed. From the remaining, a card is drawn at random. Find the probability that the card drawn is

(i) a black queen

(ii) a red card

(iii) a ten

(iv) a picture card ( jacks, queens and kings are picture cards)

**35.** A right-angled triangle whose sides are 15 cm and 20 cm, is made to revolve about its hypotenuse. Find the volume and surface area of the double cone so formed. [take, $\pi = 3.14$]

*Or*

A solid toy is in the form of a hemisphere surmounted by a right circular cone. Height of the cone is 4 cm and the diameter of the base is 8 cm. If a right circular cylinder circumscribes the solid. Find how much more space it will cover?

# Section-E

**Case study based questions are compulsory**

**36.** To conduct Sports Day activities in your rectangular shaped school ground $ABCD$, lines have been drawn with chalk powder at a distance of 1 m each, 100 flower pots have been placed at a distance of 1 m from each other along $AD$, as shown in figure.

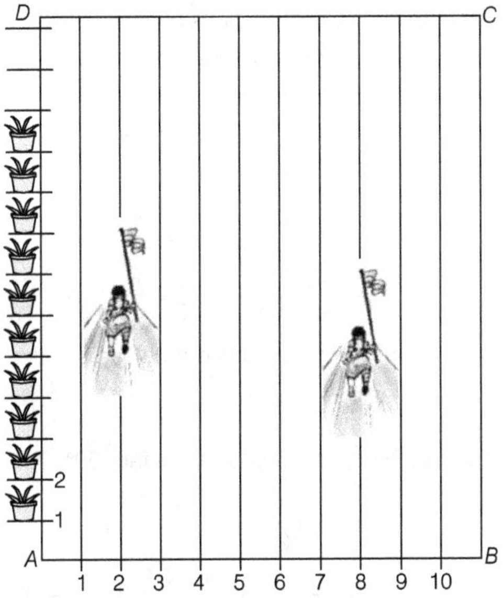


Niharika runs $\frac{1}{4}$th the distance $AD$ on the 2nd line and posts a green flag. Preet runs $\frac{1}{5}$th the distance $AD$ on the 8th line and posts a red flag.

On the basis of above information, answer the following questions.

(i) Write the coordinates of green flag. (1)

(ii) Write the coordinates of red flag. (1)

(iii) Find the distance between both the flags. (2)

*Or*

If Rashmi has to post a blue flag exactly half way between the line segment joining the flags, then find the coordinates of that point. (2)

**37.** A regular morning walk, schedule can help you to reduce weight. You can take care of many health problems concerning your heart, joints, mental health, lung capacity, immune system and body strength just by walking. To improve the health two friends Vicky and Love went to the walk on concrete track. (Shown in figure). In the figure, $AOB$ is a flower bed in the shape of a sector of a circle of radius 40 m and $\angle AOB = 60°$. Also a 15 m wide concrete track is made as shown in the figure.

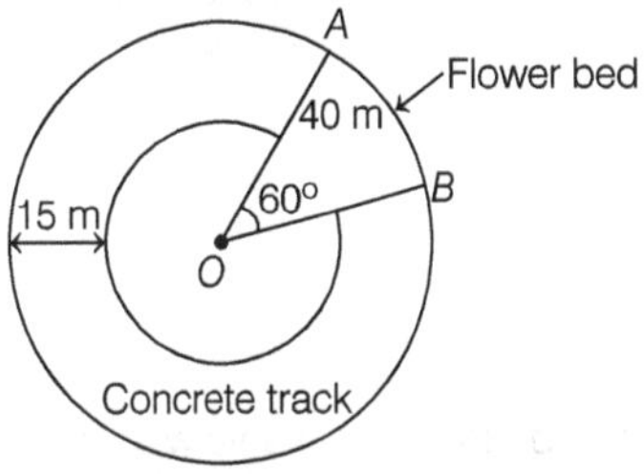


On the basis of above information, answer the following questions.

(i) Find the radius of inner circle. (1)

(ii) Write the formula to find the area of sector. (1)

(iii) Find the area of the sector $AOB$. (2)

*Or* If instead of flower bed there had been a complete circular concrete track, then find the area of the concrete region. (2)

**38.** Anil, a student of class X goes to Ganga rivers with his father. When he saw a boat in the river, he wanted to sit in the boat. So he made his father Ramesh is ready to sit with him on the boat. In this order, Anil is sitting on a boat which is upstream at a speed of 6 km/h and downstream at a speed of 14 km/h. When Anil is on the boat, some questions arise in his mind.

**On the basis of above information, answer the following questions.**

(i) What is the speed (in km/h) of the boat in still water? (1)

(ii) What is the speed (in km/h) of stream? (1)

(iii) Find the average speed of Anil, if he travels 5 km upstream and 10 km downstream. (2)

*Or*

What is the ratio between the speed of the boat and speed of the water current respectively? (2)

# SOLUTIONS

**1.** (c) We know that

HCF × LCM = Product of two numbers

$\Rightarrow \quad 5\times 99\times a = 45\times 55$

$\Rightarrow \quad a = \frac{45\times 55}{5\times 99} = 5$

**2.** (d) $1350 = 2\times 3\times 3\times 3\times 5\times 5$

$= 2\times 3^3\times 5^2$

**3.** (d) Let $E$ be the event Sania winning the match, then

$P(E) = 0.63$ [given]

$\therefore$ $P$ (Sania losing the match) $= P(\text{not } E) = P(\bar{E})$

$= 1 - P(E) = 1 - 0.63$

$= 0.37$

**4.** (a) It is clear that curve cut the $X$-axis at only one point. Hence, the number of zeroes of $p(x)$ is 1.

**5.** (b) Given polynomial is $p(x) = 4x^2 + 2x - 5a$.

Since, 2 is a zero of polynomial.

$\therefore \quad p(2) = 0$

$\Rightarrow \quad 4(2)^2 + 2(2) - 5a = 0$

$\Rightarrow \quad 16 + 4 - 5a = 0$

$\Rightarrow \quad 5a = 20$

$\Rightarrow \quad a = 4$

**6.** (b) Now, $7 + 5\sqrt{8} = 7 + 10\sqrt{2}$

Since, $\sqrt{2}$ is irrational number.

Therefore, $7 + 10\sqrt{2}$ is irrational number.

**7.** (b) Let the points are $P(20, 15)$ and origin $O(0, 0)$.

$\therefore$ Distance between two points

$= \sqrt{(0-20)^2 + (0-15)^2}$

$= \sqrt{(-20)^2 + (-15)^2}$

$= \sqrt{400 + 225} = \sqrt{625} = 25$ units

**8.** (c) Given, $(x_1, y_1) = (-7, 9)$ and $(x_2, y_2) = (-3, 5)$

$\therefore \quad x = \frac{x_1 + x_2}{2} = \frac{-7-3}{2} = \frac{-10}{2} = -5$

and $\quad y = \frac{y_1 + y_2}{2} = \frac{9+5}{2} = \frac{14}{2} = 7$

$\therefore$ Mid-point is $(-5, 7)$.

**9.** (d) The given equations can be rewritten as

$2x + ky - 1 = 0$ and $3x - 5y - 7 = 0$.

On comparing with $a_1x + b_1y + c_1 = 0$

and $a_2x + b_2y + c_2 = 0$, we get

$a_1 = 2, b_1 = k, c_1 = -1$

and $\quad a_2 = 3, b_2 = -5, c_2 = -7$

For unique solution,

$\frac{a_1}{a_2} \neq \frac{b_1}{b_2} \Rightarrow \frac{2}{3} \neq \frac{k}{-5} \Rightarrow k \neq \frac{-10}{3}$

Thus, given lines have a unique solution for all real values of $k$, except $\frac{-10}{3}$.

**10.** (b) $2\sin^2 30^\circ - 3\cos^2 45^\circ + \tan^2 60^\circ$

$= 2\times\left(\frac{1}{2}\right)^2 - 3\left(\frac{1}{\sqrt{2}}\right)^2 + (\sqrt{3})^2$

$= \frac{2}{4} - \frac{3}{2} + 3 = \frac{1}{2} - \frac{3}{2} + 3 = -1 + 3 = 2$

**11.** (d) Let the length of rod be $BC$ and length of shadow is $AB$.

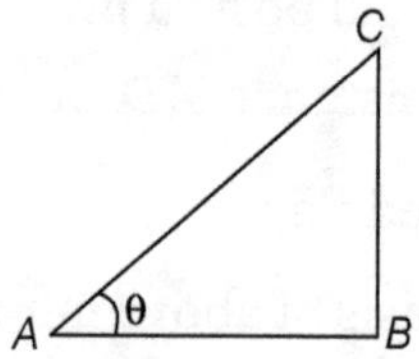


Then, $\frac{BC}{AB} = \frac{\sqrt{3}}{1}$ (given)

Let $\theta$ be the angle of elevation of Sun make.

Then, $\tan\theta = \frac{BC}{AB} = \frac{\sqrt{3}}{1}$

$\Rightarrow \quad \theta = 60^\circ$

**12.** (b) Let $O$ be the centre of the circle of radius 21 cm such that an arc $APB$ subtends 90° angle at the centre.

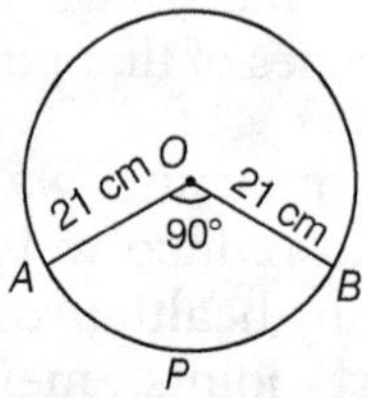

$\therefore$ Area of sector $OAPB = \frac{\theta}{360^\circ} \times \pi r^2$

$= \frac{90^\circ}{360^\circ} \times \frac{22}{7} \times 21 \times 21$

$= \frac{1}{4} \times 22 \times 3 \times 21$

$= \frac{1386}{4} = 346.5 \text{ cm}^2$

**13.** (a) In $\Delta ABC$ and $\Delta PQR$,

$\because \quad \frac{3}{4.5} = \frac{5}{7.5} = \frac{4}{6} = \frac{2}{3}$

$\therefore \quad \frac{AC}{PR} = \frac{AB}{PQ} = \frac{BC}{RQ}$

So, by SSS similarity criteria, $\Delta ABC \sim \Delta PQR$.

**14.** (b) In 1 h, distance covered by wheel = 30 km

In 1 min, distance covered by wheel

$= \frac{30 \times 1000}{60} = 500$ m

Number of revolutions made in 1 min

$= \frac{\text{Distance covered by wheel}}{\text{Circumference of the wheel}}$

$= \frac{500}{2 \times \frac{22}{7} \times \frac{20}{100}} = \frac{500 \times 7 \times 100}{2 \times 22 \times 20}$

$= \frac{50 \times 25 \times 7}{22} = \frac{625 \times 7}{11}$

= 398 (approx)

**15.** (d) Given, $a = 5, d = -7$ and $n = 6$

We know that

$a_n = a + (n-1)d$

$\therefore \quad a_6 = 5 + (6-1)(-7) = 5 + 5(-7) = 5 - 35 = -30$

**16.** (c) Given, $a = 10$ and $d = 7$

We know that,

$a_n = a + (n-1)d$

$\therefore \quad a_1 = 10 + (1-1)(7) = 10$

$a_2 = 10 + (1)(7) = 17$

$a_3 = 10 + (2)(7) = 24$

and $\quad a_4 = 10 + (3)(7) = 31$

**17.** (b) Let the number be $x$.

Then according to the given condition,

$2x^2 + x = 21 \Rightarrow 2x^2 + x - 21 = 0$

**18.** (a) (a) Given that $x^2 - 5x + 6 = 0$

Put $x = 3$, we get

$(3)^2 - 5(3) + 6 = 9 - 15 + 6 = 0$

Hence, $x = 3$ is a root of the equation.

(b) $-x^2 + 3x - 3 = 0$

Put $x = 3$, we get

$-(3)^2 + 3(3) - 3 = -9 + 9 - 3 = -3 \neq 0$

Hence, $x = 3$ is not a root of the equation.

(c) $\sqrt{2}x^2 - \frac{3}{\sqrt{2}}x + 1 = 0$

Put $x = 3$, we get

$\sqrt{2}(3)^2 - \frac{3(3)}{\sqrt{2}} + 1$

$\Rightarrow \quad 9\sqrt{2} - \frac{9}{\sqrt{2}} + 1 \neq 0$

Hence, $x = 3$ is not a root of the equation.

(d) $3x^2 - 3x + 3 = 0$

Put $x = 3$, we get

$3(3)^2 - 3(3) + 3 = 27 - 9 + 3 = 21 \neq 0.$

Hence, $x = 3$ is not a root of the equation.

**19.** (c) Taking first two terms,

common difference $= 2k + 1 - k = k + 1$

Taking second and third terms,

common difference $= 5k - 2 - 2k - 1 = 3k - 3$

Since, the terms are in AP.

$\therefore \quad k + 1 = 3k - 3$

$\Rightarrow \quad -2k = -4 \Rightarrow k = 2$

So, the given Assertion is true.

We know that sum of $n$ terms of an AP

$= \frac{n}{2}[2a + (n-1)d] \neq \frac{n}{2}[a + (n-1)d]$

So, the given Reason is false.

**20.** (c) Given, $x^3 + x = 0$

$\Rightarrow \quad x(x^2 + 1) = 0$

$\Rightarrow \quad x = 0$ or $x = \sqrt{-1}$

So, the polynomial has only one real zero i.e. 0.

$\because x^3 + x$ is a cubic polynomial with degree 3 and has only one real zero.

So, the given Reason is false.

**21.** Let $AB$ be a tangent drawn from point $B$ to a circle with centre $O$ such that $AB = 12$ cm and $OB = 13$ cm.

We know that, the tangent at any point of a circle is perpendicular to the radius through the point of contact.

$\therefore$ In $\Delta AOB$, $OA \perp AB$

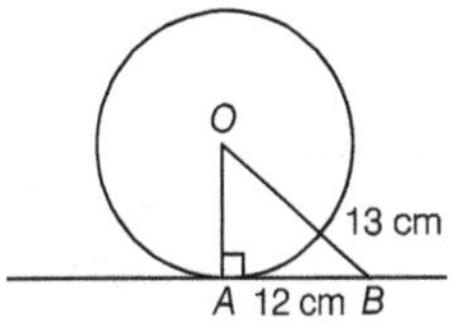


(1)

Now, in right angled $\Delta OAB$,

$OB^2 = OA^2 + AB^2$

$\Rightarrow \quad (13)^2 = OA^2 + (12)^2$

$\Rightarrow \quad 169 = OA^2 + 144$

$\Rightarrow \quad OA^2 = 169 - 144 = 25 \Rightarrow OA = 5$ cm

Hence, the radius of the required circle is 5 cm. (1)

**22.** LHS $= \tan^2\theta + \cot^2\theta + 2$

$= (1+\tan^2\theta) + (1+\cot^2\theta) = \sec^2\theta + \text{cosec}^2\theta$ (1)

$= \frac{1}{\cos^2\theta} + \frac{1}{\sin^2\theta} = \frac{\sin^2\theta + \cos^2\theta}{\cos^2\theta\sin^2\theta}$

$= \frac{1}{\cos^2\theta\sin^2\theta} = \frac{1}{\cos^2\theta}\cdot\frac{1}{\sin^2\theta}$

$= \sec^2\theta\,\text{cosec}^2\theta =$ RHS **Hence proved.** (1)

*Or*

LHS $= (\text{cosec}\,A - \sin A)(\sec A - \cos A)$

$= \left(\frac{1}{\sin A} - \sin A\right)\left(\frac{1}{\cos A} - \cos A\right)$ (1)

$= \frac{1-\sin^2 A}{\sin A} \times \frac{1-\cos^2 A}{\cos A} = \frac{\cos^2 A}{\sin A} \times \frac{\sin^2 A}{\cos A}$

$= \cos A \sin A =$ RHS **Hence proved.** (1)

**23.** Yes, we know that, if $\alpha$ and $\beta$ are the zeroes of a quadratic polynomial, then the quadratic polynomial

$= x^2 -$ (sum of zeroes) $x +$ product of zeroes (1)

$\therefore$ Required polynomial $= x^2 - (-3)x + 2$

$= x^2 + 3x + 2$ (1)

**24.** Table for product of observation and frequency

| $x_i$ | $f_i$ | $f_i x_i$ |
|---|---|---|
| 2 | 3 | 6 |
| 4 | 2 | 8 |
| 6 | 3 | 18 |
| 10 | 1 | 10 |
| $p+5$ | 2 | $2p+10$ |
| | $n = \Sigma f_i = 11$ | $\Sigma f_i x_i = 2p + 52$ |

(1)

We have, $n = \Sigma f_i = 11$ and $\Sigma f_i x_i = 2p + 52$

$\therefore$ Mean $= \frac{\Sigma f_i x_i}{n}$

$\Rightarrow 6 = \frac{2p+52}{11}$

$\Rightarrow 66 = 2p + 52 \Rightarrow 14 = 2p$

$\therefore p = 7$ (1)

**25.** Given, equation is $\frac{x+3}{x-2} - \frac{1-x}{x} = \frac{17}{4}$

$\Rightarrow \frac{x(x+3) - (1-x)(x-2)}{x(x-2)} = \frac{17}{4}$

$\Rightarrow 4[x^2 + 3x - (x - 2 - x^2 + 2x)] = 17(x^2 - 2x)$

$\Rightarrow 4x^2 + 12x - 12x + 8 + 4x^2 = 17x^2 - 34x$

$\Rightarrow 8x^2 - 17x^2 + 34x + 8 = 0$

$\Rightarrow 9x^2 - 34x - 8 = 0$

[dividing both sides by $-1$] (1)

$\Rightarrow 9x^2 - 36x + 2x - 8 = 0$

[by factorisation]

$\Rightarrow 9x(x-4) + 2(x-4) = 0$

$\Rightarrow (x-4)(9x+2) = 0$

$\Rightarrow x - 4 = 0$ or $9x + 2 = 0$

$\therefore x = 4$ or $x = \frac{-2}{9}$

Hence, the required roots of the given equation are 4 and $\frac{-2}{9}$. (1)

***Or***

Since, $-4$ is a root of the equation

$x^2 + px - 4 = 0$

$\therefore (-4)^2 + p \times (-4) - 4 = 0$

[$\because$ a root always satisfies the equation]

$\Rightarrow 16 - 4p - 4 = 0$

$\Rightarrow 4p = 12$

$\Rightarrow p = 3$ (1)

The equation $x^2 + px + k = 0$ has equal roots.

Here, $a = 1$, $b = p$ and $c = k$

$\therefore$ Discriminant $= 0 \Rightarrow b^2 - 4ac = 0$

$\Rightarrow p^2 - 4k = 0 \Rightarrow 9 - 4k = 0$

$\therefore k = \frac{9}{4}$ (1)

**26.** The given numbers are $7, 10\frac{1}{2}, 14, \ldots, 84$.

$\because 10\frac{1}{2} - 7 = 14 - 10\frac{1}{2} = \ldots = \frac{7}{2}$

$\therefore$ The given numbers forms an AP. (1/2)

Here, first term, $a = 7$,

common difference, $d = \frac{7}{2}$

and last term, $l = a_n = 84$

$\because a_n = a + (n-1)d$

$\therefore 84 = 7 + (n-1)\frac{7}{2}$ $\left[\because a = 7 \text{ and } d = \frac{7}{2}\right]$

$\Rightarrow \frac{7}{2}(n-1) = 84 - 7$ (1)

$\Rightarrow \frac{7}{2}(n-1) = 77$

$\Rightarrow n - 1 = 77 \times \frac{2}{7}$

$\Rightarrow n - 1 = 22 \Rightarrow n = 23$ (1/2)

$\because$ Sum of $n$ terms of an AP, $S_n = \frac{n}{2}(a + l)$

$\therefore$ Sum of 23 terms, $S_{23} = \frac{23}{2}(7 + 84) = \frac{23}{2} \times 91$

$= \frac{2093}{2} = 1046\frac{1}{2}$ (1)

**27.** $\text{LHS} = \sin^6\theta + \cos^6\theta + 3\sin^2\theta\cos^2\theta$

$= (\sin^2\theta)^3 + (\cos^2\theta)^3 + 3\sin^2\theta\cos^2\theta$

$= (\sin^2\theta + \cos^2\theta)^3 - 3\sin^2\theta\cos^2\theta$

$(\sin^2\theta + \cos^2\theta) + 3\sin^2\theta\cos^2\theta$

$[\because a^3 + b^3 = (a+b)^3 - 3ab(a+b)]$ (1)

$= (1)^3 - 3\sin^2\theta\cos^2\theta(1) + 3\sin^2\theta\cos^2\theta$

$= 1 - 3\sin^2\theta\cos^2\theta + 3\sin^2\theta\cos^2\theta = 1$

= RHS **Hence proved.** (2)

*Or*

$$\text{LHS} = \frac{\tan\theta}{1-\cot\theta} + \frac{\cot\theta}{1-\tan\theta}$$

$$= \frac{\frac{\sin\theta}{\cos\theta}}{1-\frac{\cos\theta}{\sin\theta}} + \frac{\frac{\cos\theta}{\sin\theta}}{1-\frac{\sin\theta}{\cos\theta}}$$ (1)

$$= \frac{\sin^2\theta}{\cos\theta(\sin\theta - \cos\theta)} + \frac{\cos^2\theta}{\sin\theta(\cos\theta - \sin\theta)}$$

$$= \frac{1}{\sin\theta - \cos\theta}\left(\frac{\sin^2\theta}{\cos\theta} - \frac{\cos^2\theta}{\sin\theta}\right)$$ (1)

$$= \frac{1}{\sin\theta - \cos\theta} \times \frac{\sin^3\theta - \cos^3\theta}{\sin\theta\cos\theta}$$

$$= \frac{(\sin\theta - \cos\theta)(\sin^2\theta + \cos^2\theta + \sin\theta\cos\theta)}{(\sin\theta - \cos\theta)\sin\theta\cos\theta}$$

$[\because a^3 - b^3 = (a-b)(a^2 + b^2 + ab)]$

$$= \frac{1 + \sin\theta\cos\theta}{\sin\theta\cos\theta} = \frac{1}{\sin\theta\cos\theta} + 1$$

$= \sec\theta \operatorname{cosec}\theta + 1 = \text{RHS}$ **Hence proved.** (1)

**28.** It is given that on dividing 444 by the required number, there is a remainder of 7. This means that $444 - 7 = 437$ is exactly divisible by the required number. In other words required number is a factor of 391. (1/2)

Similarly, required positive integer is a factor of $486 - 11 = 475$ and $604 - 15 = 589$.

Clearly, required number is the HCF of 437, 475 and 589. (1)

Using the factor tree the prime factorisations of 437, 475 and 589 are as follows

$$437 = 19 \times 23,\ 475 = 5^2 \times 19 \text{ and } 589 = 19 \times 31$$

Hence, required number = 19 (1½)

**29.** We know that tangents drawn from external point to the circle are equal in length.

Here, $P$ is an external point.

$\therefore \quad PS = PT = 4\text{ cm}$

So, $\angle PTS = \angle PST$

[$\because$ angle opposite to equal sides are equal] (1)

In $\Delta PTS$, we have

$\angle PTS + \angle PST + \angle TPS = 180°$

[by angle sum property of triangle]

$\Rightarrow \quad \angle PTS + \angle PTS + 60° = 180°$

[$\because \angle PST = \angle PTS$ and $\angle TPS = 60°$]

$\Rightarrow \quad 2\angle PTS = 180° - 60°$

$\Rightarrow \quad 2\angle PTS = 120°$

$\Rightarrow \quad \angle PTS = \frac{120°}{2} = 60°$ (1)

$\therefore \Delta PTS$ is an equilateral triangle.

Hence, $TS = 4$ cm

Here, infinite lines of same length $TS$ can be drawn in a circle. (1)

*Or*

**Given** $AB$ is a diameter of the circle with centre $O$ and $DC$ is the tangent of circle and $\angle BAC = 30°$.

**To prove** $BC = BD$

**Construction** Join $O$ to $C$.

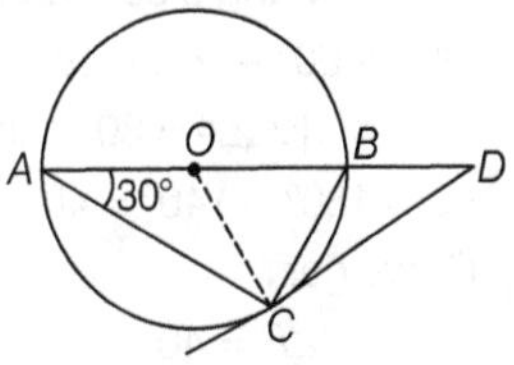


(1)

**Proof** Since, $OC \perp CD$

[$\because$ the tangent at any point of a circle is perpendicular to the radius through the point of contact]

$\therefore \quad \angle OCB + \angle BCD = 90°$

Now, $OC = OA$ [radii]

$\Rightarrow \quad \angle OCA = \angle OAC$

[angles opposite to equal sides are equal]

$\therefore \quad \angle OCA = 30°$

Now, $\angle ACB = 90°$ [angle in a semi-circle]

$\therefore \quad \angle OCA + \angle OCB = 90°$

$\Rightarrow \quad \angle OCB = 60°$

and $\angle BCD = 30°$ (1)

In $\Delta ACD$, $\angle ACD + \angle CAD + \angle ADC = 180°$

$\Rightarrow \quad 120° + 30° + \angle ADC = 180°$

$\Rightarrow \quad \angle ADC = 30°$

$\therefore$ In $\Delta BCD$,

$\angle BCD = \angle BDC = 30°$

$\therefore \quad BC = BD$ **Hence proved.** (1)

**30.** The highest frequency in the given data is 15, whose modal class is 50-100.

Here, $l = 50$, $f = 15$, $f_1 = 10$, $f_2 = 7$ and $h = 50$ (1)

$\because \quad \text{Mode} = l + \dfrac{f - f_1}{2f - f_1 - f_2} \times h$

$= 50 + \dfrac{15 - 10}{2 \times 15 - 10 - 7} \times 50$

$= 50 + \dfrac{5 \times 50}{30 - 17}$

$= 50 + \dfrac{250}{13}$

$= 50 + 19.23 = 69.23$ (2)

**31.** In $\Delta ABC$ and $\Delta RQP$,

$\dfrac{AB}{RQ} = \dfrac{3.8}{7.6} = \dfrac{1}{2}, \dfrac{BC}{QP} = \dfrac{6}{12} = \dfrac{1}{2}$ and $\dfrac{CA}{PR} = \dfrac{3\sqrt{3}}{6\sqrt{3}} = \dfrac{1}{2}$

$\because \quad \dfrac{AB}{RQ} = \dfrac{BC}{QP} = \dfrac{CA}{PR} = \dfrac{1}{2}$

$\therefore \quad \Delta ABC \sim \Delta RQP$ [by SSS similarity criterion]

So, $\angle C = \angle P$ ...(i)

[$\because$ corresponding angles of similar triangles are equal] (1½)

In $\Delta ABC$, $\angle A + \angle B + \angle C = 180°$

[by angle sum property of a triangle]

$\Rightarrow \quad 80° + 60° + \angle C = 180°$

[$\because \angle A = 80°$ and $\angle B = 60°$, given]

$\Rightarrow \quad \angle C = 180° - 140° = 40°$

From Eq. (i), we get

$\angle P = 40°$ (1½)

**32.** Let $AB$ be the tower of height $h$ m, $C$ and $D$ be the position of car at an angle of depression of 30° and 60°, respectively. Also, let the speed of car be $x$ km/min and $y$ min will be taken by the car to cover distance $BD$. (1)

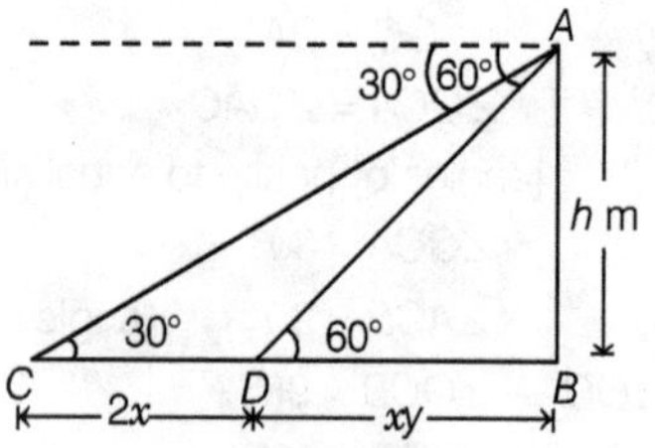


Then, $CD = 2x$ km

[$\because$ time taken to cover distance $CD$ is 2 min and distance = speed × time] (1)

and $BD = xy$ km

Now, in $\Delta ABC$, we have

$\tan 30° = \dfrac{AB}{BC}$ $\left[\because \tan\theta = \dfrac{\text{perpendicular}}{\text{base}}\right]$

$\dfrac{1}{\sqrt{3}} = \dfrac{AB}{BD + CD}$ $\left[\because \tan 30° = \dfrac{1}{\sqrt{3}}\right]$ (1)

$\Rightarrow \quad \dfrac{1}{\sqrt{3}} = \dfrac{h}{2x + xy}$

$\Rightarrow \quad \dfrac{1}{\sqrt{3}} = \dfrac{h}{x(2 + y)}$ ...(i)

and in $\Delta ABD$, we have

$\tan 60° = \dfrac{AB}{BD} \Rightarrow \sqrt{3} = \dfrac{h}{xy}$

$\Rightarrow \quad \dfrac{h}{x} = \sqrt{3}y$ [$\because \tan 60° = \sqrt{3}$] (1)

On substituting the value of $\dfrac{h}{x}$ in Eq. (i), we get

$\dfrac{1}{\sqrt{3}} = \dfrac{\sqrt{3}y}{2 + y}$

$\Rightarrow \quad 2 + y = 3y$

$\Rightarrow \quad 2 = 2y \Rightarrow y = 1$ min

Hence, the car will take 1 min to reach the foot of the tower. (1)

**33.** We have, $BC^2 = AC \times DC$

$\Rightarrow \quad BC \times BC = AC \times DC$

$\Rightarrow \quad \dfrac{BC}{DC} = \dfrac{AC}{BC}$ (1)

In $\Delta ABC$ and $\Delta BDC$,

$\dfrac{BC}{DC} = \dfrac{AC}{BC}$

and $\angle C = \angle C$ (common) (1)

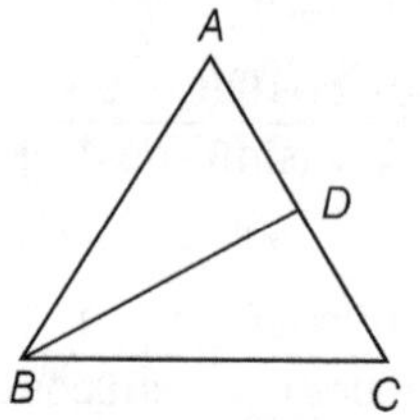


$\therefore \Delta ABC \sim \Delta BDC$ [by SAS similarity criterian] (1)

$\Rightarrow \quad \dfrac{AC}{BC} = \dfrac{AB}{BD}$

$\Rightarrow \quad \dfrac{AC}{BC} = \dfrac{AC}{BD}$ [$\because AB = AC$]

$\Rightarrow \quad BD = BC$ **Hence proved.** (2)

**34.** Total number of outcomes in a single throw of two dice = 6 × 6 = 36

(i) Possible doublets are (1, 1), (2, 2), (3, 3), (4, 4), (5, 5) and (6, 6).

Number of favourable outcomes = 6

$\therefore$ $P$ (getting a doublet) $= \dfrac{6}{36} = \dfrac{1}{6}$ (1)

(ii) Possible outcomes for a number less than 3 on each die, are (1, 1), (1, 2), (2, 1) and (2, 2)

Number of favourable outcomes = 4

$\therefore$ $P$ (getting a number less than 3 on each die)

$= \dfrac{4}{36} = \dfrac{1}{9}$ (1)

(iii) Possible outcomes for getting an odd number as a sum are (1, 2), (2, 1), (1, 4), (4, 1), (1, 6), (6, 1), (2, 3), (3, 2), (2, 5), (5, 2), (3, 4), (4, 3), (3, 6), (6, 3), (4, 5), (5, 4), (5, 6) and (6, 5)

Number of favourable outcomes = 18

$\therefore$ $P$ getting (an odd number as a sum)

$$= \frac{18}{36} = \frac{1}{2} \quad (1\frac{1}{2})$$

(iv) Possible outcomes for getting an odd number on a die and a number less than or equal to 4 on other die

= (1, 1), (1, 2), (1, 3), (1, 4), (1, 5), (2, 1), (2, 3), (2, 5), (3, 1), (3, 2), (3, 3), (3, 4), (3, 5), (4, 1), (4, 3), (4, 5), (5, 1), (5, 2), (5, 3) and (5, 4)

Number of favourable outcomes = 20

$\therefore$ Required probability $= \frac{20}{36} = \frac{5}{9}$ $(1\frac{1}{2})$

*Or*

Total number of cards = 52

$\therefore$ Total number of possible outcomes = 52

Number of cards that removed $= 4 \times 2 = 8$

$\therefore$ Total number of remaining cards $= (52 - 8)$

$= 44$ (1)

(i) $\because$ Number of black queens is 2.

$\therefore$ $P$ (getting a black queen) $= \frac{2}{44} = \frac{1}{22}$ (1)

(ii) $\because$ Number of red cards $= (26 - 8) = 18$

$\therefore$ $P$ (getting a red card) $= \frac{18}{44} = \frac{9}{22}$ (1)

(iii) $\because$ Number of tens = 4

$\therefore$ $P$ (getting a ten) $= \frac{4}{44} = \frac{1}{11}$ (1)

(iv) We know that jacks, queens and kings are picture cards.

$\therefore$ Remaining number of picture cards

$= 3 \times 2 = 6$

$\therefore$ $P$ (getting a picture card) $= \frac{6}{44} = \frac{3}{22}$ (1)

**35.** Let $BAC$ be a right-angled triangle such that $AB = 15$ cm and $AC = 20$ cm.

Using Pythagoras theorem, we have

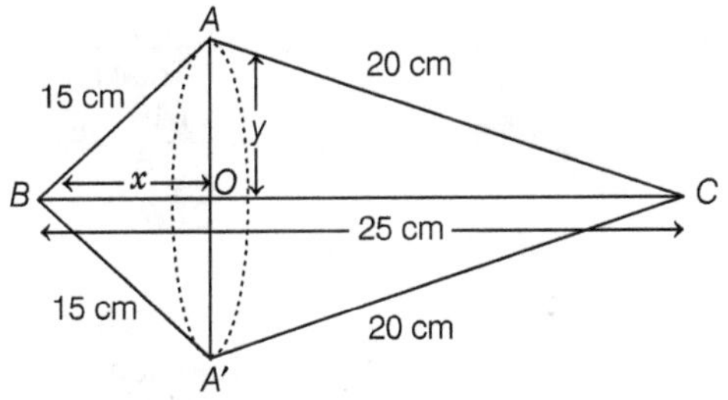


$$(BC)^2 = (AB)^2 + (AC)^2$$

$$\Rightarrow \quad (BC)^2 = 15^2 + 20^2$$

$$\Rightarrow \quad (BC)^2 = 225 + 400 = 625$$

$$\therefore \quad BC = 25 \text{ cm}$$

[taking positive square root] (1)

Let $OB = x$ and $OA = y$.

Again, using Pythagoras theorem in $\Delta OAB$ and $\Delta OAC$, we have

$$(AB)^2 = (OB)^2 + (OA)^2$$

$$\Rightarrow \quad 15^2 = x^2 + y^2$$

$$\Rightarrow \quad x^2 + y^2 = 225 \quad \ldots\text{(i)}$$

and $(AC)^2 = (OA)^2 + (OC)^2$

$$\Rightarrow \quad 20^2 = y^2 + (25 - x)^2$$

$$\Rightarrow \quad (25 - x)^2 + y^2 = 400 \quad \ldots\text{(ii)}$$

From Eq. (ii) subtracted by Eq. (i),

$$\Rightarrow \{(25 - x)^2 + y^2\} - \{x^2 + y^2\} = 400 - 225$$

$$\Rightarrow \quad (25 - x)^2 - x^2 = 175$$

$$\Rightarrow \quad (25 - x - x)(25 - x + x) = 175$$

$[\because a^2 - b^2 = (a - b)(a + b)]$

$$\Rightarrow \quad (25 - 2x) \times 25 = 175$$

$$\Rightarrow \quad 25 - 2x = 7$$

$$\Rightarrow \quad 2x = 18 \Rightarrow x = 9 \quad (1)$$

On putting $x = 9$ in Eq. (i), we get

$$81 + y^2 = 225$$

$$\Rightarrow \quad y^2 = 144$$

$$\therefore \quad y = 12 \quad \text{[taking positive square root]}$$

Thus, we have $OA = 12$ cm and $OB = 9$ cm (1)

$\therefore$ Volume of the double cone

= Volume of cone $CAA'$

+ Volume of cone $BAA'$

$$= \frac{1}{3}\pi (OA)^2 \times OC + \frac{1}{3}\pi (OA)^2 \times OB$$

$$= \frac{1}{3}\pi \times 12^2 \times 16 + \frac{1}{3}\pi \times 12^2 \times 9$$

$$= \frac{1}{3}\pi \times 144 (16 + 9)$$

$$= \frac{1}{3} \times 3.14 \times 144 \times 25 \text{ cm}^3$$

$$= 3768 \text{ cm}^3 \quad (1)$$

$\therefore$ Total surface area of the double cone

= Curved surface area of cone $CAA'$

+ Curved surface area of cone $BAA'$

$$= \pi \times OA \times AC + \pi \times OA \times AB$$

$$= (\pi \times 12 \times 20 + \pi \times 12 \times 15)$$

$$= 420\,\pi$$

$$= 420 \times 3.14$$

$$= 1318.8 \text{ cm}^2 \quad (1)$$

*Or*

Let $BPC$ be the hemisphere and $ABC$ be the cone mounted on the base of the hemisphere.

Let $EFGH$ be the right circular cylinder circumscribing the given toy.

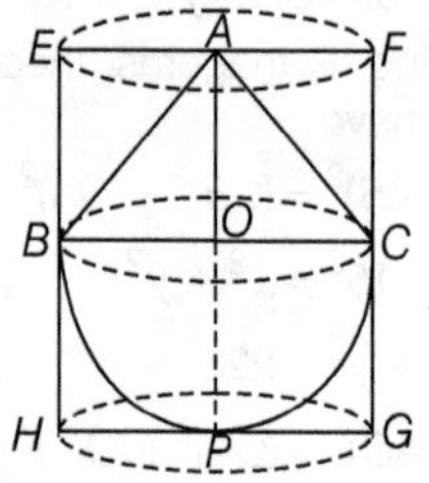


(1)

We have, height of cone, $OA = 4$ cm

Diameter of the base of the cone, $d = 8$ cm

$\therefore$ Radius of the base of cone, $r = \frac{d}{2} = \frac{8}{2} = 4$ cm

Here, $AP = AO + OP = 4 + 4 = 8$ cm (1)

Required space

= Volume of cylinder – (Volume of cone + Volume of hemisphere)

$$= \pi r^2 H - \left[\frac{1}{3}\pi r^2 h + \frac{2}{3}\pi r^3\right] = \pi r^2\left[H - \frac{1}{3}h - \frac{2}{3}r\right]$$

$$= \pi(4)^2\left[8 - \frac{1}{3}\times 4 - \frac{2}{3}\times 4\right]$$

$\left[\begin{array}{l}\text{Here, } H = AP = 8\text{ cm}\\ \text{and } h = AO = 4\text{ cm}\end{array}\right]$ (1)

$$= 16\pi\left[8 - \frac{4}{3} - \frac{8}{3}\right] = 16\pi\left[\frac{24 - 4 - 8}{3}\right]$$

$$= 16\pi \times \frac{12}{3} = 64\pi \text{ cm}^3$$

Hence, the right circular cylinder covers $64\pi$ cm$^3$ more space than the solid toy. (2)

**36.** (i) From the given figure, the position of green flag posted by Niharika is $M\left(2\times 1, \frac{1}{4}\times 100\right)$

i.e. $M(2, 25)$.

(ii) From the given figure, the position of red flag posted by Preet is $N\left(8\times 1, \frac{1}{5}\times 100\right)$

i.e. $N(8, 20)$.

(iii) $\because M = (2, 25)$ and $N = (8, 20)$

Now, $MN = \sqrt{(8-2)^2 + (20-25)^2}$

$[\because \text{distance} = \sqrt{(x_2 - x_1)^2 + (y_2 - y_1)^2}]$

$= \sqrt{(6)^2 + (-5)^2} = \sqrt{36 + 25} = \sqrt{61}$

Hence, the distance between flags is $\sqrt{61}$ m.

*Or*

(iv) Let $P$ be the position of the blue flag posted by Rashmi in the half way of line segment $MN$.

Then, coordinates of $P = \left(\frac{x_1 + x_2}{2}, \frac{y_1 + y_2}{2}\right)$

$= \left(\frac{2+8}{2}, \frac{25+20}{2}\right)$

$= \left(\frac{10}{2}, \frac{45}{2}\right) = (5, 22.5)$

Hence, the blue flag is on the 5th line at a distance of 22.5 m above it.

**37.** (i) $\because r_1 = 40$ m and $r_2 = 15$ m

$\therefore r_1 - r_2 = 40 - 15 = 25$ m

(ii) Area of sector $= \frac{\theta}{360^\circ} \times \pi r^2$

(iii) Area of sector $AOB = \frac{60^\circ}{360^\circ} \times \frac{22}{7} \times 40 \times 40$

$= \frac{1}{6} \times \frac{22}{7} \times 40 \times 40$

$= 838.09$ m$^2$

*Or*

Required area = Area of complete circle – Area of inner circle

$= \pi \times (40)^2 - \pi \times (25)^2$

$= \pi(40^2 - 25^2)$

$= \pi(40 + 25)(40 - 25)$

$= 65 \times 15 \times \pi = 975\pi$ m$^2$

**38.** (i) Let the speed of the boat in still water be $x$ km/h and speed of the stream be $y$ km/h.

Then, $x - y = 6$ ...(i)

$x + y = 14$ ...(ii)

On adding Eqs. (i) and (ii), we get

$2x = 20 \Rightarrow x = 10$

$\therefore$ Speed of the boat in still water is 10 km/h.

(ii) $\because x = 10$

On putting the value of $x$ in equation $x - y = 6$, we get

$10 - y = 6 \Rightarrow -y = 6 - 10 \Rightarrow y = 4$

$\therefore$ Speed of the stream is 4 km/h.

(iii) Time taken by Anil to travel 5 km upstream $= \frac{5}{6}$ h

Time taken by Anil to travel 10 km downstream $= \frac{10}{14}$ h

$\therefore$ Average speed $= \frac{\text{Total distance}}{\text{Total time}}$

$= \frac{5+10}{\frac{5}{6}+\frac{5}{7}} = 9.69$ km/h

*Or*

Speed of the boat = 10 km/h

Speed of the stream = 4 km/h

$\therefore$ Required ratio $= \frac{10}{4} = \frac{5}{2}$

# SAMPLE QUESTION PAPER 9

## Mathematics (Basic)

Time : **3 hrs** Max. Marks : **80**

### Instructions

1. This question paper has 5 Sections A, B, C, D and E.
2. Section A has 20 Multiple Choice Questions (MCQs) carrying 1 mark each.
3. Section B has 5 Short Answer-I (SA-I) Type Questions carrying 2 marks each.
4. Section C has 6 Short Answer-II (SA-II) Type Questions carrying 3 marks each.
5. Section D has 4 Long Answer (LA) Type Questions carrying 5 marks each.
6. Section E has 3 Case Based integrated units of assessment (4 marks each) with sub-parts of the values of 1, 1 and 2 marks each respectively.
7. All questions are compulsory. However, an internal choice in 2 questions of 2 marks, 2 questions of 3 marks and 2 questions of 5 marks has been provided. An internal choice has been provided in the 2 marks questions of Section E.
8. Draw neat figures wherever required. Take $\pi = 22/7$ wherever required if not stated.

## Section-A

**Section A consists of 20 questions of 1 mark each**

**1.** Two concentric circles are of radii 17 cm and 8 cm. Then, the length of the chord of the larger circle which touches the smaller circle is

(a) 16 (b) 36
(c) 15 (d) None of these

**2.** A card is drawn from a well-shuffled deck of 52 cards. Then, the probability that the card drawn is a black ace is

(a) $\frac{1}{52}$ (b) $\frac{1}{26}$ (c) $\frac{1}{13}$ (d) $\frac{3}{52}$

**3.** The product of the zeroes of the polynomial $3x^2 - 7x + 18$ is

(a) $-4$ (b) $\frac{7}{3}$
(c) $-\frac{7}{3}$ (d) 6

**4.** If one zero of the quadratic polynomial $kx^2 + 5x + k$ is 3, then the value of $k$ is

(a) $-\frac{3}{2}$ (b) $\frac{15}{8}$
(c) $\frac{1}{3}$ (d) $\frac{2}{3}$

**5.** The distance of point $P(6, -8)$ from the origin is
(a) 10 units (b) $\sqrt{14}$ units
(c) 2 units (d) 4 units

**6.** The centroid of a $\Delta ABC$, whose vertices are $A(1, 2)$, $B(-1, 3)$ and $C(3, -1)$ are
(a) $\left(\frac{3}{2}, 2\right)$ (b) (3, 4)
(c) $\left(1, \frac{4}{3}\right)$ (d) None of these

**7.** Coordinates of $A$ and $B$ are $(-3, a)$ and $(1, a+4)$. If mid-point of $AB$ is $(-1, 1)$, then the value of $a$ is
(a) 0 (b) $-1$ (c) $-\frac{1}{2}$ (d) 1

**8.** The discriminant of the quadratic equation $x^2 - 4x + 1 = 0$ is
(a) $2\sqrt{3}$ (b) 12 (c) 15 (d) $-8$

**9.** In the given figure, $DE \| BC$. If $AD = x$, $DB = x - 2$, $AE = x + 2$ and $EC = x - 1$, then the value of $x$ is

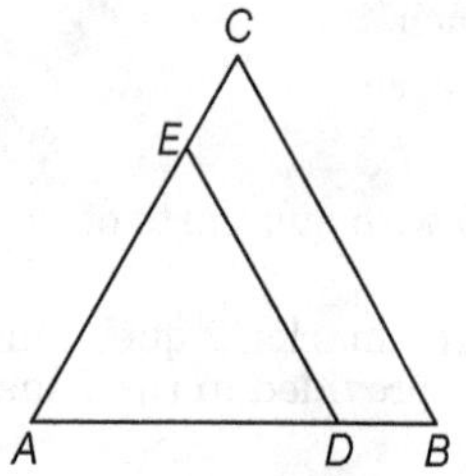


(a) 2 (b) 6 (c) 4 (d) 3

**10.** A pendulum swings through an angle of 30° and describes an arc 11.1 cm in length. The length of pendulum is
(a) 6 cm (b) 16.8 cm
(c) 8.4 cm (d) 21.19 cm

**11.** The square root of all positive integers are
(a) rational number
(b) irrational number
(c) may be rational or irrational number
(d) None of the above

**12.** If the pair of lines are coincident, then we say that pair of lines is consistent and it has a
(a) unique solution (b) no solution
(c) infinite solutions (d) None of these

**13.** If $x \cot 45° \cos 60° = \sin 30° \sin 90°$, then the value of $x$ is
(a) $\frac{1}{2}$ (b) $-1$ (c) 1 (d) 2

**14.** The prime factor of 1584 is
(a) $2^5 \times 3 \times 11$ (b) $2^3 \times 3^3 \times 11$
(c) $2^3 \times 3 \times 11^2$ (d) $2^4 \times 3^2 \times 11$

**15.** If we join two hemispheres of same radius along their bases, then we get a
(a) cone (b) cylinder
(c) cuboid (d) sphere

**16.** Two identical solid cubes of side $3a$ are joined end to end. Then, total surface area of the resulting cuboid is
(a) $8a^2$ (b) $6a^2$
(c) $90a^2$ (d) $12a^2$

**17.** The median of the data 12, 15, 17, 19, 22, 27 is
(a) 17 (b) 18 (c) $\frac{41}{2}$ (d) 19

**18.** The pair of equations $3x + 2y + 7 = 0$ and $6x + 4y + 14 = 0$ has
(a) unique solution
(b) exactly two solutions
(c) infinitely many solutions
(d) no solution

**Directions** *In the question number 19 and 20, a statement of Assertion (A) is followed by a statement of Reason (R). Choose the correct option.*

**19. Assertion (A)** In a circle of radius 6 cm, the angle of a sector is 60°, the area of the sector is $\frac{132}{7}$ cm$^2$.

**Reason (R)** Area of the circle with radius $r$ is $\pi r^2$.
(a) Both Assertion (A) and Reason (R) are true and Reason (R) is the correct explanation of Assertion (A)
(b) Both Assertion (A) and Reason (R) are true but Reason (R) is not the correct explanation of Assertion (A)
(c) Assertion (A) is true but Reason (R) is false
(d) Assertion (A) is false but Reason (R) is true

**20.** **Assertion (A)** $x^2 + 5x + 7$ has no real zeroes.

**Reason (R)** A quadratic polynomial can have at the most two zeroes.

(a) Both Assertion (A) and Reason (R) are true and Reason (R) is the correct explanation of Assertion (A)
(b) Both Assertion (A) and Reason (R) are true but Reason (R) is not the correct explanation of Assertion (A)
(c) Assertion (A) is true but Reason (R) is false
(d) Assertion (A) is false but Reason (R) is true

# Section-B

**Section B consists of 5 questions of 2 marks each**

**21.** Use elimination method to find all possible solutions of the following pair of equation

$ax + by - a + b = 0$ and $bx - ay - a - b = 0$

*Or*

Find the solution of the following system of equations by substitution method.

$1.1x + 1.5y + 2.3 = 0,\ 0.7x - 0.2y = 2$

**22.** The length of minute hand of a clock is 21 cm. Find the area swept by the minute hand in one minute.

$\left[\text{take, } \pi = \frac{22}{7}\right]$

**23.** Without solving the following quadratic equation, find the value of $p$, for which the roots are equal.

$px^2 - 4x - 3 = 0$

**24.** Find the 25th term of the AP $-5, \frac{-5}{2}, 0, \frac{5}{2}, \ldots$

*Or* Determine the AP, whose 3rd term is 5 and the 7th term is 9.

**25.** If $\alpha$ and $\beta$ are the zeroes of quadratic polynomial $p(y) = 3y^2 + 5y + 2$, then find the value of $\alpha + \alpha\beta + \beta$.

# Section-C

**Section C consists of 6 questions of 3 marks each**

**26.** A man standing on the bank of a river observes that the angle of elevation of a tree on the opposite bank is 60°. When he moves 50 m away from the bank, then he find the angle of elevation to be 30°. Calculate

(i) the width of the river.
(ii) the height of the tree.

*Or*

A vertical tower is 20 m high. A man standing at some distance from the tower knows that the cosine of the angle of elevation $\theta$ of the top of the tower is 0.53. i.e. $\cos\theta = 0.53$ How far is he standing from the foot of the tower?

**27.** If $\tan\theta = \frac{12}{5}$, find the value of $\frac{1+\sin\theta}{1-\sin\theta}$.

*Or* If $\sin(A+B) = 1$ and $\cos(A-B) = \frac{\sqrt{3}}{2}$, $0° < A + B \le 90°$, $A > B$, then find the values of $A$ and $B$.

**28.** In the given figure, $DE || BC$ and $CD || EF$, then prove that $AD^2 = AB \times AF$.

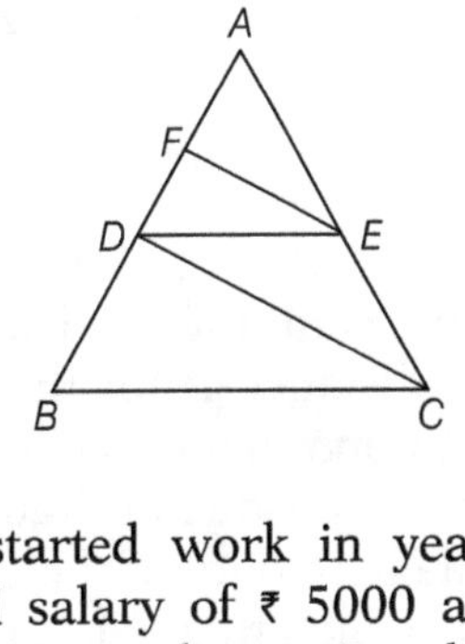


**29.** Ram started work in year 1995 at an annual salary of ₹ 5000 and received a ₹ 200 raise each year. In what year did his annual salary will reach ₹ 7000?

**30.** Solve : $(x-3)(x-4)=\frac{34}{(33)^2}$.

**31.** The mid-point of sides $AB$ and $AC$ of $\Delta ABC$ are $E(2,-1)$ and $F(0,-1)$, respectively. The coordinates of the point $A$ is $(1,-4)$. Find the centroid of $\Delta ABC$.

# Section-D

**Section D consists of 4 questions of 5 marks each**

**32.** A solid is in the shape of a cone standing on a hemisphere with both their radii being equal to 2 cm and the height of the cone is equal to its radius. Find the volume and surface area of the solid.

**33.** A card is drawn from a well-shuffled pack of 52 cards. Find the probability that the card drawn is

(i) 5 of heart or diamond

(ii) jack or queen

(iii) ace and king

(iv) a red or a king

**34.** An aeroplane flies horizontally in a fixed direction at a height of $1500\sqrt{3}$m from ground. At any time the angle of elevation from a point on a ground is 60° and after 15 s, the angle of measurement of an aeroplane becomes 30°. Find the speed of the aeroplane.

*Or* A 1.5 m tall boy is standing at some distance from a 30 m tall building. The angle of elevation from his eyes to the top of the building increases from 30° to 60° as he walks towards the building. Find the distance he walked towards the building.

**35.** $ABCD$ is a trapezium, in which $AB \parallel DC$ and its diagonals intersect each other at the point $O$. Show that $\frac{AO}{BO}=\frac{CO}{DO}$.

*Or*

In the given figure, altitudes $AD$ and $CE$ of $\Delta ABC$ intersect each other at the point $P$.

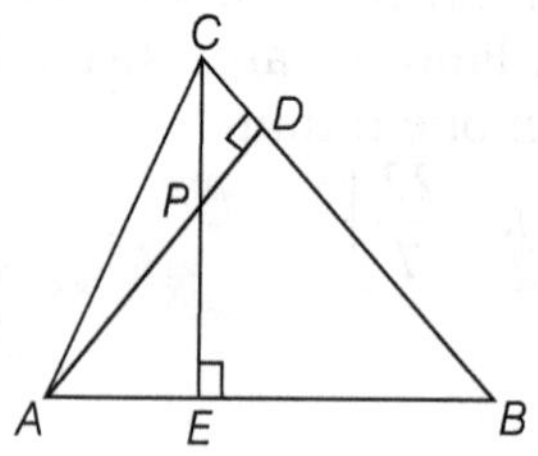


Show that

(i) $\Delta AEP \sim \Delta CDP$.

(ii) $\Delta ABD \sim \Delta CBE$.

(iii) $\Delta AEP \sim \Delta ADB$.

(iv) $\Delta PDC \sim \Delta BEC$.

# Section-E

**Case study based questions are compulsory**

**36.** People of village want to construct a road nearest to a circular village Rampur. The road cannot pass through the village. But the people want the road should be at the shortest distance from the centre of the village. Suppose, the road start from point $O$, which is outside the circular village and touch the boundary of the circular village at point $A$ such that $OA=20$ cm and also, the straight distance of the point $O$ from the centre $C$ of the village is 25 cm.

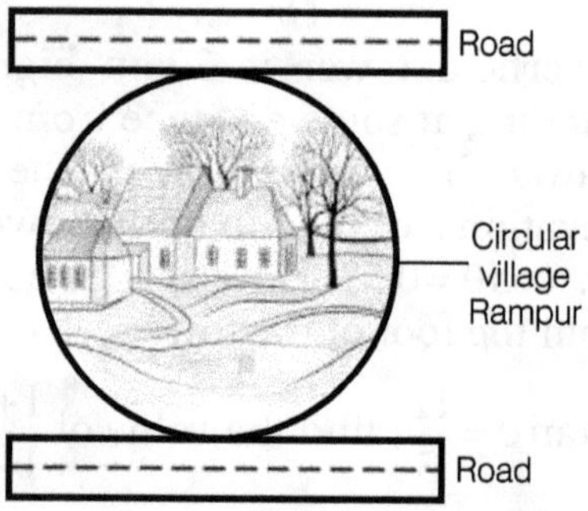

On the basis of above information, answer the following questions.

(i) Find the shortest distance of the road from the centre of the village. (1)

(ii) If a point is inside the circle, how many tangents can be drawn from that point? (1)

(iii) If two circles are externally and they do not touch, then find the number of common tangents. (2)

*Or* If $DE$ and $DF$ are tangents from the external point $D$ to the circular village. If $DE \perp DF$, then find the length of $DE$. (2)

**37.** Air pollution refers to the release of pollutants into the air that are detrimental to human health and the plant as a whole. In this order Rajasthan government, conducted a awareness programme related to environment localities of a city, the concentration of sulphur dioxide ($SO_2$) in the air (in parts per million i.e., ppm) in 24 are as following

| Concentration of $SO_2$ (in ppm) | Frequency |
|---|---|
| 0.00 - 0.02 | 2 |
| 0.02 - 0.04 | 5 |
| 0.04 - 0.06 | 4 |
| 0.06 - 0.08 | 3 |
| 0.08 - 0.10 | 4 |
| 0.10 - 0.12 | 6 |

On the basis of above information, answer the following questions.

(i) Write formula to find the mean. (1)

(ii) Write the formula to find the median. (1)

(iii) Find the mean concentration of $SO_2$. (2)

*Or*

Find the median concentration of $SO_2$. (2)

**38.** To enhance the reading skills of grade X students, the school nominates you and two of your friends to set up a class library. There are two sections- Section A and Section B of grade X. There are 32 students in section A and 36 students in section B.

On the basis of above information answer the following questions.

(i) What is the minimum number of books you will acquire for the class library, so that they can be distributed equally among students of Section A or Section B? (1)

(ii) If the product of two positive integers is equal to the product of their HCF and LCM is true, then find the HCF (32, 36). (1)

(iii) Express 5310 as product of primes. (2)

*Or* If $p$ and $q$ are positive integers such that $p = ab^2$ and $q = a^2b$, where $a$ and $b$ are prime numbers, then find the LCM$(p, q)$. (2)

# SOLUTIONS

**1.** (d) Let $O$ be the centre of concentric circles of radii 17 cm and 8 cm, respectively.

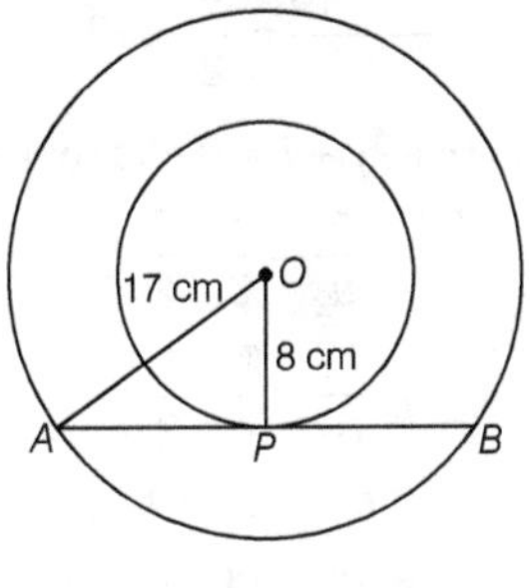


Let $AB$ be a chord of the larger circle touching the smaller circle at $P$.

Then, $AP = PB$ and $OP \perp AB$.

Now, in $\Delta OPA$, we have

$$OA^2 = OP^2 + AP^2 \quad \text{[by Pythagoras theorem]}$$

$\Rightarrow$ $(17)^2 = (8)^2 + AP^2 \Rightarrow 289 = 64 + AP^2$

$\Rightarrow$ $AP^2 = 225$

$\Rightarrow$ $AP = 15\text{ cm}$

$\therefore$ $AB = 2AP = 2 \times 15 = 30\text{ cm}$

**2.** (b) Well-shuffling ensures equally likely outcomes.
Total number of outcomes =52
There are two black aces one of each suit.
∴ The number of favourable outcomes to the event an ace = 2

$\therefore P(\text{an ace})=\frac{2}{52}=\frac{1}{26}$

**3.** (d) Let $p(x)=3x^2-7x+18$

Now, product of zeroes $=\frac{\text{Constant term}}{\text{Coefficient of } x^2}$

$=\frac{18}{3}=6$

**4.** (a) Since, 3 is a zero of $kx^2+5x+k$.

$\therefore\ k(3)^2+5(3)+k=0$

$\Rightarrow\ 9k+15+k=0$

$\Rightarrow\ 10k+15=0$

$\Rightarrow\ k=-\frac{15}{10}=-\frac{3}{2}$

**5.** (a) Given, points are $P(6,-8)$ and origin $O(0,0)$.
Here, $(x_1,y_1)=(6,-8)$ and $(x_2,y_2)=(0,0)$

$\therefore\ OP=\sqrt{(x_2-x_1)^2+(y_2-y_1)^2}$

$=\sqrt{(0-6)^2+(0+8)^2}$

$=\sqrt{36+64}=\sqrt{100}=10$ units

**6.** (c) The centroid of a $\Delta ABC$ having vertices $A(1,2)$, $B(-1,3)$ and $C(3,-1)$ is

$G\left(\frac{1-1+3}{3},\frac{2+3-1}{3}\right)$ or $G\left(1,\frac{4}{3}\right)$

**7.** (b) Mid-point of $AB=\left(\frac{-3+1}{2},\frac{a+a+4}{2}\right)=(-1,1)$

$\Rightarrow\ (-1,a+2)=(-1,1)$

$\Rightarrow\ a+2=1\Rightarrow a=-1$

**8.** (b) Given, quadratic equation is $x^2-4x+1=0$.

On comparing with $ax^2+bx+c=0$, we get

$a=1, b=-4$ and $c=1$

$\therefore\ D=b^2-4ac=(-4)^2-4(1)(1)$

$=16-4=12$

**9.** (c) In $\Delta ABC$, we have

$DE \parallel BC$

$\therefore\ \frac{AD}{DB}=\frac{AE}{EC}$ [by Thales theorem]

$\Rightarrow\ \frac{x}{x-2}=\frac{x+2}{x-1}$

$\Rightarrow\ x(x-1)=(x-2)(x+2)$

$\Rightarrow\ x^2-x=x^2-4$

$\Rightarrow\ x=4$

**10.** (d) Here, $\theta=30^\circ$ and $l=\text{arc}=11.1$ cm

$\therefore\ l=\frac{\theta}{360^\circ}\times 2\pi r$

$\Rightarrow\ 11.1=\frac{30^\circ}{360^\circ}\times 2\times\frac{22}{7}\times r$

$\Rightarrow\ r=\frac{11.1\times 6\times 7}{22}$ cm $=21.19$ cm

**11.** (c) Clearly, $\sqrt{9}=\pm 3$, which is rational number.

Hence, square root of all positive integers may be rational or irrational number.

**12.** (c) If the pair of lines are coincident, then it has infinite number of solutions and hence, consistent.

**13.** (c) We have, $x\cot 45^\circ\cos 60^\circ=\sin 30^\circ\sin 90^\circ$

$\therefore\ x\times 1\times\frac{1}{2}=\frac{1}{2}\times 1$

$\Rightarrow\ x=1$

**14.** (d) The prime factor of 1584 is

| | |
|---|---|
| 2 | 1584 |
| 2 | 792 |
| 2 | 396 |
| 2 | 198 |
| 3 | 99 |
| 3 | 33 |
| | 11 |

$\therefore\ 1584=2^4\times 3^2\times 11$

**15.** (d) Sphere

**16.** (c) Length of the resulting cuboid = $6a$
breadth of the resulting cuboid = $3a$
and height of the resulting cuboid = $3a$

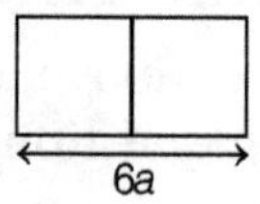


$\therefore$ Total surface area $=2(lb+bh+hl)$

$=2[6a(3a)+3a(3a)+3a(6a)]$

$=2(18a^2+9a^2+18a^2)$

$=2\times(459)^2=90a^2$

**17.** (b) For the given data, these are two middle terms, 17 and 19.

$\therefore$ Median $=\frac{17+19}{2}=\frac{36}{2}=18$

**18.** (c) Given, $3x+2y+7=0$ and $6x+4y+14=0$

Here, $\frac{a_1}{a_2}=\frac{3}{6}=\frac{1}{2}$,

$\frac{b_1}{b_2}=\frac{2}{4}=\frac{1}{2}$

and $\frac{c_1}{c_2}=\frac{7}{14}=\frac{1}{2}$

Hence, $\frac{a_1}{a_2}=\frac{b_1}{b_2}=\frac{c_1}{c_2}=\frac{1}{2}$

So, the lines representing the given pair of linear equation will coincide, therefore there are infinitely many solutions.

**19.** (b) Area of a sector $=\frac{\theta}{360^\circ}\times\pi r^2$

Here, $\theta=60^\circ$ and $r=6$ cm

$\therefore$ Area of given sector $=\frac{60^\circ}{360^\circ}\times\frac{22}{7}\times6\times6$

$=\frac{22\times6}{7}=\frac{132}{7}\text{ cm}^2$

So, the Assertion is true.

Area of a circle with radius, $r=\pi r^2$

Clearly, Reason is also true but it is not the correct explanation of Assertion.

**20.** (b) Let $p(x)=x^2+5x+7$

Put $p(x)=0 \Rightarrow x^2+5x+7=0$

On comparing $ax^2+bx+c=0$, we get

$a=1, b=5$ and $c=7$

$\therefore$ Discriminant, $d=b^2-4ac=(5)^2-4\times1\times7$

$=25-28=-3<0$

So, the given polynomial has no real roots.

Hence, the given Assertion is true.

Clearly, Reason is also true but it is not the correct explanation of given Assertion.

**21.** Given, pair of linear equations is

$ax+by=a-b$ ...(i)

and $bx-ay=a+b$ ...(ii)

On multiplying Eq. (i) by $a$, Eq. (ii) by $b$ and then adding them, we get

$a^2x+aby+b^2x-aby=a^2-ab+ba+b^2$

$\Rightarrow (a^2+b^2)x=(a^2+b^2)$

$\Rightarrow x=\frac{a^2+b^2}{a^2+b^2}=1$ (1)

On putting $x=1$ in Eq. (i), we get

$a+by=a-b \Rightarrow y=-\frac{b}{b}=-1$

Hence, $x=1$ and $y=-1$, which is the required unique solution. (1)

*Or*

Given, pair of linear equations are

$1.1x+1.5y+2.3=0$ and $0.7x-0.2y=2$

On multiplying these equations by 10, we get

$11x+15y+23=0$ ...(i)

and $7x-2y=20$ ...(ii)

From Eq. (i), $15y=-23-11x$

$\Rightarrow y=\frac{-23-11x}{15}$

On putting the value of $y$ in Eq. (ii), we get

$7x-2\left(\frac{-23-11x}{15}\right)=20$

$\Rightarrow 105x+(46+22x)=15\times20$

$\Rightarrow 127x=300-46$

$\Rightarrow 127x=254 \Rightarrow x=2$ (1)

Put $x=2$ in Eq. (ii), we get

$7(2)-2y=20$

$\Rightarrow 2y=14-20$

$\Rightarrow y=7-10$

$\Rightarrow y=-3$ (1)

**22.** The minute hand of a clock describes a circle of radius equal to its length, i.e. 21 cm in 1 h.

So, the angle described by minute hand in 60 min $=360^\circ$.

$\therefore$ Angle described by minute hand in 1 min

$=\frac{360^\circ}{60}=6^\circ$ (1)

So, the area swept by the minute hand in 1 min is the area of a sector of angle 6° in a circle of radius 21 cm.

$\therefore$ Required area $=\frac{\theta}{360^\circ}\times\pi r^2$

$=\frac{6^\circ}{360^\circ}\times\frac{22}{7}\times(21)^2$

$=\frac{1}{60}\times\frac{22}{7}\times21\times21=23.1\text{ cm}^2$ (1)

**23.** Given, quadratic equation is $px^2-4x-3=0$.

On comparing it with $ax^2+bx+c=0$, we get

$a=p, b=-4$ and $c=-3$

Since, the given equation has equal roots.

So, the discriminant $D$ will be zero. (1)

i.e. $D=b^2-4ac=0$

$\therefore (-4)^2-4\times p\times(-3)=0$

$\Rightarrow 16+12p=0 \Rightarrow 12p=-16$

$\therefore p=\frac{-16}{12}=\frac{-4}{3}$

Hence, the value of $p$ is $\frac{-4}{3}$. (1)

**24.** Given, AP is $-5, \frac{-5}{2}, 0, \frac{5}{2}, \ldots$

Here, $a=-5$

and common difference $(d)=-\frac{5}{2}-(-5)=\frac{-5}{2}+5=\frac{5}{2}$ (1)

$\therefore$ 25th term of the given AP is

$a_{25}=a+(25-1)d$ $[\because a_n=a+(n-1)d]$

$\Rightarrow a_{25}=-5+24\left(\frac{5}{2}\right)=-5+60=55$

Hence, 25th term of the given AP is 55. (1)

*Or*

Let $a$ and $d$ be the first term and common difference of an AP.

$\therefore$ $T_3 = 5$ and $T_7 = 9$

$\Rightarrow$ $a + (3-1)d = 5$ $\quad [\because a_n = a + (n-1)d]$

and $a + (7-1)d = 9$

$\Rightarrow$ $a + 2d = 5$ ...(i)

and $a + 6d = 9$ ...(ii) (1)

On subtracting Eq. (i) from Eq. (ii), we get

$$6d - 2d = 9 - 5$$

$\Rightarrow$ $4d = 4$

$\Rightarrow$ $d = 1$

On putting $d = 1$ in Eq. (i), we get

$$a + 2 \times 1 = 5 \Rightarrow a = 3$$

$\therefore$ The AP series is 3, 4, 5, 6, ... (1)

**25.** Given, polynomial is $p(y) = 3y^2 + 5y + 2$

Now sum of zeroes, $\alpha + \beta = -\dfrac{\text{Coefficient of } y}{\text{Coefficient of } y^2}$

$= -\dfrac{5}{3}$

and product of zeroes, $\alpha\beta = \dfrac{\text{Constant term}}{\text{Coefficient of } y^2}$

$= \dfrac{2}{3}$ (1)

Now, $\alpha + \alpha\beta + \beta = (\alpha + \beta) + \alpha\beta$

$= -\dfrac{5}{3} + \dfrac{2}{3} = -\dfrac{3}{3} = -1$ (1)

**26.** Let $AB = h$ be the height of the tree and $BC = x$ be the width of the river.

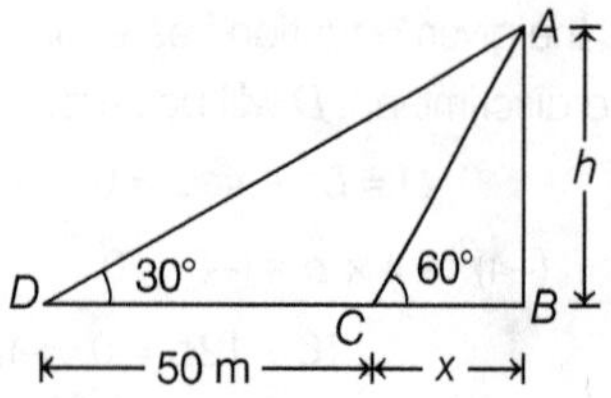


(1)

(i) In $\Delta ABC$, we have

$$\tan 60° = \frac{AB}{BC}$$

$\Rightarrow$ $\sqrt{3} = \dfrac{h}{x}$ $\quad [\because \tan 60° = \sqrt{3}]$

$\Rightarrow$ $h = \sqrt{3}x$ ...(i)

Now, in $\Delta ABD$, we have

$$\tan 30° = \frac{AB}{BD}$$

$\Rightarrow$ $\tan 30° = \dfrac{AB}{BC + CD}$

$\Rightarrow$ $\dfrac{1}{\sqrt{3}} = \dfrac{h}{x + 50}$ $\quad \left[\because \tan 30° = \dfrac{1}{\sqrt{3}}\right]$

$\Rightarrow$ $x + 50 = \sqrt{3}h$ ...(ii) (1/2)

On putting the value of $h$ from Eq. (i) to Eq. (ii), we get

$$x + 50 = \sqrt{3} \times \sqrt{3}x$$

$\Rightarrow$ $x + 50 = 3x$

$\Rightarrow$ $3x - x = 50$

$\Rightarrow$ $2x = 50$

$\Rightarrow$ $x = \dfrac{50}{2} = 25$

Hence, the width of the river is 25 m. (1)

(ii) On putting $x = 25$ in Eq. (i), we get

$$h = \sqrt{3} \times 25 = 1.732 \times 25 = 43.3 \text{ m}$$

Hence, the height of the tree is 43.3 m. (1/2)

*Or*

Given, height of tower, $AB = 20$ m

Let a man standing at the point $C$. The angle of elevation of the top of tower is $\theta$ and we have

$$\cos \theta = 0.53$$

Let distance between foot of the tower and man be $BC = x$ m.

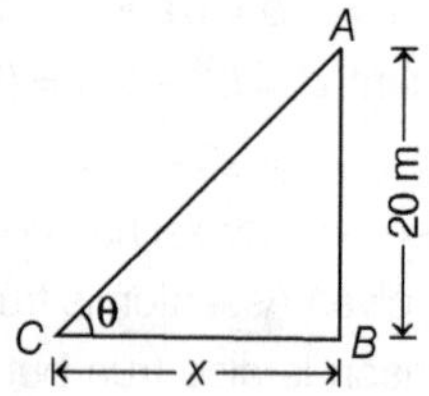


(1)

We know that

$$\sin^2\theta + \cos^2\theta = 1$$

$\Rightarrow$ $\sin\theta = \sqrt{1 - \cos^2\theta}$

$= \sqrt{1 - (0.53)^2}$ $\quad [\because \cos\theta = 0.53]$

$= \sqrt{1 - 0.281}$

$= \sqrt{0.719} = 0.85$

Now, $\tan\theta = \dfrac{\sin\theta}{\cos\theta} = \dfrac{0.85}{0.53}$ ...(i) (1)

In $\Delta ABC$, we have

$$\tan\theta = \frac{AB}{BC} = \frac{20}{x}$$

$\Rightarrow$ $x = \dfrac{20}{\tan\theta}$

$\Rightarrow$ $x = \dfrac{20 \times 0.53}{0.85}$ $\quad$ [from Eq. (i)]

$= 12.47$

Hence, the distance between man and foot of tower is 12.47 m. (1)

**27.** We have, $\tan\theta = \dfrac{12}{5}$

$\therefore$ $\sec\theta = \sqrt{1 + \tan^2\theta}$ $\quad [\because \sec^2 A = 1 + \tan^2 A]$

$= \sqrt{1 + \left(\dfrac{12}{5}\right)^2} = \sqrt{\dfrac{169}{25}} = \dfrac{13}{5}$ (1)

$\therefore \quad \dfrac{1+\sin\theta}{1-\sin\theta} = \dfrac{\sec\theta+\tan\theta}{\sec\theta-\tan\theta}$

[divide $\cos\theta$ by numerator and denominator] **(1)**

$$= \frac{\frac{13}{5}+\frac{12}{5}}{\frac{13}{5}-\frac{12}{5}} = 25 \quad \textbf{(1)}$$

*Or*

We have, $\sin(A+B)=1$

$\Rightarrow \quad \sin(A+B)=\sin 90^\circ$

$\Rightarrow \quad A+B=90^\circ \quad \ldots\text{(i)} \quad \textbf{(1)}$

and $\quad \cos(A-B)=\dfrac{\sqrt{3}}{2}$

$\Rightarrow \quad \cos(A-B)=\cos 30^\circ$

$\Rightarrow \quad A-B=30^\circ \quad \ldots\text{(ii)} \quad \textbf{(1)}$

On adding Eqs. (i) and (ii), we get

$(A+B)+(A-B)=90^\circ+30^\circ$

$\Rightarrow \quad 2A=120^\circ$

$\Rightarrow \quad A=60^\circ$

Putting $A=60^\circ$ in Eq. (i), we get

$60^\circ+B=90^\circ$

$\Rightarrow \quad B=30^\circ$

Hence, $A=60^\circ$ and $B=30^\circ$ **(1)**

**28.** In $\Delta ABC$, we have

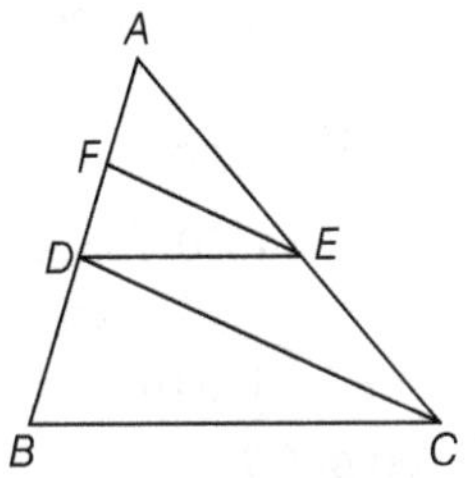


$DE \parallel BC \Rightarrow \dfrac{AB}{AD}=\dfrac{AC}{AE} \quad \ldots\text{(i)} \quad \textbf{(1)}$

In $\Delta ADC$, we have

$FE \parallel DC \Rightarrow \dfrac{AD}{AF}=\dfrac{AC}{AE} \quad \ldots\text{(ii)}$

From Eqs. (i) and (ii), we get

$\dfrac{AB}{AD}=\dfrac{AD}{AF}$

$\Rightarrow \quad AD^2 = AB \times AF$ **Hence proved.** **(2)**

**29.** Annual salary received by Ram in 1995, 1996, 1997 … is ₹ 5000, ₹ 5200, ₹ 5400.

Clearly, it is AP with first term $a=5000$ and common difference $d=5200-5000=200$

Suppose Ram's annual salary reaches to ₹ 7000 in $n$th yr. **(1)**

Then, $n$th term of the above AP, $T_n =$ ₹ 7000

$\therefore \quad a+(n-1)d=T_n$

$\Rightarrow \quad 5000+(n-1)\times 200=7000 \quad \textbf{(1)}$

$\Rightarrow \quad (n-1)\times 200=2000$

$\Rightarrow \quad n-1=\dfrac{2000}{200}=10$

$\Rightarrow \quad n=10+1=11$

Thus, 11th annual salary received by Ram will be ₹ 7000. This means that after 10 yr, i.e. in the year 2005 his annual salary will reach to ₹ 7000. **(1)**

**30.** We have,

$$(x-3)(x-4)=\frac{34}{(33)^2}$$

$\Rightarrow \quad x^2-7x+12-\dfrac{34}{(33)^2}=0$

$\Rightarrow \quad x^2-7x+\dfrac{13034}{(33)^2}=0$

$\Rightarrow \quad x^2-7x+\dfrac{98}{33}\times\dfrac{133}{33}=0 \quad \textbf{(1)}$

$\Rightarrow \quad x^2-\dfrac{231}{33}x+\dfrac{98}{33}\times\dfrac{133}{33}=0$

$\Rightarrow \quad x^2-\left(\dfrac{98}{33}+\dfrac{133}{33}\right)x+\dfrac{98}{33}\times\dfrac{133}{33}=0$

$\Rightarrow \quad x^2-\dfrac{98}{33}x-\dfrac{133}{33}x+\dfrac{98}{33}\times\dfrac{133}{33}=0$

$\Rightarrow \quad \left(x^2-\dfrac{98}{33}x\right)-\left(\dfrac{133}{33}x-\dfrac{98}{33}\times\dfrac{133}{33}\right)=0 \quad \textbf{(1)}$

$\Rightarrow \quad x\left(x-\dfrac{98}{33}\right)-\dfrac{133}{33}\left(x-\dfrac{98}{33}\right)=0$

$\Rightarrow \quad \left(x-\dfrac{98}{33}\right)\left(x-\dfrac{133}{33}\right)=0$

$\Rightarrow \quad x=\dfrac{98}{33} \text{ or } x=\dfrac{133}{33} \quad \textbf{(1)}$

**31.** Given, the mid-point of sides $AB$ and $AC$ of $\Delta ABC$ are $E(2,-1)$ and $F(0,-1)$, respectively and coordinate of $A$ is $(1,-4)$.

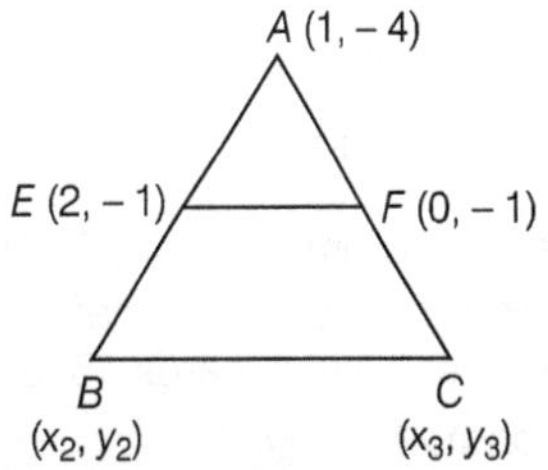


**(1)**

Let $A(1,-4)$, $B(x_2, y_2)$ and $C(x_3, y_3)$.

$\because \quad E$ is the mid-point of $AB$.

$2=\dfrac{1+x_2}{2}, \; -1=\dfrac{-4+y_2}{2}$

$\Rightarrow \quad x_2=4-1, \; y_2=-2+4$

$\Rightarrow \quad x_2=3, \; y_2=2 \quad \textbf{(1)}$

Similarly, $F$ is mid-point of $AC$.

$\Rightarrow \quad 0=\frac{1+x_3}{2}, \ -1=\frac{-4+y_3}{2}$

$\Rightarrow \quad x_3=-1, \ y_3=2$

So, the coordinates of the centroid of a triangle whose vertices are $(1,-4)$, $(3,2)$ and $(-1,2)$ are

$$\left(\frac{1+3+(-1)}{3}, \frac{-4+2+2}{3}\right) \text{ or } (1, 0)$$ (1)

**32.** Given, radius of cone, $r_1 = 2$ cm

Height of cone, $h_1 = 2$ cm

Radius of hemisphere, $r_2 = 2$ cm

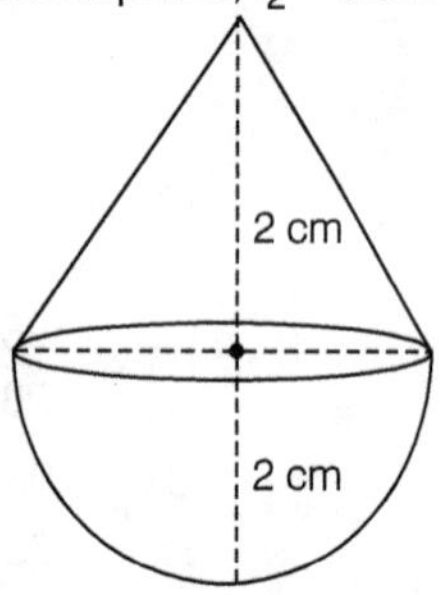


(1)

Let $V$ and $S$ be the volume and surface area of the solid.

Then, $V$ = volume of cone + volume of hemisphere

$= \frac{1}{3}\pi r_1^2 h_1 + \frac{2}{3}\pi r_2^3$ (1)

$= \frac{1}{3}\pi[(2)^2 \times 2 + 2 \times (2)^3]$

$= \frac{1}{3}\pi(8+16) = \frac{24}{3}\pi$

$= 8\pi \text{ cm}^3$ (1)

and $S$ = Curved surface area of cone + Curved surface area of hemisphere

$= \pi r_1 l + 2\pi r_1^2 = \pi(r_1 l + 2r_1^2)$ (1)

$= \pi[2 \times \sqrt{h_1^2 + r_1^2} + 2 \times (2)^2]$

$= \pi(2 \times \sqrt{2^2 + 2^2} + 8)$

$= \pi(2 \times 2\sqrt{2} + 8)$

$= 4\pi(\sqrt{2} + 2) \text{ cm}^2$ (1)

**33.** A card is drawn from a well-shuffled pack of 52 cards.

$\therefore$ Number of possible outcomes = 52 (1)

(i) There are 2 such cards (5 of heart and 5 of diamond).

$\therefore$ $P$ (drawn card is 5 of heart or diamond)

$= \frac{2}{52} = \frac{1}{26}$ (1)

(ii) There are total 8 such cards (4 jack and 4 queen).

$\therefore$ $P$ (drawn card is a jack or queen) $= \frac{8}{52} = \frac{2}{13}$ (1)

(iii) There is no card, which is an ace as well as king.

$\therefore$ $P$ (drawn card is ace and king) $= \frac{0}{52} = 0$ (1)

(iv) There are total 28 such cards (26 red cards and 2 black kings).

$\therefore$ $P$ (drawn card is a red or a king) $= \frac{28}{52} = \frac{7}{13}$ (1)

**34.** Let $A$ be the position of an aeroplane which is flying at a height $1500\sqrt{3}$ m from the ground,

i.e. $AB = 1500\sqrt{3}$ m and angle of elevation from point $P$ be $60°$ i.e. $\angle APB = 60°$. (1)

After 15 s, aeroplane reaches at point $A'$, then angle of elevation from point $P$ be $\angle A'PB' = 30°$ and $AB = A'B' = 1500\sqrt{3}$ m.

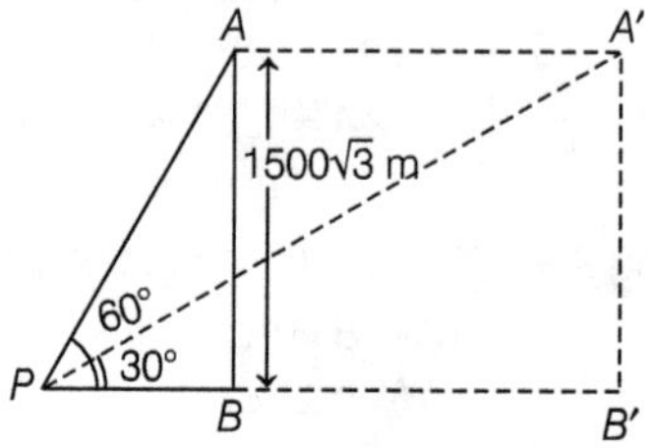


(1)

In right angled $\Delta A'B'P$,

$\tan 30° = \frac{A'B'}{PB'} = \frac{AB}{PB'}$ $[\because A'B' = AB]$

$\Rightarrow \quad \frac{1}{\sqrt{3}} = \frac{1500\sqrt{3}}{PB'}$ $\left[\because \tan 30° = \frac{1}{\sqrt{3}}\right]$

$\Rightarrow \quad PB' = 1500\sqrt{3} \times \sqrt{3}$ [using cross-multiplication]

$\Rightarrow \quad PB' = 4500$ m (1)

In right angled $\Delta APB$,

$\tan 60° = \frac{AB}{PB}$

$\Rightarrow \quad \sqrt{3} = \frac{1500\sqrt{3}}{PB}$ $[\because \tan 60° = \sqrt{3}]$

$\Rightarrow \quad PB = \frac{1500\sqrt{3}}{\sqrt{3}}$

$= 1500$ m (1)

Distance travelled by aeroplane in 15 s,

$BB' = PB' - PB = (4500 - 1500)$ m

$= 3000$ m

Now, speed of aeroplane

$= \frac{\text{Distance covered in 15 s}}{\text{Time taken to cover the distance}}$

$= \frac{3000}{15}$

$= 200$ m/s

Hence, the speed of aeroplane is 200 m/s. (1)

*Or*

Let $AB = 30$ m be the height of the building, $DC = 1.5$ m be the length of the boy. The point $D$ be the boy eyes. The angle of elevations are $\angle BDF = 30^\circ$ and $\angle BEF = 60^\circ$.

Let $DE = x$ and $EF = y$

Now, $BF = AB - AF = 30 - 1.5 = 28.5$

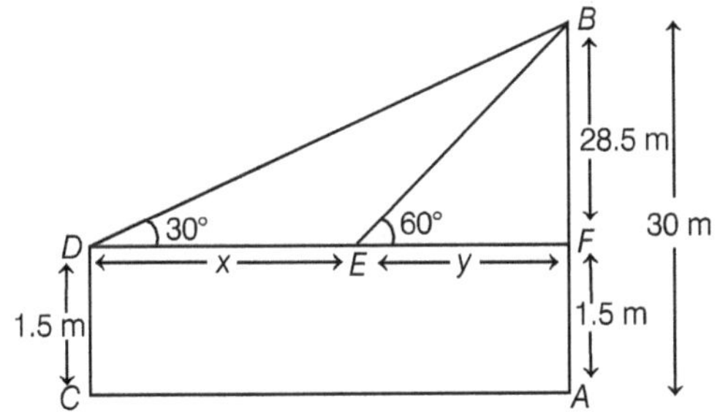


(1)

In right angled $\Delta BDF$,

$$\tan 30^\circ = \frac{BF}{DF}$$

$$\Rightarrow \quad \frac{1}{\sqrt{3}} = \frac{28.5}{x+y}$$

$$\Rightarrow \quad x + y = 28.5\sqrt{3} \quad \text{...(i) (1)}$$

Again, in right angled $\Delta BEF$,

$$\tan 60^\circ = \frac{BF}{EF}$$

$$\Rightarrow \quad \sqrt{3} = \frac{28.5}{y}$$

$$\Rightarrow \quad y = \frac{28.5}{\sqrt{3}} \text{ m} \quad \text{...(ii) (1)}$$

Putting $y = \frac{28.5}{\sqrt{3}}$ in Eq. (i), we get

$$x + \frac{28.5}{\sqrt{3}} = 28.5\sqrt{3}$$

$$\Rightarrow \quad x = 28.5\left(\sqrt{3} - \frac{1}{\sqrt{3}}\right) = 28.5\left(\frac{3-1}{\sqrt{3}}\right)$$

$$= \frac{28.5 \times 2}{\sqrt{3}} \times \frac{\sqrt{3}}{\sqrt{3}} = \frac{57\sqrt{3}}{3} = 19\sqrt{3} \text{ m}$$

Hence, the distance between two elevations is $19\sqrt{3}$ m. (2)

**35.** **Given** $ABCD$ is a trapezium in which $AB \parallel CD$.

Diagonals $AC$ and $BD$ intersect each other at $O$.

**To prove** $\frac{AO}{BO} = \frac{CO}{DO}$

**Construction** Draw $EOF \parallel AB$, also parallel to $CD$.

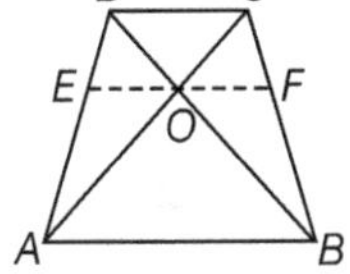


(1)

**Proof** In $\Delta ACD$, $OE \parallel CD$ [by construction]

$$\Rightarrow \quad \frac{AE}{ED} = \frac{AO}{OC} \quad \text{...(i) (1)}$$

[by basic proportionality theorem]

In $\Delta ABD$, $OE \parallel BA$ [by construction]

$$\Rightarrow \quad \frac{ED}{AE} = \frac{OD}{OB}$$

[by basic proportionality theorem]

$$\Rightarrow \quad \frac{AE}{ED} = \frac{OB}{OD}$$

[taking reciprocal of the terms] ...(ii) (1)

From Eqs. (i) and (ii), we get

$$\frac{AO}{OC} = \frac{OB}{OD}$$

$$\therefore \quad \frac{AO}{BO} = \frac{CO}{DO}$$

**Hence proved.** (2)

*Or*

Given, $AD$ and $CE$ are altitudes which intersect each other at the point $P$. (1)

(i) In $\Delta AEP$ and $\Delta CDP$,

$\angle AEP = \angle CDP$ [each 90°]

and $\angle APE = \angle CPD$ [vertically opposite angles]

$\therefore$ $\Delta AEP \sim \Delta CDP$ [by AA similarity criterion] (1)

(ii) In $\Delta ABD$ and $\Delta CBE$,

$\angle ADB = \angle CEB$ [each 90°]

and $\angle ABD = \angle CBE$ [common angle]

$\therefore$ $\Delta ABD \sim \Delta CBE$ [by AA similarity criterion] (1)

(iii) In $\Delta AEP$ and $\Delta ADB$,

$\angle AEP = \angle ADB$ [each 90°]

and $\angle PAE = \angle BAD$ [common angle]

$\therefore$ $\Delta AEP \sim \Delta ADB$ [by AA similarity criterion] (1)

(iv) In $\Delta PDC$ and $\Delta BEC$,

$\angle PDC = \angle BEC$ [each 90°]

and $\angle PCD = \angle BCE$ [common angle]

$\therefore$ $\Delta PDC \sim \Delta BEC$ [by AA similarity criterion]

**Hence proved.** (1)

**36.** (i) Given, $OA = 20$ cm and $OC = 25$ cm

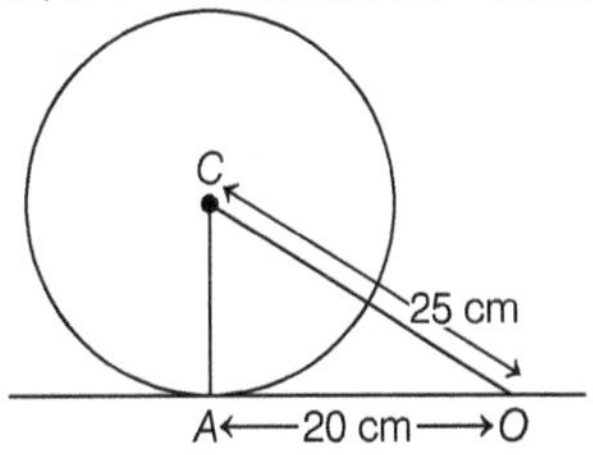


We know that the tangent at any point of a circle is perpendicular to the radius through the point of contact.

$\therefore$ In $\Delta OAC$, $AC \perp OA$

In right angled $\Delta OAC$,

$$OC^2 = OA^2 + AC^2$$

[by Pythagoras theorem]

$\Rightarrow \quad (25)^2 = (20)^2 + AC^2$

$\Rightarrow \quad 625 = 400 + AC^2$

$\Rightarrow \quad AC^2 = 225 \Rightarrow AC = 15\text{ cm}$

(ii) In a point is inside the circle, then no tangent can be drawn.

(iii)

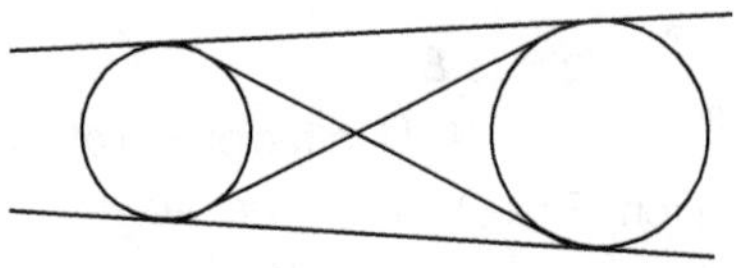

It is clear that four common tangents can be drawn, when the two circles does not touch externally.

*Or*

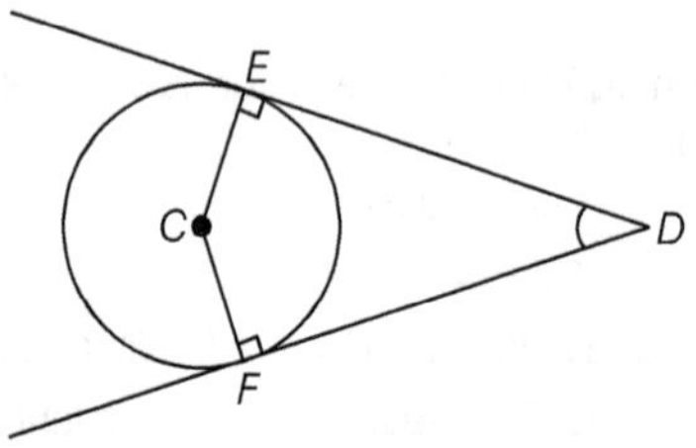


$\because DE \perp DF$, $\angle EDF = 90°$

and we know, $CE \perp ED$ and $CF \perp FD$

Also, $\quad CF = CE$

$\therefore$ *FCED* is a square.

$\Rightarrow \quad CE = CF = FD = DE$

$\therefore \quad DE = 15\text{ cm} \quad [\because \text{radius} = 15\text{ cm}]$

**37.** (i) Mean $(\bar{X}) = \dfrac{\Sigma f_i x_i}{\Sigma f_i}$

(ii) Median $= l + \left\{\dfrac{\frac{N}{2} - c \cdot f}{f}\right\} \times h$

(iii) The table for given distribution is

| Concentration of $SO_2$ (in ppm) | Frequency ($f_i$) | Cumulative frequency ($cf$) | Class marks ($x_i$) | $f_i x_i$ |
|---|---|---|---|---|
| 0.00 - 0.02 | 2 | 2 | 0.01 | 0.02 |
| 0.02 - 0.04 | 5 | 7 | 0.03 | 0.15 |
| 0.04 - 0.06 | 4 | 11 ($cf$) | 0.05 | 0.20 |
| 0.06 - 0.08 | 3 ($f$) | 14 | 0.07 | 0.21 |
| 0.08 - 0.10 | 4 | 18 | 0.09 | 0.36 |
| 0.10 - 0.12 | 6 | 24 | 0.11 | 0.66 |
| Total | $\Sigma f_i = 24$ | | | $\Sigma f_i u_i = 1.60$ |

Here, $\Sigma f_i x_i = 1.60$ and $\Sigma f_i = 24$

$\therefore$ Mean concentration of $SO_2 = \dfrac{\Sigma f_i x_i}{\Sigma f_i} = \dfrac{1.60}{24}$

$= 0.066$ (approx.)

*Or*

(iv) Here, $N = 24 \Rightarrow \dfrac{N}{2} = 12$

The cumulative frequency just greater than 12 is 14 and corresponding class interval is 0.06 - 0.08.

Here, $l = 0.06$, $cf = 11$, $f = 3$ and $h = 0.02$

$\therefore$ Median $= l + \left\{\dfrac{\frac{N}{2} - cf}{f}\right\} \times h$

$= 0.06 + \left\{\dfrac{\frac{24}{2} - 11}{3}\right\} \times 0.02$

$= 0.06 + \left\{\dfrac{12 - 11}{3}\right\} \times 0.02$

$= 0.06 + \dfrac{0.02}{3}$

$= 0.06 + 0.006$

$= 0.066$ (approx.)

**38.** (i) Given, number of students in Section A = 32

Number of students in Section B = 36

The minimum number of books acquire for the class library = LCM of (32, 36)

$= 2 \times 2 \times 2 \times 2 \times 2 \times 3 \times 3$

$= 2^5 \times 3^2$

$= 32 \times 9 = 288$

(ii) Given, product of the two numbers

= LCM × HCF

$\therefore \quad 32 \times 36 = \text{LCM }(32, 36) \times \text{HCF }(32, 36)$

$\Rightarrow \quad 32 \times 36 = 288 \times \text{HCF }(32, 36)$

$\Rightarrow$ HCF (32, 36) $= \dfrac{32 \times 36}{288} = 4$

(iii) Factor tree of 5310 is

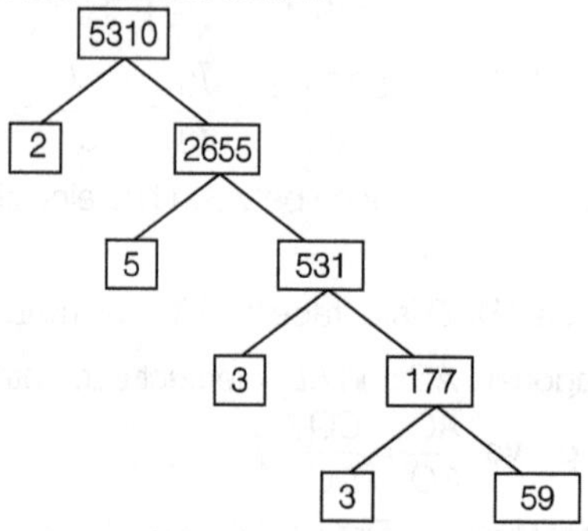


$\therefore 5310 = 2 \times 3^2 \times 5 \times 59$

*Or*

Given, $p = ab^2$ and $q = a^2b$

LCM $(p, q)$ = Product of the greatest power of each prime factor involved in the numbers, with highest power $= a^2 \times b^2$

# SAMPLE QUESTION PAPER 10

## Mathematics (Basic)

Time : **3 hrs** Max. Marks : **80**

### Instructions

1. This question paper has 5 Sections A, B, C, D and E.
2. Section A has 20 Multiple Choice Questions (MCQs) carrying 1 mark each.
3. Section B has 5 Short Answer-I (SA-I) Type Questions carrying 2 marks each.
4. Section C has 6 Short Answer-II (SA-II) Type Questions carrying 3 marks each.
5. Section D has 4 Long Answer (LA) Type Questions carrying 5 marks each.
6. Section E has 3 Case Based integrated units of assessment (4 marks each) with sub-parts of the values of 1, 1 and 2 marks each respectively.
7. All questions are compulsory. However, an internal choice in 2 questions of 2 marks, 2 questions of 3 marks and 2 questions of 5 marks has been provided. An internal choice has been provided in the 2 marks questions of Section E.
8. Draw neat figures wherever required. Take $\pi = 22/7$ wherever required if not stated.

## Section-A

**Section A consists of 20 questions of 1 mark each**

**1.** The HCF of 95 and 152 is

(a) 1 (b) 17 (c) 13 (d) 19

**2.** The sum of the exponents of the prime factors in the prime factorisation of 196 is

(a) 2 (b) 4 (c) 6 (d) 8

**3.** A month is selected at random in a year, the probability that it is March or October is

(a) $\frac{1}{3}$ (b) $\frac{1}{4}$ (c) $\frac{1}{6}$ (d) $\frac{1}{2}$

**4.** A die is thrown once, the probability of getting a prime number is

(a) $\frac{1}{3}$ (b) $\frac{1}{4}$ (c) $\frac{1}{6}$ (d) $\frac{1}{2}$

**5.** If $\alpha$ and $\beta$ are zeroes of the polynomial $p(x) = 4x^2 + 3x + 7$, then the value of $\frac{1}{\alpha} + \frac{1}{\beta}$ is

(a) $-\frac{7}{3}$ (b) $\frac{7}{3}$ (c) $-\frac{3}{7}$ (d) $-\frac{3}{4}$

**6.** If the centre of a circle is (4, –1) and one end of the diameter is (2, 0), then the coordinate of the other end is

(a) (10, –3) (b) (6, – 2)
(c) (2, –1) (d) (–6, 1)

**7.** The ratio in which $Y$-axis divides the line segment joining the points $P(-4, 5)$ and $Q(3, -7)$ is

(a) $\frac{4}{3}$ (b) $\frac{5}{7}$ (c) $\frac{7}{3}$ (d) $\frac{3}{5}$

**8.** If the system of equations $5x + 2y = k$ and $10x + 4y = 3$ has infinitely many solutions, then the value of $k$ is

(a) $\frac{3}{2}$ (b) $\frac{1}{2}$ (c) $\frac{1}{3}$ (d) 2

**9.** In $\Delta DEW$, $AB \parallel EW$. If $AD = 2$ cm, $DE = 6$ cm and $DW = 15$ cm, then the value of $DB$ is

(a) 2 cm (b) 5 cm (c) 9 cm (d) 13 cm

**10.** The value of $\frac{4}{\cot^2 30°} + \frac{1}{\sin^2 60°} - \cos^2 45°$ is

(a) $\frac{29}{6}$ (b) $\frac{77}{6}$ (c) $\frac{13}{6}$ (d) $\frac{29}{12}$

**11.** If $\sec\theta + \tan\theta = x$, then the value of $\sec\theta - \tan\theta$ in terms of $x$ is

(a) $\frac{1}{x}$ (b) $x^2$ (c) $\frac{x-1}{x}$ (d) $x$

**12.** The expression for the common difference of an AP whose first term is $a$ and $n$th term is $b$, is

(a) $\frac{a-b}{n}$ (b) $\frac{b-a}{n}$ (c) $\frac{b}{a}$ (d) $\frac{b-a}{n-1}$

**13.** $AB$ is a chord of the circle and $AOC$ is its diameter such that $\angle BAC = 60°$. If $CP$ is the tangent to the circle at the point $C$, then $\angle BCP$ is equal to

(a) 50° (b) 60° (c) 70° (d) 80°

**14.** If the length of the shadow of a building is decreasing, then the angle of elevation is

(a) decreasing (b) increasing
(c) remains same (d) None of these

**15.** The zeroes of the polynomial $f(x) = x^2 - 2\sqrt{2}x - 16$ are

(a) $\sqrt{2}$ and $-\sqrt{2}$ (b) $4\sqrt{2}$ and $-2\sqrt{2}$
(c) $-4\sqrt{2}$ and $2\sqrt{2}$ (d) $4\sqrt{2}$ and $2\sqrt{2}$

**16.** In a $\Delta ABC$, it is given that $AB = 6$ cm, $AC = 8$ cm and $AD$ is the bisector of $A$. Then, $BD : DC$ is

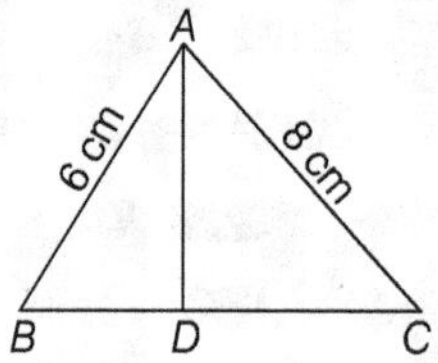


(a) 3 : 4 (b) 9 : 16
(c) 4 : 3 (d) $\sqrt{3}$ : 2

**17.** If $a = 2\ \text{cosec}^2\theta - 1$ and $b = \cot^2\theta - 3$, then $a - 2b$ is equal to

(a) 6 (b) 7 (c) –7 (d) 5

**18.** If the point $(x, y)$ is equidistant from the points (2, 1) and (1, – 2), then

(a) $x + 3y = 0$ (b) $3x + y = 0$
(c) $x + 2y = 0$ (d) $3x + 2y = 0$

**Directions** *In the question number 19 and 20, a statement of Assertion (A) is followed by a statement of Reason (R). Choose the correct option.*

**19. Assertion (A)** If $x = 3\sin^2\theta$ and $y = 3\cos^2\theta + 1$, then the value of $x + y = 4$.

**Reason (R)** For any value of $\theta$, $\sin^2\theta + \cos^2\theta = 1$.

(a) Both Assertion (A) and Reason (R) are true and Reason (R) is the correct explanation of Assertion (A)
(b) Both Assertion (A) and Reason (R) are true but Reason (R) is not the correct explanation of Assertion (A)
(c) Assertion (A) is true but Reason (R) is false
(d) Assertion (A) is false but Reason (R) is true

**20. Assertion (A)** The point (0, 7) lies on $Y$-axis.

**Reason (R)** The $x$-coordinate of the point on $Y$-axis is zero.

(a) Both Assertion (A) and Reason (R) are true and Reason (R) is the correct explanation of Assertion (A)
(b) Both Assertion (A) and Reason (R) are true but Reason (R) is not the correct explanation of Assertion (A)
(c) Assertion (A) is true but Reason (R) is false
(d) Assertion (A) is false but Reason (R) is true

# Section-B

**Section B consists of 5 questions of 2 marks each**

**21.** A letter is chosen at random from the letters of the word ACCEPTABILITIES. Find the probability that the letter chosen is a (i) vowel (ii) consonant.

*Or* Ashok buys a fish from a shop for his aquarium. The shopkeeper takes out one fish at random from a tank containing 10 male fish and 9 female fish. What is the probability that the fish taken out is a male fish?

**22.** A wheel has diameter 84 cm. Find how many complete revolutions must it take to cover 792 m.

**23.** Find the solution of the equation $\frac{2x}{x-4}+\frac{2x-5}{x-3}=\frac{25}{3}$, $x \neq 3, 4$.

*Or* If $\frac{1}{2}$ is a root of the equation $x^2+kx-\frac{5}{4}=0$, then find the value of $k$.

**24.** If the mean of $x$ and $\frac{1}{x}$ is $M$. What is the value of mean of $x^3$ and $\frac{1}{x^3}$?

**25.** Find the perimeter of the triangle formed by the points (0, 0), (2, 0) and (0, 2).

# Section-C

**Section C consists of 6 questions of 3 marks each**

**26.** If $\alpha$ and $\beta$ are the zeroes of the quadratic polynomial $f(x)=kx^2+4x+4$ such that $\alpha^2+\beta^2=24$, find the values of $k$.

**27.** Prove that $\sqrt{2}+\sqrt{5}$ is irrational, given that $\sqrt{2}$ is irrational.

**28.** Find the value of

$$\frac{\tan^2 60^\circ+4\cos^2 45^\circ+3\sec^2 30^\circ+5\cos^2 90^\circ}{\operatorname{cosec} 30^\circ+\sec 60^\circ-\cot^2 30^\circ}.$$

*Or*

Prove that $\frac{\sin\theta}{1+\cos\theta}+\frac{1+\cos\theta}{\sin\theta}=2\operatorname{cosec}\theta$.

**29.** A circle is touching the side $BC$ of $\Delta ABC$ at $P$ and touching $AB$ and $AC$ produced at $Q$ and $R$ respectively.

Prove that $AQ=\frac{1}{2}$ (Perimeter of $\Delta ABC$).

*Or*

The radii of two concentric circles are 13 cm and 8 cm. $AB$ is a diameter of the bigger circle. $BD$ is a tangent to the smaller circle touching it at $D$. Find the length $AD$.

**30.** One number of two digits is such that the product of digits is 12. If 36 is added to the number, then the places of the digits are interchanged. Find the number.

**31.** Find the value of the height $(h)$ in the given figure, at which the tennis ball must be hit, so that it will just pass over the net and land 7 m away from the base of the net.

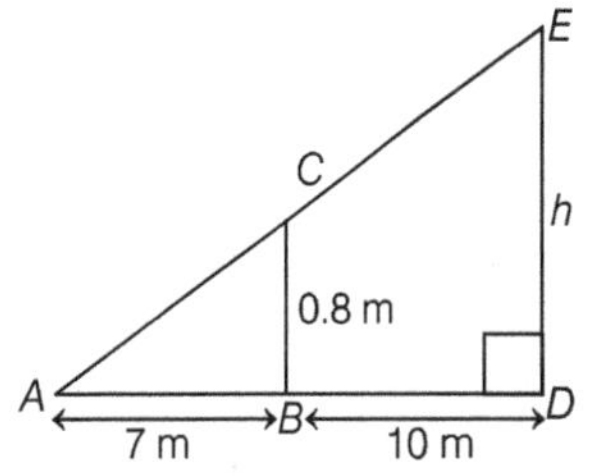

# Section-D

**Section D consists of 4 questions of 5 marks each**

**32.** From the top of a 7 m high building, the angle of elevation of the top of a cable tower is 60° and the angle of depression of its foot is 45°. Determine the height of the cable tower.

**33.** A toy is in the form of a cone mounted on a hemisphere of radius 3.5 cm. The total height of the toy is 15.5 cm. Find the total surface area of the toy.

**34.** During the medical check up of 35 students of a class, their weight were recorded as follows

| Weight (in kg) | Number of students |
|---|---|
| Less than 38 | 0 |
| Less than 40 | 3 |
| Less than 42 | 5 |
| Less than 44 | 9 |
| Less than 46 | 14 |
| Less than 48 | 28 |
| Less than 50 | 32 |
| Less than 52 | 35 |

Find the median weight of the above data.

*Or* 100 surnames were randomly picked up from a local telephone directory and the frequency distribution of the number of letters in English alphabets in the surnames was obtained as follows

| Number of letters | 0-5 | 5-10 | 10-15 | 15-20 | 20-25 |
|---|---|---|---|---|---|
| Number of surnames | 10 | 30 | 40 | 16 | 4 |

Find the median of the above data.

**35.** $CD$ and $GH$ are respectively the bisectors of $\angle ACB$ and $\angle EGF$ such that $D$ and $H$ lie on sides $AB$ and $FE$ of $\Delta ABC$ and $\Delta EFG$, respectively.

If $\Delta ABC \sim \Delta FEG$, show that

(i) $\frac{CD}{GH} = \frac{AC}{FG}$ (ii) $\Delta DCB \sim \Delta HGE$

*Or*

Sides $AB$ and $BC$ and median $AD$ of $\Delta ABC$ are respectively proportional to sides $PQ$ and $QR$ and median $PM$ of $\Delta PQR$. Show that $\Delta ABC \sim \Delta PQR$.

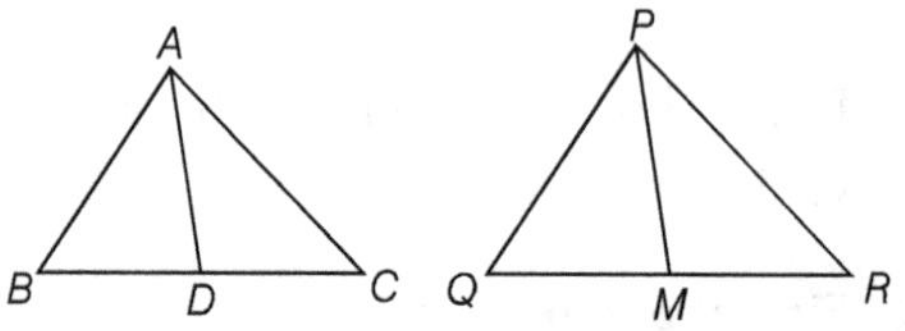


# Section-E

**Case study based questions are compulsory**

**36.** Sonu is studying in X standard. He is making a brooch and understanding areas related to circles. A brooch is made with silver wire in the form of a circle with diameter 35 mm. The wire is also used in making 5 diameters which divide the circle into 10 equal sectors.

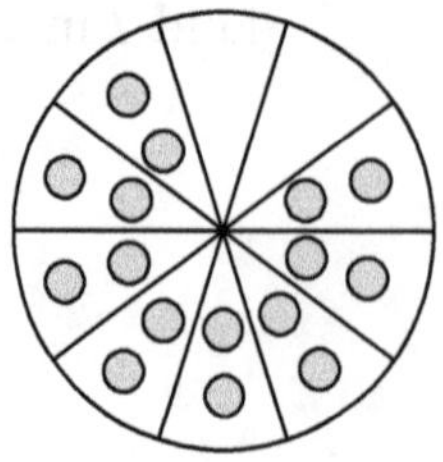

Few questions came in his mind while making the brooch. Give answers to his questions.

(i) Find the area of circle. (1)

(ii) Find the measure of angle of each sector. (1)

(iii) Find the total length of the silver wire. (2)

*Or*

Find the area of each sector of the brooch. (2)

**37.** Ram asks the labour to dig a well up to a depth of 15 m. Labour charges ₹ 100 for first metre and increase ₹ 25 for each subsequent metres. As labour was uneducated, he claims ₹ 400 for the whole work.

On the basis of above information, answer the following questions.

(i) Find the AP sequence that is formed by the labour charge. (1)

(ii) Find the labour charge to dig the well. (1)

(iii) How much money would Ram save if labour agree with ₹ 400 for the whole work? (2)

*Or* Find the sum of AP sequence that is formed by the labour charge. (2)

**38.** It is common that Government revise travel fares from time to time based on various factors such as inflation (a general increase in prices and fall in the purchasing value of money) on different types of vehicles like auto rickshaws, taxis, radio cab etc. The auto charges in a city comprise of a fixed charge together with the charge for the distance covered.

Study the following situations:

| Name of city | Distance travelled (km) | Amount paid (₹) |
|---|---|---|
| City A | 10 | 75 |
| | 15 | 110 |
| City B | 8 | 91 |
| | 14 | 145 |

**Situation 1** In city A, for a journey of 10 km, the charge paid is ₹ 75 and for a journey of 15 km, the charge paid is ₹ 110.

**Situation 2** In city B, for a journey of 8 km, the charge paid is ₹ 91 and for a journey of 14 km, the charge paid is ₹ 145.

On the basis of above information, answer the following questions.

**Refer situation 1**

(i) If the fixed charges of auto rickshaws is ₹ $x$ and the running charges be ₹ $y$ per km, then find the pair of linear equations representing this situation. (1)

(ii) A person travels a distance of 50 km. Find the amount he has to pay. (1)

**Refer situation 2**

(iii) Draw the graph of lines representing the conditions (situation 2). (2)

*Or* Solve the pair of linear equations formed (situation 2) by elimination mehtod. (2)

# SOLUTIONS

**1.** (d) Let $a = 95$ and $b = 152$

$\therefore \quad a = 5 \times 19$ and $b = 2^3 \times 19$

$\therefore$ HCF (95, 152) = 19

**2.** (b) Let $a = 196$

| | |
|---|---|
| 2 | 196 |
| 2 | 98 |
| 7 | 49 |
| 7 | 7 |
| | 1 |

$\therefore a = 2^2 \times 7^2$

$\therefore$ Required sum $= 2 + 2 = 4$

**3.** (c) There are twelve months in a year.

$\therefore$ Required probability $= \frac{2}{12} = \frac{1}{6}$

**4.** (d) When a die is thrown we get 1, 2, 3, 4, 5, 6.

Out of which there are 2, 3 and 5 prime numbers.

$\therefore$ Required probability $= \frac{3}{6} = \frac{1}{2}$

**5.** (c) We have, $\alpha + \beta = -\frac{3}{4}$ and $\alpha\beta = \frac{7}{4}$

$$\therefore \quad \frac{1}{\alpha} + \frac{1}{\beta} = \frac{\alpha+\beta}{\alpha\beta} = \frac{(-3/4)}{(7/4)} = -\frac{3}{7}$$

**6.** (b) Let the coordinates of other end of a diameter be $(x_1, y_1)$.

We know that mid-point of the end of a diameter is equal to the centre of a circle.

$$\therefore \quad \left(\frac{2+x_1}{2}, \frac{0+y_1}{2}\right) = (4, -1)$$

$$\Rightarrow \quad \left(\frac{2+x_1}{2}, \frac{y_1}{2}\right) = (4, -1)$$

On equating the coordinates, we get

$$\frac{2+x_1}{2} = 4 \text{ and } \frac{y_1}{2} = -1$$

$$\Rightarrow \quad x_1 = 8 - 2 \text{ and } y_1 = -2$$

$$\Rightarrow \quad x_1 = 6 \text{ and } y_1 = -2$$

**7.** (a) Suppose $Y$-axis divides $PQ$ in the ratio $\lambda : 1$ at point $R$. Then, the coordinates of $P$ are $\left(\frac{3\lambda - 4}{\lambda + 1}, \frac{-7\lambda + 5}{\lambda + 1}\right)$.

Since, $R$ lies on $Y$-axis.

$$\therefore \quad \frac{3\lambda - 4}{\lambda + 1} = 0 \Rightarrow 3\lambda - 4 = 0 \Rightarrow \lambda = \frac{4}{3}$$

**8.** (a) Given, system of equations is

$5x + 2y = k$ and $10x + 4y = 3$

Here $a_1 = 5, b_1 = 2, c_1 = -k$

and $a_2 = 10, b_2 = 4, c_2 = -3$

For infinitely many solutions, we must have

$$\frac{a_1}{a_2} = \frac{b_1}{b_2} = \frac{c_1}{c_2} \Rightarrow \frac{5}{10} = \frac{2}{4} = \frac{-k}{-3}$$

$$\Rightarrow \quad \frac{1}{2} = \frac{1}{2} = \frac{k}{3} \Rightarrow \frac{1}{2} = \frac{k}{3} \Rightarrow k = \frac{3}{2}$$

**9.** (b) Given, $AB \parallel EW$

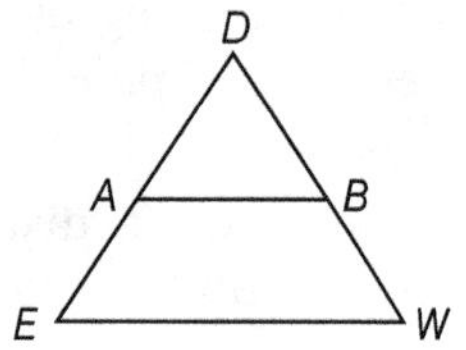


$$\therefore \quad \frac{DA}{AE} = \frac{DB}{BW}$$

[by basic proportionality theorem]

$$\Rightarrow \quad \frac{DA}{DE - DA} = \frac{DB}{DW - DB}$$

$$\Rightarrow \quad \frac{2}{6-2} = \frac{DB}{15 - DB}$$

$$\Rightarrow \quad \frac{2}{4} = \frac{DB}{15 - DB}$$

$$\Rightarrow \quad \frac{1}{2} = \frac{DB}{15 - DB}$$

$$\Rightarrow \quad 15 - DB = 2DB$$

$$\Rightarrow \quad 3DB = 15$$

$$\Rightarrow \quad DB = \frac{15}{3} = 5\text{ cm}$$

**10.** (c) $\frac{4}{\cot^2 30^\circ} + \frac{1}{\sin^2 60^\circ} - \cos^2 45^\circ$

$$= \frac{4}{(\sqrt{3})^2} + \frac{1}{\left(\frac{\sqrt{3}}{2}\right)^2} - \left(\frac{1}{\sqrt{2}}\right)^2$$

$$= \frac{4}{3} + \frac{4}{3} - \frac{1}{2} = \frac{8}{3} - \frac{1}{2} = \frac{16 - 3}{6} = \frac{13}{6}$$

**11.** (a) We know that

$$\sec^2\theta - \tan^2\theta = 1$$

$$\Rightarrow \quad (\sec\theta - \tan\theta)(\sec\theta + \tan\theta) = 1$$

$[\because a^2 - b^2 = (a - b)(a + b)]$

$$\Rightarrow \sec\theta - \tan\theta = \frac{1}{\sec\theta + \tan\theta} = \frac{1}{x}$$

$[\because \sec\theta + \tan\theta = x$, given$]$

**12.** (d) Let the common difference be $d$.

We know that $\quad a_n = a + (n - 1)d$

According to the question,

$$\Rightarrow \quad b = a + (n - 1)d$$

$$\Rightarrow \quad d = \frac{b - a}{n - 1}$$

**13.** (b) $\angle ABC = 90^\circ$

[$\because$ angle in a semi-circle is right angle]

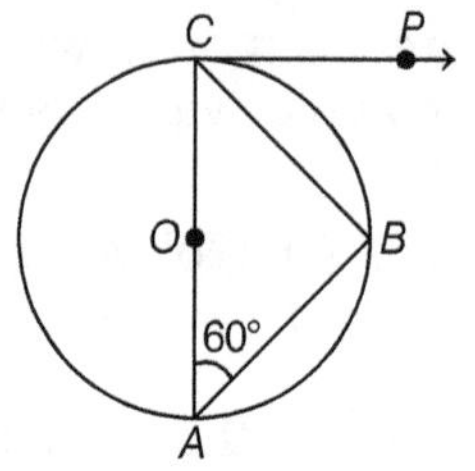


In $\Delta ABC$,

$$\angle A + \angle B + \angle C = 180^\circ$$

$$\Rightarrow \quad 60^\circ + 90^\circ + \angle C = 180^\circ$$

$$\Rightarrow \quad \angle C = 180^\circ - 150^\circ = 30^\circ$$

Now, $\quad \angle OCP = 90^\circ$

[$\because$ radius is perpendicular to the tangent at the point of contact]

$$\therefore \quad \angle BCP = 90^\circ - \angle OCB$$

$$= 90^\circ - 30^\circ = 60^\circ$$

**14.** (b) Here, $AB$ is the building and $BE$ is the initial length of the shadow.

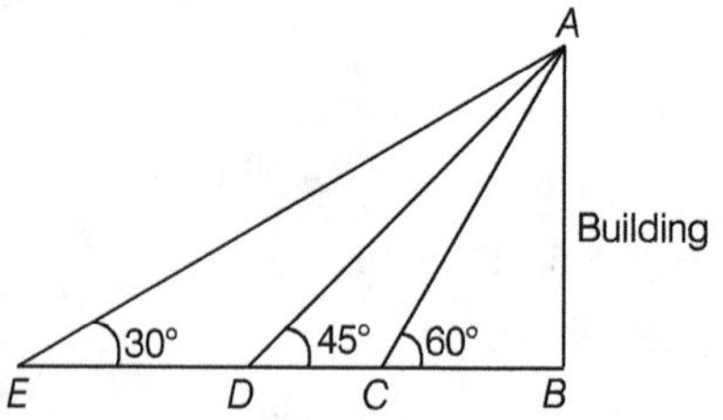


As the shadow reaches from $E$ to $C$, the angle of elevation increases from 30° to 60°.

**15.** (b) The zeroes of $f(x) = x^2 - 2\sqrt{2}x - 16$ are

$$f(x) = 0$$

i.e. $\quad x^2 - 2\sqrt{2}x - 16 = 0$

$$\Rightarrow \quad x^2 - 4\sqrt{2}x + 2\sqrt{2}x - 16 = 0$$

$$\Rightarrow \quad x(x - 4\sqrt{2}) + 2\sqrt{2}(x - 4\sqrt{2}) = 0$$

$$\Rightarrow \quad (x + 2\sqrt{2})(x - 4\sqrt{2}) = 0$$

$$\Rightarrow \quad x = 4\sqrt{2} \text{ or } x = -2\sqrt{2}$$

**16.** (a) Given, $AD$ is the bisector of $\angle A$.

By angle bisector theorem, bisector of an angle divides the opposite side in the same ratio as of two remaining sides.

$\therefore \quad \frac{BD}{DC} = \frac{AB}{AC}$

$\Rightarrow \quad \frac{BD}{DC} = \frac{6}{8}$

$\Rightarrow \quad \frac{BD}{DC} = \frac{3}{4}$

**17.** (b) We have,

$a = 2\,\text{cosec}^2\theta - 1$ and $b = \cot^2\theta - 3$

$\therefore a - 2b = (2\,\text{cosec}^2\theta - 1) - 2(\cot^2\theta - 3)$

$= 2(\text{cosec}^2\theta - \cot^2\theta) - 1 + 6$

$= 2(1) - 1 + 6 \quad [\because \text{cosec}^2 A - \cot^2 A = 1]$

$= 2 - 1 + 6 = 7$

**18.** (a) Let the points be $P(x, y)$, $A(2, 1)$ and $B(1, -2)$.

Since, $P$ is equidistant from $A$ and $B$.

$\therefore \quad AP = BP$

$\Rightarrow \quad AP^2 = BP^2$

$\Rightarrow \quad (x-2)^2 + (y-1)^2 = (x-1)^2 + (y+2)^2$

[by distance formula]

$\Rightarrow x^2 - 4x + 4 + y^2 - 2y + 1$

$= x^2 - 2x + 1 + y^2 + 4y + 4$

$\Rightarrow \quad 2x + 6y = 0$

$\Rightarrow \quad x + 3y = 0 \quad$ [dividing by 3]

**19.** (a) Given, $x = 3\sin^2\theta$ and $y = 3\cos^2\theta + 1$

$\therefore x + y = 3\sin^2\theta + 3\cos^2\theta + 1$

$= 3(\sin^2\theta + \cos^2\theta) + 1$

$= 3 + 1 = 4 \quad [\because \sin^2 A + \cos^2 A = 1]$

So, the given Assertion and Reason are true and Reason is the correct explanation of Assertion.

**20.** (a) The $x$-coordinate of the given point is zero and $y$-coordinate = 7

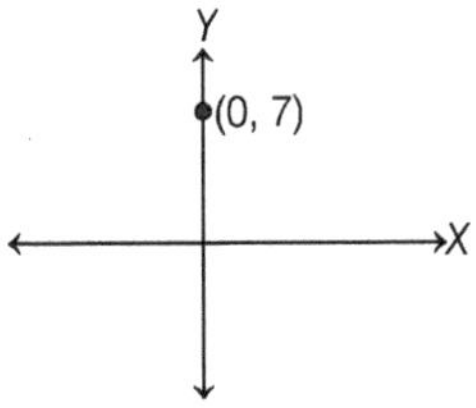


Since, the $x$-coordinate is zero, so the point lies on Y-axis.

So, the given Assertion and Reason are true and Reason is the correct explanation of Assertion.

**21.** There are 15 letters in the word ACCEPTABILITIES out of which one letter can be chosen in 15 ways.

$\therefore$ Total number of elementary events = 15 (1/2)

(i) There are 7 vowels in the word ACCEPTABILITIES. So, there are 7 ways of selecting a vowel.

$\therefore$ Probability of selecting a vowel $= \frac{7}{15}$ (1)

(ii) We have,

Probability of selecting a consonant

$= 1 -$ Probability of selecting a vowel

$= 1 - \frac{7}{15} = \frac{8}{15}$ (1/2)

*Or*

There are 19 (= 10 + 9) fish out of which one can be chosen in 19 ways.

$\therefore$ Total number of elementary events = 19

There are 10 male fish out of which one male fish can be chosen in 10 ways. (1)

$\therefore$ Favourable number of elementary events = 10

Hence, required probability $= \frac{10}{19}$ (1)

**22.** Let $r$ be the radius of the wheel.

Then, diameter = 84 cm

$\Rightarrow \quad 2r = 84$ cm

$\Rightarrow \quad r = 42$ cm

$\therefore$ Circumference of the wheel $= 2\pi r$

$= 2 \times \frac{22}{7} \times 42$

$= 264$ cm

$= 2.64$ m

$[\because 1\text{ m} = 100\text{ cm}]$ (1)

So, the wheel covers 2.64 m in one complete revolution.

$\therefore$ Total number of revolutions in covering 792 m

$= \frac{792}{2.64} = 300$ (1)

**23.** Given, equation is $\frac{2x}{x-4} + \frac{2x-5}{x-3} = \frac{25}{3}, x \neq 3, 4$

$\Rightarrow \quad \frac{2x(x-3) + (x-4)(2x-5)}{(x-4)(x-3)} = \frac{25}{3}$

$\Rightarrow \quad \frac{2x^2 - 6x + (2x^2 - 13x + 20)}{(x-4)(x-3)} = \frac{25}{3}$ (1)

$\Rightarrow \quad 3(4x^2 - 19x + 20) = 25(x^2 - 7x + 12)$

$\Rightarrow 25x^2 - 12x^2 - 175x + 57x + 300 - 60 = 0$

$\Rightarrow \quad 13x^2 - 118x + 240 = 0$

$\Rightarrow \quad 13x^2 - 78x - 40x + 240 = 0$

[by factorisation method]

$\Rightarrow \quad 13x(x-6) - 40(x-6) = 0$

$\Rightarrow \quad (13x - 40)(x-6) = 0$

$\Rightarrow \quad 13x - 40 = 0$ or $x - 6 = 0$

$\Rightarrow \quad x = \frac{40}{13}$ or $x = 6$ (1)

*Or*

Since, $\frac{1}{2}$ is a root of the quadratic equation

$x^2 + kx - \frac{5}{4} = 0$

$\therefore \quad \left(\frac{1}{2}\right)^2 + k\left(\frac{1}{2}\right) - \frac{5}{4} = 0$

$\Rightarrow \quad \frac{1}{4} + \frac{k}{2} - \frac{5}{4} = 0$ (1)

$\Rightarrow \quad \frac{1+2k-5}{4} = 0$

$\Rightarrow \quad 2k - 4 = 0 \Rightarrow 2k = 4$

$\therefore \quad k = 2$ (1)

**24.** Given, mean of $x$ and $\frac{1}{x}$ is $M$

$\Rightarrow \quad \frac{x + \frac{1}{x}}{2} = M$

$\left[\because \text{mean} = \frac{\text{sum of all observations}}{\text{total number of observations}}\right]$

$\Rightarrow \quad \frac{x^2+1}{2x} = M \Rightarrow \frac{x^2+1}{x} = 2M \Rightarrow x + \frac{1}{x} = 2M$ ...(i)

On squaring both sides of Eq. (i), we get

$\left(x + \frac{1}{x}\right)^2 = 4M^2$

$\Rightarrow \quad x^2 + \frac{1}{x^2} = 4M^2 - 2$ ...(ii) (1)

$\therefore$ Mean of $x^3$ and $\frac{1}{x^3}$ is

$= \frac{x^3 + \frac{1}{x^3}}{2} = \frac{\left(x + \frac{1}{x}\right)\left(x^2 - x \cdot \frac{1}{x} + \frac{1}{x^2}\right)}{2}$

$= \frac{2M \cdot (4M^2 - 2 - 1)}{2}$ [from Eqs. (i) and (ii)]

$= M(4M^2 - 3)$ (1)

**25.** Let $A(0, 0)$, $B(2, 0)$ and $C(0, 2)$ be the vertices of $\Delta ABC$.

$\therefore \quad AB = \sqrt{(2-0)^2 + (0-0)^2}$

$= \sqrt{4+0} = 2$ units [by distance formula]

$BC = \sqrt{(0-2)^2 + (2-0)^2}$

$= \sqrt{4+4} = \sqrt{8} = 2\sqrt{2}$ units

and $CA = \sqrt{(0-0)^2 + (0-2)^2}$

$= \sqrt{0+4} = 2$ units (1)

$\therefore$ Required perimeter $= AB + BC + CA$

$= (2 + 2\sqrt{2} + 2)$

$= (4 + 2\sqrt{2})$ units (1)

**26.** Since, $\alpha$ and $\beta$ are the zeroes of the quadratic polynomial $f(x) = kx^2 + 4x + 4$.

$\therefore \quad \alpha + \beta = -\frac{4}{k}$ and $\alpha\beta = \frac{4}{k}$ (1/2)

Now, given $\quad \alpha^2 + \beta^2 = 24$

$\Rightarrow \quad (\alpha + \beta)^2 - 2\alpha\beta = 24$

$\Rightarrow \quad \left(-\frac{4}{k}\right)^2 - 2 \times \frac{4}{k} = 24$

$\Rightarrow \quad \frac{16}{k^2} - \frac{8}{k} = 24$

$\Rightarrow \quad 16 - 8k = 24k^2$

$\Rightarrow \quad 3k^2 + k - 2 = 0$ (1)

$\Rightarrow \quad 3k^2 + 3k - 2k - 2 = 0$

$\Rightarrow \quad 3k(k+1) - 2(k+1) = 0$

$\Rightarrow \quad (k+1)(3k-2) = 0$ (1/2)

$\Rightarrow \quad k + 1 = 0$ or $3k - 2 = 0$

$\Rightarrow \quad k = -1$ or $k = \frac{2}{3}$

Hence, $k = -1$ or $k = \frac{2}{3}$ (1)

**27.** Let us assume on the contrary that $\sqrt{2} + \sqrt{5}$ is a rational number. Then, there exist coprime positive integers $a$ and $b$ such that

$\sqrt{2} + \sqrt{5} = \frac{a}{b} \Rightarrow \frac{a}{b} - \sqrt{2} = \sqrt{5}$

$\Rightarrow \quad \left(\frac{a}{b} - \sqrt{2}\right)^2 = (\sqrt{5})^2$ [squaring both sides] (1)

$\Rightarrow \quad \frac{a^2}{b^2} - \frac{2a}{b}\sqrt{2} + 2 = 5$

$\Rightarrow \quad \frac{a^2}{b^2} - 3 = \frac{2a}{b}\sqrt{2} \Rightarrow \frac{a^2 - 3b^2}{2ab} = \sqrt{2}$ (1)

$\Rightarrow \sqrt{2}$ is a rational number.

[$\because a, b$ are integers $\therefore \frac{a^2 - 3b^2}{2ab}$ is rational]

This contradicts the fact that $\sqrt{2}$ is irrational. So, our assumption is wrong.

Hence, $\sqrt{2} + \sqrt{5}$ is irrational. **Hence proved.** (1)

**28.** $\frac{\tan^2 60° + 4\cos^2 45° + 3\sec^2 30° + 5\cos^2 90°}{\operatorname{cosec} 30° + \sec 60° - \cot^2 30°}$

$= \frac{(\sqrt{3})^2 + 4\left(\frac{1}{\sqrt{2}}\right)^2 + 3\left(\frac{2}{\sqrt{3}}\right)^2 + 5(0)}{2 + 2 - (\sqrt{3})^2}$ (1)

$= \frac{3 + \frac{4}{2} + 3 \times \frac{4}{3} + 0}{4 - 3} = \frac{3 + 2 + 4}{1} = 9$ (2)

*Or*

We have,

$\text{LHS} = \frac{\sin\theta}{1 + \cos\theta} + \frac{1 + \cos\theta}{\sin\theta}$

$= \frac{\sin^2\theta + (1 + \cos\theta)^2}{(1 + \cos\theta)\sin\theta}$ (1)

$= \frac{\sin^2\theta + 1 + 2\cos\theta + \cos^2\theta}{(1 + \cos\theta)\sin\theta}$

$= \frac{(\sin^2\theta + \cos^2\theta) + 1 + 2\cos\theta}{(1 + \cos\theta)\sin\theta}$ (1)

$= \frac{1+1+2\cos\theta}{(1+\cos\theta)\sin\theta} = \frac{2+2\cos\theta}{(1+\cos\theta)\sin\theta}$

$= \frac{2(1+\cos\theta)}{(1+\cos\theta)\sin\theta} = \frac{2}{\sin\theta}$

$= 2\,\text{cosec}\,\theta = \text{RHS}$ **Hence proved.** (1)

**29.** Since, tangent from an exterior point to a circle are equal in length.

$\therefore$ $BP = BQ$ [from $B$] ...(i)

$CP = CR$ [from $C$] ...(ii)

and $AQ = AR$ [from $A$] ...(iii) (1)

From Eq. (iii), we have

$AQ = AR$

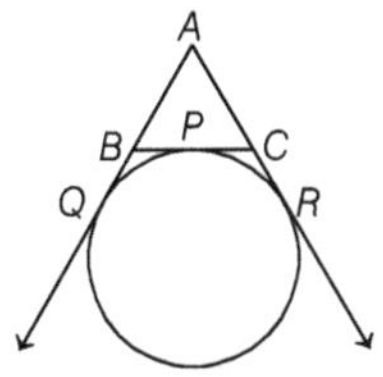


$\Rightarrow AB + BQ = AC + CR$

$\Rightarrow AB + BP = AC + CP$ [using Eqs. (i) and (ii)] ...(iv)

Now, Perimeter of $\Delta ABC = AB + BC + AC$ (1)

$\Rightarrow$ Perimeter of $\Delta ABC = AB + (BP + PC) + AC$

$\Rightarrow$ Perimeter of $\Delta ABC = (AB + BP) + (AC + PC)$

$\Rightarrow$ Perimeter of $\Delta ABC = 2(AB + BP)$ [using Eq. (iv)]

$\Rightarrow$ Perimeter of $\Delta ABC = 2(AB + BQ)$ [using Eq. (i)]

$\Rightarrow$ Perimeter of $\Delta ABC = 2AQ$

$\therefore AQ = \frac{1}{2}$(Perimeter of $\Delta ABC$) **Hence proved.** (1)

*Or*

Let the line $BD$ intersects the bigger circle at $E$.
Now, Join $AE$.

Let $O$ be the centre of the bigger circle, then $O$ is the mid-point of $AB$.

[$\because$ $AB$ is a diameter of the bigger circle]

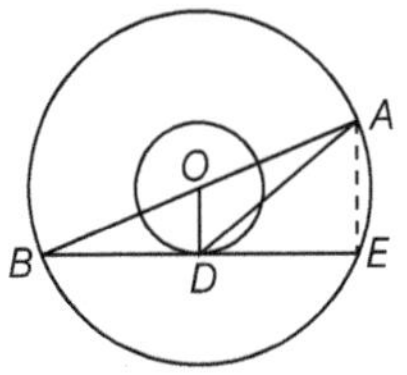


$BD$ is a tangent to the smaller circle and $OD$ is a radius through the point of contact $D$. Then,

$OD \perp BD$

$\Rightarrow$ $OD \perp BE$ (1)

Since, $OD$ is perpendicular to a chord $BE$ of bigger circle.

$\therefore$ $BD = DE$

[$\because$ perpendicular drawn from the centre to a chord bisects the chord]

$D$ is the mid-point of $BE$.

$\therefore$ In $\Delta BAE$, $O$ is the mid-point of $AB$ and $D$ is the mid-point of $BE$.

$\therefore$ $OD = \frac{1}{2}AE$

[$\because$ line segment joining the mid-points of any two sides of a triangle is half of the third side]

$\Rightarrow$ $AE = 2(OD) = 2 \times 8 = 16$ cm (1)

In right angled $\Delta OBD$, use Pythagoras theorem,

$OD^2 + BD^2 = OB^2$

$\Rightarrow$ $BD = \sqrt{OB^2 - OD^2}$

$= \sqrt{(13)^2 - (8)^2}$

$= \sqrt{169 - 64} = \sqrt{105}$

$\therefore$ $DE = BD = \sqrt{105}$ cm

In right angled $\Delta AED$, using Pythagoras theorem, we have

$AD = \sqrt{AE^2 + DE^2}$

$= \sqrt{(16)^2 + (\sqrt{105})^2}$

$= \sqrt{256 + 105} = \sqrt{361} = 19$ cm (1)

**30.** Let unit's place digit is $y$ and ten's place digit is $x$.

Then, number of two digits $= 10x + y$

$\because$ Product of digits, $xy = 12$ [given] ...(i)

Interchanging the position of digits, new number

$= 10y + x$

According to the question,

$10x + y + 36 = 10y + x$

$\Rightarrow 10x - x + y - 10y + 36 = 0$ [on transposition]

$\Rightarrow$ $9x - 9y + 36 = 0$

$\Rightarrow$ $x - y + 4 = 0$ [on dividing by 9]

$\Rightarrow$ $y = x + 4$ ...(ii) (1)

On putting the value of $y$ from Eq. (ii) in Eq. (i), we get

$x(x + 4) = 12$

$\Rightarrow$ $x^2 + 4x = 12$

$\Rightarrow$ $x^2 + 4x - 12 = 0$ [on transposition]

By using factorisation method,

$x^2 + (6-2)x - 12 = 0$

$\Rightarrow$ $x^2 + 6x - 2x - 12 = 0$ (1)

$\Rightarrow$ $x(x + 6) - 2(x + 6) = 0 \Rightarrow (x+6)(x-2) = 0$

$\Rightarrow$ $x + 6 = 0$ or $x - 2 = 0$

$\Rightarrow$ $x = -6$ or $x = 2$

$\therefore$ $x = 2$ [$\because x \neq -6$]

On putting the value of $x$ in Eq. (ii), we get

$y = x + 4 = 2 + 4 = 6$

Hence, required number of two digits $= 10x + y$

$= 10 \times 2 + 6$

$= 20 + 6$

$= 26$ (1)

**31.** Since, the height ($h$) is measured vertically. So, $\angle EDA$ is a right angle.

We assume that the net (i.e. $CB$) is vertical.

Here, $\Delta ADE$ and $\Delta ABC$ are similar.

[by AA similarity criterion]

$\therefore \quad \frac{DE}{BC} = \frac{AD}{AB}$ (1½)

$\Rightarrow \quad \frac{h}{0.8} = \frac{17}{7} \Rightarrow h = \frac{17 \times 0.8}{7} = 1.94 \text{ m}$

Hence, the height at which the ball should be hit is 2.7 m.

(1½)

**32.** Let $AD = 7$ m be the height of the building and $BC = h$ m be the height of the cable tower.

From the top of the building $D$, the angles of elevation and depression are $\angle CDE = 60°$ and $\angle EDB = 45°$.

From the point $D$, draw a line $DE \parallel AB$.

Then, $\quad \angle EDB = \angle ABD = 45°$ [alternate angles]

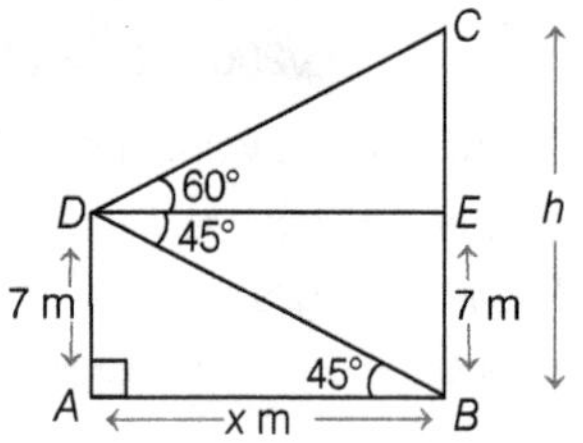


(2)

Also, let $AB = DE = x$ m be the distance between building and cable tower.

In right angled $\Delta BAD$,

$\tan 45° = \frac{AD}{AB} \quad \left[\because \tan\theta = \frac{\text{perpendicular}}{\text{base}}\right]$

$\Rightarrow \quad 1 = \frac{7}{x} \quad [\because \tan 45° = 1]$

$\Rightarrow \quad x = 7 \text{ m}$ ...(i) (1)

Now, in right angled $\Delta CED$,

$\tan 60° = \frac{CE}{DE} = \frac{CB - BE}{AB}$ (1)

$\Rightarrow \quad \sqrt{3} = \frac{h-7}{x} \quad [\because \tan 60° = \sqrt{3}]$

$\Rightarrow \quad h - 7 = x\sqrt{3}$

$\Rightarrow \quad h = x\sqrt{3} + 7$

$\Rightarrow \quad h = 7\sqrt{3} + 7$ [from Eq. (i)]

$\Rightarrow \quad h = 7(\sqrt{3} + 1) \text{ m}$

Hence, the height of the cable tower is $7(\sqrt{3} + 1)$ m.

(1)

**33.** Let $r$ be the radius of cone and hemisphere and $H$ be the height of the toy.

Given, radius of the conical and hemispherical portion, $r = 3.5$ cm

and total height of the toy, $H = 15.5$ cm

$\therefore$ Height of conical portion,

$h$ = Total height − Radius of hemispherical portion

$= 15.5 - 3.5 = 12$ cm (1)

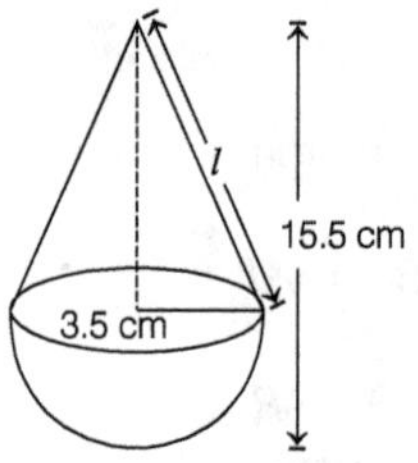


(1)

$\therefore$ Slant height of the cone, $l = \sqrt{h^2 + r^2}$

$= \sqrt{(12)^2 + (3.5)^2}$

$= \sqrt{144 + 12.25}$

$= \sqrt{156.25}$

$l = 12.5$ cm (1)

Now, total surface area of the toy

= Curved surface area of conical portion + Curved surface area of hemispherical portion

(1)

$= \pi r l + 2\pi r^2 = \pi r (l + 2r)$

$= \frac{22}{7} \times 3.5 \times (12.5 + 2 \times 3.5)$

$= \frac{22}{7} \times 3.5 \times 19.5 = 214.5 \text{ cm}^2$

Hence, the total surface area of the toy is 214.5 $\text{cm}^2$.

(1)

**34.** Here, we have cumulative frequency distribution less than types.

First we convert it into an ordinary frequency distribution, which is shown below

| **Weight** (in 1kg) | **Frequency** | **Cumulative frequency** |
|---|---|---|
| 38-40 | 3 | 3 |
| 40-42 | $5 - 3 = 2$ | 5 |
| 42-44 | $9 - 5 = 4$ | 9 |
| 44-46 | $14 - 9 = 5$ | 14 |
| 46-48 | $28 - 14 = 14$ | 28 |
| 48-50 | $32 - 28 = 4$ | 32 |
| 50-52 | $35 - 32 = 3$ | 35 |
| **Total** | $N = 35$ | |

(2)

Here, $\frac{N}{2} = \frac{35}{2} = 17.5$

Since, the cumulative frequency just greater than 17.5 is 28 and the corresponding class-interval is 46-48.

$\therefore$ Median class is 46-48. (1)

So, $l = 46$, $\frac{N}{2} = 17.5$, $f = 14$ and $cf = 14$

$$\text{Now, median} = l + \frac{\left(\frac{N}{2} - cf\right)}{f} \times h = 46 + \frac{17.5 - 14}{14} \times 2$$

$$= 46 + \frac{3.5}{7} = 46 + \frac{1}{2}$$

$$= 46 + 0.5 = 46.5 \text{ kg} \quad \textbf{(2)}$$

*Or*

The cumulative frequency table of given data is

| Number of letters | Number of surnames ($f_i$) | Cumulative frequency ($cf$) |
|---|---|---|
| 0-5 | 10 | 10 |
| 5-10 | 30 | 40 ($cf$) |
| 10-15 | 40 ($f$) | 80 |
| 15-20 | 16 | 96 |
| 20-25 | 4 | 100 |
| **Total** | $N = 100$ | |

Here, $N = 100$

$$\therefore \quad \frac{N}{2} = \frac{100}{2} = 50 \quad \textbf{(2)}$$

Since, the cumulative frequency just greater than 50 is 80 and the corresponding class interval is 10-15.

$\therefore$ Median class is 10 – 15.

$\because$ $l = 10$, $cf = 40$, $h = 5$ and $f = 40$ **(1)**

$$\text{Now, median} = l + \left(\frac{\frac{N}{2} - cf}{f}\right) \times h = 10 + \left(\frac{50 - 40}{40}\right) \times 5$$

$$= 10 + \frac{10}{40} \times 5 = 10 + \frac{5}{4}$$

$$= 10 + 1.25 = 11.25 \quad \textbf{(2)}$$

**35.** Draw $\Delta ABC$ and $\Delta FEG$ and then draw bisectors $CD$ and $GH$ of $\angle ACB$ and $\angle EGF$ such that $D$ lies on $AB$ and $H$ lies on $FE$.

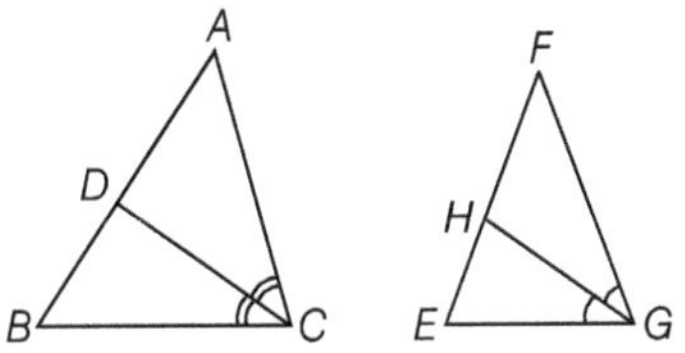


**(1)**

(i) Given, $\Delta ABC \sim \Delta FEG$

So, all corresponding angles are equal.

$\therefore \quad \angle CAB = \angle GFE$

or $\quad \angle CAD = \angle GFH$ ...(i)

and $\quad \angle ACB = \angle FGE$

$\Rightarrow \quad \frac{1}{2}\angle ACB = \frac{1}{2}\angle FGE$

[dividing both sides by 2] **(1)**

$\Rightarrow \quad \angle ACD = \angle FGH$ ...(ii)

From Eqs. (i) and (ii), we get

$\Delta ACD \sim \Delta FGH$ [by AA similarity criterion]

$\therefore \quad \frac{CD}{GH} = \frac{AC}{FG}$

[since, corresponding sides of two similar triangles are proportional] **(1)**

(ii) In $\Delta DCB$ and $\Delta HGE$,

$\angle DBC = \angle HEG$ ...(iii)

$\left[\because \quad \Delta ABC \sim \Delta FEG \quad \therefore \quad \angle ABC = \angle FEG \Rightarrow \angle DBC = \angle HEG\right]$

and $\quad \angle DCB = \angle HGE$ ...(iv) **(1)**

$\left[\because \Delta ABC \sim \Delta FEG \ \therefore \ \angle ACB = \angle FGE \Rightarrow \frac{1}{2}\angle ACB = \frac{1}{2}\angle FGE \Rightarrow \angle DCB = \angle HGE\right]$

From Eqs. (iii) and (iv),

$\Delta DCB \sim \Delta HGE$ [by AA similarity criterion] **(1)**

*Or*

**Given** $\Delta ABC$ and $\Delta PQR$ in which $AD$ and $PM$ are their medians respectively

and $\quad \frac{AB}{PQ} = \frac{BC}{QR} = \frac{AD}{PM}.$

**To prove** $\Delta ABC \sim \Delta PQR$

**Proof** We have, $\frac{AB}{PQ} = \frac{BC}{QR} = \frac{AD}{PM}$ [given]

$\Rightarrow \quad \frac{AB}{PQ} = \frac{1/2BC}{1/2QR} = \frac{AD}{PM}$

[multiplying numerator and denominator of middle term by 1/2] **(1½)**

$\Rightarrow \quad \frac{AB}{PQ} = \frac{BD}{QM} = \frac{AD}{PM}$

[since, medians $AD$ and $PM$ bisect the lines $BC$ and $QR$, respectively, i.e. $BD = 1/2BC$ and $QM = 1/2QR$]

$\Rightarrow \quad \Delta ADB \sim \Delta PMQ$ [by SSS similarity criterion]

$\therefore \quad \angle B = \angle Q$ ...(i) **(1½)**

In $\Delta ABC$ and $\Delta PQR$,

$\frac{AB}{PQ} = \frac{BC}{QR}$ [given]

and $\quad \angle B = \angle Q$ [from Eq. (i)]

$\therefore \quad \Delta ABC \sim \Delta PQR$

[by SAS similarity criterion] **Hence proved. (2)**

**36.** (i) Area of circle $= \pi r^2 = \pi\left(\frac{35}{2}\right)^2 = \frac{22}{7} \times \frac{35}{2} \times \frac{35}{2}$

$$= 11 \times 5 \times \frac{35}{2}$$

$$= \frac{1925}{2}$$

$$= 962.5 \text{ mm}^2$$

(ii) Since total circle is divided into 10 sectors

$\therefore$ Angle of each sector $= \frac{360^\circ}{10} = 36^\circ$

(iii) Circumference of circle = $\pi d$

$$= \frac{22}{7} \times 35 = 110 \text{mm}$$

$\therefore$ Total length of the silver wire = $\pi d + 5d$

$$= 110 + 5 \times 35 = 285\text{mm}$$

*Or*

Area of each sector of the brooch

$$= \frac{\theta}{360°} \times \pi r^2$$

$$= \frac{36°}{360°} \times \frac{22}{7} \left(\frac{35}{2}\right)^2 \quad \left[\because r = \frac{d}{2} = \frac{35}{2} \text{mm}\right]$$

$$= \frac{1}{10} \times \frac{22}{1} \times \frac{5}{2} \times \frac{35}{2} = \frac{11 \times 35}{2 \times 2}$$

$$= \frac{385}{4} \text{mm}^2$$

**37.** (i) For first metre, the charge is ₹ 100
i.e. first term, $a = 100$

As, there is increasing of ₹ 25 for each subsequent metres, therefore common differenece, $d = 25$

So, the AP thus formed is

100, 125, 150, ...

(ii) Labour charge to dig the well is the 15th term of AP.

We know, $a_n = a + (n-1)d$

$\therefore \quad a_{15} = 100 + (15-1)25$

$$= 100 + 14 \times 25 = 450$$

$\therefore$ Labour charge = ₹ 450

(iii) Money saved by Ram = ₹ 450 − ₹ 400 = ₹ 50

*Or*

We know that $S_n = \frac{n}{2}[2a + (n-1)d]$

Sum of 15 terms, $S_{15} = \frac{15}{2}[2 \times 100 + 14 \times 25]$

$$= \frac{15}{2}[200 + 350]$$

$$= \frac{15}{2} \times 550$$

$$= 4125$$

**38.** (i) Fixed charges = ₹ $x$ per km
and running charges = ₹ $y$ per km

$\therefore$ Running charges for 10 km = $10y$
and for 15 km = $15y$

$\therefore$ Total amount paid = Fixed charges + Running charges

$\Rightarrow \quad x + 10y = 75 \quad \ldots$(i)

and $\quad x + 15y = 110 \quad \ldots$(ii)

(ii) On subtracting Eqs.(i) and (ii), we get

$$5y = 35$$

$\Rightarrow \quad y = 7$

On substituting $y = 7$ in Eq. (i), we get

$$x + 70 = 75$$

$\Rightarrow \quad x = 5$

$\therefore$ Fixed charges = ₹ 5 per km
and running charges = ₹ 7 per km
So, for 50 km,

$$x + 50y = 5 + 50 \times 7$$
$$= 5 + 350 = 355$$

$\therefore$ Amount he has to pay is ₹ 355

(iii) Let fixed charges = ₹ $x$ per km
and running charges = ₹ $y$ per km
Running charges for 8 km = $8y$
and for 14 km = $14y$
So, the equations are

$x + 8y = 91 \quad \ldots$(i)

and $\quad x + 14y = 145 \quad \ldots$(ii)

Taking Eq. (i)

$$x + 8y = 91$$

| | | |
|---|---|---|
| **x** | 11 | 19 |
| **y** | 10 | 9 |

Now, taking Eq. (ii)

$$x + 14y = 145$$

| | | |
|---|---|---|
| **x** | 5 | 19 |
| **y** | 10 | 9 |

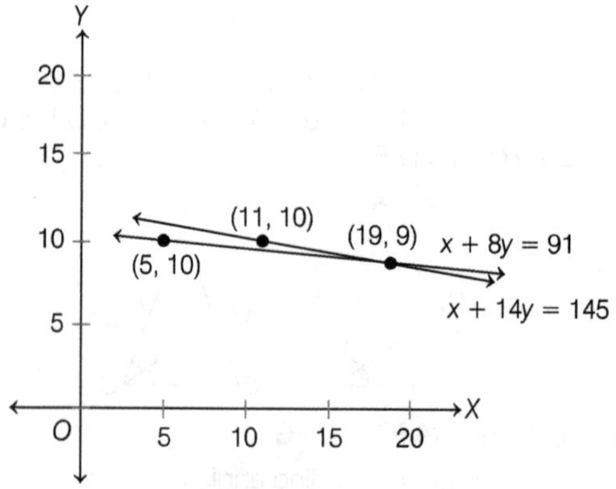


*Or*

Pair of linear equations representing the situation are

$x + 8y = 91 \quad \ldots$(i)

$x + 14y = 145 \quad \ldots$(ii)

$- \quad - \quad\quad -$

$$-6y = -54 \Rightarrow y = 9$$

On putting $y = 9$ in Eq. (i), we get

$$x + 8(9) = 91$$

$\Rightarrow \quad x = 91 - 72 = 19$

Hence, $x = 19$ and $y = 9$

**Stage 3**

# SAMPLE QUESTION PAPER 11

## Mathematics (Basic)

Time : **3 hrs** Max. Marks : **80**

## Instructions

1. This question paper has 5 Sections A, B, C, D and E.
2. Section A has 20 Multiple Choice Questions (MCQs) carrying 1 mark each.
3. Section B has 5 Short Answer-I (SA-I) Type Questions carrying 2 marks each.
4. Section C has 6 Short Answer-II (SA-II) Type Questions carrying 3 marks each.
5. Section D has 4 Long Answer (LA) Type Questions carrying 5 marks each.
6. Section E has 3 Case Based integrated units of assessment (4 marks each) with sub-parts of the values of 1, 1 and 2 marks each respectively.
7. All questions are compulsory. However, an internal choice in 2 questions of 2 marks, 2 questions of 3 marks and 2 questions of 5 marks has been provided. An internal choice has been provided in the 2 marks questions of Section E.
8. Draw neat figures wherever required. Take $\pi = 22/7$ wherever required if not stated.

## Section-A

**Section A consists of 20 questions of 1 mark each**

**1.** The product of a rational and irrational number is

(a) rational
(b) irrational
(c) can be rational and irrational
(d) None of the above

**2.** If $\frac{4}{5}$, $p$ and 2 are three consecutive terms of an AP, then the value of $p$ is

(a) $\frac{14}{5}$ (b) $\frac{3}{5}$ (c) $\frac{7}{5}$ (d) $\frac{14}{15}$

**3.** The common difference of an AP in which $a_{20} - a_{16} = 40$ is

(a) 8 (b) 10 (c) 4 (d) 6

**4.** If angle between two radii of a circle is 140°, then the angle between the tangents at the ends of the radii is

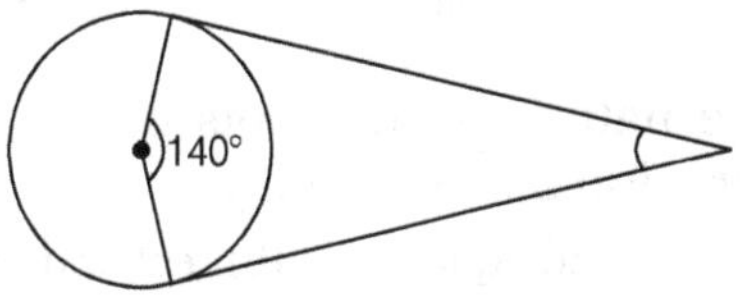


(a) 40° (b) 60° (c) 80° (d) 90°

**5.** If angle between two tangents drawn from a external point $P$ to a circle of radius $a$ with centre $O$ is 90°, then $OP$ is equal to

(a) $a$ (b) $a\sqrt{2}$
(c) $\frac{a}{2}$ (d) None of these

**6.** If $\sin A = \frac{1}{3}$, then the value of $\cos A$ is

(a) $\frac{\sqrt{2}}{4}$ (b) $\frac{2}{3}$ (c) $\frac{3\sqrt{2}}{2}$ (d) $\frac{2\sqrt{2}}{3}$

**7.** If the perimeter of a semi-circle protractor is 36 cm, then its diameter is

(a) 14 cm (b) $\frac{126}{11}$ cm (c) $\frac{63}{11}$ cm (d) 6 cm

**8.** $D$ and $E$ are the mid-points of side $AB$ and $AC$ of a $\Delta ABC$, respectively and $BC = 6$ cm. If $DE \parallel BC$, then the length (in cm) of $DE$ is

(a) 6 (b) 3 (c) 2.5 (d) 5

**9.** If a die is thrown, then the probability of getting 4 is

(a) $\frac{1}{6}$ (b) $\frac{2}{3}$ (c) 1 (d) $\frac{1}{3}$

**10.** The probability of an event that cannot happen is

(a) $\frac{1}{2}$ (b) 1 (c) 0 (d) 2

**11.** $PQ$ is a tangent drawn from a point $P$ to a circle with centre $O$ and $QOR$ is a diameter of the circle such that $\angle POR = 120°$, then $\angle OPQ$ is equal to

(a) 40° (b) 60° (c) 80° (d) 30°

**12.** The maximum volume of a cone that can be carved out of a solid hemisphere of radius $r$ is

(a) $\pi r^3$ (b) $\frac{\pi r^3}{3}$ (c) $\frac{2\pi r^3}{3}$ (d) $\frac{\pi r^3}{6}$

**13.** If the ratio of the height of a tower and the length of its shadow is $1 : \sqrt{3}$, then the angle of elevation is

(a) 60° (b) 30° (c) 45° (d) 90°

**14.** The nature of the roots of the quadratic equation $2x^2 + x + 4$ is

(a) real and equal (b) real and distinct
(c) imaginary roots (d) Can't say

**15.** The discriminant of quadratic equation $2x^2 - 6x + 1 = 0$ is

(a) 15 (b) $2\sqrt{3}$ (c) 20 (d) 28

**16.** If $\alpha$ and $\beta$ are zeroes of $p(x) = x^2 + x - 1$, then $\frac{1}{\alpha} + \frac{1}{\beta}$ is equal to

(a) −1 (b) 2 (c) 1 (d) −2

**17.** The class mark of the class 40-45 is

(a) 2.5 (b) 85 (c) 42.5 (d) 5

**18.** An ice-cream has the shape of the combination of

(a) a cylinder and a sphere
(b) a cone and a hemisphere
(c) a cylinder and a cone
(d) a cone and a cube

**Directions** *In the question number 19 and 20, a statement of Assertion (A) is followed by a statement of Reason (R). Choose the correct option.*

**19. Assertion (A)** In the given figure, $\Delta ABC \sim \Delta PQR$.

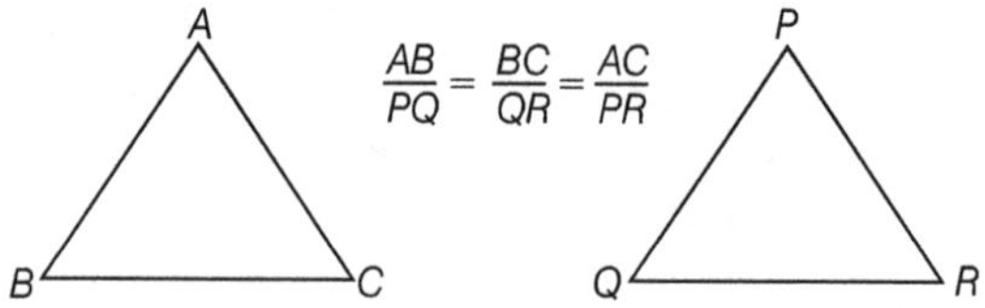


**Reason (R)** If the corresponding sides of two triangles are proportional, then they are similar.

(a) Both Assertion (A) and Reason (R) are true and Reason (R) is the correct explanation of Assertion (A)
(b) Both Assertion (A) and Reason (R) are true but Reason (R) is not the correct explanation of Assertion (A)
(c) Assertion (A) is true but Reason (R) is false
(d) Assertion (A) is false but Reason (R) is true

**20. Assertion (A)** If the circumference of two circles are in the ratio 2 : 3, then ratio of their areas is 4 : 9.

**Reason (R)** The circumference of a circle of radius $r$ is $\pi r$ and its area is $\pi r^2$.

(a) Both Assertion (A) and Reason (R) are true and Reason (R) is the correct explanation of Assertion (A)
(b) Both Assertion (A) and Reason (R) are true but Reason (R) is not the correct explanation of Assertion (A)
(c) Assertion (A) is true but Reason (R) is false
(d) Assertion (A) is false but Reason (R) is true

# Section-B

**Section B consists of 5 questions of 2 marks each**

**21.** An army contingent of 616 members is to march behind an army band of 32 members in a parade. The two groups are to march in the same number of columns. What is the maximum number of columns in which they can march?

**22.** If the points $P(4, 3)$ and $Q(x, 5)$ are on the circle with centre $O(2, 3)$, then find the value of $x$.

**23.** In a rhombus of side 10 cm, one of the diagonals is 12 cm long. Find the length of the second diagonal.

*Or* In the given figure, if $DE \parallel AQ$ and $DF \parallel AR$, then prove that $EF \parallel QR$.

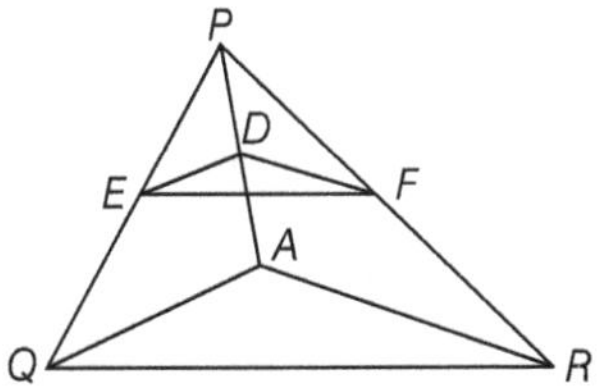


**24.** If $\frac{\cos\alpha}{\cos\beta} = m$ and $\frac{\cos\alpha}{\sin\beta} = n$, show that $(m^2 + n^2)\cos^2\beta = n^2$.

*Or*

Find acute angle $A$ and $B$, if

$\sin(A+2B) = \frac{\sqrt{3}}{2}$ and $\cos(A+4B) = 0$, $A > B$.

**25.** Jio has launched two new mobile hand sets: set A and set B. Set A is cheaper as compared to set B but set B has built-in device to recharge the battery with auto-cut power supply when it is fully charged. In a lot, there are 250 pieces of set A and 100 pieces of set B. If a mobile is picked at random.

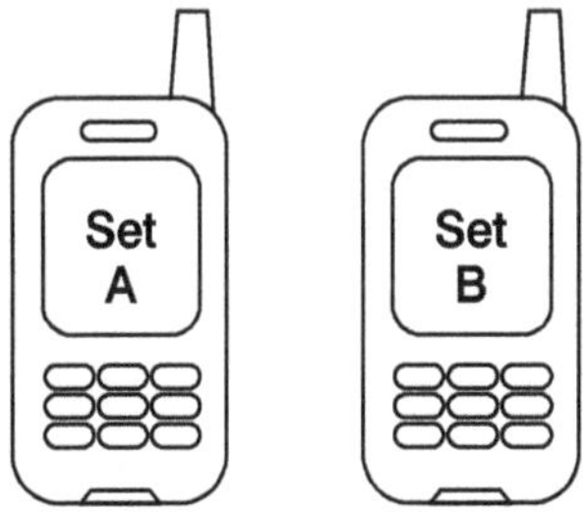


Then,

(i) find the probability of getting set A.

(ii) find the probability of getting set B.

# Section-C

**Section C consists of 6 questions of 3 marks each**

**26.** Find the value of $k$ for which the given equation has equal roots.

$$(k-12)x^2 + 2(k-12)x + 2 = 0$$

*Or*

Find the value of $x$ in the following equation $\frac{16}{x} - 1 = \frac{15}{x+1}$, $x \neq 0, -1$.

**27.** Which term of the AP 3, 15, 27, 39, ... will be 120 more than its 21st term?

*Or*

Find the sum of last ten terms of the AP series 8, 10, 12, 14, ......, 126.

**28.** The given figure shows two parallel tangents $XY$ and $X'Y'$ at the points $A$ and $B$, respectively to the circle with centre $O$.

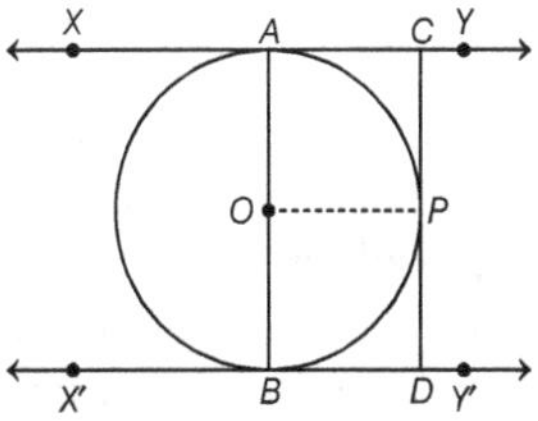


Another tangent $CD$ is drawn parallel to $AB$ at the point $P$. Show that a circle with $P$ as centre and $OP$ as radius will pass through $C$ and $D$.

**29.** If $\tan\theta - \cot\theta = a$ and $\cos\theta + \sin\theta = b$, then show that $(a^2+4)(b^2-1)^2 = 4$.

**30.** Find the greatest number that will divide 445, 572 and 699 leaving remainders 4, 5 and 6, respectively.

**31.** Circular footpath of width 2 m is constructed at the rate of ₹ 20 per $m^2$ around a circular park of radius 1500 m. Find the total cost of construction of the footpath. [take $\pi = 3.14$]

# Section-D

**Section D consists of 4 questions of 5 marks each**

**32.** The following frequency distribution shows the daily savings of 64 children in a locality

| Daily savings (in ₹) | 1-3 | 3-5 | 5-7 | 7-9 | 9-11 | 11-13 | 13-15 |
|---|---|---|---|---|---|---|---|
| Number of children | 7 | 6 | $x$ | 13 | $y$ | 5 | 4 |

If mean savings is 8, then find the missing frequencies $x$ and $y$.

*Or* An incomplete distribution is given as follows

| Class interval | Frequency |
|---|---|
| 0-10 | 10 |
| 10-20 | 20 |
| 20-30 | ? |
| 30-40 | 40 |
| 40-50 | ? |
| 50-60 | 25 |
| 60-70 | 15 |

The median value is 35 and the sum of all the frequencies is 170. Using the median formula, fill up the missing frequencies.

**33.** From the given figures, find $\angle P$.

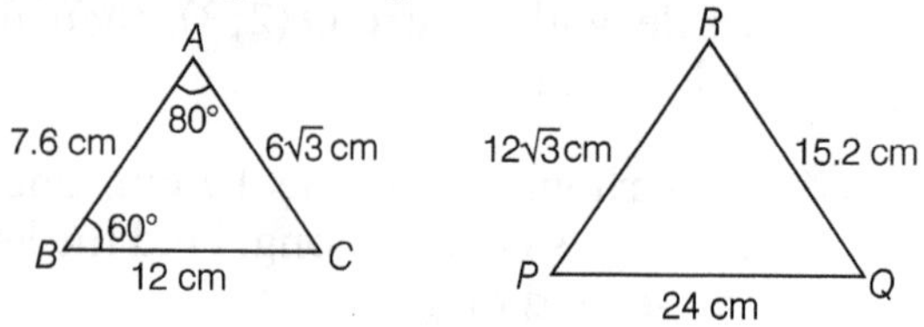


**34.** Sum of the areas of two squares is 117 $m^2$. If the difference of their perimeters is 12 m, find the sides of both squares.

**35.** As observed from the top of a 75 m high lighthouse from the sea-level, the angles of depression of two ships are 30° and 45°. If one ship is exactly behind the other on the same side of the lighthouse, find the distance between the two ships.

*Or* The angle of elevation of the top of a building from the foot of the tower is 30° and the angle of elevation of the top of the tower from the foot of the building is 60°. If the tower is 50 m high, find the height of the building.

# Section-E

**Case study based questions are compulsory**

**36.** Adventure camps are the perfect place for the children to practice decision making for themselves without parents and teachers guiding their every move. Some students of a school reached for adventure at Sakleshpur. At the camp, the waiters served some students with a welcome drink in a cylindrical glass and some students in a hemispherical cup whose dimensions are shown below.

After that they went for a jungle trek. The jungle trek was enjoyable but tiring. As dusk fell, it was time to take shelter. Each group of four students was given a canvas of area 551 m². Each group had to make a conical tent to accommodate all the four students. Assuming that all the stitching and wasting incurred while cutting, would amount to 1 m², the students put the tents. The radius of the tent is 7 m.

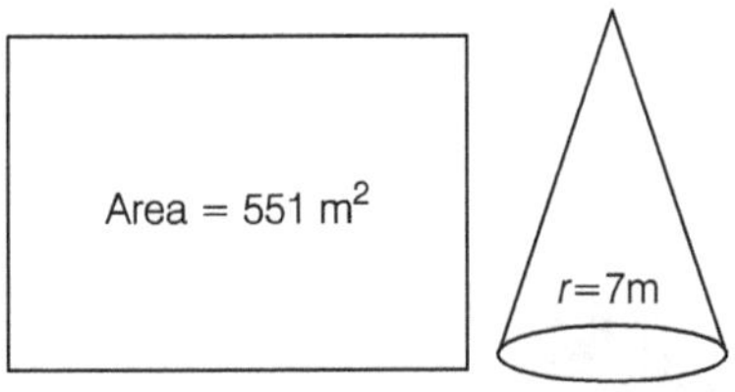


On the basis of above information, answer the following questions.

(i) Find the volume of cylindrical cup. (1)

(ii) Find the volume of hemispherical cup. (1)

(iii) Find the height of the conical tent prepared to accommodate four students. (2)

*Or* How much space on the ground is occupied by each student in the conical tent? (2)

**37.** The below picture are few natural examples of parabolic shape which is represented by a quadratic polynomial. A parabolic arch is an arch in the shape of a parabola.

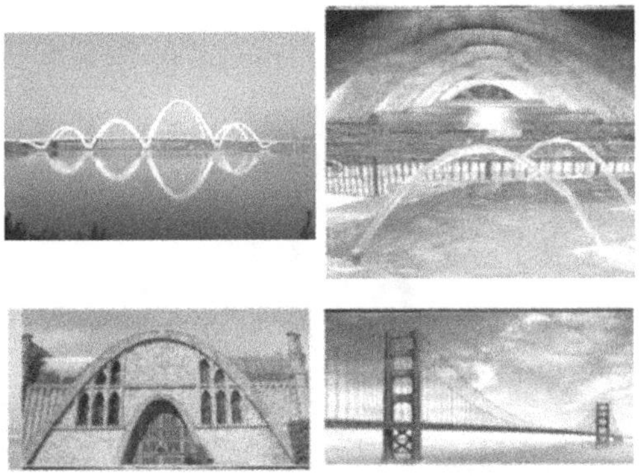

In structures, their curve represents an efficient method of load and so can be found in bridges and in architecture in a variety of forms.

On the basis of above information, answer the following questions.

(i) Write the standard form of quadratic polynomial. (1)

(ii) Draw the graph of polynomial $y(x) = x^2 + 1$. (1)

(iii) If $\alpha$ and $\frac{1}{\alpha}$ are the zeroes of the quadratic polynomial $2x^2 - x + 8k$, then find the value of $k$. (2)

*Or* If the sum of the roots is $-p$ and product of the roots is $-\frac{1}{p}$, then find the quadratic polynomial. (2)

**38.** The Chief Minister of Delhi launched the 'Switch Delhi', an electric vehicle mass awareness campaign in the National Capital. The government has also issued tenders for setting up 100 charging stations across the city. Each station will have five charging points. For demo charging station is set up along a straight line and has charging points at $A\left(\frac{-7}{3}, 0\right)$, $B\left(0, \frac{7}{4}\right)$, $C(3,4)$, $D(7, 7)$ and $E(x, y)$. Also, the distance between $C$ and $E$ is 10 units.

On the basis of above information, answer the following questions.

(i) Find the distance between $C$ and $D$. (1)

(ii) Are the points $C$, $D$ and $E$ collinear? Explain. (1)

(iii) Find the value of $x + y$. (2)

*Or* Find the ratio in which $B$ divides $AC$. (2)

# ANSWERS

**1.** (b) **2.** (c) **3.** (b) **4.** (a) **5.** (b) **6.** (d) **7.** (a) **8.** (b) **9.** (a) **10.** (c)

**11.** (d) **12.** (b) **13.** (b) **14.** (c) **15.** (d) **16.** (c) **17.** (c) **18.** (b) **19.** (a) **20.** (c)

**21.** 8

**22.** 2

**23.** 16 cm

**24.** *Or* $A = 30°, B = 15°$

**25.** (i) $\frac{5}{7}$ (ii) $\frac{2}{7}$

**26.** 14 Or $\pm 4$

**27.** 31st term *Or* 1170

**30.** 63

**31.** ₹ 377051.2

**32.** $x = 9$ and $y = 20$ *Or* Missing frequency of the class 20-30 is 35 and the class 40-50 is 25

**33.** $\angle P = 40°$

**34.** 9 m and 6 m

**35.** $75(\sqrt{3} - 1)$ m *Or* $16\frac{2}{3}$ m

**36.** (i) 404.25 $cm^3$ (ii) 89.83 $cm^3$ (iii) 24 m *Or* 38.5 $m^2$

**37.** (i) $ax^2 + bx + c$ (iii) $k = \frac{1}{4}$ *Or* $k\left(x^2 + px - \frac{1}{p}\right)$

**38.** (i) 5 units (ii) Yes (iii) 21 *Or* 7 : 9

*Scan this QR code from your mobile phone to get the explanations of this paper.*

# SAMPLE QUESTION PAPER 12

## Mathematics (Basic)

Time : **3 hrs** Max. Marks : **80**

### Instructions

1. This question paper has 5 Sections A, B, C, D and E.
2. Section A has 20 Multiple Choice Questions (MCQs) carrying 1 mark each.
3. Section B has 5 Short Answer-I (SA-I) Type Questions carrying 2 marks each.
4. Section C has 6 Short Answer-II (SA-II) Type Questions carrying 3 marks each.
5. Section D has 4 Long Answer (LA) Type Questions carrying 5 marks each.
6. Section E has 3 Case Based integrated units of assessment (4 marks each) with sub-parts of the values of 1, 1 and 2 marks each respectively.
7. All questions are compulsory. However, an internal choice in 2 questions of 2 marks, 2 questions of 3 marks and 2 questions of 5 marks has been provided. An internal choice has been provided in the 2 marks questions of Section E.
8. Draw neat figures wherever required. Take $\pi = 22/7$ wherever required if not stated.

## Section-A

**Section A consists of 20 questions of 1 mark each**

**1.** Express 450 as a product of its primes.

(a) $2\times3^2\times5$ (b) $2\times3\times5$
(c) $2\times3^2\times5^2$ (d) $2\times3\times5^2$

**2.** In the given figure, if $\Delta EDC \sim \Delta EBA$, $\angle BEC = 115°$ and $\angle EDC = 70°$. Then, $\angle DEC$ is equal to

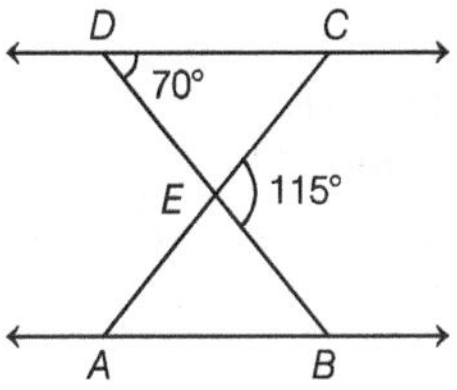


(a) 75° (b) 65° (c) 115° (d) 80°

**3.** A bag contains 5 red balls, 8 white balls, 4 green balls and 7 black balls. If one ball is drawn at random, then the probability that it is black is

(a) $\frac{5}{24}$ (b) $\frac{1}{3}$ (c) $\frac{1}{6}$ (d) $\frac{7}{24}$

**4.** If the system of equations $x+2y=5$, $3x+ky-15=0$ has no solution, then the value of $k$ is

(a) $-6$ (b) $6$ (c) $R-\{-6\}$ (d) $R-\{6\}$

**5.** The distance of the point $P(4, 7)$ from the origin (approx) is

(a) 8 units (b) 3 units
(c) 11 units (d) 6 units

**6.** The mid-point of the line segment joining the points $(-6, 9)$ and $(-2, 5)$ is

(a) $(-4, 7)$ (b) $(-2, 2)$
(c) $\left(-\frac{8}{3}, \frac{14}{3}\right)$ (d) $(-8, 14)$

**7.** The point which divides the line segment joining the points $A(0, 6)$ and $B(6, 0)$ internally in the ratio 1 : 3 is

(a) (18, 6) (b) (6, 18)
(c) $\left(\frac{3}{2}, \frac{9}{2}\right)$ (d) None of these

**8.** In a $\Delta ABC$, right angled at $A$, if $AB = 5$, $AC = 12$ and $BC = 13$, then the value of $\sin B$ is

(a) $\frac{5}{12}$ (b) $\frac{13}{5}$ (c) $\frac{5}{13}$ (d) $\frac{12}{13}$

**9.** If $2 \sin 2\theta = \sqrt{3}$, such that $0° < \theta < 90°$, then the value of $\theta$ is

(a) 60° (b) 30° (c) 45° (d) 15°

**10.** Three cubes each of side 5 cm are joined end to end. The surface area of the resulting solid is

(a) 250 $cm^2$ (b) 150 $cm^2$
(c) 350 $cm^2$ (d) 170 $cm^2$

**11.** How many terms are there in the sequence 4, 7, 10, 13, ......, 112?

(a) 37 (b) 32 (c) 36 (d) 35

**12.** For some integer $n$, the odd integer is represented as

(a) $n$ (b) $2n$ (c) $n+1$ (d) $2n+1$

**13.** In the given figure, $\Delta PMN \sim \Delta PQR$ and $PM = 3$ cm, $PQ = 4$ cm and $PN = 6$ cm, then $PR$ is equal to

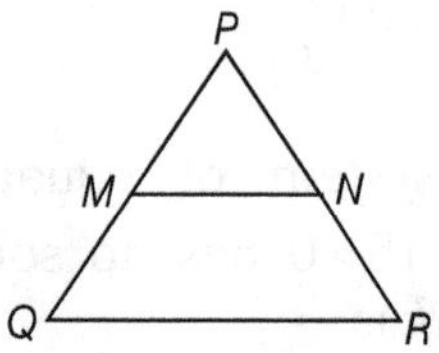


(a) 4.5 cm (b) 10 cm (c) 8 cm (d) 2 cm

**14.** The area of a sector of a circle with radius 6 cm, if the angle of the sector is 60°, is

(a) $\frac{132}{7}$ $cm^2$ (b) $\frac{44}{7}$ $cm^2$
(c) $\frac{88}{7}$ $cm^2$ (d) $\frac{152}{7}$ $cm^2$

**15.** In a circle of radius 7 cm, an arc subtends an angle of 30° at the centre. The length of the arc is

(a) 20 cm (b) $\frac{11}{3}$ cm
(c) $\frac{154}{13}$ cm (d) 44 cm

**16.** A solid cylinder of radius $r$ and height $h$ is placed over another cylinder of same height and radius. The total surface area of the shape so formed is

(a) $2\pi rh + \pi r^2$ (b) $4\pi rh + 4\pi r^2$
(c) $4\pi rh + 2\pi r^2$ (d) $2\pi rh + 2\pi r^2$

**17.** If we throw two coins in the air, then the probability of getting both tails will be

(a) $\frac{1}{2}$ (b) 0
(c) 1 (d) $\frac{1}{4}$

**18.** Which of the following are not similar figures?

(a) Squares
(b) Circles
(c) Equilateral triangles
(d) Isosceles triangle

**Directions** *In the question number 19 and 20, a statement of Assertion (A) is followed by a statement of Reason (R). Choose the correct option.*

**19. Assertion (A)** 3 is an example of a rational number.

**Reason (R)** The square roots of all positive integers are irrational numbers.

(a) Both Assertion (A) and Reason (R) are true and Reason (R) is the correct explanation of Assertion (A)
(b) Both Assertion (A) and Reason (R) are true but Reason (R) is not the correct explanation of Assertion (A)
(c) Assertion (A) is true but Reason (R) is false
(d) Assertion (A) is false but Reason (R) is true

**20.** **Assertion (A)** The probability of an event that cannot happen is equal to zero.

**Reason (R)** The probability lies between 0 and 1. Hence, it cannot be negative.

(a) Both Assertion (A) and Reason (R) are true and Reason (R) is the correct explanation of Assertion (A)
(b) Both Assertion (A) and Reason (R) are true but Reason (R) is not the correct explanation of Assertion (A)
(c) Assertion (A) is true but Reason (R) is false
(d) Assertion (A) is false but Reason (R) is true

# Section-B

**Section B consists of 5 questions of 2 marks each**

**21.** Find the mean of the following distribution.

| x | 10 | 30 | 50 | 70 | 89 |
|---|---|---|---|---|---|
| f | 7 | 8 | 10 | 15 | 10 |

**22.** A bag contains 5 red balls and some blue balls. If the probability of drawing a blue ball is double that of a red ball, find the number of blue balls in the bag.

*Or*

A game consists of tossing a one rupee coin 3 times and noting its outcome each time. Hanif wins if all the tosses give the same result i.e. three heads or three tails, and loses otherwise. Calculate the probability that Hanif will lose the game.

**23.** In the given figure, if $PA$ and $PB$ are tangents to the circle with centre $O$, such that $\angle APB = 50°$. Then, find $\angle OAB$.

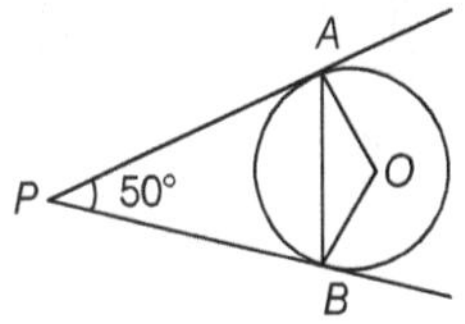


**24.** If $\tan\theta + \cot\theta = 2$, find the value of $\tan^2\theta + \cot^2\theta$.

*Or* If $\cos\theta = \frac{3}{5}$, where $0 < \theta < 90°$, then find the value of $\cot\theta + \operatorname{cosec}\theta$.

**25.** An arc of a circle is of length $5\pi$ cm and the sector if bounds has an area of $20\pi$ cm$^2$. Find the radius of the circle.

# Section-C

**Section C consists of 6 questions of 3 marks each**

**26.** If $\tan\theta = \frac{12}{5}$, where $0 < \theta < 90°$, then find the value of $\frac{1+\sin\theta}{1-\sin\theta}$.

**27.** Prove that $5 - 2\sqrt{3}$ is an irrational number.

*Or* If HCF of (180, 252 and 324) = 36, then find the LCM of (180, 252 and 324).

**28.** Point $P$ divides the line segment joining the points $A(2, 1)$ and $B(5, -8)$ such that $\frac{AP}{AB} = \frac{1}{3}$. If $P$ lies on the line $2x - y + k = 0$, find the value of $k$.

**29.** Solve the following quadratic equation by factorisation method

$$4x^2 - 2(a^2 + b^2)x + a^2b^2 = 0.$$

**30.** The 10th term of an AP is 52 and 16th term is 82. Find the 32th term and the general term.

**31.** In a two-digit number, the ten's digit is thrice of units digit. If 36 is subtracted from the number, then digits are interchanged. Find the number.

*Or* If tangents $PA$ and $PB$ from a point $P$ to a circle with centre $O$ are inclined to each other at angle of 70°, then find the value of $\angle POA$.

## Section-D

**Section D consists of 4 questions of 5 marks each**

**32.** A pole 5 m high is fixed on the top of a tower. The angle of elevation of the top of the pole observed from a point $A$ on the ground is $60^\circ$ and the angle of depression of point $A$ from the top of the tower is $45^\circ$. Find the height of the tower.

**33.** In the given figure, two chords $AB$ and $CD$ intersect each other at the point $P$.

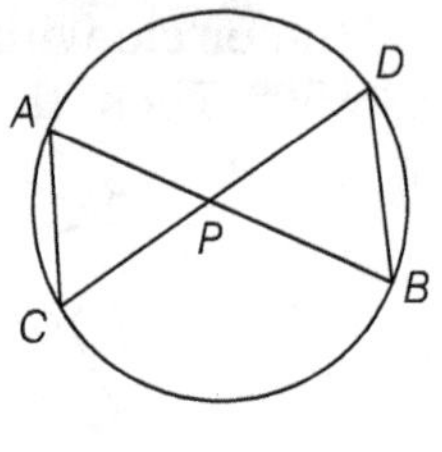


Prove that

(i) $\Delta APC \sim \Delta DPB$ (ii) $AP \cdot PB = CP \cdot DP$.

*Or*

Show that if the diagonals of a quadrilateral divide each other proportionally, then it is a trapezium.

**34.** The radii of two concentric circles are 13 cm and 8 cm. $AB$ is a diameter of the bigger circle. $BD$ is a tangent to the smaller circle touching it at $D$. Find the length $AD$.

**35.** The sum of areas of two squares is $468\text{ m}^2$. If difference of their perimeters is 24 m, then find their sides of both squares.

*Or*

Solve $(x-3)(x-4) = \dfrac{34}{(33)^2}$.

## Section-E

**Case study based questions are compulsory**

**36.** The Great Stupa at Sanchi is one of the oldest stone structures in India, and an important monument of Indian Architecture.

It was originally commissioned by the emperor Ashoka in the 3rd century *BCE*. Its nucleus was a simple hemispherical brick structure built over the relics of the Buddha. It is a perfect example of combination of solid figures. A big hemispherical dome with a cuboidal structure mounted on it.

(take $\pi = \dfrac{22}{7}$)

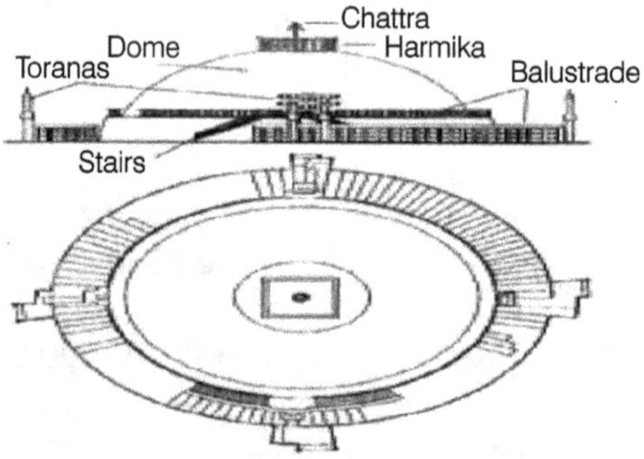


On the basis of above information, answer the following questions.

(i) Calculate the volume of the hemispherical dome, if the height of the dome is 21 m. (1)

(ii) Find the volume of the cuboidal shaped top with dimensions $8\text{ m} \times 6\text{ m} \times 4\text{ m}$. (1)

(iii) Find the total surface area of the combined figure i.e. hemispherical dome with radius 14 m and cuboidal shaped top with dimensions $8\text{ m} \times 6\text{ m} \times 4\text{ m}$. (2)

*Or* Find the cost of cloth required at the rate of ₹ $80/\text{m}^2$ to cover the hemispherical dome, if the radius of its base is 14 m. (2)

**37. Electricity Energy Consumption**

Electricity energy consumption is the form of energy consumption that uses electric energy. Global electricity consumption continues to increase faster than world population, leading to an increase in the average amount of electricity consumed per person (per capita electricity consumption).

| | | | |
|---|---|---|---|
| Tariff | : LT-Residential | Bill Number | : 384756 |
| Type of Supply | : Single Phase | Connected Load | : 3 kW |
| Meter Reading Date | : 31-11-13 | Meter Reading | : 65789 |
| Previous Reading Date | : 31-10-13 | Previous Meter Reading | : 65500 |
| | | Units Consumed | : 289 |

A survey is conducted for 56 families of a Colony A. The following tables gives the weekly consumption of electricity of these families.

| Weekly consumption (in units) | 0-10 | 10-20 | 20-30 | 30-40 | 40-50 | 50-60 |
|---|---|---|---|---|---|---|
| Number of families | 16 | 12 | 18 | 6 | 4 | 0 |

The similar survey is conducted for 80 families of Colony B and the data is recorded as below :

| Weekly consumption (in units) | 0-10 | 10-20 | 20-30 | 30-40 | 40-50 | 50-60 |
|---|---|---|---|---|---|---|
| Number of families | 0 | 5 | 10 | 20 | 40 | 5 |

On the basis of above information, answer the following questions.

**Refer to data received from Colony A**

(i) Find the mean weekly consumption. (1)

(ii) Find the modal class of the above data. (1)

**Refer to data received from Colony B**

(iii) Find the median weekly consumption. (2)

*Or*

Find the modal weekly consumption. (2)

**38.** In a soccer match, the path of the soccer ball in a kick is recorded as shown in the following graph.

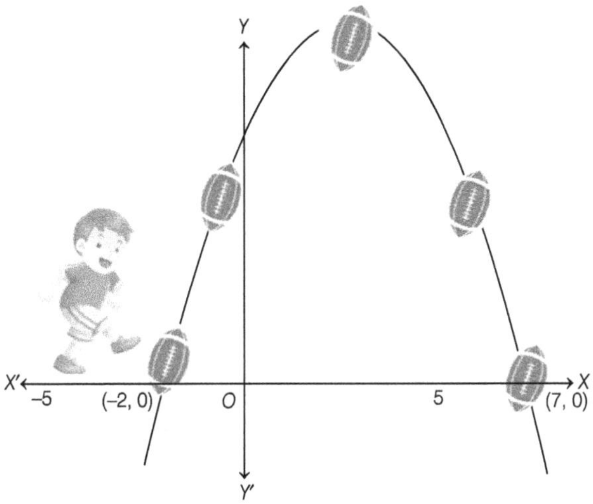


On the basis of above information, answer the following questions.

(i) What is the shape of the path of the soccer ball. (1)

(ii) Find the zeroes of the polynomial, represented in the given graph. (1)

(iii) Which of the following polynomials has −2 and −3 as its zeroes?

(a) $x^2 - 5x - 5$

(b) $x^2 + 5x - 6$

(c) $x^2 + 6x - 5$

(d) $x^2 + 5x + 6$ (2)

*Or*

For what value of $x$, the value of the polynomial $f(x) = (x-3)2+9$ is 8? (2)

# ANSWERS

**1.** (c) **2.** (b) **3.** (d) **4.** (b) **5.** (a) **6.** (a) **7.** (c) **8.** (d) **9.** (b) **10.** (c)

**11.** (a) **12.** (d) **13.** (c) **14.** (a) **15.** (b) **16.** (c) **17.** (d) **18.** (d) **19.** (c) **20.** (b)

**21.** 55

**22.** 10 *Or* $\frac{3}{4}$

**23.** 25°

**24.** 2 *Or* 2

**25.** 8 cm

**26.** 25

**27.** *Or* 11340

**28.** –8

**29.** $x = \frac{a^2}{2}$ or $x = \frac{b^2}{2}$

**30.** $a_{32} = 162$ and $a_n = 5n + 2$

**31.** 62 *Or* 55°

**32.** 6.83 m

**34.** 19 cm

**35.** Side of first square = 18 m and side of second square = 12 m *Or* $x = \frac{98}{33}$ or $x = \frac{133}{33}$

**36.** (i) 19404 $m^3$ (ii) 192 $m^3$ (iii) 1392 $m^2$ *Or* ₹ 98560

**37.** (i) 19.64 units (ii) 20-30 (iii) 41.25 units *Or* 43.6 units

**38.** (i) Parabola (ii) –2 and 7 (iii) (d) *Or* $\frac{5}{2}$

Scan this QR code from your mobile phone to get the explanations of this paper.

# SAMPLE QUESTION PAPER 13

## Mathematics (Basic)

Time : **3 hrs** Max. Marks : **80**

### Instructions

1. This question paper has 5 Sections A, B, C, D and E.
2. Section A has 20 Multiple Choice Questions (MCQs) carrying 1 mark each.
3. Section B has 5 Short Answer-I (SA-I) Type Questions carrying 2 marks each.
4. Section C has 6 Short Answer-II (SA-II) Type Questions carrying 3 marks each.
5. Section D has 4 Long Answer (LA) Type Questions carrying 5 marks each.
6. Section E has 3 Case Based integrated units of assessment (4 marks each) with sub-parts of the values of 1, 1 and 2 marks each respectively.
7. All questions are compulsory. However, an internal choice in 2 questions of 2 marks, 2 questions of 3 marks and 2 questions of 5 marks has been provided. An internal choice has been provided in the 2 marks questions of Section E.
8. Draw neat figures wherever required. Take $\pi = 22/7$ wherever required if not stated.

## Section-A

**Section A consists of 20 questions of 1 mark each**

**1.** If the LCM of $a$ and 18 is 36 and the HCF of $a$ and 18 is 2, then the value of $a$ is

(a) 1 (b) 4
(c) 2 (d) None of these

**2.** If median $=139$ units and mean $=136.50$ units, then the mode is

(a) 140.25 units
(b) 131.5 units
(c) 144 units
(d) 138.16 units

**3.** In the given figure, two equal circles touch each other at $T$, if $QP = 4.5$ cm, then $PR$ is equal to

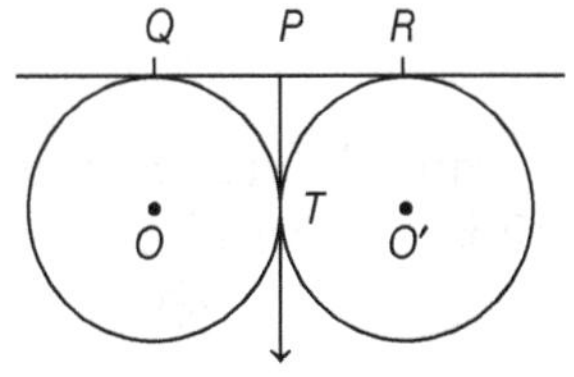


(a) 2.5 cm (b) 4.5 cm
(c) 9 cm (d) 2.2 cm

**4.** The LCM of 510 and 92 is

(a) 23460 (b) 46920 (c) 15640 (d) 7820

**5.** If the points $A(5, p)$, $B(1, 5)$, $C(2, 1)$ and $D(6, 2)$ form a square $ABCD$, then the value of $p$ is

(a) 8 (b) 6 (c) 4 (d) 2

**6.** If three points $(0, 0)$, $(3, \sqrt{3})$ and $(3, \lambda)$ form an equilateral triangle, then the value of $\lambda$ is

(a) 3 (b) $\sqrt{2}$
(c) 6 (d) $\sqrt{3}$

**7.** The ratio if the line segment joining the points $(-3, -4)$ and $(1, 2)$ is divided by $X$-axis is

(a) 2 : 1 (b) 1 : 3
(c) 1 : 2 (d) 3 : 1

**8.** If the equation $9x^2 + 6kx + 4 = 0$ has equal roots, then the value of $k$ is

(a) ± 4 (b) ± 1
(c) ± 2 (d) ± 6

**9.** The nature of the roots of the equation $4x^2 - 12x - 9 = 0$ is

(a) real and equal (b) real and distinct
(c) imaginary (d) None of these

**10.** If $\cos B = \frac{1}{3}$, then the value of $\cot B$ is

(a) $\sqrt{8}$ (b) $\frac{\sqrt{8}}{3}$ (c) $\frac{3}{\sqrt{8}}$ (d) $\frac{1}{\sqrt{8}}$

**11.** The area of the sector of a circle whose radius is 14 cm and angle of sector is 45° is

(a) 11 $cm^2$ (b) 77 $cm^2$
(c) 85 $cm^2$ (d) 65 $cm^2$

**12.** The probability that it will rain tomorrow is 0.85. Then, the probability that it will not rain tomorrow, is

(a) 0.15 (b) 1.70 (c) 1 (d) 0.42

**13.** The common difference of an AP whose $n$th term is $a_n = 3n + 7$ is

(a) 3 (b) 6 (c) 4 (d) 7

**14.** Which of the following is not irrational?

(a) $(2+\sqrt{5})$ (b) $(2-\sqrt{5})$
(c) $2\sqrt{5}$ (d) $(2-\sqrt{5})(2+\sqrt{5})$

**15.** In the given figure, $\Delta ABC \sim \Delta PQR$. The value of $x$ is

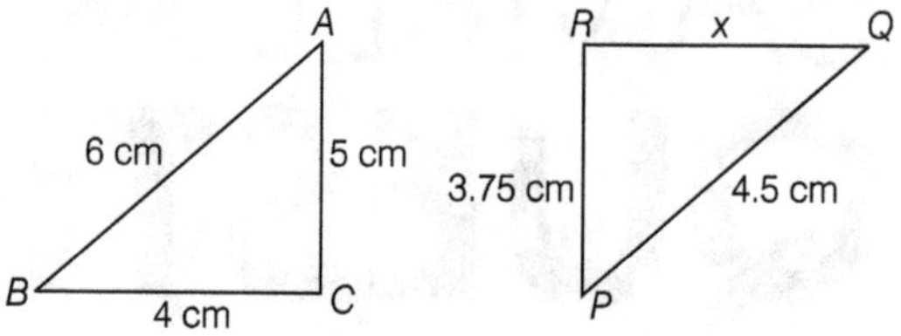


(a) 2.5 cm (b) 3.5 cm
(c) 2.75 cm (d) 3 cm

**16.** The pair of equations $x = 0$ and $x = 3$ has

(a) no solution
(b) unique/one solution
(c) two solutions
(d) infinitely many solutions

**17.** In the given figure, $DE \parallel AB$. Which of the following is true?

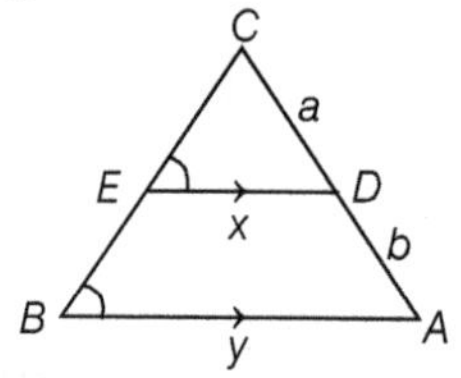


(a) $x = \frac{a+b}{ay}$ (b) $\frac{x}{y} = \frac{a}{b}$
(c) $y = \frac{ax}{a+b}$ (d) $x = \frac{ay}{a+b}$

**18.** In the given figure, $DE \parallel BC$. If $AD = 6$ cm, $DB = 8$ cm and $AE = 12$ cm. Then, the value of $EC$ is

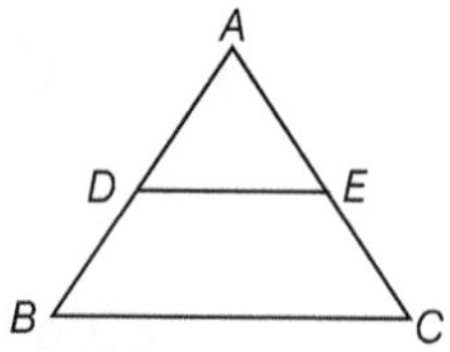


(a) 16 cm (b) 8 cm (c) 6 cm (d) 12 cm

**Directions** *In the question number 19 and 20, a statement of Assertion (A) is followed by a statement of Reason (R). Choose the correct option.*

**19. Assertion (A)** The value of $k$ for which the system of linear equations $kx - y = 2$ and $6x - 2y = 3$ has a unique solution is 3.

**Reason (R)** The graph of linear equations $a_1x + b_1y + c_1 = 0$ and $a_2x + b_2y + c_2 = 0$ gives a pair of intersecting lines, if $\frac{a_1}{a_2} \neq \frac{b_1}{b_2}$.

(a) Both Assertion (A) and Reason (R) are true and Reason (R) is the correct explanation of Assertion (A)
(b) Both Assertion (A) and Reason (R) are true but Reason (R) is not the correct explanation of Assertion (A)
(c) Assertion (A) is true but Reason (R) is false
(d) Assertion (A) is false but Reason (R) is true

**20.** **Assertion (A)** If a line divides any two sides of a triangle in the same ratio, then the line is parallel to the third side.

**Reason (R)** Line segment joining the mid-point of any two sides of a triangle is parallel to the third side.

(a) Both Assertion (A) and Reason (R) are true and Reason (R) is the correct explanation of Assertion (A)
(b) Both Assertion (A) and Reason (R) are true but Reason (R) is not the correct explanation of Assertion (A)
(c) Assertion (A) is true but Reason (R) is false
(d) Assertion (A) is false but Reason (R) is true

# Section-B

**Section B consists of 5 questions of 2 marks each**

**21.** 1000 tickets of a lottery were sold and there are 5 prizes on these tickets. If Pawan has purchased one lottery ticket, what is the probability of winning a prize?

**22.** A child has a block in the shape of a cube with one letter written on each face as shown below :

| | | | | | |
|---|---|---|---|---|---|
| A | B | C | A | E | A |

The cube is thrown once. What is the probability of getting (i) $A$ ? (ii) $D$?

*Or* A bag contains 5 red balls, 8 white balls, 4 green balls and 7 black balls. If one ball is drawn at random, find the probability that it is

(i) black (ii) red

**23.** Prove that the tangents at the extremities of any chord make equal angles with the chord.

**24.** If $\tan\theta = \frac{1}{\sqrt{3}}$, evaluate $\frac{\text{cosec}^2\theta - \sec^2\theta}{\text{cosec}^2\theta + \sec^2\theta}$.

*Or*

Prove that $\frac{\sin\theta}{1-\cos\theta} = \text{cosec}\theta + \cot\theta$.

**25.** In the given figure, the incircle of $\Delta ABC$ touches the sides $BC$, $CA$ and $AB$ at $D, E$ and $F$ respectively. Show that

$$AF + BD + CE = AE + BF + CD = \frac{1}{2}(\text{Perimeter of } \Delta ABC)$$

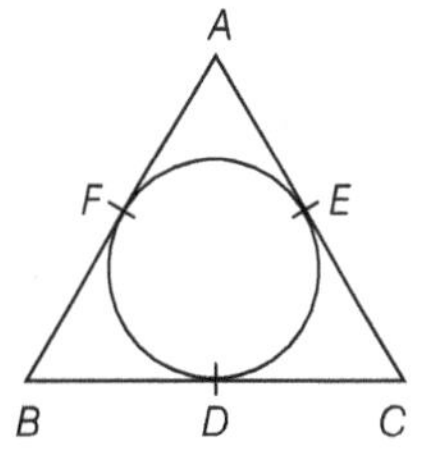


# Section-C

**Section C consists of 6 questions of 3 marks each**

**26.** If $\sec\theta + \tan\theta = p$, then show that $\frac{p^2-1}{p^2+1} = \sin\theta$.

*Or*

Show that $2(\sin^6\theta + \cos^6\theta) - 3(\sin^4\theta + \cos^4\theta) + 1 = 0$

**27.** A Sweet seller has 420 kaju barfis and 130 badam barfis. She wants to stack them in such a way that each stack has the same number and they take up the least area of the tray. What is the maximum number of barfis that can be placed in each stack for this purpose?

*Or* Prove that $3 - 2\sqrt{5}$ is irrational.

**28.** Three vertices of a parallelogram $ABCD$ are $A(3,-4)$, $B(-1,-3)$ and $C(-6,2)$. Find the coordinates of vertex $D$ and find the length of sides of the parallelogram.

**29.** Solve the quadratic equation

$$\frac{x}{x+1}+\frac{x+1}{x}=\frac{34}{15},\ x\neq 0,\ x\neq -1,$$

by factorisation method.

**30.** The area of a rectangle gets reduced by 80 sq units, if its length is reduced by 5 units and the breadth is increased by 2 units. If we increase the length by 10 units and decrease the breadth by 5 units, the area is increased by 50 sq units. Find the length and breadth of the rectangle.

**31.** Determine the height of a mountain, if the elevation of its top at an unknown distance from the base is 60° and at a distance 10 km further off from the mountain, along the same line, the angle of elevation is 30°.

## Section-D

**Section D consists of 4 questions of 5 marks each**

**32.** Find the zeroes of the quadratic polynomial $2x^2-3x+1$ and verify the relationship between the zeroes and the coefficients. Now, form a quadratic polynomial whose zeroes are double the zeroes of the given polynomial.

**33.** Find the median from the following table.

| Marks below | 10 | 20 | 30 | 40 | 50 | 60 | 70 | 80 |
|---|---|---|---|---|---|---|---|---|
| Number of students | 15 | 35 | 60 | 84 | 96 | 127 | 198 | 251 |

*Or* The following table shows the ages of the patients admitted in a hospital during a year

| Age (in years) | Number of patients |
|---|---|
| 5-15 | 6 |
| 15-25 | 11 |
| 25-35 | 21 |
| 35-45 | 23 |
| 45-55 | 14 |
| 55-65 | 5 |

Find the mode and the mean of the data given above. Compare and interpret the two measures of central tendency.

**34.** $ABCD$ is a trapezium with $AB \parallel DC$. $E$ and $F$ are two points on non-parallel sides $AD$ and $BC$ respectively, such that $EF$ is parallel to $AB$.

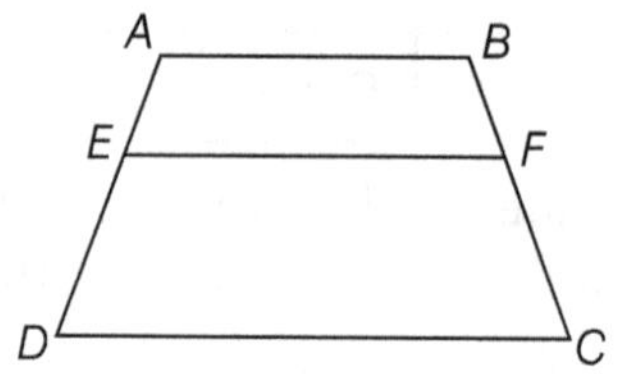


Show that $\frac{AE}{ED}=\frac{BF}{FC}$.

**35.** A toy is in the form of a cone mounted on a hemisphere of radius 7 cm. The total height of the toy is 33 cm. Find the total surface area of the toy.

*Or*

A utensil is in the form of hemispherical bowl, in which a hollow cylinder is kept on it. The radius of sphere is 7 cm and the height of utensil is 13 cm. Find the capacity of utensil.

# Section-E

**Case study based questions are compulsory**

**36.** A mathematics teacher of class X write three sequence on black board and ask some questions with the students which are based on above sequences.

On the basis of above information, answer the following questions.

(i) Which sequence is not an arithmetic progression? (1)

(ii) Write the formula to find the general term of an AP. (1)

(iii) If the last term of sequence III is 78, then find the sum of all the terms. (2)

*Or*

How many term of sequence I must be added to get the sum 245. (2)

**37.** Rekha is studying in X standard, she is observing a flag staff on a tower of height 20 m.

At a point on the ground, the angle of elevation of the foot and top of the flag are 45° and 60° as shown in the figure.

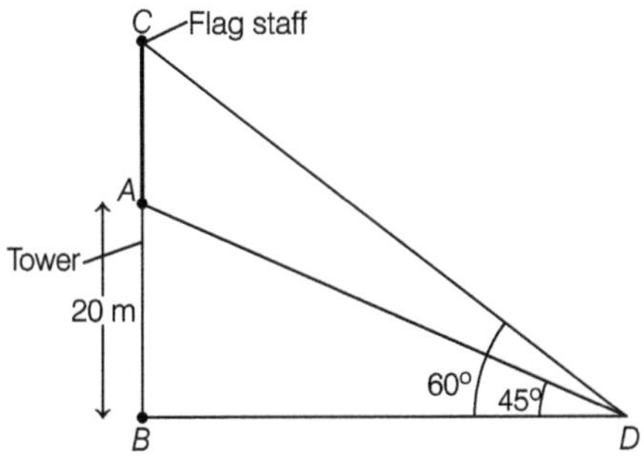


Few questions arise in her mind while she is observing the flag staff.

On the basis of above information, answer the following questions.

(i) What is the length of $BD$? (1)

(ii) What is the length of $AD$? (1)

(iii) What is the length of the flag staff? (2)

*Or*

The length of (flag staff + tower) and its shadow are in the ratio $1 : \sqrt{3}$. Then, find the angle of elevation of the Sun. (2)

**38.** A drain cover is a cover with holes in it or a grating used to cover a water drain. It allows the drainage but in the same time it prevents bigger objects to be flushed in the drain. In this order to manage drainage system, a drain cover is made from a circular metal plate of diameter 40 cm having 440 holes of diameter 1 cm each drilled in it. These holes are equally divided into 8 sectors of the circular plate as shown in figure.

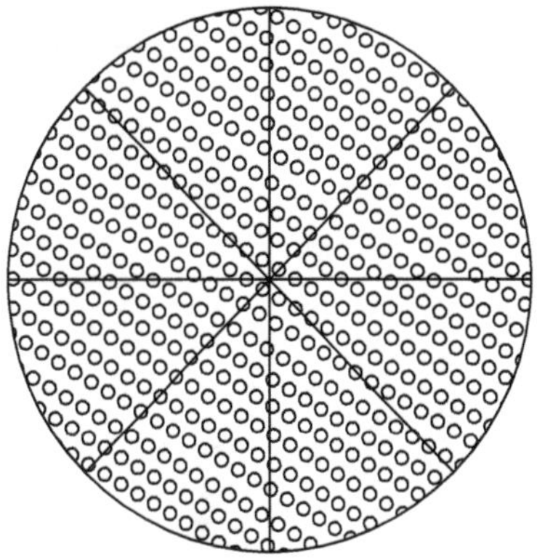

On the basis of above information, answer the following questions.

(i) Find half the circumference of the circular plate. (1)

(ii) Find the area occupied by all the holes. (1)

(iii) Find the arc length of the sector, if the sector is making an angle Of 60° at the centre. (2)

*Or* If the area enclosed by each sector is equal, then find the area of the sector of the plate considering the holes in it. (2)

# ANSWERS

**1.** (b) **2.** (c) **3.** (b) **4.** (a) **5.** (b) **6.** (d) **7.** (a) **8.** (c) **9.** (b) **10.** (d)
**11.** (b) **12.** (a) **13.** (a) **14.** (d) **15.** (d) **16.** (a) **17.** (d) **18.** (a) **19.** (d) **20.** (b)

**21.** 0.005

**22.** (i) $\frac{1}{2}$ (ii) 0 *Or* (i) $\frac{7}{24}$ (ii) $\frac{5}{24}$

**24.** $\frac{1}{2}$

**27.** 10

**28.** (2, −1) and length of sides are $\sqrt{17}$ units, $\sqrt{17}$ units, $\sqrt{50}$ units and $\sqrt{50}$ units.

**29.** $x = \frac{3}{2}, -\frac{5}{2}$

**30.** Length = 40 units and breadth = 30 units

**31.** $5\sqrt{3}$ km

**32.** $1, \frac{1}{2}; x^2 - 3x + 2$

**33.** 59.52 *Or* Mode = 36.8 yr and mean = 35.57 yr

**35.** 900.24 $cm^2$ *Or* 1642.67 $cm^3$

**36.** (i) Sequence II (ii) $T_n = a + (n-1)d$ (iii) 645 *Or* 10 terms

**37.** (i) 20 m (ii) 28.28 m (iii) 14.64 m *Or* 30°

**38.** (i) $20\pi$ cm (ii) $110\pi$ $cm^2$ (iii) $\frac{20}{3}\pi$ cm *Or* $\frac{145}{4}\pi$ $cm^2$

*Scan this QR code from your mobile phone to get the explanations of this paper.*

# SAMPLE QUESTION PAPER 14

## Mathematics (Basic)

Time : **3 hrs** Max. Marks : **80**

### Instructions

1. This question paper has 5 Sections A, B, C, D and E.
2. Section A has 20 Multiple Choice Questions (MCQs) carrying 1 mark each.
3. Section B has 5 Short Answer-I (SA-I) Type Questions carrying 2 marks each.
4. Section C has 6 Short Answer-II (SA-II) Type Questions carrying 3 marks each.
5. Section D has 4 Long Answer (LA) Type Questions carrying 5 marks each.
6. Section E has 3 Case Based integrated units of assessment (4 marks each) with sub-parts of the values of 1, 1 and 2 marks each respectively.
7. All questions are compulsory. However, an internal choice in 2 questions of 2 marks, 2 questions of 3 marks and 2 questions of 5 marks has been provided. An internal choice has been provided in the 2 marks questions of Section E.
8. Draw neat figures wherever required. Take $\pi = 22/7$ wherever required if not stated.

## Section-A

**Section A consists of 20 questions of 1 mark each**

**1.** If 2 is a zero of polynomial $p(x) = ax^2 + 2(a+1) - 3$, then the value of $a$ is

(a) $\frac{1}{3}$ (b) $\frac{1}{4}$ (c) $\frac{1}{6}$ (d) $\frac{1}{2}$

**2.** The pair of equations $y = 1$ and $y = 4$ has

(a) no solution
(b) one solution
(c) two solutions
(d) infinitely many solutions

**3.** If $x = 1$ is a common root of the equations $ax^2 + ax + 3 = 0$ and $x^2 + x + b = 0$, then $ab$ is equal to

(a) $-\frac{3}{2}$ (b) $-2$
(c) $-\frac{7}{2}$ (d) 3

**4.** The term of the given AP $2, -1, -4, -7, \ldots$ is $-40$, is

(a) 13 (b) 15 (c) 12 (d) 14

**5.** In the given figure, value of $\angle x$ is

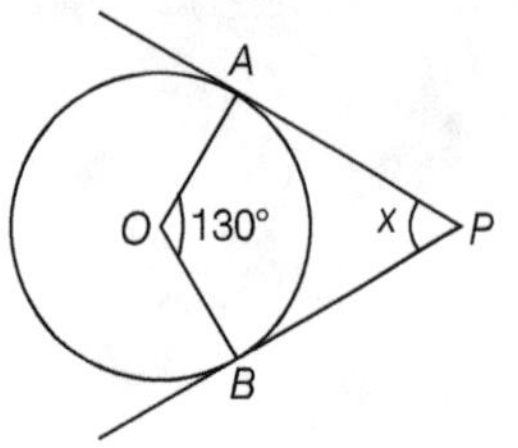


(a) 80° (b) 60°
(c) 50° (d) 90°

**6.** When two dice are thrown together, then the probability of getting a number always greater than 4 on the second die is

(a) $\frac{1}{6}$ (b) $\frac{2}{9}$ (c) $\frac{5}{18}$ (d) $\frac{1}{3}$

**7.** The discriminant of the equation $4x^2 - 12x + 9 = 0$ is

(a) 100 (b) 0 (c) 288 (d) $\sqrt{288}$

**8.** If $2\cos 3\theta = \sqrt{3}$, then the angle $\theta$ is

(a) 10° (b) 30° (c) 20° (d) 15°

**9.** If $\sin A = \frac{2}{5}$, then the value of $5 + 4\cot^2 A$ is

(a) $5 + 2\sqrt{21}$ (b) $\frac{121}{21}$
(c) 26 (d) $\frac{41}{4}$

**10.** Card marked with numbers 2 to 90 are placed in a box and mixed thoroughly. One card is drawn at random from the box. The probability that the card drawn, shows a two-digit number is

(a) $\frac{80}{89}$ (b) $\frac{79}{89}$ (c) $\frac{82}{89}$ (d) $\frac{81}{89}$

**11.** Two alarm clocks ring their alarms at regular intervals of 50 s and 48 s. If they first beep together at 12 noon, at what time will they beep again for the first time?

(a) 12 : 20 pm (b) 12 : 12 pm
(c) 12 : 11 pm (d) None of these

**12.** It is given that, $\Delta ABC \sim \Delta EDF$ such that $AB = 5$ cm, $AC = 7$ cm, $DF = 15$ cm and $DE = 12$ cm, then the sum of the remaining sides of the triangles is

(a) 23.05 cm (b) 16.8 cm
(c) 6.25 cm (d) 24 cm

**13.** If the points $A(-2,5)$ and $B(4,3)$ are equidistant from the $Y$-axis, then the coordinates of that point are

(a) (0, – 1) (b) (0, 1)
(c) (1, 0) (d) None of these

**14.** In $\Delta ABC$, $DE \parallel BC$, $\frac{AD}{DB} = \frac{6}{10}$ and $AC = 56$ cm, then the value of $AE$ is

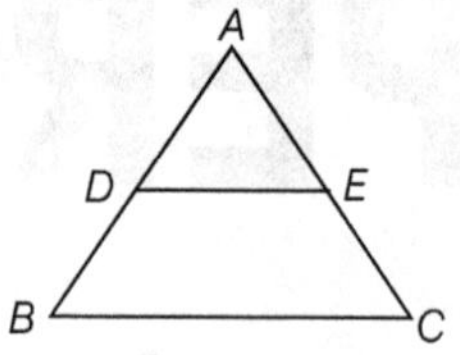


(a) 20 cm (b) 24 cm (c) 21 cm (d) 23 cm

**15.** If $C(-2, 1)$ is the mid-point of the line joining $A(-6, p)$ and $B(2, p+6)$, then the value of $p$ is

(a) 2 (b) –2 (c) 0 (d) 4

**16.** Name the criteria of similarity by which following triangles are similar.

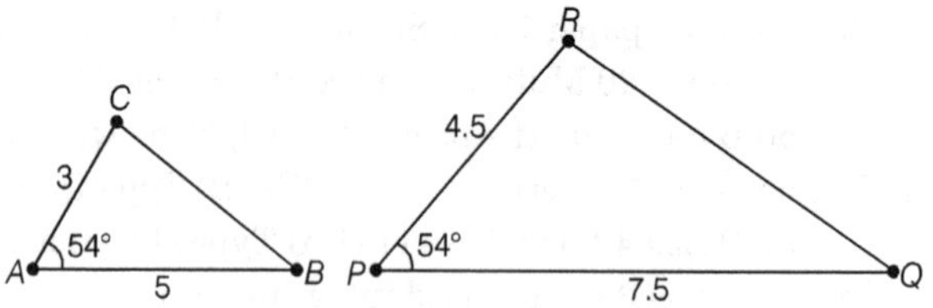


(a) SSS (b) SAS (c) AAA (d) ASA

**17.** Number of tangents drawn at a point of the circle is/are

(a) infinite (b) one (c) two (d) none

**18.** A race track is in the form of a circular ring whose outer and inner circumference are 396 m and 352 m respectively. The width of the track is

(a) 56 m (b) 7 m (c) 59.5 m (d) 18 m

**Directions** *In the question number 19 and 20, a statement of Assertion (A) is followed by a statement of Reason (R). Choose the correct option.*

**19. Assertion (A)** The length of the minute hand of a clock is 5 cm. Then, the area swept by the minute hand in 10 min is $\frac{275}{42}$ cm$^2$.

**Reason (R)** The length of an arc of a sector of angle $\theta$ and radius $r$ is given by $l = \frac{\theta}{360°} \times 2\pi r$.

(a) Both Assertion (A) and Reason (R) are true and Reason (R) is the correct explanation of Assertion (A)
(b) Both Assertion (A) and Reason (R) are true but Reason (R) is not the correct explanation of Assertion (A)
(c) Assertion (A) is true but Reason (R) is false
(d) Assertion (A) is false but Reason (R) is true

**20.** **Assertion (A)** The volume of two spheres are in the ratio 27 : 8, then the surface area is in the ratio 3 : 2.

**Reason (R)** Volume of sphere $= \frac{4}{3}\pi r^3$ and its surface area is $4\pi r^2$.

(a) Both Assertion (A) and Reason (R) are true and Reason (R) is the correct explanation of Assertion (A)
(b) Both Assertion (A) and Reason (R) are true but Reason (R) is not the correct explanation of Assertion (A)
(c) Assertion (A) is true but Reason (R) is false
(d) Assertion (A) is false but Reason (R) is true

## Section-B

**Section B consists of 5 questions of 2 marks each**

**21.** In the given figure, $PQ \parallel CB$ and $PR \parallel CD$.

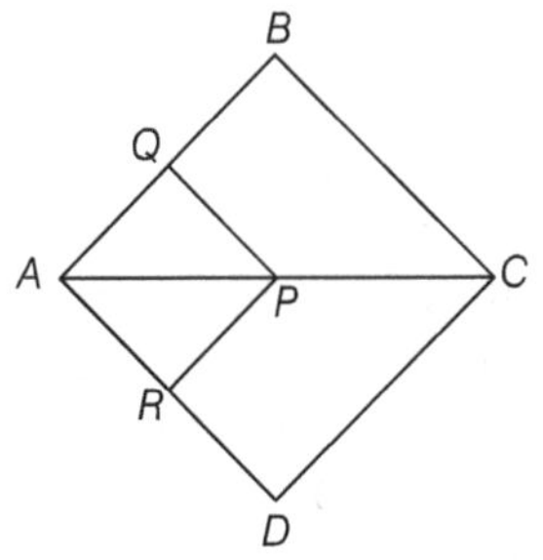


Prove that

(i) $\frac{AR}{AD} = \frac{AQ}{AB}$ (ii) $\frac{QB}{AQ} = \frac{RD}{AR}$.

*Or* In the given figure, $\angle ABC = 90°$ and $BD \perp AC$.

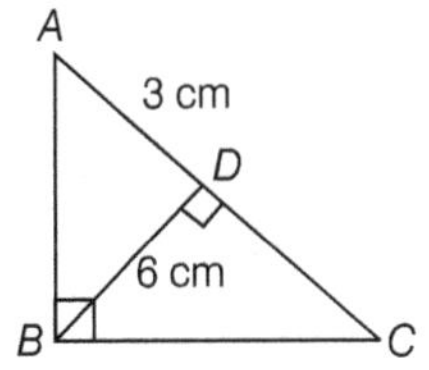


If $BD = 6$ cm and $AD = 3$ cm, then find the value of $CD$.

**22.** Express the number 140 as a product of its prime factors (using tree method).

**23.** Prove that $\frac{\tan A + \cot A}{\tan B + \cot B} = \frac{\sin B \cos B}{\sin A \cos A}$.

*Or*

Evaluate $2\tan^2 45° + \cos^2 60° - \sin^2 60°$.

**24.** If the mode of the following series is 54, then find the value of $f$.

| Class interval | 0-15 | 15-30 | 30-45 | 45-60 | 60-75 | 75-90 |
|---|---|---|---|---|---|---|
| Frequency | 3 | 5 | $f$ | 16 | 12 | 7 |

**25.** Ramesh, Anupriya and Laxmi were fighting to get first chance in a game. Ramesh says, "Let us toss two coins. If both heads appear, Anupriya will take first chance, if both tails appear, Laxmi will get it and if one head and one tail appear, I will get the chance". What is the probability of Ramesh, Anupriya and Laxmi getting the first chance?

## Section-C

**Section C consists of 6 questions of 3 marks each**

**26.** Find the largest number that divides 1251, 9377 and 15628 leaving remainders 1, 2 and 3 respectively.

**27.** Prove that

$$\left(\frac{1+\tan^2 A}{1+\cot^2 A}\right) = \left(\frac{1-\tan A}{1-\cot A}\right)^2 = \tan^2 A.$$

*Or* Prove that

$$\sec^4\theta(1-\sin^4\theta) - 2\tan^2\theta = 1.$$

**28.** Without solving the following quadratic equation, find the value of $m$ for which the given equation has real and equal roots.

$$x^2 + 2(m-1)x + (m+5) = 0$$

**29.** If the length of an arc of a circle of radius $r$ is equal to that of an arc of a circle of radius $2r$, then the angle of the corresponding sector of the first circle is double the angle of the corresponding sector of the other circle. Is this statement false? Why?

*Or* The area of a circular playground is $22176 \text{ m}^2$. Find the cost of fencing this playground at the rate of ₹ 60 per m.

**30.** The 4th term of an AP, is 22 and 15th term is 66. Find the first term and the common difference. Hence, find the sum of the series to 8 terms.

**31.** In $\Delta ABC$, $D$ and $E$ are points on the sides $AB$ and $AC$ respectively, such that $DE \parallel BC$. If $AD = 4x - 3$, $AE = 8x - 7$, $BD = 3x - 1$ and $CE = 5x - 3$, then find the value of $x$.

# Section-D

**Section D consists of 4 questions of 5 marks each**

**32.** Find the unknown entries $m, n, o, p, q$ and $r$ in the following distribution of heights of students in a class and the total number of students is 50.

| **Height** (in cm) | 150 -155 | 155 -160 | 160 -165 | 165 -170 | 170 -175 | 175 -180 |
|---|---|---|---|---|---|---|
| **Frequency** | 12 | $n$ | 10 | $p$ | $q$ | 2 |
| **Cumulative frequency** | $m$ | 25 | $o$ | 43 | 48 | $r$ |

*Or*

The following table gives weekly wages in rupees of workers in a certain commercial organization. The frequency of class 49-52 is missing. It is known that the mean of the frequency distribution is 47.2. Find the missing frequency.

| **Weekly wages (₹)** | 40-43 | 43-46 | 46-49 | 49-52 | 52-55 |
|---|---|---|---|---|---|
| **Number of workers** | 31 | 58 | 60 | ? | 27 |

**33.** The ratio of incomes of two friends Jasmine and Aman is 9 : 7 and the ratio of their expenditures is 4: 3. If each of them saves ₹ 6000 per month, find their monthly incomes. Also, if each of them donates 2% of her/his income to a charity working for old age destitutes, find the resulting savings of each.

**34.** An aeroplane is flying with the speed of box 600 km/h along a straight road towards a point on the road. At any time, the angle of elevation from that point to the angle of elevation is 30°. After 6 s, the angle of elevation from that point to the aeroplane becomes 60°. Find the vertical height of an aeroplane.

*Or*

The tangent of angle of elevation from any point to the top of the tower is 7/4. Moving 25 m towards the tower, the tangent of angle of elevation becomes 7/3. Find the height of the tower.

**35.** In the given figure, $O$ is the centre of a circle with radius 5 cm. If $T$ is a point such that $OT = 13$ cm, then find the length of $AB$.

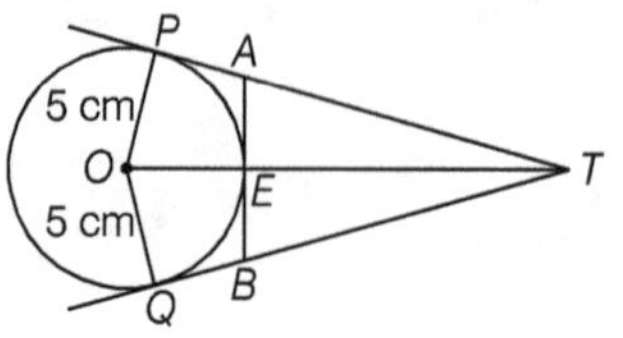

# Section-E

**Case study based questions are compulsory**

**36.** A parking shed is in the shape of a cuboid surmounted by a half cylinder. The base of the shed is of dimension 20 m × 15 m, and the height of the cubodial portion is 10 m. In the shed, there are cars and bikes. The cars in the shed occupy a total space of 1200 $m^3$ and there are 250 bikes, each of them occupy about 0.5 $m^3$ space on an average.

On the basis of above information, answer the following questions.

(i) Find the total height of the shed. (1)

(ii) Find the volume of cuboidal portion. (1)

(iii) Find the volume of the air, when there are cars and bikes in the shed (ignore the air inside the cars). (2)

*Or* Find the total surface area of the shed. (2)

**37.** Basketball and soccer are played with a spherical ball. Even though an athlete dribbles the ball in both sports, a basketball player uses his hands and a soccer player uses his feet. Usually, soccer is played outdoors on a large field and basketball is played indoor on a court made out of wood. The projectile (path traced) of soccer ball and basketball are in the form of parabola representing quadratic polynomial.

On the basis of above information, answer the following questions.

(i) Write the general form of a quadratic polynomial. (1)

(ii) How many zeroes do the following polynomial has? (1)

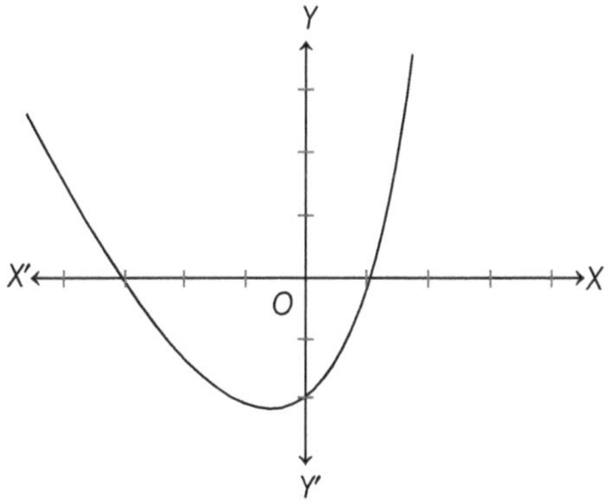


(iii) If one zero of the quadratic polynomial $(k-1)x^2 + kx + 1$ is $-4$, then find the value of $k$. (2)

*Or*

Find the quadratic polynomial, whose sum of zeroes is $-\frac{1}{4}$ and product of zeroes is $\frac{1}{4}$. (2)

**38.** To raise social awareness about hazards of cancer, an organisation decided to start a campaign. 5 students were asked to prepare campaign banners in the shape of a triangle. The vertices of the triangle are $A(0, 6)$, $B(6, 6)$ and $C(1, 1)$.

On the basis of above information, answer the following questions.

(i) Find the coordinates of centroid of $\Delta ABC$. (1)

(ii) If $S$ be the mid-point of the line joining $A$ and $B$, then find the coordinates of $S$ and distance of $AB$. (2)

*Or*

If $T$ be the mid-point of the line joining $C$ and $B$, then find the coordinates of $T$ and distance of $CB$. (2)

(iii) If $U$ be the mid-point of the line joining $C$ and $A$, then find the coordinates of $U$. (1)

# ANSWERS

| | | | | | | | | | |
|---|---|---|---|---|---|---|---|---|---|
| **1.** (c) | **2.** (a) | **3.** (d) | **4.** (b) | **5.** (c) | **6.** (d) | **7.** (b) | **8.** (a) | **9.** (c) | **10.** (d) |
| **11.** (a) | **12.** (a) | **13.** (b) | **14.** (c) | **15.** (b) | **16.** (b) | **17.** (b) | **18.** (b) | **19.** (d) | **20.** (d) |

**21.** *Or* 12 cm **22.** $2^2 \times 5 \times 7$ **23.** *Or* $\frac{3}{2}$ **24.** 10

**25.** $\frac{1}{2}, \frac{1}{4}, \frac{1}{4}$ **26.** 625 **28.** $-1$ and 4 **29.** No *Or* ₹ 31680

**30.** $a = 10, d = 4, S_8 = 192$ **31.** 1

**32.** $m = 12,\ n = 13, o = 35,\ p = 8, q = 5$ and $r = 50$. *Or* 44

**33.** Income of Jasmine = ` 54000 and income of Aman = ₹ 42000

Resulting saving of Jasmine = ₹ 4920 and resulting saving of Aman = ₹ 5160

**34.** $\frac{\sqrt{3}}{2}$ km *Or* 175 m

**35.** $\frac{20}{3}$ cm

**36.** (i) 17.5 m (ii) 3000 $m^3$ (iii) 3442.85 $m^3$ *Or* 1648.21 $m^2$

**37.** (i) $ax^2 + bx + c = 0$ (ii) 2 (iii) $\frac{5}{4}$ *Or* $x^2 + \frac{1}{4}x + \frac{1}{4}$

**38.** (i) $\left(\frac{7}{3}, \frac{13}{3}\right)$ (ii) (3, 6), 6 units *Or* $\left(\frac{7}{2}, \frac{7}{2}\right)$, $5\sqrt{2}$ units (iii) $\left(\frac{1}{2}, \frac{7}{2}\right)$

Scan this QR code from your mobile phone to get the explanations of this paper.

# SAMPLE QUESTION PAPER 15

## Mathematics (Basic)

Time : **3 hrs** Max. Marks : **80**

### Instructions

1. This question paper has 5 Sections A, B, C, D and E.
2. Section A has 20 Multiple Choice Questions (MCQs) carrying 1 mark each.
3. Section B has 5 Short Answer-I (SA-I) Type Questions carrying 2 marks each.
4. Section C has 6 Short Answer-II (SA-II) Type Questions carrying 3 marks each.
5. Section D has 4 Long Answer (LA) Type Questions carrying 5 marks each.
6. Section E has 3 Case Based integrated units of assessment (4 marks each) with sub-parts of the values of 1, 1 and 2 marks each respectively.
7. All questions are compulsory. However, an internal choice in 2 questions of 2 marks, 2 questions of 3 marks and 2 questions of 5 marks has been provided. An internal choice has been provided in the 2 marks questions of Section E.
8. Draw neat figures wherever required. Take $\pi = 22/7$ wherever required if not stated.

## Section-A

**Section A consists of 20 questions of 1 mark each**

**1.** The least number that is divisible by all the numbers from 1 to 10 (both inclusive) is

(a) 1260 (b) 2520 (c) 3780 (d) 1890

**2.** The nature of roots of the quadratic equation $2x^2 - \sqrt{5}x + 1 = 0$ is

(a) real, unequal and rational
(b) real and equal
(c) imaginary
(d) real, unequal and irrational

**3.** For what value of $k$, do the equations $3x - y + 8 = 0$ and $6x - ky = -16$ represent coincident lines?

(a) $\{R\} - 2$ (b) $\{R\} - \{-2\}$
(c) $-2$ (d) 2

**4.** In the given figure, the graph of a polynomial $p(x)$ is shown as below

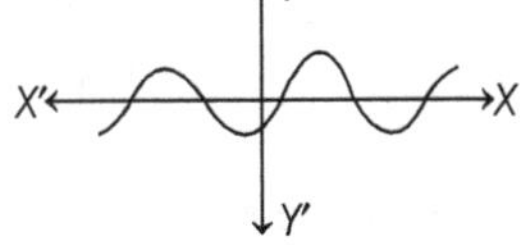


The number of zeroes of $p(x)$ is

(a) 3 (b) 1
(c) 2 (d) 5

**5.** If point $P$, which internally divides the line segment joining the points $A(-2, 1)$ and $B(1, 4)$ in the ratio 2 : 1, then the coordinates of point $P$ is

(a) (1.5, 2) (b) (0, 3)
(c) (−1, 2) (d) (− 0.5, 2.5)

**6.** The similarity criterion, such that $\frac{AB}{PQ} = \frac{AC}{PR}$, $\angle A = \angle P$, if $\Delta ABC \sim \Delta PQR$ is

(a) ASA (b) SAS (c) AA (d) SSS

**7.** In the given figure, $PA$ and $PB$ are tangents draw from point $P$ outside the circle and $OP$ is the perpendicular bisector of $AB$ such that $PA = 10$ cm and $\angle APB = 60°$, then the length of chord $AB$ is

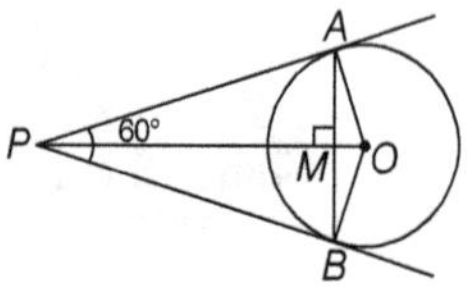


(a) 5 cm (b) 10 cm (c) 8 cm (d) $5\sqrt{3}$ cm

**8.** If $7\sin^2\theta + 3\cos^2\theta = 4$, then $\sec\theta + \operatorname{cosec}\theta$ is equal to

(a) $\frac{7}{2\sqrt{3}}$ (b) $\frac{\sqrt{3}+1}{2}$ (c) $\frac{2}{\sqrt{3}} + 2$ (d) $\frac{\sqrt{6}+2}{2\sqrt{2}}$

**9.** If $\tan\theta = \frac{a}{b}$, then the value of $\sec\theta$ is

(a) $\frac{b}{a}$ (b) $\frac{\sqrt{a^2+b^2}}{b}$
(c) $\frac{\sqrt{a^2-b^2}}{b}$ (d) $\frac{b\sqrt{a^2+b^2}}{a^2+b^2}$

**10.** The probability of getting a multiple of 3 in a single throw of a die is

(a) $\frac{1}{6}$ (b) $\frac{1}{2}$ (c) $\frac{2}{3}$ (d) $\frac{1}{3}$

**11.** If the Sun's angle of elevation is 30° and height of the pole is 8m, then the length of the shadow is

(a) 16 m (b) $\frac{16\sqrt{3}}{3}$ m
(c) $\frac{8}{\sqrt{3}}$ m (d) $8\sqrt{3}$ m

**12.** If one root of the equation $(k-1)x^2 - 10x + 4 = 0$ is the reciprocal of the other, then the value of $k$ is

(a) 5 (b) −3
(c) −9 (d) 11

**13.** The sum of the roots of the equation $3x^2 - 10x + 5 = 0$ is

(a) 8 (b) $\frac{10}{3}$ (c) $\frac{5}{3}$ (d) $-\frac{5}{3}$

**14.** A tangent $PQ$ at a point $P$ of a circle of radius 6 cm meets a line through the centre $O$ at a point $Q$, so that $OQ = 10$ cm. The length of $PQ$ is

(a) 3 cm (b) $2\sqrt{34}$ cm
(c) 8 cm (d) 5 cm

**15.** A cylinder and a cone are of same base radius and of same height. The ratio of the volume of cylinder to that of the cone is

(a) 1 : 1 (b) 2 : 3 (c) 3 : 4 (d) 3 : 1

**16.** If $Q\left(\frac{a}{3}, -4\right)$ is the mid-point of the segment joining the points $P(6, -5)$ and $R(2, -3)$, then the value of $a$ is

(a) 12 (b) −6 (c) −12 (d) −4

**17.** In $\Delta ABC \sim \Delta DEF$ such that $AB = 9.1$ cm and $DE = 6.5$ cm. If the perimeter of $\Delta DEF$ is 25 cm, then the perimeter of $\Delta ABC$ is

(a) 36 cm (b) 30 cm (c) 34 cm (d) 35 cm

**18.** $\sqrt{2}$ times the distance between (0, 5) and (−5, 0) is

(a) $10\sqrt{2}$ (b) 10
(c) $2\sqrt{5}$ (d) $5\sqrt{2}$

**Directions** *In the question number 19 and 20, a statement of Assertion (A) is followed by a statement of Reason (R). Choose the correct option.*

**19. Assertion (A)** The point (0, 8) lies on $Y$-axis.

**Reason (R)** The $y$-coordinate of the point on $X$-axis is zero.

(a) Both Assertion (A) and Reason (R) are true and Reason (R) is the correct explanation of Assertion (A)
(b) Both Assertion (A) and Reason (R) are true but Reason (R) is not the correct explanation of Assertion (A)
(c) Assertion (A) is true but Reason (R) is false
(d) Assertion (A) is false but Reason (R) is true

**20. Assertion (A)** In an equilateral triangle of side $4\sqrt{2}$ cm, the length of the altitude is 5 cm.

**Reason (R)** If a ladder 8 m long reaches a window 4 m above the ground, then the distance of the foot of the ladder from the base of the wall is $4\sqrt{3}$ m.

(a) Both Assertion (A) and Reason (R) are true and Reason (R) is the correct explanation of Assertion (A)
(b) Both Assertion (A) and Reason (R) are true but Reason (R) is not the correct explanation of Assertion (A)
(c) Assertion (A) is true but Reason (R) is false
(d) Assertion (A) is false but Reason (R) is true

## Section-B

**Section B consists of 5 questions of 2 marks each**

**21.** Find the largest number which when divides 969 and 2059, the remainder obtained are 9 and 11, respectively.

*Or* Find the LCM and HCF of the following pairs of integers and verify that LCM × HCF = product of the two numbers 26 and 91.

**22.** Solve the equation $x^2+(3-2a)x-6a=0$ by factorisation method.

**23.** Find the ratio in which the line segment joining $A(1,-5)$ and $B(-4,5)$ is divided by the $X$-axis. Also, find the coordinates of the point of division.

**24.** In the given figure, $PQR$ and $QST$ are two right angled triangles, right angled at $R$ and $T$, respectively.

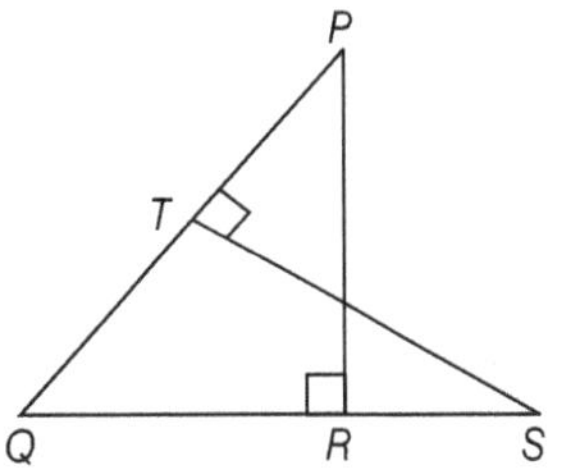


Prove that $QR \times QS = QP \times QT$.

**25.** Ramesh asks the labour to dig a well upto a depth of 10 m. Labour charges ₹ 150 for first metre and ₹ 50 for each subsequent metres. As labour was uneducated, he claims ₹ 550 for the whole work. Was labour right?

*Or*

Find the sum of first 20 even natural numbers.

## Section-C

**Section C consists of 6 questions of 3 marks each**

**26.** Find the zeroes of the polynomial $x^2+x-20$. Also, verify the relation between the coefficients and zeroes of the polynomial.

*Or* If $\alpha$ and $\beta$ are the zeroes of $f(x)=x^2+5x+6$, then find the value of $\alpha^2+\beta^2$.

**27.** Two years ago, Salim was thrice as old as his daughter and six years later, he will be four years older than twice her age. How old are they now?

*Or* Taxi charges in a city consist of fixed charges and the remaining depending upon the distance travelled in kilometres. If a person travels 60 km, he pays ₹ 490 and for travelling 90 km, he pays ₹ 700. Express the above statements with the help of simultaneous equations and hence find the fixed charge and the rate per kilometre.

**28.** Prove that $\sqrt{7}$ is an irrational number.

**29.** If $a$, $b$ and $c$ are the sides of right triangle, where $c$ is hypotenuse, then prove that the radius $r$ of the circle which touches the sides of the triangle, is given by $r=\dfrac{a+b-c}{2}$.

**30.** The given table gives the enrolment in Higher Secondary School in 1978. Find the average enrolment in HS School.

| Enrolment | Number of schools |
|---|---|
| 20-39 | 526 |
| 40-59 | 620 |
| 60-79 | 674 |
| 80-99 | 717 |
| 100-119 | 681 |
| 120-139 | 612 |
| 140-159 | 540 |
| 160-179 | 517 |
| 180-199 | 552 |
| **Total** | 5439 |

**31.** In a game, the entry fee is ₹ 5. The game consists of tossing a coin 3 times. If one or two heads show, Sweta gets her entry fee back. If she throws 3 heads, she receives double the entry fees. Otherwise she will lose.

For tossing a coin three times, find the probability that she

(i) loses the entry.

(ii) just gets her entry fee.

# Section-D

**Section D consists of 4 questions of 5 marks each**

**32.** If $\frac{\cos^4 \alpha}{\cos^2 \beta} + \frac{\sin^4 \alpha}{\sin^2 \beta} = 1$, then prove that

$$\frac{\cos^4 \beta}{\cos^2 \alpha} + \frac{\sin^4 \beta}{\sin^2 \alpha} = 1.$$

*Or*

If $3\cot A = 4$, then check whether

$\frac{1 - \tan^2 A}{1 + \tan^2 A} = \cos^2 A - \sin^2 A$ or not.

**33.** Find the sum of $n$ terms of the sequence $\{a_n\}$, where $a_n = 5 - 6n, n \in N$.

**34.** A medicine capsule is in the shape of a cylinder with two hemispheres stuck to each of its ends (see below figure). The length of the entire capsule is 14 mm and the diameter of the capsule is 5 mm. Find its surface area.

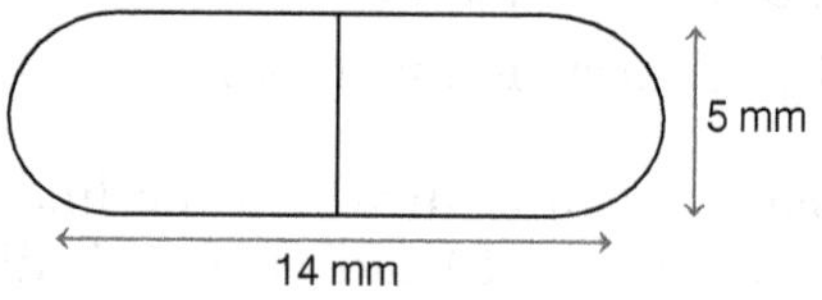


*Or* A solid toy is in the form of a hemisphere surmounted by a right circular cone. The height of this cone is 4 cm and the diameter of the base is 8 cm. Find the volume of the toy.

**35.** In the given figure, if $PQRS$ is a parallelogram and $AB || PS$, then prove that $OC || SR$.

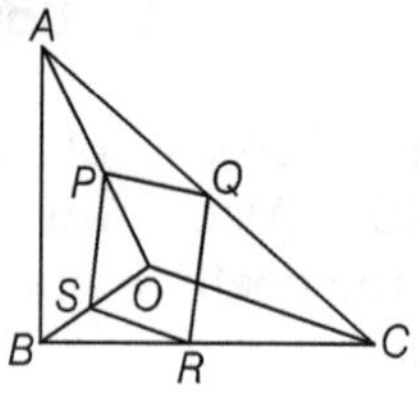

# Section-E

**Case study based questions are compulsory**

**36.** A Satellite flying at height h is watching the top of the two tallest mountains in Uttarakhand and Karnataka, then being Nanda Devi (height 7816 m) and Mullayanagiri (height 1930 m). The angles of depression from the satellite, to the top of Nanda Devi and Mullayanagiri are 30° and 60°, respectively. If the distance between the peaks of two mountains is 1937 km and the satellite is vertically above the midpoint of the distance between the two mountains.

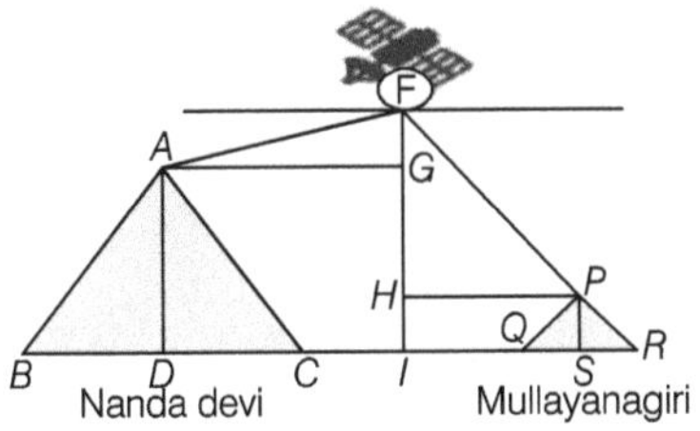


On the basis of above information, answer the following questions.

(i) Find the distance of the satellite from the top of Nanda Devi. (1)

(ii) Find the distance of the satellite from the top of Mullayanagiri. (1)

(iii) Find the distance of the satellite from the ground. (2)

*Or* If a mile stone very far away from, makes 30° to the top of Mullanyangiri montain. So, find the distance of this mile stone from the mountain. (2)

**37.** The COVID-19 pandemic, also known as coronavirus pandemic, is an ongoing pandemic of coronavirus disease caused by the transmission of severe acute respiratory syndrome coronavirus 2 (SARS-CoV-2) among humans.

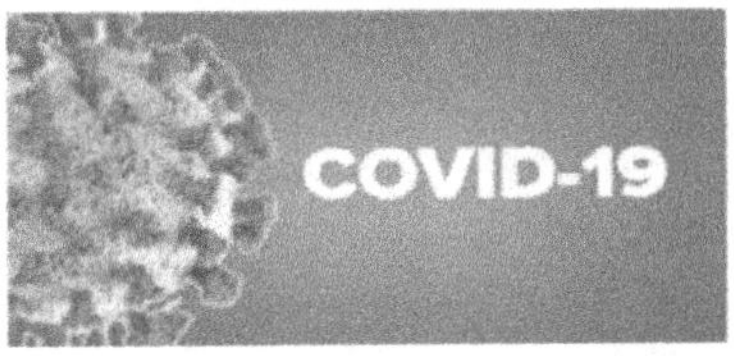


The following tables shows the age distribution of case admitted during a day in two different hospitals

**Table 1**

| Age (in years) | 5-15 | 15-25 | 25-35 | 35-45 | 45-55 | 55-65 |
|---|---|---|---|---|---|---|
| Number of cases | 6 | 11 | 21 | 23 | 14 | 5 |

**Table 2**

| Age (in years) | 5-15 | 15-25 | 25-35 | 35-45 | 45-55 | 55-65 |
|---|---|---|---|---|---|---|
| Number of cases | 8 | 16 | 10 | 42 | 24 | 12 |

On the basis of above information, answer the following questions.

**Refer to table 1**

(i) Find the upper limit of modal class. (1)

(ii) Find the mean of the given data. (1)

**Refer to table 2**

(iii) Find the mode of the given data. (2)

*Or*

Find the median of the given data. (2)

**38.** Ram bought a pendulum clock for his living room from Chandni Chowk, Delhi. The clock contains pendulum of length 20 cm. The minute hand and hour hand of the clock are 10 cm and 7 cm long, respectively and there is no second hand in the clock.

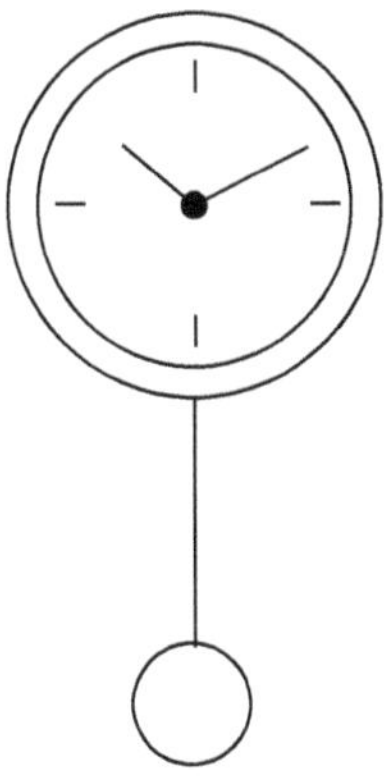

On the basis of above information, answer the following questions.

(i) Find the angle described by minute hand in 20 min. (1)

(ii) Find the area swept by the minute hand in 10 min. (1)

(iii) If the pendulum covers a distance of 30 cm in one complete oscillation, then find the angle described by the pendulum at the centre. (2)

*Or*

Find the area swept by the hour hand between 10 am and 5 pm. (2)

# ANSWERS

| | | | | | | | | | |
|---|---|---|---|---|---|---|---|---|---|
| **1.** (b) | **2.** (c) | **3.** (d) | **4.** (d) | **5.** (b) | **6.** (b) | **7.** (b) | **8.** (c) | **9.** (b) | **10.** (d) |
| **11.** (d) | **12.** (a) | **13.** (b) | **14.** (c) | **15.** (d) | **16.** (a) | **17.** (d) | **18.** (b) | **19.** (b) | **20.** (d) |

**21.** 64 *Or* LCM = 182, HCF = 13

**22.** $-3$ and $2a$

**23.** 1 : 1 and $\left(-\frac{3}{2}, 0\right)$

**25.** No *Or* 400

**26.** $x = 4, -5$ *Or* 13

**27.** Salim's age = 38 yr and his daughter's age = 14 yr *Or* Fixed charge = ₹ 70 and the rate per kilometre = ₹ 7

**30.** 107.38

**31.** (i) $\frac{1}{8}$ (ii) $\frac{3}{4}$

**32.** *Or* Yes

**33.** $n(2-3n)$

**34.** 220 $mm^2$ *Or* 201.14 $cm^3$

**36.** (i) 1118.3 km (ii) 1937 km (iii) 566.996 km *Or* $1930\sqrt{3}$ m

**37.** (i) 45 (ii) 35.4 (iii) 41.4 *Or* 40.24

**38.** (i) 120° (ii) 52.38 $cm^2$ (iii) 42.95° *Or* 89.83 $cm^2$

*Scan this QR code from your mobile phone to get the explanations of this paper.*

# Solutions to the Qualifying ROUND

## Chapter 1 Real Numbers

**1.** (*c*) Required number = HCF (1659 – 8, 2036 – 4)

$= \text{HCF } (1651, 2032) = 127$

**2.** (*b*) Required number of containers $= \dfrac{144 + 216}{\text{HCF }(144, 216)}$

$= \dfrac{360}{72} = 5$

**3.** (*c*) Let $x$ be the HCF of the numbers.

We have the numbers as $3x$, $4x$ and $5x$.

Now, LCM $(3x, 4x, 5x) = 3 \times 4 \times 5 \times x = 60x$

$\Rightarrow \quad 60x = 1200$

$\therefore \quad x = 20$

**4.** (*d*) For some integer $q$, every odd integer is of the form $2q + 1$.

**5.** (*b*) LCM $(p, q)$ = product of the greatest power of each prime factor involved in the numbers.

$= a^2b^2$

**6.** Now, LCM of (8, 15, 21) = 840

Divide 110000 by 840 and find the remainder.

$\therefore \quad 110000 = 840 \times 130 + 800$ (1)

Now, the number which is divisible by each 8, 15 and 21 and lies between 100000 and 110000, is 109200. (1)

**7.**

| | |
|---|---|
| 3 | 2475 |
| 3 | 825 |
| 5 | 275 |
| 5 | 55 |
| 11 | 11 |
| | 1 |

(1)

$\therefore$ The prime factorisation of 2475 is $3^2 \times 5^2 \times 11$. (1)

**8.** We have, $7 \times 11 \times 13 + 13$

$= 1001 + 13$

$= 1014$ (1)

Now, $1014 = 2 \times 3 \times 13 \times 13$

Thus, it is the product of prime factors.

Hence, $7 \times 11 \times 13 + 13$ is a composite number. (1)

**9.** If $8^n$ ends with 0, then it must have 5 as a factor. But $8^n = (2^3)^n = 2^{3n}$ i.e., the only prime factor of $8^n$ is 2.(1)

By using the fundamental theorem of arithmetic, every composite number can be expressed as a product of primes and this factorisation is unique apart from the order, in which the prime factors occur.

Thus, there does not exist any natural number, for which $8^n$ ends with zero. (1)

**10.** Given, Sonia takes 18 min to drive one round of the field and Ravi takes 12 min to drive one round of the field.

They both start at the same point and at the same time, and go in the same direction.

They will meet again at the starting point after the minutes equal to LCM of 18 and 12.

The prime factorisation of $18 = 2 \times 3 \times 3 = 2^1 \times 3^2$

The prime factorisation of $12 = 2 \times 2 \times 3 = 2^2 \times 3^1$ (1)

Now, LCM (18, 12) = Product of the greatest power of each prime factor involved in the numbers

$= 2^2 \times 3^2 = 4 \times 9 = 36$

Hence, after 36 min, they will meet again at the starting point. (1)

**11.** In order to arrange the books as required, we have to find the largest number that divides 96, 240 and 336 exactly. Clearly, such a number is their HCF.

Now, $96 = 2 \times 2 \times 2 \times 2 \times 2 \times 3 = 2^5 \times 3$ (1/2)

$240 = 2 \times 2 \times 2 \times 2 \times 3 \times 5 = 2^4 \times 3 \times 5$ (1/2)

$336 = 2 \times 2 \times 2 \times 2 \times 3 \times 7 = 2^4 \times 3 \times 7$ (1/2)

Hence, HCF $(96, 240, 336) = 2^4 \times 3 = 48$

So, there must be 48 books in each stack. (1/2)

**12.** For finding the maximum capacity, we have to find the HCF of 850 and 680.

Now, prime factors of numbers 850 and 680 are

$850 = 2 \times 5^2 \times 17$

and $\quad 680 = 2^3 \times 5 \times 17$ (1½)

$\therefore$ HCF of $(850, 680) = 2 \times 5 \times 17 = 170$

Hence, the capacity of the required container is 170 L. (1½)

**13.** We know that any positive integer is of the form $2q$ or $2q + 1$.

So, $n$ will be of the form $2q + 1$. $\quad [\because n \text{ is odd}]$

i.e. $n = 2q + 1$ for some integer $q$. (1)

Now, consider $n^2 - 1 = (2q+1)^2 - 1$
$= 4q^2 + 1 + 4q - 1 = 4q^2 + 4q$
$= 4q(q+1)$ (1)

Note that $q(q+1)$ is either 0 or even.

Let it be $2m$, where $m$ is a whole number.

$\therefore$ $n^2 - 1 = 4(2m) = 8m$, which is divisible by 8

Hence, $n^2 - 1$ is divisible 8, if $n$ is an odd integer. (1)

**14.** Let $7 - 5\sqrt{3}$ be a rational number.

Then, $7 - 5\sqrt{3} = \frac{p}{q}$, where $p$ and $q$ are coprime integers and $q \neq 0$.

$\therefore \quad 7 - \frac{p}{q} = 5\sqrt{3} \Rightarrow \frac{7}{5} - \frac{p}{5q} = \sqrt{3}$

Here, $\frac{p}{5q}$ is a rational number. (2½)

$\therefore \frac{7}{5} - \frac{p}{2q}$ is a rational number.

$\Rightarrow \sqrt{3}$ is a rational number.

But this contradicts the fact that $\sqrt{3}$ is an irrational number.

Hence, our assumption that $(7 - 5\sqrt{3})$ is a rational number, is not correct.

$\therefore (7 - 5\sqrt{3})$ is an irrational number. **Hence proved.** (2½)

**15.** It is given that on dividing 1251 by the required number, it leaves remainder equals to 1. Clearly, $1251 - 1 = 1250$ is exactly divisible by the required number i.e. required number is a factor of 1250. (1)

Similarly, required positive integer is a factor of $9377 - 2 = 9375$ and $15628 - 3 = 15625$ (1)

Thus, the required number is the HCF of 1250, 9375 and 15625.

$1250 = 2 \times 5^4$
$9375 = 3 \times 5^5$
and $15625 = 5^6$

$\therefore$ HCF of (1250, 9375, 15625) $= 5^4 = 625$ (2)

Hence, the required largest number is 625 which divides 1251, 9377 and 15628 leaving remainders 1, 2 and 3, respectively. (1)

## Chapter 2 Polynomials

**1.** (*b*) Zeroes of a polynomial $p(y)$ is ordinate of the point, where the graph intersects the *Y*-axis.

**2.** (*b*) Given, HCF of (6, 12) = 6 is one of the roots.

$\therefore \quad f(6) = 0$
$\Rightarrow \quad (6)^2 - 8 \times 6 + k = 0$
$\Rightarrow \quad 36 - 48 + k = 0$
$\Rightarrow \quad -12 + k = 0$
$\therefore \quad k = 12$

**3.** (*c*) By relationship of zeroes and coefficients of polynomial, we have

$a + b = \frac{5}{p}$ and $ab = \frac{q}{p}$

It is given that $a + b = ab = 10$

$\Rightarrow \quad 10 = \frac{5}{p}$ and $10 = \frac{q}{1/2}$

$\Rightarrow \quad p = \frac{1}{2}$ and $q = 5$

$\therefore \quad p = 1/2$ and $q = 5$

**4.** (*c*) Let the roots of the given polynomials be $\alpha$ and $\frac{1}{\alpha}$.

Then, product of roots $\alpha \cdot \frac{1}{\alpha} = \frac{k}{5}$

$\Rightarrow 1 = \frac{k}{5} \Rightarrow k = 5$

**5.** (*a*) We have, $p(x) = ax^2 - 3(a+2) - 4$

Since, 2 is a zero of $p(x)$.

$\therefore \quad p(2) = 0$
$\Rightarrow \quad a(2)^2 - 3(a+2) - 4 = 0$
$\Rightarrow \quad 4a - 3a - 6 - 4 = 0$
$\Rightarrow \quad a - 10 = 0$
$\Rightarrow \quad a = 10$

**6.** Let one zero of the given polynomial be $\alpha$.

Then, the other zero $= -\alpha$

Given, $f(x) = 4x^2 - 8kx - 9$

$\therefore$ Sum of zeroes $= (-\alpha) + \alpha = 0$ (1)

$\Rightarrow \quad \frac{-b}{a} = 0$

$\Rightarrow \quad \frac{8k}{4} = 0$

$\therefore \quad k = 0$ (1)

**7.** Given sum of zeroes, $S = 8$

and product of zeroes, $P = -3$ (1)

$\therefore$ Quadratic polynomial is $x^2 - Sx + P$.

i.e. $x^2 - 8x - 3$. (1)

**8.** Since, $\alpha, \beta$ are the zeroes of the given polynomial.

$\therefore \quad \alpha + \beta = -\frac{b}{a} = \frac{-5}{1} = -5$

and $\alpha\beta = \frac{c}{a} = \frac{-10}{1} = -10$ (1)

$\therefore \alpha^2 + \beta^2 = (\alpha + \beta)^2 - 2\alpha\beta$
$= (-5)^2 - 2(-10) = 25 + 20 = 45$ (1)

**9.** Given polynomial is

$7y^2 - \frac{11}{3}y - \frac{2}{3} = \frac{1}{3}(21y^2 - 11y - 2)$

$= \frac{1}{3}(21y^2 - 14y + 3y - 2)$

[by splitting the middle term]

$$= \frac{1}{3}[7y(3y-2)+1(3y-2)]$$

$$= \frac{1}{3}[(3y-2)(7y+1)]$$

$$= \left(y-\frac{2}{3}\right)(7y+1)$$

Hence, zeroes are $\frac{2}{3}$ and $\frac{-1}{7}$. (1)

To verify, we know that

Sum of zeroes $= \frac{2}{3}+\left(\frac{-1}{7}\right) = \frac{14-3}{21} = \frac{11}{21}$

Now, $\frac{-\text{Coefficient of } y}{\text{Coefficient of } y^2} = -\left(\frac{\frac{-11}{3}}{\frac{3}{7}}\right)$

$= \frac{11}{21} =$ Sum of zeroes (1/2)

Product of zeroes $= \frac{2}{3}\times\left(-\frac{1}{7}\right) = -\frac{2}{21}$

Now, $\frac{\text{Constant term}}{\text{Coefficient of } y^2} = \frac{-\frac{2}{3}}{7} = \frac{-2}{21} =$ Product of zeroes.

Hence, relationship between the zeroes and the coefficient of the polynomial is verified. (1/2)

**10.** Let $g(x) = (a^2+4)x^2+9x+4a$

Let one zero of polynomial be $\alpha$, then the other zero will be $\frac{1}{\alpha}$. (1)

Now product of zeroes,

$$\alpha\times\frac{1}{\alpha} = \frac{\text{Constant term}}{\text{Coefficient of } x^2}$$

$\Rightarrow$ $1 = \frac{4a}{a^2+4}$

$\Rightarrow$ $a^2+4 = 4a \Rightarrow a^2-4a+4=0$

$\Rightarrow$ $(a-2)^2 = 0 \Rightarrow a = 2$ (1)

**11.** It is given that $\alpha$ and $\beta$ are the zeroes of the polynomial, $f(x) = x^2-5x+k$.

Then, sum of zeroes, $\alpha+\beta = -\frac{\text{Coefficient of } x}{\text{Coefficient of } x^2}$

$= -\frac{(-5)}{1} = 5$

and product of zeroes, $\alpha\beta = \frac{\text{Constant term}}{\text{Coefficient of } x^2}$

$= \frac{k}{1} = k$ (1½)

Also given, $\alpha-\beta = 1$

On squaring both sides, we get

$(\alpha-\beta)^2 = 1^2$

$\Rightarrow$ $\alpha^2+\beta^2-2\alpha\beta = 1$

$\Rightarrow$ $(\alpha+\beta)^2-4\alpha\beta = 1 \Rightarrow (5)^2-4(k) = 1$

$\Rightarrow$ $4k = 25-1$

$\Rightarrow$ $4k = 24 \Rightarrow k = 6$ (1½)

**12.** Let the zeroes of the given polynomial be $mk$ and $nk$, where $k$ is a positive integer.

$\therefore$ Sum of zeroes $= mk+nk$

$= \frac{-\text{Coefficient of } x}{\text{Coefficient of } x^2} = \frac{-b}{a}$ ...(i)

and product of zeroes $= (mk)(nk)$

$= \frac{\text{Constant term}}{\text{Coefficient of } x^2} = \frac{b}{a}$ ...(ii) (1½)

Now, $\sqrt{\frac{m}{n}}+\sqrt{\frac{n}{m}} = \frac{\sqrt{m}}{\sqrt{n}}+\frac{\sqrt{n}}{\sqrt{m}}$

$= \frac{m+n}{\sqrt{mn}} = \frac{\frac{-b}{ak}}{\sqrt{\frac{b}{ak^2}}}$

[using Eqs. (i) and (ii)]

$= \frac{-b}{ak}\times k\sqrt{\frac{a}{b}} = -\sqrt{\frac{b}{a}}$ (1½)

**13.** Since, $\alpha$ and $\beta$ are the zeroes of $ax^2+bx+c$.

$\therefore \alpha+\beta = -\frac{b}{a}$ and $\alpha\beta = \frac{c}{a}$ (1)

To have a polynomial whose zeroes are $\frac{\alpha^2}{\beta}$ and $\frac{\beta^2}{\alpha}$.

Sum of the zeroes of required polynomial

$$= \frac{\alpha^2}{\beta}+\frac{\beta^2}{\alpha} = \frac{\alpha^3+\beta^3}{\alpha\beta}$$

$$= \frac{(\alpha+\beta)(\alpha^2+\beta^2-\alpha\beta)}{\alpha\beta}$$

$$= \frac{(\alpha+\beta)[(\alpha+\beta)^2-3\alpha\beta]}{\alpha\beta}$$

$$= \frac{\frac{-b}{a}\left(\frac{b^2}{a^2}-\frac{3c}{a}\right)}{c/a} = \frac{-b}{c}\left(\frac{b^2-3ca}{a^2}\right)$$

$$= \frac{-b}{a^2c}(b^2-3ac)$$ (2)

and the product of the zeroes of required polynomial

$$= \frac{\alpha^2}{\beta}\times\frac{\beta^2}{\alpha} = \alpha\beta = \frac{c}{a}$$

$\therefore$ Required polynomial

$= x^2 -$ (Sum of the zeroes) $x +$ Product of the zeroes

$= x^2+\frac{b}{a^2c}(b^2-3ac)x+\frac{c}{a}$ (2)

**14.** Given that $\alpha$ and $\beta$ are the zeroes of the quadratic polynomial $f(x) = kx^2+4x+4$,

Then sum of zeroes, $\alpha+\beta = -\frac{\text{Coefficient of } x}{\text{Coefficient of } x^2}$

$= -\frac{4}{k}$

and product of zeroes, $\alpha\beta = \frac{\text{Constant term}}{\text{Coefficient of } x^2} = \frac{4}{k}$ (1)

Also given, $\alpha^2 + \beta^2 = 24$

$\Rightarrow \quad (\alpha + \beta)^2 - 2\alpha\beta = 24$

$[\because \alpha^2 + \beta^2 = (\alpha + \beta)^2 - 2\alpha\beta]$

$\Rightarrow \quad \left(-\frac{4}{k}\right)^2 - 2 \times \frac{4}{k} = 24$ (1)

$\Rightarrow \quad \frac{16}{k^2} - \frac{8}{k} = 24$

$\Rightarrow \quad 16 - 8k = 24k^2$

$\Rightarrow \quad 24k^2 + 8k - 16 = 0$

$\Rightarrow \quad 3k^2 + k - 2 = 0$ [divide by 8] (1)

$\Rightarrow \quad 3k^2 + 3k - 2k - 2 = 0$

$\Rightarrow \quad 3k(k + 1) - 2(k + 1) = 0$

$\Rightarrow \quad (3k - 2)(k + 1) = 0$

$\Rightarrow \quad 3k - 2 = 0$ and $k + 1 = 0$

$\Rightarrow \quad k = \frac{2}{3}$ and $k = -1$ (2)

**15.** Given, $\alpha$ and $\beta$ are the zeroes of the polynomial $3x^2 - 6x + 4$.

Now, sum of zeroes $= \alpha + \beta = \frac{-b}{a} = \frac{-(-6)}{3} = 2$

and product of zeroes $= \alpha\beta = \frac{c}{a} = \frac{4}{3}$ (1)

Now, $\frac{\alpha}{\beta} + \frac{\beta}{\alpha} = \frac{\alpha^2 + \beta^2}{\alpha\beta} = \frac{(\alpha + \beta)^2 - 2\alpha\beta}{\alpha\beta}$

$= \frac{(2)^2 - 2 \times \frac{4}{3}}{\frac{4}{3}} = \frac{4 - \frac{8}{3}}{\frac{4}{3}} = \frac{4}{3} \times \frac{3}{4} = 1$ (1½)

and $\frac{1}{\alpha} + \frac{1}{\beta} = \frac{\alpha + \beta}{\alpha\beta} = \frac{2}{\frac{4}{3}} = \frac{3}{2}$ (1)

$\therefore \left(\frac{\alpha}{\beta} + \frac{\beta}{\alpha}\right) + 2\left(\frac{1}{\alpha} + \frac{1}{\beta}\right) + 3\alpha\beta = 1 + 2 \times \frac{3}{2} + 3 \times \frac{4}{3}$

$= 1 + 3 + 4 = 8.$ (1½)

# Chapter 3 Pair of Linear Equations in Two Variables

**1.** (a) Given pair of linear equations is

$x + 2y = 5$ and $3x + 12y = 10$

Here $a_1 = 1, b_1 = 2, c_1 = -5$

and $a_2 = 3$ $b_2 = 12$ $c_2 = -10$

Clearly $\frac{a_1}{a_2} \neq \frac{b_1}{b_2}$

Hence, pair of linear equation has unique solution.

**2.** (a) Using the condition for unique solution,

$$\frac{a_1}{a_2} \neq \frac{b_1}{b_2}$$

We find that the pair of equations

$$2x + y = 3 \text{ and } x + 2y = 5$$

has a unique solution, as

$$\frac{2}{1} \neq \frac{1}{2}$$

**3.** (c) Since, $x = -2$ and $x = 3$ are two parallel lines.

Hence, no solution exists.

**4.** (a) A pair of linear equations in two variables is said to be inconsistent, if it has no solution and their graphical representation is parallel lines.

**5.** (b) Let man's speed in still water $= x$ km/h

and rate of current $= y$ km/h

Speed of man in still water

$= \frac{1}{2}$ (rate of upstream + rate of downstream)

$= \frac{1}{2}(x - y + x + y) = \frac{1}{2}(2x) = x$

$\therefore$ Speed in still water $= \frac{1}{2}(7 + 10) = 8.5$ km/h

Rate of current $= \frac{1}{2}$ (rate of downstream − rate of upstream)

$= \frac{1}{2}(10 - 7) = 1.5$ km/h

**6.** Given equations are

$$6x - 2y + 9 = 0 \text{ and } 3x - y + 12 = 0$$

which are of the form $a_1x + b_1y + c_1 = 0$

and $a_2x + b_2y + c_2 = 0$.

Here, $a_1 = 6, b_1 = -2, c_1 = 9$

and $a_2 = 3, b_2 = -1, c_2 = 12$

Now, $\frac{a_1}{a_2} = \frac{6}{3} = \frac{2}{1}, \frac{b_1}{b_2} = \frac{-2}{-1} = \frac{2}{1}$ and $\frac{c_1}{c_2} = \frac{9}{12} = \frac{3}{4}$ (1)

$\therefore \quad \frac{a_1}{a_2} = \frac{b_1}{b_2} \neq \frac{c_1}{c_2}$

So, given system has no solution.

Hence, the graph of given equations is a pair of parallel lines. (1)

**7.** Given, $47x + 31y = 18$ ...(i)

and $31x + 47y = 60$ ...(ii)

On adding Eqs. (i) and (ii), we get

$78x + 78y = 78$ (1)

$\Rightarrow \quad x + y = 1$ [divide both sides by 78] (1)

**8.** Suppose an audio cassette costs ₹ $x$ and video cassette costs ₹ $y$.

According to the given conditions,

$7x + 3y = 1110$ ...(i)

$5x + 4y = 1350$ ...(ii)

On multiplying Eq. (i) by 4 and Eq. (ii) by 3, we get

$28x + 12y = 4440$ ...(iii)

$15x + 12y = 4050$ ...(iv)

On subtracting Eq. (iv) from Eq. (iii), we get

$$13x = 390 \Rightarrow x = \frac{390}{13} = 30 \quad (1)$$

On putting $x = 30$ in Eq. (i), we get

$$7(30) + 3y = 1110$$
$$\Rightarrow 210 + 3y = 1110$$
$$\therefore 3y = 1110 - 210 = 900$$
$$\Rightarrow y = 900 \div 3 = 300$$

Hence, cost of 1 audio cassette = ₹ 30 and cost of 1 video cassette = ₹ 300. (1)

**9.** Given pair of equations is

$$x - 2y = 8 \text{ and } 5x + 10y = c$$
$$\Rightarrow x - 2y - 8 = 0 \text{ and } 5x + 10y - c = 0$$

which is of the form $a_1x + b_1y + c_1 = 0$ and $a_2x + b_2y + c_2 = 0$.

Here, $a_1 = 1, b_1 = -2, c_1 = -8$

and $a_2 = 5, b_2 = 10, c_2 = -c$

Now, $\frac{a_1}{a_2} = \frac{1}{5}, \frac{b_1}{b_2} = \frac{-2}{10} = \frac{-1}{5}$ and $\frac{c_1}{c_2} = \frac{-8}{-c}$

$$\because \frac{a_1}{a_2} \neq \frac{b_1}{b_2} \quad (1)$$

So, for all real values of $c$, the given pair of equations has a unique solution.

Hence, the given statement is true. (1)

**10.** Given, pair of equations is $2x + 3y - 7 = 0$ and $2\alpha x + (\alpha + \beta)y - 28 = 0$, which is of the form $a_1x + b_1y + c_1 = 0$ and $a_2x + b_2y + c_2 = 0$.

The given system of equations will have infinite number of solutions, if

$$\frac{2}{2\alpha} = \frac{3}{\alpha + \beta} = \frac{7}{28} \quad (1)$$
$$\Rightarrow \frac{1}{\alpha} = \frac{3}{\alpha + \beta} = \frac{1}{4} \Rightarrow \frac{1}{\alpha} = \frac{1}{4} \text{ and } \frac{3}{\alpha + \beta} = \frac{1}{4}$$
$$\Rightarrow \alpha = 4 \text{ and } \alpha + \beta = 12 \Rightarrow \alpha = 4 \text{ and } \beta = 8$$

Hence, the given system of equations will have infinitely many solutions, if $\alpha = 4$ and $\beta = 8$. (1)

**11.** Since, $ABCD$ is a rectangle.

$$\therefore AB = CD \text{ and } AD = BC$$

[$\because$ opposite sides of the rectangle]

$$x + 3y = 13 \quad \text{...(i)}$$
$$\text{and} \quad 3x + y = 7 \quad \text{...(ii)} \; (1)$$

On multiplying Eq. (i) by 3 and subtracting Eq. (ii) from Eq. (i), we get

$$(3x + 9y) - (3x + y) = 39 - 7$$
$$\Rightarrow 8y = 32$$
$$\Rightarrow y = \frac{32}{8} = 4$$

On putting $y = 4$ in Eq. (i), we get

$$x + 3 \times 4 = 13$$
$$\Rightarrow x = 13 - 12 = 1 \quad (1)$$

**12.** Given equations are $0.4x + 0.3y = 1.7$ ... (i)

and $0.7x - 0.2y = 0.8$ ... (ii)

On multiplying each equation by 10, we get

$$4x + 3y = 17 \quad \text{... (iii)}$$
$$\text{and} \quad 7x - 2y = 8 \quad \text{...(iv)} \; (1)$$

On multiplying Eq. (iii) by 2 and Eq. (iv) by 3 and then adding, we get

$$29x = 58 \Rightarrow x = \frac{58}{29} = 2 \quad (1)$$

On putting $x = 2$ in Eq. (iv), we get

$$7 \times 2 - 2y = 8 \Rightarrow 2y = 14 - 8$$
$$\Rightarrow 2y = 6 \Rightarrow y = 3$$

Hence, $x = 2$ and $y = 3$ (1)

**13.** Let fixed charge for first three days = ₹ $x$ and extra charge for each day = ₹ $y$

According to the question,

$$x + 4y = 27 \quad \text{... (i)}$$
$$\text{and} \quad x + 2y = 21 \quad \text{... (ii)} \; (1)$$

On subtracting Eq. (ii) from Eq. (i), we get

$$x + 4y = 27$$
$$x + 2y = 21$$
$$- \quad - \quad -$$
$$2y = 6$$
$$\Rightarrow y = \frac{6}{2} = 3 \quad (1)$$

On substituting the value of $y$ in Eq. (i), we get

$$x + 4 \times 3 = 27 \Rightarrow x + 12 = 27$$
$$\therefore x = 15$$

Hence, fixed charge for first three days = ₹ 15 and extra charge for each day = ₹ 3. (1)

**14.** Let $x$ be the digit at unit's place and $y$ be the digit at ten's place of two-digit number.

Then, two-digit number = $10y + x$

According to the question,

$$x + y = 12 \quad \text{...(i)}$$

When interchanging its digits, new two-digit number = $10x + y$ (1)

According to the question,

$$(10x + y) - (10y + x) = 18$$
$$\Rightarrow 9x - 9y = 18$$
$$\Rightarrow x - y = 2 \quad \text{...(ii)}$$

On adding Eqs. (i) and (ii), we get

$$2x = 14$$
$$\Rightarrow x = 7 \quad (1)$$

On putting $x = 7$ in Eq. (i), we get

$$7 + y = 12$$
$$\Rightarrow y = 5$$

Hence, the required number is $10 \times 5 + 7 = 57$ (1)

**15.** Let the numerator and denominator of the fraction be $x$ and $y$, respectively.

$\because$ Fraction will be $\frac{x}{y}$.

$\therefore \quad y = x + 4$ ...(i) (1)

According to the question,

$$y + 1 = 8(x - 2)$$
$$\Rightarrow \quad y + 1 = 8x - 16$$
$$\Rightarrow \quad y = 8x - 17 \quad \text{...(ii) (1)}$$

On subtracting Eq. (i) from Eq. (ii), we get

$$0 = (8x - x) - 17 - 4$$
$$\Rightarrow -7x = -21 \Rightarrow x = \frac{21}{7} = 3 \quad (2)$$

So, $y = 3 + 4 = 7$ [from Eq. (i)]

Hence, required fraction $= \frac{3}{7}$ (1)

**16.** Given pair of linear equations is

$$2x + y = 4 \text{ and } 2x - y = 4$$

Table for line $2x + y = 4$ i.e. $y = 4 - 2x$ is

| $x$ | 0 | 2 |
|---|---|---|
| $y = 4 - 2x$ | 4 | 0 |
| **Points** | $A(0, 4)$ | $B(2, 0)$ |

(1)

Now, we plot all these points on a graph paper and join them to get a line $AB$.

Also, table for line $2x - y = 4$ i.e. $y = 2x - 4$ is

| $x$ | 0 | 2 |
|---|---|---|
| $y = 2x - 4$ | $-4$ | 0 |
| **Points** | $C(0, -4)$ | $B(2, 0)$ |

(1)

Now, we plot all these points on the same graph paper and join them to get a line $BC$.

Graphical representation of both lines is given below

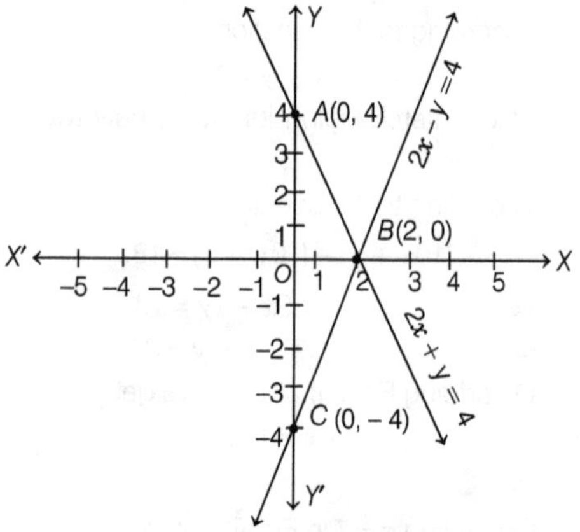


(2)

The vertices of the triangle formed by these lines and $Y$-axis are $A(0, 4)$, $B(2, 0)$ and $C(0, -4)$.

Here, $AC = OA + OC = 4 + 4 = 8$ units and $OB = 2$ units

$\therefore$ Area of $\Delta ABC = \frac{1}{2} \times \text{Base} \times \text{Altitude}$

$$= \frac{1}{2} \times AC \times OB = \frac{1}{2} \times 8 \times 2$$
$$= 8 \text{ sq units} \quad (1)$$

# Chapter 4 Quadratic Equations

**1.** (*b*) $x^2 - bx + 1 = 0$ has no real roots.

$$\therefore \quad D < 0$$
$$\Rightarrow \quad (-b)^2 - 4 \cdot 1 \cdot 1 < 0 \Rightarrow b^2 - 4 < 0$$
$$\Rightarrow \quad (b + 2)(b - 2) < 0 \Rightarrow -2 < b < 2$$

**2.** (*a*) $\because$ $p$ and $q$ are roots of the equation.

$$\therefore \quad p^2 - p^2 + q = 0 \Rightarrow q = 0$$

and $q^2 - pq + q = 0 \Rightarrow q(q - p + 1) = 0$

$$\Rightarrow \quad q = 0 \text{ or } p = q + 1 \Rightarrow p = 1$$
$$\therefore \quad p = 1 \text{ and } q = 0$$

**3.** (*c*) $D = b^2 - 4ac = k^2 - 4 \cdot k^2 \cdot 1$

$$= k^2 - 4k^2 = -3k^2 < 0$$

$D < 0$, hence equation has no real roots.

**4.** (*b*) For equal roots, $b^2 - 4ac = 0$

$$\Rightarrow \quad b^2 = 4ac \Rightarrow c = \frac{b^2}{4a}$$

**5.** Given $x = 2$ is a root of the equation $kx^2 + 2x - 3 = 0$, therefore put $x = 2$ in the given equation, we get

$$k(2)^2 + 2(2) - 3 = 0 \quad (1)$$
$$\Rightarrow \quad 4k + 4 - 3 = 0$$
$$\Rightarrow \quad 4k = -1 \Rightarrow k = -\frac{1}{4} \quad (1)$$

**6.** Given equation is $9x^2 - 3x - 2 = 0$

$$\Rightarrow \quad 9x^2 - 6x + 3x - 2 = 0 \quad (1)$$
$$\Rightarrow \quad 3x(3x - 2) + 1(3x - 2) = 0$$
$$\Rightarrow \quad (3x + 1)(3x - 2) = 0$$
$$\Rightarrow \quad x = -\frac{1}{3} \text{ and } x = \frac{2}{3} \quad (1)$$

**7.** We have, $2x^2 - 7x + 3 = 0$

On comparing it with $ax^2 + bx + c = 0$, we get

$$a = 2, b = -7 \text{ and } c = 3 \quad (1/2)$$

$\therefore$ By using quadratic formula,

$$x = \frac{-b \pm \sqrt{b^2 - 4ac}}{2a}$$
$$= \frac{-(-7) \pm \sqrt{(-7)^2 - 4 \times 2 \times 3}}{2 \times 2}$$
$$= \frac{7 \pm \sqrt{49 - 24}}{4} = \frac{7 \pm \sqrt{25}}{4} = \frac{7 \pm 5}{4}$$
$$= \frac{12}{4}, \frac{2}{4} = 3, \frac{1}{2}$$

$\therefore$ Required roots are $3, \frac{1}{2}$. (1½)

**8.** Given equation is $\sqrt{3}x^2 + 10x + 7\sqrt{3} = 0$

$\Rightarrow \quad \sqrt{3}x^2 + 3x + 7x + 7\sqrt{3} = 0$

$\Rightarrow \quad \sqrt{3}x(x + \sqrt{3}) + 7(x + \sqrt{3}) = 0$ (1)

$\Rightarrow \quad (\sqrt{3}x + 7)(x + \sqrt{3}) = 0$

$\Rightarrow \quad \sqrt{3}x + 7 = 0$ or $x + \sqrt{3} = 0$

$\Rightarrow \quad x = \frac{-7}{\sqrt{3}}$ or $x = -\sqrt{3}$

Hence, $x = -\frac{7}{\sqrt{3}}, -\sqrt{3}$ are the roots of the given equation. (1)

**9.** Given equation is $\frac{x+1}{x-1} + \frac{x-2}{x+2} = 3$

$\Rightarrow \quad \frac{(x+1)(x+2)+(x-2)(x-1)}{(x-1)(x+2)} = 3$

$\Rightarrow \quad (x+1)(x+2) + (x-2)(x-1) = 3(x-1)(x+2)$

$\Rightarrow \quad x^2 + 3x + 2 + x^2 - 3x + 2 = 3(x^2 + x - 2)$

$\Rightarrow \quad 2x^2 + 4 = 3x^2 + 3x - 6$

$\Rightarrow \quad 2x^2 + 4 - 3x^2 - 3x + 6 = 0$

$\Rightarrow \quad -x^2 - 3x + 10 = 0$ (1½)

$\Rightarrow \quad x^2 + 3x - 10 = 0$

[multiplying both sides by (–1)]

$\Rightarrow \quad x^2 + 5x - 2x - 10 = 0$

[by splitting the middle term]

$\Rightarrow \quad x(x+5) - 2(x+5) = 0$

$\Rightarrow \quad (x+5)(x-2) = 0$

$\Rightarrow \quad x + 5 = 0$ or $x - 2 = 0$

$\Rightarrow \quad x = -5$ or $x = 2$

Hence, –5 and 2 are the solutions of given equation. (1½)

**10.** Given equation is $\frac{3}{x+1} + \frac{4}{x-1} = \frac{29}{4x-1}$

$\Rightarrow \quad \frac{3(x-1) + 4(x+1)}{(x+1)(x-1)} = \frac{29}{4x-1}$

$\Rightarrow \quad \frac{7x+1}{x^2 - 1^2} = \frac{29}{4x-1}$

$\Rightarrow \quad (7x+1)(4x-1) = 29(x^2 - 1)$ (1)

$\Rightarrow \quad 28x^2 - 7x + 4x - 1 = 29x^2 - 29$

$\Rightarrow \quad x^2 + 3x - 28 = 0$

$\Rightarrow \quad x^2 + 7x - 4x - 28 = 0$

$\Rightarrow \quad x(x+7) - 4(x+7) = 0$

$\Rightarrow \quad (x-4)(x+7) = 0$ (1)

$\Rightarrow \quad x - 4 = 0$ and $x + 7 = 0$

$\Rightarrow \quad x = 4$ and $x = -7$ (1)

**11.** Given quadratic equation is

$$x^2 + \left(\frac{a}{a+b} + \frac{a+b}{a}\right)x + 1 = 0$$

$\Rightarrow \quad x^2 + \frac{ax}{a+b} + \frac{a+b}{a}x + \frac{a}{a+b} \times \frac{a+b}{a} = 0$

$\Rightarrow \quad x\left(x + \frac{a}{a+b}\right) + \frac{a+b}{a}\left(x + \frac{a}{a+b}\right) = 0$ (1½)

$\Rightarrow \quad \left(x + \frac{a}{a+b}\right)\left(x + \frac{a+b}{a}\right) = 0$

$\Rightarrow \quad x + \frac{a}{a+b} = 0$ or $x + \frac{a+b}{a} = 0$

$\Rightarrow \quad x = -\frac{a}{a+b}$ or $x = -\frac{a+b}{a}$ (1½)

**12.** Given quadratic equation is

$$(3k+1)x^2 + 2(k+1)x + 1 = 0$$

On comparing with $ax^2 + bx + c = 0$, we get

$a = 3k + 1, b = 2(k+1), c = 1$ (1)

Since, the roots are equal, so $b^2 - 4ac = 0$

$\therefore \quad [2(k+1)]^2 - 4(3k+1)(1) = 0$

$\Rightarrow \quad 4(k+1)^2 - 4(3k+1) = 0$

$\Rightarrow \quad 4(k^2 + 2k + 1) - 4(3k+1) = 0$

$\Rightarrow \quad 4(k^2 + 2k + 1 - 3k - 1) = 0$

$\Rightarrow \quad k^2 + 2k + 1 - 3k - 1 = 0$ $[\because 4 \neq 0]$

$\Rightarrow \quad k^2 - k = 0$

$\Rightarrow \quad k(k-1) = 0$

$\Rightarrow \quad k = 0$ or $k = 1$

We know that, if roots are equal, then roots will be the form of $\frac{-b}{2a}, \frac{-b}{2a}$.

Thus, roots are $\frac{-b}{2a}, \frac{-b}{2a}$. (2)

$\therefore$ Equal roots are $\frac{-(k+1)}{(3k+1)}, \frac{-(k+1)}{(3k+1)}$

When $k = 0$, equal roots are $\frac{-(0+1)}{0+1}$ and $\frac{-(0+1)}{0+1}$

i.e. – 1 and – 1.

When $k = 1$, equal roots are $\frac{-(1+1)}{3+1}$ and $\frac{-(1+1)}{3+1}$

i.e. $\frac{-1}{2}$ and $\frac{-1}{2}$ (2)

## Chapter 5 **Arithmetic Progression (AP)**

**1.** (c) $a_n = a + (n-1)d$

$\Rightarrow \quad 5 = a + (8-1)(-3)$

$\Rightarrow \quad 5 = a - 21$

$\Rightarrow \quad a = 5 + 21 = 26$

**2.** (a) Given, AP is 7, 11, 15, …, 139

$\therefore \quad a = 7, d = 11 - 7 = 4$

Since, $a_n = 139$

$\Rightarrow \quad a + (n-1)d = 139$

$\Rightarrow \quad 7 + (n-1)(4) = 139$

$\Rightarrow \quad (n-1)(4) = 132$

$\Rightarrow \quad n - 1 = 33$

$\Rightarrow \quad n = 34$

**3.** (*b*) We have to find the sum of following series : $6 + 12 + 18 + 24 + \dots$ to 30 terms

Here, $a = 6, d = 6, n = 30$

$\therefore \quad S_n = \frac{n}{2}[2a + (n-1)d]$

$\Rightarrow S_{30} = \frac{30}{2}[2 \times 6 + (30-1)(6)]$

$= 15[12 + 29 \times 6]$

$= 15(186) = 2790$

**4.** (a) Here, $a = 20$ and $d = 17 - 20 = -3$

Let $a_n < 0$. Then, $a + (n-1)d < 0$

$\therefore \quad 20 + (n-1) \times (-3) < 0$

$\Rightarrow \quad 20 < 3(n-1)$

$\Rightarrow \quad \frac{20}{3} < n - 1$

$\Rightarrow \quad n > \frac{20}{3} + 1$

$\Rightarrow \quad n > 6.6 + 1$

$\Rightarrow \quad n > 7.6$

Hence, 8th term is the first negative term.

**5.** Given AP sequence is $a_n = 4n + 5$

Now, replacing $n$ by $n + 1$, we get

$a_{n+1} = 4(n+1) + 5 = 4n + 9$ (1)

$\therefore$ Common difference, $d = a_{n+1} - a_n$

$= (4n + 9) - (4n + 5) = 4$ (1)

**6.** Given, $a = 4$ and $d = -3$

The arithmetic progression with first term $a$ and common difference $d$ is given by

$a, a + d, a + 2d, a + 3d, \dots$ (1)

i.e. $4, 4 - 3, 4 + 2 \times (-3), 4 + 3(-3)$

or $4, 1, -2, -5, \dots$ (1)

**7.** Here, $a = 3$ and $d = 15 - 3 = 12$

$\therefore$ 21st term is given by

$T_{21} = a + (21-1)d = a + 20d = 3 + 20 \times 12 = 243$

$\therefore$ Required term $= 243 + 120 = 363$ (1)

Let it will be $n$th term. Then,

$T_n = 363$

$\Rightarrow \quad a + (n-1)d = 363$

$\Rightarrow \quad 3 + (n-1) \times 12 = 363$

$\Rightarrow 3 + 12n - 12 - 363 = 0$

$\Rightarrow \quad 12n - 9 = 363 \Rightarrow 12n = 372 \Rightarrow n = 31$

Hence, 31st term is the required term. (1)

**8.** Let the four numbers be $a - 3d, a - d, a + d$ and $a + 3d$.

Then, sum = 50

$\Rightarrow \quad (a - 3d) + (a - d) + (a + d) + (a + 3d) = 50$

$\Rightarrow \quad 4a = 50 \Rightarrow a = \frac{25}{2}$ (1/2)

Given, greatest number = 4 × (least number)

$a + 3d = 4(a - 3d)$

$\Rightarrow \quad a + 3d = 4a - 12d$

$\Rightarrow \quad 3a = 15d \Rightarrow d = \frac{3}{15}a$

$\Rightarrow \quad d = \frac{3}{15} \times \frac{25}{2} \Rightarrow d = \frac{5}{2}$ (1/2)

$\therefore$ The numbers are $a - 3d = \frac{25}{2} - \frac{15}{2} = 5$

$a - d = \frac{25}{2} - \frac{5}{2} = 10, a + d = \frac{25}{2} + \frac{5}{2} = 15$

$a + 3d = \frac{25}{2} + \frac{15}{2} = 20$

Hence, the numbers are 5, 10, 15 and 20. (1)

**9.** The natural numbers between 200 and 1502 which are exactly divisible by 3 are 201, 204, 207, ..., 1497, 1500.

These numbers form an AP with first term, $a = 201$, common difference, $d = 3$ and last term $l = 1500$.

Let the number of terms be $n$.

Then, $\quad a_n = l$

$\Rightarrow \quad a + (n-1)d = 1500$

$\Rightarrow \quad 201 + (n-1)3 = 1500$ (1)

$\Rightarrow \quad 201 + 3n - 3 = 1500$

$\Rightarrow \quad 3n = 1302$

$\Rightarrow \quad n = 434$ ...(i)

Required sum $= \frac{n}{2}(a + l)$

$= \frac{434}{2}(201 + 1500)$

$= 217(1701) = 369117$

Hence, the required sum is 369117. (1)

**10.** Since, Ramkali's initial savings is ₹ 5 and further she increased her weekly savings by the same amount of ₹ 1.75, therefore her weekly savings form an AP

Here, $a =$ ₹ 5, $d =$ ₹ 1.75,

In $n$th week, her saving = ₹ 20.75

$\because$ $n$th term of an AP is $a_n = a + (n-1)d$ (1)

$\Rightarrow \quad 20.75 = 5 + (n-1) \times 1.75$

$\Rightarrow \quad (n-1) \times 1.75 = 15.75$

$\Rightarrow \quad n - 1 = \frac{15.75}{1.75} = 9$

$\Rightarrow \quad n = 9 + 1 = 10$ (1)

**11.** Here, $a = -6$ and $d = -\frac{11}{2} - (-6) = \frac{1}{2}$

Given, $-25$ is the sum of $n$ terms of this AP, where $n \in N$.

$\because \quad S_n = \frac{n}{2}[2a + (n-1)d]$

$\therefore \quad -25 = \frac{n}{2}\left[2(-6) + (n-1)\left(\frac{1}{2}\right)\right]$

$\Rightarrow \quad -50 = \frac{n(-24 + n - 1)}{2}$

$\Rightarrow \quad -50 = n\left(\frac{n-25}{2}\right)$ (1)

$\Rightarrow \quad -100 = n^2 - 25n$

$\Rightarrow \quad n^2 - 25n + 100 = 0$

$\Rightarrow \quad n^2 - 20n - 5n + 100 = 0$

[by splitting the middle term]

$\Rightarrow \quad n(n-20) - 5(n-20) = 0$

$\Rightarrow \quad (n-5)(n-20) = 0$ (1)

$\Rightarrow \quad n - 5 = 0$ or $n - 20 = 0$

$\Rightarrow \quad n = 5$ or $n = 20$

Both the values of $n$ are natural numbers.

Hence, the sum of 5 terms or 20 terms of the given AP will be $-25$. (1)

**12.** We have, $a_n = 5 - 6n, n \in N$ ...(i)

Then, $a_{n+1} = 5 - 6(n+1) = -1 - 6n$ ...(ii)

On subtracting Eq. (i) from Eq. (ii), we get

$a_{n+1} - a_n = (-1 - 6n) - (5 - 6n) = -6$ (1)

which is independent of $n$.

$\therefore \{a_n\}$ is an AP.

Also, $a_1 = 5 - 6 \times 1 = -1$ (1)

$\therefore$ Sum of $n$ terms,

$S_n = n\left(\frac{a_1 + a_n}{2}\right) = n\left(\frac{-1 + 5 - 6n}{2}\right)$ $\left[\because S_n = \frac{n}{2}(a + l)\right]$

$= n\left(\frac{4 - 6n}{2}\right)$

$= n(2 - 3n)$ (1)

**13.** In the given AP, let first term be $a$ and common difference be $d$.

Then, $T_n = a + (n-1)d$

$\Rightarrow \quad T_8 = a + (8-1)d, T_{38} = a + (38-1)d$

and $\quad T_{18} = a + (18-1)d$

$\Rightarrow \quad T_8 = (a + 7d), T_{38} = (a + 37d)$

and $\quad T_{18} = (a + 17d)$

Now, $\quad T_8 = 0 \Rightarrow a + 7d = 0$

$\Rightarrow \quad a = -7d$ ...(i) (3)

$\therefore \quad T_{38} = (-7d + 37d) = 30d$ [using Eq. (i)]

and $\quad T_{18} = (-7d + 17d) = 10d$ [using Eq. (i)]

$\therefore \quad T_{38} = 30d = 3 \times (10d) = (3 \times T_{18})$

Hence, 38th term is triple its 18th term.

**Hence proved.** (2)

**14.** Let $a$ be the first term and $d$ be the common difference of the given AP.

Then, $\quad S_1 = \frac{n}{2}[2a + (n-1)d]$ ...(i)

$S_2 = \frac{2n}{2}[2a + (2n-1)d]$ ...(ii)

and $\quad S_3 = \frac{3n}{2}[2a + (3n-1)d]$ ...(iii) (1)

Now, $S_2 - S_1 = \frac{2n}{2}[2a + (2n-1)d] - \frac{n}{2}[2a + (n-1)d]$

$= \frac{n}{2}[2\{2a + (2n-1)d\} - \{2a + (n-1)d\}]$

$= \frac{n}{2}[4a + (4n-2)d - 2a - (n-1)d]$ (2)

$= \frac{n}{2}[2a + (4n - 2 - n + 1)d]$

$= \frac{n}{2}[2a + (3n-1)d]$

$\therefore \quad 3(S_2 - S_1) = \frac{3n}{2}[2a + (3n-1)d]$ ...(iv)

From Eqs. (iii) and (iv), we have

$S_3 = 3(S_2 - S_1)$ **Hence proved.** (2)

# Chapter 6 Triangles

**1.** (a) We have, $\frac{AO}{OC} = \frac{BO}{OD} \Rightarrow \frac{3x-1}{5x-3} = \frac{2x+1}{6x-5}$

[$\because$ diagonals of a trapezium divide each other proportionally]

$\therefore (3x-1)(6x-5) = (2x+1)(5x-3)$

$\Rightarrow 18x^2 - 21x + 5 = 10x^2 - x - 3$

$\Rightarrow 8x^2 - 20x + 8 = 0$

$\Rightarrow 2x^2 - 5x + 2 = 0 \Rightarrow (x-2)(2x-1) = 0$

$\Rightarrow \quad x = 2$ or $x = \frac{1}{2}$

But $x = \frac{1}{2}$ makes $OC$ negative. Hence, $x = 2$

**2.** (d) $\Delta ABC \sim \Delta DEF$

$\therefore \quad \frac{AB}{DE} = \frac{BC}{EF} \Rightarrow \frac{1}{3} = \frac{6}{EF}$ [$\because 3AB = DE$]

$\Rightarrow \quad EF = 18$ cm

**3.** (c) Let $AB$ and $CD$ be the vertical poles.

$AB = 6$ m, $CD = 11$ m and $AC = 12$ m

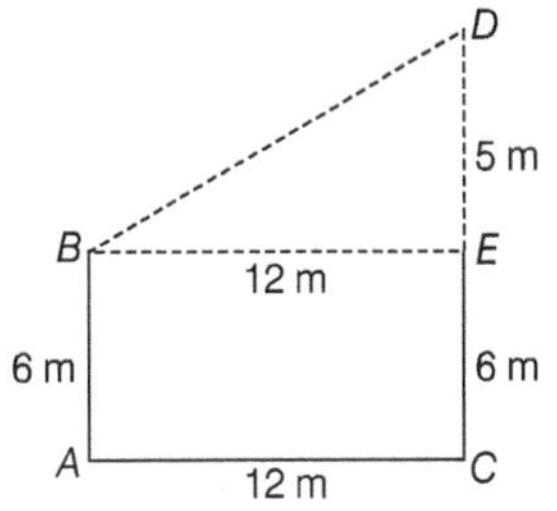

Draw $BE \parallel AC$,

$$DE = (CD - CE) = (11 - 6)\,\text{m} = 5\,\text{m}$$

In right $\Delta BED$,

$$BD^2 = BE^2 + DE^2 = 12^2 + 5^2 = 169$$

$$BD = \sqrt{169}\,\text{m} = 13\,\text{m}$$

Hence, distance between the tops = 13 m

**4.** (c) $\Delta ABC$ is equilateral, $AB = BC = CA$

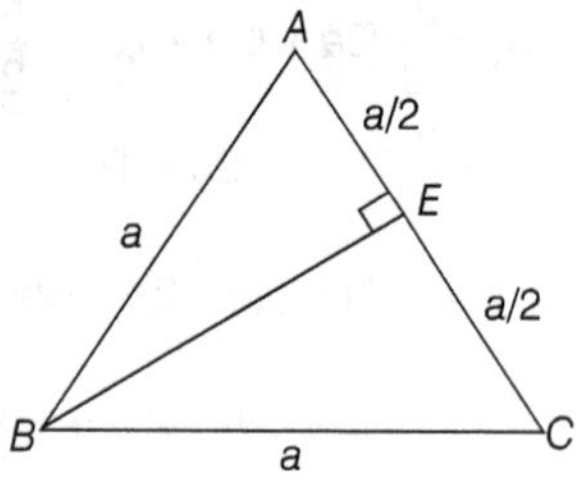


Let $AB = BC = CA = a$

$$BE^2 = a^2 - \left(\frac{a}{2}\right)^2 = \frac{3a^2}{4} \Rightarrow a^2 = \frac{4BE^2}{3}$$

$$\therefore \quad AB^2 + BC^2 + CA^2 = 3a^2 = \frac{3 \times 4BE^2}{3} = 4BE^2$$

**5.** (a) Area of $\Delta ABC = \frac{1}{2}(AB \times AC) = \frac{1}{2}bc$

Also, area of $\Delta ABC = \frac{1}{2}(BC \times AD)$

$\Rightarrow$ Area of $\Delta ABC = \frac{1}{2}\sqrt{b^2 + c^2} \times AD$

So, $\frac{1}{2}\sqrt{b^2 + c^2} \times AD = \frac{1}{2}bc$

$$\therefore \quad AD = \frac{bc}{\sqrt{b^2 + c^2}}$$

**6.** We know that the bisector of an angle of a triangle divides the opposite side in the ratio of the sides containing the angle. (1)

$\therefore BD : DC = AB : AC = \sqrt{3} : 2$ (1)

**7.** In $\Delta ABC$, we have

$PQ \parallel BC$

$\Rightarrow \frac{AQ}{QC} = \frac{AP}{PB}$ [by Thales theorem] (1)

$\Rightarrow \frac{AQ}{6} = \frac{6}{4} \Rightarrow AQ = 9\,\text{cm}$ (1)

**8.** In $\Delta BPA$, we have

$DC \parallel AP$ [given] (1/2)

Therefore, by basic proportionality theorem, we have

$\frac{BC}{CP} = \frac{BD}{DA}$ ...(i) (1/2)

In $\Delta BCA$, we have

$DE \parallel AC$ [given]

Therefore, by basic proportionality theorem, we have

$\frac{BE}{EC} = \frac{BD}{DA}$ ...(ii) (1/2)

From Eqs. (i) and (ii), we get

$\frac{BC}{CP} = \frac{BE}{EC}$ or $\frac{BE}{EC} = \frac{BC}{CP}$ **Hence proved.** (1/2)

**9.** $\angle AOB + \angle BOC = 180°$ [by linear pair axiom]

$\therefore \quad \angle AOB = 180° - \angle BOC = 180° - 125° = 55°$

$\angle DOC = \angle AOB = 55°$ [vertically opposite angles]

Now, in $\Delta COD$,

$\angle DCO = 180° - (\angle CDO + \angle COD)$

$= 180° - (70° + 55°) = 180° - 125° = 55°$ (1)

Since, $\Delta ODC \sim \Delta OBA$,

$\angle DCO = \angle OAB$ [corresponding angles of similar triangles are congruent]

But $\angle DCO = 55°$ [proved above]

and $\angle OAB = 55°$

Hence, $\angle DOC = 55°$, $\angle DCO = 55°$ and $\angle OAB = 55°$ (1)

**10.** Let the shortest side be $x$ m. Then according to the question,

Hypotenuse = $(2x + 6)$ m and 3rd side = $(2x + 4)$ m

By Pythagoras theorem,

$$(2x + 6)^2 = x^2 + (2x + 4)^2$$

$\Rightarrow \quad 4x^2 + 24x + 36 = x^2 + 4x^2 + 16x + 16$

$\Rightarrow \quad x^2 - 8x - 20 = 0$ (1)

$\Rightarrow \quad x^2 - 10x + 2x - 20 = 0$

$\Rightarrow \quad (x - 10)(x + 2) = 0$

$\Rightarrow \quad x = 10$

$\therefore$ The sides are 26 m, 10 m and 24 m. (1)

**11.** In $\Delta ACB$ and $\Delta AED$, we have

$\angle A = \angle A$ [common angle]

and $\angle C = \angle E$ [each 90°]

$\therefore \quad \Delta ACB \sim \Delta AED$ [by AA similarity criterion] (1)

In $\Delta ABC$, we have

$(AB)^2 = (BC)^2 + (AC)^2$ [by Pythagoras theorem]

$\Rightarrow (AB)^2 = (12)^2 + (5)^2 = 144 + 25 = 169$

[$\because BC = 12$ cm and $AC = 5$ cm] (1)

$\Rightarrow AB = 13\,\text{cm}$

Since, $\Delta ACB \sim \Delta AED$

$\therefore \quad \frac{AB}{AD} = \frac{BC}{DE} = \frac{AC}{AE}$

[by basic proportionality theorem]

$\Rightarrow \quad \frac{13}{3} = \frac{12}{DE} = \frac{5}{AE}$

$\Rightarrow \quad DE = \frac{36}{13}$ cm and $AE = \frac{15}{13}$ cm (1)

**12.** (i) In $\Delta ABC$ and $\Delta AED$,

$\angle ABC = \angle AED$ [given]

$\angle BAC = \angle EAD$ [common angle]

$\therefore \quad \Delta ABC \sim \Delta AED$ [by AA similarity criterion] (1)

(ii) Since, $\Delta ABC \sim \Delta AED$

$$\Rightarrow \quad \frac{AB}{AE} = \frac{BC}{ED} = \frac{AC}{AD}$$

[$\because$ corresponding sides of similar triangles are in the same ratio]

$$\Rightarrow \quad \frac{AB}{5} = \frac{7}{3}$$

[$\because$ $AE = 5$ cm, $AC = 7$ cm and $AD = 3$ cm]

$$\Rightarrow \quad 3AB = 35$$

$$\Rightarrow \quad AB = \frac{35}{3} = 11\frac{2}{3} \text{ cm} \quad (1)$$

$$\therefore \quad BD = AB - AD = 11\frac{2}{3} - 3$$

$$= 8\frac{2}{3} \text{ cm} \quad (1)$$

**13.** Given, in $\Delta PQR$, $DS \parallel QR$

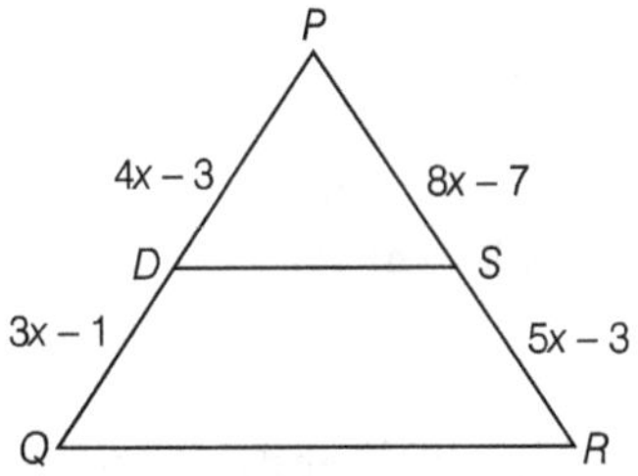


By Thale's theorem, we get

$$\frac{PD}{DQ} = \frac{PS}{SR}$$

$$\Rightarrow \quad \frac{4x-3}{3x-1} = \frac{8x-7}{5x-3}$$

$$\Rightarrow \quad (4x-3)(5x-3) = (8x-7)(3x-1)$$

$$\Rightarrow \quad 20x^2 - 12x + 9 - 15x = 24x^2 - 21x - 8x + 7 \quad (1)$$

$$\Rightarrow \quad 4x^2 - 2x - 2 = 0$$

$$\Rightarrow \quad 2x^2 - x - 1 = 0$$

$$\Rightarrow \quad 2x^2 - 2x + x - 1 = 0$$

$$\Rightarrow \quad 2x(x-1) + 1(x-1) = 0 \quad (1)$$

$$\Rightarrow \quad (x-1)(2x+1) = 0$$

$$\Rightarrow \quad x = -\frac{1}{2} \text{ or } x = 1$$

If $x = -\frac{1}{2}$, then $AD = 4 \times \left(-\frac{1}{2}\right) - 3 = -5 < 0$

[not possible]

Hence, $x = 1$ is the required value. (1)

**14. Given** A $\Delta ABC$ and $D$, $E$ are two points on $AB$ such that $AD = BE$. Also, $DP \parallel BC$ and $EQ \parallel AC$.

**To prove** $PQ \parallel AB$

**Proof** In $\Delta ABC$, $DP \parallel BC$

$$\therefore \quad \frac{AD}{DB} = \frac{AP}{PC} \quad \text{...(i) (1/2)}$$

[by Thale's theorem]

In $\Delta CBA$, $EQ \parallel AC$

$$\therefore \quad \frac{BE}{EA} = \frac{BQ}{QC} \quad \text{[by Thale's theorem] (1/2)}$$

$$\Rightarrow \quad \frac{AD}{BD} = \frac{BQ}{QC} \quad \text{...(ii) (1/2)}$$

[$\because$ $BE = AD$ and $EA = ED + DA = DE + EB = BD$]

From Eqs. (i) and (ii), we get

$$\frac{AP}{PC} = \frac{BQ}{QC}$$

$$\therefore \quad PQ \parallel AB$$

[by converse of Thale's theorem]

**Hence proved.** (1½)

**15.** (i) In $\Delta ABE$ and $\Delta ACD$,

$\angle ABE = \angle ACD$

[corresponding angles as $BE \parallel CD$]

$\angle AEB = \angle ADC$

[corresponding angles as $BE \parallel CD$] (1)

and $\angle BAE = \angle CAD$ [common angle]

$\therefore$ $\Delta ABE \sim \Delta ACD$ [by AAA similarity criterion]

$$\Rightarrow \quad \frac{BE}{CD} = \frac{AB}{AC} = \frac{8}{8+3} = \frac{8}{11} \quad (2)$$

(ii) It is a trapezium, which has 2 parallel sides $BE$ and $CD$. (2)

**16.** Draw $\Delta ABC$ and $\Delta FEG$ and then draw bisectors $CD$ and $GH$ of $\angle ACB$ and $\angle EGF$ such that $D$ lies on $AB$ and $H$ lies on $FE$.

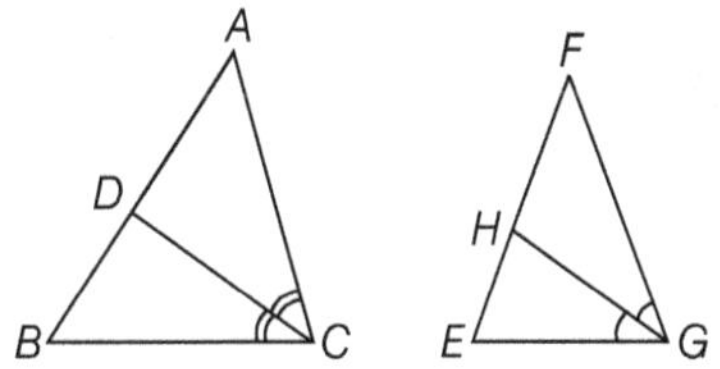


(1/2)

(i) Given, $\Delta ABC \sim \Delta FEG$

So, all corresponding angles are equal.

$\therefore$ $\angle CAB = \angle GFE$

or $\angle CAD = \angle GFH$ ...(i)

and $\angle ACB = \angle FGE$

$\Rightarrow$ $\frac{1}{2}\angle ACB = \frac{1}{2}\angle FGE$ [dividing both sides by 2]

$\Rightarrow$ $\angle ACD = \angle FGH$ ...(ii)

From Eqs. (i) and (ii),

$\Delta ACD \sim \Delta FGH$ [by AA similarity criterion]

$\therefore$ $\frac{CD}{GH} = \frac{AC}{FG}$ [since, corresponding sides of two similar triangles are proportional] (1½)

(ii) In $\Delta DCB$ and $\Delta HGE$,

$\angle DBC = \angle HEG$ ...(iii)

[$\because$ $\Delta ABC \sim \Delta FEG$

$\therefore$ $\angle ABC = \angle FEG \Rightarrow \angle DBC = \angle HEG$]

and $\angle DCB = \angle HGE$ ...(iv)

$$\left[\begin{array}{l} \because \Delta ABC \sim \Delta FEG \\ \therefore \angle ACB = \angle FGE \\ \Rightarrow \frac{1}{2}\angle ACB = \frac{1}{2}\angle FGE \Rightarrow \angle DCB = \angle HGE \end{array}\right]$$

From Eqs. (iii) and (iv),

$\Delta DCB \sim \Delta HGE$ [by AA similarity criterion] (1½)

(iii) In $\Delta DCA$ and $\Delta HGF$,

$\angle DAC = \angle HFG$ ...(v)

$$\left[\begin{array}{l} \because \Delta ABC \sim \Delta FEG \\ \therefore \angle CAB = \angle GFE \\ \Rightarrow \angle CAD = \angle GFH \text{ or } \angle DAC = \angle HFG \end{array}\right]$$

and $\angle DCA = \angle HGF$ ...(vi)

$$\left[\begin{array}{l} \because \Delta ABC \sim \Delta FEG \\ \therefore \angle ACB = \angle FGE \\ \Rightarrow \frac{1}{2}\angle ACB = \frac{1}{2}\angle FGE \Rightarrow \angle DCA = \angle HGF \end{array}\right]$$

From Eqs. (v) and (vi),

$\Delta DCA \sim \Delta HGF$ [by AA similarity criterion]

**Hence proved.** (1½)

**17.** Given, in $\Delta ABC$ and $\Delta PQR$, $AD$ and $PM$ are their medians, respectively.

$\therefore \quad \dfrac{AB}{PQ} = \dfrac{AC}{PR} = \dfrac{AD}{PM}$ ...(i)

**To prove** $\Delta ABC \sim \Delta PQR$

**Construction** Produce $AD$ to $E$ such that $AD = DE$ and produce $PM$ to $N$ such that $PM = MN$.

Join $BE$, $CE$, $QN$ and $RN$.

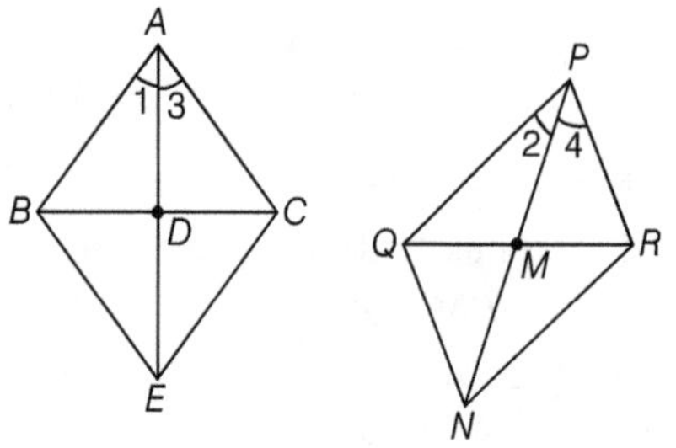


(1)

**Proof** Quadrilaterals $ABEC$ and $PQNR$ are parallelograms because their diagonals bisect each other at $D$ and $M$, respectively.

$\therefore \quad BE = AC$ and $QN = PR$

$\Rightarrow \quad \dfrac{BE}{AC} = 1$ and $\dfrac{QN}{PR} = 1$

$\Rightarrow \quad \dfrac{BE}{AC} = \dfrac{QN}{PR}$ or $\dfrac{BE}{QN} = \dfrac{AC}{PR}$

$\Rightarrow \quad \dfrac{BE}{QN} = \dfrac{AB}{PQ}$ [from Eq. (i)]

or $\quad \dfrac{AB}{PQ} = \dfrac{BE}{QN}$ ...(ii) (1)

From Eq. (i), we get

$$\frac{AB}{PQ} = \frac{AD}{PM} = \frac{2AD}{2PM} = \frac{AE}{PN}$$

[since, diagonals bisect each other]

$\Rightarrow \quad \dfrac{AB}{PQ} = \dfrac{AE}{PN}$ ...(iii) (1)

From Eqs. (ii) and (iii),

$$\frac{AB}{PQ} = \frac{BE}{QN} = \frac{AE}{PN}$$

$\Rightarrow \quad \Delta ABE \sim \Delta PQN \Rightarrow \angle 1 = \angle 2$ ...(iv)

[since, corresponding angles of two similar triangles are equal]

Similarly, we can prove that

$\Delta ACE \sim \Delta PRN \Rightarrow \angle 3 = \angle 4$ ...(v) (1)

On adding Eqs. (iv) and (v), we get

$\angle 1 + \angle 3 = \angle 2 + \angle 4$

$\Rightarrow \quad \angle BAC = \angle QPR$

and $\quad \dfrac{AB}{PQ} = \dfrac{AC}{PR}$ [from Eq. (i)]

$\therefore \quad \Delta ABC \sim \Delta PQR$ [by SAS similarity criterion]

**Hence proved.** (1)

## Chapter 7 Coordinate Geometry

**1.** (a) By distance formula, we have

$$D = \sqrt{(x_2 - x_1)^2 + (y_2 - y_1)^2}$$

$\Rightarrow \quad 3 = \sqrt{(x-2)^2 + (0-3)^2}$

$\Rightarrow \quad 9 = (x-2)^2 + (-3)^2$ [squaring both sides]

$\Rightarrow \quad 9 = (x-2)^2 + 9$

$\Rightarrow (x-2)^2 = 0 \Rightarrow x - 2 = 0$

$\therefore \quad x = 2$

**2.** (c) Let $M$ be the mid-point of $BC$, and $AM$ be the median.

Hence, coordinates of $M$ are

$$M\left(\frac{0+2}{2}, \frac{0+1}{2}\right), \text{ i.e. } M\left(1, \frac{1}{2}\right)$$

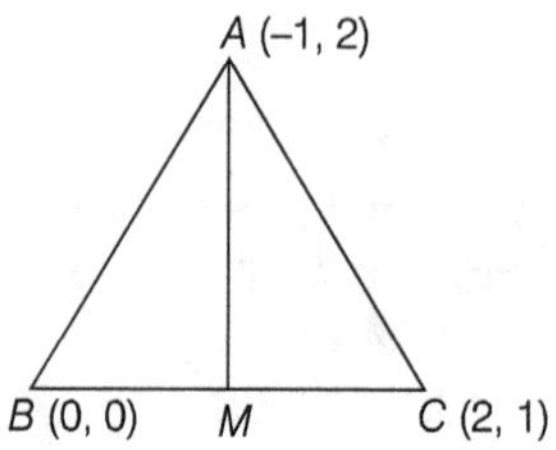


$$\therefore AM = \sqrt{(1+1)^2 + \left(\frac{1}{2} - 2\right)^2} = \sqrt{\frac{25}{4}} = \frac{5}{2} \text{ units}$$

The length of median is $\frac{5}{2}$ units.

**3.** Here, point $A$ lies on $Y$-axis, so its abscissa is zero and its ordinate is 4. So, the point $A$ on $Y$-axis is $A(0, 4)$.

Here, $A = (x_1, y_1) = (0, 4)$

and $B = (x_2, y_2) = (-3, 1)$

$\therefore AB = \sqrt{(x_2 - x_1)^2 + (y_2 - y_1)^2}$ [by distance formula]

$= \sqrt{(-3-0)^2 + (1-4)^2}$ (1)

$= \sqrt{(-3)^2 + (-3)^2}$

$= \sqrt{9+9} = \sqrt{18}$

$= 3\sqrt{2}$ units

Hence, the distance between $A$ and $B$ is $3\sqrt{2}$ units. (1)

**4.** Given points are $(k, 0)$ and $\left(7, \frac{3}{2}\right)$.

Now, coordinates of mid-point

$$= \left(\frac{k+7}{2}, \frac{0+\frac{3}{2}}{2}\right) = \left(\frac{k+7}{2}, \frac{3}{4}\right) \quad (1)$$

$\left[\because \text{coordinates of mid-point} = \left(\frac{x_1 + x_2}{2}, \frac{y_1 + y_2}{2}\right)\right]$

But coordinates of mid-point are given $\left(3, \frac{3}{4}\right)$.

$\therefore \quad \left(3, \frac{3}{4}\right) = \left(\frac{k+7}{2}, \frac{3}{4}\right)$

On comparing $x$-coordinate both sides, we get

$$3 = \frac{k+7}{2}$$

$\Rightarrow \quad k + 7 = 6$

$\therefore \quad k = -1$ (1)

**5.** Let $AB$ be a diameter of the circle having its centre at $C(1, -3)$ such that the coordinates of one end are $(4, -1)$.

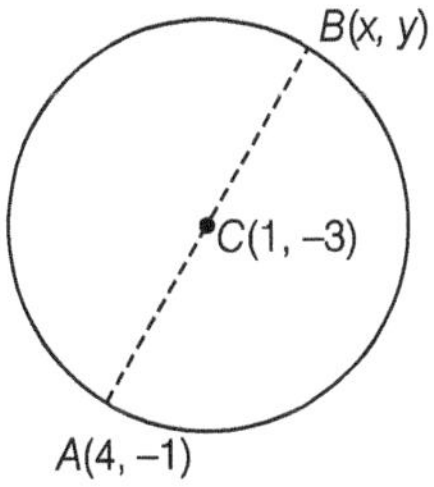


Let the coordinates of $B$ be $(x, y)$.

Since, $C$ is the mid-point of $AB$. (1)

Therefore, the coordinates of $C$ are $\left(\frac{x+4}{2}, \frac{y-1}{2}\right)$.

But the coordinates of $C$ are given as $(1, -3)$.

$\therefore \quad \frac{x+4}{2} = 1$ and $\frac{y-1}{2} = -3$

$\Rightarrow \quad x + 4 = 2$ and $y - 1 = -6$

$\Rightarrow \quad x = -2$ and $y = -5$

Hence, the coordinates of $B$ are $(-2, -5)$. (1)

**6.** Applying section formula, we get

$$\frac{3x + 4(2)}{7} = -2 \Rightarrow x = -\frac{22}{3}$$

and $\quad \frac{3y + 4(5)}{7} = 4 \Rightarrow y = \frac{8}{3}$ (1)

$\therefore \quad x^2 + y^2 = \left(\frac{-22}{3}\right)^2 + \left(\frac{8}{3}\right)^2 = \frac{548}{9}$ (1)

**7.** Let the point $A(x, y)$ be equidistant from the points $B(3, 6)$ and $C(-3, 4)$.

$\therefore \quad AB = AC$

$\Rightarrow \quad \sqrt{(x-3)^2 + (y-6)^2} = \sqrt{(x+3)^2 + (y-4)^2}$

[$\because$ by using distance formula, distance $= \sqrt{(x_2 - x_1)^2 + (y_2 - y_1)^2}$]

On squaring both sides, we get

$(x-3)^2 + (y-6)^2 = (x+3)^2 + (y-4)^2$ (1)

$\Rightarrow \quad x^2 - 6x + 9 + y^2 - 12y + 36 = x^2 + 6x + 9 + y^2 - 8y + 16$

$\Rightarrow \quad -6x - 6x - 12y + 8y + 36 - 16 = 0$

$\Rightarrow \quad -12x - 4y + 20 = 0$

$\Rightarrow \quad -4(3x + y - 5) = 0$

$\Rightarrow \quad 3x + y - 5 = 0$ [$\because -4 \neq 0$] (1)

**8.** Let the required ratio be $k : 1$, then by section formula, the coordinates of the point which divides $AB$ in the ratio $k : 1$ are $\left(\frac{-4k+1}{k+1}, \frac{5k-5}{k+1}\right)$

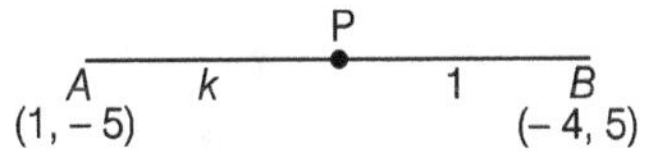


(1)

Given, point lies on the $X$-axis, and we know that on the $X$-axis, the ordinate is zero.

$\therefore \quad \frac{5k-5}{k+1} = 0 \Rightarrow 5k - 5 = 0, k = 1$

Therefore, the required ratio is 1 : 1 (1)

**9.** It is given that $P$ divides the line segment joining $A(-1, 3)$ and $B(9, 8)$ in the ratio $k : 1$.

So, coordinates of $P$ are $\left(\frac{9k-1}{k+1}, \frac{8k+3}{k+1}\right)$.

$\therefore$ Point $P\left(\frac{9k-1}{k+1}, \frac{8k+3}{k+1}\right)$ lies on the line $x - y + 2 = 0$.

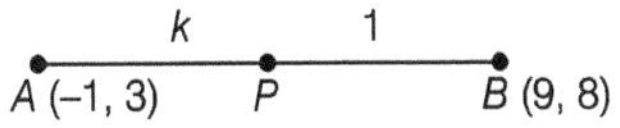


(1)

$\therefore \quad \frac{9k-1}{k+1} - \frac{8k+3}{k+1} + 2 = 0$

$\Rightarrow \quad 9k - 1 - (8k + 3) + 2(k + 1) = 0$

$\Rightarrow \quad k - 4 + 2k + 2 = 0$

$\Rightarrow \quad 3k - 2 = 0$

$\Rightarrow \quad k = \frac{2}{3}$ (1)

**10.** Let $A(3, 2)$, $B(0,5)$, $C(-3,2)$ and $D(0,-1)$ are the vertices of a square.

Now, $AB = \sqrt{(3-0)^2 + (2-5)^2} = \sqrt{9+9} = \sqrt{18}$ units [by distance formula]

$BC = \sqrt{(0+3)^2 + (5-2)^2} = \sqrt{9+9} = \sqrt{18}$ units (1)

$CD = \sqrt{(-3-0)^2 + (2+1)^2} = \sqrt{9+9} = \sqrt{18}$ units

Also, $AD = \sqrt{(3-0)^2 + (2+1)^2} = \sqrt{9+9} = \sqrt{18}$ units (1)

Here, $AB = BC = CD = DA = \sqrt{18}$ units

Also, $AC = \sqrt{(3+3)^2 + (2-2)^2} = \sqrt{36}$ units

or $BD = \sqrt{(0-0)^2 + (-1-5)^2} = \sqrt{36}$ units

$\because$ Diagonal $AC$ = Diagonal $BD$

Hence, $ABCD$ is a square. **Hence proved.** (1)

**11.** Given, $(a, b)$ is the mid-point of $AB$.

$\therefore \quad (a, b) = \left(\dfrac{10+k}{2}, \dfrac{-6+4}{2}\right)$

$\left[\because \text{ midpoint} = \left(\dfrac{x_1+x_2}{2}, \dfrac{y_1+y_2}{2}\right)\right]$

$\Rightarrow \quad (a, b) = \left(\dfrac{10+k}{2}, -1\right)$ (1)

On comparing the coordinates, we get

$a = \dfrac{10+k}{2}$ ...(i)

and $b = -1$ ...(ii)

Given, $a - 2b = 18 \Rightarrow a - 2(-1) = 18$ [from Eq. (ii)]

$\Rightarrow \quad a + 2 = 18 \Rightarrow a = 18 - 2$

$\therefore \quad a = 16$

On putting the value of $a$ in Eq. (i), we get

$16 = \dfrac{10+k}{2} \Rightarrow 10 + k = 32 \Rightarrow k = 32 - 10 = 22$ (1)

Now, $A = (10, -6)$ and $B = (22, 4)$

$\therefore$ Distance, $AB = \sqrt{(x_2 - x_1)^2 + (y_2 - y_1)^2}$

$= \sqrt{(22-10)^2 + [4-(-6)]^2}$

$= \sqrt{(12)^2 + (10)^2} = \sqrt{144+100}$

$= \sqrt{244} = 2\sqrt{61}$ units (1)

**12.** Suppose point $A$ has abscissa $= x$

then ordinate $= 2x$

$\therefore$ $A$ is $(x, 2x)$.

Take other point $(4,3)$ as $B$.

$\therefore \quad \sqrt{(4-x)^2 + (3-2x)^2} = AB$

[$\because$ by distance formula, distance $= \sqrt{(x_2-x_1)^2 + (y_2-y_1)^2}$]

$\sqrt{16 + x^2 - 8x + 9 + 4x^2 - 12x} = \sqrt{10}$ (1)

On squaring both sides, we get

$5x^2 - 20x + 25 = 10$

$\Rightarrow \quad 5x^2 - 20x + 25 - 10 = 0$

$\Rightarrow \quad 5x^2 - 20x + 15 = 0$

$\Rightarrow \quad x^2 - 4x + 3 = 0$ [divided by 5]

$\Rightarrow \quad x^2 - 3x - x + 3 = 0$

[by splitting middle term] (1)

$\Rightarrow \quad x(x-3) - 1(x-3) = 0$

$\Rightarrow \quad (x-3)(x-1) = 0$

$\therefore \quad x - 3 = 0$ or $x - 1 = 0$

$\Rightarrow \quad x = 3$ or $x = 1$

When $x = 3$, then $2x = 2 \times 3 = 6$

$\therefore$ Coordinates of $A$ are $(3, 6)$.

When $x = 1$, then $2x = 2 \times 1 = 2$

$\therefore$ Coordinate of $A$ are $(1, 2)$. (1)

Hence, coordinates of point $A$ are $(3, 6)$ and $(1, 2)$.

**13.** Let $A(4, -1)$ and $B(-2, -3)$ be the end points of line segment $AB$ and points of trisection of the line segment be $P$ and $Q$.

Then, $AP = PQ = BQ = k$ [say] (1)

Now, $PB = PQ + QB = k + k = 2k$

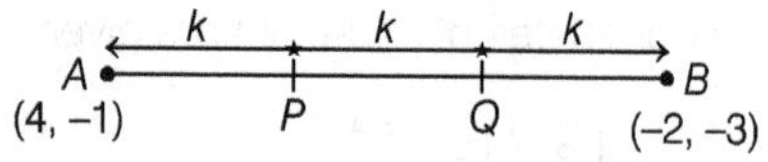


$\therefore$ $AP : PB = k : 2k = 1 : 2$ and $AQ : QB = 2k : k = 2 : 1$

Since, $P$ divides $AB$ internally in the ratio $1:2$. (1)

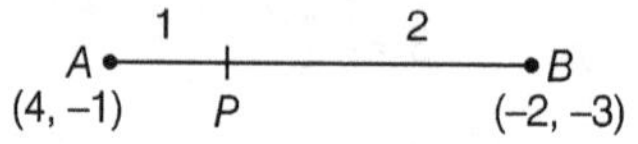


So, the coordinates of $P$

$= \left[\dfrac{1 \times (-2) + 2 \times 4}{1+2}, \dfrac{1 \times (-3) + 2 \times (-1)}{1+2}\right]$

$\left[\because \text{ using section formula i.e.} \left(\dfrac{m_1x_2 + m_2x_1}{m_1 + m_2}, \dfrac{m_1y_2 + m_2y_1}{m_1 + m_2}\right)\right]$

$= \left(\dfrac{-2+8}{3}, \dfrac{-3-2}{3}\right)$

$= \left(\dfrac{6}{3}, \dfrac{-5}{3}\right) = \left(2, -\dfrac{5}{3}\right)$

$\because$ $Q$ divides $AB$ internally in the ratio $2 : 1$. (1)

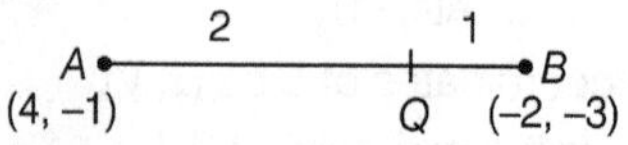


So, the coordinates of $Q$

$= \left[\dfrac{2 \times (-2) + 1 \times 4}{2+1}, \dfrac{2 \times (-3) + 1 \times (-1)}{2+1}\right]$

$= \left(\dfrac{-4+4}{3}, \dfrac{-6-1}{3}\right) = \left(0, -\dfrac{7}{3}\right)$

So, the two points of trisection are $\left(2, -\dfrac{5}{3}\right)$ and $\left(0, -\dfrac{7}{3}\right)$. (2)

**14.** Let $PQRS$ be a square with $P(-1, 2)$ and $R(3, 2)$. Let the coordinates of $Q$ be $(x, y)$.

$\because$ All sides of a square are equal.

$\therefore \quad PQ = QR$

$\Rightarrow \quad PQ^2 = QR^2$ [on squaring both sides]

$\Rightarrow (x+1)^2 + (y-2)^2 = (x-3)^2 + (y-2)^2$

[$\because$ distance $= \sqrt{(x_2 - x_1)^2 + (y_2 - y_1)^2}$] (1)

$\Rightarrow \quad (x+1)^2 = (x-3)^2$

$\Rightarrow \quad x^2 + 1 + 2x = x^2 + 9 - 6x$

$\left[\because \begin{array}{l} (a+b)^2 = a^2 + b^2 + 2ab \\ (a-b)^2 = a^2 + b^2 - 2ab \end{array}\right]$

$\Rightarrow \quad 2x + 1 = -6x + 9$

$\Rightarrow \quad 8x = 8 \Rightarrow x = 1$ ...(i)

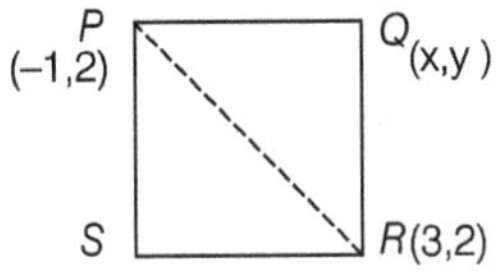


(1)

In $\Delta PQR$, $PQ^2 + QR^2 = PR^2$

[by Pythagoras theorem]

$\Rightarrow \quad (x+1)^2 + (y-2)^2 + (x-3)^2 + (y-2)^2 = (3+1)^2 + (2-2)^2$

$\Rightarrow x^2 + 1 + 2x + y^2 + 4 - 4y + x^2 + 9 - 6x + y^2 + 4 - 4y = 4^2 + 0^2$ (1)

$\Rightarrow \quad 2x^2 + 2y^2 + 2x - 6x - 4y - 4y + 1 + 4 + 9 + 4 = 16$

$\Rightarrow \quad 2x^2 + 2y^2 - 4x - 8y + 2 = 0$

$\Rightarrow \quad x^2 + y^2 - 2x - 4y + 1 = 0$ [dividing by 2] ...(ii) (1)

On putting $x = 1$ from Eq. (i) in Eq. (ii), we get

$1 + y^2 - 2 - 4y + 1 = 0$

$\Rightarrow \quad y^2 - 4y = 0$

$\Rightarrow \quad y(y-4) = 0$

$\Rightarrow \quad y = 0$ or $4$

Hence, the required vertices of square are (1, 0) and (1, 4). (1)

## Chapter 8 Introduction to Trigonometry

**1.** (*b*) $\sin\theta + \sin^2\theta = 1$

$\Rightarrow \quad \sin\theta = 1 - \sin^2\theta$

$\Rightarrow \quad \sin\theta = \cos^2\theta$ [$\because \cos^2\theta = 1 - \sin^2\theta$]

$\Rightarrow \quad \sin^2\theta = \cos^4\theta$ [squaring both sides]

$\Rightarrow \quad 1 - \cos^2\theta = \cos^4\theta$

$\Rightarrow \quad \cos^4\theta + \cos^2\theta = 1$

**2.** (*a*) We have, $\sin\theta = \frac{1}{2} \Rightarrow \theta = 30°$

Now, $\quad 3\cos\theta - 4\cos^3\theta \Rightarrow 3\cos 30° - 4\cos^3 30°$

$\Rightarrow \quad 3 \times \frac{\sqrt{3}}{2} - 4 \times \left(\frac{\sqrt{3}}{2}\right)^3$

$\Rightarrow \quad \frac{3\sqrt{3}}{2} - \frac{4 \times 3\sqrt{3}}{8} \Rightarrow \frac{3\sqrt{3}}{2} - \frac{3\sqrt{3}}{2} = 0$

**3.** (*b*) Given, $\tan\theta = \frac{12}{5}$

As, $\cos\theta = \frac{1}{\sec\theta} = \frac{1}{\sqrt{1 + \tan^2\theta}}$

$= \frac{1}{\sqrt{1 + \left(\frac{12}{5}\right)^2}} = \frac{1}{\sqrt{\frac{169}{25}}} = \frac{5}{13}$

Thus, $\frac{1 + \cos\theta}{1 - \cos\theta} = \frac{1 + \frac{5}{13}}{1 - \frac{5}{13}} = \frac{9}{4}$

**4.** (*a*) $\frac{\sin 30° - \sin 90° + 2\cos 0°}{\tan 30° \tan 60°} = \frac{\frac{1}{2} - 1 + 2 \times 1}{\frac{1}{\sqrt{3}} \times \sqrt{3}}$

$= \frac{\frac{1 - 2 + 4}{2}}{1} = \frac{3}{2}$

**5.** LHS $= \sin 3x$

$= \sin 3 \times 30° = \sin 90°$ [put $x = 30°$]

$= 1$ (1)

RHS $= 3\sin x - 4\sin^3 x$

$= 3\sin 30° - 4\sin^3 30°$

$= 3 \times \frac{1}{2} - 4 \times \left(\frac{1}{2}\right)^3$

$= \frac{3}{2} - \frac{4}{8} = \frac{3}{2} - \frac{1}{2} = \frac{2}{2} = 1$

$\therefore$ LHS = RHS **Hence verified.** (1)

**6.** Given, $\cos 2x = \cos 60° \cos 30° + \sin 60° \sin 30°$

$= \frac{1}{2} \times \frac{\sqrt{3}}{2} + \frac{\sqrt{3}}{2} \times \frac{1}{2} = \frac{\sqrt{3}}{4} + \frac{\sqrt{3}}{4} = \frac{\sqrt{3}}{2}$ (1)

$\Rightarrow \quad \cos 2x = \cos 30°$

$\Rightarrow \quad 2x = 30° \Rightarrow x = 15°$ (1)

**7.** Given, $a\cos\theta + b\sin\theta = t$, $a\sin\theta - b\cos\theta = s$

RHS $= s^2 + t^2$

$= (a\sin\theta - b\cos\theta)^2 + (a\cos\theta + b\sin\theta)^2$ (1)

$= a^2\sin^2\theta + b^2\cos^2\theta - 2ab\sin\theta\cos\theta + a^2\cos^2\theta + b^2\sin^2\theta + 2ab\sin\theta\cos\theta$

$= a^2(\sin^2\theta + \cos^2\theta) + b^2(\cos^2\theta + \sin^2\theta)$

$= a^2 + b^2 =$ LHS **Hence proved.** (1)

**8.** We have, $\cos\theta\left(\frac{1}{1 - \sin\theta} - \frac{1}{1 + \sin\theta}\right)$

$= \cos\theta\left[\frac{1 + \sin\theta - 1 + \sin\theta}{(1 - \sin\theta)(1 + \sin\theta)}\right]$

$= \cos\theta\left(\frac{2\sin\theta}{1 - \sin^2\theta}\right)$ [$\because a^2 - b^2 = (a-b)(a+b)$]

(1)

$= \cos\theta \cdot \dfrac{2\sin\theta}{\cos^2\theta} = 2\dfrac{\sin\theta}{\cos\theta}$

$= 2\tan\theta$ $\left[\because \tan\theta = \dfrac{\sin\theta}{\cos\theta}\right]$

On comparing it with $k\tan\theta$, we get

$k = 2$ (1)

**9.** Let us first draw a right $\Delta ABC$.

We know that $\sin A = \dfrac{BC}{AC} = \dfrac{3}{4}$

$\therefore$ If $BC = 3k$, then $AC = 4k$, where $k$ is a positive number.

Now, $(AC)^2 = (AB)^2 + (BC)^2$ [using Pythagoras theorem]

$\Rightarrow (AB)^2 = (AC)^2 - (BC)^2 = (4k)^2 - (3k)^2$

$= 16k^2 - 9k^2 = 7k^2$

$\Rightarrow AB = +\sqrt{7k^2} = \sqrt{7}k$

[taking positive square root]

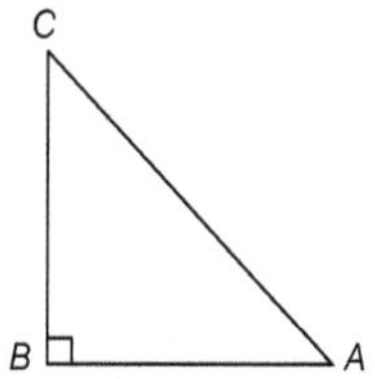


(1)

$\therefore \cos A = \dfrac{AB}{AC} = \dfrac{\sqrt{7}k}{4k} = \dfrac{\sqrt{7}}{4}$

and $\tan A = \dfrac{BC}{AB} = \dfrac{3k}{\sqrt{7}k} = \dfrac{3}{\sqrt{7}}$ (1)

**10.** LHS $= 4(\sin^4 30° + \cos^4 60°) - 3(\cos^2 45° - \sin^2 90°)$

$= 4\left\{\left(\dfrac{1}{2}\right)^4 + \left(\dfrac{1}{2}\right)^4\right\} - 3\left\{\left(\dfrac{1}{\sqrt{2}}\right)^2 - (1)^2\right\}$

$\left[\because \sin 30° = \dfrac{1}{2}, \cos 60° = \dfrac{1}{2}\right.$

$\left.\cos 45° = \dfrac{1}{\sqrt{2}} \text{ and } \sin 90° = 1\right]$

$= 4\left(\dfrac{1}{16} + \dfrac{1}{16}\right) - 3\left(\dfrac{1}{2} - 1\right)$ (1)

$= 4\left(\dfrac{1+1}{16}\right) - 3\left(\dfrac{1-2}{2}\right)$

$= 4 \times \dfrac{2}{16} - 3\left(-\dfrac{1}{2}\right) = \dfrac{1}{2} + \dfrac{3}{2}$

$= \dfrac{1+3}{2} = \dfrac{4}{2} = 2 =$ RHS **Hence proved.** (1)

**11.** LHS $= \left(\dfrac{1+\sin\theta-\cos\theta}{1+\sin\theta+\cos\theta}\right)^2$

$= \dfrac{1+\sin^2\theta+\cos^2\theta+2\sin\theta-2\cos\theta-2\sin\theta\cos\theta}{1+\sin^2\theta+\cos^2\theta+2\sin\theta+2\cos\theta+2\sin\theta\cos\theta}$

$= \dfrac{1+1+2\sin\theta-2\cos\theta(1+\sin\theta)}{1+1+2\sin\theta+2\cos\theta(1+\sin\theta)}$ (1)

$[\because \sin^2\theta + \cos^2\theta = 1]$

$= \dfrac{2+2\sin\theta-2\cos\theta(1+\sin\theta)}{2+2\sin\theta+2\cos\theta(1+\sin\theta)}$

$= \dfrac{2\{(1+\sin\theta)-\cos\theta(1+\sin\theta)\}}{2\{(1+\sin\theta)+\cos\theta(1+\sin\theta)\}}$

$= \dfrac{(1+\sin\theta)(1-\cos\theta)}{(1+\sin\theta)(1+\cos\theta)}$

$= \dfrac{1-\cos\theta}{1+\cos\theta}$

= RHS **Hence proved.** (1)

**12.** Given,

LHS $= 2\sec^2\theta - \sec^4\theta - 2\text{cosec}^2\theta + \text{cosec}^4\theta$

$= 2(\sec^2\theta) - (\sec^2\theta)^2 - 2(\text{cosec}^2\theta) + (\text{cosec}^2\theta)^2$

$= 2(1+\tan^2\theta) - (1+\tan^2\theta)^2$

$-2(1+\cot^2\theta) + (1+\cot^2\theta)^2$ (1½)

$= 2 + 2\tan^2\theta - (1 + 2\tan^2\theta + \tan^4\theta) - 2$

$-2\cot^2\theta + (1 + 2\cot^2\theta + \cot^4\theta)$

$= 2 + 2\tan^2\theta - 1 - 2\tan^2\theta - \tan^4\theta$

$-2 - 2\cot^2\theta + 1 + 2\cot^2\theta + \cot^4\theta$

$= \cot^4\theta - \tan^4\theta =$ RHS **Hence proved.** (1½)

**13.** We have, LHS $= \sec\theta + \tan^3\theta\,\text{cosec}\,\theta$

$= \sec\theta\left\{\dfrac{\sec\theta + \tan^3\theta\,\text{cosec}\,\theta}{\sec\theta}\right\}$

$= \sec\theta\left\{1 + \tan^3\theta \cdot \dfrac{\cos\theta}{\sin\theta}\right\}$

$= \sec\theta\,\{1 + \tan^3\theta \cdot \cot\theta\}$

$= \sqrt{1+\tan^2\theta}\{1+\tan^2\theta\}$

$[\because \sec\theta = \sqrt{1+\tan^2\theta}]$ (1½)

$= \{1+\tan^2\theta\}^{3/2}$

$= \{1+(1-t^2)\}^{3/2}$ $[\because \tan^2\theta = 1 - t^2]$

$= (2-t^2)^{3/2}$ **Hence proved.** (1½)

**14.** LHS $= \dfrac{2-\text{cosec}^2 A}{\text{cosec}^2 A + 2\cot A} = \dfrac{2 - \dfrac{1}{\sin^2 A}}{\dfrac{1}{\sin^2 A} + \dfrac{2\cos A}{\sin A}}$

$\left[\because \text{cosec}\, A = \dfrac{1}{\sin A} \text{ and } \cot A = \dfrac{\cos A}{\sin A}\right]$

$= \dfrac{\dfrac{2\sin^2 A - 1}{\sin^2 A}}{\dfrac{1 + 2\sin A\cos A}{\sin^2 A}}$ (1)

$= \dfrac{2\sin^2 A - 1}{\sin^2 A} \cdot \dfrac{\sin^2 A}{1 + 2\sin A\cos A}$

$$= \frac{2\sin^2 A - (\sin^2 A + \cos^2 A)}{\sin^2 A + \cos^2 A + 2\sin A\cos A}$$

$[\because \sin^2 A + \cos^2 A = 1]$

$$= \frac{2\sin^2 A - (\sin^2 A + \cos^2 A)}{(\sin A + \cos A)^2} \quad (1)$$

$$= \frac{2\sin^2 A - \sin^2 A - \cos^2 A}{(\sin A + \cos A)^2} = \frac{\sin^2 A - \cos^2 A}{(\sin A + \cos A)^2}$$

$$= \frac{(\sin A - \cos A)(\sin A + \cos A)}{(\sin A + \cos A)^2}$$

$$= \frac{\sin A - \cos A}{\sin A + \cos A} \quad [\because a^2 - b^2 = (a-b)(a+b)]$$

= RHS **Hence proved.** (1)

**15.** Given, $\sin(A + 2B) = \frac{\sqrt{3}}{2}$

$\Rightarrow \quad \sin(A + 2B) = \sin 60° \quad \left[\because \sin 60° = \frac{\sqrt{3}}{2}\right]$

$\Rightarrow \quad A + 2B = 60° \quad \ldots$ (i)

Also, $\cos(A + 4B) = 0$

$\Rightarrow \quad \cos(A + 4B) = \cos 90° \quad [\because \cos 90° = 0]$

$\Rightarrow \quad A + 4B = 90° \quad \ldots$ (ii) (1)

On subtracting Eq. (i) from Eq. (ii), we get

$A + 4B - A - 2B = 90° - 60°$

$\Rightarrow \quad 2B = 30° \Rightarrow B = \frac{30°}{2} = 15°$ (1)

Now, on putting the value of $B$ in Eq. (i), we get

$A + 2 \times 15° = 60°$

$\Rightarrow \quad A + 30° = 60 \Rightarrow A = 30°$

Hence, $A = 30°$ and $B = 15°$. (1)

**16.** LHS $= \sec^4\theta(1 - \sin^4\theta) - 2\tan^2\theta$

$= \sec^4\theta[1 - (\sin^2\theta)^2] - 2\tan^2\theta$

$= \sec^4\theta(1 - \sin^2\theta)(1 + \sin^2\theta) - 2\tan^2\theta$

$[\because (a^2 - b^2) = (a-b)(a+b)]$ (1½)

$= \sec^4\theta\cos^2\theta(1 + \sin^2\theta) - 2\tan^2\theta$

$[\because 1 - \sin^2\theta = \cos^2\theta]$

$$= \sec^2\theta(\sec^2\theta \cdot \cos^2\theta)(1 + \sin^2\theta) - \frac{2\sin^2\theta}{\cos^2\theta}$$

$\left[\because \tan\theta = \frac{\sin\theta}{\cos\theta}\right]$ (1½)

$$= \frac{1 + \sin^2\theta}{\cos^2\theta} - \frac{2\sin^2\theta}{\cos^2\theta}$$

$\left[\because \sec^2\theta = \frac{1}{\cos^2\theta} \text{ and } \sec^2\theta \cdot \cos^2\theta = 1\right]$

$$= \frac{1 + \sin^2\theta - 2\sin^2\theta}{\cos^2\theta} = \frac{1 - \sin^2\theta}{\cos^2\theta}$$

$$= \frac{\cos^2\theta}{\cos^2\theta} = 1 = \text{RHS} \quad [\because 1 - \sin^2\theta = \cos^2\theta]$$

**Hence proved.** (2)

**17.** LHS $= a^2b^2(a^2 + b^2 + 3)$

$= (\operatorname{cosec}\theta - \sin\theta)^2(\sec\theta - \cos\theta)^2$
$\{(\operatorname{cosec}\theta - \sin\theta)^2 + (\sec\theta - \cos\theta)^2 + 3\}$

$$= \left(\frac{1}{\sin\theta} - \sin\theta\right)^2\left(\frac{1}{\cos\theta} - \cos\theta\right)^2 \left\{\left(\frac{1}{\sin\theta} - \sin\theta\right)^2 + \left(\frac{1}{\cos\theta} - \cos\theta\right)^2 + 3\right\}$$

$$= \left(\frac{1 - \sin^2\theta}{\sin\theta}\right)^2\left(\frac{1 - \cos^2\theta}{\cos\theta}\right)^2 \left\{\left(\frac{1 - \sin^2\theta}{\sin\theta}\right)^2 + \left(\frac{1 - \cos^2\theta}{\cos\theta}\right)^2 + 3\right\} \quad (2½)$$

$$= \left(\frac{\cos^2\theta}{\sin\theta}\right)^2\left(\frac{\sin^2\theta}{\cos\theta}\right)^2\left\{\left(\frac{\cos^2\theta}{\sin\theta}\right)^2 + \left(\frac{\sin^2\theta}{\cos\theta}\right)^2 + 3\right\}$$

$$= \cos^2\theta\sin^2\theta\left\{\frac{\cos^6\theta + \sin^6\theta + 3\cos^2\theta\sin^2\theta}{\cos^2\theta\sin^2\theta}\right\}$$

$= \cos^6\theta + \sin^6\theta + 3\cos^2\theta\sin^2\theta$

$= (\cos^2\theta)^3 + (\sin^2\theta)^3 + 3\cos^2\theta\sin^2\theta$
$(\sin^2\theta + \cos^2\theta)$

$= (\sin^2\theta + \cos^2\theta)^3$

$= 1 = \text{RHS}$ **Hence proved.** (2½)

**18.** $$\text{LHS} = \frac{\cot^2 A(\sec A - 1)}{1 + \sin A} = \frac{\frac{\cos^2 A}{\sin^2 A}\left(\frac{1}{\cos A} - 1\right)}{1 + \sin A} \quad (1)$$

$\left[\because \cot A = \frac{\cos A}{\sin A} \text{ and } \sec A = \frac{1}{\cos A}\right]$

$$= \frac{\frac{\cos^2 A}{\sin^2 A}\left(\frac{1 - \cos A}{\cos A}\right)}{1 + \sin A} = \frac{\cos A(1 - \cos A)}{\sin^2 A(1 + \sin A)}$$

$$= \frac{\cos A(1 - \cos A)}{(1 - \cos^2 A)(1 + \sin A)} \quad (1)$$

$[\because \sin^2 A = 1 - \cos^2 A]$

$$= \frac{\cos A(1 - \cos A)}{(1 - \cos A)(1 + \cos A)(1 + \sin A)}$$

$[\because a^2 - b^2 = (a+b)(a-b)]$

$$= \frac{\cos A}{(1 + \cos A)(1 + \sin A)}$$

$$= \frac{\cos A(1 - \sin A)}{(1 + \cos A)(1 + \sin A)(1 - \sin A)} \quad (1)$$

[multiplying numerator and denominator by $(1 - \sin A)$]

$$= \frac{\cos A(1 - \sin A)}{(1 + \cos A)(1 - \sin^2 A)}$$

$[\because (a-b)(a+b) = a^2 - b^2]$ (1)

$$= \frac{\cos A(1 - \sin A)}{(1 + \cos A)\cos^2 A} \quad [\because 1 - \sin^2 A = \cos^2 A]$$

$$= \frac{1}{\cos A} \cdot \frac{(1 - \sin A)}{(1 + \cos A)}$$

**Hence proved.** (1)

## Chapter 9 **Some Applications of Trigonometry**

**1.** (*b*) Let $AB$ be the tower and $O$ be the point of observation.

Given, $AB = \frac{100}{\sqrt{3}}$ m and $OA = 100$ m

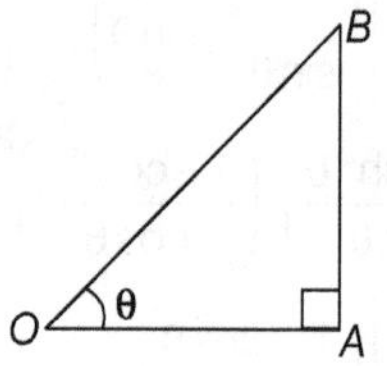


Then, $\tan\theta = \frac{AB}{OA} = \frac{\frac{100}{\sqrt{3}}}{100} = \frac{1}{\sqrt{3}} \Rightarrow \theta = 30°$

**2.** (*b*) Let $AB$ be the tower and $C, D$ be the points of observation.

Given, $\angle BCD = 30°$, $\angle BDA = 60°$, $CD = 20$ m

Let $DA = x$ m.

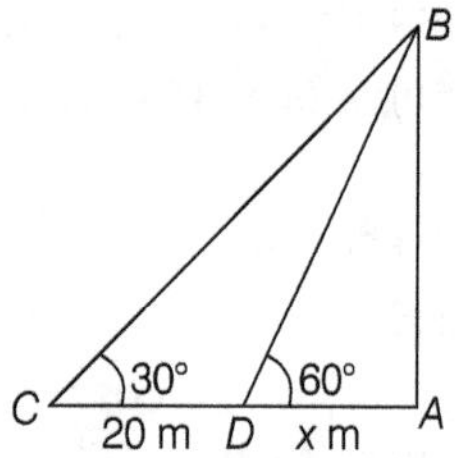


Then, $\frac{AB}{AD} = \tan 60° = \sqrt{3}$

$\Rightarrow \frac{AB}{x} = \sqrt{3}$

$\Rightarrow AB = \sqrt{3}x$

and $\frac{AB}{AC} = \tan 30°$

$\Rightarrow AB = \frac{20 + x}{\sqrt{3}}$

$\therefore \sqrt{3}x = \frac{20 + x}{\sqrt{3}}$

$\Rightarrow 3x = 20 + x \Rightarrow x = 10$ m

The height of the tower $= 10\sqrt{3}$ m

**3.** (*b*) Let $AB$ be the tower and $AC$ be the horizontal line such that $AC = 30$ m, $\angle BCA = \angle XBC = 45°$

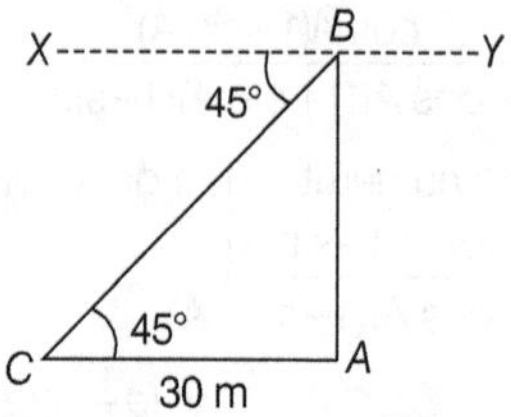


$\frac{AB}{CA} = \tan 45° = 1$

$\Rightarrow \frac{AB}{30} = 1 \Rightarrow AB = 30$ m

**4.** Let $AB = 40$ m be the height of tower and the angle of depression is

$\angle DAC = 30°$ i.e. $\angle ACB = 30°$ [alternate angles]

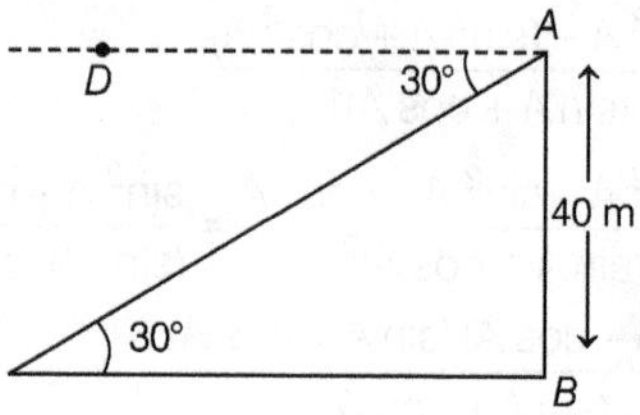


(1)

In rigth angled $\Delta ABC$, $\sin 30° = \frac{AB}{AC}$

$\Rightarrow \frac{1}{2} = \frac{40}{AC}$

$\therefore AC = 80$ m

Hence, the distance of the point from top of the tower is 80 m. (1)

**5.** Let $AB$ be the length of the shadow and height of the pole $BC = 18$ m and angle of elevation $\angle BAC = \theta$.

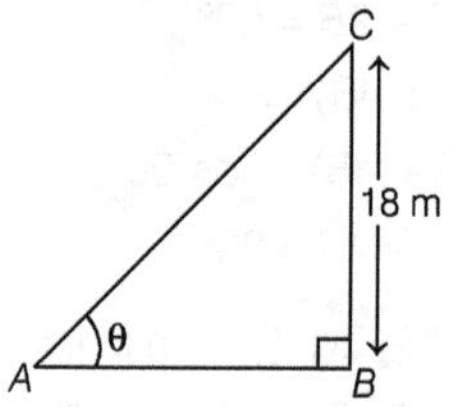


(1)

In right angled $\Delta ABC$,

$\tan\theta = \frac{BC}{AB}$ $\left[\because \tan\theta = \frac{\text{perpendicular}}{\text{base}}\right]$

$\Rightarrow \frac{6}{7} = \frac{18}{AB}$ $\left[\tan\theta = \frac{6}{7}, \text{given}\right]$

$\Rightarrow 6 \times AB = 18 \times 7$

$\Rightarrow AB = \frac{18 \times 7}{6} = 21$

Hence, the length of the shadow is 21 m. (1)

**6.** Let $AB = x$ m be the height of a tower and $CD = y$ m be the height of other tower and $\angle AEB = 45°$ and $\angle CED = 60°$.

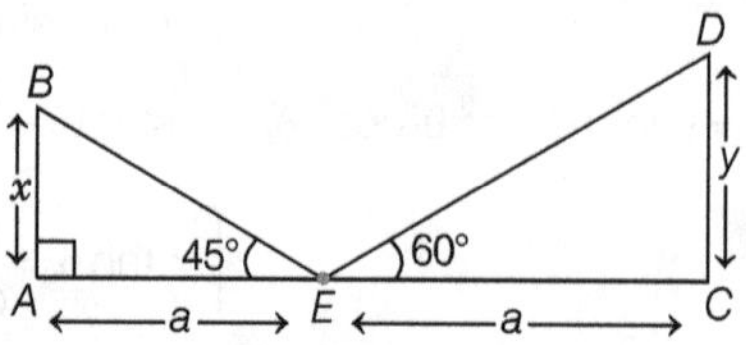


Let $E$ be the point (centre) on the line $AC$.

i.e. $AE = EC = a$

In right angled $\Delta BAE$,

$\tan 45° = \frac{AB}{AE}$ $\left[\because \tan\theta = \frac{\text{perpendicular}}{\text{base}}\right]$

$\Rightarrow \frac{x}{a} = 1$ $[\because \tan 45° = 1]$

$\Rightarrow x = a$ ...(i) (1)

Again, in right angled $\Delta DCE$, $\tan 60° = \dfrac{DC}{CE}$

$\Rightarrow$ $\sqrt{3} = \dfrac{y}{a}$ $[\because \tan 60° = \sqrt{3}]$

$\Rightarrow$ $y = \sqrt{3}a$ ...(ii)

$\therefore$ $(x + y):y = (a + \sqrt{3}a):a\sqrt{3} = (1 + \sqrt{3}):\sqrt{3}$

[by Eqs. (i) and (ii)]

Hence, the requred ratio $(x + y):y$ is $(1 + \sqrt{3}):\sqrt{3}$. (1)

**7.** Let $AB$ be the tower and $CD$ be the hill.

Then, $\angle CAD = 60°$, $\angle ACB = 30°$ and $AB = 65$ m.

Let $CD = x$ m

From right angled $\Delta BAC$,

$$\frac{AC}{AB} = \cot 30° = \sqrt{3} \Rightarrow AC = 65\sqrt{3} \text{ m}$$

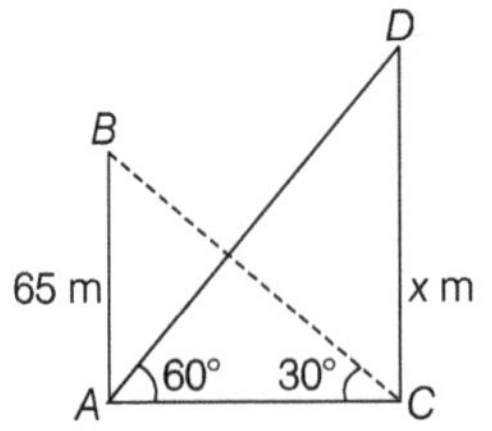


(1)

From right angled $\Delta ACD$,

$$\frac{CD}{AC} = \tan 60° = \sqrt{3} \Rightarrow CD = 65\sqrt{3} \times \sqrt{3} = 195 \text{ m}$$ (1)

**8.** Let the Sun's altitude at that time be $\theta$ and let $AB$ be the height of tower and $CB$ be the shadow of the tower such that $AB = CB$

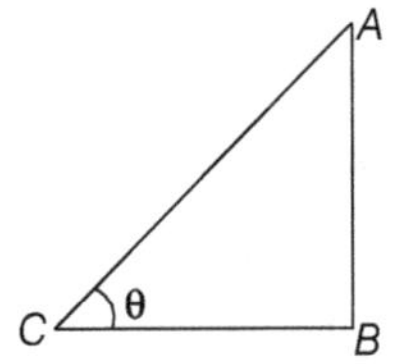


$$\therefore \tan\theta = \frac{AB}{CB} = \frac{AB}{AB} = 1 \Rightarrow \tan\theta = \tan 45° \Rightarrow \theta = 45°$$ (2)

**9.** Let $OP$ be the pedestal and $PQ$ be the statue of height 2.4 m.

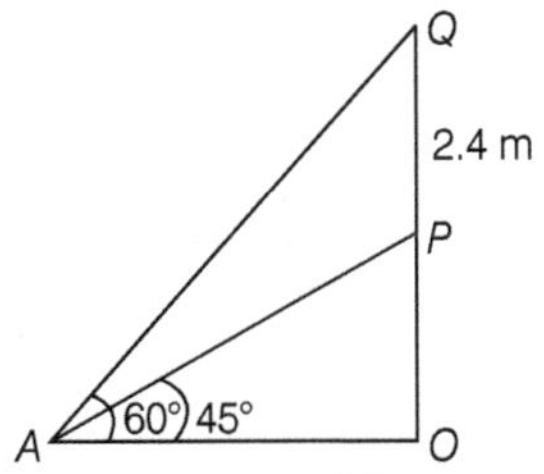


In $\Delta AOP$, $\tan 45° = \dfrac{OP}{AO}$

$\Rightarrow$ $1 = \dfrac{OP}{AO}$

$\Rightarrow$ $OA = OP$ ...(i)

and in $\Delta AOQ$, $\tan 60° = \dfrac{OQ}{AO}$

$\Rightarrow$ $\sqrt{3} = \dfrac{PQ + PO}{AO}$

$\Rightarrow$ $\sqrt{3} = \dfrac{2.4 + PO}{OP}$ [from Eq. (i)] (1)

$\Rightarrow$ $OP(\sqrt{3} - 1) = 2.4$

$\Rightarrow$ $OP = \dfrac{2.4}{(\sqrt{3} - 1)} \times \dfrac{\sqrt{3} + 1}{\sqrt{3} + 1}$

$= \dfrac{2.4 \times (\sqrt{3} + 1)}{3 - 1} = \dfrac{2.4}{2}(\sqrt{3} + 1)$

$= 1.2 \times (\sqrt{3} + 1)$ m

Hence, height of pedestal is $1.2 \times (\sqrt{3} + 1)$ m. (1)

**10.** Let $CD = h$ m be the height of the tower.

Let $A$ and $B$ be any two objects on the line.

From top of the tower say $D$, the angles of depression of objects are $\angle ODA = \alpha$ and $\angle ODB = \beta$.

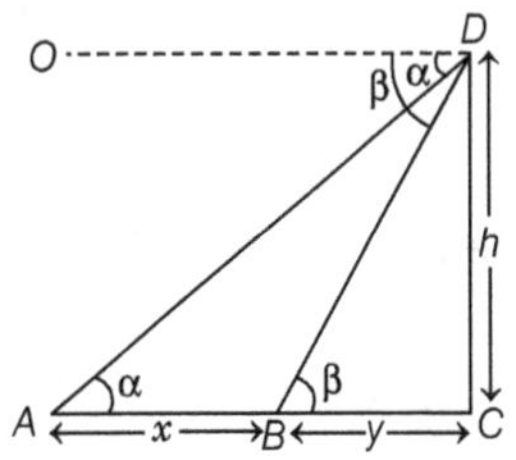


$\Rightarrow \angle DAC = \alpha$ and $\angle DBC = \beta$ [alternate angles] (1)

Let the distance between two objects

$$AB = x \text{ m and } BC = y \text{ m}$$

In right angled $\Delta ACD$,

$$\tan\alpha = \frac{CD}{AC}$$

$\Rightarrow$ $\tan\alpha = \dfrac{h}{AB + BC} \Rightarrow \tan\alpha = \dfrac{h}{x + y}$

$\Rightarrow$ $x + y = h\cot\alpha$ ...(i) (1)

In right angled $\Delta BCD$,

$$\tan\beta = \frac{CD}{BC} = \frac{h}{y}$$

$\Rightarrow$ $y = h\cot\beta$

On putting $y = h\cot\beta$ in Eq. (i), we get

$$x + h\cot\beta = h\cot\alpha$$

$\Rightarrow$ $x = h(\cot\alpha - \cot\beta)$

Hence, the distance between two objects is $h(\cot\alpha - \cot\beta)$. **Hence proved.** (1)

**11.** Let $h$ be the height of aeroplane $P$ above the road. $A$ and $B$ be two consecutive milestones and $\alpha, \beta$ be the angle of depression of two points.

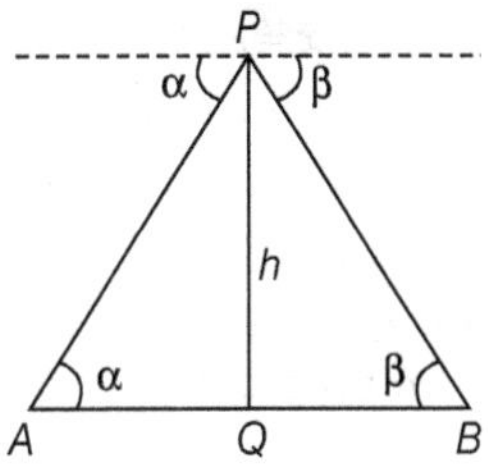

Then, $AB = 1$ mile (1)

In $\Delta AQP$, $\tan\alpha = \dfrac{PQ}{AQ}$

$\Rightarrow$ $\tan\alpha = \dfrac{h}{AQ}$

$AQ = h\cot\alpha$ ...(i)

and in $\Delta BQP$, $\tan\beta = \dfrac{PQ}{BQ} \Rightarrow \tan\beta = \dfrac{h}{BQ}$

$\Rightarrow$ $BQ = h\cot\beta$ ...(ii) (1)

On adding Eqs. (i) and (ii), we get

$$AQ + BQ = h\cot\alpha + h\cot\beta$$

$$\Rightarrow \quad AB = h\left(\frac{1}{\tan\alpha} + \frac{1}{\tan\beta}\right)$$

$$\Rightarrow \quad 1 = h\left(\frac{\tan\beta + \tan\alpha}{\tan\alpha\tan\beta}\right)$$

$$\Rightarrow \quad h = \frac{\tan\alpha\tan\beta}{\tan\alpha + \tan\beta}$$ **Hence proved.** (1)

**12.** Let $AB$ and $CD$ be two pillars of equal height $h$ m and distance between them be $BD = 100$ m.

Let $E$ be a point on the road such that $BE = x$ m, $DE = (100 - x)$ m, $\angle AEB = 60°$ and $\angle CED = 30°$.

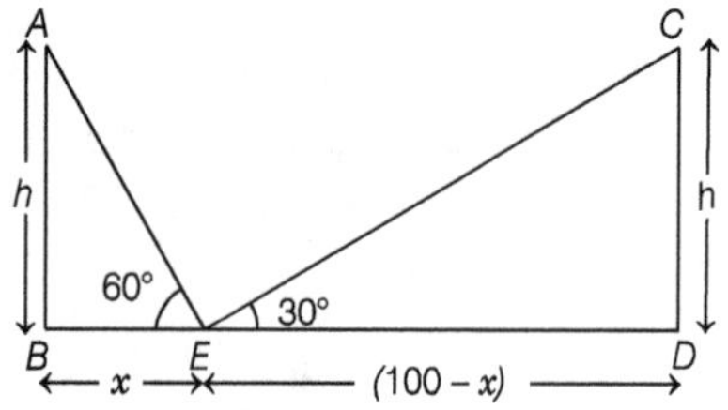


In right angled $\Delta ABE$,

$$\frac{AB}{BE} = \tan 60° \Rightarrow \frac{h}{x} = \sqrt{3} \quad [\because \tan 60° = \sqrt{3}]$$

$\Rightarrow$ $h = \sqrt{3}x$ ...(i) (1)

In right angled $\Delta CDE$,

$$\frac{CD}{DE} = \tan 30°$$

$$\Rightarrow \quad \frac{h}{100 - x} = \frac{1}{\sqrt{3}} \quad \left[\because \tan 30° = \frac{1}{\sqrt{3}}\right]$$

$\Rightarrow$ $h = \dfrac{100 - x}{\sqrt{3}}$ ...(ii) (1)

From Eqs. (i) and (ii), we get

$$\sqrt{3}x = \frac{100 - x}{\sqrt{3}}$$

$\Rightarrow$ $3x = 100 - x$

$\Rightarrow$ $4x = 100$

$\therefore$ $x = 25$

On putting $x = 25$ in Eq. (i), we get

$$h = \sqrt{3} \times 25 = 25 \times 1.732$$
$$= 43.3 \text{ m}$$

Hence, height of each pillar is 43.3 m and position of the point from the pillar making an angle of 60° is 25 m. (1)

**13.** Let initially, position of aeroplane be $A$ and after 15 s, its position be $C$.
So, $AC$ is the distance covered in 15 s.

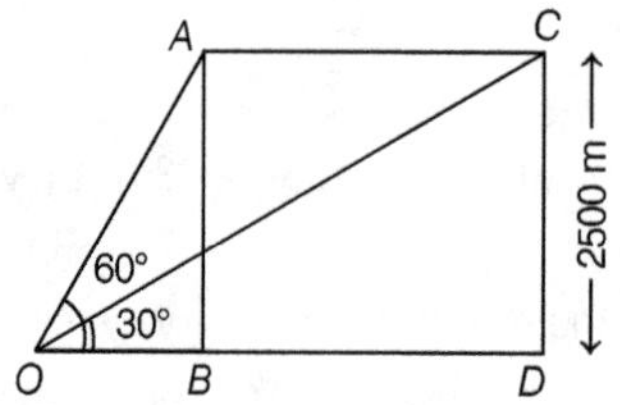


Also, $\angle AOB = 60°$, $\angle COD = 30°$, $AB = CD = 2500$ m (1)

In right angled $\Delta ABO$,

$$\frac{OB}{AB} = \cot 60° \Rightarrow \frac{OB}{2500} = \frac{1}{\sqrt{3}} \left[\because \cot 60° = \frac{1}{\sqrt{3}}\right]$$

$\Rightarrow$ $OB = \dfrac{2500}{\sqrt{3}}$ ...(i)

In right angled $\Delta CDO$,

$$\frac{OD}{CD} = \cot 30° \Rightarrow \frac{OD}{2500} = \sqrt{3}$$

$[\because \cot 30° = \sqrt{3}]$

$\Rightarrow$ $OD = 2500\sqrt{3}$ m ...(ii)

Now, $BD = OD - OB = 2500\sqrt{3} - \dfrac{2500}{\sqrt{3}}$ (1)

[from Eqs. (i) and (ii)]

$$= 2500\left(\sqrt{3} - \frac{1}{\sqrt{3}}\right)$$

$$\Rightarrow \quad BD = 2500\left(\frac{3-1}{\sqrt{3}}\right) = \frac{2500 \times 2 \times \sqrt{3}}{3}$$

$$= \frac{5000 \times 1.732}{3} = \frac{8660}{3} \text{ m}$$ (1)

Hence, $\dfrac{8660}{3}$ m distance is covered in 15 s.

$$\therefore \quad \text{Speed} = \frac{8660}{3 \times 15} \text{ m/s} = \frac{8660}{3 \times 15 \times 1000} \times 60 \times 60$$

$= 692.8$ km/h

So, the speed of aeroplane is 692.8 km/h. (2)

**14.** Let $QR$ be the surface of the lake and $P$ be point above the surface such that $PQ = 36$ m. Let $B$ represents the bird and $B'$ be its image in the lake.

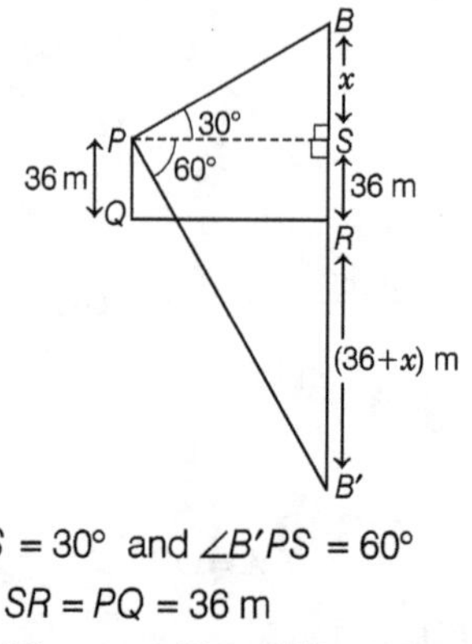


(1)

$\therefore$ $\angle BPS = 30°$ and $\angle B'PS = 60°$

Also, $SR = PQ = 36$ m

Let $BS = x \Rightarrow B'R = BR = (36 + x)$ m

$\therefore$ $B'S = SR + B'R = 36 + 36 + x = (72 + x)$ m (1)

In right angled $\Delta PSB$,

$$\frac{BS}{PS} = \tan 30^\circ$$

$\therefore$ $\frac{x}{PS} = \frac{1}{\sqrt{3}}$ $\left[\because \tan 30^\circ = \frac{1}{\sqrt{3}}\right]$

$\Rightarrow$ $PS = \sqrt{3}x$ ...(i) (1)

Again, in right angled $\Delta B'SP$,

$$\frac{B'S}{PS} = \tan 60^\circ \Rightarrow \frac{72 + x}{PS} = \sqrt{3}$$

[$\because$ $B'S = (72+x)$ m and $\tan 60^\circ = \sqrt{3}$]

$\Rightarrow$ $PS = \frac{72 + x}{\sqrt{3}}$ ...(ii) (1)

From Eqs. (i) and (ii), we get

$$\sqrt{3}x = \frac{72 + x}{\sqrt{3}} \Rightarrow \sqrt{3}\cdot\sqrt{3}x = 72 + x$$

$\Rightarrow$ $3x - x = 72 \Rightarrow 2x = 72$

$\Rightarrow$ $x = \frac{72}{2} \Rightarrow x = 36$

$\therefore$ Height of bird above surface of the lake,

$BR = BS + SR = 36 + 36 = 72$ m (1)

# Chapter 10 **Circles**

**1.** (*b*) Here, $OA \perp AP$

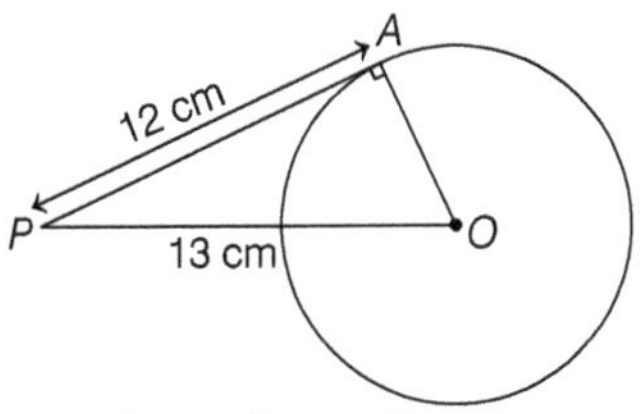


In $\Delta AOP$, $OP^2 = OA^2 + AP^2$

$\Rightarrow$ $13^2 = OA^2 + 12^2$

$\Rightarrow$ $OA^2 = 13^2 - 12^2 = 169 - 144 = 25$

$\Rightarrow$ $OA = 5$ cm

$\therefore$ Diameter $= 2 \times 5 = 10$ cm

**2.** (*a*) In quadrilateral $PBOA$,

$\angle APB + \angle AOB = 180^\circ$

$\therefore$ $\angle AOB = 180^\circ - 80^\circ = 100^\circ$

$\Rightarrow$ $\angle AOB = 100^\circ$

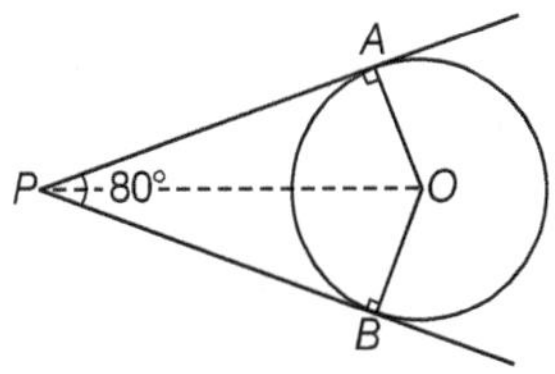


and $\angle POA = \frac{1}{2}\angle AOB$ [$\because$ $\Delta OAP \cong \Delta OBP$]

$= \frac{1}{2} \times 100^\circ = 50^\circ$

**3.** (*d*) Given, $AB$ is a diameter of circle with centre $O$.

$\angle ARB = 90^\circ$ [$\because$ angle in a semi-circle]

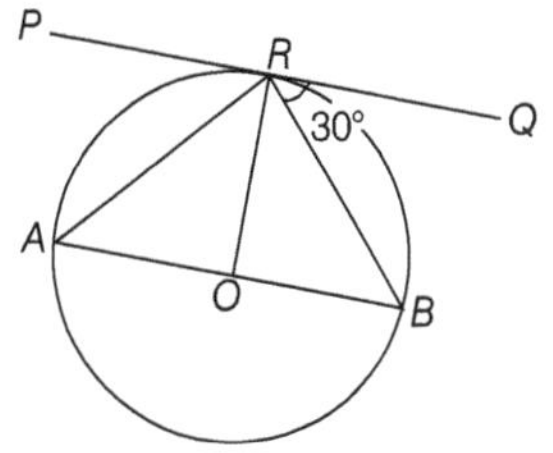


$\therefore \angle PRA + \angle ARB + \angle QRB = 180^\circ$ [linear pair]

$\Rightarrow$ $\angle PRA + 90^\circ + 30^\circ = 180^\circ$

$\therefore$ $\angle PRA = 60^\circ$

**4.** (*a*) Here, $PL = PM = 4$ cm

[tangents from an external point are equal]

$QK = QM = 5$ cm

[tangents from an external points are equal]

$RK = RL = RP - PL = 12 - 4 = 8$ cm

$\therefore$ $QR = QK + RK = 5 + 8 = 13$ cm

**5.** Since, a tangent to a circle is perpendicular to the radius through the point of contact.

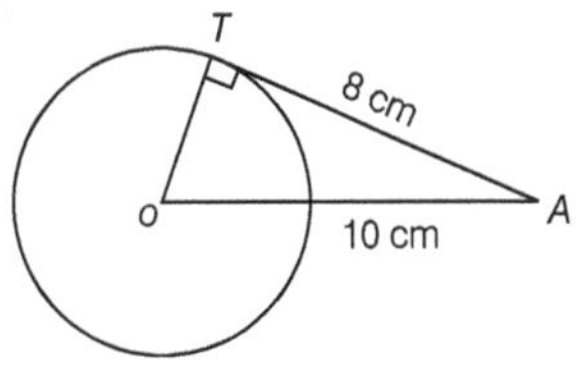


$\therefore$ $\angle OTA = 90^\circ$ (1)

Now, in right $\Delta OTA$, $OA^2 = OT^2 + AT^2$

$\Rightarrow$ $(10)^2 = OT^2 + (8)^2$

$\Rightarrow$ $OT^2 = (10)^2 - (8)^2$

$= (10 - 8)(10 + 8) = 36$

$\therefore$ $OT = +\sqrt{36} = 6$ cm (1)

[$\because$ length is always positive, so we take positive sign]

Hence, radius of circle is 6 cm.

**6.** Here, $\angle OBA = 90^\circ$

[$\because$ tangent to a circle is perpendicular to the radius through the point of contact]

$\angle AOB = 180^\circ - 130^\circ = 50^\circ$ [linear pair]

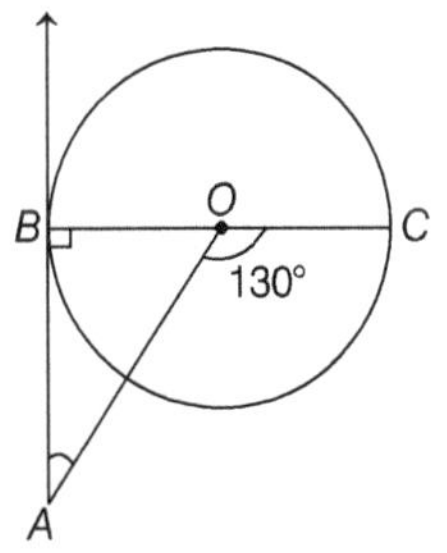


(1)

In $\Delta AOB$, $\angle OAB + \angle ABO + \angle AOB = 180^\circ$

(angle sum property of triangle)

$\Rightarrow$ $\angle OAB + 90^\circ + 50^\circ = 180^\circ$

$\Rightarrow$ $\angle OAB + 140^\circ = 180^\circ$

$\Rightarrow$ $\angle OAB = 40^\circ$ (1)

**7.** Let $OP$ be radius and $AB$ be tangent of the inner circle.

$\therefore$ $OP \perp AB$ [$\because$ tangent is perpendicular to the radius at the point of contact]

Again, let $OB$ be radius of outer circle.

Here, $OP = 3\,\text{cm}, OB = 5\,\text{cm}$

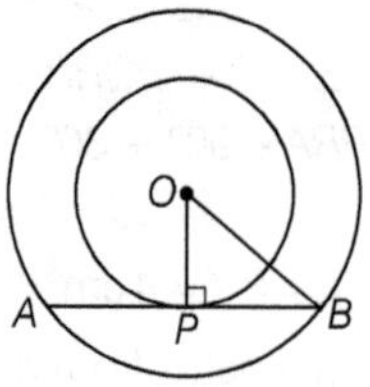


In right angled $\Delta OPB$,

$$(PB)^2 = (OB)^2 - (OP)^2$$

[by using Pythagoras theorem]

$\Rightarrow$ $PB = \sqrt{(5)^2 - (3)^2}$ (1)

[taking positive square root both sides]

$= \sqrt{25-9} = \sqrt{16} = 4\,\text{cm}$

$\therefore$ $AB = 2PB = 2 \times 4 = 8\,\text{cm}$

[$\because$ perpendicular from the centre to the chord bisects the chord]

Hence, the length of the chord of the outer circle which touches the inner circle is 8 cm. (1)

**8.** Given, $AB = AC \Rightarrow AF + FB = AE + EC$ ...(i)

Now, $BF = BD$

[$\because$ length of tangents drawn from an external point to a circle are equal]

and $CE = CD$ ...(ii)

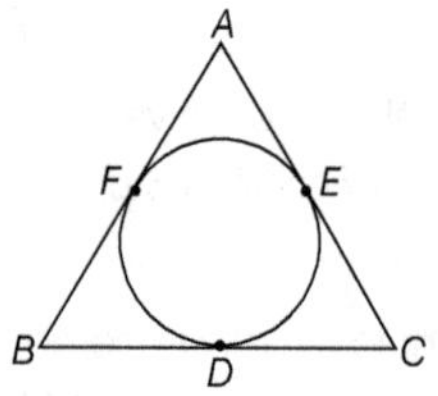


(1)

From Eqs. (i) and (ii),

$$AF + BD = AE + CD$$

$\Rightarrow$ $BD = CD$ [$\because AF = AE$]

**Hence proved.** (1)

**9. Given,** $BC = 3\,\text{cm}$, $AC = 4\,\text{cm}$

In $\Delta ACB, \angle BCA = 90°$ [angle in a semi-circle]

$\therefore$ $(AB)^2 = (AC)^2 + (BC)^2$ [by Pythagoras theorem]

$\Rightarrow$ $(AB)^2 = 4^2 + 3^2 \Rightarrow (AB)^2 = 16 + 9 \Rightarrow (AB)^2 = 25$

$\Rightarrow$ $AB = \sqrt{25} = 5\,\text{cm}$ (1)

[taking postive square root both sides]

$OA = OB$ [radius of circle]

$\Rightarrow$ $AB = OA + OB \Rightarrow 5 = OA + OA = 2OA$

$\Rightarrow$ $OA = \frac{5}{2} = 2.5\,\text{cm}$

Also given, $\Delta ACB \sim \Delta PAO$

$\therefore$ $\frac{AB}{AC} = \frac{OP}{AP} \Rightarrow \frac{5}{4} = \frac{OP}{AP}$ i.e. $\frac{OP}{AP} = \frac{5}{4}$ (1)

**10.** We know that the tangents drawn from an external point to the circle are equal.

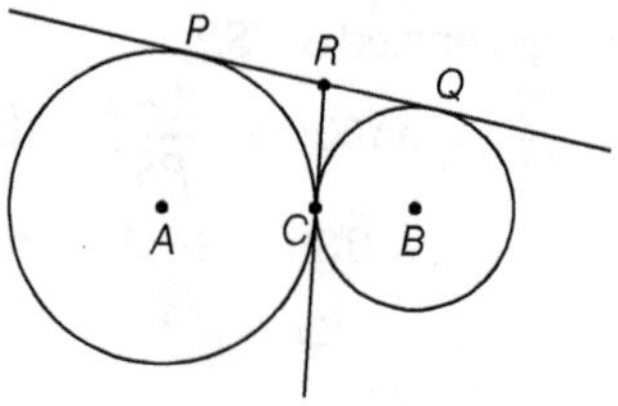


(1)

$\therefore$ $RP = RC$ and $RC = RQ$

$\Rightarrow RP = RQ$

$\Rightarrow R$ is the mid-point of $PQ$. **Hence proved.**(1)

**11.** Here, $a, b$ and $c$ are the sides of right angled $\Delta ABC$ such that $BC = a$, $CA = b$ and $AB = c$.

Let the circle touches the sides $BC$, $CA$, $AB$ at $D$, $E$ and $F$, respectively.

Then, $AE = AF$ and $BD = BF$

[$\because$ tangents drawn from an external point are equal in length]

Also, $CE = CD = r$ [$\because$ $CEOD$ is a square]

$\therefore$ $AF = b - r$ [as, $AE = b - r$]

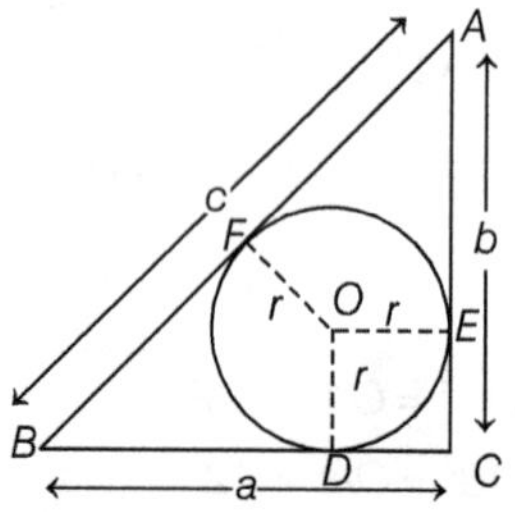


(1½)

$\Rightarrow$ $BF = a - r$ [as, $BD = a - r$]

Now, $AB = c$

$\Rightarrow$ $AF + BF = (b - r) + (a - r)$

$\Rightarrow$ $AB = b - r + a - r$

$\Rightarrow$ $c = a + b - 2r \Rightarrow 2r = a + b - c$

$\therefore$ $r = \frac{a+b-c}{2}$ **Hence proved.** (1½)

**12.** Let $PQ$ be the length of the common chord of two intersecting circles.

$\therefore$ $PQ = 30\,\text{cm}$ [given]

Diameters of two circles are 50 cm and 34 cm.

Join $AB$.

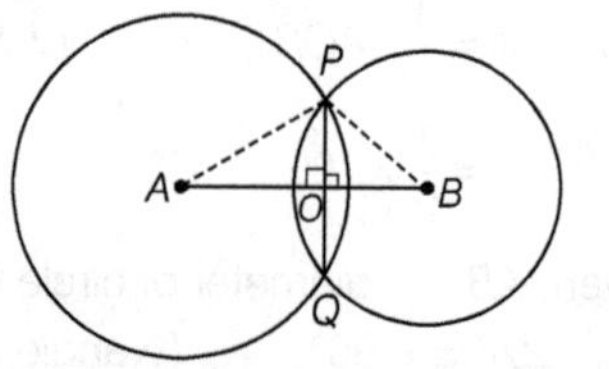

Since, $AB$ bisects the common chord $PQ$ perpendicularly.

$\therefore \quad OP = OQ = \frac{1}{2} \times PQ = \frac{1}{2} \times 30 = 15$ cm

Radius, $AP = \frac{1}{2} \times 50 = 25$ cm

and radius, $PB = \frac{1}{2} \times 34 = 17$ cm (1½)

In right angled $\Delta AOP$,

$OA = \sqrt{(AP)^2 - (OP)^2}$ [by using Pythagoras theorem]

$= \sqrt{(25)^2 - (15)^2}$

$= \sqrt{625 - 225} = \sqrt{400} = 20$ cm

In right angled $\Delta POB$,

$OB = \sqrt{(PB)^2 - (OP)^2} = \sqrt{(17)^2 - (15)^2}$ [by using Pythagoras theorem]

$= \sqrt{289 - 225} = \sqrt{64} = 8$ cm

$\therefore$ Distance between centres,

$AB = OA + OB = 20$ cm $+ 8$ cm $= 28$ cm (1½)

**13.** **Given** $O$ is the centre of the circle, $AB$ is diameter and $AT$ is tangent at $A$. Also, $\angle AOQ = 64°$

$\because$ $OA$ is radius and $AT$ is tangent.

$\therefore \quad \angle OAT = 90°$

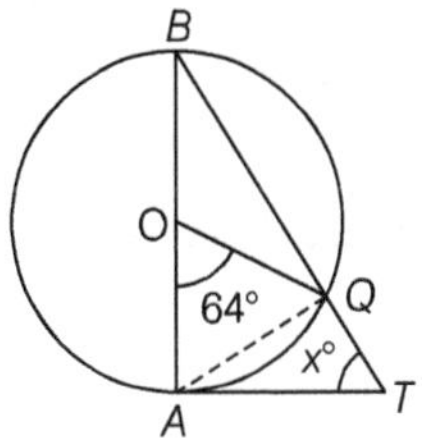


(1)

Also, $\angle AOQ = 64°$ [given]

$\therefore \quad \angle BOQ = 180° - \angle AOQ$ [linear pair axiom]

$= 180° - 64° = 116°$ ...(i)

But $OB = OQ$ [radii]

$\Rightarrow \angle OQB = \angle OBQ$

[$\because$ angles opposite to equal sides of a triangle are equal]

But $\angle OBQ + \angle OQB + \angle BOQ = 180°$

[by angle sum property of a triangle] (1)

$\Rightarrow \angle OBQ + \angle OQB = 180° - 116° = 64°$ [using Eq. (i)]

$\Rightarrow \angle OBQ + \angle OBQ = 64°$

$\Rightarrow \quad \angle OBQ = 32°$ [$\because \angle OBQ = \angle OQB$]

$\therefore \quad \angle OQB = 32°$

Now, in $\Delta BAT$, $\angle ABT + \angle BAT + \angle ATB = 180°$

$\Rightarrow \quad 32° + 90° + x° = 180°$ [$\because \angle BAT = \angle OAT = 90°$]

$\Rightarrow \quad x° = 180° - 32° - 90°$

$\Rightarrow \quad x° = 58°$ (1)

**14.** **Given** A circle with centre $O$. $PA$ and $PB$ are tangents to the circle from $P$, outside the circle such that $\angle APB = 120°$.

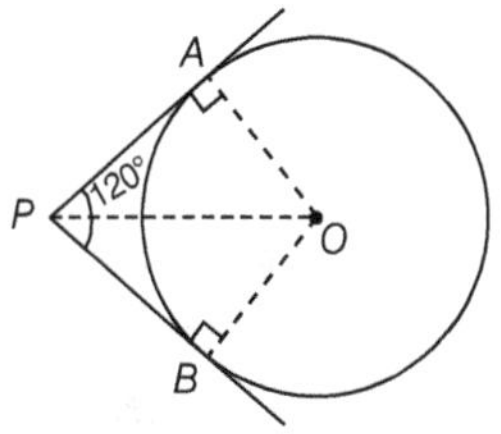


**To prove** $OP = 2\,AP$

**Construction** Join $OA$, $OB$ and $OP$. (1)

**Proof** In $\Delta PAO$ and $\Delta PBO$,

$PA = PB$

[$\because$ tangents drawn to a circle from an external point are equal in length]

$OP = OP$ [common sides]

$\angle OAP = \angle OBP = 90°$

[$\because$ tangent is perpendicular to the radius at the point of contact]

$\therefore \quad \Delta PAO \cong \Delta PBO$ [by RHS congruency rule]

Then, $\angle OPA = \angle OPB = \frac{1}{2} \angle APB = \frac{1}{2} \times 120° = 60°$ (1)

In right angled $\Delta OAP$, $\frac{AP}{OP} = \cos 60° = \frac{1}{2}$

$\left[\because \frac{\text{base}}{\text{hypotenuse}} = \cos\theta \text{ and } \cos 60° = \frac{1}{2}\right]$

$\Rightarrow \quad OP = 2AP$ **Hence proved.** (1)

**15.** In $\Delta AOC$, $OA = OC$ [radii of the same circle]

$\therefore \quad \angle ACO = \angle CAO$ [$\because$ angles opposite to equal sides of a triangle are equal]

$\Rightarrow \angle ACO = \angle CAO = 30°$

[$\because \angle CAO = \angle CAB = 30°$, given] ...(i) (1)

Also, $\angle ACB = 90°$ [angle in semi-circle]

$\therefore \quad \angle OCB = \angle ACB - \angle ACO = 90° - 30° = 60°$

[from Eq. (i)]

In $\Delta COB$, $OC = OB$ [radii of the same circle]

$\therefore \quad \angle OBC = \angle OCB = 60°$

[$\because$ angles opposite to equal sides of a triangle are equal] ...(ii)

Now, $OC \perp CQ$ (1)

[$\because$ tangent at any point of a circle is perpendicular to radius through the point of contact]

$\therefore \quad \angle OCQ = 90°$

Now, $\angle BCQ = \angle OCQ - \angle OCB$

$= 90° - 60° = 30°$ [from Eq. (ii)] ...(iii)

Also, $\angle OBC + \angle CBQ = 180°$ [linear pair]

$\Rightarrow \quad 60° + \angle CBQ = 180°$ [from Eq. (ii)]

$\therefore \quad \angle CBQ = 120°$ ...(iv)

In $\Delta CBQ$, $\angle BCQ + \angle CBQ + \angle CQB = 180°$ (1)

[$\because$ sum of all angles of a triangle is 180°]

$\Rightarrow$ $30° + 120° + \angle CQB = 180°$ [from Eqs. (iii) and (iv)]

$\Rightarrow$ $\angle CQB = 30°$

$\therefore$ $\angle CQA = \angle CQB = 30°$

and $\angle CBA = \angle OBC = 60°$ [from Eq. (ii)]

Hence, $\angle CQA = 30°$ and $\angle CBA = 60°$ (2)

**16.** Let $PQ$ and $PR$ are two tangents drawn from an external point $P$ to a circle with centre $O$.

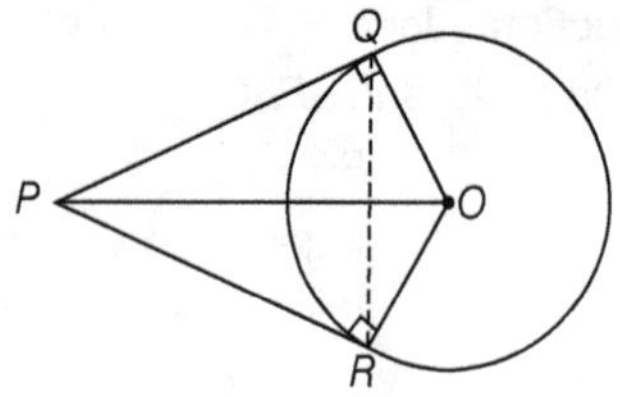


**To prove** $\angle QOR = 180° - \angle QPR$

$\Rightarrow$ $\angle QOR + \angle QPR = 180°$ (1)

**Proof** In right angled $\Delta OQP$ and $\Delta ORP$,

$PQ = PR$

[$\because$ tangents drawn from an external point are equal in length]

$OQ = OR$ [radii of same circle]

$OP = OP$ [common]

$\therefore$ $\Delta OQP \cong \Delta ORP$ [by SSS congruency] (1)

Then, $\angle QPO = \angle RPO$ [by CPCT]

and $\angle POQ = \angle POR$ [by CPCT]

$\Rightarrow$ $\left.\begin{array}{l}\angle QPR = 2\angle OPQ\\ \angle QOR = 2\angle POQ\end{array}\right\}$ ...(i)

In $\Delta OPQ$, $\angle QPO + \angle QOP = 90°$ [$\because \angle PQO = 90°$]

$\Rightarrow$ $\angle QOP = 90° - \angle QPO$ (1)

$\Rightarrow$ $2\angle QOP = 180° - 2\angle QPO$

[multiplying by 2 both sides]

$\Rightarrow$ $\angle QOR = 180° - \angle QPR$ [from Eq. (i)]

$\Rightarrow$ $\angle QOR + \angle QPR = 180°$ **Hence proved.** (2)

**17.** Given, $PT$ and $PAB$ be a tangent and a secant, respectively of a circle.

Also, $PT = 6$ cm and $AB = 5$ cm.

Join $OT$, $OA$ and $OP$. Draw $OC \perp AB$. (1)

Let radius of circle be $r$.

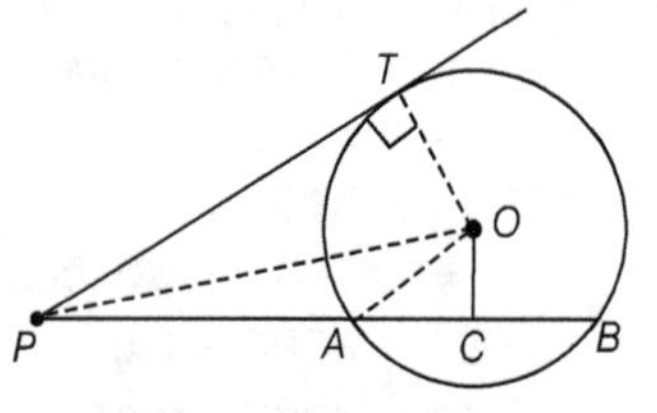


$\because$ $OT \perp PT$ [$\because$ tangent is perpendicular to the radius at the point of contact]

In right angled $\Delta OTP$,

$(OP)^2 = (PT)^2 + (OT)^2$ [by Pythagoras theorem]

$\Rightarrow$ $(OP)^2 = 6^2 + r^2$

$\Rightarrow$ $(OP)^2 - r^2 = 36$

$\Rightarrow$ $(OP)^2 - (OA)^2 = 36$ [$\because OA = OT = r$]...(i)

Also, in right angled $\Delta OCA$,

$(OA)^2 = (OC)^2 + (AC)^2$ [by Pythagoras theorem] (1)

On putting the value of $OA^2$ in Eq. (i), we get

$(OP)^2 - (OC^2 + AC^2) = 36$

$\Rightarrow$ $(OP)^2 - (OC)^2 - (AC)^2 = 36$

$\Rightarrow$ $(PC)^2 - (AC)^2 = 36$

[$\because$ in $\Delta OCP$, $(OP)^2 - (OC)^2 = (PC)^2$]

$\Rightarrow$ $(PC - AC)(PC + AC) = 36$

[$a^2 - b^2 = (a-b)(a+b)$]

$\Rightarrow$ $AP\,(PC + BC) = 36$

[$\because$ $AC = BC$, as perpendicular from centre to the chord bisects the chord] (1)

$\Rightarrow$ $AP\,(PB) = 36$

$\Rightarrow$ $AP\,(AP + AB) = 36$

$\Rightarrow$ $AP\,(AP + 5) = 36$ [$\because AB = 5$ cm]

$\Rightarrow$ $AP^2 + 5AP - 36 = 0$

$\Rightarrow$ $(AP + 9)(AP - 4) = 0$

$\Rightarrow$ $AP = 4$ or $-9$

Hence, $AP = 4$ cm [$\because$ side cannot be negative] (2)

## Chapter 11 Areas Related to Circles

**1.** (*d*) Given, $2\pi r = 44$

$\Rightarrow$ $2 \times \frac{22}{7} \times r = 44$

$\Rightarrow$ $r = 7$ cm

The central angle of a quadrant of a circle is 90°.

$\therefore$ Area of quadrant $= \frac{\theta}{360°} \times \pi r^2$

$= \frac{90°}{360°} \times \frac{22}{7} \times 7 \times 7 = \frac{77}{2}\text{ cm}^2$

**2.** (*b*) Area of the segment, $\frac{\pi r^2\theta}{360°} - \frac{1}{2}r^2\sin\theta$

$= \frac{\frac{22}{7} \times 21 \times 21 \times 60°}{360°} - \frac{1}{2} \times 21 \times 21 \times \sin 60°$

$= 231 - 191 = 40\text{ cm}^2$

**3.** (*d*) Circumference of the wheel $= 2\pi r$

$= 2 \times \frac{22}{7} \times 14$ cm

$= 88$ cm

Distance covered in 50 complete rotation is

$88 \times 50 = 4400$ cm

**4.** (a) Let $r$ m and $R$ m be the radii of the inner and outer boundaries.

Then, $2\pi r = 437$ and $2\pi R = 503$

$$\Rightarrow \quad r = \frac{437}{2\pi} \text{ and } R = \frac{503}{2\pi}$$

$$\text{Width of the track} = (R - r)\text{ m} = \frac{503 - 437}{2\pi}\text{ m}$$

$$= \frac{66}{2 \times \frac{22}{7}}\text{ m} = \frac{66 \times 7}{44}\text{ m} = 10.5\text{ m}$$

**5.** (c) Given, circumference = Area

$$\Rightarrow \quad 2\pi r = \pi r^2 \Rightarrow r = 2 \text{ units}$$

**6.** Length of the minute hand

= Radius of a circle ($r$) = 14 cm

Area swept in 1 h = Area of sector = $\frac{\pi r^2 \theta}{360°}$ (1)

$$= \frac{\pi r^2 \times 360°}{360°} = \pi r^2 = \frac{22}{7} \times 14 \times 14 \quad [\because \theta = 360°]$$

$$= 22 \times 28 = 616 \text{ cm}^2$$

Hence, the area swept out by the minute hand in 1 h is 616 $\text{cm}^2$. (1)

**7.** Let radius of protractor, $r = 3.5$ cm

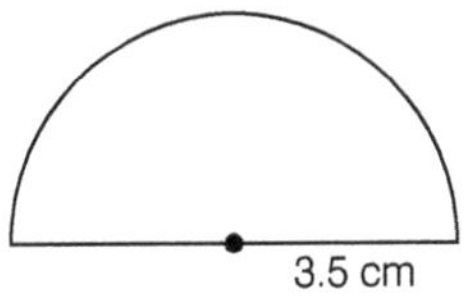


(1)

Then, perimeter of protractor = $\pi r + 2r$

$$= \frac{22}{7} \times 3.5 + 2 \times 3.5$$

$$= 11 + 7 = 18 \text{ cm} \quad (1)$$

**8.** Let the radius of the circle be $r$ units.

Area of the given circle = $\pi r^2$

The radius when halved = $\frac{r}{2}$

New area of the circle = $\pi\left(\frac{r}{2}\right)^2 = \frac{\pi r^2}{4}$ (1)

$\therefore$ Required ratio = $\frac{\pi r^2}{4} : \pi r^2 = 1 : 4$

Hence, the ratio of area of the new circle to the given circle is 1 : 4. (1)

**9.** Given, umbrella to be a flat circle. So, the central angle of an umbrella is 360°.

Since, umbrella has 8 ribs.

$\therefore$ Angle between two ribs = $\frac{360°}{8} = 45°$ (1)

Area between two ribs

= Area of one sector of the umbrella

$$= \frac{\theta}{360°} \times \pi r^2 = \frac{45°}{360°} \times \frac{22}{7} \times (45)^2 \quad [\because r = 45, \text{ given}]$$

$$= \frac{22}{7 \times 8}(45)^2 = \frac{22275}{28} \text{ cm}^2 \quad (1)$$

**10.** Distance covered in 1 s = 1.1 m

Distance covered in 88 s

$= 1.1 \times 88 = 96.8$ m [$\because$ 1 min 28 s = 60 + 28 = 88 s]

$= 9680$ cm [$\because$ 1 m = 100 cm] (1)

Now, distance covered in one revolution

$$= 2\pi r = \frac{22}{7} \times 77 \quad [\because \text{diameter} = 2r = 77 \text{ cm}]$$

$$= 22 \times 11 = 242 \text{ cm}$$

Hence, the number of complete revolutions

$$= \frac{9680}{242} = 40 \quad (1)$$

**11.** Let $ABCD$ be a rectangular field of dimensions 20 m × 16 m.

Suppose, a cow is tied at a point $A$ and length of the rope, $AE = 14\text{ m} = r$ [say]

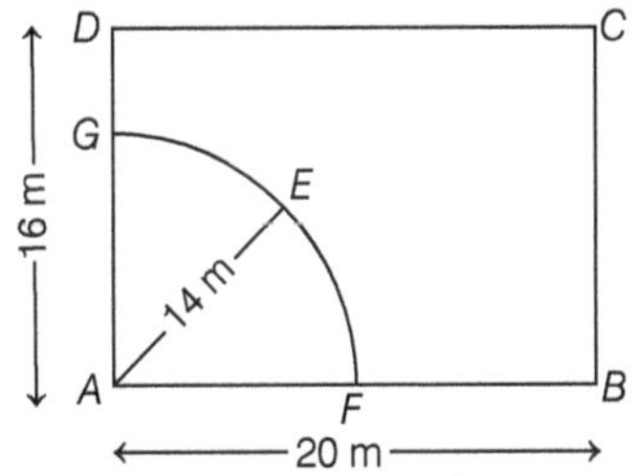


$\therefore$ Area of the field in which the cow graze

$$= \text{Area of sector } AFEG = \frac{\pi r^2 \theta}{360°} = \frac{\pi (14)^2 \cdot 90°}{360°} \quad (1)$$

[$\because$ $\theta = 90°$ i.e. shape of the field is rectangular]

$$= \pi \times 196 \times \frac{1}{4} = \frac{22}{7} \times 196 \times \frac{1}{4} = 154 \text{ m}^2 \quad (1)$$

**12.** Let the radius of the circle be $r$ cm.

Given, circumference – diameter = 24.6 cm

or $\quad 2\pi r - 2r = 24.6$

$\Rightarrow \quad \pi r - r = 12.3$

$\Rightarrow \quad r(\pi - 1) = 12.3 \Rightarrow r = \frac{12.3}{2.14}$

$\Rightarrow \quad r = 5.74$ (1½)

$\therefore$ Circumference of circle = $2\pi r$

$= 2 \times 3.14 \times 5.74$

$= 36.04$ cm (1½)

**13.** Given, radius of quadrant, $r = 3.5$ cm

Area of quadrant $OACB = \frac{1}{4} \times$ Area of circle

$$= \frac{1}{4} \times \pi r^2 \quad (1½)$$

$$= \frac{1}{4} \times \frac{22}{7} \times (3.5)^2$$

$$= \frac{1}{4} \times \frac{22}{7} \times 3.5 \times 3.5$$

$$= \frac{269.5}{28} = 9.625 \text{ cm}^2 \quad (1½)$$

**14.** Given, $\angle AOB = \angle COD = 30°$, $r_1 = OC = 7$ cm and $r_2 = OB = 21$ cm

$\therefore$ Area of sector $COD = \dfrac{\theta \pi r_1^2}{360°} = \dfrac{30°}{360°} \times \dfrac{22}{7} \times (7)^2$

$= \dfrac{1}{12} \times \dfrac{22}{7} \times 7 \times 7$

$= \dfrac{77}{6} = 12.83 \text{ cm}^2$ (1½)

and area of sector $OAB = \dfrac{\theta \pi r_2^2}{360°} = \dfrac{30°}{360°} \times \dfrac{22}{7} \times (21)^2$

$= \dfrac{1}{12} \times \dfrac{22}{7} \times 21 \times 21 = \dfrac{693}{6}$

$= 115.50 \text{ cm}^2$ (1½)

**15.** Given, diameter of circle, $d = 35$ mm

$\therefore$ Circumference of circle $= \pi d$ [$\because d = 2r$]

$= \dfrac{22}{7} \times 35 = 110$ mm

Now, length of 5 diameters $= 5 \times 35 = 175$ mm (1)

(i) Total length of the silver wire $= \pi d + 5d$

$= 110 + 175$

$= 285$ mm (1)

(ii) Here, we see that total circle is divided into 10 sectors.

$\therefore$ Angle of each sector $= \dfrac{360°}{10} = 36°$

Then, area of each sector of the brooch

$= \dfrac{\theta}{360°} \times \pi r^2$

$= \dfrac{36°}{360°} \times \dfrac{22}{7}\left(\dfrac{35}{2}\right)^2$ $\left[\because r = \dfrac{d}{2} = \dfrac{35}{2} \text{ mm}\right]$

$= \dfrac{1}{10} \times \dfrac{22}{1} \times \dfrac{5}{2} \times \dfrac{35}{2}$

$= \dfrac{11 \times 35}{2 \times 2} = \dfrac{385}{4} \text{ mm}^2$ (1)

**16.** Given, radius of circle = 40 m and angle of sector = 60°

Area of the sector $AOB = \dfrac{60°}{360°} \times 3.14 \times (40)^2$

$= \dfrac{1}{6} \times 3.14 \times 1600$

$= \dfrac{2512}{3} \text{ m}^2$

(1)

Amount spent for making the flower bed at the rate of ₹2.40 per m$^2$ $=$ ₹ $2.40 \times \dfrac{2512}{3}$

$=$ ₹ 2009.60

Angles for the major sectors of both the circle at $O$ is same, i.e. 300°.

Radius of inner circle $= 40 - 15 = 25$ m (1)

Area of concrete track

$= \left\{\dfrac{300°}{360°} \times \pi \times (40)^2 - \dfrac{300°}{360°} \times \pi \times (25^2)\right\}$

[$\because$ area of track = area of outer sector – area of inner sector]

$= \dfrac{5}{6} \times \pi \times (1600 - 625)$

$= \dfrac{5}{6} \times 3.14 \times 975$

$= 2551.25 \text{ m}^2$ (2)

Amount spent for making the concrete track at the rate of ₹ 20 per m$^2$ $= 20 \times 2551.25 =$ ₹ 51025

Thus, the total amount spent for both the jobs

$=$ ₹2009.60 + ₹ 51025

$=$ ₹ 53034.60 (1)

**17.** Given, chord $AB$ subtends an angle 60° at the centre.

$\therefore$ $\angle AOB = 60°$ and $OA = OB$ [radii of circle]

$\therefore$ $\angle OBA = \angle OAB = x$ [say]

[$\because$ angles opposite to equal sides are also equal]

In $\Delta AOB$,

$\angle AOB + \angle OBA + \angle OAB = 180°$

[by angle sum property of triangle]

$\Rightarrow$ $60° + x + x = 180°$

$\Rightarrow$ $2x = 180° - 60°$

$\Rightarrow$ $x = \dfrac{120°}{2} = 60°$

$\Rightarrow$ $\angle OBA = \angle OAB = 60° = \angle AOB$ (2)

$\therefore \Delta AOB$ is an equilateral triangle.

Now, area of $\Delta AOB = \dfrac{\sqrt{3}}{4} \times (15)^2$

[$\because$ area of equilateral triangle $= \dfrac{\sqrt{3}}{4}$ (side)$^2$]

$= 56.25 \times 1.73 = 97.3125 \text{ cm}^2$ (1)

Area of sector $OACBO = \dfrac{\theta}{360°} \times \pi r^2$

$= \dfrac{60°}{360°} \times 3.14 \times (15)^2$

$= \dfrac{3.14 \times 225}{6} = \dfrac{706.5}{6}$

$= 117.75 \text{ cm}^2$ (1)

$\therefore$ Area of minor segment $ACBDA$

= Area of sector $OACBO$ – Area of $\Delta AOB$

$= 117.75 - 97.3125$

$= 20.4375 \text{ cm}^2$

Now, area of major segment

= Area of circle – Area of minor segment

$= \pi (15)^2 - 20.4375$

$= 3.14 \times 225 - 20.4375$

$= 706.5 - 20.4375$

$= 686.0625 \text{ cm}^2$ (1)

## Chapter 12 Surface Areas and Volumes

**1.** (c) Diameter of the base = 21 cm

$\therefore$ Radius of the base $= \frac{21}{2}$ cm

Height of the cylinder = 14 cm

Curved surface area of the cylinder $= 2\pi rh$

$$= 2 \times \frac{22}{7} \times \frac{21}{2} \times 14$$

$$= 924 \text{ cm}^2$$

**2.** (b) Given, cylindrical vessel contains = 49.896 L

$\therefore$ Volume, $V = \pi r^2 h = 49.896 \times 1000 \text{ cm}^3$

$= 49896 \text{ cm}^3$

Also given, curved surface area $= \frac{9504}{2} \text{ cm}^2$

$\Rightarrow \quad 2\pi rh = 4752$

$\Rightarrow \quad \frac{\pi r^2 h}{2\pi rh} = \frac{49896}{4752} \Rightarrow r = \frac{49896}{4752} \times 2$

$r = 21$ cm, $h = 36$ cm

Now, total surface area $= 2\pi r(h + r)$

$$= 2 \times \frac{22}{7} \times 21 \times 57$$

$$= 7524 \text{ cm}^2$$

**3.** (a) Mass = Volume × Density $= \pi(R + r)(R - r)h \times D$

$[\because$ volume of hollow pipe $= \frac{22}{7}(R^2 - r^2)h]$

$$= \frac{22}{7}\left(\frac{4.5}{2} + 2\right)\left(\frac{4.5}{2} - 2\right) \times 77 \times 8 \text{ gm}$$

$$= \left(\frac{22}{7} \times \frac{8.5}{2} \times \frac{0.5}{2} \times 77 \times 8\right) \text{ gm}$$

$= 2057$ gm $= 2.057$ kg

**4.** (b) Given, radius = 56 cm

Curved surface area of cone = 12320 cm$^2$

$\Rightarrow \quad \pi rl = 12320$

$\Rightarrow \quad \frac{22}{7} \times 56 \times l = 12320 \Rightarrow l = \frac{12320 \times 7}{22 \times 56} = 70$ cm

Therefore, the slant height of the right circular cone is 70 cm.

**5.** Given, radius of cylinder = 12 cm

and height of water raised in cylinder = 6.75 cm

$\therefore$ Volume of water raised $= \pi r^2 h$

$= \pi \times 12 \times 12 \times 6.75$ cm$^3$

Let the radius of spherical iron piece be $R$ cm. (1)

$\because$ Volume of sphere = Volume of water raised

$\Rightarrow \quad \frac{4}{3}\pi R^3 = \pi \times 12 \times 12 \times 6.75$

$\Rightarrow \quad R^3 = \frac{\pi \times 12 \times 12 \times 6.75 \times 3}{4\pi}$

$\Rightarrow \quad R^3 = 729 \Rightarrow R = \sqrt[3]{729} = 9$ cm

[$\because$ taking cube root both sides]

Hence, the radius of spherical piece is 9 cm. (1)

**6.** Given, diameter and height of the conical portion are

$d_1 = 5$ cm and $h_1 = 6$ cm.

$\therefore$ Radius, $r_1 = \frac{5}{2} = 2.5$ cm

Also, given diameter and height of a cylindrical portion are $d_2 = 3$ cm, $h_2 = 26 - 6 = 20$ cm.

$\therefore \quad$ Radius, $r_2 = \frac{3}{2} = 1.5$ cm (1)

Now, volume of the solid figure

= Volume of a cone + Volume of a cylinder

$$= \frac{1}{3}\pi r_1^2 h_1 + \pi r_2^2 h_2$$

$$= \frac{3.14 \times (2.5)^2 \times 6}{3} + 3.14 \times (1.5)^2 \times 20$$

$$= \frac{117.75}{3} + 141.3$$

$$= 39.25 + 141.3$$

$= 180.55 \text{ cm}^3$ (1)

**7.** Given, diameter of the semi-circular sheet = 28 cm

$\therefore$ Radius of the semi-circular sheet = 14 cm

Circumference of the base of the cone

$= \frac{1}{2} \times$ Circumference of the circle with radius 14 cm

$\Rightarrow \quad 2\pi r = \pi \times 14$

$\Rightarrow \quad r = 7$ cm (1)

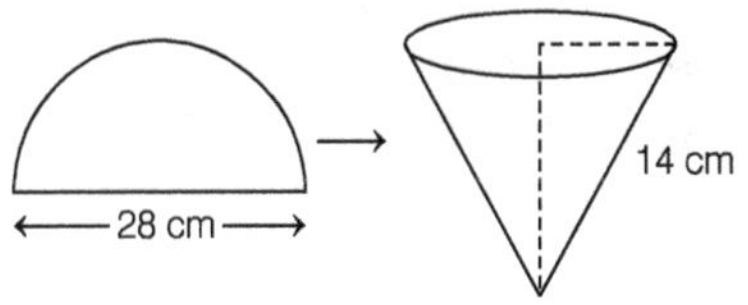


Height of the cone $= \sqrt{14^2 - 7^2}$

$= \sqrt{196 - 49} = \sqrt{147} = 12.12$ cm

$\therefore$ Capacity of cup = Volume of the conical cup

$$= \frac{1}{3}\pi r^2 h = \frac{1}{3} \times \frac{22}{7} \times (7)^2 \times 12.12$$

$= 622.16 \text{ cm}^3$ (1)

**8.** Given, diameter of hemispherical bowl, $d = 7.2$ cm

$\therefore$ Radius of hemispherical bowl,

$$r_1 = \frac{d}{2} = \frac{7.2}{2} = 3.6 \text{ cm}$$

Now, volume of hemispherical bowl $= \frac{2}{3} \times \pi r_1^3$

$$= \frac{2}{3} \times \pi \times (3.6)^3 \text{ cm}^3$$

Also, radius of cone,

$r_2 = 4.8$ cm [given]

Let the height of cone be $h$ cm.

$\therefore$ Volume of cone $= \frac{1}{3}\pi r_2^2 h = \frac{1}{3}\pi (4.8)^2 \times h \text{ cm}^2$

Since, the tomato sauce from hemispherical bowl is completely poured into an inverted cone. (1)

$\therefore$ Volume of hemispherical bowl = Volume of cone

$\Rightarrow \quad \frac{2}{3}\pi \times (3.6)^3 = \frac{1}{3}\pi (4.8)^2 \times h$

$\Rightarrow \quad 93.312 = 23.04\,h$

$\therefore \quad h = \frac{93.312}{23.04}$

$= 4.05$ cm

Hence, the height of the cone is 4.05 cm. (1)

**9.** Given, radius of conical vessel, $r = \frac{2}{2} = 1$ m

and height = 3.5 m

Let the rainfall be $x$ cm.

Now, volume of water on the roof

= Volume of conical vessel

$\Rightarrow \quad 22 \times 20 \times x = \frac{1}{3}\pi r^2 h$

$\Rightarrow \quad 22 \times 20 \times x = \frac{1}{3} \times \frac{22}{7} \times (1)^2 \times (3.5)$ (1)

$\therefore \quad x = \frac{1}{3} \times \frac{22}{7} \times \frac{35}{10} \times \frac{1}{22} \times \frac{1}{20}$

$= \frac{1}{120}$ m

$= \frac{1}{120} \times 100$ cm [$\because$ 1 m = 100 cm]

$= \frac{5}{6}$ cm = 0.83 cm

Hence, the rainfall is 0.83 cm. (1)

**10.** Given, side of a solid cube, $a = 7$ cm

Height of conical cavity, $h = 7$ cm

Radius of conical cavity, $r = 3$ cm

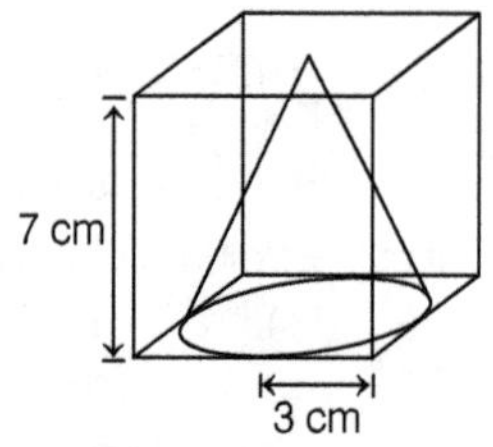


Now, volume of cube $= a^3 = (7)^3$

$= 343$ cm$^3$ (1/2)

and volume of conical cavity $= \frac{1}{3}\pi \times r^2 \times h$

$= \frac{1}{3} \times \frac{22}{7} \times 3 \times 3 \times 7$

$= 66$ cm$^3$ (1/2)

According to the question,

Volume of remaining solid

= Volume of cube – Volume of conical cavity

$= 343 - 66 = 277$ cm$^3$

Hence, the required volume of solid is 277 cm$^3$. (1)

**11.** Given, vessel is a combination of hollow hemisphere and a hollow cylinder.

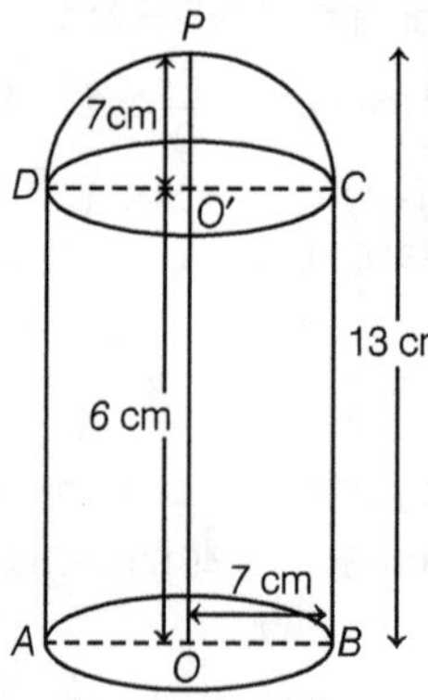


So, curved surface area of the vessel is equal to the curved surface areas of cylinder and hemisphere.

Also, we have

Diameter, $AB = DC = 14$ cm

Radius, $OB = O'C = O'P = \frac{AB}{2} = \frac{14}{2} = 7$ cm (1)

and total height, $PO = 13$ cm

$\therefore \quad OO' = PO - O'P = 13 - 7 = 6$ cm (1)

Radius of hemisphere = Height of hemisphere = 7 cm

Now, the inner curved surface area of the vessel

= Curved surface area of cylinder

+ Curved surface area of hemisphere

$= 2\pi rh + 2\pi r^2$

$= 2 \times \frac{22}{7} \times 7 \times 6 + 2 \times \frac{22}{7} \times (7)^2$

$= 44 \times 6 + 44 \times 7 = 44 \times (6 + 7)$

$= 44 \times 13 = 572$ cm$^2$ (1)

**12.** Given, radius of the cylinder, $R = 3$ cm

and height of the cylinder, $H = 5$ cm

Aslo, radius of the cone, $r = \frac{3}{2}$ cm

and hight of the cone, $h = \frac{8}{9}$ cm

$\therefore$ Volume of metal $A$ = Volume of the cylinder

– Volume of the cone

$= \pi \times (3)^2 \times 5 - \frac{1}{3} \times \pi \times \left(\frac{3}{2}\right)^2 \times \frac{8}{9}$

$= \pi\left(45 - \frac{2}{3}\right) = \frac{133}{3}\pi$ cm$^3$ (1)

and volume of metal $B$ = Capacity of the conical hole

$= \frac{1}{3}\pi \times \left(\frac{3}{2}\right)^2 \times \frac{8}{9} = \frac{2}{3}\pi$ cm$^3$ (1)

Hence, ratio of the volume of the metal $A$ to the volume of the metal $B = \frac{\frac{133}{3}\pi}{\frac{2\pi}{3}} = \frac{133}{2} = 66.5 : 1.$ (1)

**13.** Given, internal radius of the hollow hemispherical vessel $(r_1) = 35$ cm

External radius of the hollow hemispherical vessel $(r_2) = 39$ cm (1)

Volume of the vessel $= \frac{2}{3}\pi r_1^3$

$= \frac{2}{3} \times \frac{22}{7} \times 35 \times 35 \times 35$

$= \frac{269500}{3}$ cm$^3$

$= 89833.33$ cm$^3$ (1)

Curved surface area of the vessel $= 2\pi r_2^2$

$= 2 \times \frac{22}{7} \times (39)^2$

$= 9560.57$ cm$^2$ (1)

**14.** Given, base radius = 8 cm, height $(h) = 15$ cm

$\therefore$ Slant height $(l) = \sqrt{r^2 + h^2} = \sqrt{8^2 + 15^2} = 17$ cm (1)

$\therefore$ Curved surface area of the cap $= \pi rl$

$= \frac{22}{7} \times 8 \times 17$

$= 427.42$ cm$^2$ (1)

$\therefore$ Curved surface area of 10 such caps $= 427.42 \times 10$

$= 4274.2$ cm$^2$

Hence, the area of sheet required is 4274.2 cm$^2$. (1)

**15.** Given, toy is formed by combination of a cone and a hemisphere.

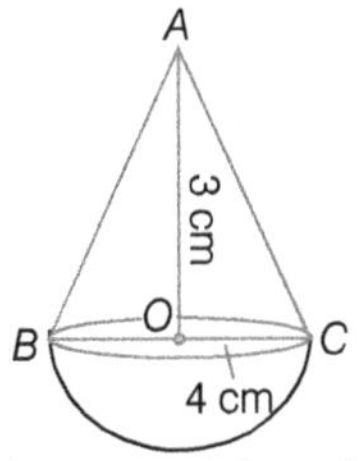


Here, radius of cone = radius of sphere = 4 cm

and height of cone, $h = 3$ cm (1)

Now, in right angled $\Delta AOC$,

$AC = \sqrt{AO^2 + OC^2}$ [by Pythagoras theorem]

$= \sqrt{3^2 + 4^2} = \sqrt{9 + 16}$

$= \sqrt{25} = 5$ cm

$\therefore$ Slant height of a cone, $l = AC = 5$ cm (1)

Now, curved surface area of conical portion $= \pi rl$

$= 3.14 \times 4 \times 5$

$= 62.8$ cm$^2$

and curved surface area of hemispherical portion

$= 2\pi r^2$

$= 2 \times 3.14 \times (4)^2$

$= 6.28 \times 16$

$= 100.48$ cm$^2$

$\therefore$ Required surface area of toy

= Curved surface area of conical portion + Curved surface area of the hemispherical portion

$= 62.8 + 100.48 = 163.28$ cm$^2$ (1)

Now, volume of conical portion $= \frac{1}{3}\pi r^2 h$

$= \frac{1}{3} \times 3.14 \times (4)^2 \times 3$

$= \frac{3.14 \times 16 \times 3}{3}$

$= \frac{150.72}{3} = 50.24$ cm$^3$

and volume of hemispherical portion $= \frac{2}{3}\pi r^3$

$= \frac{2}{3} \times 3.14 \times (4)^3 = \frac{6.28 \times 64}{3} = \frac{401.92}{3} = 133.97$ cm$^3$

$\therefore$ Required volume of toy = Volume of conical portion + Volume of hemispherical portion

$= 50.24 + 133.97 = 184.21$ cm$^3$ (2)

**16.** Let $r$ be the radius of the base of the building.

It is given that the height of the building is equal to the diameter of the base.

$\therefore$ Height of the building $= 2r$

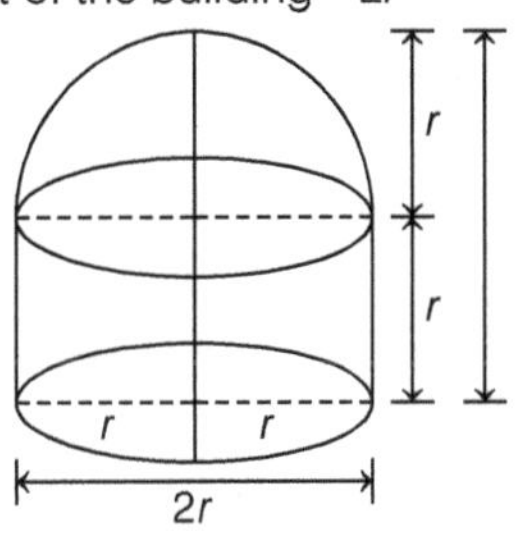


Also, height of the vaulted dome $= r$

Therefore, height of the cylindrical portion of the building $= 2r - r = r$ (1)

$\therefore$ Volume of the building = Volume of the cylinder + Volume of the hemisphere

$\Rightarrow \quad 17.7 = \pi r^3 + \frac{2}{3}\pi r^3$ (1)

[$\because$ volume of the building = quantity of air in building = 17.7 m$^3$]

$\Rightarrow \quad \frac{5}{3}\pi r^3 = 17.7 \Rightarrow r^3 = \frac{17.7 \times 3 \times 7}{5 \times 22} = \frac{17.7 \times 21}{110}$

$\Rightarrow \quad r = \left(\frac{17.7 \times 21}{110}\right)^{1/3}$

[taking cube root on both sides] (2)

$\therefore$ Height of the building $= 2r$

$= 2 \times \left(\frac{17.7 \times 21}{110}\right)^{1/3}$

$= 3$ m (approx.) (1)

**17.** Given, $h$ = Length of the cylindrical neck = 9 cm

$r$ = Radius of cylindrical neck = $\frac{3}{2}$ = 1.5 cm

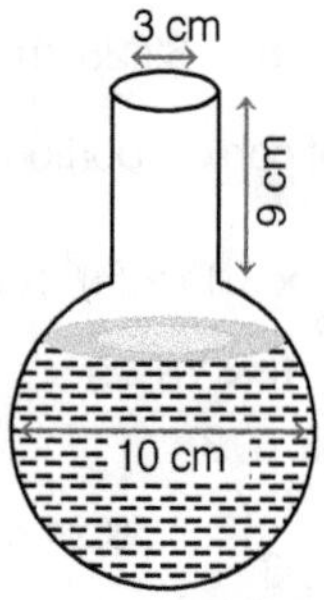


(1)

Now, volume of the cylindrical neck,

$V_1 = \pi r^2 h = \pi \times (1.5)^2 \times 9$

$= 20.25\pi \text{ cm}^3$ (1½)

Volume of the spherical part,

$V_2 = \frac{4}{3}\pi r^3 = \frac{4}{3}\pi \times \left(\frac{10}{2}\right)^3 = 166.66\,\pi \text{ cm}^3$ (1½)

$\therefore$ The water stored in the vessel $= V_1 + V_2$

$= (20.25\pi + 166.66\pi)\text{cm}^3$

$= 186.91\pi \text{ cm}^3$ (1)

## Chapter 13 **Statistics**

**1.** (c) Sum of five numbers = 5 × Mean of the numbers

$= 10 \times 5 = 50$

Since, each number is decreased by 3, then the sum is decreased by $3 \times 5 = 15$

$\therefore$ Mean of new numbers $= \frac{50 - 15}{5} = 7$

**2.** (c) Since, median is the middle most item and each item is increased by 2, the new median will be $20 + 2 = 22$.

**3.** (b) Now, $\Sigma f = 4 + 5 + y + 1 + 2 = 12 + y$

$\Sigma fx = 4 + 10 + 3y + 4 + 10 = 28 + 3y$

$\therefore$ Mean $= \frac{\Sigma fx}{\Sigma f} \Rightarrow 2.6 = \frac{28 + 3y}{12 + y}$

$\Rightarrow 26(12 + y) = 10(28 + 3y) \Rightarrow y = 8$

**4.** (a) Given, median = 145 and mean = 148.5

$\therefore$ Mode = 3 (Median) − 2(Mean)

$= 3 \times 145 - 2 \times 148.5$

$= 435 - 297 = 138$

**5.** (a) Arithmetic mean

$= \frac{1+2+3+4+5+6+7+8+9+10}{10} = 5.5$

**6.** $\because$ Mean $= \frac{x_1 + x_2 + \ldots + x_n}{n}$

$\therefore \frac{6 + 6 + 2x + 5 + 8 + 3x}{4} = 20$ [$\because$ mean = 20] (1)

$\Rightarrow 25 + 5x = 80$

$\Rightarrow 5x = 80 - 25 \Rightarrow x = 11$ (1)

**7.** If each observation is increased by 5, then the required new mean is also increased by 5.

Thus, the new mean is 17. (2)

**8.** Let assumed mean, $A = 145$

Table for deviation is given below

| Height (in cm) | Number of girls ($f_i$) | Class marks $x_i$ | $d_i = x_i - A$ | $f_i d_i$ |
|---|---|---|---|---|
| 120-130 | 2 | 125 | −20 | −40 |
| 130-140 | 8 | 135 | −10 | −80 |
| 140-150 | 12 | 145 = $A$ | 0 | 0 |
| 150-160 | 20 | 155 | 10 | 200 |
| 160-170 | 8 | 165 | 20 | 160 |
| **Total** | $\Sigma f_i = 50$ | | | $\Sigma f_i d_i = 240$ |

(1)

Here, $\Sigma f_i = 50$ and $\Sigma f_i d_i = 240$

$\therefore$ Mean, $\bar{x} = A + \frac{\Sigma f_i d_i}{\Sigma f_i}$

$= 145 + \frac{240}{50} = 145 + 4.8 = 149.8$ (1)

**9.** Here inclusive classes are given. Therefore, for determining median, inclusive class limits need to be converted into continuous class as shown in the table given below

| Given classes | Class boundaries | Frequency | cf |
|---|---|---|---|
| 130-139 | 129.5-139.5 | 4 | 4 |
| 140-149 | 139.5-149.5 | 9 | 13 |
| 150-159 | 149.5-159.5 | 18 | 31 |
| 160-169 | 159.5-169.5 | 28 | 59 |
| 170-179 | 169.5-179.5 | 24 | 83 |
| 180-189 | 179.5-189.5 | 10 | 93 |
| 190-199 | 189.5-199.5 | 7 | 100 |

(1)

Here, $n = 100$

So, $\frac{n}{2} = \frac{100}{2} = 50$

Cumulative frequency just greater than 50 is 59 corresponding to the class 159.5 − 169.5

$\therefore l = 159.5, \frac{n}{2} = 50, f = 28, cf = 31$ and $h = 10$

$\because$ Median $= l + \frac{\frac{n}{2} - cf}{f} \times h$

$= 159.5 + \frac{50 - 31}{28} \times 10$

$= 159.5 + \frac{190}{28} = 159.5 + 6.79 = 166.29$ (1)

**10.** We observe that the class 1500-2000 has the maximum frequency 40.

So, it is the modal class such that

$l = 1500, h = 500, f_1 = 40, f_0 = 24$ and $f_2 = 33$ (1/2)

$$\therefore \text{ Mode} = l + \left(\frac{f_1 - f_0}{2f_1 - f_0 - f_2}\right) \times h \quad (1/2)$$

$$= 1500 + \left(\frac{40-24}{80-24-33}\right) \times 500$$

$$= 1500 + \frac{16}{23} \times 500$$

$$= 1500 + 347.826 = 1847.825 \quad (1)$$

**11.** Let assumed mean be $A = 50$.

Table for deviation is given below

| Class interval | Frequency ($f_i$) | Mid value ($x_i$) | $d_i = x_i - A$ | $f_i d_i$ |
|---|---|---|---|---|
| 0-20 | 17 | 10 | −40 | −680 |
| 20-40 | $f_1$ | 30 | −20 | $-20f_1$ |
| 40-60 | 32 | 50 | 0 | 0 |
| 60-80 | $f_2$ | 70 | 20 | $20f_2$ |
| 80-100 | 19 | 90 | 40 | 760 |
| Total | $N = \Sigma f_i = 68 + f_1 + f_2$ | | | $\Sigma f_i d_i = 80 - 20f_1 + 20f_2$ |

(1)

We have, $N = \Sigma f_i = 120$ [given]

$\Rightarrow \quad 68 + f_1 + f_2 = 120$

$\Rightarrow \quad f_1 + f_2 = 52$ ...(i) (1)

But mean = 50 [given]

$$\therefore \quad A + \frac{\Sigma f_i d_i}{\Sigma f_i} = 50$$

$$\Rightarrow \quad 50 + \frac{80 - 20f_1 + 20f_2}{120} = 50$$

$$\Rightarrow 50 + 20 \times \left(\frac{4 - f_1 + f_2}{120}\right) = 50$$

$$\Rightarrow \quad 50 + \frac{4 - f_1 + f_2}{6} = 50 \Rightarrow \frac{4 - f_1 + f_2}{6} = 0$$

$\Rightarrow \quad 4 - f_1 + f_2 = 0$

$\therefore \quad f_1 - f_2 = 4$ ...(ii)

On solving Eqs. (i) and (ii), we get

$f_1 = 28$ and $f_2 = 24$ (1)

**12.** Classes are not continuous, hence we make them continuous by adding 0.5 to the upper limits and subtracting 0.5 from the lower limits.

| Class interval | Frequency | Cumulative frequency |
|---|---|---|
| 0-5.5 | 13 | 13 |
| 5.5-11.5 | 10 | 23 |
| 11.5-17.5 | 15 | 38 |
| 17.5-23.5 | 08 | 46 |
| 23.5-29.5 | 11 | 57 |
| Total | $\Sigma f = 57$ | |

(1½)

Class interval cannot be negative. Hence, the first class interval is starting from 0.

Now to find median we calculate $\frac{\Sigma f}{2} = \frac{57}{2} = 28.5$

$\therefore$ Median class is 11.5-17.5.

So, the upper limit is 17.5. (1½)

**13.** We will use the deviation method to find mean.

Let assumed mean $A = 70$.

So, $d_i = x_i - 70$ (1½)

| Literacy rate (in %) | Frequency ($f_i$) | Class mark ($x_i$) | $d_i = x_i - 70$ | $f_i d_i$ |
|---|---|---|---|---|
| 45-55 | 3 | 50 | −20 | −60 |
| 55-65 | 10 | 60 | −10 | −100 |
| 65-75 | 11 | 70 | 0 | 0 |
| 75-85 | 8 | 80 | 10 | 80 |
| 85-95 | 3 | 90 | 20 | 60 |
| Total | $\Sigma f_i = 35$ | | | $\Sigma f d_i = -20$ |

(2)

$$\therefore \text{ Mean } (\bar{x}) = A + \frac{\Sigma f d_i}{\Sigma f_i}$$

$$= 70 + \frac{-20}{35} = 70 - 0.57 = 69.43\% \quad (1½)$$

**14.** Table for cumulative frequency is given below

| Class interval | Frequency | Cumulative frequency |
|---|---|---|
| 0-6 | 4 | $4 + 0 = 4$ |
| 6-12 | $x$ | $4 + x = (4 + x)$ |
| 12-18 | 5 | $5 + (4 + x) = 9 + x$ |
| 18-24 | $y$ | $y + (9 + x) = 9 + x + y$ |
| 24-30 | 1 | $1 + (9 + x + y) = 10 + x + y$ |

(1)

Since, $N = 20$

$\therefore \quad 10 + x + y = 20$

$\Rightarrow \quad x + y = 20 - 10$

$\Rightarrow \quad x + y = 10$ ...(i)

Also, we have, median = 14.4

which lies in the class interval 12-18.

$\therefore$ The median class is 12-18, such that

$l = 12, f = 5, C = 4 + x$ and $h = 6$

$$\therefore \quad \text{Median} = l + \left(\frac{\frac{N}{2} - C}{f}\right) \times h \quad (1½)$$

$$\Rightarrow \quad 14.4 = 12 + \left[\frac{10 - (4 + x)}{5}\right] \times 6$$

$$\Rightarrow \quad 14.4 - 12 = \frac{6 - x}{5} \times 6$$

$$\Rightarrow \quad 2.4 = \frac{36 - 6x}{5}$$

$\Rightarrow \quad 12 = 36 - 6x$

$\Rightarrow \quad 6x = 24$

$\Rightarrow \quad x = 4$ (1½)

Now, put the value of $x$ in Eq. (i), we get

$$4+y=10 \Rightarrow y=10-4=6$$

Thus, $x=4$ and $y=6$ (1)

**15.** Let assumed mean be $A=35$.

Table for deviation and their product with corresponding frequency is given below

| Class interval | $x_i$ | $f_i$ | $cf$ | $d_i = x_i - A$ | $f_i d_i$ |
|---|---|---|---|---|---|
| 0-10 | 5 | 3 | $3+0=3$ | −30 | −90 |
| 10-20 | 15 | 4 | $4+3=7$ | −20 | −80 |
| 20-30 | 25 | 7 | $7+7=14$ | −10 | −70 |
| 30-40 | $35=A$ | 15 | $15+14=29$ | 0 | 0 |
| 40-50 | 45 | 10 | $10+29=39$ | 10 | 100 |
| 50-60 | 55 | 7 | $7+39=46$ | 20 | 140 |
| 60-70 | 65 | 4 | $4+46=50$ | 30 | 120 |
| **Total** | | $\Sigma f_i = 50$ | | | $\Sigma f_i d_i = 120$ |

(2)

Here, $\Sigma f_i = 50, \Sigma f_i d_i = 120$

(i) Mean $= A + \dfrac{\Sigma f_i d_i}{\Sigma f_i}$

$$\text{Mean} = 35 + \left(\frac{120}{50}\right) = 35 + \frac{12}{5} = 35 + 2.4 = 37.4$$ (1)

(ii) **To find the mode**

Here, greatest frequency = 15

∴ Modal class = 30-40

Here, $l=30, f_1=15, f_0=7, f_2=10$ and $h=10$

$$\therefore \text{Mode} = l + \left(\frac{f_1 - f_0}{2f_1 - f_0 - f_2}\right) \times h = 30 + \left(\frac{8}{30-17}\right) \times 10$$

$$= 30 + \frac{8}{13} \times 10 = 30 + \frac{80}{13}$$

$$= 30 + 6.15 = 36.15$$ (1)

(iii) **To find the median**

Here, $N = 50$

Now, $\dfrac{N}{2} = \dfrac{50}{2} = 25$

∴ Median class is 30-40.

Here, $l=30, C=14, f=15$ and $h=10$

$$\therefore \text{Median} = l + \left(\frac{\frac{N}{2} - C}{f}\right) \times h = 30 + \left(\frac{25-14}{15}\right) \times 10$$

$$= 30 + \left(\frac{11}{15}\right) \times 10 = 30 + \frac{22}{3} = 30 + 7.3 = 37.3$$ (1)

# Chapter 14 Probability

**1.** (*b*) Out of the given numbers, multiples of 5 are 5, 10, 15, 20, 25.

Then, the number of favourable outcomes = 5

$$\therefore P\text{ (getting a multiple of 5)} = \frac{5}{25} = \frac{1}{5}$$

**2.** (*b*) Total number of balls = 15

Number of non white balls = 10

$$P(E) = \frac{10}{15} = \frac{2}{3}$$

**3.** (*b*) Average of the given numbers

$$= \frac{3+5+5+7+7+7+9+9+9+9}{10} = \frac{70}{10} = 7$$

$$\therefore P\text{ (selecting 7)} = \frac{3}{10}$$

**4.** (*b*) Possible outcomes are 1, 2, 3, 4, 5, 6.

Favourable outcomes are 1, 2, 3, 4.

$$\therefore P\text{ (getting a number less than 5)} = \frac{4}{6} = \frac{2}{3}$$

**5.** (i) Probability of a sure event = 1

(ii) Probability of an event which is impossible = 0

(iii) Range of probability of an event $E$ is $0 \le P(E) \le 1$. (2)

**6.** Two dice can be thrown in $6 \times 6 = 36$ ways

Let $E$ be the event of getting numbers on the two dice whose product is 12. (1)

Then, favourable outcomes to '$E$'

$= \{(2, 6), (6, 2), (3, 4), (4, 3)\}$, $n(E) = 4$

$$P(E) = \frac{n(E)}{n(S)} = \frac{4}{36} = \frac{1}{9}$$ (1)

**7.** Let $E$ be the event of two students not having the same birthday.

Then, $P(E) = 0.992$

$\because P(E) + P(\bar{E}) = 1$

$\therefore P(\bar{E}) = 1 - 0.992 = 0.008$ (1)

So, the probability of two students having the same birthday is 0.008. (1)

**8.** Total possible outcomes = 17

Odd numbered cards are 1, 3, 5, 7, 9, 11, 13, 15, 17 = 9

$$\therefore P\text{ (getting an odd numbered card)} = \frac{9}{17}$$ (2)

**9.** An ordinary year has 365 days, i.e. 52 weeks and 1 day. It can be any of the 7 days of the week.

$$\therefore P\text{ (the day is Sunday)} = \frac{1}{7}$$ (1)

Hence, the probability that an ordinary year has 53 Sundays is $\frac{1}{7}$. (1)

**10.** Total number of marbles in the box = 5 + 8 + 4 = 17

(i) Probability of taking out a red marble

$$= \frac{\text{Number of red marbles}}{\text{Total number of marbles}} = \frac{5}{17}$$

(ii) Probability of taking out a white marble

$$= \frac{\text{Number of white marbles}}{\text{Total number of marbles}} = \frac{8}{17}$$ (1)

(iii) Probability of taking out a marble which is not a green marble

$$= \frac{\text{Either red or white marble}}{\text{Total number of marbles}} = \frac{5+8}{17} = \frac{13}{17}$$ (1)

**11.** Total number of pens
= Number of good pens + Number of defective pens
= 132 + 12 = 144
Let $E$ be the event of selecting a good pen.
Then, number of outcomes favourable to $E$ = 132 (1)
∴ Probability of selecting a good pen,
$$P(E) = \frac{\text{Number of good pens}}{\text{Total number of pens}} = \frac{132}{144} = \frac{11}{12} \quad (1)$$

**12.** Total possible outcomes are 3, 4, 5 ..., 25 = 23
Prime numbers in the given numbers are
3, 5, 7, 11, 13, 17, 19, 23 (1)
Total favourable outcomes = 8
$$P\text{ (getting a prime number)} = \frac{8}{23} \quad (1)$$

**13.** (i) Total number of outcomes = 35
Out of the given numbers, multiple of 7 are 7, 14, 21, 28, 35
Total number of favourable outcomes = 5
$$\therefore P\text{ (getting a multiple of 7)} = \frac{5}{35} = \frac{1}{7} \quad (1\tfrac{1}{2})$$
(ii) Out of the given numbers, multiples of 3 are 3, 6, 9, 12, 15, 18, 21, 24, 27, 30, 33 = 11
Multiples of 5 are 5, 10, 15, 20, 25, 30, 35 = 7
Multiples of 3 and 5 both are 15, 30 = 2
Total number of favourable outcomes
= 11 + 7 − 2 = 16
$$\therefore P\text{ (getting a multiple of 3 or 5)} = \frac{16}{35} \quad (1\tfrac{1}{2})$$

**14.** (i) Possible outcomes are 1, 2, 3, ..., 90.
∴ Total number of possible outcomes = 90
Two-digit numbers from 1 to 90 are 10, 11, 12, ..., 90.
Thus, the number of favourable ways of 'getting a two-digit number' = 81
$$P(E) = \frac{\text{Number of outcomes favourable to } E}{\text{Total number of outcomes}}$$
$$\therefore P\text{ (a two-digit number)} = \frac{81}{90} = \frac{9}{10}$$
*Or*
One-digit numbers from 1 to 90 are 1, 2, 3, 4, 5, 6, 7, 8, 9. Thus, the number of favourable ways of 'getting a one-digit number' = 9
$$\therefore P\text{ (a one-digit number)} = \frac{9}{90} = \frac{1}{10}$$
$P$ (not a one-digit number)
= 1 − $P$ (a one-digit number)
$$\Rightarrow P\text{ (a two-digit number)} = 1 - \frac{1}{10} = \frac{9}{10} \quad (1)$$
(ii) Perfect square numbers from 1 to 90 are 1, 4, 9, 16, 25, 36, 49, 64, 81. Thus, the number of favourable ways of 'getting a perfect square number' = 9
$$\text{Hence, } P\text{ (a perfect square number)} = \frac{9}{90} = \frac{1}{10} \quad (1)$$
(iii) Number divisible by 5, from 1 to 90 are 5, 10, 15, 20, 25, 30, 35, 40, 45, 50, 55, 60, 65, 70, 75, 80, 85, 90
Thus, the number of favourable ways of 'getting a number divisible by 5' = 18
$$\text{Hence, } P\text{ (a number divisible by 5)} = \frac{18}{90} = \frac{1}{5} \quad (1)$$

**15.** Given sides of rectangle are $l = 3$ m and $b = 2$ m
Area of the rectangle = $l \times b = 3\text{ m} \times 2\text{ m} = 6\text{ m}^2$
Area of the circle having diameter 1 m
$\left[\text{i.e. radius} = \frac{1}{2}\text{ m}\right]$
$$= \pi\left(\frac{1}{2}\right)^2 = \frac{\pi}{4}\text{ m}^2 \quad (1)$$
$P$ (dice will land inside the circle)
$$= \frac{\text{Favourable area region}}{\text{Total area}}$$
$$= \frac{\text{Area of the circle}}{\text{Area of the rectangle}} = \frac{\frac{\pi}{4}}{6} = \frac{\pi}{4 \times 6} = \frac{\pi}{24} \quad (2)$$

**16.** Two dice are thrown simultaneously.
So, number of possible outcomes = 36
(i) ∵ Sum of the numbers appearing on the dice is 7.
∴ Possible ways are (1, 6), (2, 5), (3, 4), (4, 3), (5, 2) and (6, 1).
Thus, number of favourable outcomes = 6
$$\text{Hence, required probability} = \frac{6}{36} = \frac{1}{6} \quad (1)$$
(ii) ∵ Sum of the numbers appearing on the dice is a prime number, i.e. 2, 3, 5, 7 and 11.
∴ Possible ways are (1, 1), (1, 2), (2, 1), (1, 4), (2, 3), (3, 2), (4,1), (1, 6), (2, 5), (3, 4), (4, 3), (5, 2), (6, 1), (5, 6) and (6, 5).
Thus, number of favourable outcomes = 15
$$\text{Hence, required probability} = \frac{15}{36} = \frac{5}{12} \quad (1)$$
(iii) ∵ Sum of the numbers appearing on the dice is 1, which is not possible. So, its probability is zero. (1)

**17.** There are 17 cards, numbered 1, 2, 3, 4, 5 ..., 17, in a box.
Out of 17 cards, one card can be drawn in 17 ways.
∴ Total number of possible outcomes = 17
(i) There are 9 odd numbered cards, namely 1, 3, 5, 7, 9, 11, 13, 15 and 17.
∴ Number of favourable outcomes = 9
Hence, $P$ (getting an odd number)
$$= \frac{\text{Number of favourable outcomes}}{\text{Total number of outcomes}} = \frac{9}{17} \quad (1)$$
(ii) There are 7 prime numbered cards, namely 2, 3, 5, 7, 11, 13 and 17.
∴ Number of favourable outcomes = 7
Hence, $P$ (getting a prime number)
$$= \frac{\text{Number of favourable outcomes}}{\text{Total number of outcomes}} = \frac{7}{17} \quad (1)$$

(iii) If a number is divisible by 3, then it is a multiple of 3. There are 5 cards, which are multiple of 3, namely 3, 6, 9, 12, and 15.

$\therefore$ Number of favourable outcomes = 5

Hence, $P$ (getting a card bearing a number divisible by 3)

$= \dfrac{\text{Number of favourable outcomes}}{\text{Total number of outcomes}} = \dfrac{5}{17}$ (1)

(iv) If a number is divisible by 2 and 3 both, then it is a multiple of 6. In cards bearing numbers 1, 2, 3, 4, ..., 17, there are only 2 cards which bear a number divisible by 2 and 3 both, i.e. by 6, namely 6 and 12.

$\therefore$ Number of favourable outcomes = 2

Hence, $P$ (getting a card bearing number divisible by 2 and 3 both)

$= \dfrac{\text{Number of favourable outcomes}}{\text{Total number of outcomes}} = \dfrac{2}{17}$ (1)

(v) There are 7 numbered cards, which are multiple of 3 or 5 namely, 3, 5, 6, 9, 10, 12 and 15.

$\therefore$ Number of favourable outcomes = 7

Hence, $P$ (getting a card bearing a number multiple of 3 or 5)

$= \dfrac{\text{Number of favourable outcomes}}{\text{Total number of outcomes}} = \dfrac{7}{17}$ (1)

**18.** Total number of cards in one deck of cards is 52.

$\therefore$ Total number of possible outcomes = 52 (1)

(i) Let $E_1$ = Event of getting a king of red colour

$\therefore$ Number of outcomes favourable to $E_1 = 2$

[$\because$ there are four kings in a deck of playing cards out of which two are red and two are black]

Hence, probability of getting a king of red colour,

$$P(E_1) = \frac{2}{52} = \frac{1}{26} \quad (1)$$

(ii) Let $E_2$ = Event of getting a face card

$\therefore$ Number of outcomes favourable to $E_2 = 12$

[$\because$ in a deck of cards, there are 12 face cards, namely 4 kings, 4 jacks, 4 queens]

Hence, probability of getting a face card,

$$P(E_2) = \frac{12}{52} = \frac{3}{13} \quad (1)$$

(iii) Let $E_3$ = Event of getting a red face card

$\therefore$ Number of outcomes favourable to $E_3 = 6$

[$\because$ in a deck of cards, there are 12 face cards out of which 6 are red and 6 are black]

Hence, probability of getting a red face card,

$$P(E_3) = \frac{6}{52} = \frac{3}{26} \quad (1)$$

(iv) Let $E_4$ = Event of getting a jack of heart

$\therefore$ Number of outcomes favourable to $E_4 = 1$

[$\because$ there are four jack cards in a deck, namely 1 of heart, 1 of club, 1 of spade and 1 of diamond]

Hence, probability of getting a jack of heart,

$$P(E_4) = \frac{1}{52} \quad (1)$$

**19.** When two coins are tossed, then possible outcomes are $HH, HT, TH, TT$

$\therefore$ Total number of outcomes = 4 (1)

(i) Let $E_1$ be the event that Neha gets first chance.

$\therefore$ Number of outcomes favourable to $E_1$ (i.e. $HT, TH$) = 2

Hence, $P(E_1)$

$= \dfrac{\text{Number of favourable outcomes}}{\text{Total number of outcomes}}$

$= \dfrac{2}{4} = \dfrac{1}{2}$ (1)

(ii) Let $E_2$ be the event that Lata gets first chance.

$\therefore$ Number of outcomes favourable to $E_2$ (i.e. H H)

Hence, $P(E_2) = \dfrac{1}{4}$ (1)

(iii) Let $E_3$ be the event that Sonia gets first chance.

$\therefore$ Number of outcomes favourable to $E_3$ (i.e. $TT$)

Hence, $P(E_3) = \dfrac{1}{4}$ (1)

(iv) No, as the number of cases favourable to each one of them is not equal. (1)

# LATEST
# CBSE SAMPLE PAPER

*A Sample Question Paper for CBSE Class X Issued by CBSE*

## Mathematics (Basic)

Time : **3 hrs** Max. Marks : **80**

### Instructions

1. This question paper has 5 Sections A, B, C, D and E.
2. Section A has 20 Multiple Choice Questions (MCQs) carrying 1 mark each.
3. Section B has 5 Short Answer-I (SA-I) Type Questions carrying 2 marks each.
4. Section C has 6 Short Answer-II (SA-II) Type Questions carrying 3 marks each.
5. Section D has 4 Long Answer (LA) Type Questions carrying 5 marks each.
6. Section E has 3 Case Based integrated units of assessment (4 marks each) with sub-parts of the values of 1, 1 and 2 marks each respectively.
7. All questions are compulsory. However, an internal choice in 2 questions of 2 marks, 2 questions of 3 marks and 2 questions of 5 marks has been provided. An internal choice has been provided in the 2 marks questions of Section E.
8. Draw neat figures wherever required. Take $\pi = 22/7$ wherever required if not stated.

## Section-A

**Section A consists of 20 questions of 1 mark each**

**1.** If two positive integers $p$ and $q$ can be expressed as $p = ab^2$ and $q = a^3b$; $a, b$ being prime numbers, then LCM $(p, q)$ is

(a) $ab$ (b) $a^2b^2$ (c) $a^3b^2$ (d) $a^3b^3$

**2.** What is the greatest possible speed at which a man can walk 52 km and 91 km in an exact number of hours?

(a) 17 km/h (b) 7 km/h
(c) 13 km/h (d) 26 km/h

**3.** If one zero of the quadratic polynomial $x^2 + 3x + k$ is 2, then the value of $k$ is

(a) 10 (b) $-10$ (c) 5 (d) $-5$

**4.** Graphically, the pair of equations given by $6x - 3y + 10 = 0$, $2x - y + 9 = 0$ represents two lines which are

(a) intersecting at exactly one point
(b) parallel
(c) coincident
(d) intersecting at exactly two points

**5.** If the quadratic equation $x^2 + 4x + k = 0$ has real and equal roots, then

(a) $k < 4$ (b) $k > 4$
(c) $k = 4$ (d) $k \geq 4$

**6.** The perimeter of a triangle with vertices (0, 4), (0, 0) and (3, 0) is

(a) 5 units (b) 12 units
(c) 11 units (d) $(7+\sqrt{5})$ units

**7.** If in triangles $ABC$ and $EDF$, $\frac{AB}{DE}=\frac{BC}{FD}$, then they will be similar, when

(a) $\angle B=\angle E$ (b) $\angle A=\angle D$
(c) $\angle B=\angle D$ (d) $\angle A=\angle F$

**8.** In which ratio the $Y$-axis divides the line segment joining the points $(5, -6)$ and $(-1, -4)$?

(a) 1 : 5 (b) 5 : 1 (c) 1 : 1 (d) 1 : 2

**9.** In the figure, if $PA$ and $PB$ are tangents to the circle with centre $O$ such that $\angle APB=50^\circ$, then $\angle OAB$ is equal to

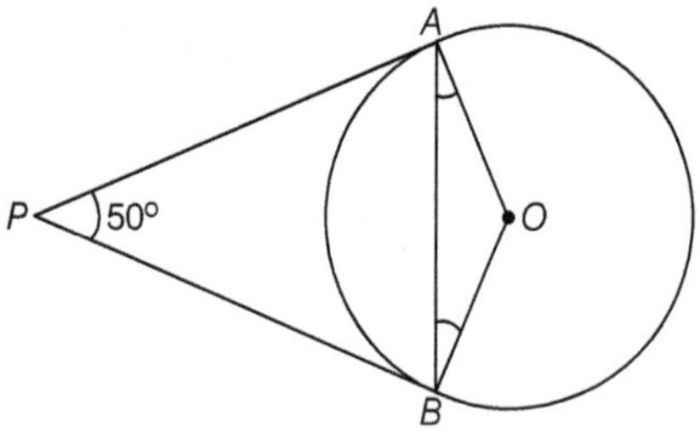


(a) 25° (b) 30° (c) 40° (d) 50°

**10.** If $\sin A=\frac{1}{2}$, then the value of $\sec A$ is

(a) $\frac{2}{\sqrt{3}}$ (b) $\frac{1}{\sqrt{3}}$ (c) $\sqrt{3}$ (d) 1

**11.** $\sqrt{3}\cos^2 A+\sqrt{3}\sin^2 A$ is equal to

(a) 1 (b) $\frac{1}{\sqrt{3}}$ (c) $\sqrt{3}$ (d) 0

**12.** The value of $\cos 1^\circ \cos 2^\circ \cos 3^\circ \cos 4^\circ \ldots\ldots \cos 90^\circ$ is

(a) 1 (b) 0 (c) $-1$ (d) 2

**13.** If the perimeter of a circle is equal to that of a square, then the ratio of their areas is

(a) 22 : 7 (b) 14 : 11
(c) 7 : 22 (d) 11 : 14

**14.** If the radii of two circles are in the ratio of 4 : 3, then their areas are in the ratio of

(a) 4 : 3 (b) 8 : 3
(c) 16 : 9 (d) 9 : 16

**15.** The total surface area of a solid hemisphere of radius 7 cm is

(a) $447\pi$ cm$^2$ (b) $239\pi$ cm$^2$
(c) $174\pi$ cm$^2$ (d) $147\pi$ cm$^2$

**16.** For the following distribution:

| Class | 0-5 | 5-10 | 10-15 | 15-20 | 20-25 |
|---|---|---|---|---|---|
| Frequency | 10 | 15 | 12 | 20 | 9 |

the upper limit of the modal class is

(a) 10 (b) 15 (c) 20 (d) 25

**17.** If the mean of the following distribution is 2.6, then the value of $y$ is

| Variable ($x$) | 1 | 2 | 3 | 4 | 5 |
|---|---|---|---|---|---|
| Frequency | 4 | 5 | $y$ | 1 | 2 |

(a) 3 (b) 8 (c) 13 (d) 24

**18.** A card is selected at random from a well shuffled deck of 52 cards. The probability of its being a red face card is

(a) $\frac{3}{26}$ (b) $\frac{3}{13}$ (c) $\frac{2}{13}$ (d) $\frac{1}{2}$

**Directions** *In the question number 19 and 20, a statement of Assertion (A) is followed by a statement of Reason (R). Choose the correct option.*

**19. Assertion (A)** If HCF of 510 and 92 is 2, then the LCM of 510 and 92 is 32460.

**Reason (R)** As HCF $(a, b)\times$ LCM $(a, b)=a\times b$

(a) Both Assertion (A) and Reason (R) are true and Reason (R) is the correct explanation of Assertion (A)
(b) Both Assertion (A) and Reason (R) are true but Reason (R) is not the correct explanation of Assertion (A)
(c) Assertion (A) is true but Reason (R) is false
(d) Assertion (A) is false but Reason (R) is true

**20. Assertion (A)** The ratio in which the line segment joining $(2, -3)$ and $(5, 6)$ internally divided by $X$-axis is 1 : 2.

**Reason (R)** As formula for the internal division is $\left(\frac{mx_2+nx_1}{m+n}, \frac{my_2+ny_1}{m+n}\right)$.

(a) Both Assertion (A) and Reason (R) are true and Reason (R) is the correct explanation of Assertion (A)
(b) Both Assertion (A) and Reason (R) are true but Reason (R) is not the correct explanation of Assertion (A)
(c) Assertion (A) is true but Reason (R) is false
(d) Assertion (A) is false but Reason (R) is true

# Section-B

**Section B consists of 5 questions of 2 marks each**

**21.** For what values of $k$ will the following pair of linear equations have infinitely many solutions?

$$kx + 3y - (k - 3) = 0$$
$$12x + ky - k = 0$$

**22.** In the figure, altitudes $AD$ and $CE$ of $\Delta ABC$ intersect each other at the point $P$.

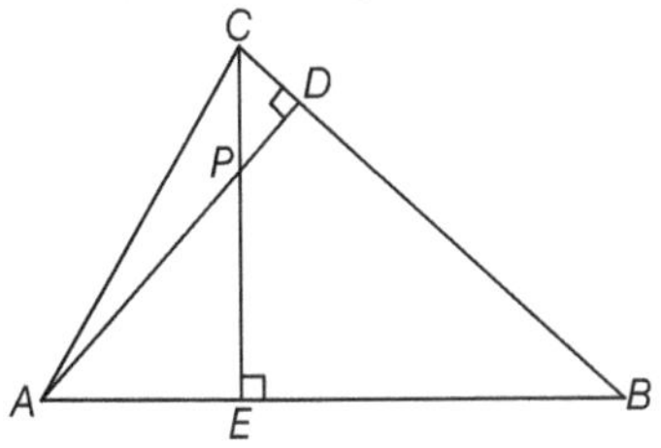


Show that

(i) $\Delta ABD \sim \Delta CBE$ (ii) $\Delta PDC \sim \Delta BEC$

*Or*

In the figure, $DE \parallel AC$ and $DF \parallel AE$.

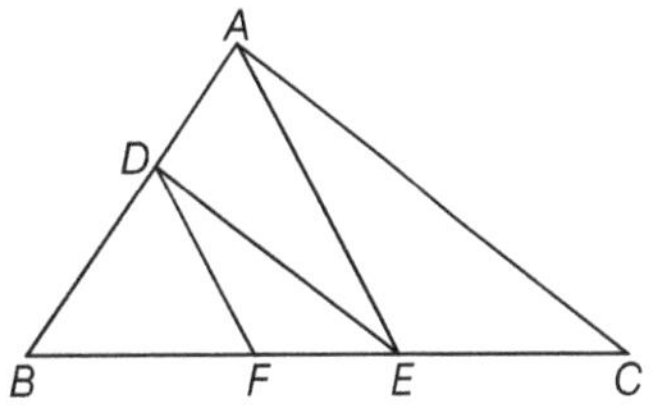


Prove that $\dfrac{BF}{FE} = \dfrac{BE}{EC}$.

**23.** Two concentric circles are of radii 5 cm and 3 cm. Find the length of the chord of the larger circle which touches the smaller circle.

**24.** If $\cot\theta = \dfrac{7}{8}$, evaluate $\dfrac{(1+\sin\theta)(1-\sin\theta)}{(1+\cos\theta)(1-\cos\theta)}$

**25.** Find the perimeter of a quadrant of a circle of radius 14 cm.

*Or* Find the diameter of a circle whose area is equal to the sum of the areas of the two circles of radii 24 cm and 7 cm.

# Section-C

**Section C consists of 6 questions of 3 marks each**

**26.** Prove that $\sqrt{5}$ is an irrational number.

**27.** Find the zeroes of the quadratic polynomial $6x^2 - 3 - 7x$ and verify the relationship between the zeroes and the coefficients.

**28.** A shopkeeper gives books on rent for reading. She takes a fixed charge for the first two days, and an additional charge for each day thereafter. Latika paid ₹ 22 for a book kept for six days, while Anand paid ₹ 16 for the book kept for four days. Find the fixed charges and the charge for each extra day.

*Or* Places $A$ and $B$ are 100 km apart on a highway. One car starts from $A$ and another from $B$ at the same time. If the cars travel in the same direction at different speeds, they meet in 5 h. If they travel towards each other, they meet in 1 h. What are the speeds of the two cars?

**29.** In the figure, $PQ$ is a chord of length 8 cm of a circle of radius 5 cm. The tangents at $P$ and $Q$ intersect at a point $T$. Find the length $TP$.

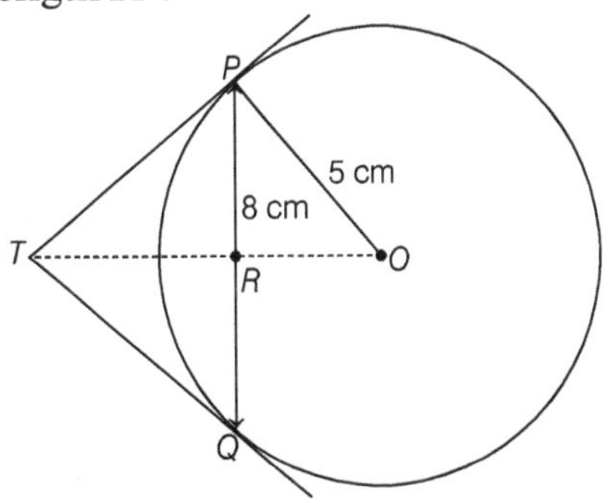


**30.** Prove that
$$\frac{\tan\theta}{1-\cot\theta} + \frac{\cot\theta}{1-\tan\theta} = 1 + \sec\theta \operatorname{cosec}\theta.$$

*Or* If $\sin\theta + \cos\theta = \sqrt{3}$, then prove that $\tan\theta + \cot\theta = 1$.

**31.** Two dice are thrown at the same time. What is the probability that the sum of the two numbers appearing on the top of the dice?

(i) 8 (ii) 13 (iii) less than or equal to 12

# Section-D

**Section D consists of 4 questions of 5 marks each**

**32.** An express train takes 1 h less than a passenger train to travel 132 km between Mysore and Bangalore (without taking into consideration the time they stop at intermediate stations). If the average speed of the express train is 11km/h more than that of the passenger train, find the average speed of the two trains.

*Or* A motor boat whose speed is 18 km/h in still water takes 1 h more to go 24 km upstream than to return downstream to the same spot. Find the speed of the stream.

**33.** Prove that if a line is drawn parallel to one side of a triangle to intersect the other two sides in distinct points, the other two sides are divided in the same ratio. In the figure, find $EC$ if $\frac{AD}{DB} = \frac{AE}{EC}$ using the above theorem.

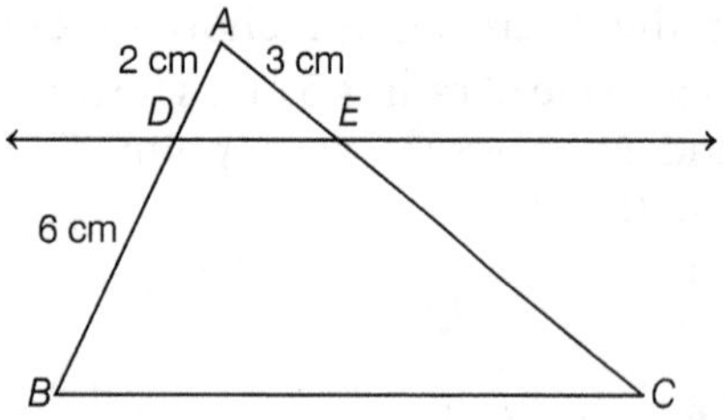


**34.** A pen stand made of wood is in the shape of a cuboid with four conical depressions to hold pens.

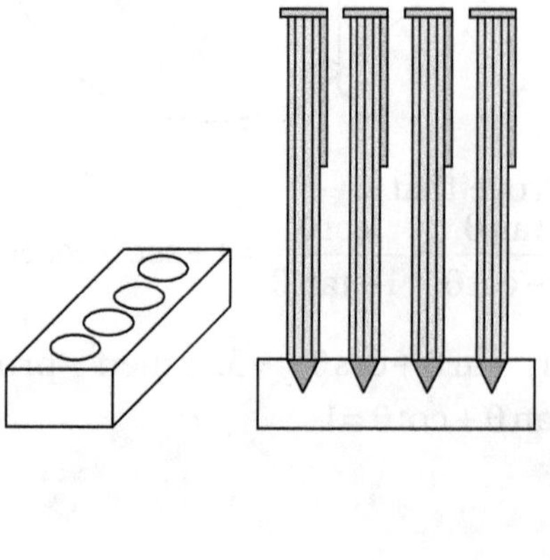

The dimensions of the cuboid are 15 cm by 10 cm by 3.5 cm. The radius of each of the depressions is 0.5 cm and the depth is 1.4 cm. Find the volume of wood in the entire stand.

*Or*

Ramesh made a bird-bath for his garden in the shape of a cylinder with a hemispherical depression at one end. The height of the cylinder is 1.45 m and its radius is 30 cm. Find the total surface area of the bird-bath.

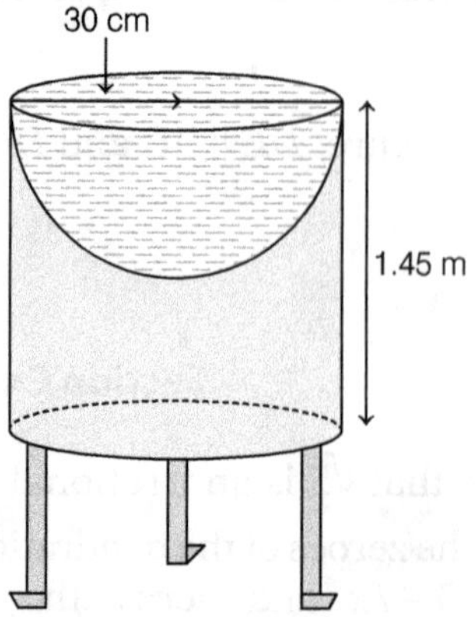


**35.** A life insurance agent found the following data for distribution of ages of 100 policy holders. Calculate the median age, if policies are given only to persons having age 18 yr onwards but less than 60 yr.

| Age (in years) | Number of policy holders |
|---|---|
| Below 20 | 2 |
| 20-25 | 4 |
| 25-30 | 18 |
| 30-35 | 21 |
| 35-40 | 33 |
| 40-45 | 11 |
| 45-50 | 3 |
| 50-55 | 6 |
| 55-60 | 2 |

# Section-E

**Case study based questions are compulsory**

**36.** In the month of April to June 2022, the exports of passenger cars from India increased by 26% in the corresponding quarter of 2021-22, as per a report. A car manufacturing company planned to produce 1800 cars in 4th year and 2600 cars in 8th year. Assuming that the production increases uniformly by a fixed number every year.

Based on the above information, answer the following questions.

(i) Find the production in the 1st year. (1)

(ii) Find the production in the 12th year. (1)

(iii) Find the total production in first 10 year. (2)

*Or*

In which year the total production will reach to 31200 cars? (2)

**37.** In a GPS, The lines that run East-West are known as lines of latitude, and the lines running North-South are known as lines of longitude. The latitude and the longitude of a place are its coordinates and the distance formula is used to find the distance between two places. The distance between two parallel lines is approximately 150 km. A family from Uttar Pradesh planned a round trip from Lucknow ($L$) to Puri ($P$) *via.* Bhuj ($B$) and Nashik ($N$) as shown in the given figure below.

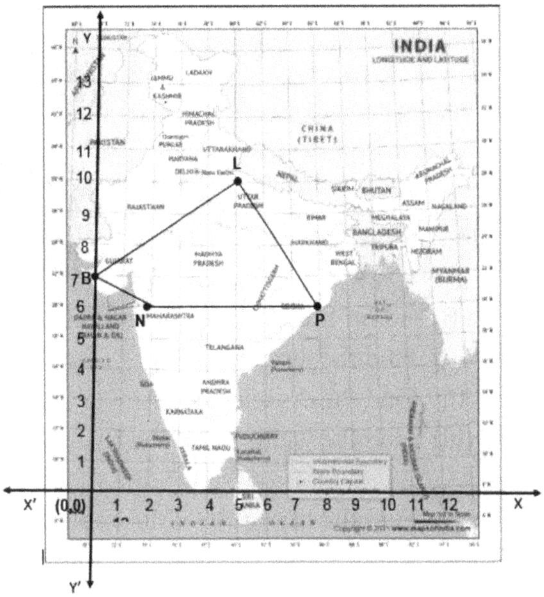


Based on the above information, answer the following questions using the coordinate geometry.

(i) Find the distance between Lucknow ($L$) to Bhuj ($B$). (1)

(ii) If Kota ($K$), internally divide the line segment joining Lucknow ($L$) to Bhuj ($B$) into 3:2, then find the coordinate of Kota ($K$). (1)

(iii) Name the type of triangle formed by the places Lucknow ($L$), Nashik ($N$) and Puri ($P$). (2)

*Or*

Find a place (point) on the longitude ($Y$-axis) which is equidistant from the points Lucknow ($L$) and Puri ($P$). (2)

**38.** Lakshaman Jhula is located 5 km North-East of the city of Rishikesh in the Indian state of Uttarakhand. The bridge connects the villages of Tapovan to Jonk. Tapovan is in Tehri Garhwal district, on the West bank of the river, while Jonk is in Pauri Garhwal district, on the East bank.

Lakshman Jhula is a pedestrian bridge also used by motorbikes. It is a landmark of Rishikesh. A group of Class X students visited Rishikesh in Uttarakhand on a trip. They observed from a point (P) on a river bridge that the angles of depression of opposite banks of the river are 60° and 30° respectively. The height of the bridge is about 18 m from the river.

Based on the above information, answer the following questions.

(i) Find the distance $PA$. (1)

(ii) Find the distance $PB$. (1)

(iii) Find the width $AB$ of the river. (2)

*Or*

Find the height $BQ$ if the angle of the elevation of $Q$ from $P$ be 30°. (2)

# SOLUTIONS

**1.** (c) Given, $p = ab^2 = a \times b \times b$

$$q = a^3b = a \times a \times a \times b$$

To find the LCM, we list all prime factors of $ab^2$ and $a^3b$.

$\therefore$ LCM $(ab^2, a^3b) = a \times a \times a \times b \times b$

$$= a^3b^2$$

**2.** (c) The greatest possible speed at which a man can walk 52 km and 91 km in an exact number of hours

$$= \text{HCF } (52, 91)$$

Prime factors of $52 = 2 \times 2 \times 13$

Prime factors of $91 = 7 \times 13$

$\therefore$ HCF (52, 91) = 13

So, the required speed = 13 km/h

**3.** (b) Let $p(x) = x^2 + 3x + k$

$\because$ 2 is a zero of the polynomial.

$\therefore \quad p(2) = 0$

$\Rightarrow \quad 2^2 + 3(2) + k = 0$

$\Rightarrow \quad 4 + 6 + k = 0$

$\Rightarrow \quad k = -10$

**4.** (b) Given, pair of linear equation is $6x - 3y + 10 = 0$ and $2x - y + 9 = 0$.

Now, let us find atleast two solutions of each of the above equations, as shown in the following tables.

Table for line $6x - 3y + 10 = 0$

| | | |
|---|---|---|
| $x$ | 0 | $-\frac{5}{3}$ |
| $y$ | $\frac{10}{3}$ | 0 |
| **Points** | $A\left(0, \frac{10}{3}\right)$ | $B\left(-\frac{5}{3}, 0\right)$ |

Table for line $2x - y + 9 = 0$

| | | |
|---|---|---|
| $x$ | 0 | $-\frac{9}{2}$ |
| $y$ | 9 | 0 |
| **Points** | $C(0, 9)$ | $D\left(-\frac{9}{2}, 0\right)$ |

Now, plot the points $A\left(0, \frac{10}{3}\right)$, $B\left(-\frac{5}{3}, 0\right)$ on a graph paper and join them to get the line $AB$.

Similarly, plot the points $C(0, 9)$ and $D\left(-\frac{9}{2}, 0\right)$ and join them to get the line $CD$.

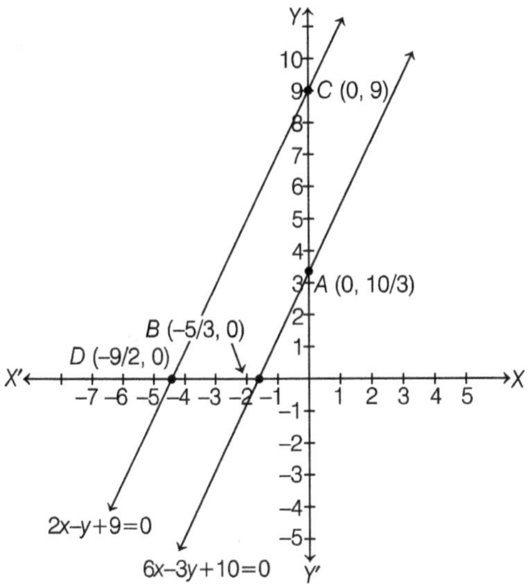


From the graph, it is clear that lines represented by the equations $2x - y + 9 = 0$ and $6x - 3y + 10 = 0$ are parallel.

**5.** (c) Given equation is $x^2 + 4x + k = 0$

On comparing it with $ax^2 + bx + c = 0$, we get

$$a = 1, b = 4, c = k$$

We know, for real and equal roots, discriminant $D = 0$

$\Rightarrow \quad 4^2 - 4(1)(k) = 0 \qquad [\because D = b^2 - 4ac]$

$\Rightarrow \quad 16 - 4k = 0 \Rightarrow 4k = 16 \Rightarrow k = 4$

**6.** (b) Let the given coordinates are $A(0, 0)$, $B(3, 0)$ and $C(0, 4)$.

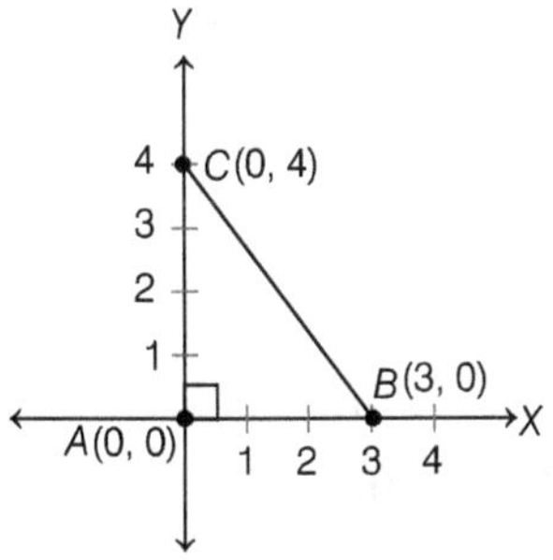


$AB = 3$ units,

$AC = 4$ units

and $BC = \sqrt{(0-3)^2 + (4-0)^2}$

$= \sqrt{9 + 16} = \sqrt{25} = 5$ units

So, perimeter of $\Delta ABC = AB + BC + CA$

$= 3 + 5 + 4$

$= 12$ units

**7.** (c) Given, $\frac{AB}{DE} = \frac{BC}{FD}$

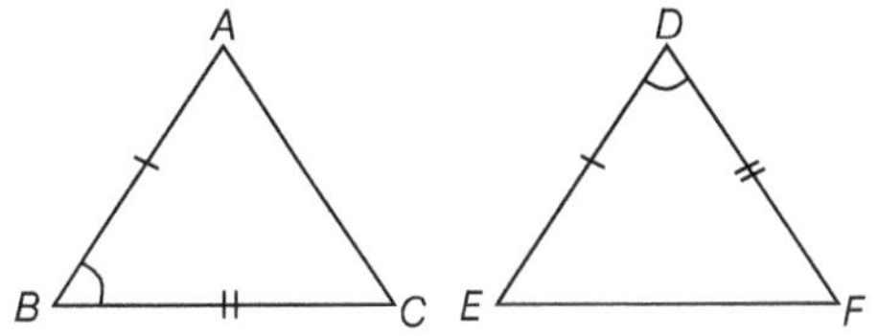

Here, $\Delta ABC \sim \Delta EDF$ [by SAS similarity criterion]

Since, sides including $\angle B$ and $\angle D$ are proportional, so if $\angle B = \angle D$

**8.** (b) On $Y$-axis, $x$-coordinate of a point is zero. Let a point $P(0, y)$ divides the line segment joining the points $A(5, -6)$ and $B(-1, -4)$ in the ratio $m : n$.

By section formula, we get

$$P(0, y) = \left(\frac{-1m + 5n}{m + n}, \frac{-4m - 6n}{m + n}\right)$$

So, $\quad 0 = \frac{-m + 5n}{m + n} \Rightarrow -m + 5n = 0$

$\Rightarrow \quad 5n = m \Rightarrow \frac{m}{n} = \frac{5}{1}$

So, the $Y$-axis divides the line segment joining the points $A(5, -6)$ and $B(-1, -4)$ in the ratio 5 : 1.

**9.** (a) Since, $PA$ and $PB$ are tangents drawn from the external point $P$ to the circle.

$\therefore \quad PA = PB$

[$\because$ length of tangents drawn from an external point to the circle are equal]

In $\Delta PAB$, $\quad PA = PB$

$\Rightarrow \quad \angle PBA = \angle PAB \qquad \dots$(i)

[$\because$ angles opposite to equal sides are equal]

In $\Delta PAB$,

$$\angle BPA + \angle PAB + \angle ABP = 180^\circ$$

$\Rightarrow \angle PAB + \angle ABP = 180^\circ - 50^\circ = 130^\circ$

$\Rightarrow \quad \angle PAB = \frac{130^\circ}{2} = 65^\circ \qquad$ [using Eq. (i)]

We know that radius is perpendicular to the tangent at the point of contact.

$\therefore \quad \angle OAP = 90^\circ \qquad [\because OA \perp AP]$

$\Rightarrow \quad \angle OAB + \angle BAP = 90^\circ$

$\Rightarrow \quad \angle OAB + 65^\circ = 90^\circ$

$\Rightarrow \quad \angle OAB = 25^\circ$

Hence, $\angle OAB$ is equal to $25^\circ$.

**10.** (a) Let us first draw a right angled $\Delta ABC$.

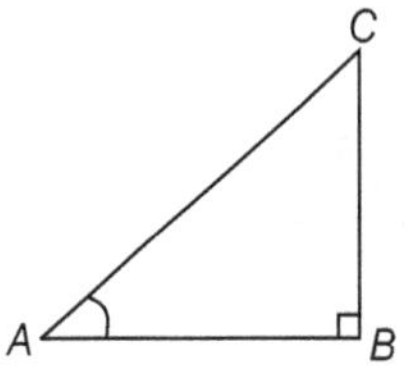

We know that $\sin A = \frac{BC}{AC} = \frac{1}{2}$

Let $BC = k$ and $AC = 2k$, where $k$ is a positive number.

Now, by using the Pythagoras theorem, we have

$$AC^2 = AB^2 + BC^2$$

$$\Rightarrow \quad (2k)^2 = AB^2 + (k)^2$$

$$\Rightarrow \quad AB^2 = 4k^2 - k^2$$

$$\Rightarrow \quad AB^2 = 3k^2 \Rightarrow AB = k\sqrt{3}$$

So, $\sec A = \frac{AC}{AB} = \frac{2k}{k\sqrt{3}} = \frac{2}{\sqrt{3}}$

**11.** (c) $\sqrt{3}\cos^2 A + \sqrt{3}\sin^2 A = \sqrt{3}(\cos^2 A + \sin^2 A)$

$$= \sqrt{3} \quad [\because \sin^2 A + \cos^2 A = 1]$$

**12.** (b) $\cos 1^\circ \cos 2^\circ \cos 3^\circ \ldots \cos 90^\circ$

$= 0$ [$\because \cos 90^\circ = 0$ and the product of any number by zero is zero itself]

**13.** (b) Let the radius of a circle be $r$ and the length of the side of a square be $a$.

Circumference of the circle $= 2\pi r$

Perimeter of the square $= 4a$

According to the question,

$$2\pi r = 4a$$

$$\Rightarrow \quad 2 \times \frac{22}{7} \times r = 4a$$

$$\Rightarrow \quad \frac{11}{7} \times r = a$$

$$\Rightarrow \quad r = \frac{7}{11}a \quad \ldots(\text{i})$$

Now, area of the circle $= \pi r^2 = \frac{22}{7} \times \left(\frac{7}{11}a\right)^2$ [using Eq. (i)]

and area of the square $= a^2$

So, the required ratio is $\frac{\frac{22}{7} \times \left(\frac{7}{11}a\right)^2}{a^2} = \frac{22}{7} \times \frac{7}{11} \times \frac{7}{11}$

$$= \frac{14}{11}$$

**14.** (c) Let the radius of two circles be $r_1$ and $r_2$ respectively.

Given, $\frac{r_1}{r_2} = \frac{4}{3}$

Let $\frac{r_1}{r_2} = \frac{4k}{3k}$

Then, $r_1 = 4k$ and $r_2 = 3k$

Area of first circle $= \pi r_1^2 = \pi(4k)^2$

Area of second circle $= \pi r_2^2 = \pi(3k)^2$

$\therefore$ Required ratio $= \frac{\pi r_1^2}{\pi r_2^2} = \frac{(4k)^2}{(3k)^2}$

$$= \left(\frac{4}{3}\right)^2 = \frac{16}{9}$$

**15.** (d) Total surface area of a hemisphere $= 3\pi r^2$

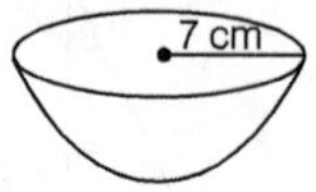


$$= 3\pi \times 7 \times 7$$

$$= 147\,\pi \text{ cm}^2$$

**16.** (c) The class with the maximum frequency is the modal class, which is 15-20 for the given data with a frequency of 20.

The lower limit is 15 and the upper limit is 20.

Hence, the upper limit of the modal class is 20.

**17.** (b) $\Sigma f_i x_i = 4 \times 1 + 5 \times 2 + y \times 3 + 1 \times 4 + 2 \times 5$

$$= 4 + 10 + 3y + 4 + 10 = 28 + 3y$$

$$\Sigma f_i = 4 + 5 + y + 1 + 2 = 12 + y$$

$\because$ Mean $= \frac{\Sigma f_i x_i}{\Sigma f_i}$

$$\Rightarrow \quad \frac{28 + 3y}{12 + y} = 2.6 \quad [\text{given, mean} = 2.6]$$

$$\Rightarrow \quad 28 + 3y = 2.6(12 + y)$$

$$\Rightarrow \quad 28 + 3y = 312 + 2.6y \Rightarrow 0.4y = 32$$

$$\Rightarrow \quad y = \frac{32}{4} = 8$$

**18.** (a) Total number of outcomes = 52

Total number of red face card

= 3 cards of diamonds + 3 cards of hearts

= 6

$\therefore$ Probability, $P = \frac{\text{Favourable outcomes}}{\text{Total number of outcomes}}$

$$= \frac{6}{52} = \frac{3}{26}$$

**19.** (d) We know that

$$\text{HCF}(a, b) \times \text{LCM}(a, b) = a \times b \quad \ldots(\text{i})$$

So, if HCF of 510 and 92 is 2, then

LCM of 510 and 92 $= \frac{510 \times 92}{\text{HCF}(510, 92)}$ [using Eq. (i)]

$$= \frac{46920}{2} = 23460 \neq 32460$$

So, the given Assertion is false and Reason is true.

**20.** (a) The $y$-coordinate of the point which lies on $X$-axis is zero.

So, let point $P(x, 0)$ divides the line segment joining $A(2, -3)$ and $B(5, 6)$ internally in the ratio $m_1 : m_2$.

By section formula,

$$(x, 0) = \left(\frac{m_1(5) + m_2(2)}{m_1 + m_2}, \frac{m_1(6) + m_2(-3)}{m_1 + m_2}\right)$$

$$\Rightarrow \quad 0 = \frac{6m_1 - 3m_2}{m_1 + m_2}$$

$$\Rightarrow \quad 6m_1 - 3m_2 = 0$$

$$\Rightarrow \quad 6m_1 = 3m_2$$

$$\Rightarrow \quad 2m_1 = m_2$$

$$\Rightarrow \quad \frac{m_1}{m_2} = \frac{1}{2}$$

So, the given Assertion is correct.

Also, the Reason is also true and it is the correct explanation of Assertion.

**21.** Given equations are,

$$kx + 3y - (k - 3) = 0$$

and $$12x + ky - k = 0$$

For a pair of linear equations to have infinitely many solutions

$$\frac{a_1}{a_2} = \frac{b_1}{b_2} = \frac{c_1}{c_2}$$

$$\Rightarrow \quad \frac{k}{12} = \frac{3}{k} = \frac{-(k-3)}{-k}$$

$$\Rightarrow \quad \frac{k}{12} = \frac{3}{k} = \frac{k-3}{k}$$

$$\Rightarrow \quad \frac{k}{12} = \frac{3}{k} \quad \ldots(i)$$

$$\Rightarrow \quad k^2 = 36 \Rightarrow k = \sqrt{36} = \pm 6 \quad (1)$$

Also, $$\frac{3}{k} = \frac{k-3}{k} \quad \ldots(ii)$$

$$\Rightarrow \quad 3k = k^2 - 3k \Rightarrow k^2 - 6k = 0$$

$$\Rightarrow \quad k(k-6) = 0 \Rightarrow k = 0, k = 6$$

Therefore, the value of $k$, that satisfies both the conditions, (i) and (ii) is 6. (1)

**22.** (i) In $\Delta ABD$ and $\Delta CBE$,

$\angle ADB = \angle CEB = 90°$

$\angle ABD = \angle CBE$ [common angle]

$\Rightarrow \Delta ABD \sim \Delta CBE$ [AA criterion] (1)

(ii) In $\Delta PDC$ and $\Delta BEC$,

$\angle PDC = \angle BEC = 90°$

$\angle PCD = \angle BCE$ [common angle]

$\Rightarrow \Delta PDC \sim \Delta BEC$ [AA criterion] (1)

*Or*

In $\Delta ABC$, $DE \parallel AC$

$$\therefore \quad \frac{BD}{AD} = \frac{BE}{EC} \quad \ldots(i)$$

[using basic proportionality theorem]

In $\Delta ABE$, $DF \parallel AE$

$$\therefore \quad \frac{BD}{AD} = \frac{BF}{FE} \quad \ldots(ii)$$

[using basic proportionality theorem] (1)

From Eqs. (i) and (ii), we get

$$\frac{BD}{AD} = \frac{BE}{EC} = \frac{BF}{FE}$$

Thus, $$\frac{BF}{FE} = \frac{BE}{EC}$$ **Hence proved.** (1)

**23.** Let $O$ be the centre of the concentric circles of radii 5 cm and 3 cm, respectively.

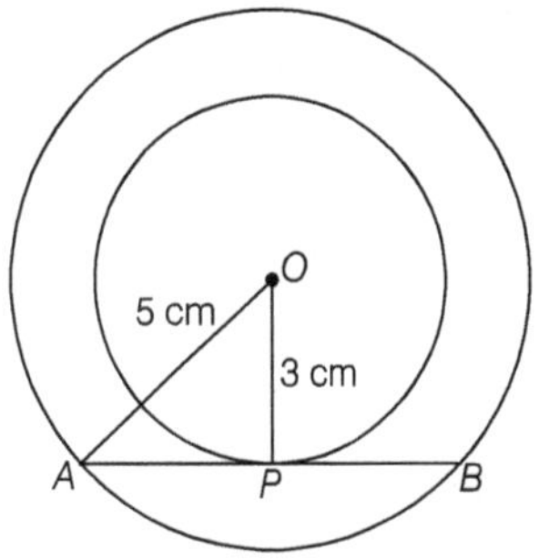


Let $AB$ be a chord of the larger circle touching the smaller circle at $P$.

So, $OP \perp AB$

[∵ tangent to a circle is perpendicular to the radius through the point of contact] (1)

Since, $AB$ is a chord and $OP \perp AB$.

So, $AP = PB$

[∵ perpendicular from the centre bisects the chord] ...(i)

Applying Pythagoras theorem in $\Delta OPA$, we have

$$OA^2 = OP^2 + AP^2$$

$$\Rightarrow \quad (5)^2 = (3)^2 + AP^2 \Rightarrow 25 - 9 = AP^2$$

$$\Rightarrow \quad AP^2 = 16 \Rightarrow AP = 4\text{ cm}$$

$$\therefore \quad AB = 2AP = 8\text{ cm} \quad \text{[using Eq. (i)]} \quad (1)$$

**24.** Given, $\cot\theta = \frac{7}{8}$

Now, $$\frac{(1+\sin\theta)(1-\sin\theta)}{(1+\cos\theta)(1-\cos\theta)} = \frac{1^2 - \sin^2\theta}{1^2 - \cos^2\theta}$$

[using identity, $(a+b)(a-b) = a^2 - b^2$]

$$= \frac{\cos^2\theta}{\sin^2\theta}$$

[∵ $\sin^2\theta + \cos^2\theta = 1 \therefore \sin^2\theta = 1 - \cos^2\theta$ or $\cos^2\theta = 1 - \sin^2\theta$] (1)

$$= \left(\frac{\cos\theta}{\sin\theta}\right)^2$$

$$= \cot^2\theta \quad \left[\because \frac{\cos\theta}{\sin\theta} = \cot\theta\right]$$

$$= \left(\frac{7}{8}\right)^2 = \frac{49}{64}$$

$\left[\text{given, } \cot\theta = \frac{7}{8}\right]$ (1)

**25.** Let $r = 14$ cm

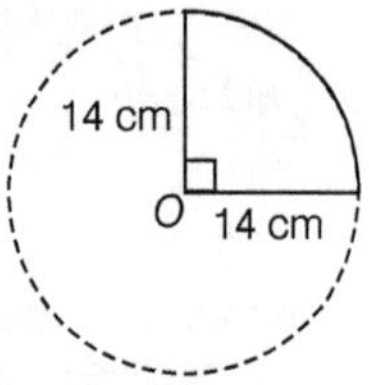


We know that

Perimeter of quadrant

$= 2r + \frac{1}{4}$ circumference of circle (1)

$= 2r + \frac{1}{4} \times 2\pi r$

$= 2 \times 14 + \frac{1}{2} \times \frac{22}{7} \times 14$

$= 28 + 22$

$= 50$ cm (1)

*Or*

Let $r_1 = 24$ cm and $r_2 = 7$ cm

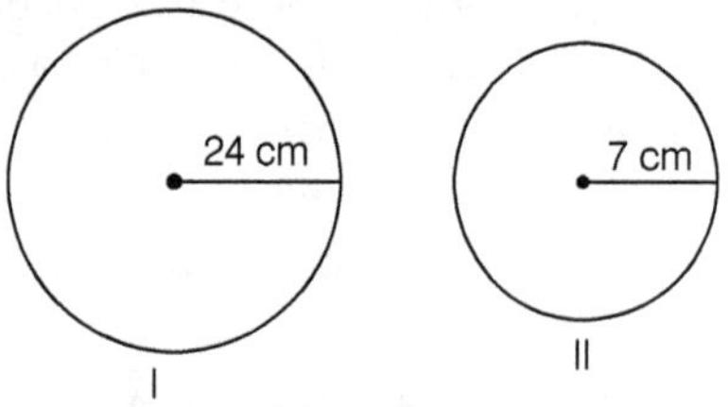


Area of I circle $= \pi r_1^2$

$= \pi(24)^2$

$= 576\,\pi\ \text{cm}^2$ ... (i)

Area of II circle $= \pi r_2^2$

$= \pi(7)^2 = 49\pi\ \text{cm}^2$ ...(ii) (1)

Let $R$ be the radius of a circle whose area is equal to the sum of the areas of two circles.

Area of the circle = Area of I circle + Area of II circle

$\therefore \quad \pi R^2 = 576\pi + 49\pi$

[using Eqs. (i) and (ii)]

$\Rightarrow \quad \pi R^2 = 625\,\pi$

$\Rightarrow \quad R^2 = 625$

$\Rightarrow \quad R = 25$ cm

Thus, diameter of the circle $= 2R = 50$ cm. (1)

**26.** Let us assume to the contrary, that $\sqrt{5}$ is rational. Then we can find $a$ and $b (b \neq 0)$ such that

$\sqrt{5} = \frac{a}{b}$ (assuming that $a$ and $b$ are co-primes)

So, $a = \sqrt{5}b$

Squaring both sides, we get

$a^2 = 5b^2$ ...(i)

Here 5 is a prime number that divides $a^2$, then 5 divides a also.

[using the theorem, if $p$ is a prime number and if $p$ divides $a^2$, then $p$ divides $a$, where $a$ is a positive integer] (1)

Thus, 5 is a factor of $a$.

Since, 5 is a factor of $a$, we can write $a = 5c$

[where $c$ is a constant]

Substituting $a = 5c$ in Eq. (i),

$(5c)^2 = 5b^2$

$\Rightarrow \quad 25c^2 = 5b^2 \Rightarrow 5c^2 = b^2$ (1)

This means 5 divides $b^2$, so 5 divides $b$ also.

Hence, $a$ and $b$ have atleast 5 as a common factor.

But this contradicts the fact that $a$ and $b$ are co-prime. This is the contradiction to our assumption that $p$ and $q$ are co-primes.

So, $\sqrt{5}$ is not a rational number.

Therefore, $\sqrt{5}$ is irrational. **Hence proved.** (1)

**27.** Let the given polynomial

$f(x) = 6x^2 - 3 - 7x = 6x^2 - 7x - 3$

$= 6x^2 - 9x + 2x - 3$

$= 3x(2x - 3) + 1(2x - 3)$

$= (2x - 3)(3x + 1)$ (1)

For zeroes, $\quad f(x) = 0$

$\Rightarrow \quad (2x - 3)(3x + 1) = 0$

$\Rightarrow 2x - 3 = 0$ or $3x + 1 = 0$

$\Rightarrow \quad x = \frac{3}{2}$ or $x = -\frac{1}{3}$

Therefore, the zeroes of $6x^2 - 3 - 7x$ are $\frac{3}{2}, -\frac{1}{3}$. (1)

Now, sum of zeroes $= \frac{3}{2} - \frac{1}{3} = \frac{9-2}{6} = \frac{7}{6}$

$= -\left(\frac{-7}{6}\right) = -\frac{\text{Coefficient of } x}{\text{Coefficient of } x^2}$

Product of zeroes $= \frac{3}{2} \times \frac{-1}{3} = \frac{-1}{2} = \frac{-3}{6}$

$= \frac{\text{Constant term}}{\text{Coefficient of } x^2}$

Therefore, the relationship between zeroes and their coefficients is verified. (1)

**28.** Let the fixed charge be ₹ $x$ and additional charge be ₹$y$ per day.

Since, shopkeeper takes a fixed charge for the first two days and an additional charge for each day thereafter.

So, number of days, book kept by Latika can written as,

$6 = 2$(fixed charge) + 4(additional charge)

Hence, total charge $= x + 4y = 22$ ...(i)

Similarly, number of days, book kept by Anand can be written as,

$4 = 2(\text{fixed charge}) + 2(\text{additional charge})$

Hence, total charge $= x + 2y = 16$ ...(ii) (1)

Subtracting Eq. (ii) from Eq. (i), we get

$(x + 4y) - (x + 2y) = 22 - 16$

$\Rightarrow \quad 4y - 2y = 6$

$\Rightarrow \quad 2y = 6 \Rightarrow y = 3$ (1)

Substituting $y = 3$ in Eq. (i), we get

$x + 4(3) = 22 \Rightarrow x = 22 - 12 = 10$

Therefore, fixed charge = ₹ 10

and additional charge = ₹ 3 per day. (1)

*Or*

Let the speeds of the cars which start from $A$ and $B$ be $x$ km/hr and $y$ km/hr respectively.

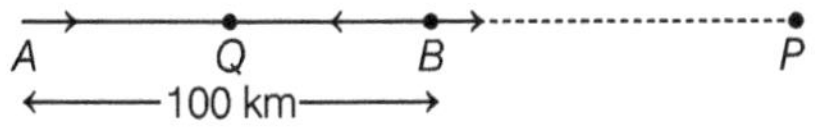


Let $P$ be the meeting point if they travel in the same direction and $Q$ be the meeting point if they travel towards each other. (1)

Given, $\quad AB = 100$ km

$\Rightarrow \quad AP - BP = 100$

$\Rightarrow \quad 5x - 5y = 100$

[using, distance = speed × time]

$\Rightarrow \quad x - y = 20$ ...(i)

Also, $\quad AB = AQ + BQ = 100$

$\Rightarrow \quad x + y = 100$ ...(ii) (1)

Adding Eqs. (i) and (ii), we get,

$x - y + x + y = 20 + 100$

$\Rightarrow \quad 2x = 120$

$\Rightarrow \quad x = 60$

Substituting $x = 60$ in Eq. (ii), we get

$60 + y = 100$

$\Rightarrow \quad y = 40$

Therefore, the speed of the first car is 60 km/hr and the speed of the second car is 40 km/hr. (1)

**29.** In the figure, $TP = TQ$

[∵ the lengths of tangents drawn from an external point are equal]

$\Rightarrow \Delta TPQ$ is isosceles.

Then, $\angle TQP = \angle TPQ$

and $TO$ is the angle bisector of $\angle PTQ$.

Also, $TO$ bisects $PQ$ at $R$ which gives $PR = RQ = 4$ cm.

So, $\quad OT \perp PQ$

[∵ line joining the centre of a circle to the mid-point of a chord is always perpendicular to the chord] (1)

So, in $\Delta ORP$,

$OR = \sqrt{OP^2 - PR^2} = \sqrt{5^2 - 4^2} = 3$ cm

Now, $\angle TPR + \angle RPO = 90° = \angle TPR + \angle PTR$

[∵ $\angle TPR + \angle PTR = 180° - \angle TRP = 180° - 90° = 90°$]

$\Rightarrow \quad \angle RPO = \angle PTR$ (1)

In $\Delta TRP$ and $\Delta PRO$,

$\angle TRP = \angle PRO = 90°$

$\angle PTR = \angle RPO$

$\Rightarrow \quad \Delta TRP \sim \Delta PRO$ [by AA rule]

So, $\quad \dfrac{TP}{PO} = \dfrac{RP}{RO}$

$\Rightarrow \quad \dfrac{TP}{5} = \dfrac{4}{3} \Rightarrow TP = \dfrac{20}{3}$ cm (1)

**30.** To prove

$\dfrac{\tan\theta}{1-\cot\theta} + \dfrac{\cot\theta}{1-\tan\theta} = 1 + \sec\theta\,\text{cosec}\,\theta$

$\text{LHS} = \dfrac{\tan\theta}{1-\cot\theta} + \dfrac{\cot\theta}{1-\tan\theta} = \dfrac{\tan\theta}{1-\dfrac{1}{\tan\theta}} + \dfrac{\dfrac{1}{\tan\theta}}{1-\tan\theta}$ (1)

$= \dfrac{\tan^2\theta}{\tan\theta - 1} + \dfrac{1}{\tan\theta(1-\tan\theta)} = \dfrac{\tan^3\theta - 1}{\tan\theta(-1+\tan\theta)}$

$= \dfrac{(\tan\theta - 1)(\tan^2\theta + \tan\theta + 1)}{\tan\theta(\tan\theta - 1)}$

[using identity $a^3 - b^3 = (a-b)(a^2 + b^2 + ab)$] (1)

$= \dfrac{\tan^2\theta + \tan\theta + 1}{\tan\theta} = \tan\theta + 1 + \cot\theta$

$= 1 + \dfrac{\sin\theta}{\cos\theta} + \dfrac{\cos\theta}{\sin\theta}$

$= 1 + \dfrac{\sin^2\theta + \cos^2\theta}{\cos\theta\sin\theta} = 1 + \dfrac{1}{\sin\theta\cos\theta}$

[∵ $\sin^2\theta + \cos^2\theta = 1$]

$= 1 + \sec\theta\,\text{cosec}\,\theta = \text{RHS}$ **Hence proved.** (1)

*Or*

Given, $\sin\theta + \cos\theta = \sqrt{3}$

Squaring both sides, we get

$(\sin\theta + \cos\theta)^2 = (\sqrt{3})^2$

$\Rightarrow \sin^2\theta + \cos^2\theta + 2\sin\theta\cos\theta = 3$

$\Rightarrow \quad 1 + 2\sin\theta\cos\theta = 3$

[∵ $\sin^2\theta + \cos^2\theta = 1$]

$\Rightarrow \quad 2\sin\theta\cos\theta = 2$

$\Rightarrow \quad \sin\theta\cos\theta = 1$ ...(i) (1½)

Now, $\text{LHS} = \tan\theta + \cot\theta = \dfrac{\sin\theta}{\cos\theta} + \dfrac{\cos\theta}{\sin\theta}$

$= \dfrac{\sin^2\theta + \cos^2\theta}{\sin\theta\cos\theta} = \dfrac{1}{\sin\theta\cos\theta}$

$= 1 = \text{RHS}$ [using Eq. (i)]

**Hence proved.** (1½)

**31.** The possible outcomes of the experiment are

| | | | | | |
|---|---|---|---|---|---|
| (1, 1) | (1, 2) | (1, 3) | (1, 4) | (1, 5) | (1, 6) |
| (2, 1) | (2, 2) | (2, 3) | (2, 4) | (2, 5) | (2, 6) |
| (3, 1) | (3, 2) | (3, 3) | (3, 4) | (3, 5) | (3, 6) |
| (4, 1) | (4, 2) | (4, 3) | (4, 4) | (4, 5) | (4, 6) |
| (5, 1) | (5, 2) | (5, 3) | (5, 4) | (5, 5) | (5, 6) |
| (6, 1) | (6, 2) | (6, 3) | (6, 4) | (6, 5) | (6, 6) |

So, the total number of possible outcomes

$= 6 \times 6 = 36$

(i) The outcomes favourable to the event 'the sum of two numbers is 8' denoted by $E$ are (2, 6), (3, 5), (4, 4), (5, 3), (6, 2) i.e., the number of outcomes favourable to $E = 5$

Hence, $P(E) = \frac{5}{36}$ **(1)**

(ii) As there is no outcome favourable to the event $F$, 'the sum of two numbers is 13'.

So, $P(F) = \frac{0}{36} = 0$ **(1)**

(iii) All the outcomes are favourable to the event $G$, 'sum of two numbers $\le 12$'.

So, $P(G) = \frac{36}{36} = 1.$ **(1)**

**32.** Let the average speed of passenger train $= x$ km/hr

and the average speed of express train

$= (x + 11)$ km/h

According to the question, time taken by the express train to cover 132 km is 1 h less than the passenger train to cover the same distance.

$\therefore \quad \frac{132}{x} - \frac{132}{x + 11} = 1$ **(1½)**

$\Rightarrow \quad \frac{132(x + 11) - 132x}{x(x + 11)} = 1$

$\Rightarrow \quad \frac{132 \times 11}{x(x + 11)} = 1$

$\Rightarrow \quad 1452 = x^2 + 11x$

$\Rightarrow \quad x^2 + 11x - 1452 = 0$ **(1½)**

$\Rightarrow x^2 + 44x - 33x - 1452 = 0$

$\Rightarrow \quad x(x + 44) - 33(x + 44) = 0$

$\Rightarrow \quad (x + 44)(x - 33) = 0$

$\Rightarrow \quad (x + 44)(x - 33) = 0$

$\Rightarrow \quad x = -44, x = 33$

As the speed cannot be negative, the speed of the passenger train is 33 km/h and the speed of the express train is $33 + 11 = 44$ km/h. **(2)**

*Or*

Let the speed of the stream $= x$ km/h

So, the speed of the boat in upstream $= (18 - x)$ km/h

and the speed of the boat in downstream

$= (18 + x)$ km/h

According to the question, time taken by the boat to cover 24 km upstream is 1 h more than to return downstream to the same spot. **(1½)**

$\therefore \quad \frac{24}{18 - x} - \frac{24}{18 + x} = 1$

$\Rightarrow \quad 24\left[\frac{1}{18 - x} - \frac{1}{18 + x}\right] = 1$

$\Rightarrow \quad 24\left[\frac{18 + x - 18 + x}{(18)^2 - x^2}\right] = 1$

$\Rightarrow \quad 24 \times (2x) = 324 - x^2$ **(1½)**

$\Rightarrow \quad x^2 + 48x - 324 = 0$

$\Rightarrow \quad x^2 + 54x - 6x - 324 = 0$

$\Rightarrow \quad x(x + 54) - 6(x + 54) = 0$

$\Rightarrow \quad (x + 54)(x - 6) = 0 \Rightarrow x = -54$ or $x = 6$

As the speed can't be negative, the speed of the stream is 6 km/h. **(2)**

**33. Given** A line is drawn parallel to one side $BC$ of a $\Delta ABC$ to intersect the other two sides $AB$ and $AC$ at distinct point $D$ and $E$, respectively.

**To prove** $\frac{AD}{DB} = \frac{AE}{EC}$.

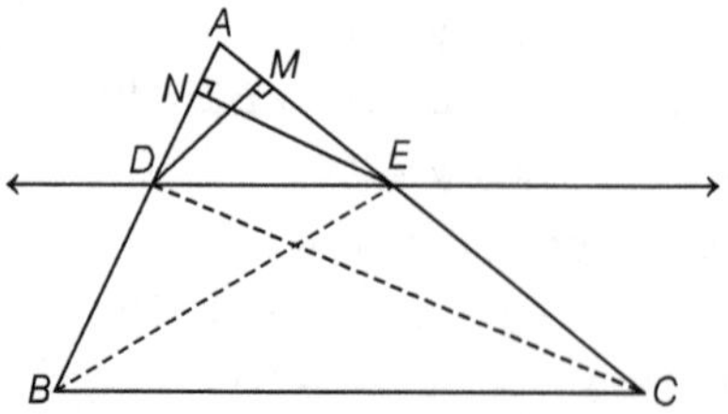


**(1)**

**Construction** Draw $DM \perp AC$ and $EN \perp AB$ and join $BE$ and $CD$.

**Proof** Area of $\Delta ADE = \frac{1}{2} \times$ Base $\times$ Height

So, $\quad ar(\Delta ADE) = \frac{1}{2}(AD \times EN)$

Similarly, $ar(\Delta BDE) = \frac{1}{2} DB \times EN$

$ar(\Delta ADE) = \frac{1}{2} AE \times DM$

and $\quad ar(\Delta DEC) = \frac{1}{2} EC \times DM$ **(1)**

$\therefore \quad \frac{ar(\Delta ADE)}{ar(\Delta BDE)} = \frac{\frac{1}{2} AD \times EN}{\frac{1}{2} DB \times EN} = \frac{AD}{DB}$ ...(i)

and $\quad \frac{ar(\Delta ADE)}{ar(\Delta DEC)} = \frac{\frac{1}{2} AE \times DM}{\frac{1}{2} EC \times DM} = \frac{AE}{EC}$ ...(ii) **(1)**

As the $\Delta BDE$ and $\Delta DEC$ are on the same base $DE$ and between the same parallels $BC$ and $DE$.

So, $ar(\Delta BDE) = ar(\Delta DEC)$ ...(iii)

From Eqs. (i), (ii) and (iii), we get

$$\frac{AD}{DB} = \frac{AE}{EC}$$ **Hence proved.** (1)

Now, in the figure,

$AD = 2$ cm, $DB = 6$ cm and $AE = 3$ cm

$\because \quad \frac{AD}{DB} = \frac{AE}{EC}$

$\Rightarrow \quad \frac{2}{6} = \frac{3}{EC}$

$\Rightarrow \quad EC = 9$ cm (1)

**34.** Given, dimensions of the cuboid

i.e. $L = 15$ cm, $B = 10$ cm and $H = 3.5$ cm

Radius of conical depression, $(r) = 0.5$ cm

Depth of conical depression $(h) = 1.4$ cm

Volume of one conical depression $= \frac{1}{3}\pi r^2 h$

$= \frac{1}{3} \times \frac{22}{7} \times (0.5)^2 \times 1.4 = 0.366 \text{ cm}^3$ (1)

So, volume of 4 conical depressions $= 4 \times 0.366$

$= 1.464 \text{ cm}^3$ (1)

Now, volume of cuboid $= L \times B \times H$

$= 15 \times 10 \times 3.5$

$= 525 \text{ cm}^3$ (1)

So, the volume of wood in the entire stand

= Volume of cuboid

− Volume of 4 conical depressions

$= 525 - 1.464$

$= 523.54 \text{ cm}^3$ (2)

*Or*

Let $h$ be the height of the cylinder and $r$ be the common radius of cylinder and hemisphere.

Then, the total surface area

= Curved surface area of hemisphere

+ Curved surface area of cylinder

+ Area of the circle at the bottom (1½)

$= 2\pi r^2 + 2\pi rh + \pi r^2$

$= \pi r(2r + 2h + r)$

$= \pi r(3r + 2h)$ (1½)

$= \frac{22}{7} \times 30(3 \times 30 + 2 \times 145)$

[$\because r = 30$ cm and $h = 1.45$ m $= 145$ cm]

$= \frac{22}{7} \times 30 \times 380$

$= 35828.57 \text{ cm}^2$

$= 3.58 \text{ m}^2$ (2)

**35.**

| Class Interval | Number of Policy holders (*f*) | Cumulative frequency (*cf*) |
|---|---|---|
| Below 20 | 2 | 2 |
| 20-25 | 4 | 6 |
| 25-30 | 18 | 24 |
| 30-35 | 21 | 45 |
| 35-40 | 33 | 78 |
| 40-45 | 11 | 89 |
| 45-50 | 3 | 92 |
| 50-55 | 6 | 98 |
| 55-60 | 2 | 100 |

(2)

Here, total observations, $N = 100 \Rightarrow \frac{N}{2} = 50$

Since, the cumulative frequency just greater than 50 is 78 and the corresponding class interval is 35-40.

$\therefore$ Median class = 35 − 40

So, class size, $h = 5$,

lower limit of median class, $l = 35$,

frequency of median class, $f = 33$

and cumulative frequency of class preceding the median class, $cf = 45$ (1)

Now, median $= l + \left(\frac{\frac{N}{2} - cf}{f}\right) \times h$

$= 35 + \left(\frac{50 - 45}{33}\right) \times 5$

$= 35 + \frac{25}{33} = 35 + 0.76 = 35.76$

$\therefore$ Median age = 35.76 yr. (2)

**36.** (i) Since the production increases uniformly by a fixed number every year, so the number of cars manufactured in 1st, 2nd, 3rd ...... years will form an AP.

We know, general term of an AP, $a_n = a + (n-1)d$

Given, company would produce 1800 cars in 4th year and 2600 cars in 8th year.

$\therefore \quad a_4 = a + (4-1)d = a + 3d = 1800$ ...(i)

$a_8 = a + (8-1)d = a + 7d = 2600$ ...(ii)

Subtracting Eq. (i) from Eq. (ii), we get

$(a + 7d) - (a + 3d) = 2600 - 1800$

$\Rightarrow \quad 4d = 800$

$\Rightarrow \quad d = 200$

Substituting $d = 200$ in Eq. (i), we get

$a + 3(200) = 1800$

$\Rightarrow \quad a = 1800 - 600$

$\Rightarrow \quad a = 1200$

So, production in 1st yr $= a = 1200$

(ii) Production in 12th yr $= a_{12} = a + (12-1)d$

$= 1200 + 11 \times 200$

$= 1200 + 2200 = 3400$

(iii) Total production in first 10 yr,

$$S_{10} = \frac{10}{2}[2 \times 1200 + (10-1)200]$$

$$\left[\because S_n = \frac{n}{2}(2a + (n-1)d\right]$$

$\Rightarrow \quad S_{10} = 5[2400 + 1800] = 5 \times 4200 = 21000$

*Or*

Let in $n$ years the production will reach to 31200 cars.

We know that $S_n = \frac{n}{2}[2a + (n-1)d]$

$\Rightarrow \quad 31200 = \frac{n}{2}[2 \times 1200 + (n-1)200]$

$\Rightarrow \quad 31200 = n[1200 + 100n - 100]$

$\Rightarrow \quad 31200 = 100n[12 + n - 1]$

$\Rightarrow \quad 312 = n[11 + n]$

$\Rightarrow \quad n^2 + 11n - 312 = 0$

$\Rightarrow n^2 + 24n - 13n - 312 = 0$

$\Rightarrow n(n+24) - 13(n+24) = 0$

$\Rightarrow \quad (n+24)(n-13) = 0$

$\Rightarrow \quad n = -24$ or $n = 13$

As, $n$ can't be negative, so $n = 13$.

Hence, in 13th yr the total production will reach to 31200 cars.

**37.** (i) Coordinates of Bhuj ($B$) are (0, 7)
and coordinates of Lucknow ($L$) are (5, 10).

So, the distance between Lucknow ($L$) and Bhuj ($B$),

$LB = \sqrt{(x_2 - x_1)^2 + (y_2 - y_1)^2}$

$= \sqrt{(0-5)^2 + (7-10)^2}$

$= \sqrt{25 + 9}$

$= \sqrt{34}$ units

(ii) Using section formula, coordinate of Kota ($K$)

$$= \left(\frac{m_1x_2 + m_2x_1}{m_1 + m_2}, \frac{m_1y_2 + m_2y_1}{m_1 + m_2}\right)$$

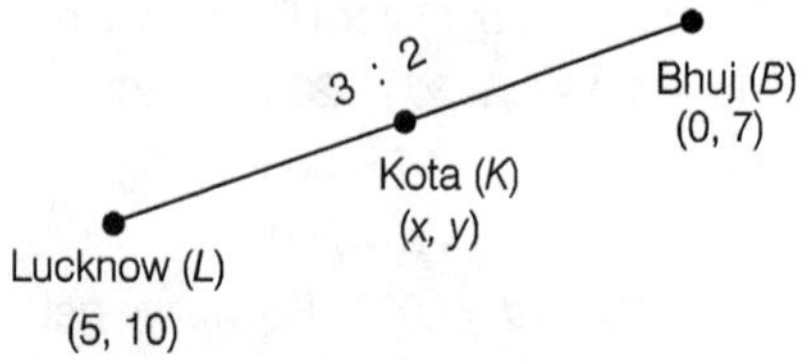


Here, $m_1 = 3$ and $m_2 = 2$

$$\Rightarrow K(x, y) = \left(\frac{3 \times 0 + 2 \times 5}{3+2}, \frac{3 \times 7 + 2 \times 10}{3+2}\right)$$

$$= \left(\frac{10}{5}, \frac{21+20}{5}\right) = (2, 8.2)$$

(iii) Coordinates of $L$ are (5, 10)
Coordinates of $P$ are (8, 6)
Coordinates of $N$ are (2, 6)

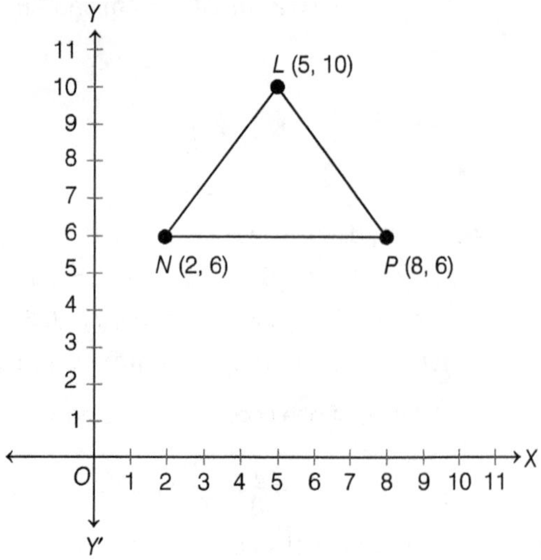


$LN = \sqrt{(5-2)^2 + (10-6)^2} = \sqrt{3^2 + 4^2}$

$= \sqrt{25} = 5$ units

$NP = \sqrt{(8-2)^2 + (6-6)^2} = 6$ units

$PL = \sqrt{(5-8)^2 + (10-6)^2} = \sqrt{3^2 + 4^2}$

$= \sqrt{25} = 5$ units

$\because LN = PL \neq NP$

$\therefore \Delta LNP$ is an isoceles triangle.

*Or*

As the point on $Y$-axis has abscissa = 0.

Let the point on the $Y$-axis which is equidistant from the points $L$ (5, 10) and $P$ (8, 6) be $A(0, y)$

Then, $LA = PA$

$\Rightarrow \sqrt{(0-5)^2 + (y-10)^2} = \sqrt{(0-8)^2 + (y-6)^2}$

$\Rightarrow \quad \sqrt{25 + (y-10)^2} = \sqrt{64 + (y-6)^2}$

Squaring both sides,

$25 + (y-10)^2 = 64 + (y-6)^2$

$\Rightarrow 25 + y^2 + 100 - 20y = 64 + y^2 + 36 - 12y$

$\Rightarrow \quad 125 - 20y = 100 - 12y$

$\Rightarrow \quad 8y = 25$

$\Rightarrow \quad y = \frac{25}{8}$

So, the coordinates of point on $Y$-axis is $\left(0, \frac{25}{8}\right)$.

**38.** (i) $\angle A = \angle P = 60°$ [alternate interior angles]

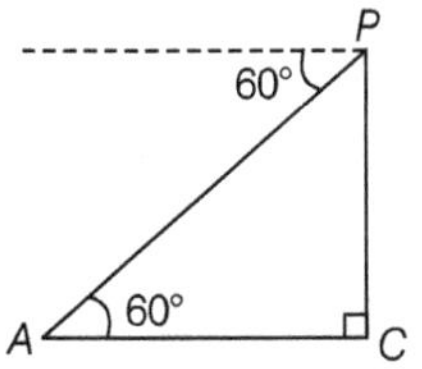


In right angled $\Delta PCA$,

$$\sin 60° = \frac{PC}{PA} \quad \text{[height of the bridge]}$$

$$\Rightarrow \quad \frac{\sqrt{3}}{2} = \frac{18}{PA}$$

[∵ $PC = 18\text{ m}$ = height of bridge from the river]

$$\Rightarrow \quad PA = \frac{36}{\sqrt{3}}$$

$$\Rightarrow \quad PA = 12\sqrt{3}\text{ m}$$

(ii) $\angle PBC = \angle BPR = 30°$

[alternate interior angles]

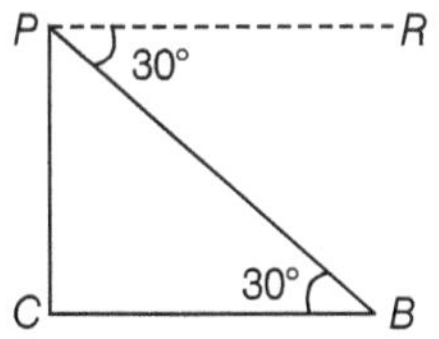


In right angled $\Delta PCB$,

$$\sin 30° = \frac{PC}{PB}$$

$$\Rightarrow \quad \frac{1}{2} = \frac{18}{PB}$$

$$\Rightarrow \quad PB = 36\text{ m}$$

(iii) In $\Delta PCA$,

$$\tan 60° = \frac{PC}{AC}$$

$$\Rightarrow \quad \sqrt{3} = \frac{18}{AC}$$

$$\Rightarrow \quad AC = \frac{18}{\sqrt{3}} = 6\sqrt{3}\text{ m}$$

In $\Delta PCB$,

$$\tan 30° = \frac{PC}{BC}$$

$$\Rightarrow \quad \frac{1}{\sqrt{3}} = \frac{18}{BC}$$

$$\Rightarrow \quad BC = 18\sqrt{3}\text{ m}$$

∴ Width $AB$ of the river $= AC + BC$

$$= 6\sqrt{3} + 18\sqrt{3}$$

$$= 24\sqrt{3}\text{ m}$$

*Or*

$RB = PC = 18\text{ m}$ and $PR = CB = 18\sqrt{3}\text{ m}$

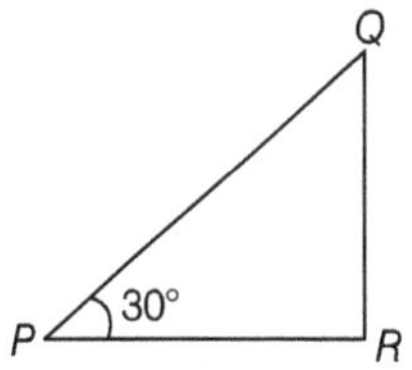


In right angled $\Delta PRQ$,

$$\tan 30° = \frac{QR}{PR}$$

$$\Rightarrow \quad \frac{1}{\sqrt{3}} = \frac{QR}{18\sqrt{3}} \quad [\because PR = BC]$$

$$\Rightarrow \quad QR = 18\text{ m}$$

So, height $BQ = QR + RB$

$$= 18 + 18 \quad [\because BR = PC]$$

$$= 36\text{ m}$$

# ONE DAY BEFORE EXAM*

## Mathematics (Basic)

Time : **3 hrs** Max. Marks : **80**

### Instructions

1. This question paper has 5 Sections A, B, C, D and E.
2. Section A has 20 Multiple Choice Questions (MCQs) carrying 1 mark each.
3. Section B has 5 Short Answer-I (SA-I) Type Questions carrying 2 marks each.
4. Section C has 6 Short Answer-II (SA-II) Type Questions carrying 3 marks each.
5. Section D has 4 Long Answer (LA) Type Questions carrying 5 marks each.
6. Section E has 3 Case Based integrated units of assessment (4 marks each) with sub-parts of the values of 1, 1 and 2 marks each respectively.
7. All questions are compulsory. However, an internal choice in 2 questions of 2 marks, 2 questions of 3 marks and 2 questions of 5 marks has been provided. An internal choice has been provided in the 2 marks questions of Section E.
8. Draw neat figures wherever required. Take $\pi = 22/7$ wherever required if not stated.

## Section-A

**Section A consists of 20 questions of 1 mark each**

**1.** A sector is cut from a circle of diameter 21 cm. If the angle of the sector is $150°$, then its area is

(a) $27.5 \text{ cm}^2$ (b) $144 \text{ cm}^2$
(c) $55 \text{ cm}^2$ (d) $288 \text{ cm}^2$

**2.** If $P(x, 6)$ is the mid-point of the line segment joining $A(6, 5)$ and $B(4, y)$, then the value of $y$ is

(a) 6 (b) 5 (c) 7 (d) 8

**3.** The system of equations $x + 2y + 5 = 0$ and $-3x - 6y + 1 = 0$ has

(a) a unique solution
(b) exactly two solutions
(c) infinitely many solutions
(d) no solution

**4.** An acute angle $\theta$, for which $\sin\theta + \cos\theta$ takes the greatest value, is

(a) 30° (b) 90° (c) 60° (d) 45°

* *To boost the confidence at last moment, students can advised to attempt this sample paper only a day before the exam.*

**5.** The value of $\sin 60° \cos 30° + \cos 60° \sin 30°$ is

(a) 1 (b) $\sqrt{3}$ (c) $\frac{\sqrt{3}}{2}$ (d) $\frac{1}{2}$

**6.** If the distance between the points $(4, p)$ and $(1, 0)$ is 5, then the value of $p$ is

(a) $\pm\sqrt{20}$ units (b) $\pm 4$ units
(c) 0 unit (d) $\pm 3$ units

**7.** One card is drawn at random from a well-shuffled deck of 52 cards. The probability of selecting a card is

(a) $\frac{1}{2}$ (b) 1 (c) $\frac{1}{52}$ (d) 0

**8.** If $(x-3)$ is a factor of the polynomial $3x^2 + 2x - k$, then value of $k$ is

(a) 31 (b) 32 (c) 33 (d) 30

**9.** If 3 chairs and 1 table cost ₹ 1500 and 6 chairs and 1 table costs ₹ 2400, then the linear equations to represent this situation is

(a) $x + 3y = 1500$ and $6x - y = 2400$
(b) $3x - y = 1500$ and $6x - y = 2400$
(c) $3x + y = 1500$ and $6x + y = 2400$
(d) $x - y = 1500$ and $x + y = 2400$

**10.** Two triangles are similar, if their corresponding angles are ......... and their corresponding sides are in the same ....... .

(a) equal, equal (b) equal, ratio
(c) not equal, ratio (d) None of these

**11.** If one of the zeroes of the quadratic polynomial $x^2 - 3x + k$ is 2, then the value of $k$ is

(a) 10 (b) 2 (c) −7 (d) −2

**12.** If in two triangles $\Delta DEF$ and $\Delta PQR$, $\angle D = \angle Q$ and $\angle R = \angle E$, then which of the following is not true?

(a) $\frac{EF}{PR} = \frac{DF}{PQ}$ (b) $\frac{DE}{PQ} = \frac{EF}{RP}$
(c) $\frac{DE}{QR} = \frac{DF}{PQ}$ (d) $\frac{EF}{RP} = \frac{DE}{QR}$

**13.** Which of the following is not a quadratic equation?

(a) $x^2 + 5x - 3 = 0$ (b) $x^2 + x^3 + 7 = 0$
(c) $3 + x + x^2 = 0$ (d) $x^2 - 36 = 0$

**14.** The equation $12x^2 + 4kx + 3 = 0$ has real and equal roots, if

(a) $k = \pm 2$ (b) $k = \pm 9$
(c) $k = 4$ (d) $k = \pm 3$

**15.** If $a$, $b$, $c$ are in AP, then $\frac{a-b}{b-c}$ is equal to

(a) $\frac{b}{a}$ (b) 1 (c) $\frac{a}{c}$ (d) $\frac{c}{a}$

**16.** The $n$th term of an AP 5, 2, −1, −4, ... is

(a) $5 - 3n$ (b) $5n - 3$
(c) $8 - 3n$ (d) $2 - 3n$

**17.** If the volume of a cube is 1728 cm$^3$, the length of its edge is equal to

(a) 7 cm (b) 12 cm
(c) 18 cm (d) 19 cm

**18.** If two tangents inclined at an angle 60° are drawn to a circle of radius 3 cm, the length of each tangent is equal to

(a) 3 cm (b) 6 cm (c) $\frac{\sqrt{3}}{2}$ cm (d) $3\sqrt{3}$ cm

**Directions** *In the question number 19 and 20, a statement of Assertion (A) is followed by a statement of Reason (R). Choose the correct option.*

**19. Assertion (A)** The graph of the linear equations $3x + 2y = 12$ and $5x - 2y = 4$ gives a pair of intersecting lines.

**Reason (R)** The graph of the linear equations $a_1x + b_1y + c_1 = 0$ and $a_2x + b_2y + c_2 = 0$ gives a pair of intersecting lines, if $\frac{a_1}{a_2} \neq \frac{b_1}{b_2}$.

(a) Both Assertion (A) and Reason (R) are true and Reason (R) is the correct explanation of Assertion (A)
(b) Both Assertion (A) and Reason (R) are true but Reason (R) is not the correct explanation of Assertion (A)
(c) Assertion (A) is true but Reason (R) is false
(d) Assertion (A) is false but Reason (R) is true

**20. Assertion (A)** All equilateral triangle are similar.

**Reason (R)** Two triangle are said to be similar, if their corresponding angles are equal and length of corresponding sides are proportional.

(a) Both Assertion (A) and Reason (R) are true and Reason (R) is the correct explanation of Assertion (A)
(b) Both Assertion (A) and Reason (R) are true but Reason (R) is not the correct explanation of Assertion (A)
(c) Assertion (A) is true but Reason (R) is false
(d) Assertion (A) is false but Reason (R) is true

# Section-B

**Section B consists of 5 questions of 2 marks each**

**21.** Find the LCM and HCF of 12, 15 and 21 by applying the prime factorisation method.

**22.** Prove that $\dfrac{\sin\theta - 2\sin^3\theta}{2\cos^3\theta - \cos\theta} = \tan\theta$.

**23.** Which term of the AP 3, 15, 27, 39, ... will be 120 more than its 21st term?

**24.** Without solving the following quadratic equation, find the value of $m$ for which the given equation has real and equal roots.

$$x^2 + (m-1)x + 2(m+5) = 0$$

*Or* For what value(s) of '$a$' quadratic equation $30ax^2 - 6x + 1 = 0$ has no real roots?

**25.** Compute the Arithmetic Mean for the following data

| Mark obtained | Number of students |
|---|---|
| 0-10 | 14 |
| 10-20 | 8 |
| 20-30 | 15 |
| 30-40 | 21 |
| 40-50 | 9 |
| 50-60 | 8 |

*Or*

Given below is a cumulative frequency distribution showing the marks secured by 50 students of a class.

| Marks | Below 20 | Below 40 | Below 60 | Below 80 | Below 100 |
|---|---|---|---|---|---|
| Number of students | 17 | 22 | 29 | 37 | 50 |

Form the frequency distribution table for the above data.

# Section-C

**Section C consists of 6 questions of 3 marks each**

**26.** At the foot of a mountain the elevation of its summit is 45°. After ascending 1000 m towards the mountain up a slope of 30° inclination, the elevation is found to be 60°. Find the height of the mountain.

*Or*

The two palm trees are of equal heights and are standing opposite each other on either side of the river, which is 80 m wide. From a point $O$ between them on the river the angles of elevation of the top of the trees are 60° and 30°, respectively. Find the height of the trees and the distances of the point $O$ from the trees.

**27.** In the figure, quadrilateral $ABCD$ is circumscribing a circle with centre $O$ and $AD \perp AB$. If radius of incircle is 10 cm, then the value of $x$ is

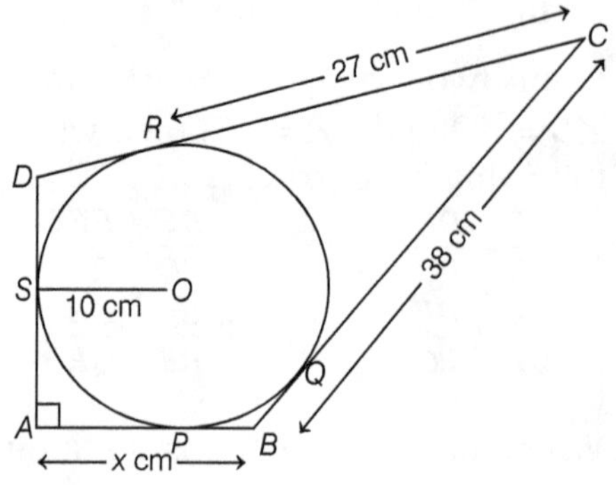

*Or*

If $PQ = 28$ cm, then find the perimeter of $\Delta PLM$.

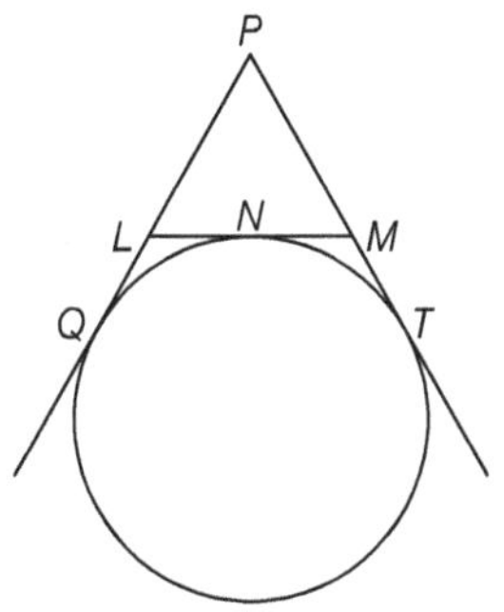


**28.** Sides $AB$ and $BC$ and median $AD$ of $\Delta ABC$ are respectively proportional to sides $PQ$ and $QR$ and median $PM$ of $\Delta PQR$. Show that $\Delta ABC \sim \Delta PQR$.

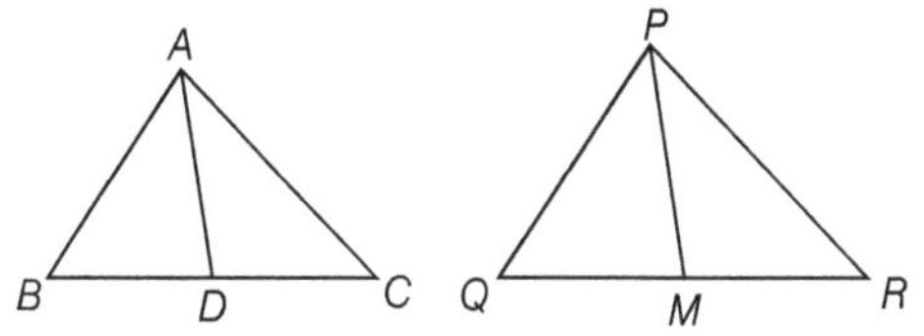


**29.** Find the zeroes of the quadratic polynomial $9x^2 - 6x + 1$ and verify the relationship between the zeroes and its coefficients.

**30.** Three different coins are tossed together. Find the probability of getting

(i) exactly two heads (ii) atleast two heads

(iii) atleast two tails

**31.** Find the area of the sector of a circle with radius 14 cm and of angle 60°. Also, find the area of the corresponding major sector. [take $\pi = 3.14$]

# Section-D

**Section D consists of 4 questions of 5 marks each**

**32.** In the given figure, $\angle AEF = \angle AFE$ and $E$ is the mid-point of $CA$. Prove that $\dfrac{BD}{CD} = \dfrac{BF}{CE}$.

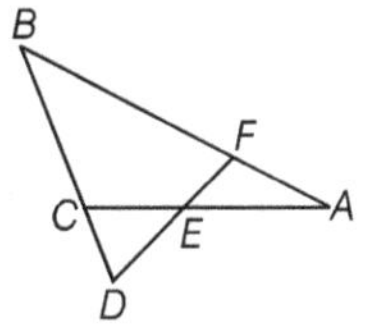


**33.** The following table gives the height of trees

| Height (Less than) | 7 | 14 | 21 | 28 | 35 | 42 | 49 | 56 |
|---|---|---|---|---|---|---|---|---|
| Number of trees | 26 | 57 | 92 | 134 | 216 | 287 | 341 | 360 |

Find the median.

**34.** If $3\cot A = 4$, check whether

$$\frac{1-\tan^2 A}{1+\tan^2 A} = \cos^2 A - \sin^2 A \text{ or not.}$$

*Or* Prove that $(\tan^2 A - \tan^2 B)$

$$= \frac{(\sin^2 A - \sin^2 B)}{\cos^2 A \cos^2 B} = \frac{\cos^2 B - \cos^2 A}{\cos^2 B \cos^2 A}.$$

**35.** Rachel, an engineering student was asked to make a model shaped like a cylinder with two cones attached at its two ends by using a thin aluminium sheet. The diameter of the model is 3 cm and its length is 12 cm. If each cone has a height of 2 cm, then find the volume of air contained in the model that Rachel made. (Assume the outer and inner dimensions of the model to be nearly the same.)

*Or* Two same conical hole have been made on both ends of a solid right circular cylinder. The height of the cylinder is 10 cm and the diameter of its base is 8 cm. If the diameter and depth of the hole are 6 cm and 4 cm respectively, then find the total surface area of remaining solid.

## Section-E

**Case study based questions are compulsory**

**36.** Amit is planning to buy a house and the layout is given below. The design and the measurement has been made such that areas of two bedrooms and kitchen together is 95 sq m.

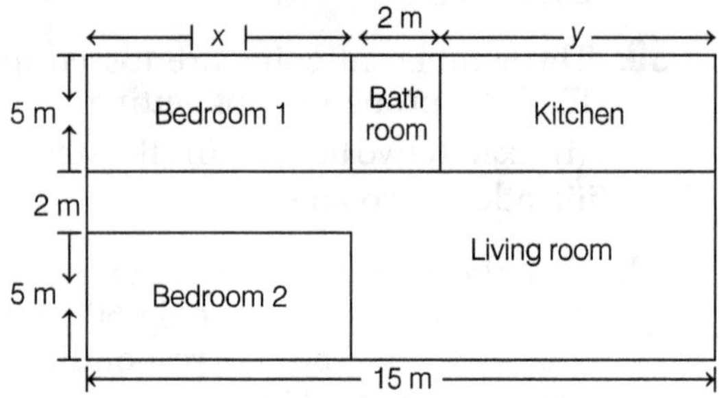


Based on the above information, answer the following questions:

(i) Form the pair of linear equations in two variables from this situation. (1)

(ii) Find the length of the outer boundary of the layout. (1)

(iii) Find the area of living room in the layout. (2)

*Or*

Find the cost of laying tiles in kitchen at the rate of ₹ 50 per sq m. (2)

**37.** Raman and Vishnu are friends living on the same street in Laxmi Nagar. Vishnu's house is at the intersection of one street with another street on which there is a cafe. They both work in the same office and that is not far from Vishnu's house. Suppose the office is situated at the point *O*, i.e. the origin. Raman's house is at point *A*. Vishnu's house is at point *B* and cafe is at point *C*.

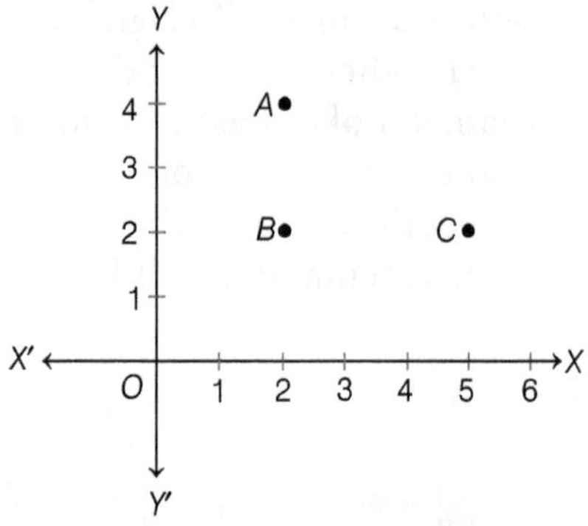


Based on the above information, answer the following questions:

(i) How far is Raman's house from Vishnu's house? (1)

(ii) How far is the office from cafe? (1)

(iii) Find the perimeter of the triangle formed by Raman's, Vishnu's house and the cafe. (2)

*Or* There is a tower between the line joining *A* and *C* which divides *AC* in the ratio 2 : 3. Find the coordinates of the tower. (2)

**38.** A seminar is being conducted by an Educational Organisation, where the participants will be educators of different subjects. The number of participants in Hindi, English and Mathematics are 60, 84 and 108 respectively.

Based on the above information answer the following questions.

(i) In each room the same number of participants are to be seated and all of them being in the same subject, hence find maximum number participants that can accommodated in each room. (1)

(ii) What is the minimum number of rooms required during the event? (1)

(iii) Find the product of HCF and LCM of 60, 84 and 108. (2)

*Or*

What is the largest number that divides 70 and 125, having remainder 5 and 8 respectively? (2)

# SOLUTIONS

**1.** (b) Given, radius of the circle, $r = \frac{21}{2}$ cm

and angle of sector, $\theta = 150°$

$\therefore$ Area of the sector $= \frac{\theta°}{360°} \times \pi r^2$

$$= \frac{150°}{360°} \times \frac{22}{7} \times \left(\frac{21}{2}\right)^2$$

$$= \frac{5}{12} \times \frac{22}{7} \times \frac{21}{2} \times \frac{21}{2}$$

$$= 144.38 \approx 144 \text{ cm}^2$$

**2.** (c) We have, $P$ is the mid-point of $A$ and $B$.

$\therefore \quad \left(\frac{6+4}{2}, \frac{5+y}{2}\right) = (x, 6)$

$\Rightarrow \quad \left(5, \frac{5+y}{2}\right) = (x, 6)$

$\Rightarrow \quad x = 5$ and $\frac{5+y}{2} = 6$

$\Rightarrow \quad x = 5$ and $y = 7$

**3.** (d) Here, $\frac{a_1}{a_2} = \frac{1}{-3}$, $\frac{b_1}{b_2} = \frac{2}{-6} = \frac{1}{-3}$ and $\frac{c_1}{c_2} = \frac{5}{1}$

As, $\quad \frac{a_1}{a_2} = \frac{b_1}{b_2} \neq \frac{c_1}{c_2}$.

Hence, the given system has no solution.

**4.** (d) For $\theta = 45°$,

$$\sin 45° + \cos 45° = \frac{1}{\sqrt{2}} + \frac{1}{\sqrt{2}} = \frac{2}{\sqrt{2}}$$

$$= \sqrt{2} = 1.414 \text{ (greatest value)}$$

**5.** (a) $\sin 60° \cos 30° + \cos 60° \sin 30°$

$$= \frac{\sqrt{3}}{2} \times \frac{\sqrt{3}}{2} + \frac{1}{2} \times \frac{1}{2}$$

$$= \frac{3}{4} + \frac{1}{4} = \frac{4}{4} = 1$$

**6.** (b) Distance between $(4, p)$ and $(1, 0)$,

$$\sqrt{(4-1)^2 + (p-0)^2} = 5$$

On squaring both sides, we get

$$(4-1)^2 + p^2 = 25$$

$\Rightarrow \quad 9 + p^2 = 25$

$\Rightarrow \quad p^2 = 25 - 9 = 16$

$\Rightarrow \quad p = \pm 4$ units

**7.** (c) Total number of possible outcomes in a deck of cards = 52.

Number of favourable outcomes of selecting a card = 1

$\therefore$ Required probability $= \frac{1}{52}$

**8.** (c) Let $p(x) = 3x^2 + 2x - k$

Since, $(x-3)$ is a factor of $p(x)$.

$\therefore \quad p(3) = 0$

$\Rightarrow \quad 3(3)^2 + 2(3) - k = 0$

$\Rightarrow \quad 27 + 6 - k = 0$

$\Rightarrow \quad k = 33$

**9.** (c) We have, the cost of 1 chair = ₹ $x$

and the cost of 1 table = ₹ $y$

Then, according to the given situation

$$3x + y = 1500$$

and $\quad 6x + y = 2400$

**10.** (b) Two triangles are similar, if their corresponding angles are equal and their corresponding sides are in the same ratio.

**11.** (b) Let $p(x) = x^2 - 3x + k$

$\because$ 2 is a zero of $p(x)$.

$\therefore \quad f(2) = 0 \Rightarrow (2)^2 - 3(2) + k = 0$

$\Rightarrow 4 - 6 + k = 0 \Rightarrow k = 2$

**12.** (b) Given, $\angle D = \angle Q$ and $\angle R = \angle E$

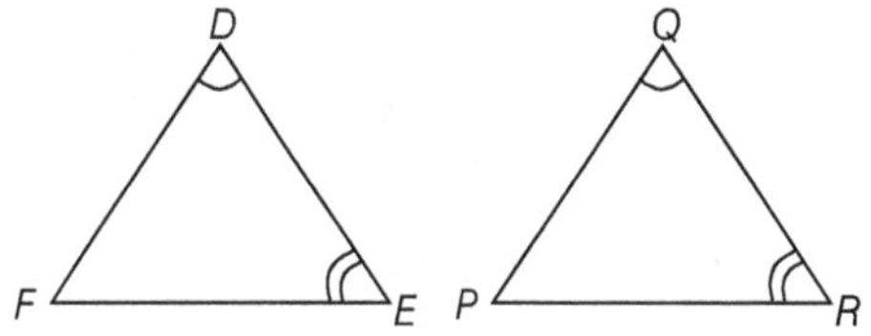


$\therefore \quad \Delta DEF \sim \Delta QRP$ [by AA rule]

$\therefore \quad \frac{DF}{QP} = \frac{ED}{RQ} = \frac{FE}{PR}$

Hence, except option (b), all options are true.

**13.** (b) Since, equation $x^2 + x^3 + 7 = 0$ has degree 3.

**14.** (d) Here, $a = 12$, $b = 4k$ and $c = 3$

$\because$ The given equation has real and equal roots.

$\therefore$ Discriminant, $d = b^2 - 4ac = 0$

$\Rightarrow \quad (4k)^2 - 4(12)(3) = 0$

$\Rightarrow \quad 16k^2 - 144 = 0$

$\Rightarrow \quad k^2 = 9$

$\Rightarrow \quad k = \pm 3$

**15.** (b) Since, $a$, $b$, $c$ are in AP.

$\therefore \quad b - a = c - b$

$\Rightarrow \quad \frac{b-a}{c-b} = 1$

$\Rightarrow \quad \frac{a-b}{b-c} = 1$

**16.** (c) Here, $a = 5$, $d = 2 - 5 = -3$

We know,

$$a_n = a + (n-1)d$$

$\Rightarrow \quad a_n = 5 + (n-1)(-3)$

$\Rightarrow \quad a_n = 5 + 3 - 3n = 8 - 3n$

**17.** (b) We know, volume of a cube with edge, $a = a^3$

$\Rightarrow a^3 = 1728 \Rightarrow a = \sqrt[3]{1728} \Rightarrow a = 12$ cm

**18.** (d) In $\Delta POR$ and $\Delta OQR$,

$OP = OQ$ [radius of circle]

$\angle OPR = \angle OQR$ [each 90°]

and $PR = QR$ [$\because$ pair of tangents drawn from a outside point to a circle are equal in length]

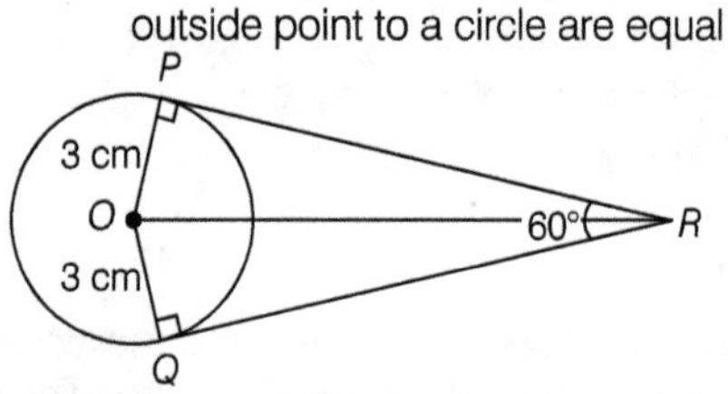


So, $\Delta POR$ and $\Delta QOR$ are congruent.

[by SAS congruency]

Therefore, $\angle QRO = \frac{60°}{2} = 30°$

In right angled $\Delta OPR$,

$$\tan 30° = \frac{OP}{PR} \Rightarrow \frac{1}{\sqrt{3}} = \frac{3}{PR}$$

$$\Rightarrow RP = 3\sqrt{3} \text{ cm} = QR$$

**19.** (a) Given, $3x + 2y = 12$ and $5x - 2y = 4$

$$\frac{a_1}{a_2} = \frac{3}{5} \text{ and } \frac{b_1}{b_2} = \frac{2}{-2} = -1$$

We know for intersecting lines $\frac{a_1}{a_2} \neq \frac{b_1}{b_2}$.

$\because \frac{a_1}{a_2} \neq \frac{b_1}{b_2}$, so the lines are intersecting.

So, the given Assertion is true.

Clearly, Reason is also true and it is the correct explanation of Assertion.

**20.** (a) Two equilateral triangle are similar, if their sides are proportional.

$\because$ In equilateral triangle, each angle are equal and sides are also equal.

Therefore, all equilateral triangle are similar.

$\therefore$ Both Assertion and Reason are true and Reason is the correct explanation of Assertion.

**21.** The prime factors of 12, 15 and 21 are

$12 = 2 \times 2 \times 3 = 2^2 \times 3$

$15 = 3 \times 5$ and $21 = 3 \times 7$ (1)

$\therefore$ HCF (12, 15, 21) = 3 (1/2)

So, LCM (12, 15 and 21) $= 2^2 \times 3^1 \times 5^1 \times 7^1$

$= 4 \times 3 \times 5 \times 7 = 420$ (1/2)

**22.** LHS $= \frac{\sin\theta - 2\sin^3\theta}{2\cos^3\theta - \cos\theta} = \frac{\sin\theta(1 - 2\sin^2\theta)}{\cos\theta(2\cos^2\theta - 1)}$ (1)

$= \tan\theta \cdot \frac{[1 - 2(1 - \cos^2\theta)]}{(2\cos^2\theta - 1)}$ [$\because \sin^2 A = 1 - \cos^2 A$]

$= \tan\theta \cdot \frac{(2\cos^2\theta - 1)}{(2\cos^2\theta - 1)} = \tan\theta = $ RHS

**Hence proved.** (1)

**23.** Here, $a = 3$ and $d = 15 - 3 = 12$

$\therefore$ 21st term is given by

$T_{21} = a + (21 - 1)d$ [$\because T_n = a + (n - 1)d$]

$= a + 20d = 3 + 20 \times 12 = 243$

$\therefore$ Required term $= 243 + 120 = 363$

Let it be $n$th term. (1)

Then, $T_n = 363$

$\Rightarrow a + (n - 1)d = 363$

$\Rightarrow 3 + (n - 1) \times 12 = 363$

$\Rightarrow 3 + 12n - 12 = 363$

$\Rightarrow 12n - 9 = 363 \Rightarrow 12n = 372$

$\therefore n = 31$

Hence, 31st term is the required term. (1)

**24.** Given, quadratic equation is

$$x^2 + (m - 1)x + 2(m + 5) = 0$$

On comparing it with $ax^2 + bx + c = 0$, we get

$$a = 1, b = m - 1 \text{ and } c = 2(m + 5)$$

Since, the given equation has real and equal roots.

So, the discriminant will be zero.

i.e. $b^2 - 4ac = 0$

$\Rightarrow [(m - 1)^2] - 4 \times 1 \times 2(m + 5) = 0$

$\Rightarrow m^2 + 1 - 2m - 8(m + 5) = 0$

[$\because (a - b)^2 = a^2 + b^2 - 2ab$] (1)

$\Rightarrow m^2 + 1 - 2m - 8m - 40 = 0$

$\Rightarrow m^2 - 10m - 39 = 0$

$\Rightarrow m^2 - 13m + 3m - 39 = 0$

[splitting the middle term]

$\Rightarrow m(m - 13) + 3(m - 13) = 0$

$\Rightarrow (m + 3)(m - 13) = 0$

$\Rightarrow m + 3 = 0$ or $m - 13 = 0$

$\therefore m = -3$ or $m = 13$

Hence, the values of $m$ are $-3$ and 13. (1)

*Or*

Given, quadratic equation is $30ax^2 - 6x + 1 = 0$.

On comparing with $Ax^2 + Bx + C = 0$, we get

$$A = 30a, B = -6 \text{ and } C = 1$$

The condition that given roots have no real value (1)

i.e. $B^2 - 4AC < 0$

$\Rightarrow (-6)^2 - 4 \times 30a \times 1 < 0$

$\Rightarrow 36 - 120a < 0$

$\Rightarrow 120a > 36$

$\Rightarrow a > \frac{36}{120}$

$\Rightarrow a > \frac{3}{10}$ (1)

**25.** Let assumed mean $(A) = 35$

| Class | Frequency $(f_i)$ | Mid-value $(x_i)$ | $d_i = x_i - A = x_i - 35$ | $f_i d_i$ |
|---|---|---|---|---|
| 0-10 | 14 | 5 | −30 | −420 |
| 10-20 | 8 | 15 | −20 | −160 |
| 20-30 | 15 | 25 | −10 | −150 |
| 30-40 | 21 | 35 = A | 0 | 0 |
| 40-50 | 9 | 45 | 10 | 90 |
| 50-60 | 8 | 55 | 20 | 160 |
| | $\Sigma f_i = 75$ | | | $\Sigma f_i d_i = -480$ |

(1)

$\therefore$ Mean, $\bar{x} = A + \dfrac{\Sigma f_i d_i}{\Sigma f_i}$

$= 35 + \dfrac{(-480)}{75}$

$= 35 - 6.4 = 28.6$ (1)

*Or*

Here, we observe that, 17 students have scored marks below 20, it lies between class interval 0-20 and 22 students have scored marks below 40, so $22 - 17 = 5$ students lies in the class interval 20-40, continuing in the same manner, we get the frequency distribution table for above data as follows (1)

| Marks | Number of students |
|---|---|
| 0-20 | 17 |
| 20-40 | 22 − 17 = 5 |
| 40-60 | 29 − 22 = 7 |
| 60-80 | 37 − 29 = 8 |
| 80-100 | 50 − 37 = 13 |

(1)

**26.** Let $AD$ be the height of the mountain and $B$ be the point on the foot of mountain.

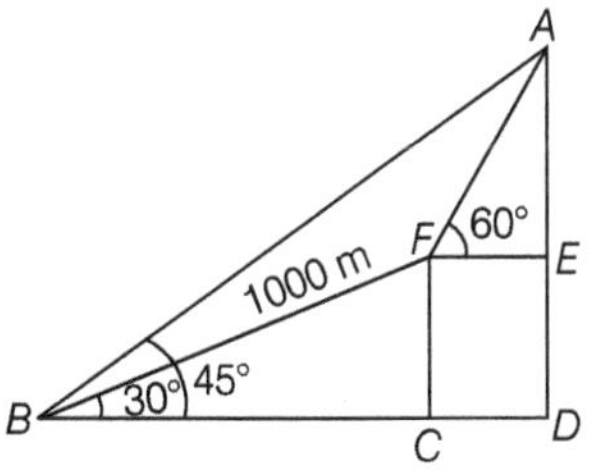


Also, given $BF = 1000$ m,

$\angle CBF = 30°$ and $\angle ABD = 45°$

$\therefore \quad \angle ABF = 45° - 30° = 15°$

In $\Delta AFE$, $\angle FAE = 180° - (90° + 60°) = 30°$

In $\Delta ABD$, $\angle BAD = 180° - (90° + 45°)$

$\Rightarrow \angle BAF + \angle FAE = 180° - 135° = 45°$

$\Rightarrow \quad \angle BAF = 45° - 30° = 15° \quad [\because \angle FAE = 30°]$

$\therefore \quad AF = FB = 1000$ m

[since, $FAB$ is an isosceles triangle] (1)

Now, in $\Delta CBF$,

$\sin 30° = \dfrac{CF}{FB} \Rightarrow \dfrac{1}{2} = \dfrac{CF}{1000}$

$\Rightarrow \quad CF = \dfrac{1000}{2} = 500$ m

Again, in $\Delta EAF$,

$\sin 60° = \dfrac{AE}{FA} \Rightarrow \dfrac{\sqrt{3}}{2} = \dfrac{AE}{1000}$

$\Rightarrow \quad AE = \dfrac{1000\sqrt{3}}{2} = 500\sqrt{3}$ m (1)

For height of mountain,

$AD = AE + DE$

$= 500\sqrt{3} + 500 \quad [\because DE = FC]$

$= 500(\sqrt{3} + 1) = 500 \times 2.73$

$= 1365 \quad [\because \sqrt{3} = 1.73]$

Hence, the height of mountain is 1365 m. (1)

*Or*

Let $AB$ and $CD$ be the positions of palm trees having equal height.

i.e. $AB = CD = h$

Let the river be $BD = 80$ m.

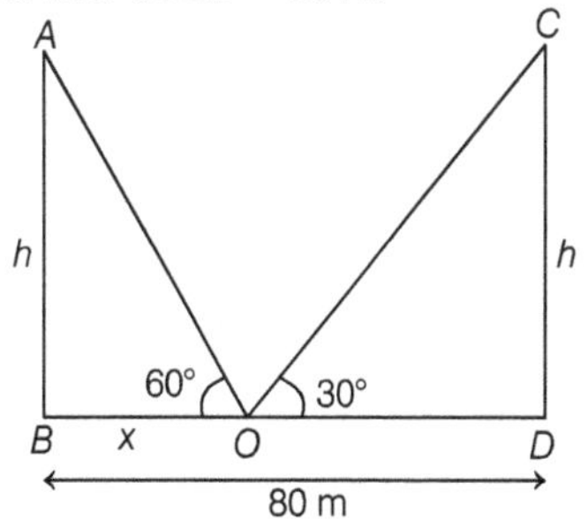


Let $BO = x$

Then, $BD - OD = x \Rightarrow OD = 80 - x$ (1)

In $\Delta ABO$,

$\tan 60° = h / x$

$\sqrt{3} = h / x$

$h = \sqrt{3}x$ ... (i)

and in $\Delta CDO$,

$\tan 30° = h / (80 - x)$

$\Rightarrow \quad 1/\sqrt{3} = h / (80 - x)$

$\Rightarrow \quad h = \dfrac{80 - x}{\sqrt{3}}$ ...(ii)

From Eqs. (i) and (ii), we get

$\sqrt{3}x = \dfrac{80 - x}{\sqrt{3}}$

$\Rightarrow \quad 3x + x = 80$

$\Rightarrow \quad x = 20$ (1)

On putting $x = 20$ in Eq. (i), we get

$h = \sqrt{3} \times 20 = 1.73 \times 20 = 34.6$ m

$\therefore$ The height of the trees, $h = 34.6$ m

Also, $BO = x = 20$ m

Now, $DO = 80 - x = 80 - 20 = 60$ m

Hence, height of the tree is 34.6 and distance of the point $O$ from the trees are 20 m and 60 m. (1)

**27.** Given, inradius of circle, $r = 10$ cm.

Draw a line perpendicular from centre to the tangent line $AB$.

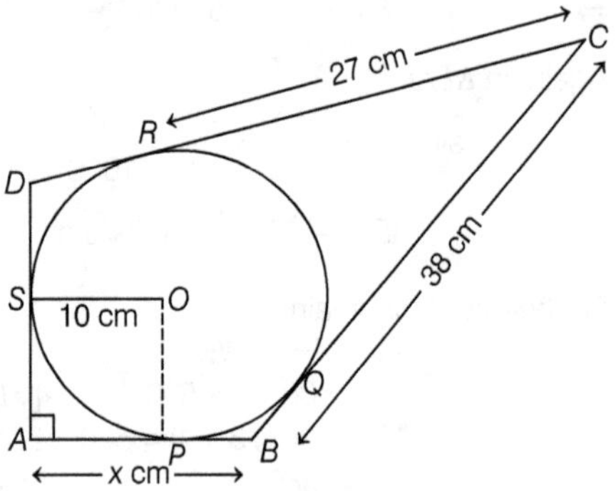


(1)

$$\angle A = \angle OPA = \angle OSA = 90^\circ$$

[$\because$ all lines in quadrilateral $APOS$ are perpendicular]

Hence, $\angle SOP = 90^\circ$

Also, $AP = AS$

[$\because$ pair of tangents drawn from an outside point to a circle are equal in length] (1)

Hence, $OSAP$ is a square.

$$AP = OS = 10 \text{ cm}$$
$$CR = CQ = 27 \text{ cm}$$

Now, $BQ = BC - CQ$
$= 38 - 27 = 11$ cm

Here, $BP = BQ = 11$ cm

$\therefore$ $x = AB = AP + BP$
$= 10 + 11$
$= 21$ cm (1)

*Or*

We have, $PQ = 28$ cm

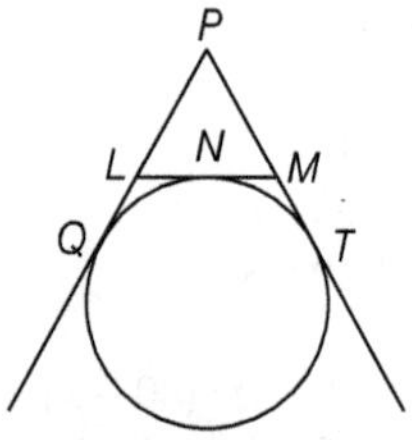


(1)

By using the theorem, that the pair of tangents drawn from an external point to a circle are equal in lengths.

$\therefore$ $PQ = PT, LQ = LN$ and $NM = MT$ ...(i)

Consider, $PQ = PT$

$\Rightarrow$ $PL + LQ = PM + MT$

$\Rightarrow$ $PL + LN = PM + NM$ [using Eq. (i)] ...(ii) (1)

Now, perimeter of $\Delta PLM$

$= PL + LM + PM$
$= PL + LN + NM + PM$
$= PL + LN + PL + LN$ [using Eq. (ii)]
$= 2(PL + LN)$
$= 2 \times (PQ)$

[$\because PL + LN = PL + LQ = PQ$]

$= 2 \times 28$
$= 56$ cm (1)

**28.** Given $\Delta ABC$ and $\Delta PQR$ in which $AD$ and $PM$ are their medians respectively and $\frac{AB}{PQ} = \frac{BC}{QR} = \frac{AD}{PM}$.

**To prove** $\Delta ABC \sim \Delta PQR$

**Proof** We have, $\frac{AB}{PQ} = \frac{BC}{QR} = \frac{AD}{PM}$ [given]

$\Rightarrow$ $\frac{AB}{PQ} = \frac{\frac{1}{2}BC}{\frac{1}{2}QR} = \frac{AD}{PM}$ (1)

[multiplying numerator and denominator of middle term by $\frac{1}{2}$]

$\Rightarrow$ $\frac{AB}{PQ} = \frac{BD}{QM} = \frac{AD}{PM}$

[$\because$ medians $AD$ and $PM$ bisect the lines $BC$ and $QR$, respectively, *i.e.* $BD = \frac{1}{2}BC$ and $QM = \frac{1}{2}QR$]

$\Rightarrow$ $\Delta ADB \sim \Delta PMQ$

[by SSS similarity criterion]

$\therefore$ $\angle B = \angle Q$ ...(i) (1)

In $\Delta ABC$ and $\Delta PQR$,

$\frac{AB}{PQ} = \frac{BC}{QR}$ [given]

and $\angle B = \angle Q$ [from Eq. (i)]

$\therefore$ $\Delta ABC \sim \Delta PQR$

[by SAS similarity criterion]

**Hence proved.** (1)

**29.** Let $p(x) = 9x^2 - 6x + 1$
$= 9x^2 - 3x - 3x + 1$
$= 3x(3x - 1) - 1(3x - 1)$
$= (3x - 1)(3x - 1) = (3x - 1)^2$ (1)

For zeroes of $p(x)$,

$p(x) = 0$

$\Rightarrow$ $(3x - 1)^2 = 0$

$\Rightarrow$ $(3x - 1)(3x - 1) = 0$

$\Rightarrow$ $3x = 1$, also $3x - 1$

$\Rightarrow$ $x = \frac{1}{3}$, also $x = \frac{1}{3}$

So, the zeroes of $p(x)$ are $\frac{1}{3}, \frac{1}{3}$. (1)

Now, sum of zeroes $= \frac{1}{3} + \frac{1}{3} = \frac{2}{3}$
$= \frac{-\text{Coefficient of } x}{\text{Coefficient of } x^2}$

and product of zeroes $= \left(\frac{1}{3}\right)\left(\frac{1}{3}\right) = \frac{1}{9}$
$= \frac{\text{Constant term}}{\text{Coefficient of } x^2}$

Hence, the relationship between the zeroes and the coefficients is verified. (1)

**30.** Total outcomes,

{*HHH, HHT, HTH, THH, TTH, THT, HTT, TTT*}

$\therefore$ Total number of outcomes = 8

(i) The outcomes favourable to event are

{HHT, HTH, THH}

∴ P(exactly two heads)

$= \dfrac{\text{Number of favourable outcomes}}{\text{Total number of outcomes}} = \dfrac{3}{8}$ (1)

(ii) The outcomes favourable to event are

{HHH, HHT, HTH, THH}

∴ P(atleast two heads)

$= \dfrac{\text{Number of favourable outcomes}}{\text{Total number of outcomes}} = \dfrac{4}{8} = \dfrac{1}{2}$ (1)

(iii) The outcomes favourable to event are

{TTH, THT, HTT, TTT}

∴ P(atleast two tails)

$= \dfrac{\text{Number of favourable outcomes}}{\text{Total number of outcomes}} = \dfrac{4}{8} = \dfrac{1}{2}$ (1)

**31.** Area of the sector $= \dfrac{\theta}{360^\circ} \times \pi r^2$

$= \dfrac{60^\circ}{360^\circ} \times 3.14 \times 14 \times 14$

$= 102.57 \text{ cm}^2$

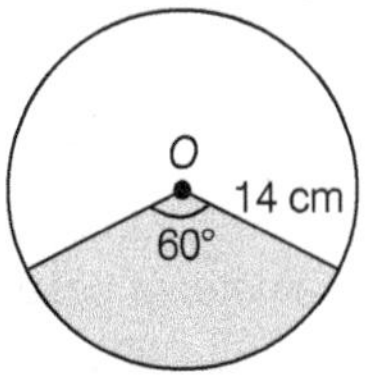


(2)

∴ Area of the corresponding major sector

$= \pi r^2 -$ area of sector

$= 3.14 \times 14 \times 14 - 102.57$

$= 615.44 - 102.57 = 512.87 \text{ cm}^2$ (1)

**32. Given** $\angle AEF = \angle AFE$ **and** $E$ **is the mid-point of** $CA$.

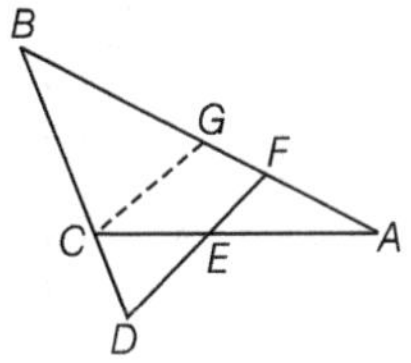


(1)

**To prove** $\dfrac{BD}{CD} = \dfrac{BF}{CE}$

**Construction** Draw a line $CG$ parallel to $DF$.

**Proof** Given, $\angle AEF = \angle AFE$ and $E$ is mid-point of $CA$.

∴ $CE = AE = \dfrac{AC}{2}$ ...(i) (1)

In $\Delta BDF$, $CG \parallel DF$

By basic proportionality theorem,

$\dfrac{BD}{CD} = \dfrac{BF}{GF}$ ...(ii) (1)

In $\Delta AFE$, $\angle AEF = \angle AFE$ [given]

⇒ $AF = AE$

[since, sides opposite to equal angles are equal]

⇒ $AF = AE = CE$ [from Eq. (i)] ...(iii)

In $\Delta ACG$, $E$ is the mid-point of $AC$ and $EF \parallel CG$.

⇒ $FG = AF$ [∵ $AE = CE$] ...(iv) (1)

From Eqs. (ii), (iii) and (iv),

$\dfrac{BD}{CD} = \dfrac{BF}{CE}$ [∵ $GF = AF = CE$]

**Hence proved.** (1)

**33.** Given, distribution is cumulative frequency distribution of less than type.

To convert the table in the interval as shown below:

| Height | Frequency | Cumulative frequency |
|---|---|---|
| 0-7 | 26 | 26 |
| 7-14 | 57 − 26 = 31 | 57 |
| 14-21 | 92 − 57 = 35 | 92 |
| 21-28 | 134 − 92 = 42 | 134 |
| 28-35 | 216 − 134 = 82 | 216 |
| 35-42 | 287 − 216 = 71 | 287 |
| 42-49 | 341 − 287 = 54 | 341 |
| 49-56 | 360 − 341 = 19 | 360 |
| **Total** | $N = 360$ | |

(2)

Here, $\dfrac{N}{2} = \dfrac{360}{2} = 180$

Since, the cumulative frequency just greater than 180 is 216 and the corresponding class interval is 28-35.

∴ Median class = 28 − 35, $l = 28$, $h = 7$,

$cf = 134$, $f = 82$ (1)

∵ Median $= l + \dfrac{\left\{\dfrac{N}{2} - cf\right\}}{f} \times h$

$= 28 + \left\{\dfrac{180 - 134}{82}\right\} \times 7$

$= 28 + \left\{\dfrac{46 \times 7}{82}\right\} = 28 + \dfrac{322}{82}$

$= 28 + 3.92 = 31.92$ (2)

**34.** Given, $3\cot A = 4 \Rightarrow \cot A = \dfrac{4}{3} \Rightarrow \dfrac{AB}{BC} = \dfrac{4}{3}$

Let $AB = 4k$, $BC = 3k$

In right angled $\Delta ABC$,

$AC^2 = AB^2 + BC^2$ [by Pythagoras theorem]

$= (3k)^2 + (4k)^2$

$= 9k^2 + 16k^2 = 25k^2$

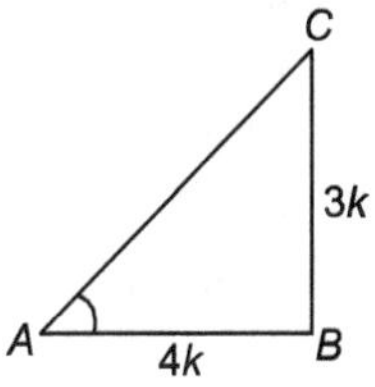


(1)

$\therefore \quad AC = 5k \quad$ [$\because$ side cannot be '–' ve]

Now, $\tan A = \dfrac{1}{\cot A} = \dfrac{3}{4} \quad \left[\because \cot A = \dfrac{4}{3}\right]$

$\cos A = \dfrac{AB}{AC} = \dfrac{4}{5}$ (1)

and $\sin A = \dfrac{BC}{AC} = \dfrac{3}{5}$

$\text{LHS} = \dfrac{1-\tan^2 A}{1+\tan^2 A}$

$= \dfrac{1-\left(\dfrac{3}{4}\right)^2}{1+\left(\dfrac{3}{4}\right)^2} = \dfrac{\dfrac{16-9}{16}}{\dfrac{16+9}{16}} = \dfrac{7}{25}$ ...(i) (1)

and $\text{RHS} = \cos^2 A - \sin^2 A = \left(\dfrac{4}{5}\right)^2 - \left(\dfrac{3}{5}\right)^2$

$= \dfrac{16-9}{25} = \dfrac{7}{25}$ ...(ii)

From Eqs. (i) and (ii), we get

LHS = RHS (2)

*Or*

$\text{LHS} = \tan^2 A - \tan^2 B = \dfrac{\sin^2 A}{\cos^2 A} - \dfrac{\sin^2 B}{\cos^2 B}$ (1)

$\left[\because \tan\theta = \dfrac{\sin\theta}{\cos\theta}\right]$

$= \dfrac{\sin^2 A \cos^2 B - \cos^2 A \sin^2 B}{\cos^2 A \cos^2 B}$

$= \dfrac{\sin^2 A(1-\sin^2 B) - (1-\sin^2 A)\sin^2 B}{\cos^2 A \cos^2 B}$

$[\because \cos^2\theta = 1-\sin^2\theta]$ (1)

$= \dfrac{\left[\begin{array}{r}\sin^2 A - \sin^2 A\sin^2 B - \sin^2 B \\ + \sin^2 A \sin^2 B\end{array}\right]}{\cos^2 A \cos^2 B}$

$= \dfrac{\sin^2 A - \sin^2 B}{\cos^2 A \cos^2 B}$ = Mid-term (1)

$= \dfrac{(1-\cos^2 A)-(1-\cos^2 B)}{\cos^2 A \cos^2 B} \quad [\because \sin^2\theta = 1-\cos^2\theta]$

$= \dfrac{1-\cos^2 A - 1 + \cos^2 B}{\cos^2 A \cos^2 B} = \dfrac{\cos^2 B - \cos^2 A}{\cos^2 A \cos^2 B}$

= RHS **Hence proved.** (2)

**35.** Given, model is a combination of a cylinder and two cones. Clearly, volume of the air will be equal to the sum of the volumes of two cones and one cylinder.

We have, diameter of the model, $BC = ED = 3$ cm

$\therefore$ Radius of cone = Radius of cylinder, $r = \dfrac{3}{2} = 1.5$ cm (1)

Length of cone, $h_1 = 2$ cm

Total length of the model, $AF = 12$ cm

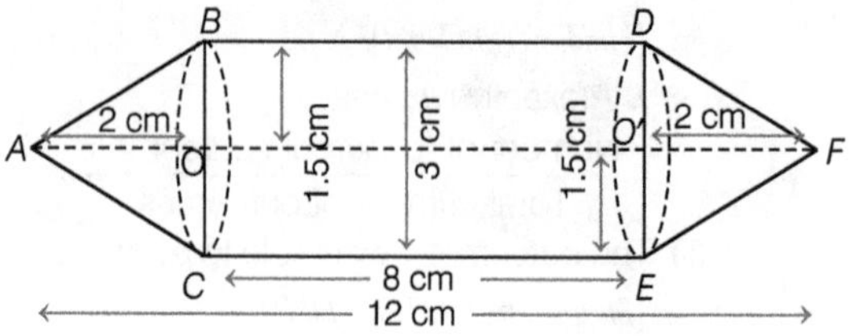


(1)

$\therefore$ Length of the cylinder, $OO' = AF - (AO + O'F)$

$= 12 - (2+2)$

$= 8 \text{ cm} = h_2$ (1)

Now, volume of the air inside the model

= Volume of air inside (cone + cylinder + cone)

$= \left(\dfrac{1}{3}\pi r^2 h_1 + \pi r^2 h_2 + \dfrac{1}{3}\pi r^2 h_1\right)$

$= \dfrac{1}{3}\pi r^2 (h_1 + 3h_2 + h_1)$

$= \dfrac{1}{3} \times \dfrac{22}{7} \times 1.5 \times 1.5\,(2 + 3 \times 8 + 2)$

$= \dfrac{22}{7} \times \dfrac{2.25}{3} \times (2 + 24 + 2)$

$= \dfrac{22}{7} \times 0.75 \times 28 = 22 \times 3 = 66 \text{ cm}^3$ (2)

*Or*

For cylinder, diameter of base = 8 cm

$\therefore$ Radius of base $(R) = \dfrac{\text{Diameter}}{2} = \dfrac{8}{2} = 4$ cm

and height $(H) = 10$ cm

$\therefore$ Curved surface area of cylinder

$= 2\pi RH = 2\pi \times 4 \times 10$

$= 80\pi \text{ cm}^2$ (1)

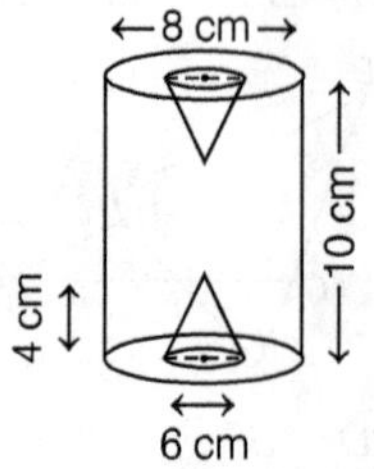


For cone, diameter of base = 6 cm (1)

$\therefore$ Radius of base $(r) = \dfrac{\text{Diameter}}{2} = \dfrac{6}{2} = 3$ cm

Depth of conical hole, $h = 4$ cm

$\therefore$ Slant height, $l = \sqrt{r^2 + h^2}$

$= \sqrt{3^2 + 4^2} = \sqrt{9+16}$

$= \sqrt{25} = 5$ cm (1)

CSA of cone $= \pi rl = \pi \times 3 \times 5 = 15\pi \text{ cm}^2$

Area of remaining ends of cylinder

= 2 (Area of base of cylinder – Area of base of cone)

$= 2(\pi R^2 - \pi r^2) = 2\pi[R^2 - r^2] = 2\pi(4^2 - 3^2)$

$= 14\pi \text{ cm}^2$

Total surface area of remaining solid shape
= CSA of cylinder + CSA of both cones
+ Area of remaining ends of cylinder
$= 80\pi + 2 \times 15\pi + 2 \times 7\pi = 80\pi + 30\pi + 14\pi$
$= 124\pi \text{ cm}^2$ (2)

**36.** (i) From the given figure we see that area of two bedrooms $= 2(5x) = 10x \text{ m}^2$

Area of kitchen $= 5 \times y = 5y \text{ m}^2$

According to the question,

Area of the two bedrooms and area of kitchen $= 95 \text{ m}^2$

$\therefore \quad 10x + 5y = 95$

$\Rightarrow \quad 2x + y = 19$ [divide both sides by 5] ... (i)

Also, length of the home = 15 m

$\therefore \quad x + 2 + y = 15$

$\Rightarrow \quad x + y = 13$ ... (ii)

Hence, pair of linear equations is

$2x + y = 19$ and $x + y = 13$

(ii) The length of the outer boundary of the layout

$= 2(l + b) = 2(15 + 12)$ [$\because b = 5 + 2 + 5 = 12$m]

$= 2(27)$

$= 54$ m

(iii) On solving Eqs. (i) and (ii), we get

$x = 6$ and $y = 7$

$\therefore$ Area of each bedroom $= 5 \times x = 5 \times 6 = 30 \text{ m}^2$

Area of living room

$= 15 \times (5 + 2) -$ Area of bedroom 2

$= 15 \times 7 - 5 \times 6$

$= 105 - 30 = 75 \text{ m}^2$

*Or*

Since, area of kitchen $= 5 \times y$

$= 5 \times 7 = 35 \text{ m}^2$

But, it is also given, the cost of laying tiles in kitchen at the rate of ₹50 per m$^2$.

$\therefore$ Total cost of laying tiles in the kitchen $= 35 \times 50$

= ₹ 1750

**37.** (i) Coordinates of $A = (2, 4)$

Coordinates of $B = (2, 2)$

Coordinates of $C = (5, 2)$

$\therefore \; AB = 4 - 2 = 2$ units

(ii) $OC = \sqrt{(5-0)^2 + (2-0)^2}$

$= \sqrt{25 + 4} = \sqrt{29}$ units

(iii) $AB = 2$ units

$BC = 5 - 2 = 3$ units

and $AC = \sqrt{(5-2)^2 + (2-4)^2}$

$= \sqrt{(3)^2 + (-2)^2}$

$= \sqrt{9 + 4} = \sqrt{13}$ units

$\therefore$ Perimeter of $\Delta ABC = AB + BC + CA$

$= 2 + 3 + \sqrt{13}$

$= 5 + \sqrt{13}$ units

*Or*

Using section formula, coordinates of tower are

$\left(\frac{2 \times 5 + 3 \times 2}{2 + 3}, \frac{2 \times 2 + 3 \times 4}{2 + 3}\right)$

$= \left(\frac{10 + 6}{5}, \frac{4 + 12}{5}\right) = \left(\frac{16}{5}, \frac{16}{5}\right)$

**38.** (i) Given, number of students in each subject are Hindi = 60, English = 84 and Mathematics = 108.

The prime factors of each subject students are

$60 = 2 \times 2 \times 3 \times 5 = 2^2 \times 3 \times 5$

$84 = 2 \times 2 \times 3 \times 7 = 2^2 \times 3 \times 7$

$108 = 2 \times 2 \times 3 \times 3 \times 3 = 2^2 \times 3^3$

The maximum number of participants that can accommodated in each room

= HCF (60, 84, 108)

= Product of the smallest power of each common prime factor involved in the numbers

$= 2^2 \times 3 = 12$

(ii) The minimum number of rooms required during the event is

$\frac{\text{Total number of participants}}{12} = \frac{252}{12} = 21$

(iii) LCM of (60, 84, 108)

= Product of the greatest power of each prime factor involved in the numbers with highest power

$= 2^2 \times 3^3 \times 5 \times 7$

$= 4 \times 27 \times 35$

$= 3780$

Now, HCF (60, 84, 108) $\times$ LCM (60, 84, 108)

$= 12 \times 3780$

$= 45360$

*Or*

Let the largest number be $x$.

Then, the number will completely divide $(70 - 5)$ and $(125 - 8)$ i.e. 65 and 117.

$65 = 13 \times 5$

$117 = 13 \times 3 \times 3$

$\therefore \; x =$ HCF (65 and 117) = 13

CPSIA information can be obtained
at www.ICGtesting.com
Printed in the USA
LVHW061206300623
751014LV00008B/76

9 789327 195583